THE INSIDERS'® GUIDE TO

Yellowstone & GRAND TETON

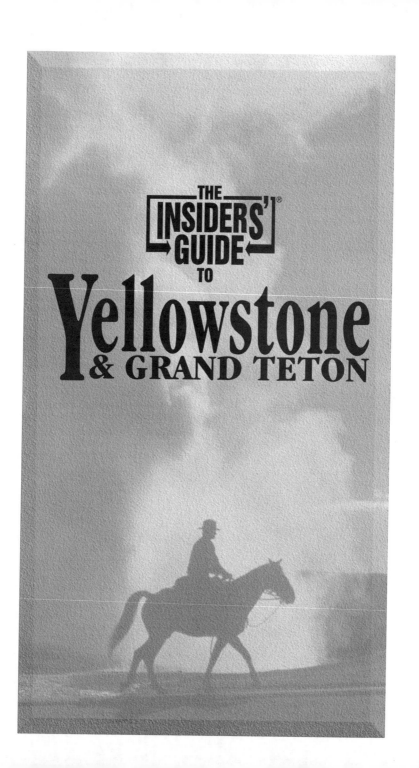

THE INSIDERS' GUIDE® TO

Yellowstone & GRAND TETON

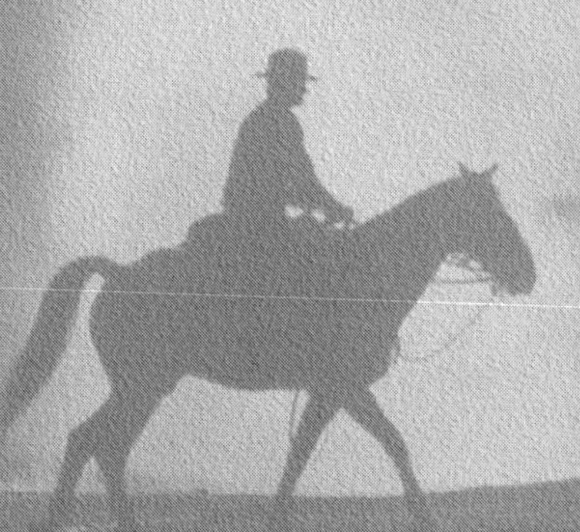

The Insiders' Guide®
An imprint of Falcon® Publishing, Inc.
A Landmark Communications company
P.O. Box 1718
Helena, MT 59624
(800) 582-2665
www.insiders.com

Co-published and marketed by:
The Post Register
333 Northgate Mile
Idaho Falls, ID 83401
(208) 522-1800
www.idahonews.com

•

Sales and Marketing: Falcon Publishing, Inc.
P.O. Box 1718
Helena, MT 59624
(800) 582-2665
www.falcon.com

•

Advertising: Scott Stawski, Advertising Director
The Post Register
333 Northgae Mile
Idaho Falls, ID 83401
(208) 522-1800
sstawski@idahonews.com

•

SECOND EDITION
2nd printing

•

•

Printed in the United States of America

•

Publications from *The Insiders' Guide*® series are available at special discounts for bulk purchases for sales promotions, premiums, or fundraisings. Special editions, including personalized covers, can be created in large quantities for special needs. For more information, please contact Falcon Publishing.

ISBN 1-57380-130-5

Preface

Yellowstone. For those who call this region home, the word conjures up a wealth of images almost too chaotic and lovely to hold on to. Yellowstone is the name of a park, but the word also denotes a region that sprawls from that park in all directions, encompassing an area the size of Maine. Yellowstone and Grand Teton Natonal Parks contain only 14 percent of the wild and near-wild lands comprising Greater Yellowstone. The region holds pieces of Montana, Wyoming and Idaho, parts of seven national forests and three wildlife refuges, along with 3.3 million acres of private land. Nearly one-third is protected wilderness.

The 3 million tourists who visit Yellowstone and Grand Teton National Parks annually make these places anomalous in Greater Yellowstone. This is not a region of crowds and traffic jams. It's a region of wildness. That's why this book doesn't stop at the parks' borders: We want you to know the real Yellowstone country.

Scraping its skies are peaks in the Beartooth Mountains, the Gallatins and Madisons, Centennials and Lionheads. Then there are the Tetons, Salt Rivers, Gros Ventre and Wyoming ranges, Wind Rivers and Absarokas. The Grand Teton is the second-highest mountain in Yellowstone country at 13,770 feet, but dozens of peaks soar to more than 12,000 feet. Beneath these peaks are broad swaths of open valley and tight, forested canyons. Waterfalls froth the many rivers, including the Snake, Green and Yellowstone. These rivers' trickling headwaters begin within a few miles of each other on the Yellowstone Plateau, destined for the Pacific and the gulfs of California and Mexico.

Along river valleys are the towns: quiet agricultural communities like Ashton, Idaho, and booming tourist meccas like West Yellowstone, Montana, and Cody and Jackson, Wyoming. There are also the towns caught awkwardly between: neither the backwater mountain villages they were nor yet the tourist-serving communities they're becoming. We even have cities such as Idaho Falls and Bozeman, many of whose inhabitants have come seeking a balance between the benefits of civilization and the wild loveliness they can almost see from their backyards.

As our communities grow, we find ourselves constantly defining what it means to be Westerners. Part of what tourism in this region does is glorify and revel in the Western myth. We do it in our art, our cuisine, our dress and our architecture.

It's great fun, this pioneer, cowboy and mountain man thing, but it's also serious business: What we glorify, if it ever truly existed, can't last. We caretake the remnants of a larger-than-life time in this nation's history.

Surviving, and sometimes thriving, in the shadow of human growth are the wilder inhabitants of this region. Grizzly bears, black bears and wolves, the largest elk herds and trumpeter swan populations in the lower 48, moose and bison and bald eagles. In fact, nearly all of the species that ambled, flew or swam in Greater Yellowstone 300 years ago can still be found here. This is true no place else in the continental United States.

Mysteriously percolating beneath it all is a Silly Putty™ mass of semimolten rock. Where you live, magma is probably more than 20 miles deep; here it's less than 4. This helps create the estimated 10,000 thermal features in Yellowstone National Park, including its signature steamworks display, Old Faithful. Most geysers are little things that spit and sputter, but six in Yellowstone National Park erupt 100 feet or higher on a predictable basis. Old Faithful erupts every 50 to 100 minutes. Steamboat Geyser may not erupt for decades, but when it does it can spew water 380 feet into the air. The rest of Yellowstone's thermal features are steaming pools, hissing fumaroles, bubbling mud pots and warm seeps. Many of these are colored in rainbow hues, courtesy of bacteria and algae which have adapted themselves to live where you could not set foot. Yellowstone National Park boasts the last relatively intact large geothermal basin in the world not commercially developed — and therefore relatively undamaged — by humans. In winter, the warmth of the thermal basins shelters oases of plant life. Winter temperatures can reach 65 below zero, and snow depths of 6 feet or more are common in some areas. Yet delicate mosses, grasses and even flowers grow in the steamy warmth of geyser basins and hot springs.

Come explore. But before you do, consider Yellowstone Lake — a fine metaphor for our hope, as you visit our home, that you'll come to appreciate the complexities and drama of Yellowstone. Clear, sparkling and ringed by lodgepole forests, the largest mountain lake in the lower 48 is lovely to view and to photograph. If that's all you did there, you would leave enriched. But what if you knew what scientists recently discovered: This 330-foot-deep pool of ice-clear water hides a bubble of semimolten rock, perhaps as little as a mile beneath its floor? What if you learned that myriad underwater geysers and steam vents turn the lake's depths into a hell of constant mudslides, with temperatures that vary hundreds of degrees within a few yards? What if you discovered that tiny, otherworldly creatures have adapted to live in that hell?

Or what if you caught a Mackinaw trout out of those clear waters and learned that the fish you're holding is featured on local "Most Wanted" posters? Planted in these drainages decades ago, voracious Mackinaws, or lake trout, threaten the survival of native cutthroats. Rangers are collecting data on lake trout colonization of these waters. Anglers who catch these fish are asked to help by killing and then showing them to staff at nearby ranger stations and visitors centers.

We wrote this book because we treasure the Greater Yellowstone region. It's flamboyantly Western and determinedly wild; it's huge and lovely and yet so poorly understood. Look hard, and Yellowstone country's size and grandeur won't disguise the fact that it's fragile. We wrote because we want to help you enjoy and understand this place; we believe that as you do, you will come to treasure it, too. To endure in this shrinking world, fragile places must be treasured. Please, dive deep.

About the Authors

Candace Burns

Candace Burns was raised in Washington, Idaho and Montana, with a brief stop in St. Paul, Minnesota. Ask her where she grew up, though, and she'll say, "Salmon, Idaho," where she has lived and worked for the past 23 years. An award-winning journalist, she has been the central Idaho correspondent to the Idaho Falls *Post Register* for more than 10 years. She also has written for *The Christian Science Monitor*, *High Country News* and numerous Northwest publications. She has driven through blizzards, climbed high mountain peaks, tracked wolves, ridden the range and shot the rapids of the Salmon River looking for the people and places that best tell the story of Idaho's wild heart.

Candace currently writes from her home in Salmon. Since moving to town, she has owned and operated a preschool and served as the central Idaho stringer for an Idaho Falls television station. When she can break away from writing deadlines, she works as an assistant midwife.

A single mother for 19 years, Candace has one daughter, Syringa, a dog, a cat and a rambling yard. Now living in an empty nest, she has watched the isolated ranching, logging and mining community grow from a wild frontier town into a bustling but tamer recreation destination. She has a passion for children, gardening, camping, crumbling log cabins, one-room schoolhouses, hiking, backpacking, dancing, exploring and listening to old-timers tell tales of the Old West.

Jo Deurbrouck

Jo's earliest memories are flavored with the tang of pine and sage. Her parents supplied this gift, but with it came a misconception: The family did so much weekend camping, hiking, fishing and rockhounding that their middle child decided the world consisted of glorious wilderness, interrupted — very occasionally — by farms or a town.

When the family drove south and east to their new home in Oklahoma City the 10-year-old discovered the truth. Drawn by mountains and memories, an older Jo wandered back West. She thought she would return to her native Washington. But instead she found the Northern Rockies of Idaho, a region where even today her childhood picture is nearly accurate.

Jo currently resides in Idaho Falls, on the edge of Greater Yellowstone. She and her husband ski, kayak, climb and hike some of the nation's loveliest wildlands, much of it barely a shout from their door. From the sage-covered hilltop behind their old farmhouse Jo can count eight mountain ranges.

Like many Northern Rockies residents, Jo works as a guide. Every summer she pilots raft-loads of adventurous visitors down Idaho's world-class whitewater rivers. In winter she stokes the woodstove and sits down to write.

Acknowledgments

Candace Burns

Researching and writing this book was fun — a little like hunting for and then collecting Easter eggs. I couldn't have found them by myself, though. It was the people of Greater Yellowstone — the stranger at the lunch counter next to me, the garrulous motel clerk, the helpful waitress and the busy shop owner — who steered me toward the information that I needed, and more.

Wherever I went by phone or by car, individuals gladly shared their passion for the roles they play in Greater Yellowstone communities. To those often anonymous individuals, I give thanks not only for valuable information but for taking time out from their busy lives to answer questions and to share their stories. Included in the long list of those who helped with this book are individuals at chambers of commerce throughout Greater Yellowstone. Almost all were models of Western hospitality, never once groaning when they picked up the phone and heard me say for the umpteenth time, "Hi, this is Candace Burns."

Countless individuals with the National Park Service answered my endless questions. Thanks go to them and to the many individuals inside and outside the parks who took the time to read through and fact-check individual sections of this book. A special thanks to Charissa Reid for wading through the whole thing.

To other authors who have gone before us, I extend my gratitude. Among them are Aubrey Haines, T. Scott Bryan, Mark C. Marschall, George Wuerthner, Seymour L. Fishbein and Lee Whittlesey.

Thanks to my longtime friend, Nance Myers, who opened her home to me and offered her bed whenever I was in her neck of the woods.

To Eileen Myers, project editor, thank you for your steady patience and calm approach under any imaginable pressures.

Special thanks go to coauthor Jo Deurbrouck for her constant sense of humor and her keen ability to zero in on a problem, then dissect, bisect and reassemble it into order. Her writing and insight have been a delight, her determination and enthusiasm an inspiration.

To Dean Miller, my mentor and managing editor of the Idaho Falls *Post Register*, I extend gratitude for nurturing the writer in me and for making me believe that I could write this book — a piece at a time. He said I would cuss him, and I did.

To my parents, Jim Burns and Kinnie Thrall, who taught me at an early age the value of the written word. To my friend Pam Dahle who didn't give up on me when I dropped out of her life for weeks at a time.

To my friend and greatest supporter, Pat Marcuson, I give a special thanks. Pat put me back together when stress scattered me to the winds. He filled my woodbox, helped weed my garden, mowed my lawn and cooked meals while I kept the midnight oil burning. More than that, he waited patiently for *The Insiders' Guide® to Yellowstone* to vacate the front seat of my life.

Jo Deurbrouck

Revisiting a bookful of businesses, attractions and visitors centers has reminded me that Greater Yellowstone residents are good people living in what can be a hard place. Many businesses closed or changed dramatically since I spoke with them a year ago. New ones have opened, determined to succeed.

So the first round of thanks goes to all of you who answered the phone or looked up from the sales counter to see a woman, pen poised over notebook, blurting, "Hi, I'm Jo Deurbrouck from Insiders' Guide. Do you have a minute?" I'm grateful at how seldom, even though you were busy or had problems of your own, you said no.

Updating a book you helped write is humbling: Every day you learn ways you missed the mark the first time. So grateful thanks go to the people who took time to read and comment — usually gently — upon the first edition. The accuracy and, in many cases, the fun in this book come from you. If anything's still not right, well, that'd be me. Special thanks to these readers: Mammoth District Naturalist Brian Suderman, who assisted with several sections; Ken Pierce of the U.S. Geologic Survey, who helped me sound like I paid attention in college geology courses; and geologists Grant Meyer and Bob Christiansen for being graceful about the fact that I didn't. The expertise of biologist Linda Wallace shows. So does that of outfitters, guides and sporting goods shop staff who improved sections on climbing, biking, fishing, hiking, cross-country skiing, rafting and snowmobiling. Local Realtors who critiqued our Area Overview and Real Estate chapters also deserve thanks. Three people read and commented upon the first edition almost in its entirety, for nothing but this thanks. These people were Yellowstone National Park ranger Charissa Reid, Executive Director of the Grand Teton Natural History Association Sharlene Milligan and Jackson Hole amateur historian, factoid collector and geyser lover Jesse O'Connor. Jesse, I'm waiting to buy your book.

Some of the best ideas in this book came from other authors. They are too numerous to mention here, but you'll find their books listed in our Resources section, both as a way of saying thanks and because I hope others will find them as useful as I do. Thanks is also owed to the journalists and feature writers whose ideas probably snuck in without my noticing.

Finally, at the risk of overlooking some, kitchen sink thank-yous go to Karen Connelly of the Jackson Hole Chamber of Commerce; the helpful and informative staff at the Jackson Hole/Greater Yellowstone Information Center in Jackson; the knowledgeable folks at Idaho Falls' Eastern Idaho Visitor Information Center; the Rexburg Chamber of Commerce; Dean Miller of the *Post Register* for giving this project more of his attention and energy than we had any right to, and for becoming the friend and colleague I've wished for; the *Post Register's* Bill Hathaway for his Insider info about Idaho Falls and St. Anthony; *Post Register* photo editor Monte LaOrange for making the book look good; Ed Brashier of Harriman State Park; U.S. Forest Service and National Park Service personnel too numerous to name; Marv Hoyt of the Greater Yellowstone Coalition; authors Jerry Painter and Tony Huegel for providing information and/or text; project editor Eileen Myers for her steady support in the hurricane that followed the hurricane; Falcon editor Erin Turner for making room on her plate; Marilynne Manguba, who passes along useful information; Bob and Arlene Deurbrouck for last year's Yellowstone journey; Candace Burns for knowing what I never learn — when to button your lip. For my husband and friend, Barry Rabin, a private thank you.

DEAN MILLER
Managing Editor

Maybe you're hoping to hear a wolf howl. City lights have lost their luster and you'd like to rest your eyes on things beautiful and wild.

By picking up this book, newly revised for 1999, you've increased the chances that you'll find your Yellowstone moment or Grand Teton grin without getting lost and without having to dig through stacks of brochures and maps or library books. This is the only comprehensive guide to the two parks and the three-state region that surrounds them.

Projects like this are a specialty of the Post Register. The Brady family's newspaper has spent more than 100 years chronicling life in and around America's oldest national park. On this project, we teamed up with the region's biggest publisher of outdoor guides: Falcon Publishing Inc. of Helena, Montana.

And we hired two competent outdoors women, Candace Burns and Jo Deurbrouck, to do the digging for you. They have crisscrossed the region by car, on foot and on horseback, by snowmobile, bike, skis, kayak, snowshoes and canoe.

This book is where you start if you're hoping to take in a mountain sunset or spy on wildlife. Use it to find your ideal day or two on horseback, on a snowmobile or on skis, or to find the right spot to wade a trout stream or raft whitewater.

About that wolf howl: get your imagination going by visiting the Yellowstone section of our web page: www.idahonews.com. Click on the paw print and close your eyes. You'll get the picture.

333 Northgate Mile
Idaho Falls, ID 83401

P.O. Box 1800
Idaho Falls, ID 83403

208-522-1800

Fax: 208-529-3142

Happy Trails!

Dean Miller

Table of Contents

Directory of Maps

Greater Yellowstone

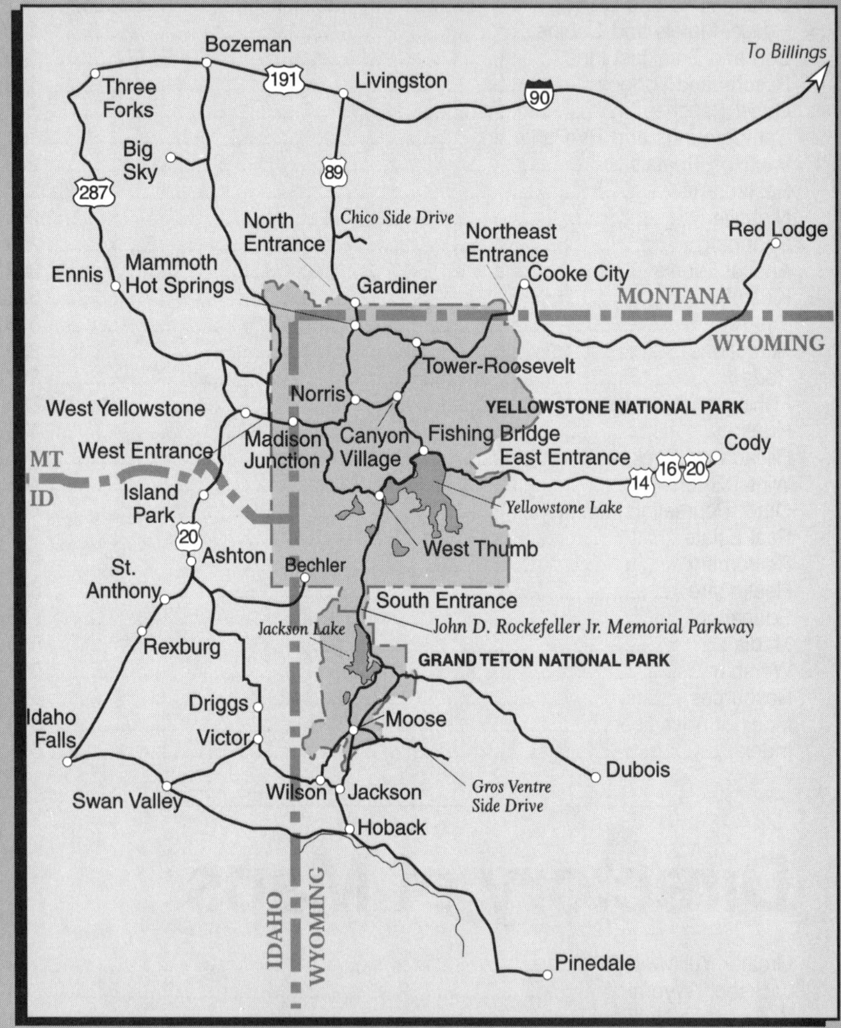

Jackson

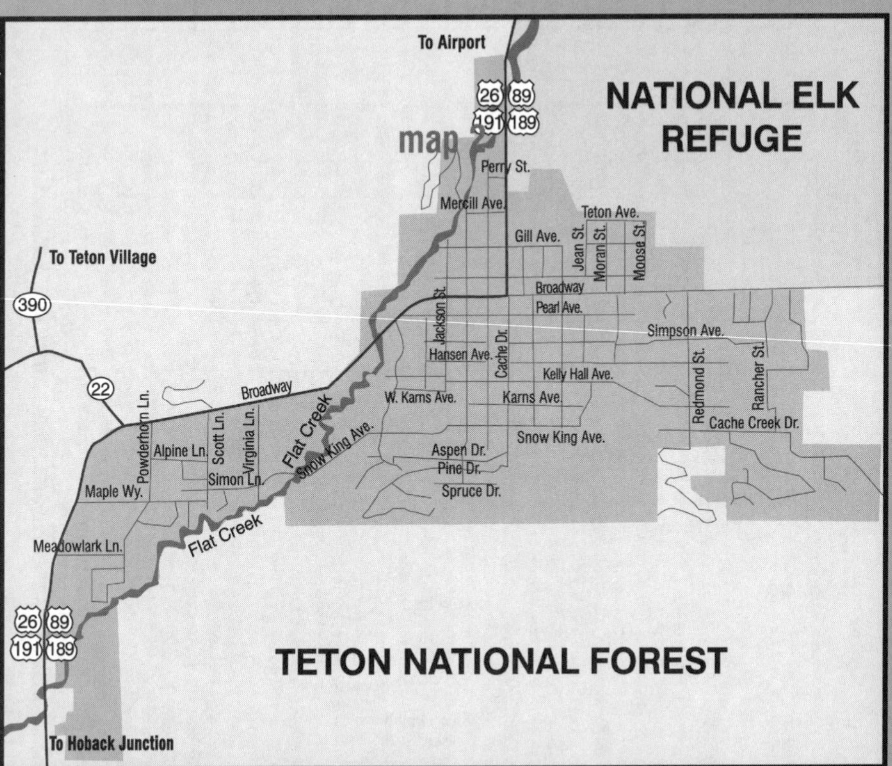

To Airport
NATIONAL ELK REFUGE
26
89
191
189
map 2
Perry St.
Mercill Ave.
Teton Ave.
Gill Ave.
Jean St.
Moran St.
Moose St.
To Teton Village
390
Broadway
Pearl Ave.
Jackson St.
Simpson Ave.
Cache Dr.
Hansen Ave.
22
Kelly Hall Ave.
Redmond St.
Rancher St.
Broadway
Flat Creek
W. Karns Ave.
Karns Ave.
Powderhorn Ln.
Scott Ln.
Virginia Ln.
Snow King Ave.
Cache Creek Dr.
Alpine Ln.
Snow King Ave.
Aspen Dr.
Simon Ln.
Pine Dr.
Maple Wy.
Spruce Dr.
Flat Creek
Meadowlark Ln.
26
89
191
189
TETON NATIONAL FOREST
To Hoback Junction

Yellowstone National Park

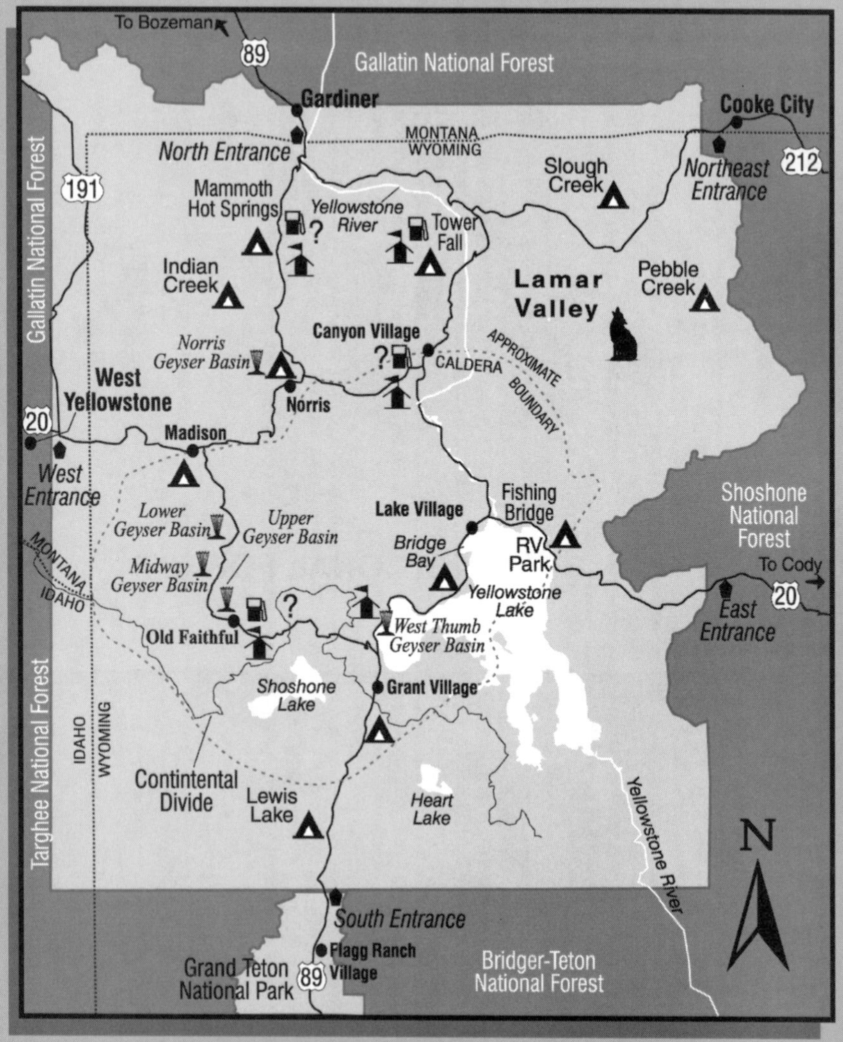

Grand Teton National Park

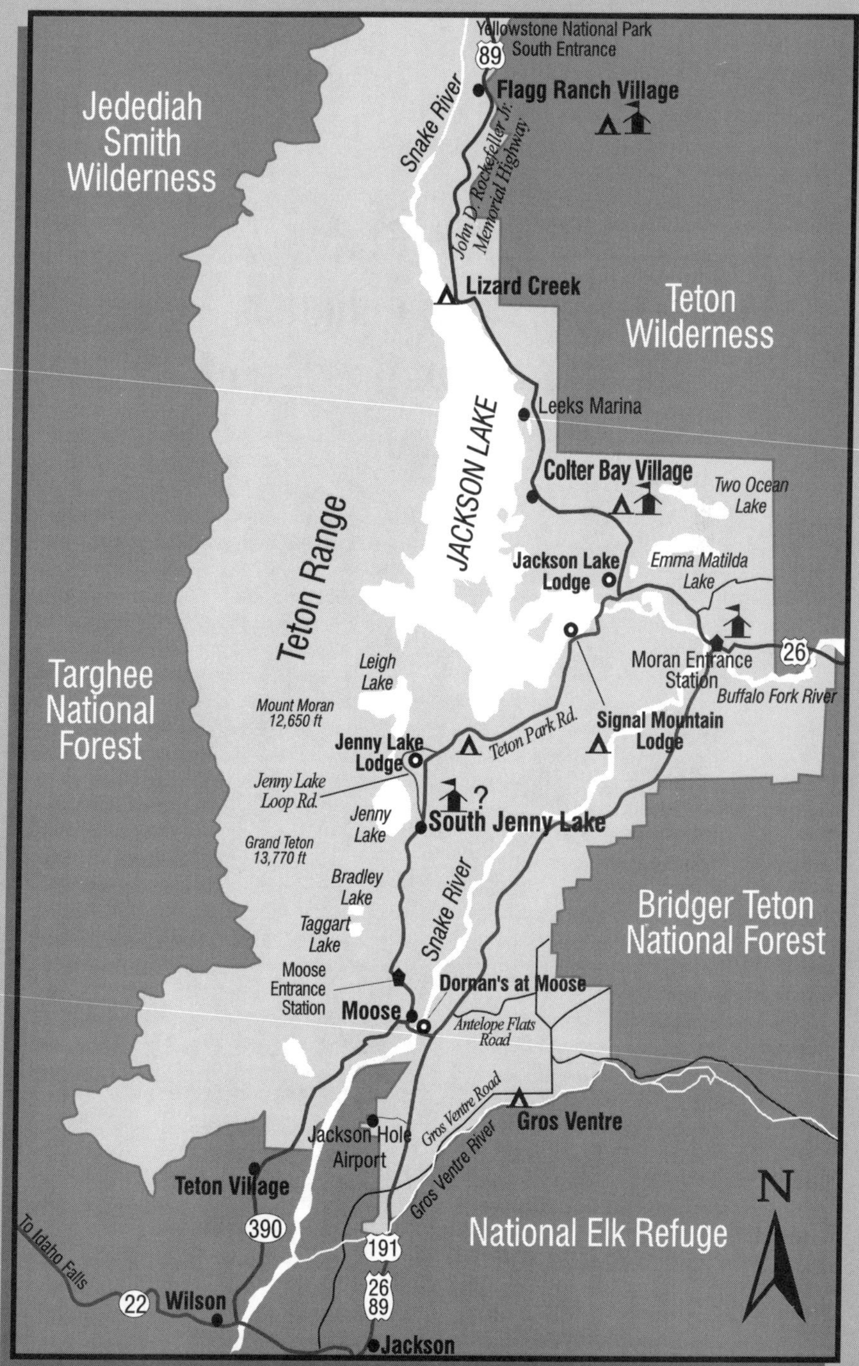

Yellowstone National Park
South Entrance
89
Flagg Ranch Village
Snake River
John D. Rockefeller Jr. Memorial Highway
Jedediah Smith Wilderness
Lizard Creek
Teton Wilderness
Leeks Marina
JACKSON LAKE
Colter Bay Village
Two Ocean Lake
Teton Range
Jackson Lake Lodge
Emma Matilda Lake
26
Moran Entrance Station
Buffalo Fork River
Targhee National Forest
Leigh Lake
Mount Moran
12,650 ft
Signal Mountain Lodge
Teton Park Rd.
Jenny Lake Lodge
Jenny Lake Loop Rd.
Jenny Lake
South Jenny Lake
Grand Teton
13,770 ft
Bradley Lake
Snake River
Taggart Lake
Bridger Teton National Forest
Moose Entrance Station
Dornan's at Moose
Moose
Antelope Flats Road
Gros Ventre Road
Gros Ventre
Jackson Hole Airport
Gros Ventre River
Teton Village
N
390
National Elk Refuge
191
To Idaho Falls
22
Wilson
26
89
Jackson

Inside the Greater Yellowstone outline is an area about the size of Maine.

How to Use This Book

Yellowstone National Park is the heart of this book because it's the heart of Greater Yellowstone, an often-disputed area that surrounds the park. It's a region often defined like a dot-to-dot picture by its perimeter towns: Lander, Dubois and Cody, Wyoming; Red Lodge, Livingston, Bozeman and Ennis, Montana; and Island Park, Ashton, Rexburg and Idaho Falls, Idaho. In this book, we have excluded both Lander and Dubois, Wyoming, simply because we had to rein it in somehow.

Inside the Greater Yellowstone outline is an area about the size of Maine. It includes two national parks, parts of three states, seven national forests, 10 counties, three national wildlife refuges and five state parks. In the Area Overview, History and Our Natural World chapters, we tell you about the land and its inhabitants — both wild and civilized. We urge you to read these three chapters first so you know more about us when you arrive. Being better informed can also help you decide which places you'd like to visit. In ambiance and philosophy, Jackson is planets apart from Cooke City, as West Yellowstone is from Cody. Reading about the land and its people first will add an extra dimension when you start checking out the Nightlife, Restaurants and Shopping chapters, for example.

Although we know most visitors to this region are headed for the national parks and Jackson, we also know there are as many fun things to do and places to stay outside the parks as inside them. That's why we've included at least a few sights and accommodations even for towns at the very edge of Greater Yellowstone. So remember, in each chapter we start with the big three: Yellowstone and Grand Teton National Parks and then Jackson Hole. Then we move just outside the parks' borders and generally work our way out to the Greater Yellowstone perimeter. Outside the parks and Jackson Hole, geographical listings occur in this order: Southwestern Montana, Eastern Idaho and Northwestern Wyoming.

Beneath each geographical heading, entries are listed alphabetically. Under Eastern Idaho, in each chapter we start with Teton Valley, which includes the towns of Driggs, Victor and Tetonia, Idaho, and Alta, Wyoming. After Teton Valley, we cover Swan Valley, which lies along the South Fork of the Snake River (here we include Alpine, Wyoming, technically above Swan Valley). From there we go to Island Park and Ashton, then heading south on U.S. Highway 20, we cover the Rexburg area next, including nearby St. Anthony. Finally, we list the Idaho Falls area, which includes Ririe and Rigby.

Because four different routes lead from the Montana perimeter of Greater Yellowstone into Yellowstone Park, we have listed Southwestern Montana entries in a particular pattern. First we list the entrance communities in order of visitor numbers: West Yellowstone first, then Gardiner and Cooke City. Next we jump north to Bozeman, which includes the towns of Gallatin Gateway and Belgrade. After Bozeman we follow U.S. Highway 191 south to Big Sky in the Gallatin River Canyon between Bozeman and West Yellowstone. Next we follow U.S. Highway 89 from Livingston, which encompasses the entire Paradise Valley, including the tiny towns of Emigrant and Pray. The third route takes you along U.S. Highway 287 from Ennis to Cameron past Hebgen Lake to West

Photo: Gary Thain, Post Register

Discovering the thrill of Tetonia Teton performing ceremonial dance is just one of many possibilities when using the Insiders' Guide to Yellowstone.

Yellowstone. Included in this geographic area are a few listings for Virginia City, a restored mining town. Finally, we list the Red Lodge area.

In Northwestern Wyoming, organizing information is easy, since U.S. Highway 20 is (almost) the only road with services and accommodations leading from Cody into Yellowstone Park. There are a couple of exceptions. In some cases, you'll find Buffalo Valley, Wyoming, accommodations listed with Grand Teton National Park instead of with other Northwestern Wyoming listings, since the valley is immediately east of the park's Moran entrance. And Jackson Hole, Wyoming, listings are grouped together right after Grand Teton National Park listings in each chapter, to make it more convenient for its many visitors to find the information they need. There is another exception: In the Camping and RV Parks chapter, you'll find a couple of Forest Service campgrounds listed on Wyo. Highway 296, sometimes referred to in this book as the Chief Joseph Highway. In the Shopping chapter, entries are first organized geographically, then by category. The Annual Events chapter is organized as a calendar of events. And in Kidstuff, you'll find an A-to-Z list of fun things to see and do geared to the younger set.

Throughout this book we remind you that Greater Yellowstone has three area codes: 307 in Wyoming and all of Grand Teton and Yellowstone national parks, 208 in Idaho and 406 in Montana.

In each chapter, we whisper a few Insiders' Tips, and in some chapters we've included Close-ups — stories about people, places, events and animals we think rate closer inspection, such as dude ranches and the Cody Nite Rodeo.

The broad scope of this book means that we're probably the only travel guide you'll need while you explore Greater Yellowstone, whether you're looking for wildlife in a geyser basin in Yellowstone or looking for a motel off I-15 in Idaho Falls' spud fields. We're pretty proud of that. We hope you'll take this book to bed with you, carry it in your car, read it on the plane, study it by flashlight in your sleeping bag, mark it and dog-ear it until it resembles a well-used telephone directory. And we hope the information in this book will lead you to a rich and memorable visit to Greater Yellowstone.

We'll be updating this guide periodically, and we want to hear from you if we've missed something you think absolutely must be included in this book. Drop us a line at Falcon Press, P.O. Box 1718, Helena, MT 59624. Or visit *The Insiders' Guide® to Yellowstone* at www.insiders.com/yellowstone, where you'll find a comment form on the site.

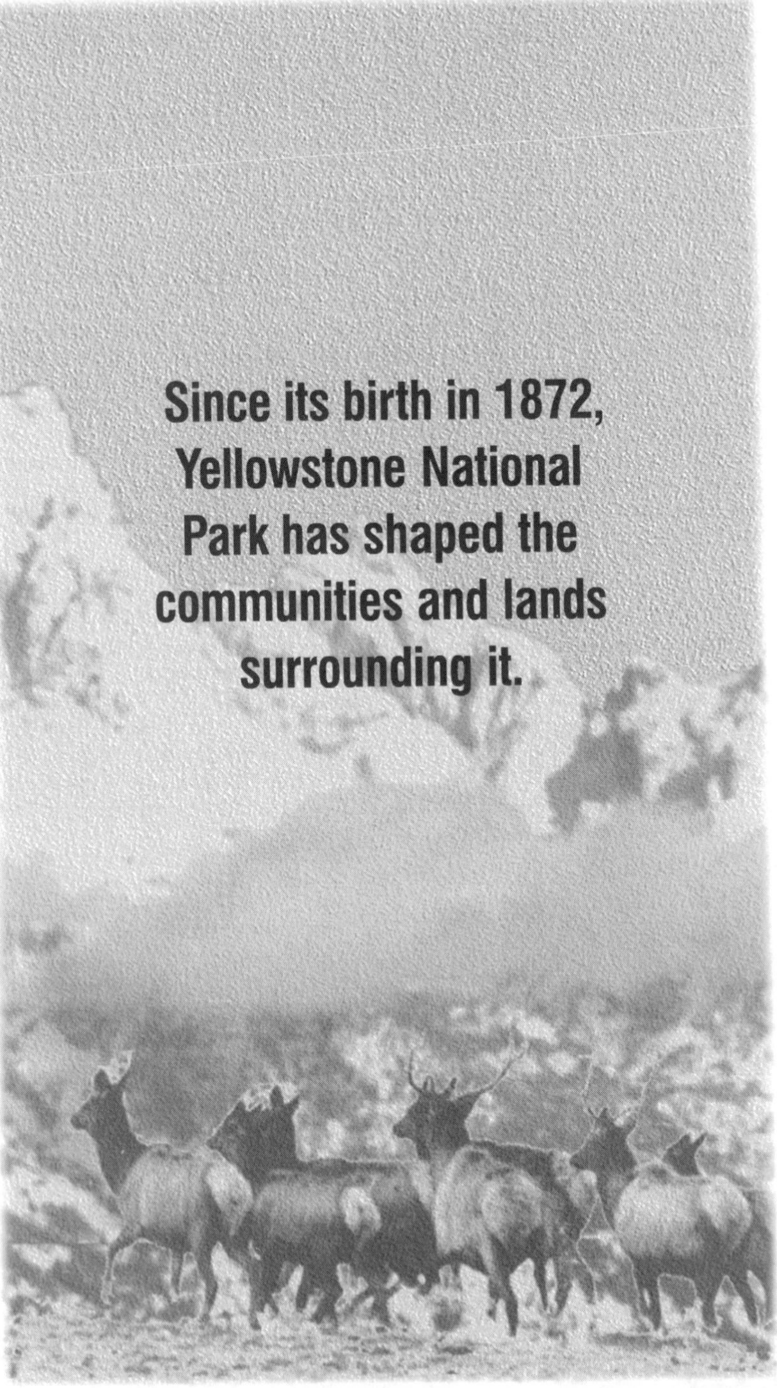
Since its birth in 1872,
Yellowstone National
Park has shaped the
communities and lands
surrounding it.

History

At the heart of Greater Yellowstone is our first national park, the very visible political, economic and ecological engine that drives the region. Since its birth in 1872, Yellowstone National Park has shaped the communities and lands surrounding it. For example, Yellowstone National Park gave birth to the national forest reserve system in 1891 when proponents pushed for an expanded park to protect migrating wildlife. The national forests that evolved from that effort are a big piece of the Greater Yellowstone ecosystem as well as a big part of the foundation on which surrounding communities have built their economies.

Grand Teton National Park to the south of Yellowstone also grew out of the Greater Yellowstone movement, an idea first conceived more than a century ago by Gen. Phillip Sheridan. Pieced together and fought over for decades, Grand Teton's history is intertwined with that of Yellowstone National Park and Jackson Hole.

Surrounding Yellowstone and Grand Teton National Parks, individual communities honor their own historic roots. Some, like Jackson and Driggs, sprang up during a brief but intense period of fur trading. Others, like Virginia City and Cooke City, grew out of gold rushes. Bozeman, in the heart of the fertile Gallatin Valley, was settled by ranchers and farmers who in turn supplied the miners with food. A few, such as Idaho Falls, started as ferry crossings and stayed on. Other towns, like West Yellowstone and Gardiner, sprang up on the parks' borders to serve visitors and park employees. Since their beginnings, all have been shaped by our two national parks and the wild national forest lands that surround them.

Because Greater Yellowstone is so huge, diverse and complex, in this chapter we'll zoom in on the history of Yellowstone National Park as it relates to the region, and especially as it relates to Grand Teton National Park. In our Area Overview chapter, we tell you briefly about the histories of the region's individual communities.

In the Beginning

In 1997, Yellowstone National Park celebrated 125 years of "the best idea America ever had." But when Nathaniel P. Langford, the park's first superintendent, was handed the reins of Yellowstone in 1872, he might well have asked, "What's the big idea?" Like a rare diamond, Yellowstone was cut out of the wilderness to be preserved and protected for the "benefit and enjoyment of the people." The park came with no instructions, no rules, no budget, no official name and no ideas about what a national park should be. Park officials, politicians and conservationists have been struggling ever since to define and redefine Yellowstone National Park. If history has taught managers one thing, it's that wild land, corralled only by legal boundaries, defies definition and management.

Take the subterranean world where the fiery innards of the earth bubble and steam, a constant reminder of the intense pressure and subsequent volcanic eruption that created the Yellowstone caldera 600,000 years ago. While Mother Nature's boiling cauldron beneath causes park managers some concern, above ground it presents subtle management dilemmas. Take the Opal Terrace at Mammoth Hot Springs. This gleaming white travertine expanse grows a foot a year. In 1947, officials let it take over a tennis court. Today, though, it threatens a historic house designed in 1908 by renowned park architect Robert Reamer. Managers have bought time by erecting a berm between house and terrace.

There are other park features confounding managers of the 2.2-million-acre park. Elk, bison, wolves and grizzlies, all brought back from the edge of extinction in this region, now spill out of the park onto national forest and private lands. Elk eat ranchers' hay and range grass outside the park, while wolves and grizzlies kill livestock. Bison tear down fences and, like elk, carry brucellosis, a disease that causes cattle to abort. At the same time, elk that leave the park each fall bring thousands of hunters and millions of dollars to Greater Yellowstone communities in Idaho, Wyoming and Montana. These same communities depend on visitors who increasingly come to watch wildlife in the park. From the outside, development creeps into wildlife habitat and threatens to interrupt or degrade the edges of the ecosystem.

If Yellowstone is the engine that drives Greater Yellowstone and the sprawling neighbor whose pets roam into others' backyards, it is also an ideological battleground. Some believed this gem's greatest beauty lay in its undisturbed ruggedness. Others saw opportunity swimming in the blue waters of hot springs. In the 1880s and 1890s, railroads and concessionaires fought to build empires in Yellowstone National Park. In the 1920s, irrigators in Wyoming, Montana and Idaho campaigned to raid Yellowstone National Park waters. Philosophical and political camps courted Congress like suitors vying for the hand of a maiden princess. Each time, park defenders narrowly won the battles.

Yellowstone National Park's little neighbor, Grand Teton National Park, is no less a study in the science of ecology married to the realities of politics. Because Teton Park was pieced together through decades of hard-fought political battles, some call it a bastardized national park. Within its boundaries, Grand Teton not only allows livestock grazing, but it also contains dude ranches, a commercial airport and a major highway. It is also the only national park that allows elk hunting. Within the boundaries of this 310,000-acre park are 103 private tracts of land. Jackson Lake, the largest in Grand Teton, was dammed in the early 1900s to supply irrigation water to eastern Idaho farmers. In the 1980s the lake was emptied and the dam raised to hold more water. Grand Teton also allows water-skiing and rafting on some of its waters.

Today, Grand Teton is still dealing with issues — often controversial — born of its patchwork past. For example, a proposed expansion of the Jackson Airport, which exists on land leased to the county by Grand Teton Park, more fits the needs of Jackson business people than the best interests of a national park. With each year that passes, private inholdings become more valuable and less attainable by the Park Service. Development on those properties threatens to mar the park's natural landscape. All but one of the grazing leases extended to leaseholders when Grand Teton Park added valley land to its boundaries in 1950 would have been terminated in 1997. But the leases were extended by the park superintendent because of open space concerns. Their home ranches and hay lands lie on the edge of Jackson and provide a pastoral landscape uninterrupted by buildings — a vanishing commodity in the midst of rampant development. Without summer range to graze their cattle, the ranch operations would no longer be profitable. If these ranchers sell their land, homes would likely sprout amidst the ranchlands.

Since its earliest days, theorists have struggled with grand ideas while front-line Yellowstone managers struggled with a paradox: how to impose some kind of civilized order to protect the primitive value of the park. With no budget and no laws to back them, civilian superintendents were hard-pressed.

INSIDERS' TIP

Interested in Western history? The 237,000-square-foot Buffalo Bill Historical Center in Cody, Wyoming, is a treasure trove of Western art and artifacts. See our Attractions chapter for more about the BBHC.

The Top of Mt. Washburn, Yellowstone National Park.
Reached via Union Pacific.

Photo: Courtesy Robert Bower

An early postcard depicts travel to the top of Mount Washburn and Yellowstone visitors.

When Army troops brought order in 1886, they paved the way for a whole new set of battles: the fight to protect lands outside the park from development. They won the first round in 1891 with the formation of the forest reserves. In 1898, they scored more points when the reserves received administrative funding from Congress. In 1905, President Theodore Roosevelt furthered protection of wildlands by creating the U.S. Forest Service. In 1964, park supporters won further protection of many forest lands through the Wilderness Act. In January 1998, the Forest Service announced a moratorium on all logging and road-building across 33 million acres of national forest at the time unprotected from commercial activity. Forest officials said managers needed a "sort of time out" to assess which lands need to be protected for recreation and which set aside for logging and other uses. But as conservationists march against environmentally unfriendly development on public lands, homes and fences on private property push into Greater Yellowstone's valleys and canyons.

Each generation's advances have made their mark on the park. Consider this: It's possible to sit at a family dinner with some kin who toured the park on horseback, some who were in the first cars to ply its roads and others who first "visited" the park via the Internet. Changeless as Old Faithful may be, our experience of it has changed rapidly. Earlier in the century, bicyclists and car owners clamored outside the gates for admittance to the park. In 1915, when automobiles finally drove through Yellowstone National Park gates, they carried 51,895 visitors — more than twice as many as the year before. More visitors brought bigger management problems, and the battle to balance public pleasure with wilderness protection — always a dilemma — began in earnest.

With no formula for finding that balance, Yellowstone became a laboratory in which managers learned by trial and error. Officials are still grappling with how best to prevent visitors from loving the wilderness to death. Because it is a protected and relatively intact ecosystem, the park has also become a laboratory for learning about wildlife, wildfire, wilderness and ecosystem management.

Finally, Yellowstone is a land of inspiration. Artists have tried to capture it in paintings, sketches and photographs. And writers have filled the pages of more than 8,000 books and articles about it. Studying the multihued Grand Canyon of the Yellowstone River at sunset or gazing at geysers through the foggy mists of winter inspires awe. Everywhere you turn in the park is a blessed reminder that this mysterious place is truly wild, uncontrollable and full of surprises.

Trappers and Miners and Discovery

Our history of Yellowstone and Grand Teton parks begins with the white man's first glimpses of this remarkable land. Before white men pénetrated its mountains, though, other humans roamed this land as long ago as 10,000 years. Those Paleo Indians eventually led to the Native American tribes found in the region by early explorers. By the time Meriwether Lewis and William Clark made their expedition in 1805, the Shoshone-Bannock, the Crow and the Blackfeet tribes inhabited different areas of Greater Yellowstone. In addition, the Nez Perce, Gros Ventre and Arapahoes regularly traveled through it. A band of Shoshone called Sheepeaters were the only Native Americans to call today's Yellowstone National Park home year-round.

Isolated from civilization, and protected naturally by the rugged mountains that ringed it, the Yellowstone Plateau remained pretty much a mystery to Euro-Americans into the 1860s. By then, word of its fantastic spouting geysers and fuming hot springs had trickled eastward. But descriptions of the rumbling earth beneath its scorched crust and the sulphurous gases billowing from below were received with the same skepticism as modern-day reports of UFO sightings.

Word of the mysterious country may first have reached Washington, D.C., in 1805, the same year Lewis and Clark led their expedition up the Missouri River north of Greater Yellowstone. Officially named by Lewis and Clark that same year, the Yellowstone River was apparently first given its moniker by Native Americans, then translated by French fur trappers. The name refers to the golden sandstone cliffs of the river's lower course. On Lewis and Clark's return trip in 1806, the expedition split up, and Clark set out to find the headwaters of the Yellowstone River. He never made it. Instead, he crossed through the beaver-rich Gallatin Valley near present-day Bozeman, then over into the Livingston area. From there he and his men built canoes and traveled down the Yellowstone to the Missouri River, missing the Mammoth Terraces by only 50 miles.

John Colter, a veteran of the Lewis and Clark Expedition, is credited by many historians as being the first white man to enter Yellowstone. In the winter of 1807-08, Colter made an epic 500-mile trip from the Bighorn River to the Shoshone River near present-day Cody, down to the Wind River and west into Jackson Hole. From there, he apparently crossed into Teton Valley, then headed up onto the Yellowstone Plateau and back over what was later named Colter Pass into the Bighorn Basin. But Colter and other trappers who followed were often uneducated and held little influence with anyone other than their fellow mountain men. Later mountain men like Jim Bridger, an accomplished storyteller (with little else to do, spinning yarns became an art around trapper campfires), probably didn't help the Yellowstone cause any. Bridger had a reputation for fantastic embellishment.

If folks back East weren't heeding stories about eerie geysers, they did listen closely to tales of a country crawling with beaver. By the 1820s, large brigades of trappers had worked their way into Yellowstone country. In 1818, a brigade led by Donald MacKenzie found its way to the headwaters of the Snake River. In 1822, William Ashley, who popularized the mountain-man rendezvous, led 100 men west. After wintering at the mouth of the Yellowstone River, many of them headed south through the Bighorn Basin, then into Jackson Hole. Among Ashley's men were notables like Bridger, Jedediah Smith, Thomas Fitzpatrick, William Sublette and David Jackson, who wintered in "the Hole," hence Jackson's Hole, a place that remained largely unpopulated until the 1870s.

Canadian, American and English fur trading companies vied with one another for beaver pelts made precious by European hat fashions. Competition among trappers was fierce, so fierce that some vowed to trap areas into "deserts," leaving no beaver for their competitors. The pelts were worth as much as $6 apiece. But the price of adventure was higher. Living by their wits, they fought the elements

Photo: Courtesy Robert Bower

The track of the Oregon Short Line (Union Pacific) reached Yellowstone National Park's western gateway in 1908 and brought visitors to the park for 60 years.

and unfriendly Indians. It's no wonder they looked forward each year to the rendezvous, which began in 1825. At this annual event held on the Green River and in Pierre's Hole (present-day Driggs, Idaho), all mountain men and Indians gathered with their pelts at a prearranged spot where they traded their furs for another year's supplies. For a week or more mountain men and Native Americans celebrated. They drank, caroused, feasted, swapped stories and ran horse races.

While towns, mountains, wildernesses and rivers have been named after these early trappers, it may be Osborne Russell who left behind the greatest legacy. A farm boy from Maine, Russell was one of the few literate trappers. His journals, published in 1955 as *Journals of a Trapper*, describe the country and give glimpses of his life from 1834 to 1843. Russell came to Yellowstone country with the Columbia River Fishing and Trading Company led by Nathaniel Wyeth, a Boston ice merchant. Wyeth led 40 men with freighting goods to a rendezvous on Ham's Fork of the Green River. When he arrived, he found another supplier had beaten him there. Stuck with wagons full of unmarketable goods, Wyeth continued on and established Fort Hall, site of today's Shoshone-Bannock Indian Reservation south of Blackfoot, Idaho.

About the time beaver were disappearing, wagonloads of settlers took up their epic migration along the Oregon Trail to the south. The discovery of gold in California brought even more people, who eventually fanned out into Washington, Idaho and Montana. Looking for their own mother lode, they scoured the streams of the Rockies. Here and there prospectors hit pay dirt outside the present-day park. To the north in Virginia City, Montana, miners found gold — lots of it — in 1863. Three years later, they found another strike to the west at Leesburg, Idaho. In 1870, two years before Yellowstone would become the nation's first national park, Bart Henderson and four partners staked their claims to a strike in what would become Cooke City, Montana.

Providence protected the heart of Yellowstone country from gold discoveries. Like trapping brigades hunting beaver, disillusioned miners came from the California and Colorado gold fields. Southerners and Easterners came to escape economic depression and the aftermath of the Civil War. A few penetrated the mountains that surrounded the Yellowstone Plateau. Walter DeLacy and his

41-man prospecting party followed the Snake River from Jackson Hole, searching for gold at the river's headwaters. They found only steaming holes, yawning river canyons and thundering waterfalls. Disappointed, they moved on.

Some folks gave up looking for gold and found a way to earn a living by supplying miners with food, firewood, lumber and other necessities. A few ranched and raised beef or garden produce. Others milked cows and supplied dairy products. Still others did laundry or ran hotels, saloons and stores. In 1868, the Bottler Brothers took up the first homestead in the Yellowstone Valley across from a small strike at Emigrant Gulch. To the west of the park at Henry's Lake, Gilman Sawtell established a ranch at Staley's Springs. Sawtell made a booming business of spearing trout from the lake, packing them in ice then hauling them by wagon over Raynolds Pass to Virginia City, where he sold them to miners. A handful of men built toll bridges and ferries at strategic places on area rivers. In 1871, Collins Baronett built a bridge across the Yellowstone River near Lamar Junction, then charged

Yellowstone Fires of 1988

Talk to residents in communities surrounding Yellowstone National Park and many of them still smolder at the mention of the fires of 1988. Fueled by more than 100 years worth of dead and fallen trees and fanned by high winds, there was no stopping the fires that stormed like an angry army across Yellowstone National Park. Thousands of people and countless planes, helicopters, bulldozers and tanker trucks tried. The federal government spent $120 million in the attempt. Despite those efforts, 56 fires burned 1.4 million acres in Yellowstone National Park and adjacent Forest Service lands from mid-June until mid-October. One million of those acres were within the park. In the end it was Mother Nature herself who put out the fires she had mostly started. Snowfall finally doused the flames firefighters had vainly battled all summer.

The lightning-ignited fires (three of them were man-caused) caught everyone by surprise. The largest fire since 1972, when a let-burn policy was instituted in the park, had been 7,600 acres. From 1972 until 1988, 235 naturally caused fires occurred in the park. With no attempts to suppress them, they charred an average of only 240 acres each. Until 1988, the largest fire in the park's 125-year history had been 18,000 acres.

In their wake, the blazes left much of the park's forest lands blackened and its meadows burned. When spring came Mother Nature showed her amazing powers of regeneration. Amidst the charred logs that littered the landscape, bright green spears of grass poked up through the ground. Wildflowers followed. As people watched for other signs of hope, they weren't disappointed. Tiny lodgepole seedlings, unlocked by the fire's heat, sprouted by the gazillions. Without the fire most of the seeds would have stayed locked up inside the cones, unable to sprout. Some lodgepole cones need the heat of fire to make them open so that the seeds can do their job. At the same time fire was opening cones, it was also sweeping away clutter on the ground, creating an open space where the seedlings could grow. Scientists have since learned that a mosiaic of fire behavior had created a patchwork of plant communities that is much more typical Of a healthy lodgepole pine community.

— continued on next page

In the meantime, the former forest lands, now opened to light, are providing more feed for rodents, birds and larger mammals. Since the fires of '88, other interesting surprises have come to light. For example, aspen groves, which usually regenerate only from underground suckers, sprouted by the trillions from suckers and from seeds. During the fires people feared wildlife populations would be devastated. But a post-fire count turned up only about 350 animals burned by fire. That winter, though, about 8,000 elk died, partially because their winter forage had burned, but also because the drought had prevented its growth.

Eleven years after the devastating fires, scientists are still watching the park to learn more about fire and its role in the ecosystem. It has become a laboratory for watching natural processes at work. As they struggle with the adverse effects of 100 years of fire suppression in national forests throughout the Rockies, they hope that Yellowstone's story will give them clues about how to handle fire outside the park.

Photo: Courtesy Robert Bower

A firefighter sprays down the roof of the Old Faithful Inn.

Cooke City miners $1 per man or mule to cross his bridge. To the west, Matt Taylor built a toll bridge across the Snake River at Eagle Rock (present-day Idaho Falls) in 1863. Much later, in 1894, Bill Menor built a ferry crossing on the Snake River near Moose in Jackson Hole. For those who wanted to stay, there were plenty of ways to eke out a living.

The Explorers

Inch by inch, word of Yellowstone crawled eastward across the plains and rivers. And one by one, exploratory expeditions turned back before they had reached the plateau. The U.S. Corps of Topographical Engineers failed in two attempts during the 1850s. Capt. William F. Raynolds of the corps traveled the southern and western outskirts of today's Yellowstone National Park in 1859, looking for a route over the rugged mountains. By the time he reached today's Targhee Pass, inclement weather and a tight schedule forced Raynolds to forgo the exploration and instead head north to the Three Forks of the Missouri River. In 1865, Father Francis Kuppens trekked into Yellowstone with a band of Piegan Indians. Impressed with the country, he told Acting Territorial Governor Thomas Meagher about it in such glowing terms that he organized an expedition in 1867. But when Meagher died mysteriously the expedition was abandoned.

The heart of Yellowstone seemed to defy discovery until 1869, when David E. Folsom, Charles W. Cook and William Peterson headed out from Bozeman on July 12. That winter, Folsom worked in Helena for Henry D. Washburn, surveyor general for the Montana Territory. Intrigued by Folsom's stories of Yellowstone, Washburn was itching to explore the fantastic country the next summer. Under military escort, he and a collection of men left Bozeman and followed Folsom's trail. Nathaniel Langford, a newly appointed agent for Jay Cooke of the Northern Pacific Railroad, was among the party. History suggests that it was Langford who promoted the expedition. Cooke, curious to know more about Yellowstone country, may even have helped finance it. The party's troubles began after they chose to follow the east side of Yellowstone Lake. They ran into tree thickets, bogs, uncrossable rivers and unstable ground before stumbling onto Old Faithful just as it was erupting. Along the way, they literally lost one of their party, Truman C. Everts, whose ultimate rescue stands out in history as a tale of man's ability to survive. When two men from the expedition finally found Everts 37 days later crawling up a hillside, they at first mistook him for a wounded bear. His diet of thistle roots had reduced him to a skeletal shadow. The balls of his frostbitten feet were worn to the bone, and he had burned his thigh in a hot spring. Miraculously, Everts survived his wilderness experience.

The story of the Washburn expedition swept through newspapers across the country, but it was Langford who, through a series of lectures in the East, stirred up real interest in Yellowstone. Ferdinand V. Hayden, head of the U.S. Geological Survey of the Territories, was the next explorer to catch Yellowstone fever. Hayden pulled enough congressional strings to secure $40,000 for a full-blown expedition that included topographers, scientists, artists Thomas Moran and Henry Elliott and photographer William H. Jackson. Traveling by train in mid-May of 1871, Hayden set up a rendezvous camp in Ogden, Utah. On June 11, the party rode north to Fort Hall, then on to Bozeman where they were joined at the last minute by another expedition led by Capt. John W. Barlow of the Army Corps of Engineers. The two parties spent just over a month in what is now Yellowstone National Park.

It was Hayden who first publicly pressed for a national park that would preserve a piece of the frontier for everyone. Historians suggest Jay Cooke encouraged the idea. Cooke foresaw Yellowstone as a tourist destination that would attract visitors from around the world. Their vehicle would be his train. Armed with Moran's colorful paintings and the best of Jackson's photographs, Hayden had no trouble pushing the park through Congress. On March 1, 1872, President Ulysses S. Grant signed the as-yet-unnamed park into being.

Railroads

Full of wonders so incredible that newspapermen refused to publish early accounts of it for fear of being called liars, Yellowstone became a magnet for explorers and exploiters alike. From the north, east, south and west, railroads raced to lay their tracks to Yellowstone's boundaries — inside them if they could. First came the Northern Pacific.

Delayed for a decade by an economic depression, it was 1882 before sweaty crews pounded the last spike in the rails that led to Livingston, Montana. From that budding railroad town, the tracks turned south and stopped 3 miles short of the park boundary at Cinnabar. A cantankerous miner, who refused to relinquish claims blocking the railroad's path, prevented it from going all the way to Gardiner. Finally, in 1903 the Northern Pacific rolled into Gardiner. That same year, President Theodore Roosevelt dedicated the monumental 50-foot-high Roosevelt Arch at Gardiner's park entrance.

While the tracks stopped at the park's boundary, the railroads' power did not. Well-connected to Washington, D.C., officials of the Northern Pacific had enough political clout to seat and unseat park superintendents like Langford and Philetus W. Norris. But they couldn't accomplish their greatest desire: to ram those railroad tracks right through the

INSIDERS' TIP

Jackson may have been the first and the only town in the nation to have an all-woman government, including the sheriff. When Mayor Grace Miller and her four-woman council took over in 1920, they found the city coffers held only $200. Within two weeks, they had collected $2,000, which they immediately applied to community improvements.

4509. Fishing Cone, Yellowstone Lake, Yellowstone National Park

Photo: Courtesy Robert Bower

Yellowstone visitors fishing from the fishing cone on Yellowstone Lake as depicted on a postcard from the early tourist years of the park.

park. For more than a decade, Northern Pacific officials fought, fussed and finagled to get the job done, but Yellowstone National Park supporters like Sen. George Graham Vest of Missouri blocked their path. The congressional battle over the rails was costly. It prevented other bills from passing — bills that would have granted more money and better management to the park.

While the Northern Pacific fought park supporters in one arena, in another the railroad was one of the park's greatest allies. The Northern Pacific and later railroads advertised the scenic wonders and brought America to its first national park. Those who came fell in love with Yellowstone and returned home among its growing throng of supporters.

Until 1901, when the Burlington Northern reached Cody at the East Entrance, and 1908 when the Oregon Short Line pulled into West Yellowstone, the Northern Pacific hauled almost all tourists who came from the East. In 1927, well after rail travel had declined, the Chicago, Milwaukee and St. Paul Railroad built a 40-mile line to Gallatin Gateway, where it erected the huge and very grand Gallatin Gateway Inn. (See both our Restaurants and Hotels, Motels and Cabins chapters for more information on this restored inn.) The Chicago and Northwestern Railroad served Lander, Wyoming, 150 miles southeast of Yellowstone National Park, after the advent of the automobile. From Lander, tour buses took visitors to the Tetons and to Yellowstone National Park.

The affordable Ford, carrying families, tents and supplies, eventually put a dent in railroad profits — so much so that by World War II some began to call it quits. The Oregon Short Line held on until 1959.

Taking Care of Tourists in the Wilderness

By the time the Northern Pacific reached Cinnabar, the National Hotel at Mammoth was unfinished but ready to receive guests. As the park's road system grew under the supervision of the Army Corps of Engineers, the Northern Pacific began to sell its customers a coupon package for touring the park. While in the park, coupon holders could stay at hotels and ride on stages owned by concessionaires that were Northern Pacific affiliates. After a night at the National Hotel, they would pile into a caravan of four-horse, 11-passenger stagecoaches spaced 500 feet apart to help reduce the dust. Packed into the stagecoaches for the day, passengers were at the mercy of the drivers, many of whom were creative cussers as well as inveterate storytellers. A few were drunks to boot. Most gave good tours. The stagecoach rides were not only bumpy, dusty and crowded, but also dangerous, with frequent runaways, occasional wrecks and at least four holdups.

For six glorious days, coupon holders explored, gawked, dined, danced and bumped through the wilderness before returning to Mammoth and then the train terminal. Along the route, accommodations ranged from rustic, to say the least, to downright civilized as hotels sprang up to meet the needs of the region's latest visitors. Until 1891 when the modern Fountain Hotel was built, tourists spent the first night at the Firehole Hotel, where the tiny rooms held two beds and had canvas walls. At other places visitors slept like sardines on the plank floors of primitive hotels with broken windows. The Fountain, on the other hand, housed 350 guests, had steam heat and electric lights and used hot spring water for baths. The Lake and Canyon hotels, two other lavishly grand hotels built from 1889 to 1891, also became regular stops. The Canyon, which measured a mile around its base, burned in 1959 after its demolition had begun. Old Faithful, the queen of park hotels with its giant Douglas fir and rock construction, didn't rise from the wilderness floor until 1903.

In addition to the geysers, there was another attraction. By the 1880s, bears had come out of the forest to feed at hotel dumps. Each evening, spectators gathered on benches to watch as hotel keepers fed them garbage. Eventually a mounted ranger gave lectures to the crowds while the bears ate garbage. All but one of the hotel shows stopped in the 1930s after one black bear chased another into the grandstand.

In 1893, William Wallace Wylie, a school superintendent from Bozeman, was granted a two-year permit to operate tent camps in Yellowstone National Park. The candy-striped tents, Wylie's hallmark, were staffed by college students and teachers. Wylie's camps had sleeping tents clustered around huge kitchen, dining and reception tents. To the chagrin of other concessionaires, Wylie offered a seven-day tour for $35, while the Yellowstone Park Association, a concessionaire owned by Northern Pacific Railroad interests, charged $50 for six days. His employees, as well as those of park hotels, also interpreted park features. Another group of travelers, contemptuously called "sagebrushers," came well-equipped from neighboring states in their own horse-drawn wagons and bypassed hotels and tent camps altogether.

Order in the Park

From 1872 to 1886, civilian superintendents struggled to maintain order despite the fact that Congress underfunded park management and there were no laws on the books to discourage lawlessness. Hunters blatantly killed elk by the thousands, while would-be concessionaires squatted at major attractions. Visitors hacked away at geysers and hauled the pieces home in satchels. They carted off whole petrified trees and skinny-dipped in hot springs. They stuffed geysers with logs, rocks, handkerchiefs, clothes, everything — then sat back and watched them blow. Why wouldn't they? There was nobody there to tell them otherwise. Nathaniel Langford, who was superintendent from 1872 until 1877, made three quick trips to the park and wrote one report during his tenure.

His successor, Philetus W. Norris, served until 1882. An energetic pioneer-scientist, he managed to get enough money from Congress to build the Norris Road to some of the geyser basins. He also collected crates of geo-

INSIDERS' TIP

Western novelist Owen Wister, author of *The Virginian*, first came to Jackson Hole in 1887 as a big-game hunter and returned for years after that. Many of his characters are said to have been fashioned after Jackson Hole old-timers.

logical and biological specimens, which he shipped to the Smithsonian. Three more civilians served from 1882 until 1886, but apathy and avarice combined to create lawlessness so scandalous that Congress refused to fund the park in 1886. Fortunately, two years earlier Sen. George Graham Vest of Missouri had won passage of the Civil Sundry Appropriations Bill, which allowed the Secretary of the Interior to request military assistance in protecting the park.

The military's presence brought almost immediate order to the park. Even without the enforcement provisions of the Lacey Act of 1894, the soldiers doggedly pursued would-be poachers using secret telegraph codes and informers to catch up with them. By the 1890s they operated from a network of 19 outposts supplemented with 16 snowshoe cabins for winter patrols. The Lacey Act, promoted by an outdoor journalist who witnessed the capture of a notorious bison poacher, made it a federal offense to break park laws. It called for stiff fines and lengthy imprisonment for serious violations.

In 1916, when the National Park Service was established, political shenanigans kept the 450-soldier post at Mammoth for two more years. The much smaller 50-ranger staff couldn't compensate for the loss of the soldiers, who trekked 5 miles to Gardiner where they found alcohol, brothels and venereal disease.

When the Park Service finally took over, many of the soldiers became rangers. By the 1930s, there were about 71 rangers, 29 of them year-round. They checked cars at the entrance gates, patrolled popular areas on foot or horseback and highways by motorcycle. They fought forest fires, investigated accidents, administered first aid, took care of problem bears, checked campgrounds and did paperwork. During the off-season, full-time rangers caught up on maintenance, worked the buffalo herd, put up hay for horses, bison and elk, patrolled the park's perimeter and killed predators such as the wolf and coyote. In winter, they manned outposts and patrolled the park on skis.

Horace Albright, Yellowstone National Park superintendent from 1919 to 1929 (a period when visitation jumped from 62,000 to 260,000 per year), cracked down on lawbreakers including bootleggers and speeders. He also began an official interpretive branch of rangers. And he built a strong alliance with concessionaires who, he said, provided the services that the park's poor funding could not. The relationship between the park and concessionaires was one of mutual dependence. As long as the concessionaires paid their 4 percent to the park, Albright was happy.

The Car Paves the Way for Millions

Car owners honked their horns at park gates for four years before getting the green light. When the gates opened in 1915, more than 50,000 mostly middle-class Americans flooded into Yellowstone National Park. Unlike the upper class who had ridden the rails in style with trunks full of clothes for dinner and dancing, these working people loaded their aunts, uncles, brothers, cousins and children into Fords and packed for fun. They strapped tents, washtubs, pots, pans, chairs and bedding to their cars, tucked a few extra tires and some gasoline into the trunks, and headed west on the Yellowstone Highway. In 1911, just one year after Henry Ford put motorized wheels under America's appetite for adventure, a "pathfinder crew" from the Minnesota Automobile Association scouted out a practical route from St. Paul to Bozeman. Pieced together with two-rut rural and county roads, the road roughly followed today's Interstates 90 and 94. Plate-sized orange circles painted on rocks, barns, logs and fenceposts marked the route. That same year, another crew blazed a route from Yellowstone to Glacier National Park in northern Montana.

Inside the park, stagecoach drivers and transportation concessionaires cussed the coughing, sputtering, lurching contraptions, saying they'd not only scare the horses but they'd also be the ruination of Yellowstone. Transportation through the park was big business for three companies: the Yellowstone and Monida of West Yellowstone, the Cody-Sylvan Pass Stagecoach Company of Pahaska Tepee and The Yellowstone Transportation Company out of Gardiner. Together they owned a formidable fleet of wagons and

Greater Yellowstone Benchmarks

Research by Teri Anderson of the Idaho Falls Post Register

1805-06 — The Lewis and Clark Expedition passes west and east through Greater Yellowstone, missing the Mammoth Hot Springs by 50 miles.

1807 — John Colter explores the area that will eventually become Yellowstone National Park.

1820s to 1840s – Fur trappers scour Greater Yellowstone, trapping beaver for their pelts, which were used for hats in Europe and the Eastern United States.

1869 — Cook-Folsom-Peterson Expedition of 1869 enters Yellowstone National Park, seeing geysers and hot pools. The three men return to Montana territory with tales that many doubted.

1870 — Gen. Henry Washburn and Nathaniel Langford, who later became the first superintendent of the park, are among the members of the official exploration party. Old Faithful is discovered and named.

1871 — The Hayden Expedition including artist Thomas Moran and photographer William Jackson, penetrates today's Yellowstone National Park. Moran's paintings and Jackson's photos help convince Congress to preserve the area.

March 1, 1872 — President Ulysses S. Grant signs the National Park Act, which creates Yellowstone National Park. It is the first national park in the world.

1877 — The Nez Perce Indians, led by Chief Joseph, pass through Yellowstone during a retreat after they were routed in a series of summer battles, losing 300 people. The retreat is later hailed as a masterful tactical display.

1882 — Gen. Phillip Sheridan tours Yellowstone National Park. Appalled by wildlife slaughter in the park, he plants the first seeds for Greater Yellowstone idea by promoting park expansion to encompass wildlife migratory and wintering grounds.

1883 — Chester A. Arthur becomes first U.S. President to visit Yellowstone National Park.

1885 — The Army Corps of Engineers completes Yellowstone National Park's Golden Gate Bridge.

1886 — The U.S. Army takes over Yellowstone National Park's administration.

1888 — Excelsior Geyser, which erupted up to 300 feet in height, resumes major eruptions.

1891 — Congress passes the Forest Reserve Act, and President Benjamin Harrison creates the Yellowstone National Park Timberland Preserve, precursor to today's national forests and a key component of Greater Yellowstone.

1894 — The Lacey Act is passed to "protect the birds and animals in Yellowstone National Park, and to punish crimes in said park." The act led to the end of hunting, with heavy penalties for poaching game in Yellowstone.

1895 — Army begins predator control by poisoning coyotes.

1900 — About 9,000 people visit the park this year.

1897 — President Grover Cleveland creates the Teton Forest Reserve, which encompasses much of today's Jackson Hole and Grand Teton National Park.

— continued on next page

1901 to mid-1950s — The world's largest trout hatchery operates on the shores of Yellowstone Lake.

1902 — Park officials count only 22 bison.

1903 — President Theodore Roosevelt dedicates the Roosevelt Arch on August 24.

1904 — Old Faithful Inn, the world's largest log hostelry, opens.

1905 — President Theodore Roosevelt creates the U.S. Forest Service and appoints Gifford Pinchot as its first director.

1915 — First automobiles are officially allowed to enter Yellowstone.

1915 — Charles Hamilton acquires Klamer's Store.

1916 — President Woodrow Wilson signs Act of Congress on August 25 creating the National Park Service as a bureau of the Department of the Interior. Shortly thereafter, civilian superintendents are appointed, replacing the park's military overseers.

1927 to 1943 — John D. Rockefeller, hoping to help create Grand Teton Park, buys thousands of acres of private land in Jackson Hole.

1929 — Congress creates Grand Teton National Park, which includes only the Teton Mountains.

1932 — Pelican control practices come to a halt in Yellowstone National Park. Hundreds of eggs were removed, and scores of young pelicans were killed between 1924 and 1932.

1941 — Park officials end bear feeding shows at Canyon. The shows, during which the bears were fed garbage, began as a way to entertain visitors during the days when the Army controlled the park.

1943 — President Franklin Roosevelt creates the 221,000-acre Jackson Hole National Monument.

1946 — Bison are fed their last hay at the Buffalo Ranch in Lamar Valley.

1948 — Yellowstone National Park visitation exceeds 1 million for the first time.

1950 — Jackson Hole National Monument is incorporated into Grand Teton Park.

1950 — Yellowstone National Park officials remove debris from Morning Glory Pool. Among the debris is $90 in coins, towels and clothes and 100 handkerchiefs.

1958 — Canyon Hotel closes.

1959 — Earthquake causes considerable damage, including a rock slide at Golden Gate Bridge. The quake's epicenter is at Hebgen Lake, Montana.

1965 — For the first time, the number of park visitors exceeds 2 million.

1973 – Yellowstone National Park managers institute catch-and-release fishing.

1988 — Fires sweep the park.

1997 — Yellowstone turns 125 years old with an average of 30,000 to 40,000 visitors each day of the summer.

---

coaches, more than 1,000 horses, and employed huge crews of drivers, blacksmiths, freighters and herd tenders.

Cars not only drove all the horses and stagecoaches off park roads, but they also forced the restructuring of Yellowstone concessionaires. In the fall of 1916, National Park Service Director Stephen T. Mather called the concessionaires to Washington, D.C. The reorganization forced concessionaires to make major investments just when World War I was keeping Americans closer to home. The Yellowstone Park Transportation Company, suddenly designated as the sole park transportation concessionaire, had to buy 116 motor buses. Frank J. Haynes, owner of several hotels and other businesses, had to sell them all and become the photographic concessionaire. The Yellowstone Park Hotel Company became the sole hotel concessionaire, while Wylie Permanent Camps merged with Shaw and Powell. Because cars could carry visitors much farther in a day, several of the hotels, tent camps and lunch stations were abandoned.

Concessionaires

Let's take a minute to talk about concessionaires. While they reaped big benefits as co-conductors of the region's economic engine, national events more than once took the steam from their smokestacks. From 1900 to 1929, concessionaire profits were high — in some cases outrageously high. For some, though, profits were barely enough to offset the lean years of the Great Depression and World War II. Gas and tire rationing, combined with the scarcity of men, dried visitor numbers to a trickle. In 1943, only 64,000 visitors toured Yellowstone National Park, the lowest number since 1919, and down from 561,000 in 1941.

Concessionaires boarded up their facilities and left them to weather the harsh elements of Yellowstone during the war years. Already crying for repairs and upgrades before the war, they were fairly screaming for attention by 1946 when 815,000 war-weary Americans swarmed into the park. The park's chief concessionaire, The Yellowstone Park Company, wasn't prepared, and the owners, strapped for cash, were reluctant to spend money on improvements. Complaints about poor service, bad food, wretched housing and overpriced accommodations filtered into congressional offices, newspapers and public meetings. Wyoming state officials were so concerned about the deplorable state of the region's economic engine that in 1955 they made a bid to buy out the park's chief concessionaire.

Operating in a crisis mode, the National Park Service set out to deal with its biggest dilemma since the creation of Yellowstone National Park — the rising flood of humanity. In 1955, the Park Service outlined a 10-year plan for updating park facilities and called it Mission 66. Roads, restrooms and campgrounds threatened to crumble under the strain of the increased use which had risen to more than a million each year. The Park Service and concessionaires would share the cost of construction and renovations to concession facilities. A period of growth and construction followed. Power and telephone lines were updated, and an FM radio communication system was installed. Permanent and seasonal housing was improved and expanded for the growing staff. And a grade school and clinic were built at Mammoth.

Meanwhile, the Yellowstone Park Company searched desperately for a buyer. In 1966 they found one: the Goldfield Corporation which later became entangled with a conglomerate calling itself General Host. Concession facilities and service spiraled downward for the next decade. In fact, conditions at park hotels and restaurants owned by General Host were so wretched and drew so many complaints that in 1976 the Interior Department began an in-depth study of the park's concessions. The results prompted the government to cancel General Host's franchise in 1979. Despite the fact that the company failed to invest $10 million in its facilities as agreed, General Host sold its holdings to the U.S. government for $19 million — a profit of nearly $13 million.

Trans World Corporation took over the company and operated as TWA Services on a two-year trial basis. The company did such a good job that it was granted a 30-year lease. In the 1980s, a 10-year restoration project

INSIDERS' TIP

In August 1877, the Nez Perce's Chief Joseph led 800 men, women and children and 2,000 horses through Yellowstone National Park in a desperate attempt to reach Canada. At the end of his 1,500-mile flight, which included 18 engagements and four major battles, Chief Joseph made his famous speech: "Hear me, my chiefs! I am tired. My heart is sick and sad. From where the sun now stands I will fight no more forever." He was only 40 miles from the Canadian border.

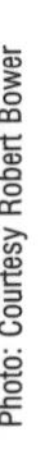
Photo: Courtesy Robert Bower

Keefer Island sits in the middle of the Snake River in downtown Idaho Falls — a piece of history essentially untouched by time.

brought the Lake Hotel back to life. And new accommodations, including a lodge at Grant Village, were built. TWA Services has since sold its lease to AmFac Parks and Resorts.

Wildlife, Wildfire and Wilderness Management Changes Definition

At the same time park managers grappled with ways to manage millions of people more closely, they began to realize that less management was in order for the wild pieces of Yellowstone. In the mid-1950s, they quit stocking the park's lakes and streams with fish. Since 1889, folks in federal fisheries agencies had stocked lakes with exotic fish while robbing native spawning beds to stock other streams across the country. In the 1970s, state managers outside the park followed the new trend toward natural fisheries. They also popularized and instituted catch-and-release fishing. Park managers today are committed to the animals that feed on fish — their needs come before those of visiting anglers.

Bear management also changed. By 1941, when park officials ended the last of the organized feeding shows, the bears had become more than a nuisance. They hung out on roads and held visitors up for tidbits of food. They lurked around campgrounds, broke into kitchens and tore apart cars looking for food. Like spoiled children with a big bite, they were quick to express their displeasure with uncooperative visitors. While feeding shows were officially stopped, visitors who knew where and when to look could find park dumps crawling with black bears and grizzlies.

Finally, in the 1960s, rangers figured out how to get rid of the visitors' favorite attraction. They cleaned up and closed the dumps, and devised bearproof trashcans. They removed and relocated the most aggressive bears and shooed the rest off to fend for themselves in the wild. For decades, critics showered park managers with acrimony. But, the bears not only survived, they thrived. Now managers grapple with ways to keep humans from bothering bears.

Elk, killed by the thousands each winter when poachers ruled Yellowstone, quickly multiplied under park protection. In the 1950s studies now disputed determined that the park's northern range could support 5,000 elk without being overgrazed. Today about 18,000 graze the same range, and overgrazing debates rage among managers. Before natural predators had made a comeback, managers were hard-pressed to find socially acceptable ways of checking the herd's growth. In the 1960s, they trapped and relocated thousands of elk, shot even more and used hunting seasons outside park boundaries to try to control the rest.

In that same decade, bison, which now number about 2,200, were released from their display pens, weaned from their winter ration of supplemental hay and turned loose to roam in the park. By 1900, bison numbers had dwindled to an alarming 25. Managers rounded them up, brought in breeding stock and began raising buffalo like cattle. Park employees raised hay in the Lamar Valley and fed it to the bison. They castrated all but a few of the males and kept some of the craggy creatures penned for display until their historic release.

These days you'll see bison wandering at will. In winter, especially severe winters, they migrate out of the park. Because they carry brucellosis, a venereal disease that causes cattle to abort, Montana passed a law in 1995 that allows the State Department of Livestock to capture and slaughter bison that leave the park. During the winter of 1995-96, more than 400 bison were destroyed. The following winter more than 1,000 were killed outside the park. Another estimated 500 died during that exceptionally severe winter. The bison wars, heated up by that year's death toll, aren't likely to subside soon.

The same year that Montanans began shooting stray buffalo, the U.S. Fish and Wildlife Service won a 20-year battle to put wolves back in the ecosystem. Ranchers, who fought wolf reintroduction with a vengeance, aren't so anxious for their recovery. Wolves were exterminated early in the century by park managers in order to protect elk and bison as well as livestock outside the park. Like their prey, wolves wander out of Yellowstone National Park. Already some have tangled with livestock.

Even fire was set free. In 1972, park managers implemented a "let-burn" policy for naturally caused fires. They suspected that the forest's health depended on fire to clean and prune it. That policy caused a firestorm of criticism in 1988 when dozens of major fires and countless smaller ones swept through Yellowstone National Park, leaving half of it burned to a crisp. Out of the blackened rubble rose some of this century's greatest lessons in the miracles of Mother Nature. Eleven years after the fire, scientists are still watching carefully and learning from the process of regrowth in Yellowstone.

Greater Yellowstone and the Battle for Grand Teton National Park

As early as 1882, Gen. Phillip Sheridan proposed a Greater Yellowstone — expansion of Yellowstone National Park to protect the winter range of its wildlife in general and its elk in particular. That Greater Yellowstone movement led to the piecemeal creation of the controversial Grand Teton National Park. The process took 33 years (from 1917 to 1950) to complete, although several small parcels have been added to the park since 1950.

The Greater Yellowstone movement didn't take off until 1917 when a 1,200-square-mile addition to Yellowstone National Park was proposed to the south. The addition, which encompassed lands already publicly held by the Forest Service, would have followed more natural boundaries: the Absaroka Range ridge to the Buffalo Fork of the Snake River, then west, south of Jackson, Leigh and Jenny lakes. In 1918, the expansion looked like it would pass Congress. But I.H. Larom, a recent graduate of Princeton University and a dude rancher

INSIDERS' TIP

For more about Yellowstone National Park's history, read *The Yellowstone Story* by Aubrey L. Haines.

near Cody, got wind of the movement and spurred the Wyoming Legislature into opposing the bill. For the next decade, efforts to expand Yellowstone were bound up in political knots tied mostly by livestock interests who used parts of the area for grazing. Wyoming officials were also concerned about turning National Forest lands over to the Park Service. A percentage of the receipts from grazing fees on forest lands helped pay for the operation of local schools. And Forest Service officials weren't happy about the prospect of having to deny cattlemen grazing rights.

In 1928, Sen. Gerald P. Nye apparently took Congress by surprise when he introduced a bill, not for the expansion of Yellowstone National Park but for the creation of a whole new park: Grand Teton National Park. The new park would encompass only the beautiful Teton Mountains, too steep and high for use by livestock interests. The bill passed and was signed into law on February 26, 1929. It was a beginning.

John D. Rockefeller Jr. was one person who wanted to see the whole area protected from commercial development. To that end, he formed the Snake River Land Company and bought up 35,000 acres ($2 million worth) of private bottom lands to donate to Grand Teton Park. What history books won't tell you, but local Jackson historians will, is that it was a group of local citizens that roped Rockefeller into the land purchases. According to local historians, Horace Albright, then former superintendent of Yellowstone National Park and retired director of the National Park Service, met with two ranchers, a banker and two others on July 26, 1936, in the Maude Noble Cabin at Menor's Ferry. The ranchers had learned that taking in dudes was more profitable than raising livestock in this high-elevation country. They saw that rampant and sloppy development could destroy the landscape of the pastoral life that high-paying Easterners sought on their dude ranches. Farsighted, they aimed to turn "the Hole" into a living museum of ranching and recreation. In addition to preserving the mountains and lakes, these ranchers wanted to protect their view of the Tetons.

Rockefeller bought the land between 1927 and 1943, but congressional and local opposition prevented Rockefeller from transferring the land to public ownership until 1949. Impatient with the stalemate, Rockefeller forced the issue by threatening in 1943 to sell the land on the open market. President Franklin Roosevelt made a decision: He set aside the 221,000-acre Jackson Hole National Monument by presidential decree.

Roosevelt's move began a whole new war. First, Congress passed a bill abolishing the monument, but Roosevelt vetoed it. Next, the state of Wyoming sued the Grand Teton National Park superintendent — and lost. Then Congress cut funding for the monument's maintenance. Finally, in 1950, all parties reached a compromise: The federal government would reimburse Teton County for taxes lost through the transfers from private to federal ownership. (Nearly 97 percent of Teton County is in federal ownership.) Livestock grazing in Grand Teton would be allowed for the lifetime of the existing leaseholders' heirs. Other existing uses would be allowed to continue. That same year, the Jackson Hole Monument was incorporated into Grand Teton Park.

Jackson Hole, inhabited by fur trappers from the 1820s to the 1840s, was settled in earnest by Mormons in the 1880s. From the late 1870s to the mid-1880s, horse thieves called the Hole home. The outlaws, led by William C. Teton Jackson and Harry Thompson, stole horses in Idaho and Utah, drove them to Jackson Hole for re-branding, then kept them in the remote valley until the brands healed. In 1885, Jackson was arrested, convicted and sent to prison. By the mid-1880s Jackson Hole was populated by others: tenacious farmers and ranchers clinging to their hard-won high-elevation land. By 1909, the

INSIDERS' TIP

Ask at the Old Faithful Inn about its regular historical tours of this monumental log and rock hotel built at the turn of the century.

town of Jackson claimed 200 residents, while the Jackson Hole population neared 1,500 inhabitants who picked up their mail at nine different post offices. By 1990, Jackson's permanent population had reached about 4,500, and the economy was based almost solely on recreation in nearby Grand Teton Park.

As in Yellowstone National Park, Grand Teton struggles to control burgeoning elk and bison populations. A bunch of 16 bison owned by Lawrence Rockefeller on his ranch near Moran grew to 380 and now roam the park. Rockefeller's fences couldn't contain them. By the spring of 1998, authorities expected their numbers to exceed 400 — the limit determined by park officials. Elk numbers are also growing and an in-park hunt each fall is failing to stabilize the population. The presence of wolves may influence herd population as the wolves establish themselves in the park ecosystem.

The Greater Yellowstone Ecosystem — And Beyond

Like a tiny seed that falls on fertile ground, the concept of a Greater Yellowstone Ecosystem was planted while Yellowstone National Park was still in its infancy. In the past 15 years it has grown so much that it's difficult to determine just when it sprouted into an idea big enough to be studied and named.

In 1983, when the Greater Yellowstone Coalition formed at the Teton Science School in Jackson, the concept, when spoken and promoted, was a dirty word. Now it rolls off unlikely tongues throughout the ecosystem and has been adopted by federal and state agencies. The Greater Yellowstone Coalition, a conservation organization headquartered in Bozeman, is one of the most successful environmental organizations in the country. The coalition leads conservation efforts to protect the ecosystem, monitoring, studying, coordinating and agitating for change every step of the way.

As technology and affluence allow man to creep closer to the park with ever more destructive tools, patrolling Yellowstone's legal boundaries is no longer enough. Just outside the park's boundaries, development threatens the ecosystem's waters and the park's thermal features. In 1990, for example, the Church Universal and Triumphant, a religious group headquartered near Gardiner, wanted to tap a geothermal feature on their land. Concerned because thermal areas in the United States and other countries have been ruined by outside tampering with connected systems, authorities studied the problem and determined that geothermal tapping outside the park could damage geothermal features inside it.

A proposed open pit-gold mine near Cooke City was blocked in 1996 by President Bill Clinton. Other development is crowding the park: oil and gas drilling, logging, mining, water and hydroelectric projects promoted by the National Energy Act of 1978, recreational resort and home developments and poaching.

Within park boundaries, authorities have their own management issues. Since the early 1970s, when Yellowstone National Park began opening from mid-December through February, winter use of Yellowstone National Park has increased so dramatically that streams of snowmobiles fill parts of the park with pollution on some days. Conservation groups have sued the park, which is working on an environmental impact statement to study and remedy the problems. The solutions won't come easily. West Yellowstone, the Snowmobile Capital of the World, would fall into instant and serious economic depression if snowmobiles were banned from the park.

For years, the Park Service has been studying ways to minimize traffic and control crowds on the park's dilapidated highways. The only seeming alternatives — limiting numbers or using buses — are unpopular. Other infrastructure, like the sewage system at Old Faithful, is decaying. In the meantime, federal budgets are declining.

Pine beetle epidemics that have infiltrated lodgepole stands in the park are now deemed good for the ecosystem and are no longer combatted with insecticides. But exotic weeds creeping into the park are a different story. And while fish are no longer planted, cutthroat-threatening lake trout released into Yellowstone Lake are caught and killed whenever possible.

Managing this 18-million-acre system, divided into three states, seven national forests, two national parks, three wildlife refuges, countless counties and even more towns, is the possibly impossible challenge of the future. In order to do so, each agency, and people in general, may somehow have to embrace a definition full of compromises that moves toward the wild center while maintaining communities and economies on the edges.

Since Yellowstone was first discovered, its challenges have always been about managing people — inside and outside the parks — and protecting the park. Much of that management has been dependent upon ever-changing politics often fanned by journalistic pens. That's as true today as it was in 1872, when Nathaniel Langford was named the first superintendent of what is now hailed by some as America's best idea. As national park managers and other residents of Greater Yellowstone look to the future, history will someday tell how successfully all grasped the idea of Yellowstone National Park and its little sister to the south, Grand Teton National Park.

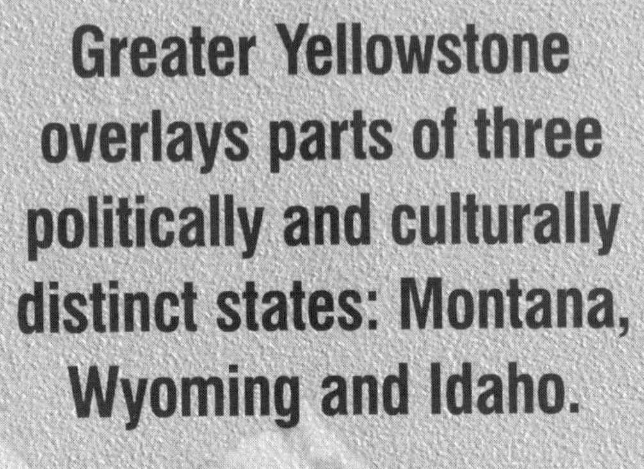
Greater Yellowstone
overlays parts of three
politically and culturally
distinct states: Montana,
Wyoming and Idaho.

Area Overview

Like your grandmother's handmade quilt, Greater Yellowstone consists of both pattern and piece. For many residents, the pieces — especially theirs — are easier to see. But look more closely: The pattern that connects us is rich indeed.

Greater Yellowstone overlays parts of three states: Montana, Wyoming and Idaho. Within each state exist politically and culturally distinct groups, most of whom rely on the land for their living or their lifestyle. In many cases, what would help one group make a living — for instance, diverting water from the Snake River to irrigate farmland — interferes with the livelihood or lifestyle of other groups, such as fishing guides and recreational boaters who feel they would be better served by an untapped, undammed river. And vice versa.

But state and economic pieces are just the beginning. Our region centers on two national parks, which are in turn buffered by parts of seven national forests. No single agency oversees these entities — each is managed independently and for different ends. National parks, for instance, are managed primarily for preservation of their special qualities and for visitor enjoyment. National forests are supposed to balance interests that range from recreation and timber to ranching and mining. Within each national forest are several ranger districts; each may strive for that balance in a different way. Then there are the Bureau of Land Management, which oversees some federal rangelands, and the Bureau of Reclamation, which has jurisdiction over some water-use issues associated with dams it built here. The U.S. Fish and Wildlife Service has partial jurisdiction here, too. Each state also has a fish and game agency and a state parks supervisory agency.

Like we said, pieces are easy to see. What about the pattern? It exists, of course, within the pieces themselves. Every dividing issue contains a thread of connection.

Dividing and Connecting

At the center of the pattern lies Yellowstone National Park. The simplest way Yellowstone acts upon us is through physical barriers. The park is nearly ringed by mountain ranges. Northeast of its boundary lie the Beartooth Mountains, with 29 peaks above 10,000 feet. The eastern border is walled by the Absarokas. The Madisons, Centennials and Lionheads lie off Yellowstone's west boundary like coral reefs guarding a tropical atoll. The park's southern reaches are squeezed between the Teton Range to the southwest and the lower Absarokas to the southeast. The only southern access is the valley through which the Snake River exits, a valley whose walls pinch inhospitably together about 60 miles from the south border of Yellowstone. Access from the east is over rugged mountain passes. The broad Yellowstone Valley sweeps north out of the park through Gardiner, marking what was once the only easy way into Yellowstone.

While in our time Yellowstone National Park's rugged mountain encirclement is a recreational plus, not long ago it was a formidable barrier. Communities on opposite sides of that near bracelet of mountains might as well have been worlds apart rather than a mere 70 or 80 miles. This isolation has fostered the characteristic independence and pride of Yellowstone region communities.

Through our region flow 17 rivers, including the Yellowstone, Snake, Madison, Gallatin, Clarks Fork, Henry's Fork and Salt. All carry the most precious cargo in the arid West, the water that allows communities to grow, ranchers to run cattle and farmers to irrigate fields.

Most of these rivers have carved valleys through otherwise inhospitably rugged country. So, to a striking degree, where our rivers go, so go our roads. And before the roads came the railroads, which needed to follow rivers both for the paths they had carved and for access to the water that ran railroad steam engines. And, of course, where road and rail made supply and commerce possible, towns sprang up, each connected to the others by the threads of transport that created them in the first place.

Idaho Falls, on the southwestern edge of Greater Yellowstone, is so located in large part because a 19th-century entrepreneur built first a ferry and then a bridge at one of the Snake River's few possible fording spots, charging travelers a toll to cross. In lovely Swan Valley, near Idaho Falls, the South Fork of the Snake and the rugged terrain on its west bank have created a string of tiny communities on the east side with uninhabited wilderness a stone's throw across the river.

Climate is another thread that both defines the pieces and pulls them together. At one time, this region's long, snowy winters fell between neighboring communities like thick white curtains. Mountain passes became impassable or nearly so. For instance, in the early days of automobiles, the one-day motor trip between Jackson and Victor, less than 30 miles apart but on opposite sides of 8,200-foot-tall Teton Pass, sometimes became a two-day ordeal. Old photos show teams of horses dragging vehicles up the sharp incline between high walls of snow.

But climatological challenges can also connect us. When Teton Pass closes, both Jackson, Wyoming, and Idaho's Teton Valley feel the pinch. People stuck on either side find willing help from locals who have been stuck a few times themselves. When the Snake River and her tributaries flooded with snowmelt in the spring of 1997, communities up and down the river corridor reached out to each other, often offering assistance they were only too likely to need themselves if the water continued to rise.

Not all of the region's shaping forces have been physical: Economic factors exist as well. The economic force of Yellowstone National Park predated nearly all the communities that surround it. It has cut many towns from whole cloth and shaped the basic weave of others. For instance, Gardiner is not a booming tourist town, partly because once the railroads quit operation, its northern location was off the beaten track. Gardiner's main role from the beginning has been to supply those who ran the park from Mammoth, including army troops and the Park Service. On the other hand, West Yellowstone has always been a tourist staging area for expeditions into the park, originally because the main railroad stop was built here. Cody and Jackson have also been staging areas for both Grand Teton and Yellowstone parks. For all three, this has meant a prosperity otherwise unlikely — a prosperity not shared, in general, by nearby communities.

The Big Pieces: State Lines

Greater Yellowstone communities are connected and know it, but residents tend to focus on differences more than connections. Added to that tendency are the very real physical, economic and cultural distances between our communities. All this makes larger identities, like those that fall along state lines in other areas, as hard to see as the pattern on a quilt wrapped around your own shoulders. Residents of Yellowstone country find their sense of place in their town or valley or county more than in their state. Nevertheless, we're going to make rough sketches of those big pieces.

Eastern Idaho

As every successful Idaho politician knows, this is a state held together, if it's held together at all, by a fierce belief in individual freedom, in each person's and each community's right to do exactly what they please, thank you. In eastern Idaho, that breaks locals into three main camps.

There are the descendants of Mormon homesteaders who cleared sage and irrigated the desert and who still feel an intense but not always careful ownership of the land they were born to. Theirs are mostly the valley towns, such as Rexburg and Rigby, where agriculture can, with hard work, be made to pay.

In more mountainous areas like Island Park live descendants of mountain men and hardscrabble ranchers, remembering the old days and living precariously off the tourist trade. They work as hunting and fishing guides; they're horse packers and shopkeepers. Some have become developers, subdividing their own or their neighbors' ranches. In larger towns like Idaho Falls, these children and grandchildren of farmers and pioneers have become urbanized, but that doesn't mean the school teacher you meet in the grocery store line doesn't drive out to the old homestead on weekends to check on the cattle. Rural roots run deep here.

Then there are the newcomers, often former urbanites. In eastern Idaho, they're drawn by recreational opportunities and high-tech jobs spawned by the INEEL, a national laboratory that is home to research and radiation, near Idaho Falls. Others are modem cowboys — professionals who fled big city office buildings for the luxury of jacking into the whole wide world from tiny Driggs, Idaho. Logging, mining, agriculture and ranching have been traditional Idaho occupations, but more and more Yellowstone country Idahoans see their future in tourism and natural resource conservation. The loudest voices in favor of conservation tend to be these newcomers, frantic to preserve the opportunity for rural clean living that drew them here.

A few towns, like Rexburg, are so homogenous they appear not to need struggle. This Mormon community has neatly gridded streets that seem to reflect an underlying, neatly planned and executed reality. Some communities, like Driggs, seem better defined by their internal differences than by any solidarity between the cowboy-hatted descendants of Mormon homesteaders and the folks Teton Valley old timers call "move-ins." Move-ins are the mountain-loving lifestyle seekers and recreational property owners who populate the valley in increasing numbers and make up the third recognizable camp of eastern Idaho residents. Many in this group are older, retired or retiring. The spare time they have to devote to issues that matter to them, as well as their often substantial financial resources, make their voices loud in proportion to their numbers. They too tend to be conservation-minded.

Idaho as a whole is a state that cheerfully embraces contradiction: Idahoans vote Republican in large part because we love to hate government and government regulation. Yet 64 percent of Idaho is federal land, and federal subsidies were until recently a standard line item in many farm budgets. Not all subsidies come in the form of cash. Much of the state's ranching and agriculture are made financially viable through federal subsidized power, water and public-land grazing. Historically, Idaho has received more federal dollars than its residents paid in taxes. The descendants of homesteaders and miners owe the land their grandfathers farmed to 19th-century homesteading laws that passed out parcels to anyone who could hold onto them.

More contradiction: Idaho is a poor state; its average annual income ranks below three-fourths of the nation. Yet the state's birthrate is high — ninth in the United States. And even more: Historically the state has seen itself as heavily dependent on agriculture for its livelihood, yet only 15 percent of Idaho's land is agricultural. The title of one of the most on-target books on contemporary Idaho says it all in the title: *Paradox Politics*.

Southwestern Montana and Northwestern Wyoming

In some ways, Montana and Wyoming are similar to Idaho. All three are largely rural and sparsely populated. And both have been settled by the descendants of trappers, miners, cattlemen and homesteaders. For nearly a century they lived unnoticed in the land that nobody wanted. Now it is the land that everybody wants.

All three states are so close to their frontier roots that here and there you'll find folks who still haul their water, live without electricity or telephones and heat their homes with wood stoves. Even those natives who now plug into the Internet remember the days when rural economies were supplemented with "making do" and "doing without." Back then, the closest thing to recreation for many of them was packing a picnic for a day of gathering the winter's wood in the mountains.

Like Idahoans, Wyoming and Montana residents share their states with the federal government. Forty-nine percent of Wyoming's lands are under federal ownership, while 28 percent of Montana's are federal. Tally the federal lands in Wyoming's and Montana's shares of Greater Yellowstone, and the number rises to more than 50 percent.

As in Idaho, each community has been shaped by the region's topography. Gardiner, Montana, sits in a narrow canyon on the edge of Yellowstone National Park, while the county seat at Livingston enjoys a wider space connected to the Paradise Valley. Pinched off from the valley where ranches and agriculture prop up local economies, Gardiner's residents have always had to turn to mining and the park for

INSIDERS' TIP

Idaho's state gemstone is the star garnet, a translucent red stone that reveals a ghostly pattern of rays at some angles.

Photo: Randy Hayes, Post Register

A recent deep snowpack in the Teton Mountain Range exceeded a 30-year high as copious amounts of moisture fed the growing levels.

employment. Livingston not only has its own diverse economy, but also is close enough to Bozeman for residents to commute. East of Gardiner, the Beartooth Mountains cut Cooke City off from Red Lodge and Billings. Cooke City's children are educated in a one-room schoolhouse; residents go to "town" (Livingston, Billings or Cody) several times a year and stock up on supplies, especially before the long, cold winter sets in. Cody residents, isolated from the rest of Wyoming by the Big Horn Mountains, party in Red Lodge and do business in Billings.

The states share other similarities, such as a flood of Southerners moving in after the Civil War. From there, though, their roots stray. While eastern Idaho was mainly Mormon, Montana was dominated by the Irish Catholics who worked the mines in Butte and Anaconda. Butte miners gave birth to the labor movement in the West when they struck back at their employers, the heavy-handed Copper Kings that dominated Montana politics and publications until the 1950s.

The states' politics differ, too. Idaho and Wyoming have traditionally been Republican states. Until recently, Montana has been Democratic.

And just as Montanans gave birth to the labor movement, Wyoming suffragists were on the forefront of women's rights. In 1869 — about a half-century before the 19th amendment was added to the U.S. Constitution giving women the right to vote — William Bright introduced the bill in Wyoming. Bright's wife, Julia, supported women's suffrage. The first woman in the nation to cast her vote was 70-year-old Louisa A. Swain on September 6, 1870, in Laramie, Wyoming. Not bad for a state whose logo is a cowboy riding a bucking bronc.

Montana is a state divided into west and east, mountains and plains. In the western third, the towering Rockies hide immense chunks of wilderness softened by trees and separated by valleys. Tumbling out of the mountains and winding their way through the valleys are rivers and streams — 32,000 miles of them — flowing either to the Pacific or Atlantic oceans. The Yellowstone River, which begins in the heart of Yellowstone National Park, slips through Montana's mountains then veers off into the plains until it joins the Missouri River. Montana's 147,138 square miles hold nine national forests and 3,331,881 acres of wilderness.

Wyoming ranks 50th in population with 481,000 people. That's nearly five residents for every square mile. Like Montana, Wyoming is divided into west and east, mountains and plains. Included in its boundaries are most of Yellowstone National Park, Grand Teton National Park, five national forests and millions of acres of Bureau of Land Management lands. What eastern Wyoming lacks in precipitation, it makes up for in rich oil and gas reserves resting below the sagebrush-covered landscape. Three-quarters of the state records an average precipitation of less than 16 inches. Pockets like the Bighorn Basin, where Cody is, average less than 8 inches.

When it comes to education, Wyoming walks away from its neighbors. In 1997, 89 percent of Wyoming's residents were high-school graduates — fifth in the country. Idaho ranked 13th with 86 percent, and Montana ranked 19th with 85 percent. In 1994, Wyoming ranked second in the nation when it came to per capita expenditure on education. Montana ranked 35th, and Idaho ranked 41st that same year.

Blurring State Lines: A Greater Yellowstone

The crowning contradiction of our three states is also our crowning glory: our two lovely, tourist-flooded national parks. Yellowstone National Park lies in all three, but we claim our respective pieces with proud but awkward shrugs. Grand Teton National Park lies in Wyoming, but the "backside" of the Tetons faces Idaho.

There are more traffic jams on a typical summer day in Yellowstone than there are in a month in Idaho Falls, Greater Yellowstone's largest community at about 50,000 inhabitants. More than 3 million visitors flood through the two parks each year. That's more than the combined populations of Idaho, Montana and Wyoming. Yet barely a stone's throw from those crowded summer roads and tourist services is wilderness that, for most of us, is the well-loved signature of this region. Learning to see the connections is a challenge for land agencies, environmental groups, residents and tourists — a 100-year-old challenge that began with the formation of Yellowstone National Park.

The borders of the nation's first national park were established in 1872, at a time when surrounding lands were virtually uninhabited. Geologic wonders awed many who saw them into desiring their preservation. These wonders were geysers and hot springs, spectacular waterfalls and the Grand Canyon of the Yellowstone. The plentiful wildlife was of secondary interest.

In the late 19th century, Yellowstone National Park was patrolled first by soldiers and then, after the creation of the National Park Service, by rangers (see our History chapter). But protective rules were few and vague, and the protectors' numbers small. The nation had never promised to preserve such a vast chunk of land before. Nobody was quite sure how to go about it. And anyway, the vast teeming forests seemed too large to damage, a generous gift to later generations — or an irritating waste of good resources, depending on how you looked at things. Back then most locals hated the idea of declaring off-limits such rich resources so near their back doors.

Only 10 years after its creation, the truth had become obvious: Yellowstone needed help. Poachers were killing off the park's elk and bison at an impressive rate. By 1902, 22 bison made up the nation's only remaining wild herd.

Civil War General Philip Sheridan, traveling through the park in 1882, saw the mayhem and was horrified. Poaching was only part of the problem. Already ranches and homesteads were encroaching on lands necessary to the survival of Yellowstone's wildlife. Elk and bison summered on the Yellowstone Plateau, but they had to drop to more hospi-

INSIDERS' TIP

The famous Idaho potato is a variety called Russet Burbank.

table elevations to survive the harsh winters. Sheridan proposed extending the borders of Yellowstone to the east and south. This action would have protected some wildlife migration routes and low elevation wintering areas.

Enlarging park boundaries would also have hampered poachers, whose operations were most profitable in winter, when the animals were outside the park wallowing in shoulder-deep snow, helpless to escape hunters' guns. Stories from Yellowstone travelers of this period tell of bison and elk carcasses littering the land. Bison were stripped of their hides, but elk died simply for their ivories, residual tusks that had become coveted symbols of a fraternal organization known as the Elks Lodge. Sheridan's call to action was a bit before its time, but eventually the concerns he raised became the hottest topic in the region.

The first attempts to address this issue in the late 1800s led to the formation of the National Forest system, which surrounded Yellowstone with public lands that would otherwise have been homesteaded. Other attempts to pull critical habitat under the Yellowstone umbrella eventually resulted in creation of Grand Teton National Park and the adjacent National Elk Refuge.

A Unified Whole

The results of successful wildlife protection made even more clear Yellowstone National Park's inescapable connection to the region. As elk and bison herds began to regain numbers, winters found them once again heading up the Yellowstone Valley to Gardiner and down the Snake River into Jackson Hole. Except now those areas were ranch and farm land. These animals competed with cattle for winter forage, ate farmers' hay and broke down fences. They still do. Today in Gardiner, you fence your trees if you want to keep them alive. In Jackson Hole, you fence your haystacks. At one time it was more serious. Ranchers barely eking an existence could be starved out by the additional demands of hungry elk. For these locals, there was no escaping the basic connection between Yellowstone country, its wildlife and its people. These ranchers fed starving elk in winter not only out of kindness but in order to survive themselves.

Recent lessons are even more complicated. One in Montana revolves around a disease, brucellosis, carried by Yellowstone bison and elk. Most experts believe the illness won't jump from Yellowstone wildlife to Montana cattle. But the state's ranchers can't forget the tremendous cost they would bear if the unlikely occurred. Brucellosis makes cattle abort their fetuses; western Montana's ranch economy relies on "cow-calf" operations that produce a yearly crop of calves — calves which lose their value if Montana loses its brucellosis-free certification. Whether from political paranoia, as some argue, or justifiable protection of the livelihoods of Montana ranchers, as others stoutly assert, Yellowstone bison are killed every year because some of their number carry this disease. Another sticky issue has been the reintroduction of wolves to Yellowstone National Park. Wolves don't know park boundaries either, and as they leave the park in search of prey (occasionally in the form of livestock), conflict hounds their trail.

The phrase "Greater Yellowstone Ecosystem" first appeared in print around 1979, a new name to help us talk about our region as a quilted whole as well as a wad of political and economic pieces. Frank Craighead is credited with coining the term in his book, *Track of the Grizzly*. The Craighead brothers conducted bear research in Yellowstone. For Frank, the Greater Yellowstone Ecosystem equated roughly with the ranges of Yellowstone grizzlies. This would have made Greater Yellowstone twice the size of the park itself, or about 4.5 million acres.

INSIDERS' TIP

Despite Montana's vast mineral wealth — it's known as the Treasure State — the state's economy is more strongly tied to agriculture than mining. Only Texas has more cultivated farmland.

The idea of an organic whole — a Greater Yellowstone defined by its rivers, mountains and wildlife rather than by political boundaries — caught like brush fire. Now we have organizations such as the Greater Yellowstone Coalition and the Yellowstone Hotspot Association, which promote, each in its own way, a picture of our region as an inescapable whole instead of three states, two national parks, seven national forests, miscellaneous private lands and human communities.

The transition has not been easy and is by no means complete. As you travel Yellowstone country, most of the communities you'll pass are struggling to hang on to traditional extractive economies — logging, ranching and mining — while trying to face this new ethic of ecosystem interdependence. Tourism has been one critical answer, but tourism's impact is not always positive. Many ranching families in Jackson, for instance, bemoan the good old days when their sleepy little town supplied few jobs but lots of peace and quiet. Others point out that although Jackson has plenty of jobs in tourist service industries, most don't pay well, particularly in light of the town's high cost of living.

Desirability aside, tourism can't be every Greater Yellowstone community's solution. In many towns with less desirable locations or with access difficulties, the only jobs available are those that make it difficult to worry about the intricate interlocking of ecosystems. If your weekly paycheck is signed by the owner of a sawmill, you may question how much timber we should be pulling from the lodgepole forests, especially when you notice how the creek outside of town runs brown when it once ran clear. But how can you vote to stop logging in the mountains behind your house? That's voting yourself out of food on the table.

To complicate matters, the survival of this sprawling region depends on an even larger interdependence. Salmon, which bring tourist dollars and which once provided a booming fishing industry, must travel down the Snake River through four states, then out into the Pacific Ocean. This means Idaho fisheries are impacted by Washington coast sea lions and, much more importantly, by federal dams hundreds of miles beyond the state's borders. For many residents, the pattern rapidly grows too big, too complicated to care too much about.

An ecosystem is an area that functions as a self-contained unit. The Greater Yellowstone Coalition is our region's most effective proponent of an ecosystem-based approach to living and working in Yellowstone country. They believe it's possible to draw a line around "the contiguous mountainous region in and around Yellowstone National Park," roughly 18 million acres, and treat that area as a self-contained, organic whole.

Most residents of Greater Yellowstone buy into the ecosystem approach to some degree. It's hard not to. A glance at a map shows us that our political boundaries ignore the natural ones of mountain range and river valley. We understand that brucellosis-bearing bison killed in Montana after they wander outside the protection of Yellowstone National Park didn't know they crossed a state line. They were merely following the biological imperative to feed themselves in winter. Greater Yellowstone residents do not, however, agree on what should be done about the fact that political and ecological boundaries make liars of each other. The arguments run through our newspapers and enliven talk at our bars; they make and break political careers. The future of our region will draw its shape largely from how — indeed, whether — we can resolve this complex issue.

Climate

If the human climate around here sometimes seems a little raucous and fragmented,

INSIDERS' TIP

Greater Yellowstone encompasses the intersection of three wild Western states: Idaho, the most populous with more than 1 million people; Montana, with around 850,000; and Wyoming, the ninth-largest in the nation geographically, with only 481,000 residents.

it only mirrors a larger pattern. For instance, a single local forecast tells you little about the weather across the region.

Most of our weather patterns originate in the moist air of the Pacific Northwest. But as the air stream sweeps across the mountain ranges of Washington and Idaho, it loses moisture. This makes our climate cool and dry. In winter, arctic air masses can sag down from Canada into parts of Greater Yellowstone, bringing clear weather and bone-aching cold.

In general, western Greater Yellowstone has higher winter precipitation and milder temperatures brought by Pacific Northwest weather patterns. The eastern side of our region gets cooler, drier weather. There, January can bite with the arctic fierceness of a Great Plains winter.

Mountain Weather

For each 1,000-foot elevation gain, expect temperature to drop more than 3 degrees. This can mean that November rainfall in Idaho Falls is a blizzard on nearby Pine Creek Pass. Our dry air also creates temperature variation: Dry air undergoes greater temperature fluctuation than humid air, since water cools and heats more slowly than air. The temperature difference between midday and midnight can be as much as 50 degrees, and a small cloud obscuring the sun can make you pull on a jacket, even in summer.

Two other local weather anomalies are inversions and orographic effects. Inversions happen as cold air drains down mountainsides to pool in the valleys. These cold-air pools can become trapped beneath a layer of warmer air. Inversion is why West Yellowstone is often the coldest spot in the nation in winter. It's also why towns such as Jackson have to breathe their own woodsmoke and car exhaust for prolonged periods every winter: Trapped beneath a warm air blanket that acts much like a ceiling, pollutants can't escape as they do in summer.

The second mountain-induced weather-maker is responsible for significantly higher precipitation in Yellowstone country towns that tuck up to the feet of mountains, especially on west-facing slopes. Air climbing over a mountain range cools. Because cool air can't hold as much moisture as warmer air, suspended water vapor forms into droplets. This creates orographic effects such as the cottonball clouds that form over mountains. Valleys in the east side of mountain ranges can be dry and sunny while rain or snow falls just over yonder.

There is a third way in which landscape creates our weather: wind. River corridors, mountain passes and wide-open valleys can whip up surprisingly forceful winds. Livingston, Montana, is known for its gusty weather. Average wind speeds in that town are 21 mph. Idaho Falls on the upper Snake River Plain is more likely to experience winter road closures from drifting snow than from snow depths. We've seen drifts form so quickly on wind-scoured Antelope Flats near Idaho Falls that even 500 yards behind a snow plow the road surface is again buried.

What all this should mean to a smart visitor is this: Dress in layers and plan for weather variation as the day progresses or as you travel. Rain and wind protection are a must here. And even in summer you'll want to carry something warm for evenings or unexpected clouds. If you're driving, don't expect the weather to be the same when you get out of the car as it was where you climbed in, especially if you're going to move from one elevation to another or from one mountain valley to another.

The Best Time to Come

That depends on you.

INSIDERS' TIP

Yellowstone Ecosystem Studies sells a beautifully detailed 39-inch by 26-inch map of the Greater Yellowstone Ecosystem for $25. To order, call Y.E.S. at (406) 587-7758; fax at (406) 587-7590; or write Y.E.S. at P.O. Box 6640, Bozeman, Montana 59771.

Spring brings snowmelt and mud to our mountain towns and early green to valley communities. Rivers usually run big and muddy from late May through July. All this means that in early summer, the fishing isn't generally too hot, the mosquitos are swarming, and the high country is not easily reachable due to slow snowmelt and swollen, difficult creek crossings. However, the weather is pleasantly cool, and lower-elevation wildflower meadows can be breathtaking.

Summer in the high country is short; it usually runs from mid-July through mid-August. Our biggest tourist crowds show up then, as does our most stable, warm weather (don't take stable to mean it can't snow anywhere in Yellowstone country anytime though). Wildflowers burst out in the higher elevations. Down low, farmers' markets begin to fill with local produce. Recreational gardeners watch the news for frost warnings starting around the first week of September.

Fall means stable high-pressure systems which bring cool, clear days bracketed by chilly nights. Aspens and cottonwoods begin to glow gold as early as September at higher elevations; down low they turn by late October. Lower valleys are still enjoying fall weather as the mountain towns slip into winter. This means that if you stay low, you enjoy shirt-sleeve weather and the sight of lovely snow-dusted peaks silhouetted against brilliant blue skies. Up in Grand Teton and Yellowstone parks, fall usually means sweater weather until the sun sets. Then it gets cold.

Most of Yellowstone country tucks under its snow blanket by late November or early December, with the most consistently snowy weather sweeping through in January and February. The coldest months are December through February; you'll enjoy the best skiing from mid-January through late March or early April. Many towns in the region don't expect to see dry pavement between late December and late February. Then the snow melts, mud season begins, and locals wait impatiently for trails and backroads to become navigable so they can shake late-winter blahs under spring's big blue sky.

The Communities

Jackson Hole, Wyoming

In Jackson, you may discover an overwhelming, previously unsuspected desire to own a cowboy hat or a fringed leather jacket. Luckily, you're in cowboy consumer heaven. Jackson has come up with more uniquely Western ways to spend your money than you probably knew existed. It's all here, from fine Western art galleries to fine restaurants that feature game and trout. You'll discover shops selling antler chandeliers, shearling jackets and handmade, custom fitted cowboy hats. And the Million Dollar Cowboy Bar will serve you in the saddle (literally, since their bar stools are saddles).

But locals are quick to point out that the rawhide glitz overlays a real Wyoming town in a valley peopled by folks who wave at each other from behind the wheels of pickups, whose grandparents moved here before the days of RVs, condos and quad chair lifts. Tourist activity also tends to obscure the other group that calls the Hole home: the Gore-Tex-clad hardbodies drawn by nearly endless opportunities for extreme outdoor sports, as well as the pleasures and benefits of what local historian Jesse O'Connor calls "mountain living." If Jacksonites look fit and healthy to you, it's because they are.

What's really fun about Jackson is that it's all three of these at once. The glitz is hard to miss, but if you want to see the quiet Jackson,

INSIDERS' TIP

In 1922 a Rigby boy showed his high school teacher a design for transmitting pictures electronically. His name was Philo T. Farnsworth, and at least around here, he's credited with being the father of modern television. A fellow graduate of Rigby High School was well-known writer Vardis Fisher, author of *The Mountain Man*.

the little town in the big valley surrounded by mountains and the windswept state of Wyoming, come in spring or fall, in the "shoulder" seasons. The endorphin seekers are always there if you look for them: They wait on you at restaurants and wrap your purchases at local boutiques. They own ski shops and teach kayaking lessons. They are climbing guides and seasonal rangers.

Jackson, so close to the wild bounty of the Tetons, was once a town of trappers, outlaws and poachers. Determined homesteaders also eked a bare living, irrigating hayfields with the waters of the Snake and Gros Ventre rivers, running cattle on the fertile valley floor and trying to raise a few crops before the inevitable early freeze. From the beginning, Jackson seemed to know it had to become a tourist town or flounder. Now it's the bustling seat of Teton County, Wyoming. Jackson's population is around 6,000, just under half that of the county itself. In summer, the steady flow of tourists and short term residents swamps locals into invisibility.

Most of the county is filled by Jackson Hole, a 48-mile-long, 20-mile-wide valley that encompasses much of Grand Teton National Park and extends nearly as far south as Hoback Junction. Jackson takes its name from this, the largest high-mountain valley in the lower 48.

Other communities in Teton County, none of which are incorporated, include Wilson, at the foot of Teton Pass, and Teton Village, less a town than a cluster of ski-related services at the base of Jackson Hole Mountain Resort. In or at the edges of Grand Teton National Park are the tiny communities of Moose, Kelly and Moran. Alta and Grand Targhee Ski and Summer Resort are also in Teton County, although mountain barriers mean that the towns closest to them are in Idaho, not Wyoming. (That's why you'll find descriptions of their services and attractions in this book listed with Teton Valley, Idaho, instead of Teton County, Wyoming.)

Jackson has some of the lowest unemployment in the state (around 2.3 percent in

1997) to complement its service-oriented economy. The government provides jobs, too, since supervisory headquarters for the Bridger-Teton National Forest are located here, as well as a district office of Wyoming Game and Fish. National Park Service jobs number in the hundreds in summer; park concessionaires account for more than a thousand.

Unfortunately housing is the priciest in the state. Median rent in 1998 was more than $800 per month; a typical price for a single-family home is currently around $250,000.

Recreational opportunities in the area are almost limitless, but tend to focus on downhill skiing at Jackson Hole and Grand Targhee, backcountry skiing and snowboarding on Teton Pass, mountain biking, hiking and technical mountaineering in the Tetons, wildlife watching, and rafting, kayaking, canoeing and fishing on the Upper Snake and tributaries.

Surrounding Areas

Southwestern Montana

West Yellowstone, Montana

Since 1908, when the Union Pacific Railroad's Oregon Short Line chugged up to the Yellowstone National Park border, West Yellowstone has had one purpose: to serve Yellowstone National Park tourists. Now a booming year-round mecca for tourists and recreationists, "West," as the 1,000 residents like to call their town, has been shaped by four dominant forces: Yellowstone National Park, the national forests that surround it, the climate and snowmobiles.

Until the mid-1960s, when the snowmobile rode into the picture, West was a "100-day town" that rose to frenetic activity each summer, then fell into quiet seclusion when winter blew in 6 feet or more of snow. The town's population swelled and shrank with the seasons. These days, cross-country skiers and snowmobilers add four months of bustling winter business to the town's economy.

In November, the town belongs to the quiet swish of champion cross-country ski and biathlete teams in training. From Christmas until mid-March, snow-machines rule. On a winter's morning, you might hear a thousand snowmobiles idling (there are 1,600 rental snow-machines in West — enough to match every motel room) before they blast off into Yellowstone National Park. Or they can drive straight from their motel rooms to more than 1,000 miles of groomed trails that lead into national forest lands bordering West Yellowstone's city limits (see our Winter Sports chapter).

Come March, locals are left alone to await the spring thaw. Some escape to a much-needed vacation. Others sweep the dust off their store counters, fatten up their inventories and prepare to make hay while the sun shines. In West Yellowstone, the sun always shines brightest from Memorial Day until Labor Day. The 2 million visitors who pass through West Yellowstone on their way to and from the park also fish, hike, bike and backpack in and around the park.

While some locals cuss the commotion created by snowmobiles, it was their advent that dragged West Yellowstone from an unorganized frontier community into the well-ordered town it now is. Snow machines forced the town fathers to incorporate in the late 1960s so the vehicles could navigate city streets. The new business and increased prosperity doubled the town's population and brought its first high school, meaning parents no longer had to send their teenage children to board in Bozeman. About the same time, newcomers steered the town toward a sewer system to replace existing cesspools. In the early '80s, city fathers passed a 3 percent city tax — the first commu-

INSIDERS' TIP

The single largest contributor to Wyoming's economy is oil. More than 50 percent of the Rockies' crude is extracted from Wyoming wells. Natural gas, coal and soda ash also exist in notable quantities.

Photo: Steve Fischbach, Post Register

Yellowstone country is a snowmobilers' paradise throughout winter.

nity tax in the state — to improve and build its infrastructure.

Ironically, the very public lands that have turned West Yellowstone into a recreation mecca now squeeze the town's bulging boundaries. West Yellowstone sprang up amidst National Forest lands. To establish property for the growing town, the Madison National Forest (now Gallatin National Forest) set aside 500 acres for a townsite. Land is scarce, and the rush for recreational homesites is on. Property prices have skyrocketed, and housing is scarce and expensive. Huge businesses like the Yellowstone IMAX Theater, the Grizzly Discovery Center (see our Attractions chapter), giant RV parks and new motels have been built on the year-round economy. Once a town too poor to live in, many say West Yellowstone is quickly becoming a town too expensive to live in.

Public land policies — and particularly those in the park — will determine West Yellowstone's future. Officials are concerned about pollution from snowmobiles and winter disturbance to wildlife. There is talk of dramatically curtailing snowmobiling, and murmurings persist about limiting park visitor numbers. If the town's population once rose and fell with the seasons, West Yellowstone's fortune has always followed the park's visitation. Townsfolk pay close attention to each new park superintendent, knowing that the policy he sets can make them or break them.

Gardiner, Montana

Ten years ago we might have told you Gardiner was a town that refused to be tamed by the prospect of tourist dollars. Still unincorporated, Gardiner has only recently begun to make an obvious bid for tourist trade. Towering new motels have risen to replace aging cabins popular with Europeans but disdained by many Americans. Behind the modern structures you'll see remnants of the frontier border town that is going, going, almost gone. You'll see simple homes and dirt streets — reminders that the 1,000 or so residents of this blue-collar town have relied more on serving the park and its concessionaires than on catering to the tourists who visit it.

Gardiner began as a supply town and stopping-off place for Yellowstone National Park visitors in 1872, when the park was created. In 1883, when the Northern Pacific Railroad pushed its Park Branch Line as far as Cinnabar 3 miles away, Gardiner got another economic boost. It also got its share of ruffians who followed the rails hoping for work. Three years later, when Army troops took over management of the park at Mammoth, the number of saloons and brothels in Gardiner took a big leap. In 1903, when the Park Branch Line finally rolled into town (a cantankerous miner held claims that blocked its path for 17 years), Gardiner burst into bloom. Stagecoaches, wagons and outfitters with horses hustled to meet trainloads of visitors with trunkloads of clothes.

Originally the grand entrance (a huge stone arch stands as a reminder) for tourists traveling to Yellowstone National Park via the railroad, the northern park entrance at Gardiner now ranks third in visitor numbers. It is the park's only year-round vehicle entrance. Just 5 miles from Mammoth, where permanent park employees live all year, Gardiner is home to the warehouses of AmFac Resorts, Yellowstone's main concessionaire. Five miles to the northeast is Jardine, the site of a gold mine that has teased the town with a century of boom and bust. Down the canyon, a few ranches add a tiny trickle to the local economy. Farther down the canyon is Livingston, the county seat and a growing center for writers, artists and actors. Between lies the Paradise Valley, where ranchers are quietly giving way to retirees and wealthy urban refugees including actors such as Peter Fonda, Jeff Bridges and Dennis Quaid. To the south is Yellowstone National Park, the capricious benefactor that Gardiner residents love and hate.

The relationship between Mammoth and Gardiner runs deeper than that of employer and employee. Mammoth high schoolers attend classes in Gardiner. And Gardiner parents take their children to the doctor at the Mammoth Clinic. In winter, elk and bison from the burgeoning park herds (they're the biggest in the nation), flow out of the park to their winter range in and around Gardiner, where the altitude is only a mile high and feed is easier to find. Some wander through town and down the Yellowstone River Canyon. Others stay on summer and winter, mercilessly pruning ornamental trees and shrubs. Living with the elk is a part of living with park policy. Some residents like having an elk peer through their picture windows and others don't. They're good for business, bad for gardens.

Like West Yellowstone and Cooke City, Gardiner is hemmed in by public lands. You'll find river rafting and fishing on the Yellowstone River that cuts through town. And you'll find hiking in and out of the park. In the fall, you'll also find hunting, especially a late hunt used to thin the park's elk herd.

Cooke City and Silver Gate, Montana

Before Yellowstone became a national park, miners had already dug into the hillsides and discovered gold in Shoofly, today's Cooke City, at the park's northeast entrance. If those miners had had their way, the Northern Pacific Railroad would have laid its tracks from Gardiner across the park to Cooke City. They didn't, though. And when the mines finally closed in the 1950s, Cooke City withered to fewer than 20 year-round residents. The rest catered to tourists during the summer and moved elsewhere to work for the winter.

During the winter, Cooke City is at the end of the road, connected to the rest of the world only by the road through the park to Gardiner. The town sits at 7,600 feet, where snow buries it, locking winter residents in. To the east the 11,000-foot Beartooth Highway to Red Lodge and Billings closes mid-October. About November 1, crews clearing the Chief Joseph Highway (Wyo. Highway 296) to Cody, stop plowing at the Montana state line about 10 miles east of Cooke City.

INSIDERS' TIP

You have almost certainly eaten Idaho potatoes many times: J.R. Simplot, Idaho's "Potato King" and one of the state's two richest men, supplies McDonald's restaurants with more than half the french fries the fast-food giant serves.

Like West Yellowstone, snowmobiles have shot winter life into Cooke City, noted for its off-trail snowmobiling opportunities. Motels and a few cafes stay open through the winter to accommodate visitors. During the summer, Cooke City's population grows from 90 to about 300, and Main Street is crowded with cars and people. Off Main Street, cabins and log houses cling helter-skelter to the hillside.

In the mid-1990s, the New World Mine loomed on the mountain above town. The proposed open-pit gold mine, halted by President Clinton, would have changed Cooke City — and possibly the park — forever. But Congress paid claim holders and the mining company a large sum of money to give up their mining rights.

In addition to snowmobiling and cross-country skiing, Cooke City is a mecca for hikers, backpackers, anglers and hunters. You'll also find a few mountain bikers. In the fall and spring, it's also a good place to see bears. And any time of year, wolves can be spotted in the Lamar Valley in the northeast corner of the park. Reintroduced to the park in 1995, the wolves have become a growing tourist attraction and have produced a noticeable trickle of wolf-watching visitors who stop into Cooke City fall through spring after a day of wildlife viewing.

Silver Gate, which is actually the town closest to Yellowstone National Park's northeast entrance, is much smaller than Cooke City. It has mostly motels and a cafe for services, none of which are open for the winter. Silver Gate was laid out in the 1930s with covenants that dictated a rustic theme. Few folks here stay through the winter, and they go to Cooke City 3 miles east for gas, grub and gab.

Cooke City is what some locals like to call a "dog" town. It has so few full-time residents they can be easily tracked by noting the whereabouts of their dogs. You'll know Old Joe is at the Miner's Saloon when you see his dog lying outside the door.

Bozeman, Montana

Bozeman is a cowtown with big growing pains — such big pains that three candidates promoting planned growth with high impact fees ousted incumbent commissioners in the 1997 election. From 1990 to 1995, Bozeman's population grew nearly 4 percent per year. And experts expect Bozeman to be the fastest growing town in the state during the next few years.

Headquartered in Bozeman is the Greater Yellowstone Coalition, an environmental group that has worked with other local planning authorities since 1983. Today, they are scrambling to keep tabs on development in Greater Yellowstone. And they're looking for ways to maintain wide open spaces and wildlife habitat.

Separated from Yellowstone National Park by 93 miles, Bozeman is the seat of Gallatin County, population 61,000. It is also the epicenter from which development is seeping into some of the wild parts of Greater Yellowstone.

Featured in a 1998 *New York Times* article as a flourishing arts center, Bozeman boasts a menu of cultural options that include ballet, live theater, a symphony orchestra, the Emerson Cultural Center, and more. Bozeman was established in 1864, when trailblazer John Bozeman promoted his route from the Oregon Trail to the Montana gold fields in Virginia City, Montana. The fertile Gallatin Valley, through which the trail ran, became a supply source for miners, ranchers and Yellowstone National Park expeditions. But it wasn't until the 1900s, when the Milwaukee Railroad built a cross-country line with a spur leading to Gallatin Gateway for Yellowstone National Park tourists, that Bozeman joined other towns as a Yellowstone connection.

Today, Gallatin Field Airport is a main connection to Yellowstone. It's also an important link to the outside world. Each Monday morning, traffic carrying air commuters flows toward the airport where buyers for $9,000-plus "car condos" exceed the supply of garages.

Home of Montana State University, Bozeman's population has mushroomed into 28,000 full-time residents with an average personal income of about $20,000 — almost the same as those who live in Cody, Wyoming. Bozeman offers a wide array of recreation opportunities, including the Bridger Bowl Ski Area to the north and Big Sky Ski Area to the south. The city also is near a rainbow of blue-ribbon trout streams and millions of acres of national forest and wilderness lands. Additionally,

Yellowstone National Park is just 90 miles to the south of the Gallatin Valley. In town, businessmen ski around Lindley Park during lunch or jog on the old railroad bed. Evenings, residents may attend a performance of the Bozeman Symphony Orchestra or a play at the Emerson Cultural Center. This combination of amenities has attracted a growing number of newcomers who want to protect the paradise they have found.

Big Sky, Montana

People come to Big Sky to play. Summer or winter, Big Sky and the Gallatin Canyon are a recreation destination lined with Forest Service campgrounds, trailheads and hiking and biking trails. Groups of horseback riders file out through the sagebrush beside the river, while others play golf or tennis in the Big Sky resort complex. Come winter, they trade their horses and bikes for skis and snowmobiles. And the snow-laden meadows and mountains hum with people playing.

Unincorporated as a town and run by a board of directors, Big Sky Ski and Summer Resort is former newscaster Chet Huntley's dream. When the resort opened in 1974, the celebration turned into a memorial service for Huntley, who had just died of lung cancer. Back then those who followed Huntley's dream lived in tents because there was no place else to live.

Big Sky was once a ranch tucked into a quiet draw of lush alpine meadows in the Madison Mountain Range. Now it is a winter and summer resort, with three "villages" separated by several miles of road. At Mountain Village, the heart of the Big Sky resort, condominiums, hotels and lodges cling to the base of Lone Mountain, 9 miles west of the Gallatin Canyon Road (U.S. Highway 191). Two more villages several miles down the road hold homes and mini-commercial centers. Banners advertise condo rentals and the Chamber of Commerce operates on an answering machine.

In the narrow canyon below, the Gallatin River runs like a ribbon from Yellowstone National Park. Before Big Sky came about, a few dude ranches and stage stops clung to the blue-ribbon trout stream, hoping to snag those driving the road to Yellowstone. The old guest ranches still show visitors a good western time and business owners in the canyon still cater to both Yellowstone and Big Sky visitors. In 1998, nearly 90 children, grades K through 8, attended school in Big Sky, while teenagers commuted to Bozeman for high school.

In the past six years, Big Sky has doubled its runs and lift capacity to accommodate 19,000 skiers per hour. Big Sky is one of eight ski areas slated for expansion or construction in Greater Yellowstone.

Livingston, Montana

Just months after the Northern Pacific Railroad rolled into town in 1882, Livingston had sprung into a full-blown town boasting six hotels and restaurants, four stores, five feed stables, two butcher shops, two liquor stores, a lumber yard and 30 saloons. Livingston has since found much of its fortune in the rails (and rivers) that run through it, despite the fact that automobiles coupled with cheap gas and a booming post-World War II economy dried up passenger rail service to the park, and eventually to Livingston. Always a headquarters for repairing ailing locomotives, the town today hosts the Livingston Rebuild Center, where locomotive engines from around the world are repaired.

Downtown, you'll find things looking pretty much the same as they did before World War II. It's not an accident. Influenced by a thriving community of internationally famous writers,

INSIDERS' TIP

Sandhill cranes, blessed (or perhaps cursed) with a call that resembles the working of unoiled machinery, fly into Teton Valley as many as 17,000 strong each September to stage their journey south.

Photo: Robert Bower, Post Register

This irrigaton system hydrates a potato field west of Idaho Falls, Idaho, helping to grow one of the state's agricultural staples.

artists and actors, residents have made it a point to preserve their downtown heritage. (In 1997, when the U.S. Postal Service tried to move the Livingston post office from downtown, it took only four days for 1,500 citizens to sign a petition, contact their congressmen and stop the move.)

Livingston is so well-kept, in fact, that more than one movie has been set in and around the town. In the summer of 1997, both Robert Redford's *The Horse Whisperer* and Dennis Quaid's *Everything That Rises* were shot in the Livingston area. Parts of Redford's *A River Runs Through It* were also filmed here.

Home of the Federation of Flyfishers, Livingston is a town quietly melding the old and the new Wests into its vision of paradise. On a summer's evening, you might find folks from every social strata sipping wine, tasting hors d'oeuvres and viewing art in one of three summer gallery walks. Afterwards, those same people might adjourn to the Stockman Bar for a steak in a small restaurant at the back of the bar. Or you might find some of them gathering down the street at the Livingston Bar and Grille, owned by Russell Chatham, an internationally known Western impressionist painter who calls Livingston home. Around the corner is the Cowboy Connection, a small shop that sells Old West cowboy memorabilia. (See our Restaurants and Shopping chapters for more about these.)

Livingston, population 7,500, has an economy based on Montana Rail Link, the Livingston Rebuild Center, agriculture, a lumber mill, fly tying, outfitting, guiding and tourism. The number of motel rooms, though, is a clue that tourism doesn't rank as high as in, say, Cody. Livingston offers 600 beds, while Cody, just slightly bigger than Livingston, claims more than 1,300 beds within its city limits.

Red Lodge, Montana

The poverty of the past is now the pride of this town. Because residents lacked the money to fix up or raze old buildings, most of Red Lodge's downtown has been put on the National Register of Historic Places. When the coal mines shut down in the 1940s, Red Lodge suffered through decades of bleak existence before building a tourism-based economy. Planners started with Red Lodge Mountain Ski Area and added recreation options to their menu. The town is now a playground for Billings and Cody residents. In turn, Red Lodge residents go to Cody and Billings for fun.

A tight-knit community with houses huddled shoulder to shoulder like men trying to block out the cold, Red Lodge, population 2,000, sits between the Beartooth and the Pryor mountains. The mile-high town still holds the charm of bygone days when coal mining was the economic mainstay. Red Lodge sprang up in the 1880s after the discovery of coal, a commodity badly needed by copper smelters in Anaconda and Butte, Montana, and by the Northern Pacific Railroad for its coal-fired locomotives. Hundreds of European miners moved into Red Lodge, each nationality carving out an ethnic neighborhood: Little Italy, Finn Town and separate sections for the Scot, Irish, English, Welsh, German, Scandinavian and Slavic populations. When most of the mines closed in the 1930s, some residents took up bootlegging during Prohibition. Their moonshine, which they labeled "syrup," was so good it was marketed as far away as Chicago and San Francisco.

Today, the ethnic lines have blurred, and the average per capita personal income of Carbon County's 8,000 residents is about $17,000. The division these days stands between old-timers, who have weathered tough times, and newcomers, who have brought their money and new ways with them. On one side of the town's main street, mountain-biking, climbing, hiking recreationists hang out at a local coffee bar where they pay $2.50 for a cup of cappuccino. Across the street, retired cowboys drink 50¢-a-cup java at the coffee shop. One group eats exotic pasta dishes. The other eats chicken-fried steak.

To the south is the Beartooth Highway, which leads over a 11,000-foot summit to Yellowstone National Park. Charles Kuralt once called it the most beautiful drive in America (and nobody in Red Lodge will let you forget it). Depending on the weather, it is closed from October 15 until June 1. In the summer, though, the Beartooth Mountains are a paradise of hiking, backpacking and fishing. And Red Lodge residents are doing their darnedest to capitalize on them.

Eastern Idaho

"A lot of state, this Idaho, that I didn't know about," former Idaho resident Ernest Hemingway once said.

Most Idahoans could say the same thing. After all, their home contains nearly 84,000 square miles, but only 1.2 million people. The last state to be "discovered" by Euro-Americans boasts nearly 16,000 miles of fishable streams and rivers, more than 2,000 natural lakes, 11 national forests and five wilderness

INSIDERS' TIP

Where is the Upper Snake? That depends. The Upper Snake River begins in Yellowstone National Park, flows south to Grand Teton National Park and Jackson Lake, ending at Palisades Reservoir below Jackson Hole. Some weather forecasters (not locals) refer to the Henry's Fork as the Upper Snake, probably because, confusingly, it flows through the eastern part of the broad valley that spans southern Idaho, and which Idahoans call the Upper Snake River Plain. Idaho Falls sits on Idaho's Upper Snake River Plain. The mainstem of the Snake River flows through Idaho Falls.

areas. Idaho contains more wilderness than any state except Alaska, more forest lands (more than 40 percent of Idaho is national forest) and more running water and whitewater. Not bad for a state best known as the home of a lowly tuber, the potato.

Teton Valley, Idaho

Teton Valley, often called Teton Basin by residents, once went by a different name, Pierre's Hole. "Hole" is the name trappers gave to a high valley surrounded by mountains: The former Pierre's Hole is a 20-mile-long valley ringed by the Big Holes to the west, the Tetons to the east and the Snake River range to the south. To the north, the valley gradually widens as it carries the trout-filled Teton River toward its meeting with the equally legendary Henry's Fork of the Snake.

The name Pierre's Hole is the only remnant of the wild, mountain-man days of the early 1800s, when the area was home to trappers and Indians. Gone is the raucous annual mountain-man rendezvous where trappers traded their winter's furs for supplies and a good party. Teton Valley's next wave of inhabitants were determined Mormon ranchers who arrived in the 1880s, first in Driggs (now Teton County seat), then in Victor, Tetonia and nearly a dozen tiny communities that in turn disappeared, existing today only in locals' memories. Valley towns like Sam, Judkins, Clementsville and Bates aren't even dots on maps anymore. All that's left of little Cedron is a tiny rangeland cemetery.

Teton County residents have made their living from ranching and some agriculture, (mostly seed potatoes, which can tolerate the short growing season). But tourism and real-estate development are supplanting traditional employment. Teton Valley grew more than 50 percent between 1990 and 1996, bumping local population to more than 5,000. Although growth has been substantial and steady since the early '70s, the latest jumps are striking. New home construction has also jumped: About 150 new homes were built between 1985 and 1990, but between 1990 and 1994, more than 400 went up.

Fuel for the local tourist and recreational housing boom is Grand Targhee Ski and Summer Resort, up winding Ski Hill Road and over the border in Wyoming. Grand Targhee was a homegrown ski hill, built with the help of grants to create jobs for locals. It boasts spectacular powder and striking views of cloud-shrouded Grand Teton from the top of lovely, but perhaps unimaginatively named, Fred's Mountain. Now the ski hill belongs to a corporation that owns several resorts; it's likely that under new leadership Grand Targhee will become more a destination resort and less a locals' hill.

Another impetus for rapid growth and tourist interest is that booming Jackson is literally "over the hill," as Jackson commuters say. Barely 22 miles — but several thousand feet of elevation gain and loss on Teton Pass — separates Victor, Idaho, in Teton Valley from Jackson, Wyoming, in Jackson Hole. And as the cost of housing in Jackson has become more and more expensive, Teton Valley has become more attractive to less well-heeled Jacksonites.

Teton Valley in general and Driggs in particular have the reputation of being "granola" heaven. Around here granola has become a term for a health-food-munching, late-'90s version of the hippie. Besides the descendants of Mormon ranchers, the most influential group in the valley may be these folks. They are artists, craftspeople, writers, construction workers and restaurant owners. They are fiercely protective of the little mountain valley they've adopted.

Locals say that one of the things all valley residents share, though, no matter how they make a living or how many generations their families can claim here, is concern for the environment and this region on the cusp of irrevocable change. Concern about change

INSIDERS' TIP

You'll find only one television for public use in Yellowstone National Park. It's in the lounge at the Mammoth Hotel.

shows in the way residents keep a close eye on their elected officials. The elections of November 1996 resulted in an 86-percent voter turnout and the turnover of every single local office.

Outside of politics, recreational opportunities include skiing, especially at Grand Targhee and in backcountry reachable from Teton Pass. Snowmobilers frequent nearby Pine Creek Pass. Fishing on the Teton River is first-class. Hiking, mountain biking and camping opportunities abound.

Swan Valley, Idaho, and Star Valley, Wyoming

Both Swan Valley and its largest town are named for the lovely and endangered trumpeter swans who frequent the area. The South Fork of the Snake, yet another of eastern Idaho's premier fly-fishing rivers, runs the valley's length. The river is lined with cottonwoods, overflown by bald eagles, paralleled by highway and punctuated by little towns. The town of Swan Valley has about 150 residents; Irwin just up the road has about 110. Farther south, the even-tinier town of Palisades doesn't exist for some map makers, but its residents know that's where they live.

The local Mormon church is the largest structure in the valley, testifying to the strong Mormon influence here. Residents have made their livings as ranchers, but following an east Idaho trend, tourist dollars are becoming more important. Anglers floating the South Fork, boaters headed up to 20-mile-long Palisades Reservoir and tourists looking for a pretty route to Teton Valley or Jackson all leave behind a few bucks. Right now the area still lacks the range of tourist facilities that would make Swan Valley a destination in its own right. Area accommodations are limited mostly to RV spots, cabins and a couple of small roadside motels. One notable exception is an elegant little fishing lodge at Palisades Creek (see our Fishing and Watersports chapter).

The area has few restaurants, and we dare you to find an afternoon's worth of shopping in the valley. In fact, the most complete cluster of tourist services in the valley isn't in what locals consider to be Swan Valley at all: It's at the head of Palisades Reservoir in Alpine, Wyoming. Alpine is technically in Star Valley. Here you'll find several lodging and dining options, as well as winter snowmobiling and summer powerboating on the reservoir. What both valleys have in undisputed plenty is the lovely, trout-filled Snake, a long green swath of fertile range edged on both sides with nearly unroaded mountains, spectacular hiking up the side drainages and wildlife-watching opportunities along the river corridor. We suspect that in the none-to-distant future, locals will remember the quiet valley of today with nostalgia.

Island Park, Idaho

We've heard three stories about how this town was named. One is that a local railroad-tie camp in the 1920s happened to be nearly surrounded by streams: Tom Creek, Split Creek, Chick Creek, Little Warm River and the Buffalo River. The result was nearly an island. A second story says that in the late 1890s, the local stop for the Yellowstone stage was a natural clearing in the midst of heavy forest, and that a tiny village grew up around the stage stop, an island of people among the trees. Not right, says early resident Charles Pond: He explains that the town was named for the stands of timber that ride like islands on the sage-dotted plain.

However the town got its pretty name, Island Park didn't need its moniker to make it unusual. This is a town with a 33-mile-long main street and fewer than 250 year-round residents. It's also a town contained entirely

INSIDERS' TIP

Avalanches closed Teton Pass between Victor, Idaho, and Wilson, Wyoming, 31 days during the heavy snow winter of 1996-97.

Photo: Robert Bower, Post Register

Eastern Idaho is one of the nation's leading wheat-growing regions. The loose volcanic soil and abundance of irrigation water make the dry and warm climate ideal for grain crops.

within one of the world's largest known calderas (a caldera is a collapsed lava dome). A similar structure exists in nearby Yellowstone National Park. Island Park's caldera is over a million years old and roughly 18 miles wide by 33 miles long. Even if you know it's there, evidence of the massive feature is hard to see. Geologists say that Sawtelle Peak, nearly 10,000 feet tall, is a section of what was once the caldera rim.

The 1860s saw the first settlement here as trappers moved in to harvest the area's furbearers. But it wasn't until Yellowstone became a national park in 1872 that the area began to boom. At first, stage lines ran through Island Park into Yellowstone. A railroad line was completed in 1908.

Along the highway corridor you'll see treeless swaths cut into the forest, clearcuts from the not-too-distant days of heavy logging. More apparent, though, are the regular clusters of tourist services. Businesses along U.S. Highway 20 are waiting to feed you, rent you the toys you need to play in their playground, guide you to the best hunting and fishing, put you up for the night or the summer, or sell you your dream cabin. Don't look for a lot of retail here, though. Nobody's here to shop.

Island Park is eastern Idaho's outdoor playground. Idaho Falls residents who own recreational cabins most likely own them here; another big contingent hails from Salt Lake City. Rexburg and St. Anthony families headed out for weekend camping trips often drive this way. Island Park Reservoir, dammed into existence in 1938, is a favorite with local powerboaters. It has five boat launch sites (see our Fishing and Watersports chapter).

In winter Idaho snowmobilers deluge the area's 200 miles of groomed snowmobile trails. These trails connect with Lionhead and West Yellowstone trails to make a total of more than 1,000 miles of groomed snowmobile heaven. The area is laced with more than 40 miles of groomed cross-country ski trails, including trails in lovely 16,000-acre Harriman State Park, winter home of moose and hundreds of trumpeter swans.

Much more than locally famous, though, is the fishing. Henry's Lake is 8 square miles of clear, cold mountain water, practically jumping with landlocked kokanee salmon, rainbow, cutthroat and a natural hybrid locals call cutt-bow. About half of the Henry's Lake fishery are natural spawners. The occasional 30-incher surprises no one. The Henry's Fork of the Snake, home to rainbow, brook trout and cutthroat, is world-class fly-fishing water. In fishing season, waders are almost obligatory attire for the well-dressed in Island Park.

Ashton, Idaho, Area

Ashton is Fremont County's second-largest town, with around 1,100 inhabitants. This little burg, the sidewalks of which always seem to have just been rolled up, clings to the top of the Upper Snake River Plain just before you climb onto the Yellowstone Plateau.

Despite its altitude-pinched growing season of about 86 days, Ashton is farm country. The self-proclaimed seed-potato capital of the world has produced certified seed stock for nearly 100 years. Many of the 40-plus area potato farmers are third- and fourth-generation seed-potato growers. As is true farther down the valley, farmers enjoy a productive combination of rich volcanic soil (naturally low in pathogens) and low humidity, coupled with plentiful irrigation water.

Although farming is arguably the mainstay in Ashton now, tourism was her impetus. A railroad spur ran from here to West Yellowstone, for decades shuttling tourists into the nation's first national park. Tourism is still important, but it's not creating a boom economy: Ashton seems to sleep in summer and hibernate in winter.

One telling Fremont County fact is that its residents don't leave. Between 1990 and 1994, less than 1 percent of the population emigrated. Perhaps their unique location keeps them home: Fremont County borders both Wyoming and Montana and, because it's practically next door to Yellowstone, gets credit as Idaho's gateway to that national park. Nearly 29 square miles of the county are water, and almost 60 percent of the land area is federally owned. At Aspen Acres, Ashton's aspen-studded golf course, an occasional plodding bear obstacle reminds local golfers that they may live in settled farmland, but they abut wild, wild country.

Other recreational opportunities are as close as the 25-mile-long Mesa Falls Scenic Byway, which begins right outside town and provides hiking, sightseeing and fishing opportunities. Nearby Bechler is Yellowstone National Park's only backcountry entrance (until recently it was also the park's only free entrance, but a couple of years ago the Park Service began to charge the hikers and horsepackers who enter the park at Bechler). A short whitewater stretch on the Fall River, runnable only in spring because a private hydroelectric project diverts much of the water other times of year, is a favorite of local kayakers and rafters.

Rexburg, Idaho

It's hard to imagine a more wholesome town. The streets run ruler-straight through a clean, old-fashioned downtown district. Pretty trees shade frame houses. Lawns are green. Ricks College, owned by the Mormon church and named for one of the town's founding fathers, occupies a scenic hill above town. Irrigated farmland stretches away in all directions. In 1994, Rexburg had no reported cases of murder, no robberies, two cases of arson and 40 burglaries in a county with a population of 23,000.

Rexburg is pretty both by design and by disaster. First, it was settled by Mormons in 1883. The church believed that ideal communities could be created to foster the best in communal support, and Rexburg, like many eastern Idaho towns, was one of its experiments. Second, and more ironically, part of Rexburg's shiny-penny look belongs to the tragedy that nearly washed it away. On June 5, 1976, the newly completed Teton Dam collapsed; millions of cubic yards of it and 80

INSIDERS' TIP

Even in summer, nighttime temperatures around freezing are not uncommon in Yellowstone country's higher altitudes. Plan to dress warmly.

billion gallons of water rampaged down the valley and right through Rexburg. The flood claimed lives, stripped topsoil and destroyed homes. It caused $800 million in damage. Locals still break their town's history into two pieces: "before the flood" and "after the flood." There aren't many buildings in the lower areas of Rexburg that haven't had substantial attention paid them since 1976. Many had to be completely rebuilt. (From 1960 to 1969, about 700 new houses were built in Madison County, but between 1970 and 1979, the decade of the flood, the number soared to four times that many.)

Rexburg is a short drive from spectacular outdoor recreation in the Big Holes, the Tetons, the St. Anthony Dunes area and Island Park. It also puts on a pretty good party every year for the International Folk Dance Festival in July (see our Annual Events chapter).

Near Rexburg, but actually a county seat in its own right, is little St. Anthony, population 3,800. It's a town easily overlooked unless you're from there — or unless you've attended the traditional Free Fishermen's Breakfast on Memorial Day Weekend. Or unless you know about the anomalous sand dunes 12 miles west of town that are the winter home of 2,500 elk and the summer playground of four-wheelers and dirt bikers (see our Attractions chapter). St. Anthony is bisected by the world-class trout waters of the Henry's Fork of the Snake River.

Idaho Falls, Idaho

Greater Yellowstone's largest community, population about 50,000, is also probably its least tourism-dependent. Situated on the broad Snake River Plain some 90 miles from Jackson, its mountains are all low-horizon mirages. Agriculture thrives in the rich volcanic soil created eons ago after the hotspot now underlying Yellowstone National Park wandered east across the Snake River Plain. Canal systems bring the plentiful water of the Snake to fields of potatoes and grain. Idaho Falls is also a retail hub for the approximately 200,000 people of the upper Snake River Valley.

The biggest single factor in the local economy, though, is the Idaho National Engineering and Environmental Laboratory (INEEL). During the nation's nuclear heyday, the INEEL and its reactors employed more than 10,000 people in mostly engineering and technical professions. Although it was recently downsized, the facility still accounts for some 38 percent of all jobs in Bonneville County. The laboratory has been responsible for an unusually high standard of living for county residents — not long ago the highest in the state — and for dramatic waves of well-educated recreation hounds who came here to pursue their technical careers because outdoor play opportunities are unrivaled at other technical sites.

The Mormon church and "the site," as locals call the INEEL, make Bonneville County home to two nearly unconnected communities. Sixty percent of county residents are Mormon, mostly descended from homesteading pioneers. These people tend to value their community and feel a strong connection to the land. Their stewardship, however, is not as gentle as recreation and lifestyle-oriented newcomers might like. Many are still tied to parcels claimed by their ancestors under homesteading laws. Then there are the techies and other imports, possessive of the play opportunities here and, since they've already arrived, begrudging the next influx for the impact it will have on skiing, fishing, hiking and mountain biking opportunities. "Community" for many imports means co-workers and perhaps the next-door neighbors. For others, it's the people they ski with.

Idaho Falls is surrounded by satellite communities that are even more strongly Mormon and rooted in agri-business — towns like Iona, Ammon, Ucon, Rigby and Ririe. Time spent in these communities is like a peek into the area's

INSIDERS' TIP

Island Park has more year-round resident trumpeter swans than people (around 350 swans and 250 people).

Photo: Robert Bower, Post Register

A small band of elk head toward winter range in Jackson Hole.

past. In little Iona, street names like Rockwood, Steele and Olsen document the original homesteaders — and the current phone book's listings.

Recreation generally involves a drive to Teton Valley or Swan Valley, to Island Park or Jackson or Yellowstone. Within a 90-minute drive in various directions lie world-class fly fishing, great powder skiing at Grand Targhee Ski and Summer Resort and nearly endless hiking and cross-country skiing. There is snowmobiling, especially at the snow-machine meccas of Island Park and West Yellowstone, mountain biking in the Big Holes, and foot/horseback access to Yellowstone National Park from the park's only backcountry entrance, at Bechler, near Ashton.

Northwestern Wyoming

Cody, Wyoming

The banner above the entrance to the Cody High School says it all: "Make Dust or Eat Dust." Cody residents have been making dust since the 1880s when Col. William F. "Buffalo Bill" Cody rode into the Big Horn Basin and decided to call it home. He had a vision, and Cody is it: A thriving tourist destination with a diverse economy.

Renowned as a hunter, guide and scout for the army during the Indian wars, Cody became an international showman who took the West to the East. On the road, he nurtured his vision, sent his money home and built his dream. In 1902, he bankrolled the construction of the Irma Hotel, the same year the North Fork Road from town to the east entrance of Yellowstone National Park was completed. That same year the Burlington Northern (induced by Buffalo Bill himself) laid tracks to Cody. To accommodate guests, he built two lodges along the North Fork Road. Then he hired guides to take guests into the park.

Cody's link to the park had been established. But that wasn't enough for Buffalo Bill's town. Next he helped convince President Teddy Roosevelt to form a Bureau of Reclamation that would build dams and reservoirs to irrigate arid Western lands. In 1910, the Buffalo Bill Dam (the highest in the world at the time) blocked the North Fork of the Shoshone River and brought life to the dry lands of the Big Horn Basin — and to Cody's dream of a prosperous community.

Liquid gold — rich oil and gas deposits — in the Oregon Basin has since greased the wheels of progress. Like Buffalo Bill, oil and gas patriarchs sank money into their town, funding facilities and infrastructure. Today, Cody is a town more than comfortable with its history. Residents have capitalized on their founder's name and adopted his showy style, using both to celebrate their Western lifestyle through well-organized and widely marketed annual events. The Cody Nite Rodeo, begun 60 years ago as a tourist attraction, is today's version of Cody's Wild West Show (see our Spectator Sports chapter). The Buffalo Bill Historical Center (see our Attractions chapter), a 237,000-square-foot museum that attracts 250,000 visitors each year, is the hub of the community. Downtown offers cosmopolitan shopping and dining.

Despite Cody's population of only 8,600, its Yellowstone Regional Airport offers daily direct flights from Denver and Salt Lake City at competitive fares (see our Getting Around chapter).

A vigorous chamber of commerce (founded in 1900) is the engine that drives the town. As Cody had envisioned, his town has a diverse economy based on agriculture, oil and mining, tourism, a gypsum plant, timber and healthcare as well as federal and state employment. Marathon Oil is the major private employer with about 300 workers. The per capita personal income of Park County's 25,000-plus residents is $19,426, about the same as residents of Gallatin County in Montana but considerably higher than in Carbon, Park and Madison counties in Montana.

Far from Yellowstone National Park and its migrating herds (it's 53 miles), Cody's economic welfare lies largely in the policies of nearby public lands including park, National Forest and Bureau of Land Management lands. Merchants can — and will — easily measure their losses caused by four recent years of road construction on the east entrance road. They have weathered the construction and look forward to increased traffic flow and more visitors because of the new road. In addition, 82 percent of Park County is public land, and 50 percent of the county lies in wilderness, unreachable except on horseback or by foot. The town's growing recreation economy relies on these lands for hiking, bicycling, hunting, fishing, camping, rafting, snowmobiling and skiing. Its resource extraction industries also rely on public land policy.

This region contains the last nearly intact ecosystem in the contiguous 48 states. The variety of creatures here is astounding, including once-common animals that now exist in few other places.

Our Natural World

It happens the first time you see the ponderous swagger of a grizzly, the jagged grandeur of the Grand Teton dressed in tattered clouds, or the improbable loveliness of Yellowstone's Opalescent Pool: You're hooked. And you realize that those interesting restaurants, cozy bed and breakfast inns and picturesque ski resorts — in fact, all the great tourist attractions Yellowstone country offers — are just at the surface of things. Underneath is the really glamorous stuff. This region hosts natural wonders so unique that descriptions by Yellowstone's first explorers weren't believed, so rare and fine that the people who saw them wanted this place preserved forever. This chapter is about these Greater Yellowstone wonders — what makes them tick and how they came to be.

We've included only the most wonderful of wonders: the animals, mountain terrain and hydrothermal fireworks that seem to stand out in people's minds both before they arrive and after they leave. We'll tell you about the Yellowstone hot spot and the park's hydrothermal magic. We'll tell you a bit about the rugged landscape of this region and how it formed, as well as the plant communities upon which the rest of life depends.

We give much of our space, though, to the wildlife. This region contains the last nearly intact ecosystem in the contiguous 48 states. The variety of creatures here is astounding, including once-common animals that now exist in few other places.

Grizzlies, bald eagles, gray wolves, bighorn sheep and bison live together in this one place much as they once did across the West. One reason wildlife is worth looking for here is that, with some effort on your part, it can often be found. Because Greater Yellowstone hosts so many visitors each year, some of its creatures have learned to tolerate humans, especially in the region's two national parks. So although the wildlife here is wild — which means it's often elusive and always deserves your cautious respect — some creatures are easier to view in Greater Yellowstone than in any of their other wild homes.

Our Geothermal Features: The Yellowstone Hot Spot

Geologists believe the earth consists mostly of molten and semimolten rock, so what looks like solid land to us actually are thin plates riding like vast life rafts on a fiery, plastic ocean. Where they meet, one plate slips under another, and the diving edge melts back into the molten sea. Sometimes they slide, in fits and starts, past each other. From the human perspective, this giant-scale rearranging of the planet's surface happens in agonizing slow motion — inches or less a year — except for the sudden corrections that are earthquakes and the sudden release of melted plate material that probably triggers some volcanic eruptions.

Geologists further theorize that there are places in this semimolten ball that circulate heat from deep within the earth like a vertical, fiery-hot El Niño. The ball and its current of heat don't move, but the life rafts above do. This means residents of life rafts currently passing over one of these "hot spots" are going to experience weird phenomena — as weird as in, say, Yellowstone National Park, where between 150 and 200 geysers spout steam and hot water into the air; where a scientific team can dig 265 feet into the earth and encounter temperatures in excess of 400 degrees; where 107 known groups of hot springs percolate; and where, all told, there are at least 10,000 individual thermal features. Like a pot on a hot stove, Yellowstone National Park simmers and steams.

One mark of a good theory is the number of questions it can answer. The hot-spot theory addresses questions such as, "Why does the park radiate enough heat to melt 19 tons of ice every second?" and "Why is there a path of old volcanic activity stretching across what is now the Snake River Plain of southern Idaho and leading straight to Yellowstone National Park — a path consisting of craters and dead volcanoes?" It also explains why volcanoes get younger the closer they are to Yellowstone and why, just west of the massive collapsed lava hump of the Yellowstone Plateau, exists an even larger collapsed hump, which residents call the Island Park Caldera.

The hot-spot theory can't account for the wonder of Yellowstone by itself, though. A similar hot spot is thought to exist under the Hawaiian Islands, and they don't have an Old Faithful or a Mammoth Hot Springs. The missing ingredients are water and the geologic plumbing to carry it. Yellowstone's unique features are hydrothermic ("hydro" means water, and "thermic," heat). Groundwater is plentiful here, and volcanic rock is porous. The water percolates into the rock, getting increasingly warm and pressurized as it descends. Pressure keeps water liquid, even in an increasingly superheated state; in some cases temperatures probably exceed 500 degrees. This heated water may penetrate as deeply as 2 miles. How hot it gets and how it returns to the surface determine what sort of hydrothermal feature you see.

Hot Springs

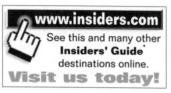

In one sense, all hydrothermal features in the park are hot springs because they all involve heated water, but the phrase usually refers to two kinds of features: the trickling springs that form terraced hillsides like those at Mammoth and pools of warm or even boiling water like Doublet Pool, Blue Star Spring and Crested Pool in Yellowstone National Park's Upper Geyser Basin.

At Mammoth and places like it, the subterranean water runs through calcium carbonate (limestone), dissolving the mineral as it goes. When the solution reaches the surface and trickles downslope, calcium carbonate is deposited to create those pale, lumpy walls and terraces you see. The resulting material is called travertine; it's similar in composition to marble.

Hot springs pools in Yellowstone are often lovely shades of blue, black or green. The blue color comes from the water and the sinter that lines the walls of the pool. This coating consists mostly of silica dissolved out of the volcanic rock. The full spectrum of light enters the water, but the blue light waves bounce off the geyserite and back through the water, which is busily absorbing the longer lightwaves while allowing blue to pass.

All but the hottest springs contain or are surrounded by life: green and yellow algae mats; orange, green, red and yellow bacteria; and ephydrid flies, which feed on the bacteria. Living elements, coupled with the chemicals dissolved in the pools and the minerals that line them, make possible all the colors of the rainbow. Orange bacteria combined with water that would appear blue will create what appears to be a pool of black water. Yellow algae in what would otherwise be blue water creates a pool that appears bright green. Silica suspended in the water can soften the color to baby blue.

Geysers

Yellowstone's most famous feature is probably Old Faithful, a geyser that erupts, on average, about every 81 minutes. But only 3 percent of the park's hydrothermal features are active geysers. To be a geyser, a hot spring must occasionally or regularly eject steam and water. This requires some fairly odd plumbing: Geysers run on a combination of superheated water — water that would like to boil into steam but doesn't have room — and steam explosions.

To create superheated water and to withstand the explosions, a geyser's plumbing needs to consist of an almost vertical chimney or series of chimneys leading down 200 feet or more. The walls must be smooth and made of resistant rock. Walls will be further smoothed and strengthened by the gradual formation of sinter from silicas in the water. These chimneys must also be narrow in order to create the tremendous pressure required to hold water in a liquid state above its boiling point. Sinter helps here, too, since as it accumulates it gradually narrows the chimney walls. Eventually it can seal a geyser chimney altogether.

At the bottom of the whole plumbing system must be a constantly replenished reservoir of water, because water is what the whole system runs on. Exposed to high temperatures and violently restricted in long, narrow chimneys, water becomes superheated. The only place it can go is up, so it tries to rise. Pressure from water in the narrow chimneys above prevents this until the pressure from below becomes too great. Then up comes a bubble of steam.

At first, what you see at the geyser's mouth isn't much — maybe a surging current or a small fountain of water. But that exiting water means that there is more room available below. The pressure that corked the chimney decreases. The superheated water that was trapped beneath flashes into steam, which instantly increases in volume and has nowhere to go but up. Fast. Water above the steam explosion is flung into the air on a rising column of steam. Up at the surface, cameras click and we ooh and aah at what seems like pure magic: a hissing, roaring column of pure white that builds itself out of nothing and then disappears.

Photo: Robert Bowe, Post Register

Wind-chill temperatures near 50 degrees below zero turned Old Faithful's boiling water column into freezing fog and ice.

To comprehend the explosive force that produces that awesome geyser display, imagine this: A cup of boiling water instantly converted to steam would increase 1,700 times in volume, suddenly requiring space equivalent to two 55-gallon drums.

Mud Pots

A mud pot looks like a cauldron of paint some joker put on the stove. Below the bubbling mess, a vent extends through the surface rock, leading to a reservoir of water far below your feet. Steam from this reservoir rises through clays created as acidic ground water dissolved surrounding rock. The watery clays, forced up to the surface by steam pressure from below, burble and spit contentedly when more steam rises through them.

Some, however, explode violently. At Mud Volcano, a giant mud pot existed for a short time that could be heard a mile away when its huge clay bubbles burst. In drier periods when clay consistency becomes thicker, mud pots can hurl clay bombs up to 200 feet.

Also called mud volcanoes or paint pots, these formations have walls generally colored by minerals, not algae and bacteria as are many hot springs. Yellows come mostly from sulphur; oranges, reds, browns and blacks come from iron oxides and iron sulfides. These minerals also exist inside the mud pots themselves, accounting for the many colors splatter-painted by these bizarre formations.

Fumaroles

Like a geyser or mud pot, this hydrothermal feature runs on steam. But there's very little liquid water in the plumbing system of a fumarole, and what little there is converts to steam as fast as it reaches boiling temperatures. What you see is a smoking hole in the ground. The roaring, hissing sounds, like the "smoke," are caused by steam exiting the vent.

A Yellowstone Time Bomb?

Geologists study slow-moving phenomena — events that occurred in such a distant past they are recorded only in stone. But the ponderous rhythm of geologic time doesn't seem to apply in Yellowstone. Here the hot spot keeps things hopping. Changes large and small happen almost in the blink of a geologist's eye. New mud pots and geysers form; old ones dry up or become something else, say a hot spring or fumarole.

Thousands of tiny earthquakes are recorded here every year, and between two and 167 annually are strong enough to feel. The last major earthquake in this area created a lake and modified hydrothermic features in Yellowstone National Park, some permanently. It occurred in 1959 and measured 7.5 on the Richter scale. The epicenter was just west of the park, and the temblor was felt across 500,000 square miles. Resulting rock slides in Madison Canyon, Montana, killed 28 people. The largest slide tumbled a mountainside into the Madison River and formed Quake Lake, which still exists. The lake is narrow but long and backs up the Madison River canyon for about 4.5 miles (learn more about Quake Lake in our Attractions chapter). After the main shock, about 300 geysers in Yellowstone National Park suddenly erupted. At least 160 of these had never been known to erupt. At least one blew so violently it threw 50- and 100-pound slabs of geyserite 50 feet from its vent.

Yellowstone's petrified forests are more distant reminders of the region's potential for dramatic geologic change. Yellowstone National Park alone has about 40 square miles of petrified forest. Other patches exist beyond park boundaries, particularly in the Gallatin National Forest. These eerie sites were created when volcanic eruptions and subsequent mud and ash buried whole forests. Silica dissolved in ground water percolated through the mummified trees, preserving them right down to their cell structure, including some of their leaves, needles and cones. Specimen Ridge in Yellowstone National Park contains layer upon layer of petrified trees. One theory has it that, like a single wave rolling up a beach, volcanic material inundated forest. The resulting rich volcanic soil gave birth to new trees, which were themselves destroyed by the next wave. Another theory says that volcanic mud slides brought section after section of forest down upon lower forests, creating the appearance of successive cataclysm where there was only one. Either way, the youngest petrified trees here are about 50 million years old. Scientists call the volcanic event(s) that created these stone forests Yellowstone's first volcanic episode.

We seem to be in the middle of the second one. Scientists who study the Yellowstone hot spot say this episode's pattern includes cataclysmic eruptions on a scale that makes Mount St. Helens look like a good neighbor. These eruptions occurred along the hot spot's path through Yellowstone country at least three times, each at roughly 600,000-year intervals. It's been 600,000 years since the last one. It left a 28-mile-by-47-mile caldera, one of the largest in the world, now partially filled by Yellowstone Lake. It's thought that before the explosion, a huge lava-filled bulge formed. For years, measurements showed that, in Yellowstone National Park, the earth's surface was bulging again — the area between Old Faithful and Canyon rose about an inch a year. Then for several years, the area subsided. Recent satellite imagery indicates that it's rising once more. Some geologists have a name for that disconcerting refusal of the earth to hold still: They call it "heavy breathing."

Our Geology: The Yellowstone Plateau

Just as beautiful as the world-famous hydrothermal features are the mountain ranges, high plateaus and glacial valleys of Greater Yellowstone. The best of these attractions are outside Yellowstone National Park. The Yellowstone Plateau itself is at high elevation, about 8,000 feet, but the terrain is rolling and, with the exception of the Grand Canyon of the Yellowstone, not particularly dramatic. The region's topography is largely the work of two volcanic episodes. One occurred about 38 to 50 million years ago and formed much of what are now the Absarokas and the Gallatins. The other, which is ongoing and began about 2 million years ago, is what gave the Yellowstone Plateau its shape. It's believed that the almost flat Yellowstone Plateau formed when a gigantic magma-filled dome collapsed; the resulting caldera was leveled by eruptions of molten rock.

Basin and Range

Our most impressive mountains are not volcanic in origin. Not long, geologically speaking, before the Yellowstone Plateau was created, much of what is now the Rockies formed. Geologists theorize that the cause was the North American plate colliding with the Pacific plate near what is now the Idaho-Oregon border. The collision created the accordion-like folding you might find on a car's hood after a head-on collision — the crumpled topography of much of the western United States. But that doesn't account for all of the West's mountains. The rest, say geologists, was the work of a massive lump in the earth's mantle, directly under the North American plate. The lump caused crustal extension — a stretching of the North American plate — that in turn created lines of weakness, or faults, which allowed more folding to take place.

Of course, no geologist was around to observe the events that formed what they call "basin and range" country, but look at a good map of the Western United States. You'll see alternating rows of mountain and valley that march from west to east like a cross between an accordian and a pregnant woman's stretch marks: The theories are easy to believe. The term "basin and range" describes the terrain of parts of Nevada, Utah, Oregon, New Mexico, Arizona, Idaho, California and Wyoming. The Tetons are its eastern edge.

Most of this redecorating of the West occurred 30 to 80 million years ago, but not so the Tetons. They may be only 5 million years old. That's why, even in the middle of rugged, mountainous country, the Tetons stand out. They seem to shred the clouds and steal scalloped bites of the moon. The Grand Teton is not the tallest mountain in Greater Yellowstone — that honor, by a few dozen feet, goes to Wyoming's Gannett Peak — but its improbably steep profile and soaring leap nearly 7,000 feet from the flat valley floor make it arguably the most spectacular. Like many mountain ranges in the Rocky Mountain region, the Tetons formed along a fault, still visible on its lower slopes, a few hundred feet above the flat valley floor. This weak line allowed a massive granite block 40 miles long and 15 miles wide to rise and the valley floor to drop. The uplift was much greater than the current height

INSIDERS' TIP

You may hear some people call elk "wapiti." Wapiti is a Shoshone word for elk; the word refers to the animal's pale, cream-colored rump, from a distance its most telltale feature.

of the Teton range, perhaps by more than a mile.

Glaciation

One more sculptor had an impact on the shape of our region: ice. Geologists find evidence of two ice ages here, although they say there have been many more. The last ended a mere 13,000 years ago. Geologists believe that between 20,000 and 25,000 years ago, at the height of that last ice advance, some 90 percent of what is now Yellowstone National Park was buried under an ice blanket perhaps 3,000 feet thick. Most of the higher elevations in Greater Yellowstone were inundated.

Slow-moving glaciers ground the valleys of Greater Yellowstone into big, rounded U's. Glaciers work like massive sandpapery sponges, scouring the earth across which they slowly creep and then incorporating the dislodged sediment into themselves. The more rock and dirt they accumulate, the better shapers of land glaciers become, just as coarse sandpaper removes paint faster than fine. As the glaciers retreated, sediment that had become part of the ice blankets was transported and then deposited in valleys by meltstreams. This further leveled valley floors. The wide, flat-bottomed valley of Jackson Hole is largely composed of glacial outwash and debris.

One valley not shaped into the classic glacial U is the famous Grand Canyon of the Yellowstone. Twenty miles long and 1,000 to 1,500 feet deep, the Grand Canyon of the Yellowstone was formed by the power of water, with a little assistance from heat and ice. The rock of the canyon walls was weakened in the heat from a series of volcanic events, making it more vulnerable to the cutting force of the Yellowstone River. Then, perhaps more than once, massive ice dams formed upstream, backing up huge volumes of water. When they released, the powerful flows sliced through the weakened rock like a saw. The result is a narrow, sheer-sided canyon with almost no flat area on the valley floor. The canyon walls' golden color is a result of chemical changes from the same heat which made them so vulnerable to the river's force.

As glaciers retreated, they left behind accumulated rocks and sediment in long, low ridges. Sometimes these ridges, called moraines, became dams, and long-profiled lakes formed behind them. All of the major lakes in Grand Teton National Park, including String and Leigh lakes, are glacial moraine-dammed lakes. Some, like Jackson and Jenny lakes, also owe their existence to the scouring power of glaciers. These with their deep-gouged basins are the footprints of glaciers long gone.

High up on the mountainsides glaciers carved cirques, which are flat-bottomed, steep-sided bowls scooped out of bare rock. The Grand Teton, a steep, sharp-edged spire, is a mountain with multiple cirques scalloping its faces. Smaller glaciers were common in the Absarokas, Palisades, Centennials, Madison, Gallatin, Salt River and Hoback ranges, among others. These ranges' ice-clear mountain lakes are typically pools that have collected in glacial cirques. The Wind River and Beartooth ranges, on the other hand, are thought to have been nearly buried under ice sheets during the last glaciation, much as Yellowstone National Park was.

Greater Yellowstone still has glaciers, although they are probably not remnants of the mighty ice fields that carved this country into its lovely, rugged shape. Geologists believe those glaciers melted and these formed later. The Tetons harbor several small glaciers, including one on the Grand itself. Glaciers grow and shrink with small fluctuations in climate. Photos taken of the Grand in the late 1800s show a much larger glacier below its north face than the one you see there today. The Wind River Mountains, in the seldom-visited southeast corner of Greater Yellowstone, get the glacier prize. Their extremely high altitude has allowed the formation of at least 24 named glaciers. This range has the largest glaciers in the lower 48 states.

Our Plant Communities

We refer, as many do, to a Greater Yellowstone ecosystem, as though it were a homogeneous place. Don't let us mislead you into thinking of Greater Yellowstone as a seamless expanse. It's a crazy quilt of wet and dry zones, lowland valleys and above-treeline alpine crags. Species like elk, bison, bear and moose do move across the region with seasons and availability of food; and it is true that Greater Yellowstone's landscapes and animal and plant communities interlock like puzzle pieces. But this region is nothing if not diverse. In a moment we want to introduce you to what we believe is the third popular attraction of Greater Yellowstone: the wildlife. But first let's look at the world — or, rather, the worlds — these animals live in.

Plant communities in Greater Yellowstone vary with altitude. Other factors are important, too, like soil type or a hillside's orientation to sun and prevailing winds. But in general, look for the driest areas and longest growing seasons at the lowest elevations.

In many of Greater Yellowstone's low valleys, sagebrush and bunch grasses dominate; they are green in spring, but gray and straw-colored by midsummer. Although 30 inches of annual precipitation fall in some parts of Greater Yellowstone, these lower elevations may see only 10. About 160 species of grasses and flowers grow here, mostly in lower-elevation meadows and valleys. Grass is the preferred forage for most grazing animals, but they'll eat sage if they have to, for instance, in winter, when grasses are buried under the snowpack.

Along these same low-elevation valleys run rivers. Where you find these rivers, you'll find deciduous trees, broad-leaved species that shed their leaves in winter. The three most common are cottonwood, willow and aspen. Find any of these three species and you've also found water, either at or just below the surface.

Cottonwoods grow along river channels at lower elevations; in some areas they practically line the banks. This is a result of cottonwoods' inclination to drop their fluffy, floating seeds just in time for spring runoff. The seeds travel downstream, lodge on exposed gravel as the river recedes and begin to grow. In return for the free ride, cottonwoods stabilize river banks.

Aspen grows in pockets where groundwater accumulates rather than near sources of surface water. Aspen is important in this ecosystem because of an anomaly in its makeup: Its bark contains chlorophyll, nutritious for elk who love to browse on aspen shoots and nibble at aspen bark, especially in winter when little else is available.

Willows are among the most abundant small trees in Greater Yellowstone. At higher elevations, they take the place of cottonwoods, stabilizing riverbanks and lakes and providing cover for small animals. Willow, one of the moose's favorite food sources, is particularly common on the marshy, flat valley floors that glaciers tend to leave behind.

Scattered across Greater Yellowstone are the region's lakes and ponds, including huge bodies of water such as Montana's Quake Lake (some maps call it Earthquake Lake) and Wyoming's Yellowstone Lake, the largest high-mountain lake in the country. Also included are tiny ponds such as Kelly Hot Springs and the lakelike waters of the Snake River Oxbow in Grand Teton National Park. Then there are the natural lakes that have been enlarged by dams to store more water, including Henry's, Jackson and Hebgen, as well as man-made reservoirs such as Palisades and Island Park.

The fish-bearing waters of Greater Yellowstone make up one of the world's most productive fisheries. Pelicans and rare trumpeter swans, as well as more common waterfowl, rely on these bodies of water. So do land mammals that find shelter in water, such as otters, or that feed on its abundant plant life, such as bear and moose. Warm water from the region's hydrothermal features keeps many of these waters ice-free in winter. This benefits species like trumpeter swans that otherwise could not survive winter here. Ice-free waters also provide winter fishing for bald eagles.

At slightly higher altitudes away from the rivers, the spruce, fir and pine forests begin. Like many areas shaped by glaciation, the soil can be very thin in places, which, scientists say, is why it's heavily forested. Sounds weird, but grasses grow quickly in deep, rich soil and shade out the slow-growing trees. So forests tend to occur in shallow soils where faster-growing plants have less of an advantage. Fast drainage also helps trees because their roots extend far below the level of the grasses: Their toes can still be cool and moist when grasses are turning to crisp straw. Much of the soil of Greater Yellowstone is volcanic in origin, which can make it nutrient-rich and fertile. You can take a fair guess if the volcanic soil you're

National Elk Refuge

Much of the traditional summer range of Greater Yellowstone's elk herds is protected as national forest or national park. Their winter range, however, is nearly gone, carved up into recreational acreages, grazed by cattle or gridded into towns. Even where fertile, lower-elevation grasslands still exist untouched, they're difficult for elk to access because towns stand across the old migration routes.

Elk feeding and the National Elk Refuge in Jackson Hole exist today as an uneasy compromise between the needs of humans and those of elk. Feeding began here during the harsh winter of 1908, but it was a local effort—too little and too late to prevent hundreds of animals from dying. The next winter was, if anything, worse. Starving elk marauded ranchers' haystacks and competed with their cattle, then died in the trampled snow anyway. Ranchers, barely eking a living in the tough conditions of a Jackson Hole winter, couldn't afford the losses to their cattle. Nor could they easily dispose of the rotting corpses in the spring.

The National Elk Refuge and the funding that subsidizes its feeding program have their roots in photos taken by a man named Stephen Leek. One of Leek's most famous pictures shows, among the crumpled forms of dead elk, a desperate few still alive, stretching toward life-giving hay too high overhead to reach. The photos prompted Congress in 1912 to allot 1,000 acres and feed money to Jackson Hole's winter elk herds.

Now the refuge contains nearly 25,000 acres of prime grassland and supports a winter herd of somewhere between 7,500 and 12,000. Funding for the roughly 30 tons of alfalfa pellets the herd requires after the natural vegetation has been grazed off comes from two sources: Wyoming Game and Fish provides about half with profits from the

— **continued on next page**

Photo: Jackson Hole Chamber of Commerce

The Elk Refuge north of Jackson Hole provides a close view of elk during the winter months.

sale of hunting licenses, and local Boy Scouts provide the other half, their share generated by their annual antler auction in Jackson, Wyoming (see our Annual Events chapter). The cost of feeding one animal for the winter is about $50. Limited hunting is allowed on the refuge since the herd's size is thought to exceed habitat carrying capacity. Nature's way of controlling numbers, a combination of winter-kill and depredation by predators, appears harsher to us than the hunter's bullet.

The refuge is home to one of the area's more interesting winter attractions: a horse-drawn sleigh ride out into the huge herds of elk (see our Attractions chapter). In summer, the elk return to the high country, and the dirt Elk Refuge Road is used by joggers and mountain bikers. Ponds at the southern end of the refuge near U.S. Highway 89 host a variety of waterfowl, including the endangered and lovely trumpeter swan.

Many people don't know that more than 20 elk-feeding sites exist between the refuge and Pinedale, Wyoming. The better-known of these are one between Jackson and Hoback Junction and another near Alpine, Wyoming, at Palisades Reservoir. Additional feeding locations are necessary because the elk that winter at the refuge constitute only a portion of the Yellowstone herds, many of which seek refuge in low grasslands that have become almost totally the domain of humans.

Another thing visitors may not know is that winter feeding is controversial around here. Every human intervention impacts ecosystem balance. For instance, winter kill has always been part of the lives of Greater Yellowstone's ungulate herds. In early spring, grizzlies and other predators rely upon the ready supply of meat provided by winter-killed elk, bison and deer. Supply feed to the herds, and few will die. Then it's the grizzlies, wolves, wolverines and coyotes that suffer hardship.

For more about the National Elk Refuge, see its listing in the Attractions chapter.

---

standing on is rhyolite (so lacking in nutrients that biologist Linda Wallace says it's "like growing on glass beads") or the more fertile andesite by the trees around you. Lodgepole, which blankets much of the region, can thrive in very poor soil. Spruce, fir, aspen and Douglas fir are more demanding.

Not all of Greater Yellowstone is forested. As we said earlier, areas at low elevation with low moisture, with thick soil or poor drainage, won't easily grow trees. Trees can't thrive at extremely high elevations, either. Above tree line, as it's called, growing conditions are too harsh and the growing season too short for anything but shrubs, grasses and wildflowers. The reason plants up here are often miniature versions of species that exist below is that they don't have time to grow large: They must flower and reproduce in too short a time to mess around getting big. In fact, if a flowering plant "thinks" it doesn't have time to flower, go to seed and reproduce itself before the winter snows hit, it will skip a year's flowering and wait until the next. For this reason, most of the tiny plants above the timberline are perennials, plants that regrow from their root systems every spring, rather than annuals, which die every fall and rely on their seeds to produce next spring's plants.

But most of us spend little time at those windswept altitudes. We play in the mid-elevation forests, made up mostly of lodgepole pine. In Yellowstone National Park, 80 percent of the forested areas are lodgepole. You also find Douglas fir at lower elevations; at higher elevations grow subalpine fir, whitebark pine and Engelmann spruce. But throughout the ecosystem, the predominant evergreen is spindly, fast-growing lodgepole. Lodgepole forests cause a gamut of challenges for land managers, not the least of which is that an important part of its life cycle is fire.

Before the coming of Euro-Americans, this was fine. In fact, just as gardeners today may burn off their garden plots to make the next crop more productive, Native Americans once burned wild lands to increase the productivity of plant communities. But today many see natural forest processes like fire as wasteful at best and disastrous at worst. Land managers, managed by public opinion and economics as much as by science, have to respond to that view. Science says fire is good for lodgepoles, which are short-lived and at maturity often become host to the mountain pine beetle, then sicken and die. Fire is good for the soil: Burned wood replenishes its nutrients. Lodgepole cones, some of which are serotinous (they open in response to heat), reseed the burned area. The heat and destruction also spur production of new aspen shoots, which sprout from a communal root system that survives all but the hottest fires. So fire begins the conversion of a mature, dying forest to a vital young one.

Fire benefits other plant species as well, because a mature lodgepole forest is homogenous. The trees, all about the same age and height, grow close together, canopies overlapping. Little underbrush can grow because little sunlight breaks through. Plus, as every home gardener knows, the soil under such trees is too acidic to support most plant species. Fire makes room for a greater variety of plant species, particularly the grasses and brush that wildlife browse upon. So greater animal diversity follows the increased plant diversity.

The massive fires that swept through Greater Yellowstone in 1988 (see our History chapter) seemed tragic to many. Vast hillsides of charred trees look like destruction to us. A human lifetime is too short to make appreciation of the forest cycle easy, especially when close to half of the nation's first national park is involved. Some 400,000 acres of trees in nearby national forests also burned, so the logging industry wasn't happy either: Harvestable timber is not the endlessly available commodity it once seemed to be, so watching those forests go up in smoke hurt. But throughout Greater Yellowstone, and most strikingly in Yellowstone National Park, the lodgepole forests were and are mature — ready to burn and make room for the greater plant and animal diversity that inevitably follows this next step in the natural process.

Our Wild Inhabitants

From its lowest elevations to its highest, Greater Yellowstone is rich with wildlife. Its vast tracts of relatively wild lands contain a wide range of environments that support an even greater range of animal life. All together, Greater Yellowstone harbors seven species of ungulates (hoofed animals), two species of bears, three kinds of wild cats, three canids and about 70 smaller predator and prey species. The area is also home to 22 kinds of fish, more than 120 species of butterflies and more than 20 species of reptiles and amphibians. You will likely see one or two of Greater Yellowstone's 90,000 mule deer along roadsides. Driving in the grassy sagelands, you may spot the white-sided pronghorn antelope, the fastest North American mammal. An incredible number of bird species — more than 300 — call this area home at least part of the year. Among these are osprey, kingfisher, ouzel, American kestrel, Steller's jay, raven and magpie. Greater Yellowstone is no zoo, however. The animals are there. But what you see will be determined by luck, patience and knowledge. We can't help with the luck and the patience is all yours, but the sections that follow

INSIDERS' TIP

If you look sharp, you may see an osprey, or fish hawk, winging away from a river with a trout slung aerodynamically head-first beneath him. And if you know that birds of prey have four toes, three forward and one back, you may be puzzled. How can he hold that slippery trout any way but sideways in his talons? The answer: The osprey's third forward toe is double jointed to bend back when he holds a trout. This enables him to clasp the fish with one talon and use the other to grab hold of his perch.

Photo: Randy Hayes, Post Register

Wintering elk flee a helicopter carrying biologists who are conducting a winter survey.

provide an introduction to several of the more famous Greater Yellowstone residents. This information should help you know where to look, since wild creatures, just like humans, live where they can find food and protection. Knowing a little about an animal's needs and habits increases your chances of seeing it.

Elk

Elk are not an endangered species, although around the turn of the century their survival was questionable. Nationwide, there are about 900,000 elk, 10 times as many as in 1900. In Yellowstone country, elk numbers seem to be at an all-time high. Estimates vary, but some say that as much as 40 percent of Greater Yellowstone's 90,000 to 120,000 elk live inside Yellowstone National Park at least part of the year. But the high, snowy Yellowstone Plateau would make for hungry winters, so the elk head for lower elevations in October. Some 10,000 to 15,000 head for the sheltered northern end of Yellowstone National Park. As many as 12,000 more spend their winters at the National Elk Refuge near Jackson. Elk refuges and winter feeding areas attempt to address the problem that for nearly six months a year, elk need to live in the same sheltered, low-elevation grasslands that make good sites for towns, ranches and farms.

Bull elk begin growing their impressiv antlers early in spring (cow elk don't have an lers). The bull's antlers grow from two perm nent bones, called pedicles, that attach to t elk's skull. Antlers take about four months grow. They harden over the summer, fall winter until, dry as old wood, they snap close to the bull's head. Then the nex begins to grow. Of the four subspecies that still survive in the United States, the R Mountain elk found in Yellowstone c have the largest racks. A pair of antlers big bull may weigh 40 pounds.

Elk like green grass, so they're ofte on open grassy hillsides. In fall, when dry up, elk will eat more small, leaf and even bushes and shrubs. In w paw through the snow and eat anyt s- can find: bushes, dried grasses, tre pine pecially aspen) and lichens hanging trees.

Especially in tough winte me elk starve. Without the feeding program that began soon after the turn of the century, even more elk would die in winter, since much of what was once their winter range has been developed for human use. This means that, despite the fact that elk populations in this area are probably much lower than before the coming of Euro-Americans, herd sizes are currently maintained at artificial highs based on what remaining wildlands can support. If we left them alone, there would be many, many fewer elk in Greater Yellowstone. (To learn more about elk and the National Elk Refuge, see our Close-up in this chapter.)

Grizzly Bear

Some estimates say that in 1800, 100,000 grizzlies lived in North America. Now experts think fewer than 1,000 live in the lower 48 states, on two tiny fragments of their former ange. Grizzlies are generally solitary animals at require huge, sprawling wilderness — a -disappearing commodity. One area still e enough and wild enough to contain griz- is Yellowstone country; another is a y defined area that contains northwest- ntana's Glacier National Park and sev- ernesses jigsawed together much like Greater Yellowstone. The Greater ne grizzly population is variously es- ween 250 and 600.

ne "grizzly bear" comes from the which is often dark brown tipped ating a grizzled appearance. But fur color to identify the grizzly: and nearly black grizzlies exist. a grizzly is likely to stand 4 feet at r. Males average 400 to 600 ales, 250 to 350. Belying their ze, grizzlies can run up to 25 mph aster than you can) and can climb of trees. They can smell a car- away; their claws are more than .

heir fearsome appearance, griz- zlies rictly meat-eaters. They also eat gras lions, berries, roots and insects. Recen es indicate that, particularly in spring arly summer, up to 80 percent of a Yellow grizzly's diet may be meat. The carcasse winter-killed animals are plentiful then, and akened or infant animals even more so. owstone National Park officials say that predators, including grizzly, account for the deaths of up to 50 percent of elk calves.

Grizzlies aren't real hibernators, but they do sleep deeply through most of the winter. Real hibernators can't be awakened by disturbance, but bears can, as researchers who've visited their winter lairs know. In winter, sleeping bears lose much of the 8-inch-thick layer of fat accumulated in the fall. At times their pulses fall to eight beats per minute.

One reason the seemingly invincible grizzly is in such danger from man is that it reproduces slowly. Females don't mate until they are at least 4 or 5 years old. Mature females are only ready to mate for two or three weeks out of a year — and the bears' huge ranges make that small window of opportunity easy to miss. Plus, cubs stay with their mothers for up to four years, and only females without cubs will mate. Females typically produce one or two cubs at a time. Wildlife managers fear that we're killing grizzlies as fast as they can reproduce, despite best efforts to the contrary.

Park Service and Forest Service rangers destroy dangerous "nuisance" bears every year; others are killed in encounters with hunters or backcountry travelers, or mistaken by hunters who thought they were shooting at black bears (hunting black bears is legal; hunting grizzlies is not). One study found that between 1975 and 1988, 86 grizzlies, 39 of them females, were killed by humans in Greater Yellowstone. Despite the fact that Yellowstone grizzly numbers seem to be fairly stable, some experts say that such a small population in such an isolated wilderness pocket is too vulnerable to further habitat reduction, mismanagement or act of nature. These people predict extinction for the Yellowstone grizzlies within 100 years.

Seeing a grizzly in the wild is a privilege and a risk. It's also rare: Grizzlies in Greater Yellowstone stick generally to meadows and alpine basins in roadless areas, as far from human intrusion as they can get. And park officials help preserve their tiny island of isolation, closing trails and campsites near kills, and in certain high-use seasons closing whole areas to human traffic. Even if you're in their territory, a grizzly can scent your presence at several hundred yards and will generally retreat without your ever knowing he was near. If you want to look at grizzlies, you'll need binoculars. If you stood close enough to see a grizzly well with the unaided eye, you'd be too close, both for your safety and the bear's. Remember that bears forfeit their lives when they lose their fear of man or when they come to associate our cars, campsites and backpacks with food. (See our Close-up on bear safety in our Hunting chapter). In the parks, report grizzly sightings to the rangers.

Black Bear

They're just as likely to be brown, cinnamon or blond, but some black bears actually are black. Black bears weigh from 125 to 500 pounds and usually stand less than 3 feet at the shoulder. They have curved claws that allow them to climb trees more easily than their larger cousins, grizzlies, whose claws are nearly straight. Black bears, like grizzlies, are competent swimmers; also like grizzlies, they can run at much higher speeds than you can, belying their fat and clownish appearance. Unlike grizzlies, who generally stick to wilder country and are seldom seen by human visitors, black bears are common in forested areas across Greater Yellowstone. Some estimates place black bear numbers in Yellowstone National Park alone at 600 and Greater Yellowstone's population at more than 1,000, but read those numbers as the educated guesses they are: No serious attempt to count black bears in this region has been made in decades. Like grizzlies, cougars and other asocial, people-shy species, black bears are difficult and expensive to reliably count.

A black bear's diet consists mostly of vegetation, perhaps as much as 80 percent. Grasses are a mainstay. This means that black bears are partial to forested areas interspersed with the open meadows that grow their dinner. Bears also like bulbs, berries, and the inner bark of some trees, as well as rodents, insects and carrion. Bears are most active at night, so dusk and dawn are most likely sighting times. Most visitors don't see a black bear, but if you happen to, do not approach it except with your binoculars. Bears look pudgy and cute, but take them seriously: They're wild and potentially dangerous animals. They have been known to attack and kill humans. Those who study bear attacks on humans point out that the very rare predatory attacks —those in which the animal obviously is after meat — more typically involve black bears than grizzlies. The National Park Service asks that you report bear sightings in the parks, particularly those near areas with significant human traffic. Bears that have been taught by careless visitors that food can be found in campgrounds or cars or backpacks are moved if possible and destroyed if necessary.

For more on how to treat both yourself and the region's bears with care, please see our Close-up on bear safety in the Hunting chapter.

Moose

The moose is the largest member of the deer family. Adult males can stand 6 feet at the shoulder and weigh up to a half-ton. Like elk and deer, bull moose grow velvet-encased antlers every spring. The velvet supplies blood to the growing bone; if you could touch an antler in summer it would feel warm from the blood coursing through the velvety sheath. The velvet dries and is scraped off in late summer. Fall is the rut, a time when female moose are receptive to mating and bulls become aggressive. This is the purpose of the massive antlers — sparring and fighting over females. Agitated males will lose up to 30 percent of their body weight during the rut, which ends in mid-

INSIDERS' TIP

If you have Internet access and are interested in Greater Yellowstone's wildlife and wonders, try the following sites: www.poky.srv.net/~jjmrm/maughan.html, www.idahonews.com, www.nps.gov/grte/ or www.wyoming.com/~yellowstonejournal/TOC.html.

Photo: Robert Bower

A trumpeter swan on the Firehole River searches for food as it paddles steadily against the current.

or late November. The heavy antlers, their usefulness outlived, harden until they snap off close to the animal's head, usually sometime in December or January.

Except in early spring when males lack antlers, the distinctive shapes of these bony appendages make for easy identification of local members of the deer family. If you see antlers at all, know you're looking at a male. If the antlers are cylindrical like tree branches and point mostly upward, you're watching a deer. If the main stem of the antler branches back on a line almost parallel with the animal's back, you're seeing a bull elk. If the antlers are great, flat plates edged with fingerlike tines, the ungainly brown beast in your binoculars is a bull moose.

There are thought to be about 6,000 moose in Greater Yellowstone. Some hypothesize that the big ungulate did not historically live in significant numbers here, but was pushed into the area as man took over its preferred, lower-elevation habitat.

Moose eat twigs, pine and fir needles, and tree bark in winter, but what they like is water vegetation and the tender willow shoots that grow alongside rivers and streams. They also like aspen and new, fresh grass. Long legs make moose good water foragers. A common sight in Greater Yellowstone is a big brown body, apparently headless, hip-deep in a pond or slow-moving stream. When the big head rises above the surface, it trails water and soggy green water plants. Those long legs also make winter snows less an obstacle for moose than for many other Greater Yellowstone ungulates.

In summer, look for moose near water, especially in willow thickets, cottonwood bottoms or plant-clogged ponds. In winter, peruse south-facing hillsides where the snowpack is not so deep or among thick trees, which also keep snowpack down.

Moose are not as sedate as they may appear, particularly if they feel cornered. Bull moose in rut or cows with calves have been known to attack hikers with little provocation. Moose aren't terribly afraid of humans. They'll avoid you if they can, but if they can't escape without going through you, they're coming through. Early one morning in Gros Ventre Campground in Grand Teton National Park, we watched from behind a big tree as a young bull moose accidentally demolished a tent that had been pitched illegally out of bounds. The moose bolted through the campground, tentfly tangled in its antlers. Twice it stopped to confront humans. The animal seemed to be flipping a mental coin: heads, run some more; tails, trample the puny creature. Although it came up heads both times, we were glad for our tree.

Trumpeter Swan

In the 1930s, the trumpeter swan balanced precariously at extinction's razor edge: Fewer than 70 were known to exist in the United States. The largest waterfowl in North America, the trumpeter swan was known by the graceful curve of its neck, its snowy feathers and (unfortunately) its tasty flesh. Now about 2,500 swans make their home in Greater Yellowstone and neighboring areas in Wyoming, Montana and Idaho, and another, larger flock lives along the Pacific coast. A moratorium on hunting and egg collecting helped, but more importantly, marshy winter habitat was preserved at places like Red Rock Lakes National Wildlife Refuge in Montana and Idaho's Harriman State Park.

One negative aspect of recovery efforts involves winter feeding. As their numbers increase, trumpeter swans are overfilling the few areas we've set aside for them. Their continued recovery hinges on finding new areas, but 50 years of winter feeding at Red Rock has discouraged the flocks from seeking other winter havens farther south. They need open water to survive, and this far north that means spring water, which stays warm enough not to freeze even in the harshest winters. There aren't many such places. The winter habitat pinch is further complicated by the fact that more aggressive mute swans, imported from Europe by humans, have pushed the native trumpeters from historic haunts.

Trumpeter swans weigh about 30 pounds. They can span 8 feet from wingtip to wingtip. They fly at nearly highway speed: 50 mph. Trumpeters' black bills help set them apart from the mute swan, which is the species most commonly seen in zoos. Tundra swans, the only other species in this area, also have black bills and are most easily distinguished from trumpeters by guesswork. Only about 1 percent of swans seen around here are tundra swans, so if you guess that a black-billed swan is a trumpeter, you're probably right. (If you want to get serious about this and you have a pair of binoculars handy, look for the telltale yellow spot on the tundra swan's bill just in front of the eye.)

A few trumpeters spend the whole year here, particularly at Harriman State Park, but most migrate from Canada in October and head back north in mid-March. Swans, like Canada geese, mate for life and return to the same nesting area every year. They prefer shallow, stagnant or slow-moving water, where they feed on shallow water plants, seeds and roots. Those long necks mean that swans can reach deeper under water than ducks can, so ducks sometimes follow swans, cleaning up plant debris stirred up by the larger birds.

Because new migration patterns are key to the birds' continued recovery, you're asked to report sightings of neck-collared swans. Please note the location and date of the sighting, color of neck collar, and color and location of any dye on the bird. If you can, note also the letter and numbers on the neck collar. Call U.S. Fish and Wildlife Service at (208) 237-6616 with your sighting.

Bison

Once there were millions, traveling in herds as unstoppable as hurricanes and as lifegiving as rain for humans and other predators. The

INSIDERS' TIP

If you have an emergency, the number to call is always 911. But if it's information or non-critical assistance you need, check our Parks and Forests chapter for ranger station and Yellowstone/ Grand Teton National Park dispatch numbers. Many other government entities, from the Bureau of Land Management to the U.S. Fish and Wildlife Service, are happy to assist visitors. Find some of those numbers in our Resource chapter.

massacre of the bison herds in the 19th century was partly about hides but mostly the result of government policy. Officials guessed, correctly, that eliminating bison would starve the Plains Indians onto reservations. American bounty hunters were extremely effective. So was a policy of handing out ammunition to wagon train members and others along herds' migratory routes. By 1900 bison were nearly extinct. What is now the last wild herd in the United States grew out of the few dozen animals that remained in Yellowstone National Park at the turn of the century, coupled with an infusion of new blood from small captive populations elsewhere. Today's Yellowstone herd is about 2,200 head. A smaller herd in Jackson Hole may number as many as 400, although estimates vary. Bison also seem to be recolonizing areas adjacent to Jackson Hole.

The bison's successful recovery in Greater Yellowstone causes problems for wildlife managers, though, as the animals begin to move outside Yellowstone National Park, particularly in winter. Bison damage fences and frighten Montana ranchers concerned that cattle could contract a disease called brucellosis from their wild cousins. Studies show such contagion to be extremely unlikely — brucellosis transmission has never been documented in the wild and has only with difficulty been induced in a laboratory setting. But livestock producers worked for decades to rid themselves of the disease, which causes infected cows to abort. Without their coveted brucellosis-free status, Montana's ranchers would not be allowed to market cattle outside the state. The upshot? Bison are shot every winter as they wander beyond park boundaries, outraging some and barely satisfying others.

Weather and other factors vary the kill rate: The winter of 1997-98 saw 11 shot. The winter before, more than 1,000 bison died. Wildlife lovers and federal and state land managers often try to haze bison back into the park. Barring that, Montana Department of Livestock or the National Park Service trap wandering bison in big, plywood-sided corrals. Trapped bison are tested for exposure to brucellosis (the test doesn't show if animals are actually infected). Forty to 50 percent test positive. Near West Yellowstone, unexposed bison that are not pregnant are marked and released, usually within a day. The rest are killed. Near Gardiner, bison that test negative, pregnant or not, are held just inside the park, then released in spring to amble further into Yellowstone National Park, where some Montanans say is the only place they belong. Under the current interim management plan, the final option is to kill every bison that leaves the park. Wildlife managers, scientists, Montana's Department of Livestock, ranchers and wildlife lovers await a better solution to this politically supercharged issue.

Unlike other Greater Yellowstone ungulates, both bull and cow bison have horns, although the males' horns are larger. Horns, unlike antlers, are not shed and regrown every year — a bison keeps its horns for life. The material that makes up horn is keratin, the stuff your fingernails consist of. Rut begins early for bison, running from mid-July to mid-August. Bulls paw the ground and shove each other. Occasionally altercations become serious, but generally they involve a lot of bullying and little real force. Hikers sometimes mistake the enraged bellowing of bison bulls during the rut for grizzly bear growls.

Bison weigh up to 2,000 pounds, which slows them down not a bit: They gallop at a ground-pounding 40 mph. Most of the time, though, they seem as sedate as cattle. Like cattle, bison are grazers, eating mostly grass

INSIDERS' TIP

Do you know why the National Park Service forbids you to remove dropped elk or deer antlers from Yellowstone and Grand Teton National Parks? The antlers are an important source of calcium for other animals. Antlers are removed from the National Elk Refuge only because those grasslands are managed as grazing areas, and the heavy equipment would bog down among several thousand sets of antlers.

year-round. In winter they bulldoze through the snowpack with their big, blocky heads to reach the dried grasses and sedges below. Look for bison in large meadow areas like Hayden Valley and the Madison Plateau in summer and in lower-elevation open areas in winter. Some move into areas with thermal features in winter, taking advantage of the fact that little snow accumulates on the heated ground. This winter comfort is purchased with risk, though: Every so often a bison breaks through a thin earth shell over boiling water and dies.

Most of Greater Yellowstone's bison are found in and immediately around Yellowstone National Park. They tend to herd, so if you see one, look for more. As we said, bison look sedate and unconcerned, which may be why the most common serious human-vs.-animal encounters in Greater Yellowstone involve bison. Every year, visitors who approach too closely are trampled or gored.

Wolf

As with bison, the survival of wolves in Yellowstone hinges on politics more than biology. Wolves, once common throughout the continental United States, were systematically trapped and poisoned to the brink of extinction for their bushy, plush hides and later to make room for livestock. Unlike most species, wolves were not protected after the creation of Yellowstone National Park. If anything, extermination efforts were stepped up in the early part of the 20th century. The last known wolves in Yellowstone National Park, two pups, were killed in 1924 near Soda Butte. The last known resident wolf in Wyoming was shot in 1943.

In 1995, after nearly two decades of debate, 14 wolves were captured in Canada and reintroduced to Yellowstone National Park. Fifteen more were released in central Idaho. The next year, 38 more were released in this region, 17 in Yellowstone National Park. As expected, the new residents of Yellowstone have dispersed from the park, sometimes onto private land. Also as expected, the newcomers have killed livestock. Defenders of Wildlife reimburses ranchers for livestock depredation, which at the end of 1998 totaled 80 sheep, 11 cows or calves and one working dog. Wolves have been killed in turn, some by other wolves, some by poachers, one by burns sustained in a hot spring or geyser, several by cars or trucks and several more by either ranchers or wildlife managers. Ranchers may legally kill wolves that attack livestock on private land, and wildlife managers kill livestock-eating wolves, whether on national forest or private land. By early 1999, 60 wolves had died or been killed, 11 at the hands of federal wildlife agents. But the new wolf population seems able to sustain the losses: in the spring of 1998 alone, 42 pups were whelped.

Recently, wolves have been seen as far south as the National Wildlife Refuge near Jackson, where they prey upon the elk that find winter shelter and feed there. Biologists hope they'll cull the weak and sick out of an elk herd currently close to double its target size. Wolves were once the area's major predators.

There are no plans to introduce more wolves to Yellowstone. In fact, the fragility of the compromises that brought wolves back to ranching country is illuminated by a pending court action that would remove all transplanted wolves and offspring. In December 1998, that was roughly 120 animals.

Meanwhile, wolves have become one of the region's star attractions. You're unlikely to see a wolf, but if you want to try, the best area has been in the northeast corner of Yellowstone National Park, along the park road in the Lamar Valley. One pack there currently numbers 22; when it occasionally travels as a unit, it's easy to spot. The National Elk Refuge in winter may become a prime spotting spot, especially since many wolves are dark in color and stand out well against snow. You'll need binoculars, though; wolves keep their distance

INSIDERS' TIP

Want to see bald eagles in winter? Try Paradise Valley near Chico Hot Springs. The big birds congregate here to fish waters kept ice-free by nearby hot springs.

from humans. What should you look for? Your best bet is to find the telltale crowd, armed with spotting scopes and binoculars. Then focus your glasses and look for a gray, whitish or black German shepherd with extra long legs, an extra bushy tail and oversized feet, weighing about 125 pounds. That's the gray wolf, newly returned in a storm of controversy to Yellowstone country.

Cutthroat Trout

Cutthroats get their name from reddish-orange slashes under the lower jaw. Yellowstone's only native trout has 13 subspecies, but only two exist here: Yellowstone cutthroat and West Slope cutthroat. The West Slope variety are found primarily in Montana, but even there their numbers are sharply limited, so it's the Yellowstone cutthroat you're likely to encounter. Some believe the Snake River Finespotted cutthroat is a third Yellowstone subspecies, but Finespotted cutthroats differ from Yellowstone cutts only in appearance (the spots along their backs and sides are smaller).

All other trout in these waters — hard-fighting rainbows, long-lived massive browns and scrappy little brook trout — were imported, beginning in the 1880s. Lake trout, which grow to a truly monstrous size, are also imports, unwanted since they threaten the survival of native cutts in Yellowstone Lake and other waters. Studies have shown that when Lake trout colonize or are introduced to cutthroat habitat, the cutts gradually disappear. Lake trout were found in Yellowstone Lake, a cutthroat stronghold, for the first time in 1994.

Many fishermen hope to catch these colorful native trout, but the interest in preserving native wild fisheries is recent and still not universal. Rainbows, browns and hatchery hybrids like cutt-bows are larger than cutts and are often perceived as a tougher and therefore more satisfying catch. Cutthroats have a reputation for being foolhardy and ready to bite anything, which makes them easy to hook, and for being less feisty on a fisherman's line than, say, rainbows.

Cutthroats eat plankton when young, then mostly insects, although larger ones may eat other fish. A 4-pound cutt would be a large fish. They were once the most widely distributed trout in the West, but wild native cutthroat fisheries are becoming few and far between. Cutthroats are not very resistant to competition from non-native fish or to habitat modification like that on the South Fork of the Snake since the construction of Palisades Dam. Believing that native wild fisheries suffer when hatchery stock is introduced, Montana stocks no cutthroat in its streams. Idaho stocks Henry's Lake with cutthroat and hybrid cuttbows, but Idaho's most robust native cutt fisheries, like the South Fork of the Snake, are left alone. Wyoming regularly stocks hatchery cutthroat in its lakes and streams, which makes that state your best bet for catching cutts, if not your best bet for catching wild, native cutts.

The best places for non-anglers to see trout, including cutthroat, are the National Fish Hatcheries in Jackson Hole, Wyoming, and Ennis, Montana; smaller state-run hatcheries at Henry's Lake and Ashton, Idaho; and fish-feeding areas such as Big Springs and the Warm River, both near Island Park, Idaho. Watching has replaced fishing at Fishing Bridge in Yellowstone National Park because the water is so clear and the fish so easy to see. In fact, thousands more visit Fishing Bridge to watch fish than ever did to wet a line there.

For information on Yellowstone country's fishing opportunities, turn to our Fishing and Watersports chapter.

Bald Eagle

Its wings can stretch 7 feet from tip to tip. It may weigh 14 pounds. It eats mostly fish, which it catches itself or steals from osprey. It also eats carrion and other easy pickings, such as the young of other birds or animals. One spring, we watched a young bald eagle attack Canada goslings on the Blackfoot River. It was beaten back by the honking parents while the young skidded away across the surface of the river, proof that what appear to be easy pickings sometimes aren't.

Younger bald eagles are difficult to distinguish from brown-headed, brown-bodied golden eagles, but at about 5 years of age, bald eagles develop the signature white head and tail that leave no question. Males and females are also difficult to distinguish, but if you see a nesting pair together, the larger of the two is the female. Young birds tend to leave our area until they reach maturity, at which time they return to stay. They'll use the same nests year after year; these nests, called eyries, can be 5 feet across.

Recently the numbers of bald eagles have been on a reassuring upswing. Nearly 100 nesting pairs have been identified in the region. If you keep your eyes peeled toward the cottonwood-lined South Fork of the Snake as you drive between Ririe and Palisades Reservoir, odds are you'll see at least one of these rare birds. Two other likely spots are the Oxbow in Grand Teton National Park and Yellowstone Lake in Yellowstone National Park.

Bighorn Sheep

Greater Yellowstone probably contains the greatest remaining concentrations of bighorn sheep, some 7,700 spread across three national forests: the Shoshone, Gallatin and Bridger-Teton. A few live in Grand Teton and Yellowstone parks. In other areas of the Rocky Mountain West, bighorns have been nearly eradicated.

What has made survival and recovery difficult for the Rocky Mountain bighorn sheep, our local subspecies, is the way these creatures are bound by habit and social rules. They follow the same trails and stop like clockwork at the same salt licks, watering holes and grazing areas. Older animals lead, and younger animals learn the trails from their elders. Innovation has no place in a bighorn sheep herd. This made them easy to hunt. More recently, when cattle and domestic sheep overran traditional bighorn ranges, this characteristic social rigidity left the wild sheep completely unequipped for finding new habitat. So they stayed on overgrazed slopes and eventually starved. Bighorns are also dramatically susceptible to the diseases of domestic livestock, so where domestic sheep and bighorns have contact, bighorns rapidly begin to die.

Both male and female bighorns have horns, but the females wear only spikes. Males, as they grow older, carry an increasingly heavy, ridged rack. Some racks grow to more than 30 pounds, or about 10 percent of the animal's body weight, and curl into a complete circle on each side of the animal's head. A male bighorn's rack can weigh more than his skeleton. Rams are also equipped with a double-layered skull, thick facial skin and a powerful tendon that connects skull with spine. All this is necessary because every fall the big rams battle for ewes and social standing by hurling themselves into crashing head-to-head contact. Their bodies are adapted to take the terrible pounding, generally without significant injury. In fact, injury is not the goal of either participant. The ritual battles, which can go on for hours, involve only this head-to-head pounding.

Look for gray-bodied, white-rumped bighorn sheep on open, south-facing mountainsides, high plateaus and ridgelines. Bighorns eat mostly grasses, so you won't often see them in or near forested areas. Since they protect themselves from predators by retreating to rocky, steep terrain, bighorn grazing areas are nearly always near rocky slopes and cliffs. From a distance, which is how you're most likely to see them, bighorns are easily mistaken for deer. Look for the larger, more

INSIDERS' TIP

While you're driving, keep the kids focused on looking for wildlife with a scoring system or an alphabet search. If you're keeping score, make sure easy-to-spot critters like deer are only worth a point or two. Big scores should be awarded for bears, mountain goats, bighorn sheep and other seldom-seen species. If you do an alphabet search, kids will have to get creative with some letters: Q could be quail or a quiet deer.

prominent white patch on the rump and the stockier, barrel-bodied shape.

Easy-to-miss Residents

Many of Greater Yellowstone's most interesting creatures don't get the attention they deserve, either from visitors or this book. Some are small or quiet and therefore easy to overlook. Others are secretive or rare and unlikely to cross paths with humans.

In the easy-to-overlook-but-very-cool category are creatures such as shrews, bats, beaver, porcupine, weasel, squirrels (including a species of flying squirrel!), mink, marmot, river otter and badger. Shrews are the tiniest predator mammals, eating their weight in spiders, slugs and carrion every day. Marmots waddle when they walk, swaddled in the fat they need for their eight-month hibernation. True hibernators like marmot will not awaken even if they're starving, so it's critical that they crawl into their dens with enough fat reserves to survive the winter. It's thought that marmots constitute up to 70 percent of golden eagles' diets. Beavers are the largest rodents in the West, weighing up to 100 pounds. Once trapped nearly to extinction for their plush, water-repelling fur, beavers are recovering some of their former range. They benefit other species in Greater Yellowstone by creating ponds that control flooding and provide habitat for waterfowl, moose and others. High quality fur-felt hats are still made from beaver harvested, these days, from fur farms.

Secretive and probably very rare in Greater Yellowstone are species such as the fisher, wolverine and lynx. The fisher looks like an elongated, chocolate-colored cat with a bushy tail. It measures about 2 feet from stem to stern. The fisher seems to require old-growth forest to live. Since there's little of that left, this small predator has disappeared from most of its former range. A few fishers have been sighted in Greater Yellowstone.

Lynx live at the mercy of their partner species, the snowshoe hare. When snowshoe hare populations are healthy, generally so are lynx populations. When snowshoes become scarce, lynx starve until there are the right number of cats to prey upon the decreased hare population. This medium-sized cat weighs up to 40 pounds and is built to hunt on snow: Long legs and huge, paddled feet allow it to stay on the snow's crust in pursuit of the hare. A lynx may eat as many as 200 snowshoe hare a year, although it will also take grouse and other small birds and mammals. Lynx also seem to need old-growth forest to live, so they too are rare. Only a few lynx have been sighted in Greater Yellowstone; they're more common in Canada where more old-growth forest remains. If in your backcountry travels you see what looks like a long-legged, clown-footed bobcat, count yourself among a very lucky few.

Wolverines look a little like small bears. They weigh up to 60 pounds and walk on all fours with a rolling swagger. Wolverines don't seem to tolerate human contact well. Females have been known to abandon their carefully hidden, remote dens merely because a human passed within eyeshot. This bodes poorly for their continued survival as roads and backcountry recreation and travel become ever more popular. Most recently, recreational snowmobiling has increased dramatically in areas formerly inaccessible to motorized vehicles. Wolverines are aggressive hunters with powerful jaws. This solitary hunter has been known to take down deer nearly twice its weight, but it also eats grouse, smaller mammals and carrion. There are about three reports per year of wolverine sightings in Yellowstone National Park. Nobody knows how many wolverines the region supports — probably nobody ever will. They are believed to be quite rare.

Secretive but not so rare is the mountain lion, also known as cougar and puma. This

INSIDERS' TIP

Those burbling streams look cool and tasty, but don't drink surface water without boiling or treating it, no matter how clean it looks. Waterborne nasties like giardia await the easily tempted.

big cat, which once lived all over what is now the continental United States, can weigh 200 pounds and reach a length of more than 8 feet if you count its long, furred tail. It's practically extinct in the East, but cougar populations seem sound in the Western United States. Mostly nocturnal and very secretive, the cougar has been difficult to study. Less is known about this fairly common predator than about the wolf we once nearly eliminated from the United States. It is known that the mountain lion is one of few species besides man that will regularly kill its own kind. Mature males will kill kittens, intruding males and even females they haven't mated with. Solitary and highly effective hunters, cougar regularly kill deer and even adult elk. These big cats were hunted into invisibility in Greater Yellowstone for the same reason wolves were: to protect livestock. But unlike wolves, cougars have recovered spontaneously — leading some to speculate that perhaps they were never gone.

Secretive and sly — but as common as pennies — are coyotes. The most abundant canine in Greater Yellowstone weighs 30 to 50 pounds and is found in nearly every part of the ecosystem. Coyotes have distinguished themselves by surviving. The intense trapping and poisoning programs that eliminated wolves from the lower 48 states only made the coyote smarter. Coyotes, working in packs, occasionally take large animals like deer or bighorn sheep, but more often they live on mice, rabbits and gophers. They're smart enough not to move when you walk or drive by, so you've probably been watched by many more coyotes than you've seen. You're much more likely to hear them than see them, yipping and howling in the evenings and early morning.

Outside Yellowstone and Grand Teton parks, in which coyotes and other predators are protected with the rest of the wildlife kaleidoscope, ranchers, trappers and Wildlife Services, the little-publicized USDA agency formerly known as Animal Damage Control (ADC), regularly kill coyotes. George Wuerthner writes in *Yellowstone: A Visitors Companion* that in 1989, ADC trapped, poisoned or shot 76,000 coyotes on public and private lands in the West. The goal is to protect ranchers' livestock, which the small hunters have been known to kill.

One spring day in 1997, we hiked along a Greater Yellowstone dirt road in search of sunshine and wildlife, dogs at our heels and binoculars swinging around our necks. When looking for wildlife, you watch for movement, so we were very close to the still shape in the road before we realized what it was. The fly-blown coyote carcass was caught in an ADC trap. A nearby trap, baited with meat, lay waiting. It was, ironically, the closest we had been to one of these elusive, shy predators: We usually count ourselves lucky to glimpse a furry tail as one drops over a ditchbank or dives into shrubbery. We were on public land, but the reason for the traps was evident: 300 yards off, a rancher's herd grazed on new spring grasses. It's unlikely but not impossible that the dead coyote had at least once tasted beef.

The more you learn about the creatures that inhabit Greater Yellowstone, the issues that threaten them and the wildlife managers' efforts to preserve and control them, the more you can appreciate the complexity of this place. You are also more likely to see what you know to look for. But remember, with the exception of the big ungulates like moose and elk, most of Greater Yellowstone's inhabitants are rarely seen from the region's roads. After all, as crowded and cosmopolitan as Yellowstone National Park can seem on a busy summer day, only 3 percent of it is accessible by road. There's real wilderness out there, just beyond the sounds of car engines and camera shutters. A good wildlife guidebook, a pair of binoculars, stout hiking boots or skis and some time provide the best opportunity to see the creatures who live in it. Walk carefully, though. We're visitors here, but these animals are in the only home they have.

National forests comprise the lion's share of Greater Yellowstone, some 62 percent.

Parks and Forests

Only 19 percent of Greater Yellowstone's 18 million acres is privately owned. That small slice of the region's pie contains our towns and farms. The rest, to the eye, is an undisturbed blanket of forestland. But on maps, Greater Yellowstone's public lands are also carved up into management chunks.

Yellowstone and Grand Teton parks make up 14 percent of Greater Yellowstone; they're managed by the National Park Service, a branch of the U.S. Department of the Interior. In addition to protecting the parks' wildlife and natural features, the Park Service manages visitors — educating, policing and entertaining them.

National forests comprise the lion's share of Greater Yellowstone, some 62 percent. The region's seven national forests are managed by the U.S. Forest Service, which is a branch of the U.S. Department of Agriculture. Each forest has its own administration. National forests are managed under a multiple-use mandate that supports logging, mining, livestock grazing, oil and gas drilling along with recreation.

The Wilderness Act of 1964 protects some of the nation's wildest forest lands. Also managed by the Forest Service, these lands are supposed to be kept as pristine as possible. Logging, road building and the use of motorized equipment is prohibited in designated wilderness. In a few cases, mining can occur. Livestock grazing is also allowed. So are hunting, fishing, hiking, rafting, camping, mountain climbing, cross-country skiing and snowshoeing. Greater Yellowstone is home to some of the nation's largest wilderness areas.

Two national wildlife refuges exist within Greater Yellowstone; they are managed by the U.S. Fish and Wildlife Service. The Red Rock Lakes Wildlife Refuge, funded through duck-stamp sales, is west of West Yellowstone and was set aside primarily to protect trumpeter swans, although recreation, trapping, mining and grazing are also allowed. The National Elk Refuge near Jackson, Wyoming, protects critical winter habitat for some of the region's huge elk herds.

State parks make up 2 percent of Greater Yellowstone's lands. They're managed in Montana by the Department of Fish, Wildlife and Parks; in Idaho by the State Department of Parks; and in Wyoming by the Department of Parks and Resources. Generally state parks serve the recreational needs of visitors, providing such amenities as campgrounds, cabins and trails.

What follows is a close look at the two most famous slices of Greater Yellowstone pie, Grand Teton and Yellowstone National Parks. Look here for information about the parks' visitor services. Then take a glance at our national forests, state parks and wildlife refuges. Contact numbers are included for each.

National Parks

Yellowstone National Park

Away from the 350-plus miles of highway that cut through our first national park, Yellowstone is pretty much the same as it was in 1872, when Congress created a "public park and pleasuring ground for the benefit and enjoyment of the people." Its 2.2 million acres are still home to the 10,000 steaming, bubbling, spraying geothermal features that first made Yellowstone famous. While many of these hot springs, fumaroles, geysers and mud pots are accessible by road, the rest can only be seen by traversing the 1,000-plus miles of backcountry trails. Since relatively few visitors venture away from the main thoroughfares, Yellowstone's hiking trails lead to areas as pristine as those discovered by early explorers.

The region has other extraordinary features: rugged mountains, crystal-clear lakes and free-flowing streams (one-tenth of Yellowstone National Park is under water). The park is also home to the biggest elk herd in North America and has one of only two grizzly bear populations in the lower 48 states. In fact, Yellowstone National Park is still home to nearly all of the animal species found by early explorers.

The heart of the park is a volcanic plateau with an average elevation of about 8,000 feet. (Elevations range from 5,000 at the north entrance to 12,000 at Eagle Peak on the park's east boundary.) This means winter comes early to the park, and growing seasons are short. That's one reason you'll find only nine kinds of trees among the 1,700 plant species that grow in and around the park.

In addition, about 300 species of birds, 18 fish species and nearly 100 different mammals inhabit Yellowstone. Among them are the black bear and the endangered grizzly. Estimates of the grizzly population in Greater Yellowstone range from 280 to 610; an estimate of black bear population for Yellowstone National Park alone is around 600. That means park visitors will be lucky to see a bear of any kind. But there are plenty of other critters to see. *National Geographic* got it right when writers of a May 1998 article wrote that the wolf has replaced the grizzly as Yellowstone's marquee mammal. The predator, reintroduced to the ecosystem in 1995, is occasionally visible enough to draw crowds of people to roadside pullouts in the park. And bison and elk often graze on the edge of the road. Near the Lake Hotel, bison are so prevalent that trees in the area bear the barkless scars caused by their rubbing. At Mammoth Hot Springs, elk lounge on the lawns and live among the buildings. During fall, when the bull elk are in rut and bugling, guests staying in the Mammoth Hotel cabins have even been trapped in their rooms by belligerent bulls.

Yellowstone National Park has three concessionaires. AmFac Parks and Resorts operates all the campgrounds, hotels, restaurants, boat marinas and activities. Hamilton Stores, the longest-operating concessionaire in the park, has a total of 14 stores within the park. Within some of these stores are lunch counters and one-hour photo shops. Since 1947, Yellowstone Park Service Stations has been the concessionaire for the park's seven service stations. Besides fuel, you can find batteries, tires and towing at stations throughout the park.

In the next sections, we describe how to enter the park and how to get around once you're in. We also provide information on visitor centers and other features. See our Attractions chapter for descriptions of some of the amazing sights you can see during your visit. And read Our Natural World for introductions to some of the flora and fauna you're likely to spot in this natural playground.

Entering the Park

When you enter the park (see more about its entrances below), a ranger will give you a map and a park publication full of useful information about where to go, what to do and what not to do. Scattered throughout the park are nine visitor centers, museums and information stations as well as several ranger sta-

INSIDERS' TIP

Traveling through Grand Teton National Park with an extra hour to spend? Turn up Signal Mountain Road. This winding paved road deadends on top of Signal Mountain and leaves you staring up at Mount Moran or down at the flat valley floor and its shining scalloped braid, the Snake River.

tions staffed with friendly folks who answer questions, issue various kinds of permits and generally help visitors. Be prepared to pay a fee to get into the park. Entrance fees went up in 1997 to help offset budget cutbacks. (For more information about park fees, see the gray box.)

For general information about Yellowstone National Park, call (307) 344-7381.

National Park Entrance Fees

$20 per private car

$15 per individual snowmobile or motorcycle

$10 per single entry (bike, foot or ski)

All these passes provide entrance to both Yellowstone and Grand Teton national parks for seven days. You can purchase an annual pass, also good for both parks, for $40. Golden Eagle Passports cost $50 and offer additional benefits to the seniors who purchase them, including discounted camping fees.

Generally, Yellowstone National Park entrances are open to automobile traffic from mid-April or May 1 through November 1. The road from Gardiner to Cooke City is open year round to auto traffic. But from about November 1 until the end of May, the road deadends in Cooke City. Depending on the weather, the Beartooth Highway northeast of Cooke City closes mid-October and the Chief Joseph Highway to Cody closes about November 1. In mid-December, when the park reopens for winter recreation, snowmobilers and snowcoaches line up at the West Entrance to travel about 150 miles of groomed roads.

Inside the park roads wind mostly around the center of the park past major attractions and through villages equipped with an array of tourist amenities. The roads, which often follow those built in the 1800s, are well-marked and generally called by the names of the attractions they lead to and from, such as the Mammoth-Norris Road, the Mammoth-Tower Junction Road or the Madison-Old Faithful Road. In park lingo the central roads are called the Grand Loop, Lower Loop and Upper Loop. Tours offered by a number of companies feature these three routes.

West Entrance

West Yellowstone, Mont.

West Yellowstone, the park's No. 1 entrance (1.1 million visitors in 1996) is easily accessed by three routes: U.S. Highway 20, U.S. Highway 191 and U.S. Highway 287. During peak season in summer or winter, by car or by snowmobile, you can expect to wait in line first thing in the morning at this entrance. The town of West Yellowstone, adjacent to the park, is packed with motels, campgrounds, restaurants and attractions of its own

South Entrance

Via Grand Teton National Park

This entrance, the second-most used with 812,000 visitors in 1997, is accessed by the north-south highway through Grand Teton National Park.

North Entrance

Gardiner, Mont.

Once the main entrance, Gardiner is a relaxed town with mostly dirt streets and a distinct Western flavor. In 1997, 539,000 visitors traveled through this northern gate. It's also the only entrance kept open year round, but the road is only plowed to Cooke City 57 miles to the east. About a quarter-mile west of the actual gate is the very grand Roosevelt Arch.

East Entrance

U.S. Hwy. 20

Just east of this entrance, which admitted 277,000 visitors in 1997, is Pahaska Tepee, an

INSIDERS' TIP

In 1948, visitor numbers to Yellowstone National Park reached 1 million for the first time. They've been rising ever since.

all-in-one motel, restaurant, gas station, convenience store and guest ranch. During the summer, Pahaska features horseback rides and other recreation. During winter, this entrance is closed to auto traffic, but not to skiers and snowmobilers. Fifty-three miles to the east is Cody, Wyoming, a hopping little town with lots to do. To get to Cody you'll drive U.S. Highway 20 through the North Fork Canyon. The scenery is outstanding, and so is the fishing in the North Fork of the Shoshone River.

Northeast Entrance
Silver Gate/Cooke City

Silver Gate, which completely closes for the winter, is about 1 mile east of the Northeast Entrance and reaches a population of 100 in the summer. Cooke City, three times as big, is another 3 miles east of Silver Gate. The two are closely connected communities. Cooke City is a little old mining-turned-tourist town that has nine months of winter. Farther east is the Beartooth Highway (U.S. Highway 212), which climbs over an 11,000-foot summit. During the summer the entrance offers spectacular views and access to awesome hiking and fishing. In 1997, 204,000 people traveled through this entrance.

Visitor Centers

Yellowstone National Park's visitor centers are touchstones of information for wandering visitors, and many of them act as repositories of park legend and lore. Most have nearby amenities such as shopping, refueling and dining that are generally open from the last week in May through the first week of September. (We've noted those that stay open longer.) See the pertinent accommodations chapters for details on lodging and camping within the park. Other chapters will fill you in on stores and restaurants doing business in the park.

Each center has an extensive bookstore run by the Yellowstone Association, a nonprofit organization that has supported educational, historical and scientific projects in Yellowstone National Park since 1933. The Yellowstone Association has contributed more than $5 million to the park.

Albright Visitor Center
Mammoth Hot Springs • (307) 344-2263

Albright, open year round, may be the hoppin'est visitor center in the park. Besides friendly rangers who will answer your every question, you'll find an informative historic display, movies shown every half-hour about Yellowstone's history and fairly regular ranger-naturalist programs that originate on the center's front steps. A new exhibit upstairs features wolves and other wildlife.

Mammoth is home to the Yellowstone National Park headquarters, which is housed mostly in old Fort Yellowstone buildings. Besides the administrative buildings, Mammoth has a hotel, cabins, campground, a bar and two restaurants operated by AmFac, Yellowstone National Park's main concessionaire. Hamilton Stores, the oldest established concessionaire in the park, operates a store here. A gas station, a post office and an ice machine are among Mammoth's amenities.

Canyon Visitor Center
Canyon Village • (307) 242-2550

This place can be a zoo sometimes, simply because it is the first visitor center you'll encounter if you're entering the park via the West Entrance at West Yellowstone, Montana. Canyon Village is also a full-service stop that attracts campers, diners, shoppers and those needing gasoline. Neatly crammed into a horseshoe-shaped complex are two Hamilton Stores (one is a new nature store), a post office and a gas station. In addition, you'll find a

INSIDERS' TIP

On August 25, Yellowstone National Park summer employees celebrate Christmas in the park.

restaurant, cafeteria, fast-food places, a hotel, cabins and a campground. Laundry facilities and showers are attached to the campground office. In 1998, Canyon Visitor Center opened a special bison display.

Old Faithful Visitor Center

Old Faithful Geyser • (307) 545-2750

This old visitor center is spacious, airy and staffed by friendly individuals who know what they're talking about. A board inside the center lists the next projected eruption time for Old Faithful as well as other neighboring geysers. And a film on geothermal features is shown throughout the day. Old Faithful is a bustling place with two hotels, a lodge, more than 100 cabins, two gas stations, a post office and shower facilities. Other features include several restaurants, a couple of gift shops and two Hamilton Stores. The center is open from the end of May until November 1.

Photo: Robert Bower

Old Faithful and the mounted Ranger Patrol are still both alive and well.

Grant Visitor Center

Grant Village • (307) 242-2650

This center has a wonderful display about the Yellowstone fires of 1988. There is also a backcountry office where you must register and buy a permit for overnight camping in this part of the park. Grant Village facilities include one Hamilton General Store, a post office, showers, a laundry facility and an ice machine. You'll also find a motel-style lodge and a large campground by the lake.

Fishing Bridge Visitor Center

North Shore of Yellowstone Lake • (307) 242-2450

Designed by Seattle architect Robert Reamer, this visitor center is one of our favorites. Besides having a wonderful collection of stuffed birds from Yellowstone National Park, the center offers a spectacular view from its lakeside steps. Because it's in the middle of grizzly country, the Fishing Bridge is not the village it used to be. Still, you will find a Hamilton Store, a RV park, a gas station and a lunch counter. The village also has showers and a laundry.

Norris Geyser Basin Museum

Norris Geyser Basin • (307) 344-2812

Don't confuse the stone building on the hill above the Norris Geyser Basin with a visitor center. The building you're looking for is the small log structure across the way. Inside, you'll find an informative museum on geothermal features in the park. We recommend stopping here before venturing into the basin.

Grand Teton National Park

Geothermal springs, geysers and mud pots were the original impetus for preserving Yellowstone National Park in 1872. For Grand Teton, it was the 7,000-foot sweep of the Teton range as it flings itself upward, with no false starts, no foothills, from a flat valley floor. Those dramatic mountains and the string of glacial lakes that lie like mirrors at their feet awed 19th-century explorers. They continue to awe today's visitors.

A north/south fault that split perhaps 5 million years ago, its western side rising and its eastern side dropping, gave cataclysmic birth to the Tetons (see Attractions and Our Natural World chapters). Glaciers, water and wind have done the rest. Starting shortly after the creation of Yellowstone National Park, calls went out to protect the magnificent Tetons as well.

The first, most obvious impetus was the mountains' grandeur; the second was a growing awareness on the part of Yellowstone's admirers and managers that a significant aspect of the region's natural beauty lay in the abundant wildlife, and that Yellowstone wildlife needed more room to survive. In 1929, the rocky heart of the Teton range became a national park. Much of the valley floor was included in 1950. The last big chunk required to connect Grand Teton and Yellowstone parks was added in 1972; this chimney of prime grizzly habitat is named John D. Rockefeller Jr. Memorial Parkway. It's managed by Grand Teton National Park.

All told, the park contains 485 square miles. On its west border rises one of the youngest mountain ranges in North America. The extensive forests are fir, spruce and lodgepole pine. One of the West's most important rivers, the nearly 1,000-mile-long Snake, meanders through the park in big willow-lined curves. Like a geologic flower garden, within the park bloom eight large lakes and numerous smaller ones, most of glacial origin. Flowering on the steep peaks are active glaciers. The flat valley floor, home to moose and wintering elk, is itself the accumulated detritus of a long-past ice age.

Park Entrances and Throughways

Grand Teton National Park's piece-by-piece birth makes it a different kind of place from Yellowstone. For instance, Grand Teton National Park's roads were not designed to detour into a tourist area but rather to facilitate through-traffic, so there are fewer traffic jams than in Yellowstone. Roads don't meander about like they do in Yellowstone: In fact, the park holds only 159 paved miles of road. However, it is also true that a car tour of Grand Teton National Park leaves many of the best sights unseen. The main park road, U.S. Highway 191/89/287, enters from the north, just below Flagg Ranch Resort. It skirts the east edge of Jackson Lake before U.S. Highway 287 joins U.S. Highway 26 and veers out the Buffalo Fork Valley through the park entrance. U.S. Highway 191/26 continues south and a little west across the broad valley floor to and through the south boundary of the park and the town of Jackson, Wyoming.

In winter most park roads are closed, but the "outer loop," U.S. Highway 191/89, and its offshoot, U.S. Highway 26/287, are plowed all winter. Unplowed roads are open to skiers and snowmobilers in winter, but Grand Teton National Park receives nowhere near the winter snowmobile and skier traffic Yellowstone does. Winter is quiet in the shadows of the Tetons.

The entrance stations at Moose and Moran can provide useful information, but even better are the park's four visitor centers/ranger stations, including the tiny one at Flagg Ranch, which is technically not part of Yellowstone or Grand Teton park but is equipped to provide resources and information about both. See our descriptions of these centers in the sections that follow.

In addition to ranger services, concessionaire-run tourist services are available in various locations. The biggest clusters are at Colter Bay, Signal Mountain Lodge, Jackson Lake Lodge, Jenny Lake and in Moose. Colter Bay, Jenny Lake and Moose have Park Service visitor centers in addition to their commercial services. More limited services are available at Kelly and Leek's Marina. Limited services exist just outside the park's Moran Junction. Teton Village and Jackson offer complete services, including accommodations, gas, medical care, entertainment and dining. Flagg Ranch to the north of the park offers most services.

Besides the two concessionaire-run RV parks, Grand Teton National Park has five Park Service campgrounds. Other lodging options within the park range from canvas-walled cabins to log cabins to hotels. See our accommodations chapters for more on where to stay.

INSIDERS' TIP

While national parks and national forests are all public lands, each is governed by a different set of regulations.

Park Services and Visitors Centers

Unlike Yellowstone, which is all public land, Grand Teton National Park is checkered with private inholdings as well as lands that have been sold to the government but leased back to former owners. More than 100 privately owned tracts exist within the park boundaries, some as large as 400 acres. This means, for instance, that cattle grazing is allowed in limited areas within the national park. Jackson Hole's municipal airport is even inside Grand Teton National Park — the only airport in the country completely surrounded by national park.

All this grows from the piecemeal birth of Grand Teton National Park (see our History chapter). The main benefit to you is the range of activities. Several dude ranches (see our Resorts and Vacation Lodges, and Guest Ranches chapters) operate here, and a variety of concessionaires offer activities such as scenic raft trips, ferry rides and horseback riding. Yellowstone has one primary on-site concessionaire and two smaller ones, but Grand Teton National Park has nine. The park is also home to three visitor centers — four if you count Flagg Ranch just north of the park — all with bookstores operated by the nonprofit Grand Teton Natural History Association and all staffed by park rangers and equipped with unique interpretive displays. Luckily, you can sort all this out on the inside front page of the *Teewinot*, Grand Teton National Park's newspaper, available at entrance stations and visitor centers. Or you can call Park Dispatch at (307) 739-3300.

Here is a quick summary of what's available at the major tourist centers and park visitor centers.

Flagg Ranch Visitors Center and Flagg Ranch Resort

John D. Rockefeller Jr. Memorial Pkwy.
• (307) 543-2861, (800) 443-2311

The visitor center is a tiny log building at one end of the Flagg Ranch Resort parking lot. Staffed by a National Park Service employee, the center provides brochures, maps and information. You can select from a limited supply of books for sale here as well.

Flagg Ranch Resort is operated by a single concessionaire that offers camping, cabins and motel accommodations as well as a variety of summer and winter diversions. You are between the two national parks, each literally a few minutes' drive away. You can catch a snowcoach or snowmobile into Yellowstone National Park, go horseback riding and rafting in summer, or fish, hike and camp. The resort has laundry, grocery and dining facilities as well.

Completely surrounded by the John D. Rockefeller Jr. Memorial Parkway, Flagg Ranch offers the only tourist services between Yellowstone's south gate and Grand Teton National Park's north one.

Colter Bay Visitors Center

Colter Bay Village on Jackson Lake
• (307) 739-3594

This is our favorite visitor center, with a good selection of books and posters for sale, a backcountry ranger to provide information about and permits for backpacking expeditions and, best of all, an impressive collection of Native American arts and artifacts. On the bottom floor, the museum area often hosts a guest artist, a Native American craftsman who can show you the skills that produce his art. The village itself is run by Grand Teton Lodge Company and offers two restaurants, a laundry, gas station, public showers and a gro-

INSIDERS' TIP

Grand Teton Lodge Company, the Grand Teton National Park concessionaire that operates Jenny Lake Lodge, Jackson Lake Lodge, Colter Bay and more, was created by John D. Rockefeller Jr. to provide accommodations and visitor services to park tourists.

cery store. There's even a marina here where you can sign up for cruises or rent a canoe. Call Grand Teton Lodge Company at (307) 543-2811.

Jackson Lake Lodge

On Jackson Lake • (307) 543-2811

Jackson Lake Lodge has no park visitor center, but the headquarters for the park's largest concessionaire, Grand Teton Lodge Company (phone number listed above), is a busy place. Many services are available, including an ATM, the park's only medical clinic, a service station, swimming pool and two restaurants. You can catch bus tours, horseback rides and Snake River float trips from here. You can also pick up a *New York Times* or shop for men's and women's clothing.

Signal Mountain Lodge

On Jackson Lake • (307) 543-2831

The complex lacks a park visitor center but little else. You can eat at either of two restaurants, hang out on the deck and sip margaritas, shop for gifts or fill your gas tank (emergency gas is available year round, although technically the lodge is closed in winter). Signal Mountain also has a convenience store and marina. You can rent a craft or a buoy or hop on a guided fishing boat. You can also sign up for a scenic float trip on the nearby Snake River.

Jenny Lake Visitor Center

South Jenny Lake Area • (307) 739-3392

This center is smaller than Colter Bay and Moose visitor centers but carries the expected selection of books and posters, as well as a bird's-eye topo map of the region. The interpretive material in this visitor center addresses the formation of the Teton Range. The park's climbing rangers also have an office, just across from the main visitor center, where you can obtain information about backcountry conditions. Until a couple of years ago, you were required to register here to climb in the Tetons.

The South Jenny Lake area offers limited services, including a general store stocked with camping supplies, groceries and T-shirts; a marina run by Teton Boating Company, (307) 733-2703; and Exxum Mountain Guides, a climbing service and school, (307) 733-2297. For more information on climbing services, see our Other Recreation chapter. Teton Boating Company is the only concessionaire plying the clear waters of Jenny Lake; they can ferry you across to the unroaded side of the lake, where the Tetons rise like a wall nearly from the water's edge.

Moose Visitor Center

Near Dornan's at Moose • (307) 739-3300

Moose Visitors Center is big and busy; it's also the only park visitor center open year round. It features interpretive information about the park's wildlife and an extensive book and poster section, maintained by the nonprofit Grand Teton Natural History Association. Over the years, the association has donated to the park around $2.5 million in profits from sales of books and other items stocked in area visitor centers and ranger stations. Backcountry rangers can supply permits for backcountry travel and help you plan your trip.

Dornan's is two minutes from the visitor center. This busy little cluster of businesses includes an extremely well-stocked grocery

INSIDERS' TIP

A sixth road in the southwest corner penetrates Yellowstone National Park to Bechler Ranger Station and to Cave Falls, a scenic attraction. Popular trails lead up the Fall River and deep into the park. Horsepackers particularly like this entrance although difficult creek crossings limit the season to mostly July through September. The Cave Falls campground is not in the park but rather in the national forest outside; the main difference is that it's cheaper than park service campgrounds.

store, sporting and mountaineering goods and gift shops, boat and bike rentals, two restaurants and a package liquor store with a fine selection of wines. The service station is open year round, as are most services.

National Forests

This nation is home to 156 national forests containing 191 million acres in 44 states. Terrain ranges from high-altitude lodgepole forest, like what you find in much of our region, to ice-gilded crags, sage-covered hills and scrub juniper. What national forests have in common is that they belong to you — to all of us.

The national forest system began right here in Greater Yellowstone more than 100 years ago, which perhaps accounts for the fact that this region encompasses seven national forests that fit around Yellowstone and Teton parks like puzzle pieces.

What follows is a thumbnail sketch of Greater Yellowstone's seven national forests. These forests encompass vast reaches of land and nearly unlimited recreational opportunities. The best way to approach them is first by phone, so we provide numbers for each forest's ranger districts and its overseeing forest headquarters.

Shoshone National Forest

America's first national forest grew out of lands set aside by Congress in 1891. Shoshone National Forest is a huge swath of land along Yellowstone National Park's eastern border, extending south to well below Grand Teton National Park and north to the Montana border. Its 2.4 million acres contain more than 1,000 miles of rivers and wide sweeps of sagebrush and grassland — more than any other Greater Yellowstone national forest. Forty-five percent of the Shoshone is protected within five federal wilderness areas, making this the most wilderness-full national forest in Greater Yellowstone.

For general information, write the Forest Headquarters, 225 W. Yellowstone Ave., Cody, WY 82414, or call (307) 527-6241.

Shoshone National Forest contains two ranger districts:

- Wapiti Ranger District, 203 A Yellowstone, Cody, WY 82414, (307) 527-6921
- Wind River Ranger District, 209 Ramshorn, Dubois, WY 82513, (307) 455-2466

Bridger-Teton National Forest

Named after its most dramatic mountain range, the Tetons, and its most flamboyant 19th-century mountain man, Jim Bridger, this national forest is Greater Yellowstone's biggest. Bridger-Teton contains 3.4 million acres stretching from Yellowstone National Park's southern boundary down Grand Teton National Park's eastern edge, encircling the valley of Jackson Hole. One of its two long southern "arms" embraces the wild, glacier-sculpted Wind River range. The other stretches nearly to Utah to encompass the Salt River and Wyoming ranges. The forest is completely contained within Wyoming.

For general information, contact the headquarters for Bridger-Teton National Forest at 340 N. Cache St., Jackson, WY 83001, (307) 733-2752.

The forest contains six ranger districts, with offices scattered from middle-of-nowhere Moran just outside Grand Teton National Park to middle-of-nowhere Kemmerer near the Utah/Wyoming border:

- Jackson Ranger District, (307) 733-4755
- Kemmerer Ranger District, (307) 877-4415
- Big Piney Ranger District, (307) 276-3375
- Greys River Ranger District, (307) 886-3166

INSIDERS' TIP

Wilderness legislation currently under consideration includes attempts to both substantially increase the size of wilderness areas in the Northern Rockies and to decrease them.

- Buffalo Ranger District, (307) 543-2386
- Pinedale Ranger District, (307) 367-4326

Targhee National Forest

Greater Yellowstone is not a region easily contained by clean lines. Some would say, for instance, that nearly one-fourth of the Targhee National Forest's 1.8 million acres is not part of Yellowstone country. Others, including us, would happily fold the whole forest into Greater Yellowstone. Either way, the Targhee marks the region's western edge from Idaho's Centennial Range down to the Caribou National Forest. The Targhee owns the western view of the majestic Tetons, as Bridger-Teton National Forest owns the eastern. East, southeast and south of the Targhee is the end of wilderness — there, a mighty swath of fertile farmland gives Idaho its famous potato reputation.

The Targhee is home to two wilderness areas. The Jedediah Smith Wilderness runs along the western slopes of the Tetons. Little-known and seldom-traveled Winegar Hole Wilderness — 10,750 acres tucked against the unroaded southwest corner of Yellowstone — is prime grizzly habitat.

For general information about Targhee National Forest, contact Forest Headquarters at Box 208, St. Anthony, ID 83445, (208) 624-3151.

The forest has four district offices within Greater Yellowstone:

- Ashton Ranger District, (208) 652-7442
- Palisades Ranger District, (208) 523-1412
- Teton Basin Ranger District, (208) 354-2431
- Island Park Ranger District, (208) 558-7301

Beaverhead-Deer Lodge National Forest

In 1996, the nearly 100-square-mile Deer Lodge National Forest was folded into the Beaverhead, which was nearly twice its size. The result sprawls across much of western Montana. Arguably, only a fraction of this forestlands complex is contained within Greater Yellowstone. What lies within our region takes the Snowcrest range for its western boundary, Red Rock Lakes National Wildlife Refuge on the Montana/Idaho border as its base and the Madison range for its eastern boundary. Also included are the lovely Tobacco Root mountains near Ennis, Montana.

One of Beaverhead-Deer Lodge's most compelling features is stark contrast: With a low elevation of around 4,000 feet and a high of more than 11,000, wildlife and vegetation vary dramatically. Low areas are covered in sage and bunch grasses. Moderate elevations are heavily forested in lodgepole pine with a bit of Englemann spruce and Douglas fir. High elevations are glacier-carved studies in rock and ice.

For general information about the forest, contact Forest Headquarters at 610 N. Montana Street, Dillon, MT 59725, (406) 683-3900. The only Greater Yellowstone ranger district within this forest is the Madison Ranger District, (406) 682-4253.

Gallatin National Forest

Gallatin is the most popular national forest in Montana. It wears the Madison and Gallatin ranges on its western side, the remote and rugged Absarokas and Beartooths to the east and the Bridger range to the north. An isolated chunk of this forest encompasses Montana's Crazy Mountains. The forest sits like a hat atop Yellowstone National Park. It absorbs 2.5 million visitor days annually, more than Wyoming's massive Bridger-Teton National Forest. Two large wilderness areas protect 41 percent of the forest from most development and resource extraction.

For general information, contact Gallatin National Forest Headquarters, Federal Building, Box 130, Bozeman, MT 59771, (406) 587-6701.

Gallatin Forest also maintains five ranger districts:

- Big Timber Ranger District, (406) 932-5155
- Livingston Ranger District, (406) 222-1892

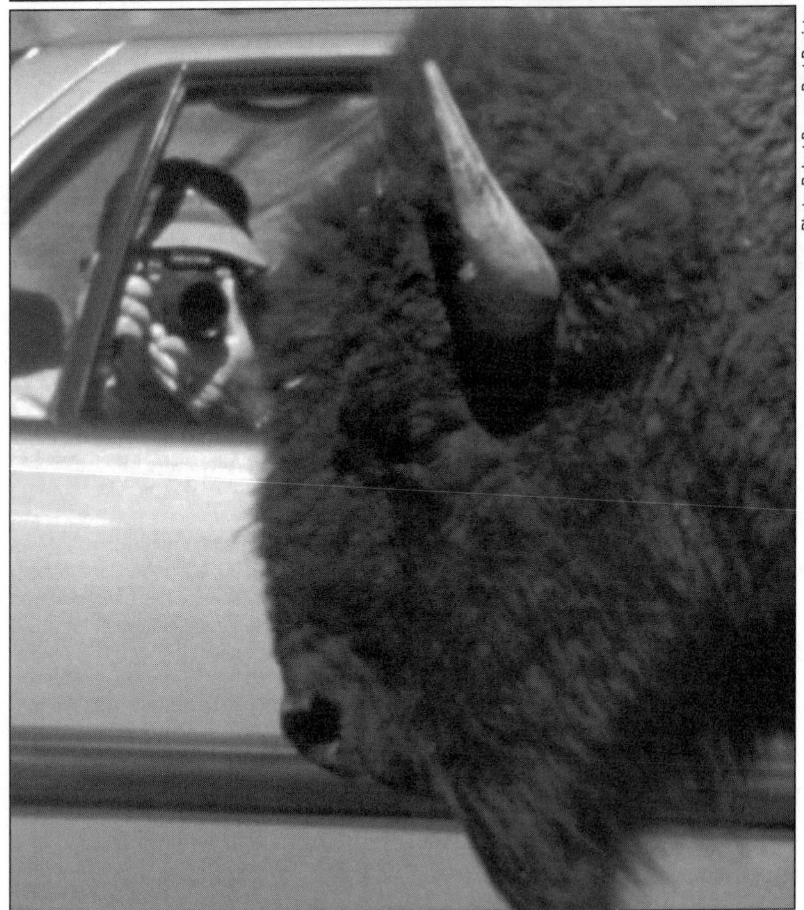

Photo: Robert Bower, Post Register

A Yellowstone park visitor gets a real close-up of a bison passing his car as they cross the highway near Flood Geyser.

- Gardiner Ranger District, (406) 848-7375
- Bozeman Ranger District, (406) 587-6920
- Hebgen Lake Ranger District, (406) 646-7369

Custer National Forest

Custer National Forest abuts Gallatin National Forest east of the Yellowstone Valley. The forest touches Yellowstone National Park's northeastern corner to the south and splits the craggy, glacier-capped Beartooths with Gallatin. It's mountainous, jagged country splashed with hundreds of trout-filled high-mountain lakes. Twenty-five peaks in Custer National Forest, most of them in the Beartooths, reach above 12,000 feet. Dozens of active glaciers survive in the thin, cold air — tiny grandchildren of the blanket of ice that covered this region more than 10,000 years ago. On its eastern side, Custer drops abruptly into prairie at about 4,000 feet above sea level.

Custer Forest Headquarters is located at 2602 First Avenue N., Box 2556, Billings, MT

59103, (406) 657-6361. Beartooth Ranger District can be reached at (406) 446-2103.

Caribou National Forest

Caribou National Forest lacks the sky-piercing crags of other Greater Yellowstone national forests — its highest point is Mead Peak at only 9,957 feet. Caribou is a long, narrow forest extending from northern Utah along the west slope of the Salt River valley and up 22-mile-long Palisades Reservoir. Away from its western edge roll the fertile volcanic farmlands of Idaho's Snake River Plain. East of the forest are the Salt and Wyoming ranges, both contained within massive Bridger-Teton National Forest. Most of the forest's 1.2 million acres lies outside what experts call Greater Yellowstone. The area within Greater Yellowstone is administered by Targhee National Forest managers.

For general information, contact Caribou Forest Headquarters at 250 S. Fourth Street, Pocatello, ID 83201, (208) 236-7500.

Caribou has four ranger districts, one of which overlaps Greater Yellowstone. For information about Greater Yellowstone's chunk of the Caribou, contact the Palisades Ranger District of the Targhee National Forest at (208) 523-1412.

National Wildlife Refuges

National Elk Refuge

When human development began to threaten critical elk and bison winter range, and building in and around the town of Jackson, Wyoming, blocked winter migration routes, the animals trapped in the northern half of Jackson Hole ravaged ranchers' hay. Then they starved in pitiful heaps. In 1912, the result of public reaction to the sight was Wyoming's National Elk Refuge, which runs along the east side of U.S. Highway 89/26 north of Jackson for about 6 miles.

The refuge is home to between 7,500 and 12,000 elk in winter, depending on whom you ask. The elk are fed when necessary to ward off starvation. They are also hunted selectively to control their numbers.

If you come by in summer, you won't see much to stop for at the National Elk Refuge. But from about November until the snow melts, the flat valley floor is home to more elk than you ever thought you'd see in one place. At the south end of the elk refuge is a visitor center with lots of local service information, educational material and interpretive displays.

See the Close-up on the National Elk Refuge in Our Natural World chapter.

Red Rock Lakes National Wildlife Refuge

If you're a bird watcher the Red Rock Lakes National Wildlife Refuge near Monida, Montana, (406) 276-3536, is a good place to hang out. A total of 232 species has been identified here, including the trumpeter swan for which the refuge was created.

The U.S. Fish and Wildlife Service established this 45,000-acre refuge in 1935 to protect and preserve trumpeter swans. About 9,000 acres of the area are lakes and ponds that are home not only to swans, but also to numerous other species.

The only way to get to this refuge is by a not-very-well-marked dirt road that leads from U.S. Highway 20 west of West Yellowstone, Montana, to Interstate 15 near Monida. The drive is beautiful and will lead you to two campgrounds.

State Parks

Buffalo Bill State Park
Yellowstone Hwy. west of Cody, Wyo.
• (307) 587-9227

This state park, established in 1957, is tucked into the North Fork Canyon. Park features include the Buffalo Bill Reservoir (8,500 surface acres) and 3,500 land acres surround-

INSIDERS' TIP

No motorized vehicles are allowed in wilderness areas. This includes snowmobiles, ORVs and mountain bikes.

ing it. The shores of the reservoir and the state park facilities changed in 1993 after the dam was raised by 25 feet.

You'll find several campgrounds, boat ramps and plenty of water for fishing and boating.

Harriman State Park

Off U.S. Hwy. 20 south of Island Park, Idaho • (208) 558-7368

Harriman State Park consists of 16,000 acres of wildlife refuge. No camping is available within the park, but plentiful camping opportunities exist in the vicinity. During summer visitors tour the Railroad Ranch buildings, 27 of which still stand. You can also fish, hike, bike and horseback ride from the onsite riding stables. In winter, cross-country skiers take over.

The park hosts plentiful wildlife, including endangered trumpeter swans. One-third of the Rocky Mountain population of these huge birds spend their winters here. You can also see bald eagles, osprey, moose, deer, coyote and more. In fall, locals head here to listen to the unearthly whistling calls of bull elk.

Facilities include a visitor center, equipped to provide information about the area's wildlife and other features, and an outdoor interpretive center that also focuses on area wildlife. The riding stables are open in summer only. The visitor center is open as a warming hut on weekends in winter.

Henry's Lake State Park

Off U.S. Hwy. 20 north of Island Park, Idaho • (208) 558-7532

This busy campground and boat ramp are easily reached from U.S. Highway 20 just north of the main business areas of Island Park. On a typical summer day, 150 to 200 vehicles may pass through the gates on their way to the boat ramp. The ramp charge for 1999 is a very reasonable $3. Attendants are available during business hours to answer your questions and keep an eye on things (see our Campgrounds and RV Parks chapter for more). The park closes from the end of October to late May.

Henry's Lake is renowned both for its prime fishing — the most common catch is the cuttbow, a volunteer hybrid of cutthroat and rainbow that grows to tackle-busting size — and for its sudden storms. Weather sweeps down from the surrounding mountain ranges, the Henry's Lake Mountains, the Centennials and the Gravelly Range. Smart boaters keep an eye on the skies.

Lewis and Clark Caverns State Park

Mont. Hwy. 2 between Cardwell and Three Forks, Mont. • (406) 287-3451

In 1937, Lewis and Clark Caverns became Montana's first state park. Below ground is the heart of this 3,034-acre park: 2 miles of limestone caverns. Above ground is a 40-space campground with several camp cabins, along with several miles of hiking trails. For a fee, rangers lead visitors through the bat-infested labyrinth each summer day. See our Attractions chapter for more information.

Madison Buffalo Jump State Park

7 miles south of the Logan Interchange on I-90, Logan, Mont. • (406) 994-6934

This primitive park encompasses a section of land that includes cliffs used for buffalo jumps by Native Americans. Primitive hiking trails lead up the rolling hills and onto the buffalo jump from which you can view the Tobacco Root Mountains. There is an interpretive shelter but no on-site staff. Entrance fees for nonresidents is $4 per car. There is no camping here, but there is a latrine.

Missouri Headwaters State Park

Mont. Hwy. 286 N., Three Forks, Mont. • (406) 994-6934

Popular with Lewis and Clark Expedition buffs as well as with anglers and boaters, this 530-acre state park is home to 23 camp sites, water spigots and a dump station. Summers, park rangers host fireside interpretive talks as well as A Weekend of Discovery late in July. Camping here costs $7, and admission is $4 per vehicle for nonresidents.

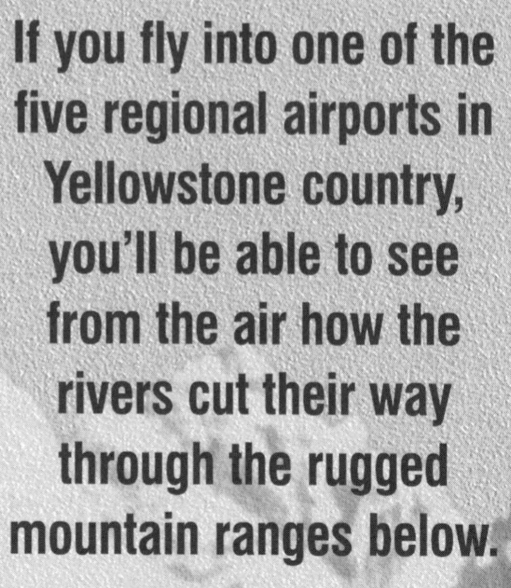

If you fly into one of the five regional airports in Yellowstone country, you'll be able to see from the air how the rivers cut their way through the rugged mountain ranges below.

Getting Here, Getting Around

If a river runs through it, chances are so does a highway.

If you fly into one of the five regional airports in Yellowstone country, you'll be able to see from the air how the rivers cut their way through the rugged mountain ranges below. Like the rivers that follow the path of least resistance, so do the highways and byways of Greater Yellowstone follow the valleys until, blocked by the towering mountains, they must climb the most obvious pass over and through them.

Once you leave the airports and the interstates, the highways leading to the heart of Yellowstone country are simple. Two-lane, uncluttered ribbons of asphalt, they connect the residents of Greater Yellowstone to each other, and to the region's two national parks. Yellowstone National Park has five entrances and 10 roads leading to those entrances. A sixth entrance deadends at a campground in the park. Grand Teton has three entrances with five roads leading to them. In this chapter, we will give you a peek at the different routes.

By Car

While Yellowstone and Grand Teton parks may be the gems of Greater Yellowstone, there is plenty to see and do outside their boundaries. Watch the dark purple majesty as the sun sets on the Madison Mountain Range. Park and picnic at the base of Emigrant Peak in the Paradise Valley near Pray, Montana. Hear the crickets chirping and the soothing sound of water, then climb into your car and keep on driving. If you're lucky, in spring or fall you'll come upon a cattle drive moving like a mirage up the highway. Cowboys aren't much on warning you about the hazards ahead, so be alert. Fresh splats of green manure smearing the highway mean livestock ahead. Getting through a cattle drive requires a bit of patience, especially if those bovine are headed the same direction as you. You've just got to creep along, maybe bang the side of your car with your hand — please don't honk your horn — and wait for those dogies to break away to the side. (Be sure to break out your cameras and camcorders to record those cowboys and that sea of hide-covered steaks bobbing ahead of your car hood.)

While cattle drives and cowboys are getting scarce these days, the area has other more common hazards to watch for along the way. From dusk 'til dawn, expect wildlife of all kinds to appear out of nowhere. Critters move about more when it's cool, and they often have to cross highways to tank up on nearby river water. If you see a sign that reads "rolling rocks," pay attention, especially after a rain or during snow melt. We came around a corner in a blizzard one night and bumped into a house-size boulder blocking the road. Smaller rocks, the kinds that can flatten a tire or empty your oil pan, are more common.

Since we're warning you about the thrills of driving to this region, a few words about mountain driving are in order. If you've never driven in the mountains before, a few of the passes in Greater Yellowstone can be downright terrifying. Take the 11,000-foot Beartooth Pass, for example. Almost daily during the summer, a vehicle full of vacationers starts up the Beartooth Highway (U.S. Highway 212) then turns around and heads back down, afraid to tackle the top. Steep, winding, narrow and without guard rails in some places, it's easy to see where you'll land (way down there) if you go over the edge. All around are scenic vistas that make heads turn and necks crane. Everywhere people are pulling off and on the road. While the pass can be terrifying to folks from flatter country, be assured that vehicles rarely go over the edge, and the view on top is worth the adrenaline. You'll see alpine meadows and lakes and snowbanks so deep the brave and the slightly crazy ski the headwalls on the Fourth of July. Speaking of snow, it can fall any time of year on the Beartooth Highway, which closes each winter, generally from mid-October until the end of May.

Winter Driving

There are a few things you need to know about getting around Yellowstone country from fall until spring. The Gardiner-to-Cooke City road is the only Yellowstone National Park road open to automobiles through the winter. Other winter travel through the park is limited to snowmobiles or snowshoeing and cross-country skiing (see our Winter Sports chapter). Inside Grand Teton National Park, U.S. Highway 26/89/191 is plowed all winter. Outside the parks, the Beartooth Highway (U.S. Highway 212) is the only one that closes for the winter. Teton Pass, on Wyo. Highway 22/33 between Targhee and Jackson, is sometimes closed temporarily because of avalanches. In eastern Idaho, roads can close in an instant due to ground blizzards, which occur when the wind whips existing snow into a swirling white curtain. Some passes, like the Chief Joseph Highway (Wyo. Highway 296), are plowed all winter, but blowing snow can quickly close them.

Later in this section we have listed phone numbers in Idaho, Wyoming and Montana that carry daily reports on winter road conditions and closures.

The valleys hold different hazards. Knee-deep snow, willows made lacy with hoarfrost and steamy fog rising from the icy waters of the Gallatin River can wrap you in a beguiling veil of winter so mesmerizing that you may forget these same conditions are a recipe for icy roads. Slippery roads drive many winter travelers to take shuttles from the airport to their recreation destination of choice. In West Yellowstone, which bills itself as the snowmobile capital of the world, only a few streets are reserved for cars. The rest are used by both cars and snow sleds. At Big Sky, Teton Village and Targhee, many of the condos are at the base of the ski hill, so who needs a car?

If you plan to drive multiple days and over long distances, we recommend packing at least a small survival kit that includes flares, a flashlight, chains, warm clothing, winter boots, matches, a candle, a small cooking pot, some emergency food, water and a blanket. You might also pack a shovel and a bag of kitty litter to be thrown on the snow for traction in case you get stuck. Winter traffic can be pretty sparse. If you venture out at night and run into car troubles, it could be a long time before help arrives. Be prepared to sit it out in comfort.

Highways and Byways

Three routes lead to West Yellowstone, the most popular entrance to our first national park. Two of them head south from Interstate 90, the east-to-west highway running across Montana. The third leads from Interstate 15, which comes up through Salt Lake City, Utah, passing near Idaho Falls on its way north.

U.S. Highway 191, the most popular northern route to Yellowstone National Park, heads through the rich agricultural fields of the Gallatin Valley, then up the narrow Gallatin Canyon past Big Sky recreation mecca and into West Yellowstone. To get to U.S. 191, take I-90 Exit 306 onto Mont. Highway 85 which turns into U.S. Highway 191 a few miles down the road. Besides taking you to Big Sky, this road follows the winding Gallatin River, a blue-ribbon fishing stream with lots of campgrounds. Dotted with lodges, rafting outfitters, fly-fishing shops, motels, restaurants and guest ranches, U.S. 191 cuts through about 20 miles of the northwestern corner of Yellowstone National Park. Commercial establishments, carved out of clearings amidst lodgepole thickets, dot the roadside as you leave the park and approach West Yellowstone.

U.S. Highway 287 also heads south through wide open spaces then into the Madison Valley, through the ranching and fishing town of Ennis, then up the Madison River Canyon, past Quake and Hebgen lakes (see our Attractions and Fishing and Watersports chapters), to West Yellowstone. Where the West Fork of the Madison River meets the main Madison River, motels, restaurants, RV parks and fly shops invite travelers to stop. There are more stopping-off places — bars, restaurants, motels and marinas — around Hebgen Lake.

If you're headed east on I-90, take Exit 274 at Three Forks then turn southwest on Mont. Highway 2 for 11 miles until you come to the U.S. 287 junction. From the west, it's I-90 Exit 256. Follow Mont. Highway 2 for 13 miles then turn south at the U.S. 287 junction. If you're

INSIDERS' TIP

In Idaho Falls, stop by the Eastern Idaho Visitor Information Center, 505 Lindsay Boulevard, (208) 523-1010. Those smart folks bundled the Chamber of Commerce, the local visitors bureau, the Bureau of Land Management and Forest Service together and stocked up with books supplied by the Grand Teton Natural History Association. The center has a vast array of informational material and several Idaho-related interpretive displays.

bound for West Yellowstone via rainbow-trout-rich Henry's Lake, turn south onto Mont. Highway 87 about a half-mile past the Wade Lake turnoff on U.S. 287. This 16-mile stretch of road bypasses Quake and Hebgen lakes and meets up with U.S. Highway 20. West Yellowstone, which sprawls in a clearing amidst the lodgepole pine, is 13 miles east of the U.S. 20 junction.

U.S. Highway 20, the third route into West Yellowstone, takes you from Idaho Falls up the Snake River Plain through pin-neat Rexburg and sleepy Ashton. Just outside Ashton, decide whether you're in a hurry or want maximum scenery. For scenery, catch the Mesa Falls Scenic Byway (it hooks up with U.S. 20 just below Island Park). On the byway you can camp, fish in the Warm River, hike and visit Upper and Lower Mesa Falls. Be warned that this road is narrow and winding, with lodgepole forest creeping nearly to pavement's edge. The direct route stays with U.S. 20, running alongside the blue-ribbon trout fishing of the Henry's Fork, to and through Island Park. You'll pass Henry's and Hebgen lakes, then wind down from the plateau and over the Montana border into West Yellowstone. Watch for the "Bison Crossing" sign for a one-of-a-kind photo opportunity.

While roads inside the parks are designed to lead you to the most outstanding natural features, they're also designed to get you in and out and across the parks from one entrance to another. For example, if you enter Yellowstone National Park at West Yellowstone, then exit the park going south, you'll take the John D. Rockefeller Jr. Memorial Parkway for just less than 8 miles before you re-enter a national park, this time Grand Teton National Park. The parkway is also called U.S. Highway 89/287/191 — we're a bit short on roads here, so we like to give each one plenty of names.

Fifty miles farther south (the same road is now called U.S. 26/89/191) you will have left Grand Teton National Park and entered cowboy playland at Jackson. We hope you take the time to drive the Teton Park Road — folks call it the inside road — which loops past glacier-formed Jenny and Leigh lakes, close beneath the spectacular Tetons. This side trip is 20 miles long and only open during the snow-free months. U.S. 89 through Grand Teton National Park is plowed to Flagg Ranch all winter.

In both national parks, you'll find other side roads to explore and many pullouts guaranteed to add hours (days, if you're smart) to travel times. See our Attractions chapter and recreational chapters to help you plan your driving.

Two popular routes bring you to the tourist mecca of Jackson from Idaho Falls, 91 miles to the west. In both cases, take U.S. Highway 26 up the South Fork of the Snake River and through Swan Valley. The South Fork flows quietly through this broad, cottonwood-swathed valley, providing more of the premier trout fishing the region is known for. Now you can take Idaho Highway 31 over scenic Pine Creek Pass and into Teton Valley, pick up Idaho Highway 33 and climb up and over Teton Pass. Make sure you stop at the top of the pass to enjoy the view down into Jackson Hole (a hole is a valley, so Jackson Hole is the whole valley, and Jackson is the valley's largest town). Your road becomes Wyo. Highway 22 as you cross the state line. Be warned that this is mountain driving at its steepest and most winding. The signs warn of a 10 percent grade, but some suspect it's steeper. Take your time. Be patient with slower vehicles.

Let's say you want to avoid Teton Pass, either because you don't like heights or because it's snowing and you want to stay low. In that case, from Swan Valley continue up the South Fork of the Snake on U.S. Highway 26 past Palisades Dam and drive along the more than 20-mile-long Palisades Reservoir. Turn with the highway at Alpine, Wyoming, and head up the upper Snake River Canyon (a.k.a. the Grand Canyon of the Snake) into Hoback Junction 13 miles south of Jackson. Several national forest campgrounds lie along the route after you pass Alpine. For the next several years, you'll also encounter highway construction. Don't be surprised at delays.

If you're approaching Yellowstone country from the east, you can take U.S. Highway 26/287 from Dubois over Togwotee Pass into Grand Teton National Park at Moran Junction. This takes you through Buffalo Valley and along the Buffalo Fork River. You won't see many people along this road, but you're almost sure to see wildlife. Around Hatchet, before you enter the park at Moran, look for inexpensive national forest campgrounds. Several guest ranches call the valley home, as well.

If you're approaching Yellowstone National Park from Cody, you'll travel the North Fork Highway (U.S. Highway 16/14/20), which leads to the East Entrance. This route follows Buffalo Bill Cody's old highway along the North Fork of the Shoshone River. It passes through Wapiti, where Cody built the Wapiti Inn, the halfway hotel used for housing guests during park tours. The highway also trails past Holy City and other awe-inspiring volcanic rock formations. If you like to fish, you'll find many pullouts and campgrounds along the river. About a dozen lodges and ranches between Cody and the park welcome drop-in dinner guests and overnighters. Pahaska Tepee, a mile east of the park entrance, has a full-blown bar and restaurant, a gift shop and convenience store, lodging, and gasoline.

Another lovely but longer route from Cody to Yellowstone National Park is the Chief Joseph Highway (Wyo. Highway 296). This wide, two-lane roadway winds its way through breathtaking alpine landscapes to the tops of mountains, into the bottom of the Clarks Fork River gorge and past Sunlight Basin. Jutting through the green carpet of grasslands, the barebones of geological evolution reveal their past. There are several Forest Service campgrounds along this lightly traveled route which intersects with the Beartooth Highway (U.S. 212) east of Cooke City and Yellowstone National Park's northeast entrance.

U.S. Highway 212, one of the prettiest summer routes to Yellowstone National Park, leaves I-90 16 miles west of Billings. It passes through Red Lodge 53 miles to the south. From Red Lodge, U.S. 212 climbs over 11,000-foot-high Beartooth Pass, dubbed by the late Charles Kuralt the most scenic drive in America. Snow and slush appear on this highway even in midsummer; in winter the highway closes from about mid-October to late May. Before passing through the northeast entrance of Yellowstone National Park, U.S. 212 cuts through the tiny mountain towns of Cooke City and Silver Gate.

To get to Yellowstone National Park's North Entrance at Gardiner, head south from I-90 on U.S. Highway 89 at Livingston. This route will take you up the open Yellowstone Valley, through Emigrant (don't blink or you'll miss it) and on to Gardiner. The fishing is good here, but campgrounds aren't as plentiful as they are along the other northern routes. Still, you'll find several reasonably priced Forest Service campgrounds near Gardiner.

Driving in the Parks

Yellowstone National Park

You've heard about Yellowstone, you've read about Yellowstone, and now you're here. Read your map. If it says the distance from Mammoth to Norris is 21 miles, count on it taking nearly an hour to drive. The speed limit in the park is 45 mph, but the average speed is 33 miles per hour and there are only 12 safe places to pass according to one park tour bus driver.

And prepare to bump, bounce and brake your way across the 350 miles of roads in the park. Since roads were first built here in the 1880s, crews have fought to keep up with the disastrous effects of harsh winters, heavy use, and insufficient funds. Expect road construction delays. And expect narrow, bumpy, potholed roads in parts of the park. Fortunately, recent years of construction have transformed some of the roads into smooth thoroughfares with actual shoulders. The biggest obstacle to smooth sailing, though, will be you and other drivers. We have seen traffic backed up for a mile while drivers stop in the middle of the road to photograph a bison by the road. "Bear jams" are worse. People park on the road and leave their cars, creating regular traffic knots. To complicate things, most drivers try to navigate the knot while craning their necks to see what all the fuss is about. While it can be frustrating at times, gawking is all a part of the national park experience.

If you look in the rear-view mirror and see a long line of vehicles behind you, pull over and let them pass. Those who live in the communities surrounding the park have to use park roads to get from one place to another. While they love to watch wildlife too, they're very often traveling through on business, not vacation. If you hit the West or North Entrances at about 8 AM, you'll find yourself waiting in line as cars creep through their turns at the gate. If you want to race through the park with barely a stop (we don't recommend it), the 142-mile Grand Loop passes almost every major attraction in Yellowstone. It goes through Mammoth to Norris, past all the major geyser basins to Madison and Old Faithful, follows the north shore of Yellowstone Lake, and takes in the Fishing Bridge before heading north to Canyon Village and Tower Falls. Even splitting your visit into a day each on the Upper Loop and the Lower Loop roads can be grueling because you'll want to hike, explore and simply stare. Several short, one-way side roads such as the Firehole Canyon and Lake drives, as well as the Blacktail Plateau Drive, provide scenic trips into interesting areas. There are many options, especially if you want to get off the beaten path. We leave the planning and the decision-making to you. Happy Trails.

Grand Teton National Park

In Grand Teton National Park, driving is easier. The park wasn't born until 1929 and didn't acquire most of its land until 1950. This means park roads are highways first and scenic attractions second, unlike the looping roads of Grand Teton's older sister to the north. What locals call the outside road, U.S. Highway 89, carries a 55-mph speed limit until you pass through a park entrance. You can drive quite a ways inside park boundaries without passing through an entrance station. In fact, it is possible to drive through Grand Teton National Park, almost from end to end, without paying a fee.

For the fast (and free) tour, hop on U.S. Highway 191/26/89 at Jackson and buzz past the National Elk Refuge. Now you're in the park, but you haven't paid yet. That's because the southern entrance station is on the inner loop road, also known as Teton Park Road, and you're on the outer loop. Continue north and east until you reach Moran Junction. Turn left here, and you'll hit Grand Teton National Park's second entrance, where you'll have to pay to continue north. Or turn right on U.S. Highway 26/287 toward Dubois, and you'll exit the park without passing an entrance station.

For the best views and a slower tour, you'll want to detour onto Teton Park Road. On Teton Park Road, which park employees call the inside road, and on U.S. Highway 89 after you pass through an entrance station, the speed limit drops to 45 mph. Generally you can expect to be able to go that fast. The tiniest loop road, Jenny Lake Loop, is also the only narrow, slow road of any significance. Wildlife and scenic wonders don't create the same kinds of congestion in Teton that they do in Yellowstone, either: Pullouts have been well-placed to coincide with the most likely places to sight wildlife or feast eyes on the Tetons. So the most important consideration in this park is not how slowly you must go, but rather how slowly you *should* go, especially if you care about wildlife, which must regularly cross roads to get to food and water. (Please see our Parks and Forests chapter for more information on touring Grand Teton National Park.)

Road and Travel Information

The National Park Service has a recorded information line for road and weather updates: weather, (307) 344-2113; road, (307) 344-2114. Or tune your radio to 1610 AM wherever you

INSIDERS' TIP

You're getting off your plane at Idaho Falls Municipal Airport, and in front of you is an expectant gathering of 10 or 20 people, or more. You are probably witnessing the near-daily event of a Mormon missionary's homecoming. Devout young Mormons leave home for two years to promote their religion around the world. Homecomings are proud and happy, often involving banners and balloons. One family last year even greeted its young returning missionary with a five-piece band.

see the roadside signs. You will hear recorded safety messages and general park information.

In Montana, call (406) 444-6339 for recorded statewide information. For the Bozeman area, call (406) 586-1313; for the Billings area, call (406) 252-2806.

In Wyoming around Cody, call (307) 587-9966. Statewide, call (888) WYO-ROAD.

In eastern Idaho from November through March, call (208) 745-7278 for a 24-hour recorded message. For a real person, call (208) 745-7781.

Highway patrol emergency numbers in Greater Yellowstone are: (800) 442-9090 in Wyoming, (208) 587-9966 in Idaho, and (406) 444-7000 in Montana.

By Air

Compared to major metropolitan areas, the airports in Greater Yellowstone are simple get-in-and-get-out facilities. There isn't one in which you couldn't holler (if you dare) from one end to the other. During summer, at the height of the tourist season, these small-town airports are bustling with planes and people. While some of these airports are on the outer fringe of Greater Yellowstone, none is more than 90 minutes from the national parks. Car rentals, shuttles and courtesy vans are standard fare at even the smallest airport during the summer months.

International Airports

Salt Lake International Airport in Utah and Logan International Airport in Billings, Montana, are the two international airports serving our region. Salt Lake, with its high volume of flights, often has the cheapest rates. Both airports are served by major carriers and car-rental companies.

Salt Lake City International Airport

776 N. Terminal Dr., Salt Lake City, Utah • (801) 575-2400

This airport serves nine large airlines: American, America West, Delta, Southwest, SkyWest, Northwest, Frontier, Continental and TWA. The commuter service Alpine, which carries people to Moab, Ely and other nearby locations, also lands here. Salt Lake City is a Delta hub.

Onsite rental car companies are Alamo, Avis, Budget, Dollar, Hertz and National. Offsite options are Advantage, Agency Rent A Car, Enterprise, Payless and Thrifty. To contact any of these companies, just call the automated airport information line above and choose the car rental menu option.

This airport, built in 1961, has received its walking papers. In 1997, 21.3 million people moved through this facility; it was built to handle half that many. That overload, combined with the fact that Salt Lake will host the 2002 Winter Olympics, has prompted plans to construct a new airport, which will be located just northwest of the current one. It is scheduled to start handling some flights as early as 2002. When the new facility is fully operational, the current airport will be torn down. Also because of the Olympics, you will encounter freeway construction as you head from the airport to downtown Salt Lake City. Construction is ongoing from Provo to downtown Salt Lake. It's slated for completion sometime in the year 2000. Expect delays and/or detours.

A shuttle operates between Salt Lake International, (801) 575-2400, and several eastern Idaho communities. Rexburg-based Salt Lake Airport Shuttle Hop (SLASH), (208) 359-3174 or (800) 359-6826, makes two runs per day at a one-way cost of less than $40. To make sure the company can offer you a ride, it adds a third run on holidays and summer weekends. Another shuttle can get you to Jackson Hole Airport and back. Jackson Hole Express, (307) 733-1719 or (800) 652-9510, charges a one-way cost of less than $50.

If you're driving, the fastest route from the Salt Lake City airport into Yellowstone country is to head north on I-15. You'll be in Idaho Falls in three hours if the weather's good, barring serious construction delays. In winter get a road report, since drifting snow closes the interstate periodically. Alternatively, you can take the scenic route, exiting I-15 at Brigham City and heading up U.S. Highway 89 to Montpelier. At Montpelier take U.S. Highway 30 to Soda Springs, then Idaho Highway 34 to Freedom and then north on U.S. Highway 89 to Alpine, Wyoming. This will bring you to the Snake River Canyon, a short, scenic drive from

Yellowstone Country's Backcountry Byways

The following passage was supplied by Tony Huegel, author of Idaho Byways: Backcountry Drives for the Whole Family. *He is also the author of similar guides for California, Utah and Colorado.*

Traffic congestion may be the single most common complaint about visiting Yellowstone National Park and its environs. Without even realizing it, you can end up gazing not so much at natural wonders as at the rear ends of lumbering RVs, tour buses and countless cars — unless you know where to find Yellowstone country's quiet and scenic, though sometimes rough, unpaved backways. Two easy dirt roads inside the park allow motorized travelers to get a feel for old Yellowstone. Both historic byways are one-way, single-lane "auto trails" that let you escape the park's often-crowded paved roads. They parallel paved primary roads, providing alluring alternatives without major detours. A bit rocky here and there, they are closed after rain and snow storms. They offer fine mountain-biking opportunities. RVs and trailers are not permitted.

The 7-mile Blacktail Plateau Road, open June through September, begins west of Phantom Lake, on the south side of the Grand Loop Road midway between Mammoth Hot Springs and Tower Junction. It follows the approximate route of the old Bannock Indian Trail of the mid-1800s. As it ascends Blacktail Deer Plateau and passes south of Crescent Hill, the views include the Gallatin Range, Electric Peak, Sepulcher Mountain,

— continued on next page

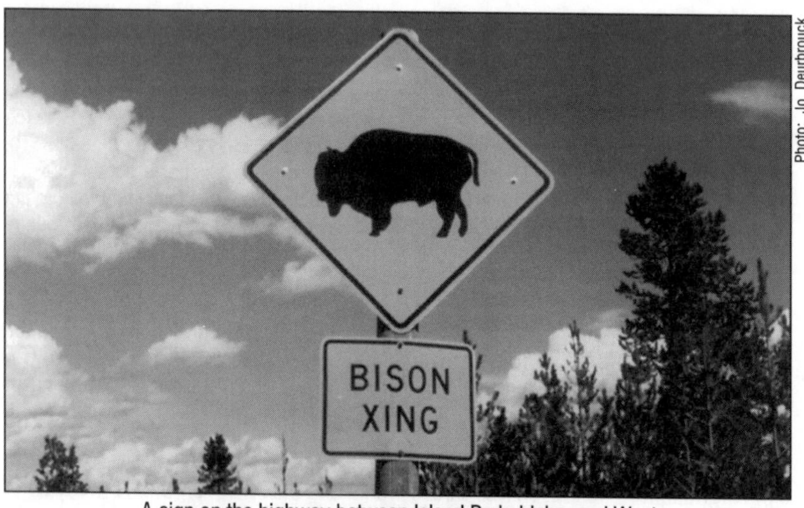

Photo: Jo Deurbrouck

A sign on the highway between Island Park, Idaho, and West Yellowstone, Montana, is a Greater Yellowstone feature.

Bunsen Peak and Antler Peak. Wildflowers bloom through June and July. Soon it passes through a mosaic of burned and unburned forests, reminders of the fires of 1988. It reconnects with the Grand Loop Road just west of the petrified tree turnoff.

High on the west rim of Gardner Canyon, the Old Gardiner Road courses for 5 miles between Mammoth Hot Springs and the park's North Entrance station, near Gardiner, Montana. It is open May through October. The 1880s stagecoach and wagon route crosses sagebrush tableland, providing panoramic views of the Gallatin Range, Gardiner and Mammoth and the traffic inching through the river canyon below. In spring and fall watch for pronghorn, elk, bison, mule deer, perhaps even bighorn sheep. The entrance to the Old Gardiner Road is a bit tricky to find. In Mammoth, drive behind the hotel and to the right of Chittenden House. Go left at the stop sign, then immediately right. You'll see the sign.

Outside Yellowstone National Park, more byways await. Just east of Cooke City, outside the park's northeast entrance, angle north from the famous Beartooth Highway at the sign for Daisy Pass. This generally easy 10-mile 4x4 loop, which can be snowy and muddy into July, will take you through glaciated Rocky Mountain scenery and over Daisy and Lulu passes, both about 9,700 feet. Below Lulu Pass, on the Fisher Creek side, you will follow a gulch through an old mining area that most recently was to have been the site of the hotly debated New World gold mine, a proposal that succumbed to environmental concerns. You'll pass the Goose Lake Jeep Trail, a rough 4x4 and hiking trail to the Absaroka-Beartooth Wilderness. Then you'll ford Fisher Creek on the way back to the highway.

Another route begins in the John D. Rockefeller Jr. Memorial Parkway, between Grand Teton and Yellowstone. The occasionally rough Reclamation Road, a.k.a. Grassy Lake Road, runs 48 miles through aspen and lodgepole pine to Ashton, Idaho, from Flagg Ranch, Wyoming, coming out at U.S. Highway 89/191/287.

Put some effort into getting off the beaten path, and traffic won't be among your Yellowstone country memories.

Jackson Hole. The scenic route is not recommended for winter travel, but it takes you past the Wellsvilles (America's steepest mountain range), scenic Bear and Gray lakes and Blackfoot Reservoir. Plan on doubling your travel time if you choose this route.

Logan International Airport

1901 Terminal Cir., Billings, Mont. • (406) 657-8495

Since 1927, when the first airplane landed at what is now its site on the Rimrocks above Billings, Logan International Airport has grown from a 192-square-foot building to the current 190,000-square-foot terminal.

Montana's only international airport, Logan is a busy transportation hub with 40 daily flights offering worldwide connections. Major carriers include Delta, Continental, Northwest and United. Regional carriers flying into Billings include Big Sky, SkyWest and Horizon. Traffic has grown from a few hundred passengers per year in the 1930s to more than 330,000 in the 1990s.

At Logan International Airport, you'll find four car rentals and two taxi services. We recommend calling ahead to reserve rental cars, especially during the summer. You can call Avis at (406) 252-8007, Budget at (406) 259-4168, Hertz at (406) 248-9151 and National at (406) 252-7626. Taxis are usually waiting curbside at the airport for incoming passengers. If for any reason you do need to call a taxi, though, call City Cab at (406) 252-8700 or Yellow Cab at (406) 245-3033.

Powder River Transportation, headquartered in Cheyenne, Wyoming, has a daily bus run between Cody, Wyoming, and Billings. In Billings, call (406) 252-4169; in Cody call (307) 527-7658. Phidippides out of Cody and Red Lodge Shuttle out of Red Lodge both operate reservation shuttles between Billings and their communities. For more information about all these shuttles, see the entries below under "When You Don't Need a Car."

If you're driving from Billings, head west 16 miles on I-90, then turn south on U.S. Highway 212. This route will take you through Red Lodge, Montana, over Beartooth Pass to Cooke City, Montana, then into the park. It takes about four hours to drive from Logan International to Yellowstone National Park. If you want to bypass the Beartooth Pass and shorten your driving time, go west on I-90, then south from Livingston, Montana, on U.S. Highway 89.

Regional Airports

Idaho Falls Municipal Airport/ Fanning Field

2140 N. Skyline Dr., Idaho Falls, Idaho • (208) 529-1221

Idaho Falls Municipal Airport opened for business in 1929 with a 1,500-foot runway and one carrier called National Park Airways. But Idaho Falls has grown up, and so has its airport. Since 1953, there have been three extensions of the longer of what are now two runways. In 1997, both underwent extensive refinishing. Now the airport accommodates jets as large as Boeing 737s. Air Force One, a 747, has touched down here twice. Idaho Falls Municipal Airport hosts more than 5,000 flights a year.

The big months for travel through the airport are July and August. April is the slowest month. Carriers are Delta's partner, SkyWest, and Horizon, which partners with Alaska Airlines and Northwest. Flights are routed through Salt Lake City or Boise, so your first flight out or last flight in is always a short hop.

Automobile rental companies at the airport are Avis, (800) 831-2847; Budget, (800) 527-0700; Hertz, (800) 654-3131; and National, (800) 227-7368. No scheduled in-town shuttle service is available, but our CART transit buses will come pick you up if you call at least a day in advance. They can get you from the airport in west Idaho Falls to Grand Teton Mall in east Idaho Falls for around $2. For information, call (208) 522-2278. CART also runs a twice-daily shuttle to Jackson for a one-way cost of around $20; for information on in-town transportation or the Jackson shuttle, call (208) 522-2278. The only taxi service in town is Easy-Way Taxi and Delivery, (208) 525-8344. Another shuttle service between here and Jackson Hole is operated by Jackson Hole Express. Its one-way rides cost about $25. Call them at (307) 733-1719 or (800) 652-9510.

Jackson Hole Airport

1250 E. Airport Rd., Jackson, Wyo. • (307) 733-7682

This little airport has one terminal and four commercial carriers. SkyWest, American, United and United Express all fly into Jackson Hole. You'll deplane from the 737, 757 or smaller propeller-driven plane onto the tarmac; the first thing you'll see is the raw, jagged skyline of the Tetons. Airport staff say it's tough tearing disembarking passengers away from that vista and moving them into the terminal. Jackson Hole Airport, 9 miles north of Jackson, is the only commercial airport in the country located inside a national park.

You're probably renting a car, but if you're not, Alltrans Inc., (307) 733-3135, meets every flight, 365 days a year. It will take you to any hotel or condo in Teton County. A round-trip transfer to Jackson costs just less than $20. You can also call Buckboard Cab, (307) 733-1112. Car rental companies at Jackson Hole

INSIDERS' TIP

Car condos are a hot item at Bozeman's Gallatin Field. For $9,400, you can buy your own garage at Car Park Garages, (406) 995-4763. Gallatin Field Car Keep at (406) 995-4517 also sells car condos.

Photo: Steve Fischbach, Post Register

This powder-hound snowmobiler gets all he bargained for.

Airport are Alamo, (800) 327-9633; Avis, (800) 831-2847; Budget, (800) 527-0700; and Hertz, (800) 654-3131.

West Yellowstone Airport
1515 Gallatin Rd., West Yellowstone, Mont. • (406) 646-7631

Built in 1965, this high-elevation airport (6,642 feet) is open only during the summer months. For three months, though, it's a hopping place serving numerous private planes and one commercial airline, SkyWest, which has three flights a day. Doris's Cantina, a Mexican restaurant in the airport, serves an array of Tex-Mex food good enough to entice West Yellowstone residents to drive the 2 miles from town (see our Restaurants chapter). Pilots can sleep overnight at an on-site campground.

At the airport, you will find two rental car companies: Budget at (406) 646-7735 and Avis at (406) 646-7635. Grayline Tours of Yellowstone offers a regular airport shuttle. Some of the hotels and motels in West Yellowstone also have courtesy phones at the airport.

Gallatin Field Airport
No. 6 Gallatin Field, Belgrade, Mont. • (406) 388-8321

It's confusing. Commonly referred to as the Bozeman airport, the Gallatin Field Airport is really in Belgrade, 8 miles north of Bozeman. If you rent a car when you land at the airport, you'll find that the most direct route to Yellowstone National Park bypasses Bozeman. This 70,000-square-foot airport has been remodeled several times since it was built in 1942, and passenger service has grown accordingly. Delta, Northwest, Horizon and SkyWest all fly into Gallatin Field, which serves about 200,000 passengers each year. Northwest, the first airline to fly into Gallatin Field in 1947, has been serving the Bozeman area for 51 years. At Gallatin Field there are a restaurant and lounge upstairs, as well as a gift store downstairs.

To reserve a rental car at the airport, call Avis at (406) 388-6414, Hertz at (406) 388-6939, Budget at (406) 388-4091 or National at (406) 388-6694. A shuttle service, 4x4 Stage, provides year-round transportation from Gallatin Field to Big Sky, West Yellowstone, Mammoth Hot Springs and the Bozeman area. (See the entry below for more information.)

Yellowstone Regional Airport
3001 Duggleby Dr., Cody, Wyo.
• (307) 587-5096

Of the 10 commercial airports in Wyoming, the Yellowstone Regional Airport is the third-busiest in the state, with five daily flights to Denver and Salt Lake City via United Express and SkyWest airlines. Despite the fact that it is a small regional airport, airfares are very competitive with those to Logan International Airport in Billings, Montana. In 1997, the 12,000-square-foot Yellowstone Regional Airport served nearly 60,000 passengers with just two gates and no concourses. You'll find a gift shop and a cafe in the airport that serves breakfast, lunch and dinner from 5 AM until 8 PM during the summer and from 5 AM until 7 PM during the winter. The cafe is a locals favorite for breakfast.

Three rental car companies have offices in the airport. To reserve a car and find out more about drop-off fees (they can be very high, especially during the summer), call Hertz at (307) 587-2914, Avis at (307) 587-5792 and Thrifty at (307) 587-8855. Phidippides, an airport transportation messenger service, offers taxi services to and from the airport as well as custom transportation to Yellowstone National Park. (See our heading below for more information.)

When You Don't Need a Car

Most visitors to Yellowstone country prefer to either drive their cars or rent at a regional airport. Others, like foreign visitors or winter travelers, want to leave the driving to someone else. If you're one of those people who quivers at the thought of navigating a mountain pass or nearly passes out when you see a road covered with black ice and blowing snow, you're not alone. Several bus companies and shuttle services in Greater Yellowstone will pick you up at the airport and drive you straight to Yellowstone and Grand Teton parks or to entrance communities surrounding the parks. Some of these same companies specialize in park tours with guides who explain things you might not otherwise learn. To find out more about these services, read on.

Yellowstone National Park and West Yellowstone, Montana

AmFac Parks and Resorts Sightseeing Tours
Mammoth Hot Springs, Yellowstone National Park • (307) 344-7311

Some people traveling through the parks without their own vehicles use Yellowstone National Park Tour buses to get around. These tours, led by trained driver/guides familiar with the park, depart from the Old Faithful Inn, Grant Village, Lake Hotel, Fishing Bridge RV Park, Canyon Lodge, Gardiner and Mammoth Hot Springs each day from mid-May until the last week of September. They follow three routes through Yellowstone National Park and cost from $22.36 to $32 per person in 1998, depending on the tour and the pickup point. (Refer to our Attractions chapter for more information).

Grand Teton National Park and Jackson Hole

Grand Teton Lodge Company
Jackson Lake Lodge, U.S. Hwy. 89
• (307) 543-2811

Grand Teton Lodge Company operates tours in the park's original tour buses (spiffed up a bit, of course), which date back to the '40s and '50s. The fanciest of the three, The Bullet, seats 20 in plush reclining seats. The company also offers daily shuttles in summer from Jackson to Jackson Lake Lodge in the park and between Colter Bay Village and Jackson Lake Lodge. The half-day Grand Teton National Park tour starts at Jackson Lake Lodge and stops at Signal Mountain Lodge, Jenny Lake, Menor's Ferry, Chapel of the Transfiguration and other historic places. These tours cost around $20, a bargain for the chance to gawk without having to watch where you're going. One-day trips begin at Jackson Lake Lodge, head north out of Grand Teton National Park and travel Yellowstone National Park's lower loop, stopping for a picnic lunch and various Yellowstone attractions before heading back down past Flagg Ranch and finishing at the lodge. These trips cost around $43 and include lunch. Robert Reed guides most of these trips; he's been at it for eight years and gets rave reviews. Tours are available mid-May to mid-October.

National Park Tours/Gray Line of Jackson Hole

1680 W. Martin Ln., Jackson, Wyo.
• (307) 733 4325, (800) 443-6133

Your tour guide stands at the front of the bus in a cowboy hat. If he's like most Gray Line guides, he's lived here for more than 10 years. He's been trained at locally famous Teton Science School in geology, history and ecology. He may even be Jack Starks, former superintendent of Grand Teton National Park. Your bus is plush: a 31-passenger vehicle with tinted windows, heating and air conditioning and a television in front so you can watch videos on fire ecology and Yellowstone history. Your seat reclines. Gray Line picks up at all hotels and condos in Jackson Hole, including those in Teton Village. Your tour may take you into Grand Teton National Park and include a scenic boat ride across Jenny Lake ($45 plus your park entrance fee). Or you may travel through Grand Teton National Park to Yellowstone National Park, spin around Yellowstone's lower loop, stopping for lunch at Old Faithful, and return to Jackson in about 10 hours ($48 plus park entrance fee, lunch not included). Both trips involve stops at scenic and historic attractions. National Park Tours/Gray Line also offers year-round custom tours and charters throughout the Intermountain Rockies. Park tours are available mid-May to October 1.

A Personal Guide Service

320 Bar Y Rd., Jackson, Wyo.
• (307) 733-1252

There are no buses here and no alternative to your car. What Art Davis and Larry Rieser do is hop in your vehicle and guide you to the best sights. Trips are catered to your interests and built to fit your schedule. Rieser has lived in Jackson Hole for 24 years. He came here to ski but fell in love and stayed. Both men are ski instructors. This company started after Rieser, in his 60s and guiding Snake River float trips for Barker-Ewing, decided the boats had gotten too heavy to haul up on a trailer. He worked for a local bus tour company one year but didn't feel that he was getting to know his guests. Davis and Rieser operate about 200 trips every summer May through October. Half-day trips in Grand Teton National Park run around $125. Daytrips up to Yellowstone run $175. The company does not accept credit cards.

Jackson's Hole Adventure

(307) 654-7849, (800) 392-3165

This is another quiet option: L.E. Schoenhals operates small, customized tours in her winterized Chevy van (with sunroof and tinted windows). You'll be one of six passengers. Schoenhals will almost certainly be your guide. Schoenhals has lived in Jackson Hole for nearly 20 years. A member of the Jackson Hole Historical Society, her main interest is pioneer history, but she can also show you great places for photos, teach you about the

INSIDERS' TIP

If you want to wander around Jackson for a few hours in summer, don't waste your time cruising for parking spaces on the streets. Head for the free municipal parking lot on N. Cache, only two blocks from town square. Or try near the elementary schools on N. Willow.

geology of the region and explain bear conservation issues in the parks. Schoenhals conducts about 200 tours per year. All start at your hotel. In summer you pay $48 plus the park entrance fee. The destination is Grand Teton National Park. A boxed picnic lunch at Jackson Lake is the high point of the trip for many. In winter, the trip is more elaborate. You pay $76 for a driving tour around Jackson Hole, a lunch stop (included in tour cost) at the spectacular National Museum of Wildlife Art and a sleighride out onto the National Elk Refuge where thousands of elk winter. There's no park entrance fee because you never enter the park.

Southwestern Montana

Grayline Tours of Yellowstone

633 Madison Ave., West Yellowstone, Mont. • Summer (406) 646-9374 or (800) 523-3102, winter (800) 733-2304

Grayline Tours of Yellowstone, a franchise of the national line, runs a shuttle between the West Yellowstone Airport and local hotels and motels. Grayline also operates park tours out of West Yellowstone and Big Sky that pick up passengers at some motels, hotels and campgrounds. Led by 25-year veteran driver Dennis Paterson, Grayline's fleet of five driver/guides is trained to answer your questions. Courteous, enthusiastic and patient, these drivers can teach you in a day what you might never figure out on your own. While all drivers are well versed in Yellowstone National Park as a whole, each has his own area of special interest including history, geology, geysers and wildlife. Grayline offers five trips: the Upper Loop, the Lower, Quake Lake and Virginia City (see our Attractions chapter) and Grand Teton National Park. The company also features a Wildlife Safari as well as individual tours for up to 12 passengers from April 18 until November 1.

In 1998, a coach tour of the Upper or Lower Loops cost $36 from West Yellowstone, while private tours started at $275. That same year a round-trip shuttle from the West Yellowstone airport to town cost $20 for the first person, plus $2.50 for each additional person.

4x4 Stage

1765 Alaska Blvd. S., Belgrade, Mont. • (406) 388-6404, (800) 517-8243

Based at the Gallatin Field Airport north of Bozeman, 4x4 Stage shuttled about 14,000 people last year from the airport to Big Sky or to Yellowstone National Park. During the winter, when travelers are heading to Yellowstone country to play in the snow, 4x4 runs four to six shuttles each day to West Yellowstone, seven trips to Big Sky and one to Mammoth Hot Springs. In the summer, when tourists feel more comfortable driving themselves, 4x4 cuts back to two daily shuttles to West Yellowstone and one tour a day through Yellowstone National Park. In addition, 4x4 Stage offers reservation tours from Bozeman through Yellowstone. The name 4x4 refers to the four-wheel-drive vans used for some Big Sky shuttles to assure getting around on steep, snowy roads.

Red Lodge Shuttle

(406) 446-2257, (888) 446-2191

Red Lodge Shuttle provides by-reservation door-to-door service between Red Lodge and the airports in Billings and Cody. If driving the Beartooth Highway to get to a trailhead or Cooke City freaks you out, call Red Lodge Shuttle. Owners Mike Vick and Nancy Immel will drop you off at trailheads in the area, including those across Beartooth Highway near

INSIDERS' TIP

In Rexburg and other Mormon communities, streets are laid out Salt Lake City-style. A typical address would read like this: 253 E. 400 N. To decipher this, just remember that addresses on a given street are derived from that street's "name." In other words, 253 is on a street labeled 400, which is east and north of the center of town. There will also be a 253 W. 400 S.

Cooke City. During the winter they provide a shuttle service from town to the Red Lodge Ski Area.

Northwestern Wyoming

Phidippides

3001 Duggleby Dr., Cody, Wyo.
• (307) 272-3232, (307) 527-6789

Frank Alvarado, a retired sheriff's deputy from California, will transport you, your lost luggage, packages, messages, you-name-it, from the Cody airport (and Cody) to almost anyplace in the region. Operating out of the airport gift shop, Phidippides offers custom tours and shuttles to Billings and almost anywhere else in the region you want to go. If you want to celebrate your 50th wedding anniversary at Old Faithful, Alvarado or one of his drivers will pick you up, take you to Old Faithful, then return a few days later to bring you back. Alvarado, who has been running his service since 1994, will deliver you to a trailhead anywhere in Yellowstone country.

If you want to see wolves and hear them howl, he will pick you up at 4 PM, supply spotting scopes and binoculars, take you to the wolves and keep you out all night so you can hear them howl. He and his drivers, who keep a fleet of two Suburbans and two 15-passenger vans on the road, carry backpacks, fishing poles and sleeping bags with them because they never know where they'll end up for the night. Alvarado charges $51 per person, $75 for two and $105 for three for a trip to Billings. He charges $1 a mile for taxi trips into Yellowstone or Grand Teton parks. Rates for custom tours vary.

Powder River Transportation

1452 Sheridan Ave., Cody, Wyo.
• (307) 527-7658

Not to be confused with Powder River Yellowstone Tours listed below, this company is headquartered in Cheyenne and has a daily three-hour run between Billings and Cody. In Cody, the pickup point is Daylight Donut. In Billings it's at the Greyhound bus station at 2502 First Avenue N. In 1998, a one-way fare cost $24, while a roundtrip ticket cost $45.60. The number for the Billings office is (406) 252-4169.

Powder River Yellowstone Tours

Cody, Wyo.
• (307) 527-6316, (800) 442-3682

From June 1 until mid-September, Powder River in Cody features daylong tours from Cody through Yellowstone National Park's Lower and Upper Loops. In 1997, Powder River transported its guests in a 46-passenger coach. The next year, it used 15-passenger vans. The 1999 season may hold a combination of both. Cody native and former park ranger Bob Richard trains the driver-guides and occasionally guides a tour when he's not busy with his own custom trips under the name of Grub Steak Expeditions. The tours leave Cody at 7:30 AM and return at 7 PM, and the driver will pick you up at your motel or campground. In 1998, the Yellowstone trip cost $49 plus tax and a $10 park entrance fee per person.

Grub Steak Expeditions

Cody, Wyo. • (307) 527-6316

Bob Richard, a former Yellowstone park ranger, specializes in custom trips of any length to the park and surrounding areas. Richard grew up in Cody guiding with his grandfather, who was one of Buffalo Bill Cody's guides. While at his grandfather's knee, Richard learned to tell a good tale. Now retired, he brings his own and his grandfather's extensive knowledge to tours tailored to suit your needs — art gallery visits, wildlife photography outings and geology expeditions, among others. Besides knowing how to get you to special park features, Richard is good at designing trips for multi-generation groups. Richard's trips are popular, so reserve your

INSIDERS' TIP

See those "Open Range" signs on the side of the highway? Open range means that cattle are not fenced away from the road. If you hit one, you are responsible for the cost of the cow.

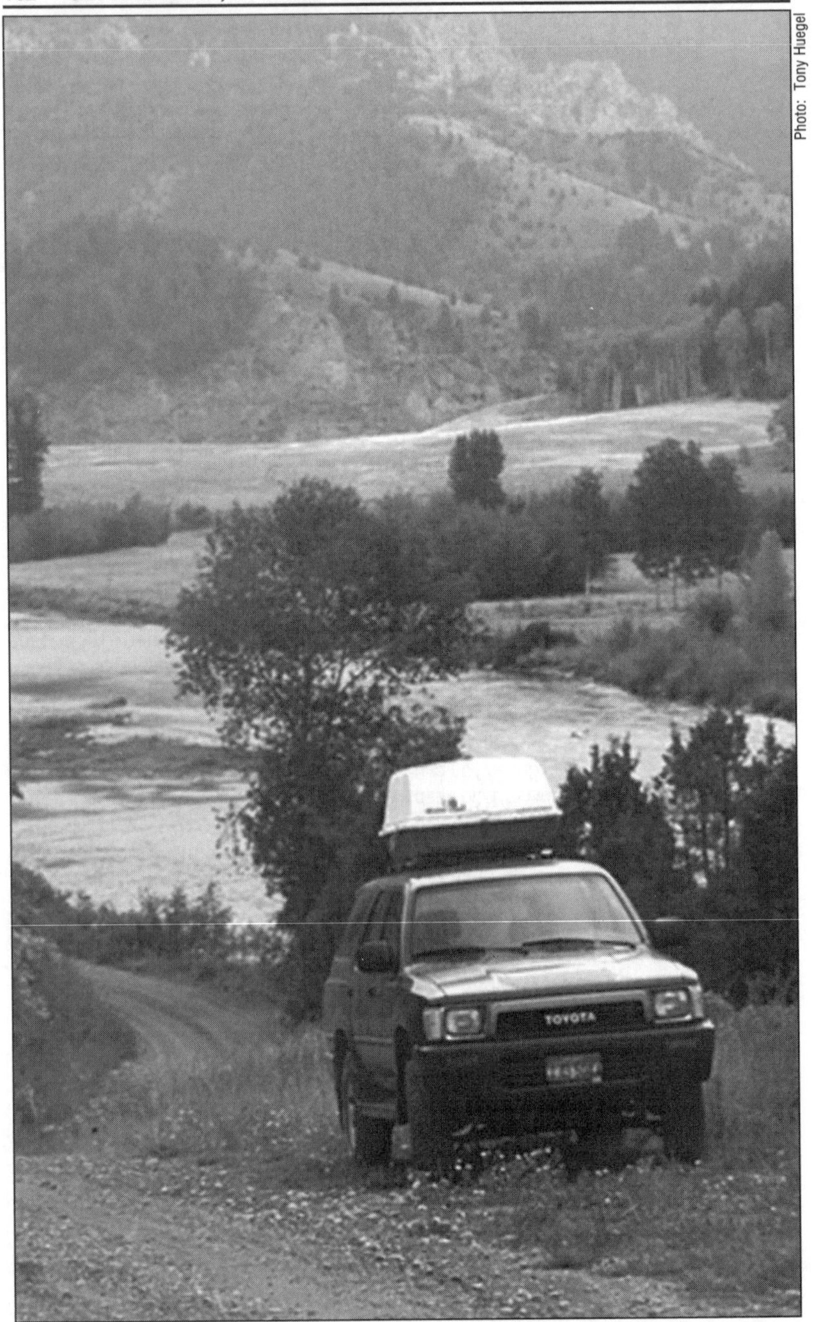

Photo: Tony Huegel

Getting off the pavement in Greater Yellowstone.

spot on his calendar well in advance by calling the number above. Richard's trips start at $275.

Yellowstone Expedition Services

Cody, Wyo. • (307) 587-5452, (888) 808-7990

The new kid on the block among Cody tour companies, Yellowstone Expedition Services operates just one six-passenger van. That's because owners Holly and Allen Moen want to be sure you get individualized attention and all your questions answered. They'll meet with you the night before to brief you on the tour and answer questions. Then they'll pick you up at your motel the next morning. Tours, which range from half-day to multi-day excursions, include narration of geothermal and volcanic activities, history and wildlife. The Moens will also pack your lunch, pay your entrance fee and bring along binoculars and spotting scopes. A full-day trip for two costs $122.50 per person. If you bring along your friends and family, the price per person drops dramatically. Since most trips are custom-designed for you, prices can vary depending upon your desires.

As you plan your trip, remember that although Greater Yellowstone is an area of low population and seasonal solitude, in summer we are full up.

Hotels, Motels and Cabins

Hotel staff in Jackson, Wyoming, tell of desperate phone calls originating 97 miles away at Old Faithful Inn in Yellowstone National Park, from travelers in search of a roof to sleep under. As you plan your trip, remember that although Greater Yellowstone is an area of low population and seasonal solitude, in summer we are full up. Even good campsites may be hard to find at the last moment. In general, this becomes truer the closer you get to Yellowstone National Park, Jackson and Grand Teton National Park.

So the word to the wise is: Make your reservations early — very early if you are planning to stay in a prime location (say, Old Faithful Inn) or at a prime time (say, July 4 or New Year's).

Yellowstone country is full of unique lodging options. Included in this book are chapters on camping, guest ranches, resorts, lodges and bed and breakfast inns. What you'll find in this chapter is a selection of the more interesting and pleasant hotel, motel and cabin accommodations available in our region. It would be impossible to include all the choices, but we've tried to cover the range of available prices and styles from posh to ultra-rustic. If you know of an establishment you feel should be included and isn't, we'd love to hear about it.

Most hotels and motels and many cabins are available year-round. If an establishment closes for one or more seasons, we've pointed that out. We also let you know if a business does not accept credit cards.

Unless noted, expect that hotel and motel rooms have cable or satellite TV and phones. You may also expect private baths in all listed options, unless noted. With almost no exceptions, the establishments we've selected offer wheelchair-accessible and nonsmoking rooms. Many provide complimentary shuttles from nearby airports. Establishments close to ski areas generally provide free shuttles to the lifts or know about convenient, low-cost transportation.

Most do not accept pets, and those that do generally told us they prefer not to advertise the fact. Most establishments also told us they could accommodate a variety of group sizes, but some are more flexible than others, of course. Especially at higher elevations, rooms may lack air conditioning; we don't address that fact in their entries, since cooling is so seldom necessary around here. Our listed cabins and hotel/motel rooms are all heated.

If any of these issues concern you, ask when you make your reservation.

Price Code

The dollar sign code that accompanies each listing represents that establishment's lowest price range for a two-person stay in the most expensive season. For most hotels and motels, this is summer; around ski areas it's winter. Most establishments offer a variety of room styles with rates that spiral up from the listed range.

$	**$25 to $49**
$$	**$50 to $75**
$$$	**$76 to $100**
$$$$	**$101 and more**

Please note that pricing information was provided by the establishments. Prices can vary during holidays and other events.

Many establishments offer at least three sets of rates: summer, winter and shoulder (fall and spring) with shoulder rates being the lowest. This makes travel in fall and spring a real bargain, with savings of more than half in many areas. In general, the closer you get to Grand Teton and Yellowstone, the more pronounced the shoulder savings.

www.insiders.com
See this and many other
Insiders' Guide
destinations online.
Visit us today!

As in most chapters, entries are organized so that accommodations in Yellowstone National Park come first. Next is Grand Teton and Jackson Hole. Surrounding areas in Montana, Idaho and Wyoming come next, in that order.

Finally, we offer a section on hostels, those traveler-friendly places that offer basic overnight amenities without taking a big bite out of your budget.

If you don't find what you're looking for here, you may be looking for something in another accommodations chapters. Many lodges and guest ranches, for instance, accept drop-in overnight traffic if they have room. Check out those chapters for more information.

Oh, and a final word about "rustic charm." Around here, that phrase gets attached to everything from falling-down cabins with no electricity to high-end hotels that happen to have log walls and Native American patterns on their plush down comforters. If your prospective host says the establishment has rustic charm, ask what that means. It may mean a handcrafted log bedstead and heritage quilts. It could mean no private bathroom, or no running water.

Hotels, Motels and Cabins

Yellowstone National Park

Before you make reservations for your stay in the park, there are a few things you ought to know. First of all, the park villages where you'll find hotels and cabins are kind of like tiny towns carved out of the wilderness. That means several things. Some of the accommodations, like the cabins at Roosevelt, may seem downright primitive to you. They're heated with wood stoves (easy-light logs are supplied), and some don't have bathrooms. This means you'll have to share a communal bathhouse with other folks in camp. We hope this information won't discourage you from staying in the cabins. If you look at them from a historic perspective and realize that some folks in Yellowstone country still live in cabins with no running water or electricity, you may be able to appreci-

INSIDERS' TIP

Island Park, Idaho, and West Yellowstone, Montana, become snowmobile heaven in winter. Accommodations book up for winter holidays faster than for summer, and you can literally end up in snowmobile traffic jams at key intersections.

TOWN SQUARE INNS
ANTLER INN · 49'ER INN · ELK COUNTRY INN

Come stay in the heart of Jackson Hole

1-800-4-TETONS

49'ER INN & SUITES

AAA ◆◆◆

30 new fireplace suites, spacious hotel rooms, beautiful suites & fireplace rooms Accommodations for all your needs.

- Cable television with HBO
- Mama Inez Mexican restaurant
- Beautiful studio suites
- Fireplace rooms available
- 30 new fireplace suites
- Pets welcome
- Suite unites
- Handicap facilities
- Winter car plug-ins
- Non-smoking rooms

W Pearl & Jackson • 4 Blks to Town Square
PO Box 1948 • Jackson, WY 83001

733-7550

1-800-451-2980 • FAX 307-733-2002

ANTLER INN

One of Jackson's finest with the premier location. Just one block west of town square.

- Large hot tub & sauna
- Cable television with HBO
- Meeting room
- Beautiful newly reconstructed rooms
- Winter car plug-ins
- Handicap facilities
- Pets welcome in some units
- Non-smoking rooms

W Pearl & Cache • 1 Blk W of Town Square
PO Box 575 • Jackson, WY 83001

733-2535

1-800-522-2406 • FAX 307-733-4158

ELK COUNTRY INN

Beautiful new log cabin or spacious rooms with loft makes this the perfect place for families

- Cable television with HBO
- Kitchenette rooms available
- Individual cabins available
- Winter car plug-ins
- Economy Rooms
- Hot tub • Ski wax room
- Large BBQ & picnic area
- Pets welcome in some rooms
- Non-smoking rooms
- Guest laundry
- RV spaces available

480 W Pearl • 4 1/2 Blks from Town Square
PO Box 1255 • Jackson, WY 83001

733-2364

1-800-483-8667 • FAX 307-733-4465

ate the charm. You might also want to know that, except at Roosevelt, a "cabin" in Yellowstone is really a basic sort of barracks-style frame building with very functional decor. Some have bathrooms and others don't.

Many of the rooms at the Old Faithful Inn, built at the turn of the century, also won't have private bathrooms. But we think the charm and privilege of being able to stay in this old inn far outweigh the inconvenience. A couple of other things you won't find in your rooms are telephones and TVs. In fact, there's only one TV available to the public in the whole park, and that's in the lounge at the Mammoth Dining Room.

Also, don't expect neatly manicured lawns with bright flowers planted here and there. This is Yellowstone, where wild grass grows up to your porch and wild animals may walk right up to your door. In fact, in the fall of 1997, a bull elk in rut refused to let cabin dwellers at Mammoth out of their rooms until he was chased off. Rut is the breeding season, and all that testosterone sometimes goes to a bull's head, making him belligerent. You may also wake up to find a bison standing in front of your porch. Please remember that even though these animals may look slow, sleepy and pettable, they can be very quick and dangerous.

Yellowstone National Park has 2,500 rooms, including 1,232 cabins. Two of the hotels listed in this section — Mammoth and the Old Faithful Snow Lodge — are open during the winter from mid-December until about the first week in March. The rest are open only during the summer months.

All these facilities are operated by the park's chief concessionaire, AmFac Parks and Resorts. For reservations at all park hotels and cabins, call AmFac Reservations at (307) 344-7311.

Canyon Lodge and Cabins

$$ • Canyon Village, Yellowstone National Park • (307) 344-7311

Built in the 1950s and '60s, the Canyon Lodge offers some standard hotel-type rooms as well as fourplex "cabins" that sleep from two to five people. All cabins have private bathrooms. Cascade Lodge (smaller than and separate from the main lodge) was built in 1993; its 30 hotel-style rooms have two double beds each. The main lodge has an activities desk in the lobby, as well as restrooms, a lounge, a gift shop and several dining options. Canyon Village is a hopping-off spot for park visitors, so expect lots of traffic and plenty of people in the village itself. The community has a visitor information center along with a Hamilton Store, a post office and a photo shop. Dunraven Lodge, a 44 room, 3-story companion to Cascade, should be open by the summer of 1999. Both lodges, decorated with rustic lodgepole furniture, offer rooms with one and two double beds. There are also a few handicapped-accessible rooms with a double and a single bed each.

Grant Village

$$$ • Grant Village, Yellowstone National Park • (307) 344-7311

Completed in 1984, Grant Village is one of Yellowstone's newest lodging facilities. In six two-story complexes that house 50 rooms each at the southern tip of Yellowstone Lake (see our Attractions chapter), you'll find regular motel-style rooms with private bathrooms with showers. All rooms have two double beds. The rooms can be a welcome relief if you've just spent days camping on the road. Nearby are two restaurants, a lounge, a gift shop and a laundry facility. Grant Village is one of the pickup spots for the Yellowstone Park Tour bus.

Lake Lodge Cabins

$ • Lake Village, Yellowstone National Park • (307) 344-7311

The Lake Lodge offers a rustic alternative to the elegance of the grand Lake Hotel. Inside the lodge, just off the huge lobby lounge with open beams and a wood floor, are a cafeteria and a gift shop. Surrounding the Lodge are 186 Western and Frontier Cabins, all with private baths. Built in the traditional barrack style of the 1950s and '60s, these cabins are clustered close together but provide a comfortable stay on the shores of Yellowstone Lake.

The cabins sleep two to five people, all in one main room with various bed combinations. Slip out of bed early in the morning, get a cup of coffee at the cafeteria, stroll to the shores of Yellowstone Lake and watch morning flood the water. Or get a head start on your laundry at the nearby facilities. The Bridge Bay Marina, headquarters for scenic cruises, guided fishing trips and boat rentals, is just a hop, skip and a jump away. (For more information on Bridge Bay Marina, read our Fishing and Watersports chapter.)

Lake Yellowstone Hotel and Cabins

$$ • Lake Village, Yellowstone National Park • (307) 344-7311

Glide into the Lake Hotel, admire the blue-tile fireplace and the sweeping staircase, then head straight for the long, elegant sunroom. Find yourself the most comfortable wicker chair facing the best view of Yellowstone Lake, sit down and gaze into the distance. Evenings, you can do your gazing to the tunes of a piano player. Anytime, you can sip mint juleps.

Built in 1891 by the Northern Pacific Railroad, the Lake Hotel was treated to reconstructive surgery in the 1920s by architect Robert Reamer (he designed the Old Faithful Inn). Reamer transformed the shoebox-shaped hotel into its current elegant state. The sunroom was his idea. So was the dining room, another grand space with Bordeaux tablecloths and plenty of windows facing the lake. This hotel, which now houses 194 guest rooms, mostly with two queen-size beds, underwent a 10-year restoration project in the 1980s. The old rooms are spacious and high-ceilinged with bathrooms, and the newer 1980s rooms follow suit. The cabins — there are 110 of them — are painted a creamy yellow; they all have private bathrooms. There is one presidential suite.

Mammoth Hot Springs Hotel and Cabins

$$ • Mammoth, Yellowstone National Park • (307) 344-7311

This year-round hotel, built in 1911 and finished in 1937, hints of the days when trips to Yellowstone were mostly accessible to the wealthy. The hotel and an annex behind it offer a total of 98 rooms during the summer and 136 rooms in winter. Most rooms have two double beds, some with an occasional single, and there are two suites. In addition to the hotel rooms, the complex has 128 cabins mostly with two double beds, but a few have an extra single. Some don't have private baths; communal facilities with toilets and showers are available. In 1998, the cabins rented for $69 and $38 respectively. Clustered behind the Mammoth dining room and lodge, these cabins are spacious, light and airy despite their 1930s vintage.

Just 5 miles from Yellowstone's North Entrance, the Mammoth Hotel is at the heart of the park's headquarters and right across the street from the Albright Visitor Center. You'll find fine dining at the Mammoth dining room (see our Restaurants chapter) and a comfortable lounge adjacent to it. At the other end of the building is a fast-food outlet. You can stock up on groceries and camping supplies at the Hamilton Store in Mammoth. The Mammoth Hotel is a pickup and drop-off point for Yellowstone Park Tour buses.

Old Faithful Inn

$$ • Old Faithful, Yellowstone National Park • (307) 344-7311

Sit on the outside balcony and sip a Bloody Mary or slurp an ice cream cone while you wait for Old Faithful to erupt right in front of the inn. Or lounge on one of the inside balconies and read a good book, write a letter or just watch people. The crown jewel of Yellowstone

INSIDERS' TIP

Area motels often can arrange activities such as horseback riding, whitewater rafting or snowmobiling. In general, lodging establishments that provide those activities themselves are found in the Resorts and Lodges chapter or in the Guest Ranches chapter.

National Park lodging, the Old Faithful Inn is worth a visit (and a tour) even if you don't stay overnight. Built of massive Douglas fir logs with a huge lobby that opens to the crow's nest 85 feet above, the turn-of-the-century inn bears testimony to the determination and ingenuity of the workers who built it. At the center of the lobby is a 14-foot-square, four-sided chimney with eight fireplaces. It's made of 500 tons of rhyolite stone. A hand-forged wrought-iron clock clings to the massive chimney and still keeps perfect time.

When the hotel opened, it had 146 rooms and was equipped with running water, electricity and steam heat. Today, the 75 remaining original rooms are much the same as they were at the turn of the century — small and dimly lit with a dangling bulb; the only thing missing is the chamber pot. Down the hall are restrooms, showers and two "bath" rooms with claw-legged tubs for guests who choose to soak. In the newer wing, 250 larger, brighter rooms each have private bathrooms. Several of the older balcony rooms, which are larger suites and overlook the geyser basin in front of the inn, are so sought-after they're reserved two years in advance. In all, the inn has 327 rooms ranging from small with no private bath that rented for $49 in 1998 to large suites for $315. Rooms range from two single beds to two doubles.

Besides the grand formal dining room, the Old Faithful Inn houses a fast-food outlet, an ice cream counter, an espresso cart, a lounge and a gift shop. Nearby, is a gas station and general store. The park's tour buses pick up passengers at the inn.

Old Faithful Lodge Cabins

$ • Old Faithful, Yellowstone National Park • (307) 344-7311

Opposite the Old Faithful Inn, on the other side of its namesake geyser, the Old Faithful Lodge is the park's modern-day answer to accommodating hordes of tourists. Inside the lodge itself are a gift shop and several dining options including a cafeteria, two snack shops and an espresso cart in the lounge. The 132 "cabins" at Old Faithful Lodge are barrack-like structures built in the '50s and '60s and range in price from $26 to $42, depending on whether or not they have private bathrooms. The rooms range from those with two singles to two double beds. There are 47 without bathrooms.

Old Faithful Snow Lodge and Cabins

$$$$ • Old Faithful, Yellowstone National Park • (307) 344-7311

During winter, the Old Faithful Snow Lodge is the happenin' hub of Yellowstone's winter wonderland and a welcome sight at the end of the snowmobile trail. Opened in 1998, the new Old Faithful Snow Lodge is the 1990s version of park splendor. Huge native-rock fireplaces, a high-ceilinged lobby, handcarved furniture, big picture windows, deep-cushioned couches and a wildlife theme combine to create a different kind of turn-of-the-21st-century elegance. All rooms have built-in armoires, some have window seats, and each has two double-size beds with comfy comforters. An additional 34 cabins feature two double beds and bathrooms. A family restaurant and a gift shop are on the premises. A nearby snack shop is open summer and winter. Cabin rates start at $73.

Roosevelt Lodge Cabins

$ • Yellowstone National Park • (307) 344-7311

Step into the Old West and early 20th-century living at the Roosevelt Lodge Cabins. Ease into one of those lodgepole rocking chairs lining the Lodge's sprawling porch, tip back your hat, prop those feet up on the porch railing and survey the landscape before you. Named after President Theodore Roosevelt, who liked to camp where the lodge now stands, the

INSIDERS' TIP

If you've never sat shoulder-deep in hot water with snow falling on your head, you owe yourself that delightfully incongruous experience; choose an establishment with a year-round, outdoor hot tub.

Roosevelt Lodge was built in 1908. Inside is a large lodgepole family-style dining room. Outside is an array of cabins that ranges from $37 to $73, depending on their amenities. The Roughrider and Rustic cabins have wood-burning stoves, and the Economy cabins have a toilet and a sink, but no shower. A few Frontier cabins come equipped with showers and toilets. Communal bathrooms and showers are scattered throughout the cabin area.

The Roosevelt Corral offers guided horseback riding, stagecoach rides and chuckwagon dinner cookouts. (For more information, see our Other Recreation chapter.) If you're planning to stay in the area, it's best to make reservations well in advance for the activities at the Roosevelt Lodge.

Grand Teton National Park

Jackson Lake Lodge, Jenny Lake Lodge, Colter Bay Village and Signal Mountain Lodge all offer cabin, hotel-style or motel-style accommodations inside the park. Just north of Grand Teton National Park is Flagg Ranch. Because these establishments also offer activities (generally at additional charge) and many visitors focus on a particular establishment's activities, you'll find them described in our Resorts and Lodges chapter. If money is a consideration, check out Colter Bay, Signal Mountain and Flagg Ranch, which are less expensive. Jackson Lake Lodge has more activities available among its horse corrals, bus tours, scenic floats and swimming pool. Lovely, rustic Jenny Lake Lodge is high-priced.

Dornan's Spur Ranch Cabins

$$$$ • 10 Moose St., Teton Park Rd. at Moose Junction, Wyo. • (307) 733-2522

Dornan's is a bustling little complex of shopping and dining opportunities, plus a small cluster of newer log cabins from which to enjoy them. Built in 1992, the cabins are situated on a flat wildflower-speckled meadow below the busy but small commercial complex. This means that even though you have access to services, including a gas station, you're not affected much. These pretty log structures also are not lined up in tidy rows; they're scattered about the meadow much as the wildflowers are. Kitchens are completely equipped. The furniture is woven rawhide, and the walls are log.

Other conveniences and amenities available at Dornan's include a well-stocked grocery store, an amazing wine selection in the liquor store, a gift shop, sports equipment rentals including mountain bikes and canoes, whitewater float trips and a tackle shop from which you can arrange guided fishing trips.

Cabins and most retail facilities are open year-round, but The Chuckwagon closes for winter.

Grand Teton Climbers Ranch

$ • Teton Park Rd. near Moose, Wyo. • (307) 733-7271

Run by the American Alpine Club, this place is bare-bones accommodations for climbers. The charge is $6 per person per night, but they'll take more if you can afford it. You get a bunk (bring your own mattress and sleeping bag) in a bare-walled cabin with a private bath, access to the roofed outdoor cooking area (bring your own stove) and to the small practice climbing wall studded with artificial handholds and footholds. The bulletin board on the office door provides weather reports and a place for you to advertise for a climbing partner if you're looking for one. There are no phones.

Luton's Log Cabins

$$$$ • U.S. Hwy. 26 at Buffalo Valley, Wyo. • (307) 543-2489

Owner Joanne Luton suggests you bring a good book. Luton's offers no activities or TV distractions from the quiet loveliness of Buffalo Valley as it borders Grand Teton National Park. There are no in-room phones (although a phone is available) and no nearby neighbors on the valley floor.

Most of her 11 duplex cabins are 7 years old; all are pleasantly designed with just enough smooth white wall to make the log and pine look magnificent. Each cabin has either one bedroom or two, plus a fully equipped kitchen, a private bath, a sitting area and a dining area. A covered porch runs the length of each cabin. Cabins were constructed with fire-killed logs from nearby forestlands. Out front, several small grassy areas are equipped with picnic tables. A volleyball court awaits the first serve. Guest laundry is available.

Joanne is a third-generation Jackson native. The ranch on which these cabins sit has been in her family since the '40s. Luton's closes December through April.

Jackson Hole

Jackson, Wyoming, and Vicinity

49'er Inn and Suites

$$ • 330 W. Pearl Ave., Jackson, Wyo. • (307) 733-7550

One good reason to stay at the 49'er is the indoor hot tub, where you can lounge in steamy comfort with 30 of your closest friends. (If you only have a few friends along, there's a conventional-size hot tub outside, too.) Even better are the fireplace rooms and suites, with their wood-burning or gas fireplaces. Amenities in the higher-priced rooms may also include refrigerators, wet bars, microwaves, coffee makers, hair dryers and more. A small fitness room is on premises.

After you enjoy your continental breakfast, you'll find that the 49'er is a short stroll from Jackson's town square and just off Broadway. It's owned by the same family that operates nearby Antler Inn (see a later entry).

The Alpenhof Lodge

$$$ • 3255 W. McCollister Dr., Teton Village, Wyo. • (307) 733-3242, (800) 732-3244

Established in 1965, the Alpenhof was the first lodge at Teton Village. It was built the same year the original ski lifts were installed. Rates are higher here in winter than in summer.

Recently remodeled, this hotel distinguishes itself by resisting the nearly universal Jackson impulse to go Western: The handmade furnishings are Bavarian. The cozy continental feel is complemented by fresh flowers scattered about, a nightly turn-down service, oversize outdoor pool (kept open in winter), a hot tub and sauna and on-call masseuses. Rooms range from comfortable to downright decadent (the bathroom in the Edelweiss Room has a heated tile floor and a heated towel rack), but all have down comforters, full baths and hair dryers. VCRs are available for rent.

Two restaurants are on premises. The Bistro is particularly pleasant. When weather allows, you can take advantage of lovely outdoor dining on a second story deck shaded by Englemann spruce and subalpine fir. The Alpenhof Dining Room specializes in continental cuisine with a Western touch. Between the two, you're covered for breakfast, lunch and dinner. Oh, did we mention you can ski to the lifts?

Anglers Inn

$$$ • 265 Millward St., Jackson, Wyo. • (307) 733-3682

Set on a quiet street that runs into sedate Flat Creek at the edge of town, Anglers Inn is still only a brisk five-minute walk from town square.

Recently remodeled, the 28 units of this popular motel feature locally made lodgepole pine furniture and pine accented walls. All rooms are outfitted with microwaves, refrigerators and ski racks with drip pads. Many have sitting areas.

Antler Inn

$$$ • 43 W. Pearl Ave., Jackson, Wyo. • (307) 733-2535

Good value for the money and only one block from Jackson's town square, the Antler Inn has 100 units ranging from cute but simple little cedar-paneled rooms with A-frame ceilings to suites with whirlpool tubs and fireplaces.

Antler Inn belongs to Clarene and Creed Law, longtime residents of the Hole. Clarene, a Wyoming state legislator, began her innkeeping career in 1962 when her father offered his life savings, $10,000, to help her start a business. She built the Antler.

Thirty-odd years later, it's obvious that Dad's trust was well-placed. If you ask locals for a good, clean, inexpensive motel, odds are pretty good they'll point you toward one of Clarene's properties.

Each room at the Antler Inn is equipped with a full bath and a winter plug-in for your car. Twenty-four newly remodeled rooms feature log furniture. Don't forget to enjoy the hotel's sauna, small fitness room and hot tub before you tuck yourself into bed.

Best Western The Inn at Jackson Hole

$$$ • 3345 W. McCollister Dr., Teton Village, Wyo. • (307) 733-2311, (800) 842-7666

Of the 83 rooms in this hotel, the hands-down winners are the loft rooms. Five have king-size beds up a spiraling oak staircase with living and kitchen areas downstairs. The other five are for larger parties, with two queen-size beds downstairs and one king-size bed up in the loft. Many rooms (not just the loft rooms) have fireplaces, and the bellman not only brings your wood but also lights the match. Room decor is classy, simple and not Western, a surprise in cowboy-to-the-hilt Jackson Hole.

Other amenities here include ski lockers, an on-site ski tune shop, a pleasant outdoor deck and pool area with three hot tubs, a massage room with on-call masseuses, laundry facilities and a restaurant.

The Inn at Jackson Hole sits at the foot of Jackson Hole Mountain Resort's lifts, so rates are lower in summer than in winter. The hotel is also on a back route into Grand Teton National Park (it's a narrow road, so no trailers or RVs are allowed).

Best Western The Lodge at Jackson Hole

$$$$ • 80 S. Scott Ln., Jackson, Wyo. • (307) 739-9703, (800) 458-3866

Locals call it "that place with all the bears." It's as good a name as any for this newer upscale hotel festooned with 33 handcarved creatures, mostly bears. Some peer in windows, others sprawl sleepily across rafters. They're the children of Afton, Wyoming, sculptor Jonathan LaBenne. Your children are gonna love them.

The building has 154 rooms on three floors. King rooms are particularly nice, with whirlpool tubs, gas fireplaces in the sitting areas, wet bars, room safes, microwaves, coffeepots and stocked fridges. TVs and VCRs are demurely recessed in armoires. Queen rooms are nearly as nice, although they don't have fireplaces and some don't have whirlpool tubs. The decor is Western.

Don't miss the pool: It's indoor/outdoor with a huge glass door that pulls down to water level to separate you from the snowy cold in winter. The door stays up in summer. Inside, pool room walls are decorated with mountain murals. Outside, views from the deck are as pleasant as any in Jackson. You look up at Snow King, the in-town ski hill.

For families, another consideration is the on-site Fun Stop Arcade; your kids get free tokens when you check in.

Although there's no restaurant on premises, nearby Gunbarrel, China Town and Bleu Moon Diner all provide room service.

Camp Creek Inn

$$ • U.S. Hwy. 189, near Hoback Junction, Wyo. • (307) 733-3099

Nine pleasant cabins look down a grassy slope to Camp Creek Inn's restaurant and bar (see our Restaurants chapter), with U.S. Highway 189 and the Hoback River beyond. Seven of the nine are cute A-frames with porches. Inside, all are pine paneled and have oversize windows, wall-to-wall carpet, lodgepole pine furniture and either one or two double beds.

Amenities include small coffee makers, refrigerators and complimentary continental breakfast in summer. In winter, when many cabins are not accessible or are closed for the season, Camp Creek Inn's cabins are easily reached from regularly plowed U.S. 189.

The folks at Camp Creek Inn also do business as Camp Creek Outfitters. In summer they can take you on guided pack and fishing trips. During hunting season they'll help you bag your deer, elk, moose or bighorn sheep. They also maintain a tackle shop and a stocked casting pond on the property.

Cowboy Village Resort

$$$ • 120 S. Flat Creek Dr., Jackson, Wyo. • (307) 733-3121, (800) 962-4988

It's a cabin village right in the middle of Jackson. Each newer cabin has a covered porch, barbecue grill and picnic table. Most floor plans are generous with sitting areas, wall-to-wall carpeting, kitchenettes (dishes not provided) and full baths. Mini-blinds screen the oversize windows. Outside, razor-edged lawns are dotted with young trees, and flower baskets riot everywhere. For best enjoyment of the pretty landscaping, make sure you ask for a unit that doesn't face the grocery store located across the street. The resort has two hot tubs and a guest laundry. In winter, check with them about snowmobiling packages.

Davy Jackson Inn

$$$$ • 85 Perry Ave., Jackson, Wyo. • (307) 739-2294, (800) 584-0532

Just like the delicate china cup from which you'll sip afternoon tea in the lobby, the Davy Jackson Inn is one-of-a-kind. Your innkeeper, Kay Minns, added some special touches to the lacy country inn she built in romping, leather-and-antler Jackson. Hallways are wide and ceilings are 10 feet high. Decorative molding tops doorways and windows.

Each of the inn's 11 rooms is unique, but all have down comforters, computer modem jacks and sitting areas. Most are equipped with an armoire to hide the television. Some have whirlpool tubs, some old-fashioned clawfoot tubs. Many are equipped with king-size beds decked with graceful lace canopies.

If your room doesn't have a whirlpool tub, don't worry: A wood-decked hot tub waits outside.

A full country breakfast is included in your room price, so in the morning be sure you wander down to the cozy dining area to enjoy food that has been featured on PBS's *Country Inn Cooking*.

Elk Refuge Inn

$$$ • 1755 U.S. Hwy. 89, National Elk Refuge, Wyo. • (307) 733-3582, (800) 544-3582

When you call to reserve one of this motel's 23 rooms, make sure you tell Craig and Elizabeth Harmening you want the second floor. These rooms have sliding glass doors from which to watch the thousands of elk who winter on the valley floor at the National Elk Refuge, but you don't even have to walk up a flight of stairs. You drive around back where a higher parking lot lets you park at your door.

These upstairs rooms are large, with kitchenettes, high-slanted ceilings and chairs on the deck. They cost about one-third more than the cinderblock-walled rooms downstairs, but it's money well spent, especially in winter when rates become significantly lower than anything comparable in Jackson proper.

Elk Refuge Inn is 2 miles from Jackson's shops, restaurants and bars. The inn can put up your horse in the corral, or if you're here to hunt, let you hang your game on the meat pole behind the motel.

Flat Creek Motel

$$$ • 1935 N. U.S. Hwy. 89, National Elk Refuge, Wyo. • (307) 733-5276, (800) 438-9338

The 72 newer rooms in this year-round motel feature refrigerators and microwaves. The facility also offers a laundry room, a hot tub and a sauna, a ski-waxing area and horse corrals in case you're traveling with a four-hooved friend. On the same property, you'll find a 24-hour gas station and convenience store — very convenient since you're a couple of miles beyond Jackson proper here. Three new motel rooms were recently added above the store. They share a semiprivate hot tub enclosed on a deck facing the refuge. The rooms can open to become one large three-bedroom, three-bathroom, two-kitchen suite.

But the main attraction is across the highway on the National Elk Refuge. In winter (when Flat Creek Motel's rates drop by more than half, by the way) thousands of elk gather and feed on the valley floor. So if you're coming to

INSIDERS' TIP

Christmas to New Year's and Presidents' Day weekend are the busiest days at the region's ski resorts. On those dates, prices for nearby lodging may be 20 percent higher than normal winter rates.

Photo: The Blacksmith Inn

Cedar siding and indoor murals by local artists — part of the charm of accommodations in Greater Yellowstone.

Jackson Hole between mid-October and May, reserve a room here and pack your binoculars.

The Golden Eagle Inn

$$ • 325 E. Broadway Ave., Jackson, Wyo. • (307) 733-2042

This older motel offers standard amenities, including a heated outdoor pool (not operative in winter). The 23 rooms are simply furnished but clean. The nifty thing about The Golden Eagle Inn is its location in a residential area several blocks from town square. You can enjoy the lower traffic volume and relative quiet and still get to your favorite restaurant or gallery in a couple minutes' walk.

The Golden Eagle, like many Jackson motels, offers truly fantastic shoulder season bargains: Prices drop by half in spring and fall.

Hoback River Resort

$$, $$$ for cabins • 11055 S. U.S. Hwy. 89, Hoback Junction, Wyo. • (307) 733-5129

If you came to Jackson looking for quiet and learned, to your surprise, that thousands of other travelers did, too, you'll love this place. It won't surprise you, for instance, that your hosts, Kathy and Mike Shidner, escaped to this sweet spot from southern California nearly nine years ago.

Located at the confluence of the Hoback and Snake rivers on a high bench overlooking the Hoback, the resort has 12 large (450 square feet) motel rooms which access a pleasant deck through sliding glass doors. For a bit more you can stay in one of the older cabins or pleasantly appointed newer cottages. Three small motel rooms are also available.

Four older cabins dating to the 1930s sit down on a low bench. Their grassy lawns dip straight into the river. They're equipped with grills, picnic tables and long, covered porches you can almost fish from.

All accommodations here are equipped with TVs but no phones. Those that have kitchens are furnished with necessary kitchen items. All have heating and private baths. Cabins are not available from October through May, but motel rooms are open all year.

The Shidners prefer to rent their cabins and cottages for a three-night minimum.

Hitching Post Lodge

$$$ • 460 E. Broadway Ave., Jackson, Wyo. • (307) 733-2606

Clustered behind a renovated cedar lodge

built in the early 1900s are the motel-cabins of Hitching Post Lodge. Lodge amenities include a heated pool (in summer only) and hot tub (in winter only); rooms are outfitted with log and pine furniture, refrigerators and microwaves. Continental breakfast is served every morning except during the slow spring and fall months in a pleasantly renovated old log house which also holds the office and reception area.

This small motel complex is on a quiet residential street a few blocks' walk from town square. Or you can hop into your car and be in the National Elk Refuge before the engine warms up.

Hostel^x

$ • 3315 McCollister Dr., Teton Village, Wyo. • (307) 733-3415

Let's say you're a skier, serious hiker or type-A sightseer, and you believe motel rooms are for sleeping in, period. Hostel^x is for you.

Rooms are plywood with simple mattresses on wooden frames and a private bath. But you can watch TV or play backgammon in the fire-warmed lounge area, mess with your skis in the waxing room, read in the library or play with your kids in Pooh Corner, the well-equipped playroom. Best of all, you can ski from the motel door, and in summer you're nearly at the entrance to Grand Teton National Park.

Winter rates at this year-round motel are best if you're traveling in groups of three or four — a group of four can stay here in expensive Teton Village for about $15 per person per night. In summer, Hostel^x offers members of hostel organizations inexpensive individual rates (see the listing under hostels in this chapter).

Inn on the Creek

$$$$ • 295 N. Millward St., Jackson, Wyo. • (307) 739-1565, (800) 669-9534

From the warm hardwood paneling to the recessed lighting and the artful disarray of the throw rugs, you'll love this inn as soon as you walk in the door. Rent one of our favorite rooms — casually luxurious with a whirlpool tub and a gas fire that flickers through the tub's steam — and we can almost guarantee you'll be hooked.

Staff say the inn is a favorite for honeymooners and couples on romantic getaways. Certainly Inn on the Creek is not a family inn, since none of the rooms are equipped with more than one queen-size bed.

The inn's back yard, a small but pleasant grassy bench, has an outdoor hot tub. Behind it is Flat Creek. All rooms are equipped with down comforters and pillows, robes and slippers; the TV and VCR are hidden in an armoire. Staff slip in nightly to turn down your bed and leave a mint on your pillow.

Afternoon tea is served in the sitting room daily. Continental breakfast is delivered to your room, as the staff know from experience you don't want to leave, even for a cup of coffee, quite yet.

Mad Dog Ranch Cabins

$$$$ • Moose-Wilson Rd., Teton Village, Wyo. • (307) 733-3729, (800) 99CABIN

Mad Dog Ranch asks that you stay a minimum of three nights during most of the year, with higher minimum stays at Christmas and in July and August. That won't be a problem, though.

Cabins are high-ceilinged, paneled with pine and bright with light from the generous windows. At night you'll cozy up to the wood stove or picnic outside on your barbecue grill. Perhaps you'll soak in the complex's outdoor hot tub.

Each of the gray-painted duplex cabins has two bedrooms, a fully equipped kitchen, wall-to-wall carpet and a long porch with a picnic table. Two newer cabins have semiprivate fenced patios and their own dishwashers, garbage disposals and washer/dryers.

INSIDERS' TIP

If you're planning a winter ski trip, ask if your lodging establishment has secure ski storage. It'll make your life easier.

You'll pay almost $100 more per night for those. If you're traveling with horses, these folks have a corral you can use.

You're a 10-minute drive from Jackson Hole Mountain Resort and about the same distance from the dining, shopping and entertainment options of Jackson.

Nowlin Creek Inn

$$$$ • 660 E. Broadway Ave., Jackson, Wyo. • (307) 733-0882, (800) 533-0882

Mark and Susan Nowlin (pronounced with a "now," as in "now and then") run a fine bed and breakfast inn barely six blocks from Jackson's central square and literally a stone's throw from the National Elk Refuge (see our Bed and Breakfast Inns chapter). Behind their lovely new country house is your cabin, built in the 1920s by Mark's grandfather and furnished with a charming, low-key eccentricity.

The cabin is equipped with two bedrooms, a full kitchen, a living room with gas fire, a TV and VCR, cordless phone and stereo. The laundry room and a large cold room off the front door store your ski gear or mountain bikes. The whimsically decorated living room is hung with a flamboyant crystal chandelier through which Jerome, a mule deer shot by Mark's dad, solemnly peers. Larger groups can expand into the basement apartment, with its bedroom, bathroom and sitting room. The yard is semiprivate, screened from the inn with a high fence. There, a covered wagon replica waits for kids to come play. The yard also comes equipped with a gas grill and Mark's full-size wire sculpture of a horse grazing the lawn (both of your hosts are artists: Susan's work is stenciled on the walls). A three-night minimum stay is requested.

Old West Cabins

$$$ • 5750 S. Hwy. 89, Jackson, Wyo. • (307) 733-0333

Six miles south of Jackson near Flat Creek and the Snake River sit two rows of cabins. They're near the highway but below it, so you won't have headlights invading your sleep at night. The nicest cabins face away from the complex toward Flat Creek and the South Elk Feeding Grounds.

Many of these rustic cabins were built in the 1930s, but they contain modern conveniences such as wall-to-wall carpeting, kitchenettes, color cable TVs, phones and on-site coin-operated laundry facilities. Morning coffee is available.

Cabins rent by the night. They are various sizes, sleeping from two to six. The grounds contain a corral for your horses and plenty of room for your kids to run and play. This is a great site for family reunions.

Ranch Inn Jackson Hole

$$$ • 45 E. Pearl Ave., Jackson, Wyo. • (307) 733-6363, (800) 348-5599

Ranch Inn is the closest motel to town square's restaurants, art galleries, clothing stores and bars. If you stay here, the action is barely a block away, and you won't have to hunt for parking. When it's time to shop, just walk out of your room.

This motel is relatively small, with only 57 rooms. But these folks still offer a range of choices. Standard rooms are just that: clean, no-frills accommodations with amenities such as free local phone calls, radio alarm clock and access to the motel's two hot tubs (one is indoors, the other out). Ranch Inn's nicest rooms have full kitchens, wood-burning fireplaces, private balconies, hair dryers and extra bathroom phones. One, which depending on the season rents for between $110 and $200, even has a large hot tub bath. Complimentary continental breakfast is served daily.

Red Lion Wyoming Inn of Jackson Hole

$$$$ • 930 W. Broadway Ave., Jackson, Wyo. • (307) 734-0035, (800) 844-0035

It's hard to walk in without admiring the massive bolted cedar beams in the entry and the oversize doors. Inside, the ponderous moose antler chandelier catches your eye. Throw rugs, Western art and leather chairs dress the lobby. A gas flame flickers quietly in the river-rock fireplace.

Wide hallways lead to guest rooms with cherry wood doors and entry ways. The 73 rooms are oversize, and the bathrooms are spacious. You'll enjoy little extra touches like pullout makeup mirrors and hair dryers. All the standard amenities you would expect are complemented by coffeepots, desks and sitting areas. All are decorated with Western art.

A few have fully equipped kitchens, some have spas, and 20 have fireplaces.

The facility offers extended continental breakfast and free guest laundry service. No smoking is allowed on the premises.

Trapper Inn

$$$ • 235 N. Cache St., Jackson, Wyo. • (307) 733-2648, (800) 341-8000

Most of the Trapper Inn's 54 rooms are standard motel fare, clean and comfortable. Nine older rooms are cozily pine paneled and pleasantly nonrectangular. In the newest of the three motel buildings are more luxurious rooms, some with fridges, microwaves and coffee makers and one with an in-room hot tub and wet bar.

The best reasons to stay here, though, aren't in your room. First, you're only a few minutes' walk from town square. Second, the people behind the desk are generally Kudars or Kudar relatives, which makes the place a Jackson institution and the person at the desk full of interesting information. Max Kudar is Trapper Inn's owner; his dad built the old motel across the street back in the days when you could play ball in the middle of that street with almost no traffic timeouts.

Twin Creek Cabins

$$$, no credit cards • Twin Creek Ranch, National Elk Refuge, Wyo. • (307) 733-3927

Susan Johansson and her family came here from Jackson in 1955. The seven cabins Susan rents date to the '20s, when Twin Creek Ranch was a working ranch and these were working buildings. One was the entertaining house, one the bunkhouse, another a storage room. They've been renovated just enough: You'll feel like you're on an old Jackson-area ranch (you are), and you'll find the furnishings old — and sometimes odd— but you'll lack no comfort. If you've never experienced the sleep-inducing radiant heat from a wood stove, you may even discover a brand-new pleasure. All cabins are fully furnished with linens, full kitchens and electric heat.

The 9-acre property abutting the National Elk Refuge offers horseshoe pits, swing sets, a large sandbox and barbecue grills for a perfect Teton cookout. Some clear nights Susan gets out her telescopes and shows guests what all that clear mountain air can do for nighttime visibility. A stocked casting pond is reserved for the kids.

Three cabins afford Teton views; the others, tucked into aspen groves, offer a feeling of green seclusion.

Johansson rents for a seven-day minimum. Her cabins are available June through mid-August. The drive into Jackson takes about 10 minutes.

Wagon Wheel Motel

$$$ • 435 Cache St., Jackson, Wyo. • (307) 733-2357, (800) 323-9279

Wagon Wheel Village is pure Jackson: unabashedly commercial, Western to the hilt and solidly rooted in Hole history. You might stay here simply for the Village's motel — 97 units with modern amenities. The Wyoming Suites, housed in two-story log buildings at the back of the property with views of Flat Creek, are the newest and most pleasant of the accommodations here. The older rooms are, well, older. All the Wyoming Suites and about a dozen of the standard rooms have gas fireplaces.

It's more likely you'll choose the Wagon Wheel for its quirky flavor. Current owner Barry Remington's grandfather won the money to buy the original nine cabins in a card game more than 50 years ago; you can still stay in eight of them. The place lights up like Christmas at night; during the day, an army of totem poles, carved wooden Indians and bears outside the gift shop make the place tough to miss. Motel staff will tell you that the you-have-to-see-it-to-believe-it lobby is probably the

INSIDERS' TIP

Spring, fall and winter motel rates are substantially less, except in winter recreation areas like West Yellowstone, Big Sky, Driggs and Teton Village where room rates can be higher even than in summer.

most photographed motel lobby in the country (we believe it).

Or you'll choose this motel for convenience. The complex includes a coin-operated laundry, gift shop, cafe, saloon, liquor store, RV park (see our Campgrounds and RV Parks chapter), hot tubs and a rafting company. The Wagon Wheel is situated directly across the street from the local visitor center.

The Wort Hotel

$$$$ • Corner of Glenwood St. and Broadway Ave., Jackson, Wyo. • (307) 733-2190, (800) 322-2727

Back in 1915, homesteader Charles J. Wort bought four lots in Jackson and started telling folks about the luxury hotel he would build there. The town stopped laughing in 1941, when Charles' sons Jess and John did it. Today, The Wort is a historic landmark. It's also a AAA four-diamond hotel, one of only three lodging establishments with that distinction in the area (the others are Jenny Lake Lodge in Grand Teton National Park and the Rusty Parrot on Flat Creek in Jackson).

Each room is unique in appearance. Most beds have down comforters, many covered in a dramatic buffalo check that manages to look luxurious and down-home at the same time. Other rooms are papered in a print designed especially for the Wort that shouldn't look classy but does: It's a faint, vertical silhouette of barbed wire.

And 20 of the 60 rooms are decorated with blown-up prints of old-time Jackson and Jacksonites obtained from the local historical society. Silver Dollar Grille, the hotel's fine-dining, casual-dress restaurant, also displays these fun old photos. On display in the adjoining Silver Dollar Bar are exactly 2,032 uncirculated silver dollars embedded in the surface of the bar (more on these in our Restaurants and Nightlife chapters, respectively).

Enjoy complete room service, indoor hot tubs and a fitness room, along with all the expected amenities of a hotel. Oh, and there is Sam, that cute, floppy teddy bear sitting on your bed: If your kids fall in love with him, don't worry — The Wort can sell you a Sam of your own.

Surrounding Areas

Southwestern Montana

West Yellowstone, Montana

Alpine Motel

$$ • 120 Madison Ave., West Yellowstone, Mont. • (406) 646-7544

After 41 years of same-family ownership, the Alpine was bought in 1997 by the owners of the Chinatown Cafe next door. This motel is small with only 12 units, all with two queen-size beds. They are very clean, cheerful, spacious, conveniently located and reasonably priced. The Alpine is open from May through October.

Best Western Cross-Winds Motor Inn

$$$ • 201 Firehole Ave., West Yellowstone, Mont. • (406) 646-9557, (800) 528-1234

There's no fuss, no muss at this compact 70-unit motel within easy walking distance of every major attraction in West Yellowstone. The rooms, decorated in darker colors that suggest sprawling and lounging are expected here, are spacious and comfortable. The Cross-Winds offers rooms with single and double queen-size beds, as well as a few king suites. A few rooms have microwaves and refrigerators.

Evenings, you can swim or soak away the day in the Cross-Winds' indoor pool and spa. Mornings, you can stroll to the motel lobby, snack on complimentary rolls and sip hot coffee. Then walk your dog or swing your child at the West Yellowstone Town Park across the street. In winter, the Cross-Winds can arrange snowmobile rentals for you on-site or ahead of time.

Best Western Executive Inn

$$$ • 236 Dunraven St. , West Yellowstone, Mont. • (406) 646-7681

Situated around a courtyard and a deliciously inviting (summer) swimming pool, this two-story, 83-room motel also has a dining room that serves breakfast and dinner, including an all-you-can-eat buffet for both meals. The rooms, cheerfully decorated with varying themes of mauve, blue or sage carpet and matching floral bedspreads, are spacious and clean. The Executive offers a variety of room sizes and combinations including family suites. Some have fireplaces. A few on the back side of the main floor have doors that open to the alley — perfect for private parking, even better for driving your snowmobile right up to the door. The Executive also has a guest laundry and exercise room.

The Executive will arrange snowmobile packages for guests wanting to sled during the winter months.

Big Western Pine Motel

$$ • 234 Firehole Ave., West Yellowstone, Mont. • (406) 646-7622, (800) 646-7622

Families return to the Big Western Pine year after year for its clean, comfortable rooms, its convenient restaurant and its cheerful management. The 45 updated rooms range from single queen-size beds to one with a combination of five queens and doubles equipped with a refrigerator and coffeepot. An outdoor pool is open summers, and an indoor spa is open year-round. The Rustler's Roost Restaurant, a favorite with locals, serves three meals a day and features wild game entrees for dinner. Winters, the Big Western Pine offers snowmobile packages. This motel also rents two reasonably priced homes by the night; one sleeps 20, and the other sleeps nine.

Brandin' Iron Inn

$$ • 201 Canyon St., West Yellowstone, Mont. • (406) 646-9411, (800) 217-4613

Park your car and head out on foot (or snowmobile, if it's wintertime.) The Brandin' Iron is right smack-dab in the middle of the action. Owned by Ventures West, the out-of-park division of Hamilton Stores in Yellowstone National Park, the Brandin' Iron has 79 spacious and recently redecorated rooms. The Brandin' Iron has almost every imaginable combination of room types, including those with single queen-size beds, double queens, king suites and kitchenettes. Each room comes with a telephone and other amenities, including a clock radio and a refrigerator. Mornings you'll find continental breakfast in the lobby along with a crackling fire in the lobby fireplace in winter.

The Brandin' Iron offers snowmobile packages for winter guests, as well as outdoor plug-ins (for car heaters) and two hot tubs in which to soothe those sore muscles. A 16-unit RV park behind the motel is open during the summer. Spaces rent for $24.75 per night.

Days Inn

$$$ • 118 Electric St., West Yellowstone, Mont. • (406) 646-7656, (800) 548-9551

The Days Inn completed a major expansion in January 1999. The motel now boasts 115 spacious rooms, most with two queen-size beds, as well as a few king suites with spas. An indoor pool with a waterslide, a hot tub and the on-site Trapper Family Restaurant make the Days Inn a convenient place to stay. The Days Inn also has conference rooms, plenty of parking and winter snowmobile packages. Children younger than 12 stay free.

Dude Motor Inn

$$ • 3 Madison Ave., West Yellowstone, Mont. • (406) 646-7301

When he was the governor of California, Ronald Reagan once stayed here while attending a governor's conference in West. The face of the Dude Motor Inn has since changed,

INSIDERS' TIP

If you like saving money on your stay in Jackson Hole, book accommodations out at Teton Village for the summer. The "hottest" months here are during ski season, so you can expect bargains when temperatures rise. In winter, stay in Jackson and grab a shuttle to Jackson Hole Mountain Resort to save big bucks on a motel bill. Some Jackson motels charge as little as half their summer rate in winter.

but its location on Boundary Street, which borders Yellowstone National Park, has not. Simple, clean and on a back street, the Dude is still only a block off Main Street. After a day in the park, bypass the Main Street traffic and slip into the Dude. In winter, cruise up to the Dude on your snow machine, dude. Bring your own machine or reserve one from the rental fleet provided by owners Dean and Leila Seely.

Most of the rooms have two queen-size beds, but you'll also find a few rooms with either kings, multiple beds or kitchenettes. The Dude has 24 rooms and 60 snowmobiles.

The Gray Wolf Inn and Suites

$$$ • 250 S. Canyon St., West Yellowstone, Mont.
• (406) 646-0000, (800) 852-8602

If you arrive at The Gray Wolf Inn after dark, you just might hear the wolves across the street at the Grizzly Discovery Center having a good howl. The 103 spacious rooms at this new-in-1997 motel are appointed with pleasing furniture, 25-inch TVs, and plush drapes and bedspreads. They're equipped with hair dryers and coffeepots. Down the hall are an indoor pool, a hot tub and sauna. Heated underground parking is a plus in winter. The rooms are attractive and include king-size beds with hide-a-bed sofas, double queens and one-bedroom suites with two queen-size beds, a hide-a-bed and a full-size kitchen. The management enhances your stay here by treating guests to a deluxe continental breakfast in the very large and comfortable lobby.

Kelly Inn West Yellowstone

$$$$ • 104 S. Canyon Ave., West Yellowstone, Mont.
• (406) 646-4544, (800) 259-4672

Frosted with a rustic theme that includes chainsaw-carved bears, raccoons and a cougar hanging from posts, peeking in windows and crouched on rooftops, the three-story Kelly Inn houses 78 spacious rooms. Plush carpet, wallpaper and curtains that accent both make these rooms soothing. Most are standards with two queen-size beds. You'll also find several deluxe rooms with either two kings or two queen-size beds with a sofa-sleeper, refrigerator and microwave. A few Jacuzzi suites are outfitted with king-size beds and sofa-sleepers, as well as microwaves, sinks, refrigerators and wet bars. Rooms on the ground floor have both interior and exterior doors, which means snowmobilers can drive their sleds right up to the outside door.

After donning their swimsuits, guests can exit through the interior door and head for the Kelly Inn's indoor swimming pool, one of the largest in West Yellowstone. Mauve tile surrounds the pool, while tables and chairs invite poolside relaxation and conversation. A sauna and whirlpool are also in the pool room. The inn serves a continental breakfast each morning in the very comfortable lobby. The Kelly Inn closes during the fall slack season. There are plug-ins for your car heater.

The Madison Hotel

$ • 139 Yellowstone Ave., West Yellowstone, Mont. • (406) 646-7745

He was a stagecoach driver and she worked at a restaurant. They married, bought a piece of ground in West Yellowstone, put up a tent hotel and then began building The Madison Hotel in 1912. Years later, owners Roxy and Dolly Bartlett were entertaining Clark Gable and other movie stars at their grand hotel. Today, the Madison Hotel is not so grand and not for those who must have amenities. It is for those who have a fascination with the olden days and love surprises. Step through the creaking latch-door and into the old pine lobby and you'll see what we mean. Straight ahead is the original log staircase. If you shut your eyes for an instant, you might be able to see a turn-of-the-century tourist floating down the stairs to lounge in the lobby and read the news.

Upstairs, you'll find an assortment of rooms with pine beds and antique dressers, plus the occasional old-fashioned sink and antique wooden medicine cabinet. The sheets are snow white and soft. But the walls are not exactly soundproof. Showers and restrooms are down the hall.

The Madison has a large gift shop and 17 newer motel rooms (with private baths) in back. If you have an adventuresome spirit, we recommend the older rooms. The rooms are nonsmoking. The Madison is open from May 28 to October 1.

Roundup Motel

$$ • 3 Madison Ave., West Yellowstone, Mont. • (406) 646-7301

Owners Dean and Leila Seely have virtually rebuilt the Roundup. The older, one-story brick motel has been replaced by a two-story structure with 37 spacious and functional rooms. But the old neon sign featuring a miniskirted cowgirl twirling two lariats still stands above the office. (The office serves both the Dude Motor Inn across the street and the Roundup.) Like the Dude, the Roundup looks across the street into Yellowstone National Park. The Roundup shares a snowmobile fleet with the Dude Motel. Most of the rooms have two queen-size beds, but this motel also has a few rooms with either kings, multiple beds or kitchenettes.

Sleepy Hollow Lodge

$$ • 124 Electric Ave., West Yellowstone, Mont. • (406) 646-7707

These 13 older cabins in mint condition will take you back to the days before neon lights came to West Yellowstone. Clustered neatly in town, the cozy cabins come in a variety of styles — some with one double bed, others with two, and a few with kitchens. All have chip-peeled lodgepole pine furniture. And each bears the name of a tied fly. Mornings, coffee, cinnamon buns, orange juice and fresh fruit await guests in the main house. A fly-tying bench is available at all times. This friendly place is open May through November and February through March. The owners don't allow smoking.

Stage Coach Inn

$$$ • 209 Madison Ave., West Yellowstone, Mont.
• (406) 646-7381, (800) 842-2882

Step into yesteryear at the Stage Coach Inn, where the lodgepole staircase and mezzanine rail remain as reminders of simpler frontier times in West Yellowstone. Built in 1948, the Stage Coach has since had several facelifts. But the best of the original building remains in the lobby, and the updated exterior still resembles the old Stage Coach Inn featured in photos throughout the inn's halls. Decorated in soothing sandstone tones with a wildlife motif, the inn's 80 rooms are simply appointed, most with two queen-size beds. Rooms in the older historic wing have one queen-size bed with no air conditioning.

A friendly, helpful staff is on hand to meet your every need. A coffee shop and a dining room are on the premises. If you're visiting in winter, we hope you packed your dancing duds. The Stage Coach has an upstairs and a downstairs bar, (see our Nightlife chapter), with dancing on the lower level. The underground garage has spaces for 24 vehicles on a first-come, first-served basis. The outside lamp poles also have plug-ins for car heaters. Like other West Yellowstone Motels, the Stage Coach features winter snowmobile packages.

Wagon Wheel Campgrounds and Cabins

$$, no credit cards • 408 Gibbon Ave., West Yellowstone, Mont.
• (406) 646-7872

The Wagon Wheel consists of eight well-maintained, spotless cabins in a cute and cozy RV park/campground shaded by mature trees. The cabins, made of logs and decorated in various themes, were built in the 1940s. They range from a honeymoon cabin with one queen-size bed to a two-story, three-bedroom cabin that sleeps seven or eight. Some have kitchenettes. The Wagon Wheel closes for the winter. For more information about the Wagon Wheel, see our Campgrounds and RV Parks chapter.

West Yellowstone Conference Hotel Holiday Inn SunSpree Resort

$$$$ • 315 Yellowstone Ave., West Yellowstone, Mont.
• (406) 646-7365, (800) 646-7365

The list of amenities at this hotel is longer even than the name itself. Besides the indoor pool, spa, sauna and exercise room just off the lobby, you'll find a refrigerator, microwave, coffee maker and hair dryer in each of the 123 rooms. Most of the rooms have either two queen-size beds or a king. But the West Yellowstone Conference Hotel also has some deluxe executive suites and two-bedroom family suites with two queen-size beds and a king.

Built in 1994, the West Yellowstone Conference Hotel Holiday Inn SunSpree Resort (we like to say this mouthful) is a popular convention center that also caters to families. That's why you'll find the latest Nintendo games in each room, too. The activities desk in the lobby is for everyone. There, someone can help you arrange bike rentals, tours, rafting, horseback riding or a day of guided fishing. In winter, you'll want to rent one of the hotel's 200 snowmobiles or reserve a ride in a snowcoach.

For you conventiongoers who insist on mixing work with your play, the Holiday Inn has 10,000 square feet of meeting space. Savor microbrews at the Iron Horse Saloon, then eat elk, buffalo or beefalo (a cross between beef and buffalo) at the Oregon Short Line Restaurant on the premises. Adults and children alike will delight in a stroll through the Oregon Short Line 1903, a beautifully restored VIP railroad car adjacent to the restaurant and saloon. (For more information, see our Attractions chapter.)

Gardiner, Montana

Absaroka Lodge

$$$ • U.S. Hwy. 89 at Yellowstone River Bridge, Gardiner, Mont.
• (406) 848-7414, (800) 755-7414

Before or after a day in Yellowstone, sit on your private balcony overlooking the Yellowstone River below and the park beyond. If it's one of the kitchen suites you're in (they cost only $10 more than the regular rooms with two queen-size beds), put dinner in the oven and let it cook while you contemplate. Nearly new and well-maintained, the Absaroka Lodge has 41 clean, comfortable, carpeted rooms with private baths and plenty of space to sprawl. All but two of the rooms have two queen-size beds.

On the lawn in front of the Lodge, park benches overlook the river and the town of Gardiner. The lodge owners will gladly help you map out a day in or out of the park, and they can arrange guided fishing or rafting trips. The Absaroka Lodge is within easy walking distance of dining and shopping in Gardiner. Three cabins with no phones offer a less expensive option; they rent for $50.

Hillcrest Cottages

$$ • U.S. Hwy. 89, Gardiner, Mont.
• (406) 848-7353, (800) 970-7353

These cute little cottages are perched on a side street just off U.S. Highway 89 on the north side of the Yellowstone River in Gardiner. Recently refurbished, each of the 15 units has either a small kitchenette or a full kitchen. Rooms range from one- to five-bed cottages, the biggest sleeping up to eight people. Sit on your cabin steps and sip coffee in the morning or a cocktail at night. Or stroll down the back street and peek behind the scenes of Gardiner. If you must, walk downtown and sample Gardiner's nightlife. Clean and simple, the Hillcrest's charm lies in the friendly, homey atmosphere provided by owners Art and Annie Bent, who will loan you cooking utensils if you have forgotten to bring your own.

Jim Bridger Court

$$ • U.S. Highway 89, Gardiner, Mont.
• (406) 848-7371

Some folks love these older cabins. Others aren't so sure. You'll have to decide for yourself. The 17 cabins at Jim Bridger Court were built in the 1930s. The well-lacquered logs and lodgepole pine furniture add charm to what would otherwise be a basic room. The bathrooms are small and functional with metal shower stalls. The cabins, arranged around a grassy courtyard, have TVs but no phones. These cabins are open from mid-May until mid-October.

Maiden Basin Inn

$$$ • 4 Maiden Basin Rd., Gardiner, Mont. • (406) 848-7080, (800) 624-3364

We weren't sure where to put this unique inn, which sits back from Mont. Highway 89, 5

INSIDERS' TIP

Several guest ranches and lodges in the Cody area will take last-minute overnight guests if they have space. Check with the Cody Chamber of Commerce, (307) 587-2777 for a list of these ranches.

miles north of Gardiner overlooking the Yellowstone Valley. Maiden Basin Inn caters to families and offers eight nonsmoking rooms, five of which include full kitchens or kitchenettes. The rooms rent by the night or week and range from a spacious studio with a kitchenette to the Yellowstone Suite with a private deck and whirlpool bath, a full kitchen and panoramic views. One unique unit without a kitchen is wheelchair-accessible.

Guests rave about the hearty continental breakfast served here. The Maiden Basin Inn is open May 15 through October. The air conditioning here is quiet, and the view of Electric Peak is stupendous.

Yellowstone River Motel

$$ • 14 Park St., Gardiner, Mont. • (406) 848-7303

Hidden behind the AmFac warehouse in Gardiner, the Yellowstone River Motel is a combination of functional Western and old-fashioned rooms. An older wing has spacious, newly carpeted rooms with knotty pine or plaster walls. Although these rooms do not have air conditioning, windows on either side of the room provide plenty of cross-ventilation for the cool mountain air in the evenings. (Some chilly nights you won't want to leave your windows open.) Rooms 109, 110 and 111 open onto an older patio overlooking the Yellowstone River. Watch otter play in the river or elk hang out in front of your room. The newer rooms are more spacious and air-conditioned. The Yellowstone River Motel has 40 units and is open from mid-April until Halloween.

Yellowstone Village Inn

$$$ • Yellowstone National Park North Gate, Gardiner, Mont. • (406) 848-7417, (800) 228-8158

The sign here says: "Elk Stay Free." So do children younger than 12. If you've been to Gardiner before, you'll know what the sign means. From late fall through spring the elk move into town, nibbling on anything that isn't protected by a very tall fence. Built in 1992, the Yellowstone Village Inn has 43 rooms, including three family condos and one suite. Most rooms, though, have either one or two queen-size beds. The inn also offers a complimentary continental breakfast and provides a guest laundry.

For recreation, in addition to an indoor pool and sauna, the Village Inn arranges horseback rides and raft trips with a local outfitter. Park bus tours are also available. Mornings, you'll find free coffee in the lobby. On cold mornings, you'll find a fire crackling in the lobby fireplace. Winters, snowmobile and snowcoach tours can be arranged as well as snowshoeing and cross-country skiing.

Cooke City, Montana

Alpine Motel

$$ • U.S. Hwy. 212, Cooke City, Mont. • (406) 838-2262

Make your reservations as early as possible at this popular 25-unit motel in snow country. Right in the middle of town, the Alpine has sparkling clean rooms ranging from singles to suites with kitchens. Most of the rooms, though, are singles or doubles with queen-size beds. You'll find newer rooms in a two-story complex built in 1993. The Alpine is open year-round.

Edelweiss Cabins

$ • 106 Main St., Cooke City, Mont. • (406) 838-2304

Five nifty cabins clustered in town — that's the Edelweiss. Three are brand new. Some have bathtubs, others have showers. All have kitchenettes. And one is handicapped-accessible. Cabins sleep from two to four people. This facility is definitely open summers, and may be open winters. If you're planning a winter visit, it's best to call ahead, as the owners may have flown to their former home — the Caribbean.

INSIDERS' TIP

When computing the cost of your room, remember that, in addition to a bed tax, most towns in Greater Yellowstone charge a 3 percent resort tax.

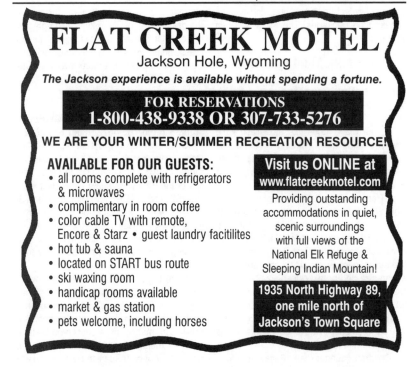

High Country Motel

$ • U.S. Hwy. 212, Cooke City, Mont.
• (406) 838-2272

Winter or summer, the High Country offers cabins and motel rooms to weary travelers and wayward snowmobilers. In summer, High Country's 15 units fill fast, often months ahead of time between mid-June and mid-August, so be sure to call ahead. You'll find an assortment of carpeted, wood-paneled rooms with either one queen-size or two double beds. From Christmas to New Year's and on Presidents' Day weekend, the units are booked almost a year in advance.

Hoosier's Motel

$$ • Main St., Cooke City, Mont.
• (406) 838-2241

You'd never guess by looking at this motel that it was built by the current owner's grandfather in 1930 — before the Beartooth Highway. That means that, besides staying in exceptionally clean, well-maintained rooms, your host will be a wealth of information about Cooke City. Hoosier's has 12 carpeted, individually heated rooms with double and queen-size beds. It closes during the winter.

Soda Butte Lodge

$$ • U.S. Hwy. 212, Cooke City, Mont.
• (406) 838-2251

In the fall of 1997, when a black bear decided to take a bath in the creek below Soda Butte Lodge, guests eating in the Lodge's restaurant left the table and crowded to the picture windows in the adjacent bar. While bears don't walk past the picture windows often, wildlife watching from the Soda Butte Lodge is a popular pastime. The lodge has an indoor pool and hot tub and 32 rooms ranging from those with one double bed to king suites. Built in 1959, Soda Butte is simple and functional.

Guests gather in the Ore House Saloon (on the premises) to watch *Monday Night Football* and other sporting events. The Prospector, an on-site restaurant, serves three squares a day, including seafood, steaks and pasta dinners. Soda Butte, a hopping place during summer, winter and early spring, also features snowmobile packages. The lodge is open year-round.

Bozeman, Montana, Area

Best Western GranTree Inn

$$$ • 1325 N. Seventh Ave., Bozeman, Mont. • (406) 587-5261, (800) 624-5865

If your plane lands late at Gallatin Field and you don't mind heading a little bit off course from the most direct route to Yellowstone National Park, the GranTree Inn is a good one-stop accommodation. At the GranTree, you'll find 103 rooms or suites from which to choose plus a restaurant, lounge, casino, an atrium, indoor pool, a guest laundry and winter plug-ins. In addition to standard motel rooms, the GranTree offers executive suites, each with a sitting area and either a king-size bed or two queen-size beds. The bridal suite features a king-size bed and a hot tub. Other niceties include hair dryers, irons and ironing boards available at the office desk. You can also bask in the atrium or bake in one of the steam units.

Children younger than 16 stay here free. And the motel offers a free airport shuttle service. The GranTree also has banquet and meeting rooms.

Blue Sky Motel

$ • 1010 E. Main St., Bozeman, Mont. • (406) 587-2311, (800) 845-9032

This exceptionally clean older 27-room motel is in mint condition. The owners have taken the winter out of their ground-floor rooms by building a glassed-in walkway that runs the motel's length and into the office where complimentary morning coffee awaits. The Blue Sky rooms range from those with one queen-size bed to suites, family rooms and kitchenettes. Other features include an indoor spa, a fax machine and winter plug-ins for cars on the premises. The Blue Sky is also right next to Bozeman's lovely Lindley Park with its lush grass, mature trees and winter Nordic ski track. On the other side of the motel is a reasonably priced family restaurant.

Gallatin Gateway Inn

$$$$ • U.S. Hwy. 191, Gallatin Gateway, Mont. • (406) 763-4672, (800) 676-3522

Once given up as a lost cause, the Gallatin Gateway Inn has risen from the rubble into its former glory as one of the grand railroad hotels of the Rocky Mountain West. Built in the late 1920s by the Chicago, Milwaukee and St. Paul Railway as a destination summer resort for Yellowstone National Park visitors, the inn echoes the tenor of the past. The only thing missing from the old days is the train and its tracks.

From the moment you walk into the 65-foot-by-40-foot foyer with its 35-foot-high ceilings you'll feel like you've stepped back in time. Arching carved and stenciled beams of Polynesian mahogany, a checkered tile floor, an assortment of fig and palm trees and two dozen 15-foot-high Spanish-style arched windows create a light, airy elegance that invites travelers to bask in the grand lounge off the foyer. A piano, silent during the day, comes to life at least one evening a week. The dining room beyond, with its double tablecloths and fresh flowers, offers award-winning fare to match its flair. The menu, which reflects the seasons, is a favorite with locals (see our Restaurants chapter).

The Gallatin Gateway Inn has 35 refurbished rooms ranging from a room for two with either a king- or queen-size bed to suites with a king-size bed and a sitting room. The price spread between a standard rate and a suite rate is slim. In addition, the inn has an outdoor swimming pool, a hot tub, tennis court

INSIDERS' TIP

What is a lodge? It's generally an establishment that supplies both accommodations and activities. It serves food, too, but not always. Sometimes "lodge" in a name just means you're out West and the innkeeper thought the word sounded cozy, folksy and fun. In this book, lodges that offer a substantial number of activities are usually found in the Resorts and Lodges chapter.

and casting pond. Be sure to ask about naturalist-guided tours into Yellowstone, as well as fly fishing guides and whitewater raft trips.

Big Sky, Montana, Area

Buck's T-4 Lodge

$$$ • U.S. Hwy. 191, Big Sky, Mont. • (406) 995-4111, (800) 822-4484

The first time we stopped at Buck's T-4, the place was teeming with people from three different parties (two wedding receptions and a reunion) going on at once. While Buck's isn't always so busy, it is a popular spot for parties of all kinds. Equipped with two restaurants, meeting and banquet facilities, a lounge, game room, gift shop and liquor store, Buck's has the space and the staff to handle large parties or individual guests. The lodge has 75 rooms ranging from standard to deluxe suites, as well as two giant hot tubs. Eight mini-suites are equipped with microwaves and refrigerators and can sleep two to four people each. Two larger suites have kitchenettes and can sleep four each. A continental breakfast comes with your room.

Buck's T-4, situated on the Gallatin Canyon Road 48 miles north of West Yellowstone and 1 mile south of the Big Sky Resort area, has a country Western atmosphere with lots of lawn and landscaped garden nooks. The lodge also has a coin-operated laundry. Inquire about snowmobile and ski packages.

Cinnamon Lodge

$$ • U.S. Hwy. 191, Big Sky, Mont. • (406) 995-4253

Casual and comfortable, the five cabins at the Cinnamon Lodge aren't for those who seek finely appointed accommodations. They are for those who like to kick back and enjoy the best of the Gallatin Canyon without dipping into their savings. Situated close to the banks of the Gallatin River, each cabin has a porch and fire grill facing the river. Decorated with an eclectic assortment of furniture and accessories, the cabins range from one room to two bedrooms with kitchenettes. The lodge serves tasty Mexican and American food in an old-fashioned log dining room. A small bar just inside the lodge entrance is a favorite hangout for locals. Cinnamon Lodge also has small RV park. During the summer, horseback riding is available through a local outfitter.

Golden Eagle Lodge

$ • Little Coyote Rd., Meadow Village, Big Sky, Mont. • (406) 995-4800, (800) 548-4488

Built in 1972 as a hostel, the Golden Eagle Lodge's very basic rooms are the best deal in Big Sky for those on a budget. Rooms sleep from two to four people and, during the slower parts of the winter, come with fantastic ski packages. For example, during the value season, a couple can sleep and ski for $128 a day. A shuttle bus stops at this year-round lodge every hour and 10 minutes during ski season.

River Rock Lodge

$$$$ • West Fork Meadows, Big Sky, Mont. • (406) 995-2295, (800) 995-9966

The log and rock entry in this upscale motel invites guests to sit a spell and relax in the deep-cushioned chairs facing a massive river-rock fireplace and chimney. Each of the 29 spacious rooms has a thick down comforter, Western art on the walls and plush furniture. Each room also has a TV and VCR, as well as a video of Robert Redford's *A River Runs Through It*. Most rooms have two queen-size beds, but there are also six kings, two handicapped-accessible rooms and a bridal suite with a TV above the fireplace — you can watch both from your king-size bed. The shower is big enough for the whole wedding party.

Livingston, Montana

Murray Hotel

$$ • 201 W. Park St., Livingston, Mont. • (406) 222-1350

The rooms and halls of this hotel in the heart of downtown Livingston ooze old times and understated class. Built in 1905 and recently refurbished, the Murray is still a favorite haunt of visiting movie stars and directors following in the footsteps of film director Sam Peckinpah, who called the Murray "home." The lobby, which has an old-fashioned tile floor and comfortably sedate furniture, is a good place to watch the world go by. Who knows who you might see? Such notables as actor

James Arness, who played *Gunsmoke's* Matt Dillon, and TV personality Barbara Walters have graced the place.

Except for two rooms, all accommodations offer private baths. All have either one or two queen-size beds.

In case you get tired of people watching, stroll into the Murray Lounge and tip a few with the locals, or wander into the Winchester Cafe, where you'll find breakfast, lunch and dinner served with style. The Murray is a must for anyone who likes to rub shoulders with the Old West.

Paradise Inn

$$ • Park Rd. and Rogers Ln., Livingston, Mont.
• (406) 222-6320, (800) 437-6291

An indoor pool, an on-site restaurant and lounge and 43 ground-floor rooms make the Paradise Inn a convenient stage stop on your way to Yellowstone National Park. Except for one room with a king-size bed, all rooms at the Paradise have either one or two queen-size beds. Thirty rooms have two outside doors. From every room, you can walk to the restaurant without going outside. In case you forgot your hair dryer or your iron, check at the office. They lend both.

Yellowstone Inn

$$ • 1515 W. Park St., Livingston, Mont.
• (406) 222-6110, (800) 826-1214.

The Yellowstone Inn came to life in 1997 when partners Paul Grossman and Tim Barnes took over the 100-room hotel/motel/convention center. Both Barnes and Grossman are former longtime managers of Chico Hot Springs. (See our Resorts and Vacation Lodges chapter for more information). Barnes and Grossman are also among the owners of Uncle Looie's, a popular Italian restaurant in Livingston (see our Restaurants chapter).

Besides remodeling every room and suite, Barnes and Grossman changed the name of the in-house restaurant from Buffalo Bill's Restaurant and Saloon to The Inn. Their chef turns out consistently good food. An indoor, atrium-like pool, where you can dine poolside, is a favorite for wedding receptions and other gala events such as the Evening of the Stars, a fund-raising dinner theater sponsored each spring by the Livingston Chamber of Commerce.

The inn offers shuttles to and from the Bozeman Airport and to Bridger Bowl Ski Area in the winter. If you know ahead of time what you want to do while you're in Livingston, the staff can make arrangements for you before you arrive.

Virginia City and Ennis, Montana, Area

El Western Motel

$$ • U.S. Hwy. 287, Ennis, Mont.
• (406) 682-4217, (800) 831-2773

If you have no other reason to go to Ennis, a stay in the cabins at the El Western may be enough. Situated on 17 lush acres south of Ennis near the Madison River, the El Western offers 29 immaculate cabins accented with mature trees, shrubs and perennial flower gardens. Using a combination of individual log cabins and duplex cabins, the El Western has an array of sleeping cabins, kitchenettes and lodges in a setting so peaceful you won't want to leave. Almost all have paintings of wildlife scenes on the exteriors and a Western motif on the inside.

In case you get cabin fever and have to go to town, Ennis is just a mile away — walk, ride your bike or go in the car. We recommend heading for the river with your fishing pole instead. The El Western is open from mid-April until mid-October. Children 10 and younger stay free.

Fairweather Inn

$ • Main St., Virginia City, Mont.
• (406) 843-5377

Stroll down the boardwalk in Virginia City and duck into the Fairweather Inn, a well-preserved Victorian-era hotel that hints of its past lives as a butcher shop, a saloon and several different hotels. Step up to the registration desk and check yourself into a room right in the heart of the Old West. From the Fairweather, which was restored and re-opened in 1946, you can walk across the street to the Bale of Hay Saloon or the Wells Fargo Cafe. Take your time, though — there's plenty to see and experience in Virginia City, the only privately restored historic town in the nation. (See our Attractions chapters for more information.) Simply appointed in Victorian decor, the rooms at the Fairweather come with or without private baths.

Madison River Cabins and RV

$ • 1403 U.S. Hwy. North. 287, Cameron, Mont. • (406) 682-4890

Resurrected from the edge of extinction, these conveniently located cabins have had reconstructive surgery inside and out. Arranged in a tidy little horseshoe, with redwood porches, a gravel driveway and islands of mature lilac bushes, the Madison River Cabins are cozy and country-style inside. The original 10 cabins range from compact one-bedrooms to a three-bedroom with a large living room and a standard-sized kitchen. All have private baths. Two newer log cabins overlooking the Madison River offer privacy, down-home Western comfort and plenty of space to accommodate six for only $120 per night.

Madison River Cabins also has nine RV spaces as well as sparkling clean restrooms and a laundry. The Crazy Lady Outpost, a grand log building surrounded by a sea of lush grass, houses a combination gift, grocery and fly shop. Fly-fishing equipment rentals and a guide service can be found at the store as well. The cabins are clean, the property tidy and the landscaping expansive. The owners have planted 80 trees and loads of lawn. Just a couple of stone's throws away is the Grizzly Bar and Grill, a lively local hangout with juicy steaks and burgers and a fun-loving crowd (see our Restaurants chapter).

Rainbow Valley Motel

$$ • U.S. Hwy. 287, Ennis, Mont. • (406) 682-4264, (800) 452-8254

You'll feel as if you're walking up to someone's ranch house when you stay at this tidy log motel surrounded by acres of lawn. Each room, paneled with knotty pine and decorated to look like an individual cabin, has its own private patio. Some have kitchens, a few have two bedrooms, and all are within hollering distance of the Madison River. Other nice touches include a heated pool, a guest laundry, a corral for your horses and a barbecue picnic area.

Rainbow Valley also has a three-bedroom, two-bath cabin that has its own deck with a spectacular view. This inviting motel has a good reputation and lots of repeat guests, so make your reservations early.

Sportsman's Lodge

$$ • U.S. Highway 287, Ennis, Mont. • (406) 682-4242

The 18 older log cabins at the Sportsman's Lodge all say, "Montana." Neatly situated in a horseshoe around the lodge's lawn, the very cozy duplex cabins are simply appointed with updated bathrooms. All are equipped with one queen-size bed and can be connected to adjoining rooms. The owners provide a corral for guests' horses. A lounge and restaurant on the premises makes it easy to kick back and relax without having to drive. An outfitter also offers horseback riding through the Sportsman's Lodge.

West Fork Cabin Camp

$ • 1475 U.S. Hwy. 287 N., Cameron, Mont. • (406) 682-4802

There is nothing fancy about the 10 housekeeping cabins at the West Fork Camp. They're just clean, comfortable and very popular with anglers, families and hunters. Cabins range from those with one queen bed to two cabins with two bedrooms that can accommodate up to five. Every cabin has a fully equipped kitchen, but you won't find telephones or TVs in your room — they interfere with the experience, says owner Gary Evans. If you must watch a football game, you can join the other guests in the lounge.

Situated on the west side of the Madison River at the West Fork bridge, West Fork Cabin Camp includes a convenience store, fly shop and guide service, laundry facilities, a shower house and raft rentals.

The facility also operates a 24-unit RV park. The spaces — they're pull-through with full hookups — rent for $17 by the night, $110 by the week and $300 for a month. Evans says it's common for people to park their RVs for at least a week at the camp, which is in the heart of blue-ribbon trout fishing. It is also close to Yellowstone National Park to the south and Virginia City and Lewis and Clark Caverns to the north (see our Attractions chapter). West

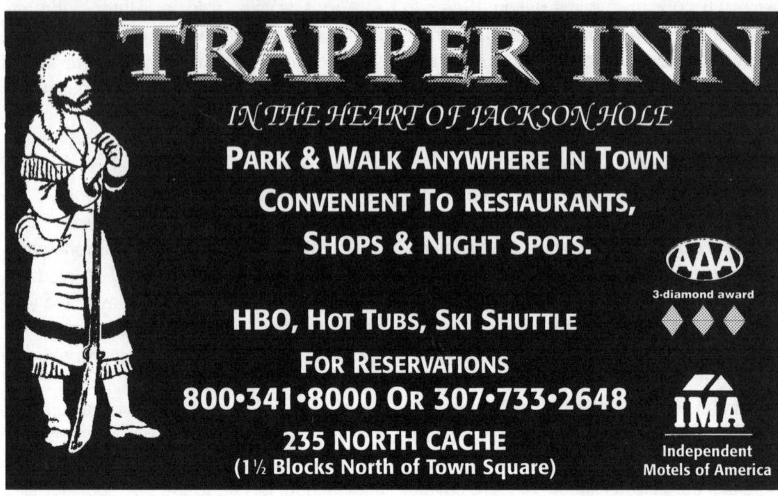

Fork Camp is open from early April through November.

Red Lodge, Montana

The Pollard

$$$ • 2 N. Broadway, Red Lodge, Mont. • (406) 446-0001, (800) POLLARD

If the brass rails leading into the Pollard Hotel say "posh" to you, you've heard them right. Stroll to the hotel's History Room (just inside the entrance to the right) and you'll see what we mean. Sink into a deep leather chair and reach for something to read. Chances are it'll be something like *On the Road with Charles Kuralt* or *Farm Boy* by Archie Lieberman, or the *New York Times FAX*. Later, you can fidget and stand in line with the other guests anxious to get their hands on today's *Wall Street Journal*. (It arrives, same-day service, at 2 PM each day.)

Built in 1893 as the Spofford Hotel, it became The Pollard in 1900 when Mr. and Mrs. Thomas Pollard took over and added 25 rooms to the existing 35. Through the years politicians, movie stars, copper kings, mountain men and notables of the day Buffalo Bill Cody and Calamity Jane graced the halls of The Pollard, a landmark among grand Rocky Mountain hotels. In 1991 the Hotel Company of Red Lodge bought The Pollard and immediately began renovating the rooms. The owners replaced all the windows, ceilings, carpets, furniture, draperies and linens. They added an exercise room, two racquetball courts and a ski storage room. The Pollard now has 38 rooms.

Most rooms have one queen-size bed. If that's all you'll need, ask about a deluxe queen with a hot tub and a balcony overlooking the gallery. (Six rooms have balconies.) Rooms are decorated with antiques, and you'll find hair dryers and telephones in the bathroom, along with two bathrobes.

Greenlee's Dining Room at The Pollard offers award-winning food with understated elegance. Breakfasts are included in the price of your room. Ask about the adventure trips offered by The Pollard. They include fly fishing, horseback riding, rock climbing and river rafting, as well as a scenic flight over Yellowstone National Park.

Yodeler Motel

$ • 601 S. Broadway Ave., Red Lodge, Mont. • (406) 446-1435

Sneak in the back door of your room at the Yodeler, then saunter out the front door. Easy access makes this chalet-looking motel a dream to drop into. And, speaking of dreaming, the Yodeler prides itself on its brand-new Mattress Mill beds made in nearby Bozeman and designed for all-night comfort. Another new feature: a new phone system with high-speed data ports for those of you who must bring your business along. Ground floor rooms are spacious and have front and back doors. Downstairs rooms are half-basement units with large daylight windows.

Eastern Idaho

Teton Valley, Idaho

Beard Mountain Ranch

$$, no credit cards • P.O. Box 84, Tetonia, ID 83452 • No phone

Trixie and Carl Beard are Teton Valley natives. In fact, nearby Beard Mountain is named after a homesteading ancestor. The little cabin they rent year round is tucked far enough off the beaten path that you could pretend you've driven back in time.

The cabin is shag-carpeted and filled with boxy, older furniture. It has a kitchen, a three-quarter bath, linens, cooking utensils and a TV without cable. It will sleep four to six people, so when you are there, the greatest number of people you're likely to see outside the mirror is five. You won't even see the ranch residents unless you go looking because the cabin is situated at the end of a private gravel road.

Trixie and husband Carl are happy to arrange horseback riding, guided or unguided fishing, hunting and packtrips for you. Carl has been a guide in the area for decades.

Best Western Teton West

$$$ • 476 N. Main St., Driggs, Idaho • (208) 354-2363, (800) 528-1234

If you want Teton Valley lodging with an indoor pool (kept warm enough for lounging, summer and winter) and a hot tub, this is the place. The best of Teton West's 40 rooms are in the newest part of the motel; they're larger and have windows looking west to the distant Big Hole Mountains. Also on-site are a guest laundry and a small conference facility.

Intermountain Lodge

$$ • 34 Ski Hill Rd., Driggs, Idaho • (208) 354-8153

The location couldn't be better: Intermountain Lodge is between Driggs and Grand Targhee Ski and Summer Resort, just outside the Targhee National Forest. The 4-acre property is screened from the highway by huge cottonwood trees. Lodging is in seven newer duplex cabins, each with a covered porch.

Amenities include a hot tub and laundry facility, plus kitchenettes in each log and pine-paneled room. The most popular rooms have queen-size log-framed bunkbeds. Managers Bob and Roberta Williams keep VCRs available for rent; they'll loan you movies from their own private collection for free. Unlike many cabin facilities in our area, Intermountain Lodge is open during the snowy months, too.

Pines Motel/Guest Haus

$ • 105 S. Main St., Driggs, Idaho • (208) 354-2774, (800) 354-2778

Leaf through the hand-embroidered guest book at John and Nancy Nielson's little establishment and the words you'll see again and again are cute, cozy and friendly. We'd add one: eccentric. Antiques, mostly from the 1920s, furnish the paneled guest rooms. Many of the showers are paneled in knotty pine. Nancy sews the curtains and matching tasseled lampshades. She also hand-stitched most of the matching quilts.

The six upstairs rooms are the nicest. Much of the building is an original two-story log cabin from the turn of the century, stuccoed over to match an addition built in the late 1930s. Some rooms face onto Main Street, motel-style. Others face an inside hallway. Most have private baths.

Don't be fooled by the small price tag: This charming little hybrid of a hotel and bed and breakfast inn lacks few amenities. Its acre of lawn contains a large hot tub, a fireplace, a gas grill, a swing set, a tree house (fun!) and a couple of hammocks. Lupine and columbine, poppies and iris surround the building. Huge willows and flowering crab apple shade the yard. Out back is a tree swing and a sandbox. Each room is scrupulously clean.

Super 8 Teton West

$$ • 133 N. Hwy. 33, Driggs, Idaho • (208) 354-8888

This is the newest of the two lodging chains in Teton Valley. These folks have 22 spacious rooms, all with small refrigerators and microwaves. A guest laundry and an indoor hot tub are available; continental breakfast is served every morning in the lobby. Rooms on each of the two floors are accessed by a central hallway. The motel plans to add 24 additional rooms in 1999.

Teton Mountain View Lodge

$$ • 510 Egbert Ave., Tetonia, Idaho • (208) 456-2741, (800) 877-TETONMT

Two nice features make this motel stand out. The first is a design that made us wonder why all motels aren't made this way. You see, the windows in the main building don't face the walkways or the parking lot — they face the pasture behind the motel. You don't need to close the curtains because there's nothing back there but grass.

The other advantage to staying at Teton Mountain View is that these folks offer unguided snowmobiling from the property in winter and are happy to hook you up with guided hunting, horseback riding and fishing in other seasons.

An enclosed hot tub is available; TV reception is via satellite.

Teton Ranch

$$$$, no credit cards • 227 E. 600 N., Tetonia, Idaho • (208) 456-2010

Only a five-minute drive from U.S. Highway 33, one of the few paved roads in Teton Valley, you'll find secluded — and affordable — luxury.

Your two "cabin" accommodations are really houses, fully furnished with Western motifs, log walls and hardwood floors. The main house is a two-story log home built in 1929. It has a rock fireplace and open-beam ceilings. Big windows invite the surrounding seclusion and scenery right into the house. In summer, up to 29 hummingbirds have been known to swarm the feeders dangling outside one window.

The smaller house is new, built in 1987. It has two porches and two bedrooms, each with private bath. A rock fireplace warms the cozy living room.

The grounds are surrounded with buck and rail fence, aspens and evergreens. The lawn is dotted with flowers, an herb garden and raspberry bushes. Enjoy a cookout on the charcoal grill — but bring your mosquito repellent in summer; there's a price to be paid for all that lush greenery!

Several paintings in the two houses are by neighbor Trixie Beard, Tetonia native. Trixie says her three favorite things to paint are the Tetons, the Tetons and mountains.

Teton Ranch rents its two lovely homes year-round. A helpful on-site manager lives in a small house on the grounds.

Trails End Motel

$ • 10 N. Main St., Victor, Idaho • (208) 787-2973, (208) 787-2771

You'll find a hodgepodge of inexpensive accommodations options here: eight cabins, two motel rooms and a three-room apartment suitable for large families or groups. The nicest choices are the four newer cabins with log interiors and full baths. All rooms are equipped with microwaves and refrigerators.

A pleasant location adjoining City Park in downtown Victor finishes out the picture. Make sure you walk across the street to the Victor Emporium for a huckleberry shake after you check in (see our Restaurants chapter for more on Victor Emporium).

Swan Valley, Idaho, and Star Valley, Wyoming

Alpen Haus Hotel

$$ •U.S. Hwy. 26 at U.S. Hwy. 89, Alpine, Wyo. • (307) 654-7545, (800) 343-6755

You won't believe it: a quaint Austrian hotel on the Idaho/Wyoming border. Alpen Haus gets its continental look from the decorative paintings on the exterior walls of its two buildings, created by an Austrian friend of owners Clarence and Dorothy Reinhart.

Rooms are larger and have balconies in Alpen Haus 1, the main hotel building. Rooms in both buildings have private baths and down comforters. Some have refrigerators, hair dryers and full baths. The honeymoon suite prom-

INSIDERS' TIP

Setting off fireworks is illegal on national forest lands.

ises inexpensive luxury with skylights, a king-size bed, a dry bar, a big-screen television and a living area with a pullout sofa. Let the staff know you're celebrating a wedding or anniversary and they'll have a bottle of champagne waiting for you.

Alpen Haus Hotel also has a gas station, a small grocery store, an ice cream parlor, a bar and restaurant, video rental, Western clothing store, laundry room and hot tub.

Now, don't think you'll be in the middle of a massive tourist complex if you make your reservations here. Alpen Haus 1 and 2 together have only 55 rooms, yet the hotel is the hoppin'est thing in tiny Alpine.

Hansen-Silver Guest Ranch

$$$ • 956 Rainey Creek Rd., Swan Valley, Idaho • (208) 483-2305, (800) 277-9041

This is a guest ranch in the summer months. But when the cabins aren't occupied by ranch guests and in winter after the guest ranch shuts down, they're available as motel-style accommodations. Choose between the duplex cabins with decks front and back and one white frame cottage. Cabins are furnished Western-style, but they're not rustic; walls are a clean white and the furniture is contemporary. Each has a private bath and queen-size bed but no TV. The cottage has a phone.

Swan Valley has little in the way of accommodations, so these cabins are a real find for those who want to enjoy the superb trout fishing on the South Fork of the Snake. Hansen-Silver Guest Ranch is only a 15-minute drive from the Spring Creek boat ramp in Swan Valley. See our Guest Ranches chapter for more.

Timberwolf Resort

$ • 3781 Swan Valley Hwy., Palisades, Idaho • (208) 483-3581

Don't let the highway sign that says you're in Irwin fool you: Locals say Irwin starts nearly 5 miles down the road. And here in Palisades the best noncamping accommodations are in Timberwolf's newer little motel cabins. Each of the units has television (no cable), a refrigerator and a private bathroom. The glossy pine-paneled walls are not overly decorated. What you're paying for are clean, simple accommodations. Outside, you have a picnic table for pleasant evening meals alfresco.

This place is one-stop shopping for travelers. On site is an RV park (it's behind your cabin; see our Campgrounds and RV parks chapter for more), a convenience store, cafe, tackle shop, liquor store, gas station and guest laundry.

These folks close up the RV park from mid-October to early May, but the cabins were recently winterized and are available year-round.

The Nordic Inn

$$ • Colonial Ln. at U.S. Hwy. 89, Alpine, Wyo. • (307) 654-7556

The Nordic Inn was a hunting camp when the Clingers, a family of Wyoming natives, bought it in 1963. Now it's a clean, cozy 10-room motel. The outdoor hot tub is screened by a lush, piney-smelling mass of hops plants. Flower beds and boxes grace the building; a long lawn slopes out to the highway.

All rooms have Pendleton blankets, pine wainscoting and bathrobes to use while you're here. All have full baths and TVs; none have phones.

Anne and Michael Clinger, mother and son, and their partner Brent Johnston live in a newer, columned Southern Colonial-style home behind the motel. They sometimes rent two huge rooms in their house to special guests.

The Nordic Inn is home to a tiny bar, decorated with memorabilia honoring Anne's late husband, Dallas Clinger, Wyoming's only World War II ace fighter pilot, and a small gift shop stocked with oddities Anne Clinger picks up in her world travels. And it houses tiny

INSIDERS' TIP

Why do they call it Jackson Hole? In fur trapper lingo, a hole was a valley. Jackson Hole was named after trapper David E. Jackson. If you want to do it as the locals do, call the town Jackson and the valley Jackson Hole.

Brenthoven's Restaurant (see our Restaurants chapter).

These folks spend their winters in New Zealand, so the Nordic Inn closes up in mid-October and reopens in June.

Island Park, Idaho

A word on Island Park accommodations: Many are cheaper in summer than in winter. They're booked for the big winter weekends — Presidents' Day, Christmas and New Year's — up to a year in advance. The reason? Island Park is a snowmobile mecca. More than 200 miles of groomed snowmobile trails ply the immediate area; these trails connect with trails in the region to bring that total to around 1,000 miles. See our Winter Sports chapter for details.

Last Chance Lodge and Hyde Outfitters Inc.

$ • 3408 N. U.S. Hwy. 20, Last Chance in Island Park, Idaho • (208) 558-7068

Clean, no-frills hotel-style accommodations are available at Last Chance Lodge. The lodge sits across U.S. 20 from the magnificent fly-fishing waters of the Henry's Fork and on the same property as Hyde Outfitters, one of the area's better-known guide services. Each room has a small TV but no phone. A few suites are available; these have kitchenettes and fireplaces. Twelve individual cabins are new in 1999. Dining options are nearby.

At Hyde Outfitters, you anglers can shop for all of life's necessities: flies, leaders, waders, hats, etc. While you're here, make sure you treat yourself to a day of fishing with Hyde's local guides in drift boats, built in nearby Idaho Falls, that bear the Hyde name (see our Fishing and Watersports chapter).

Mack's Inn Resort

$ cabin, $$ motel • U.S. Hwy. 20, Mack's Inn at Island Park, Idaho • (208) 558-7272

Thirty-eight motel rooms in two locations make up the bulk of available accommodations at Mack's Inn. One cinderblock building faces the lovely Henry's Fork, which flows past, shallow and dimpled, 10 feet from your sliding glass door. Some of these riverfront units have fireplaces and/or kitchens. The other building is tucked into the trees across the highway. These smaller rooms are simply appointed, some with fireplaces and all with private baths. You have no phone; you can rent a TV and VCR.

The 26 cabins are older, some as old as 70 years, and in varying degrees of repair. They range from simple to very rustic. All have private baths; some have fireplaces or wood stoves, and some have kitchens (but you need to supply the utensils).

The buildings, including a store, restaurant, an ice cream parlor, a game room, gift shop, and coin-operated laundry, and an RV park (see our Campgrounds and RV Parks chapter) together sprawl across 17 acres. The property also has a volleyball court, fire pits, a dinner theater (in summer), a log playground and boat rentals so you can enjoy the Henry's Fork or Big Springs area upstream (see our Attractions chapter for a must-do daytrip.)

Historic Ponds Lodge

$ • 3757 N. U.S. Hwy. 20, Ponds Lodge in Island Park, Idaho • (208) 558-7221

This place is hard to beat for convenience and comfortable cabin accommodations. Island Park facilities tend to occur in clusters; this cluster is smaller than most, but still offers, under one roof, a small grocery store (fresh fruit, even!), a selection of wines by the bottle, fishing supplies, a gift shop, a restaurant that serves breakfast, lunch and dinner and the Buffalo River Saloon. Outside are RV hookups (see our Campgrounds and RV Parks chapter) and cabins. A public laundry and shower facility are available as well.

The 25 cabins, 18 of which are winterized and available year-round, are set back from U.S. Highway 20, so you won't feel like you're living in traffic. Choose from small, inexpensive units with a single double bed, bath and tiny kitchenette, or step up to a unit with five queen-size beds, two baths and a full kitchen unit with wood stove. Cabins do not have phones, TVs or kitchen utensils/dishes, but you can leave your bedding and linens at home. Walls are pine-paneled and floors are carpeted.

The huge lodge, built in 1935 by Charles and Myna Ponds, is also available for your use. It centers around a pleasant commons area with a massive wood stove and log-frame couches and chairs. The cafe has some outdoor seating. Or you can walk down to the Buffalo River, which runs almost right next to Ponds Lodge.

Behind the lodge is a huge, rough-walled building that practically begs you to stage a family reunion or a dance. It has a low stage on one wall and big doors that open to a grassy picnic area.

Ashton, Idaho

Jessen's R.V. Park and Bed & Breakfast

$, no credit cards • 1146 S. 3400 E., Ashton, Idaho • (208) 652-3356

These pleasant little white frame cottages have TVs, propane heat, air conditioning, floral curtains and velvet-upholstered chairs. Each has its own bathroom. Each is equipped with a picnic table outside, but you'll probably spend more time in the slatted gazebo near the old white farmhouse. In late summer you can eat plums, apples and cherries right off the trees while the kids cool off in the irrigation canal that runs through the property or goof off on the trampoline and other playground equipment.

Jessen's also has two bed and breakfast rooms upstairs in the farmhouse and an RV park on the premises, so invite your whole family for an outing. The bed and breakfast inn operates all year, but the RV park and cottages are only open May through November. Reservations are recommended. (For more information, please see our Bed and Breakfast Inns and our Campgrounds and RV Parks chapters.)

Log Cabin Motel

$ • 1001 E. Main St., Ashton, Idaho • (208) 652-3956

Is it cabins or a motel? Neither. Both. The Log Cabin Motel is Ashton's niftiest accommodation and a great jump-off spot for adventures in the Bechler or Cave Falls areas of Yellowstone National Park or Island Park or the fine fishing waters of the Warm River.

Flowers hang from each cabin's roof. Hedges sprout near the doors. You can sit out front and enjoy the wildflower garden in the small complex's center, or if you rented one of two cabins that face away from the parking lot, you may contemplate an adjacent grain field.

Each cabin has cable TV, a heater and a full bath. Most of these cabins date back more than 65 years; they practically purr with quaint, old-fashioned comfort.

Owner Venis McCarthy closes up from October to early May and often finds herself full up during the summer travel months. Log Cabin Motel also has a few RV sites behind the cabin complex. Some have full hookups.

Super 8

$ • 1370 U.S. Hwy. 20, Ashton, Idaho • (208) 652-7885

This motel, completed in 1997, has a couple of pleasant extras. One is the lobby area, large and high ceilinged, made for lounging. It is warmed by a gas fire on one wall and lit by generous floor-to-ceiling windows on another. Lodgepole pine furniture lends a Western look.

Another nice touch is extra-large rooms: Several of the standard rooms are L-shaped and spacious. There are also three suites. A guest laundry, game room, 24-hour convenience store, fast-food and gift shop are on-site.

Super 8 is the only large motel chain currently in the Ashton area and in fact is the only large motel chain for many miles in any direction.

St. Anthony, Idaho

Best Western Weston Inn

$$ • 115 S. Bridge St., St. Anthony, Idaho • (208) 624-3711

Unlike most of the convenient motels along U.S. Highway 20, you can't see this one from the highway. It's screened by tall cottonwoods growing along the banks of the Henry's Fork. From your room, you may hear distant highway sounds, but if you look out the window, what you'll see is trees. The white-columned brick motel has standard amenities in addition to the convenience of its location just moments from the road. Even better is the rambling, heavily shaded park right across the street, called Clyde Keefer Memorial Park, and the fishing holes and swimming holes within walking distance along the Henry's Fork. On the same parking lot is a family-style restaurant.

Rexburg, Idaho

Best Western Cottontree Inn

$$ • 450 W. 4 S., Rexburg, Idaho
• (208) 356-4646

You'll love the lobby, with its angled glass walls and indoor garden.

With 100 rooms, this is the largest motel in town. It's also the only motel with an on-site restaurant, Frontier Pies. You'll find their menu in your room, and yes, they deliver room service. The Rexburg Chamber of Commerce rents space in the motel's conference center, so you can stroll over to pick up handy information about the area.

Nearly half the rooms have refrigerators and microwaves; many have been recently renovated. Other thoughtful touches include full-size irons and ironing boards. Hair dryers are installed in some rooms, so request one if you like that sort of thing.

Comfort Inn

$$ • 1513 W. Main St., Rexburg, Idaho
• (208) 359-1311

Conveniently located next to the second Rexburg exit from U.S. Highway 33, Comfort Inn is the newest motel in town. It has 52 standard rooms. If you're looking for a little more space, the motel offers four studio suites with microwaves and refrigerators.

The facility includes an exercise room, hot tub and indoor swimming pool. The complimentary continental breakfast will start your day right.

Days Inn

$ • 271 S. 2nd W., Rexburg, Idaho
• (208) 356-9222

These folks are right next to Mormon church-owned Ricks College; most guests who aren't heading to the national parks are parents visiting students. Days Inn bought the motel in 1993 and completely remodeled the facility. All 43 rooms have standard amenities, and some have microwaves and refrigerators. All rooms have full-size ironing boards and irons. In summer, enjoy the outdoor heated pool. Continental breakfast is free of charge; so is a copy of *USA Today* to read while you eat.

Idaho Falls, Idaho

Best Western Driftwood Inn

$$ • 575 River Pkwy., Idaho Falls, Idaho
• (208) 523-2242, (800) 939-2242

The riverside location in town is perfect, and the price is fair. Best Western Driftwood has 74 rooms, 14 with kitchenettes. All rooms are equipped with microwaves, fridges and coffee makers; outside you can swim in the heated pool (summer only) and enjoy pleasant landscaping with benches and tables. The Driftwood even supplies bicycles so you can pedal along the Snake River on paved paths.

A few special picks at the Driftwood include the four huge kitchenette units (one is a complete apartment), for between $65 and $100 per night. The six rooms in The Overhang, which looks down onto the Snake River and its magnificent man-made falls, are also pleasant.

Cavanaughs on the Falls

$$$ • 475 River Pkwy., Idaho Falls, Idaho
• (208) 523-8000, (800) 432-1005

Idaho Falls' trademark hotel and its oldest overlooks the dramatic man-made falls that *didn't* give the town its name (the name came first, then the falls). Luxury rooms are housed in the eight-story cylindrical Tower Building. Standard rooms, some small and some larger, wrap around the restaurant and large outdoor pool. If you reserve a luxury room, be sure to ask for a view of the Snake River and its falls: You'll pay a bit more, but private decks reached via generous, floor-to-ceiling sliding glass doors beg to face a river.

INSIDERS' TIP

Central reservation services generally have package deals that can save you bucks.

Luxury rooms, besides having copious amounts of empty space, may also come equipped with refrigerators, sitting areas and more. The hotel offers laundry facilities, conference rooms, a fitness room and an indoor hot tub, a full service restaurant and lounge.

Evergreen Gables Motel

$ • 3130 S. Yellowstone Hwy., Idaho Falls, Idaho • (208) 522-5410

One of the few motels in town not associated with a big chain, Evergreen Gables offers budget accommodations with a homey touch. Owners Lamont and Vaunita Lewis have done most of the renovation themselves for the last 20 years. Daughter Kami manages day-to-day operation and lives on-site. As in most budget accommodations, furniture and buildings are older, but the only amenity you might miss is air conditioning. If that matters to you, make sure you request an air-conditioned room (about half are). Some units have kitchenettes.

Most of the motel's 26 rooms face each other across a courtyard and lawn shaded by mature trees, blocked from view of the road by the office. It feels a little like you unpacked a backyard from your suitcase and tossed it out the window. Perhaps that's why Evergreen Gables is so successful as a weekly rental facility: For little more than you'd pay for one night's upscale accommodations downtown, you can stay here a week with a shady yard in which to relax every evening. The Lewises provide a couple of gas grills for your use.

Motel West

$ • 1540 W. Broadway Ave., Idaho Falls, Idaho • (208) 522-1112, (800) 582-1063

The furnishings are standard motel fare, clean and functional, but the price is good and the attached cafe, Home Town Kitchen, is a locals' favorite. (If you're a night owl, enjoy being a couple of blocks from Idaho Falls' 24-hour dining establishment, O'Brady's.)

Among the amenities are an indoor pool and hot tub, a laundry room and VCR and movie rental. Three spacious suites, rented mostly by locals celebrating anniversaries and other special events, have in-room whirlpool tubs. Rent one of these (they're cheaper than you might think) and you'll find a bottle of nonalcoholic champagne, a basket of candy and other goodies waiting when you arrive.

Shilo Inn

$$$ • 780 Lindsay Blvd., Idaho Falls, Idaho • (208) 523-0088

When the Shilo opened in 1988, it instantly became the high-end favorite in town. This independently owned and operated 161-room hotel is one of the largest facilities in town. It has the largest convention facilities in eastern Idaho.

All rooms are oversized mini-suites. Ten dollars over the base price buys you a view of the Snake River and its parklike shore — we suggest you pay it.

All rooms come with coffee makers, fridges, wet bars, microwaves, irons and ironing boards and 27-inch satellite TV. VCR and movie rentals are available. As a guest of the Shilo, you also get to use the 24-hour steam room, hot tub, sauna, indoor swimming pool and fitness center with modern aerobic equipment. You can receive faxes at no charge; also free is a full breakfast buffet and a morning newspaper to read as you eat.

The folks at the Shilo can arrange vacation packages for you. In summer ask about fishing and whitewater packages; in winter try snowmobiling. Package travel usually takes you up to Island Park or over to Jackson. Neither is more than 100 minutes away in good weather.

One huge advantage to staying at the Shilo is that, because they cater more to business travelers than tourists, weekends tend to be slower than weekdays. When accommodations closer to the parks are full up, these folks often have rooms.

Weston Quality Inn

$$ • 850 Lindsay Blvd., Idaho Falls, Idaho • (208) 523-6260, (800) 852-7829, (800) 228-5151

Rooms, ranging from a single queen to a king with a jet tub, overlook the courtyard swimming pool or look across the parking lot toward the Snake River's Porter Canal and greenbelt. Some second-floor rooms have views of the Snake River itself. A full breakfast comes with your room. Frontier Pies, the in-house family style restaurant, serves breakfast, lunch and dinner. About 90 percent of the rooms are nonsmoking.

Northwestern Wyoming

Cody, Wyoming

Best Western Sunset Motor Inn

$$$ • 1601 Eighth St., Cody, Wyo. • (307) 587-4265, (800) 624-2727

There is something unexpectedly serene about the 120 rooms, all ground-floor, at the Sunset Motor Inn. They ooze cool, soothing elegance from the creamy carpet tones to the plush bedspreads. Chances are the Sunset Motor Inn can accommodate your every need, as they have about every room combination available. Most rooms have queen-size beds, although some are king suites and one comes equipped with three queen-size beds.

A slow stroll from the Buffalo Bill Historical Center (see our Attractions chapter) and downtown, the Sunset has a list of amenities to match the soothing interiors and its sprawling, manicured lawns. Choose between an indoor pool/spa and a sunny outdoor pool. The facility also has an exercise room, a guest laundry and a children's playground. The Sunset House Family Restaurant, adjacent to the motel, serves three meals a day, breakfast and dinner buffets and offers three different dining rooms with a total seating capacity of 210.

Big Bear Motel Carter Mountain

$$ • 1701 17th Ave., Cody, Wyo. • (307) 587-4295

This older but well-maintained motel on Cody's east end specializes in two-, three- and four-bedroom family suites with kitchens. Because suite rates are so reasonable during the off-season, they're often filled. Fall, winter and early spring, a two-bedroom suite rents for $175 per week.

Cody Guest Houses

$$$$ • 1401 Rumsey Ave., Cody, Wyo. • (307) 587-6000

Why stay in a motel when you can stay in one of the seven Cody Guest Houses for as many or as few nights as you like. Owner Kathy Singer hasn't spared a dime decorating and furnishing her collection of cottages, duplex suites and homes in Cody's historic residential district. The Mayor's Inn and the Victoria House, both operated like bed and breakfasts without the breakfast or the innkeeper, are richly appointed with Victorian antiques, wallpaper, carpets and fixtures. Rent one or two rooms or the whole house. The four-bedroom Western Lodge is equally charming with its massive furniture and masculine decor. Rates for the Cody Guest Houses are competitive with motels; double occupancy rates range from $80 to $205 per night. For more information on the Cody Guest Houses, see our Vacation Rentals chapter.

Bill Cody Ranch

$$$$ • 2604 Yellowstone Hwy., Cody, Wyo. • (307) 587-6271

Even though the Bill Cody Ranch gears its schedule toward multiple-day visits, it does hang out the vacancy sign when it has room for overnight guests. If you're in the area give the Bill Cody Ranch a call, especially in the early summer and fall. Don't be surprised, though, if it's full. (For more information, see our chapter on Guest Ranches.)

Days Inn

$$$$ • 524 Yellowstone Ave., Cody, Wyo., • (307) 527-6604, (800) DAYS-INN

Clean, new and spacious, the 52 rooms at Cody's Days Inn may be a refreshing change from rustic log cabins. The rooms range from single king and queens to those with two and three queen-size beds. The Days Inn also has a couple of king suites. In addition to the huge and elaborate lobby, this motel has an indoor

INSIDERS' TIP

If your Idaho Falls motel has an address on River Parkway or Lindsay Boulevard, you'll be staying near the Snake River. Be sure to take advantage of the pleasant riverside greenbelt and parks.

pool and spa, guest laundry, and complimentary continental breakfast.

Elephant Head Lodge

$$ • Yellowstone Hwy., Wapiti, Wyo. • (307) 587-3980

Every once in a while, you'll find that this heavenly spot outside Cody has a vacancy from a last-minute cancellation. There is something about these older, tastefully modernized cabins that says "stay awhile." It's worth calling to find out if you're in the area. (For more about Elephant Head Lodge, see our Resorts and Vacation Lodges chapter.)

The Irma Hotel

$$ • 12th St. and Sheridan Ave., Cody, Wyo. • (307) 587-4221

Built in 1902 by Buffalo Bill Cody himself, The Irma Hotel is as much an attraction as an accommodation. In its heyday — heated by steam, lighted by gas, equipped with telephones in every room — The Irma was the hub of high living at the end of the Milwaukee Railroad spur. The hotel had an elegant bar, billiards, a telegraph office, a barber shop and baths. The dining room featured fresh produce, meat and dairy products from its own farm. And a livery stable sat ready to serve customers with every kind of rig and horse possible, including camp and pack outfitters to take guests hunting, fishing and sightseeing in Yellowstone National Park.

Today, The Irma is a shadow of its former self. Enough signs of the frontier days remain, though, to make a stay at this landmark a special occasion. The rooms, mostly upstairs, range from the simple to the elegant with a combination of old and new. All have private baths, and you'll find an amazing list of sleeping combinations.

Downstairs, is The Irma Restaurant, a giant dining room featuring a cherry wood bar presented to Bill Cody by the Queen of England. Adjacent to the restaurant is the Silver Saddle Bar, a favorite watering hole for tourists and locals alike.

Rainbow Park Motel

$ • 1136 17th St., Cody, Wyo. • (307) 587-6251, (800) 341-8000

This single-story, well-maintained, 40-unit brick motel wrapped U-shaped around the parking lot fills up fast. The prices are reasonable, and the rooms are clean. The Rainbow, at the east end of Sheridan Avenue, Cody's main thoroughfare, has both regular rooms and ones with kitchenettes.

Children like the small fenced, shaded playground on a grass island in the center of the parking lot. The grounds also have barbecuing facilities. On the premises is the Cody Coffee Company, a cheery little place that serves a continental-style breakfast with a great cup of coffee as well as a simple lunch (see our Restaurants chapter).

Skyline Motor Inn

$$ • 1919 17th St., Cody, Wyo. • (307) 587-4201, (800) 843-8809

Next to McDonald's, Burger King and Taco Bell at the east end of Cody, the Skyline prides itself on clean rooms — it has 46 units — and reasonable rates. The Skyline has an outdoor heated pool and a small playground.

Yellowstone Valley Inn

$$ • 3324 Yellowstone Park Hwy., Cody, Wyo. • (307) 587-3961, (888) 705-7703

This popular place midway between Cody and Yellowstone National Park has an array of accommodations and specializes in family reunions and group getaways. In addition to 15 motel rooms and 20 cabin rooms, Yellowstone Valley Inn has an RV Park and a campground, restaurant and lounge — all situated in a beautiful valley away from the hustle and bustle of town and the park. That means groups can take advantage of the various accommodation options and still be together. Each room has two double beds, and several have connecting-room possibilities. Yellowstone Valley Inn also offers guided horseback rides.

INSIDERS' TIP

Look for more cabins in our Vacation Rentals chapter.

Hostels

Backpackers' Hostel

$ • 405 W. Olive St., Bozeman, Mont. • (406) 586-4659

In the early 1990s, Jim Marshall bought a Victorian-era home in Bozeman and turned it into a 14-bunk hostel. Today, the hostel is heavily used during the summer, mostly by foreigners accustomed to the hosteling concept. Two of the bedrooms have been converted to bunk rooms. Visitors have access to two bathrooms, a kitchen and a living room. The cost is $12 per person for the bunks and $30 for the one private room at the hostel. During the winter, overnight skiers stay at this hostel. Ask about the Yellowstone Hostel Express, a shuttle service that treats travelers (four passengers is the minimum to put together a shuttle) to an overnight, round-trip tour through Yellowstone National Park to Cooke City and back to Bozeman.

The Bunkhouse

$ • 215 N. Cache St., Jackson, Wyo. • (307) 733-3668

You get a bunkbed, a locker, linens, soap and shampoo, all for about $16 per night. You also get the use of a large lounge with phone, TV with HBO, sinks and a utility area with microwave and refrigerator. Your bunk, one of 25, is semiprivate. The entire facility is about 5,000 square feet and equipped with men's and women's showers and a gear room. The Bunkhouse is in the basement of the moderately priced brick-red Anvil Motel near town square. No alcohol is permitted.

Madison Hotel West Yellowstone International Hostel

$ • 139 W. Yellowstone Ave., West Yellowstone, Montana • (406) 646-7745

The historic Madison Hotel offers hostel rates of $18 per person per night to anybody belonging to a hostel organization. (For more information, refer to the Madison Hotel entry earlier in this chapter.)

Yellowstone Yurt Hostel

$ • W. Broadway St., Cooke City, Montana • (406) 838-2349

Perched at the edge of Broadway Street, one block north of U.S. Highway 212, the Yellowstone Yurt Hostel is a semiprimitive facility that offers an alternative to Forest Service campgrounds or more expensive motels. The Yurt, owned by Jim Marshall, has six bunks (bring your own sleeping bag) and a wood stove. The $12 overnight fee entitles you to the use of a shower and a toilet on the premises. The hostel also has a primitive outside kitchen equipped with a Coleman stove. Backcountry recreationists come here summer and winter. Marshall also owns the Montana International Backpackers' Hostel in Bozeman.

Hostel^x

$ • 3315 McCollister Dr., Teton Village, Wyo. • (307) 733-3415

In winter this is an inexpensive, no-frills motel, but in summer it offers members of the American Youth Hostel Association or comparable organizations inexpensive individual rates, about $18 per person. Hostel^x sits nearly at the entrance to Grand Teton National Park with its climbing, hiking, boating and wildlife watching opportunities. See our listing under Jackson motels in this chapter for more.

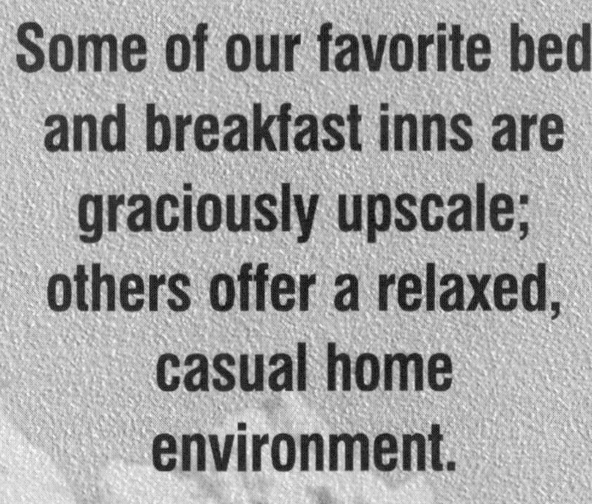

Some of our favorite bed and breakfast inns are graciously upscale; others offer a relaxed, casual home environment.

Bed and Breakfast Inns

Like this book, bed and breakfast inns are a way to get inside. Meet the innkeepers: people who moved here a decade ago, enthralled with our mountains, and people whose families have carved their livelihoods from the Northern Rockies for generations. Share your morning meals with other travelers, some with stories and travel suggestions to share and others dying to hear your stories and suggestions.

Space doesn't allow an inclusive list, and we love learning about new and wonderful places. If you don't find it described here, please tell us about your favorite Yellowstone region inn.

All the bed and breakfast inns we describe are unique. Your innkeepers often masterminded the construction. They decorated and landscaped their inn, and they live in it. It's their vision of hospitality and comfort. Relax and enjoy.

One charm of bed and breakfast inns is that amenities and policies vary. Some of our favorites are graciously upscale; others offer a relaxed, casual home environment. Some may remind you of childhood visits to grandma's house or your cousin Mary's. Others offer more unfamiliar lifestyles.

What your hosts have in common is an interest in the region you've come to see. Most have maps, brochures and books to help you plan excursions. Some will help arrange your itinerary. A few loan snowshoes, water bottles or other equipment to make excursions more comfortable.

Policies differ regarding reservations, deposits and cancellations as well as children and pets. In our opinion, the best bed and breakfast inns for children often are those in which children live; you'll find several listed here. Generally, pets aren't welcome at bed and breakfast inns. Many inns are nonsmoking. In addition, many innkeepers are happy to arrange your transportation from nearby airports with advance notice. Discuss these issues when you call.

Reservations are often required and always preferred. Most inns have cancellation policies that require you to provide generous advance notice before you change your plans. Some require minimum stays of two or more nights. Please inquire about these policies too.

For the heavy travel months of July and August, the most popular inns fill up months in advance. Some vacationers book next year's stay before they leave their inn of choice this year, particularly if they have a favorite room they want to enjoy again.

This does not mean it isn't sometimes worthwhile to drop in or attempt a reservation on short notice: Innkeepers in Yellowstone Country work within a fairly short busy season. If they get a cancellation, they're generally happy to accommodate you.

Most inns are open year round and accept major credit cards. We note exceptions for you.

Price Code

The average nightly rate for two adults during the peak summer season is indicated by the following dollar-sign chart. Please note that many bed and breakfast inns offer a range of rooms at a range of prices. Larger rooms and rooms with more spectacular views, private decks or private entrances generally cost more than the price we indicate.

$ Less than $85
$$ $85 to $115
$$$ $116 to $150
$$$$ $151 and more

Jackson Hole

Many of Jackson's best have banded together to make information gathering and reservations easy for you. Contact The Jackson Hole Bed and Breakfast Association, P.O. Box 6396, Jackson, WY 83002, (800) 542-2632, for a brochure or to ask about specific association inns. More than a dozen are represented by the association, which was formed in 1994 and is still spearheaded by Alan Blackburn, association founder and former co-manager of Moose Meadows Bed and Breakfast in Wilson.

Jackson, Wyoming, Area

The Alpine House

$$ • 285 N. Glenwood St., Jackson, Wyo. • (307) 739-1570, (800) 753-1421

After you've wandered through this sunny, uncluttered inn — an easy stroll from Jackson's downtown shopping and entertainment possibilities — you won't wonder why The Alpine House was selected as one of *Country Inns'* top 10 affordable luxuries of 1996.

Six of the seven guest rooms are upstairs, facing each other across a two-story open area that overlooks the dining and gathering areas downstairs. The warmth of exposed beams blends well with cool white walls, big windows and open space.

Rooms are not large, but each has a private bath, balcony and radiant floor heat (you'll love this feature when you step barefoot from bed on a chilly January morning). Two rooms have loft areas served by log ladders. The inn added an outdoor hot tub in 1998.

Breakfast is served buffet-style and enjoyed at several small tables scattered through the common area; so is afternoon tea. No television will draw your attention from the pleasant Scandinavian feel of your accommodations or the book you picked from the well-stocked adventure and recreational library.

Innkeepers Hans and Nancy Johnstone are both former Olympic athletes — Hans was a nordic skier and Nancy, a biathlete — and both are deeply involved in local outdoor recreation. Hans currently works with Exum Guides as a mountaineering and rock climbing guide. Their specialized knowledge of the area makes The Alpine House uniquely suited for the hard-core adventure traveler while still offering the comforts desired by the luxury vacationer.

Bentwood Bed & Breakfast

$$$$ • 4250 W. Raven Haven, Wilson, Wyo. • (307) 739-1411

Just outside Jackson, off the Village road, a 5,800-square-foot log home hides in a grove of cottonwoods. It's massive, but seems less so because of its gracious arc around the trees and flower beds at its main entrance. Bentwood is the kind of place that, if you do happen to glimpse it through the trees, might make you wonder what's behind the lace curtains that soften its imposing log presence.

Innkeepers Bill and Nell Fay would love to show you. Gracious hosts in a gracious house, the Fays offer five distinctively appointed rooms, all with private baths, porches or balconies, gas fireplaces (operated by hand-held remote!), cable TV and telephone; most have Jacuzzis. One pretty room well-suited for families features a sitting area, a queen-size Inglenook bed tucked into three walls and a loft equipped with three twin beds.

The main living area is spacious and open to the second floor. A 30-foot-high, river-rock fireplace anchors the room. Your hosts run their inn with professional hospitality: They're there when you'd like them to be, but in general, the main areas of the house are yours.

The Fays say their home is ideal for groups and conventions, which often reserve the entire house. The 3-acre property, ringed by cottonwoods, is ideal for cookouts and family get-togethers.

Moose Meadows Bed & Breakfast

$ • 1225 Green Ln., Wilson, Wyo. • (307) 733-9510

Moose Meadows is one of the most reasonably priced bed and breakfast inns in the area. It may also be the most laid-back. Owner/innkeeper Juli James invites you to share her large, Western-style house with its odd and entertaining mix of antiques, collectibles and huge elk mounts, moose antlers, mountain goats and longhorn skulls. Family pets roam the spacious house — and so should you and your children, insists the friendly innkeeper.

Juli likes to share her enthusiasm for the Western art collection hanging on the walls. You'll even eat from part of that collection: Her breakfast plates were designed by well-known Montana artist Buckeye Blake.

The antiques that furnish much of the house and the four guest rooms belonged to Juli's grandmother. Other furnishings reflect her travels and her family's accomplishments. Decorations from Africa and India are scattered about. Juli's father was once ambassador to India; a punched-steel sign on the Porch Room wall commemorates his stint as U.S. Attorney General. One daughter was the 1997 National High School Rodeo Girls' Cutting Champion. Championship belt buckles are displayed in the living room.

The house is conveniently near Wyo. Highway 22 in a small subdivision in Wilson, so guests can reach Grand Teton National Park without entering the bustle of Jackson. They can also enjoy views of the Tetons and of game-filled meadows through the house's large back and side windows or from the hot tub on the back deck.

Breakfast is a hearty sit-down affair, often featuring Wyoming game such as elk sausage. The meal is served on a big, round lazy Susan table in a dining room with Teton views.

Nowlin Creek Inn

$$$$ • 660 E. Broadway Ave., Jackson, Wyo. • (307) 733-0882, (800) 533-0882

Owners Susan and Mark Nowlin (that's NOW-lin, not NO-lin) may have the perfect location for an in-town inn. Easy to find on one of Jackson's main streets and only six blocks from the crowd-filled town square, Nowlin Creek Inn manages to feel like a quiet refuge.

Mark's great-grandfather homesteaded across the street in what is now the National Elk Refuge and was the refuge's first superintendent. Nearby Nowlin Creek carries his name.

Mark and Susan are artists and former museum curators, and their special touch adds sparkle and eccentricity to every room in this large country house. Clean white walls prevent the many fine pieces of art from diminishing each other. Offbeat chandeliers hang from vaulted ceilings. Stenciled ivy (Susan's handwork) twines across lacquered pine floors. And if you look closely, you'll notice that the window frames aren't really there: They're painted and stamped (also by Susan) onto the walls. Beyond the outdoor hot tub, a giant cowboy — once a sign on an old building downtown — waves a big welcome.

The two-story inn has five comfortable rooms, all set in corners of the house so they're flooded with light during the day and with crisp breezes at night. Three rooms have fireplaces with mantels which, like the window frames, are painted and stamped onto the drywall. The Nowlins spoil you with evening snacks and plush robes and slippers to relax in; a gourmet breakfast is served before you head out to explore Jackson or the Elk Refuge just outside the door.

The Nowlins also rent the cabin out back — built by Mark's grandfather in the 1920s and furnished with an even more exuberantly eccentric artist's touch. (See our Hotels, Motels and Cabins chapter.)

The Painted Porch Bed & Breakfast

$$$ • 3755 N. Moose-Wilson Rd., Wilson, Wyo. • (307) 733-1981

Maybe it's the white picket fence. Maybe

it's because, in the land of log, Martha MacEachern's pretty inn is a white-shuttered, porch-railed farmhouse. Or maybe it's the aspens that hiss like restless water, hiding the vague traffic noises from the Village road nearby. For whatever reason, we walked through the front gate and onto the green painted porch of this inn with a sigh of pure pleasure.

The house was built in nearby Teton Valley in 1901 by a farming family. In 1967, it was partially dismantled and brought here through Teton Pass — you know, that 10 percent-plus grade your car labored over the other day before dropping into Jackson Hole?

But the hardest thing you'll do here is pick which of the four uniquely appointed rooms you prefer. Each room has a private bath (two offer Japanese soaking tubs), cable television and Ralph Lauren bed linens, towels and comforters. But they range in feel from nouveau cowboy to sweetly sunlit.

The spacious kitchen/dining room, where the ample country breakfasts are served, is one of the most pleasant rooms in the house, with its shiny white tile counters and long dining table with fancifully painted chairs. A mass of variously colored and shaped pillows rests on a bench seat beneath the large bay window. Hmm, coffee here or out on the deck in the hammock? Another tough decision.

The Sassy Moose Inn

$$$ • 3859 Miles Rd., Wilson, Wyo. • (307) 733-1277, (800) 356-1277

Polly Kelley runs the bed and breakfast inn that her son Craig expanded six years ago on the Moose-Wilson Road (also called the Village road) between Jackson and Teton Village. Some of the nicer features Craig installed include an entrance hallway that allows guests to access rooms without passing through the common living and dining areas, and sound-damping in the walls so that one group may enjoy the television in the living area while you nap undisturbed in your room. All rooms have private baths.

One suite is particularly well-suited to a larger group. It adjoins a loft area overlooking the house's main living space. The loft is furnished with a hide-a-bed.

Polly leaves fruit and sweets out for guests during the day. In the afternoon, she provides wine and other beverages; her guests often relax together over snacks and wine to recount the day's adventures.

A Teton Tree House Bed & Breakfast

$$$ • 6175 Heck of a Hill Rd., Wilson, Wyo. • (307) 733-3233

In the stylish bed and breakfast scene in and around Jackson, you have to do something spectacular to stand out. A Teton Tree House does.

Innkeeper Denny Becker's fanciful four-story building clings like ivy to a steep hillside above Wilson. The gentle 95-stair hike from your car lands you a million miles away from busy Jackson (actually, it's only 8). From every window seat and every deck, you'll feel like you're enjoying the view from your very own tree-house retreat.

Denny, a contractor, designed and built the hybrid post-and-beam structure. His specialty is staircases, so make sure you take special note of the curving staircase, the spiral staircase and what Denny calls the staggered staircase (it takes a bit of practice to navigate). He also built the lovely long oval dining table, where you'll enjoy breakfast while watching the finches, grosbeaks and nuthatches at the window feeders enjoying theirs.

The house has six rooms of various sizes and styles. Each has deck access. Most have private decks, and all have private baths. Denny provides a cordless phone for your convenience: Take it into any room you choose, or get really silly and make your calls from the hot tub on the main deck.

INSIDERS' TIP

Most bed and breakfast inns will mail color brochures that show you what their establishments look like.

Breakfast is what Denny likes to call "full with low cholesterol:" homemade granola, lots of fresh fruit, exotic blended fruit drinks, breads and muffins and hot whole-grain cereals, but no eggs and no meat.

Most guests at A Teton Tree House are couples; it's easy to see why. We can't imagine a more romantic setting for your weekend getaway, honeymoon or second honeymoon.

Denny is open for business year-round, but he cautions that Heck of a Hill Road is not lightly named: In winter, four-wheel or front-wheel drive vehicles fare best on the well-maintained but steep, winding road.

Twin Trees Bed & Breakfast

$$ • 575 S. Willow, Jackson, Wyo. • (307) 739-9737

From the dining room window, winter guests at Twin Trees watch skiers schuss underneath the lifts at Snow King, the in-town ski area. On the Fourth of July, fireworks explode over the inn; in April, guests can sit on the comfortable porch and experience the roar and excitement of the World Championship Snowmobile Hillclimb.

Twin Trees is a gracious alternative to Jackson's downtown motels, but it's every bit as convenient. A 10-minute walk will take you to shopping and dining destinations. The bus for Teton Village, where world-class skiing awaits, picks up almost at the front door. And Snow King Resort — home to concerts, a convention center, ice rink and ski hill — is just across the street.

Innkeeper Pat Martin and her cats welcome you to an eclectically furnished house with three unique guest rooms. Down comforters and plush robes await in your small but cozy room. One room features a kimono hung on the wall and vaguely Oriental decor. Another has an arched ceiling and cushioned window seat. On summer nights, the full moon arcs past this window and lights the room. The work of local artists adorns the living and dining areas downstairs.

Amenities include an enclosed outdoor hot tub with sliding screens (so it can be opened to the cool night air), television in the living area, a lovely yard with privacy fence and a long shaded porch. Rooms have private baths but no phones.

Pat prides herself on the care she gives to her guests' dietary needs. Breakfasts — plentiful, flexible and healthful — are enjoyed at a warmly polished walnut table while Pat bustles about in the kitchen on the other side of the breakfast bar, perhaps preparing her English fruit scones.

The Wildflower Inn

$$$$ • 3725 Teton Village Rd., Wilson, Wyo. • (307) 733-4710

It's not just a name: During the summer, the driveway to Sherrie and Ken Jern's inn is lined with wildflowers. Color dances in the entry and hugs the log walls. Pots of bright blooms hang from the second-story deck.

The interior is just as pleasant — and as flower-filled. Cut flowers brighten the long table

INSIDERS' TIP

For a complete list of Wyoming Bed and Breakfast Inns, write Wyoming Homestay and Outdoor Adventures, P.O. Box 40048, Casper, WY 82604, or call (307) 237-3526.

and bay window in the dining room. Sunshine streams in through many windows, transforming the weight of log walls and river-rock fireplace into warm, elegant comfort.

Log homes are dime a dozen out here, but this house, built in 1990, has special touches. For instance, instead of synthetic chinking between logs, the Jerns chinked with wood — more laborious and more attractive. Interior log-ends were allowed to extend into the rooms, sawed into pleasant curves. The roof beams are massive and exposed. Touches like these have won Wildflower Inn awards and recognition from publications such as *National Geographic Traveler* magazine and *Glamour*.

All five guest rooms are equipped with log beds, down comforters, private baths, pedestal sinks and pleasant views. Most have small private decks. The inn is open year-round. Reservations should be made as far in advance as possible: Many people book their summer stays in January or February.

Sherrie likes to help her guests leave early for their Teton adventures, so she's happy to pack a picnic breakfast. But our guess is you'll leave the wildlife for later so you can relax over Wildflower Inn's fine fare: all your morning favorites enlivened with your host's gourmet touch. One guest favorite is the vegetable frittata — a deep-dish concoction of fresh veggies and Gruyere, Swiss and Parmesan cheeses.

Surrounding Areas

Southwestern Montana

West Yellowstone, Montana

Sportsman's High Bed and Breakfast

$$ • 750 Deer St., West Yellowstone, Mont. • (406) 646-7865

Imagine sleeping under the softest floral chintz, then rising to pen a letter as the morning sun creeps across the floor. Something outside catches your eye. It's a fat doe with her new fawn, standing for a moment among the aspen trees outside your window. All of this — and more — is real at the Sportsman's High Bed and Breakfast where owners Diana and Gary Baxter have carved their niche in paradise. Eight miles from Yellowstone National Park, Sportsman's High is also minutes away from several blue-ribbon trout streams and lakes. Just out the front door are trails for hiking, mountain biking, horseback riding and cross-country skiing, as well as hundreds of miles of groomed snowmobile trails.

In each of the five rooms at Sportsman's High, guests will find plumped feather pillows, country-fresh decor, robes, cheery bath amenities, a hair dryer, an antique desk and an assortment of guide and information books. The Bear Cabin, a one-room log cabin, offers extra privacy and charm. Diana serves a hearty breakfast at a 12-foot-long harvest table. There is a cozy upstairs sitting room for guests. Winters, the Baxters convert their bed and breakfast to a vacation rental. See our Vacation Rentals chapter information about the five other rentals owned by the Baxters.

Gardiner, Montana

Slip and Slide Bed and Breakfast

$, no credit cards • U.S. Hwy. 89, 11 mi. north of Gardiner, Mont. • (406) 848-7648

Don't let the name slip you up. This bed and breakfast is named after the Slip and Slide drainage in which the inn sits, off the highway and away from the bustle. Owners Franklin and Susan Rigler are newcomers to the bed and breakfast business, but they're old hands at hospitality. A third-generation rancher, Franklin is a hunting and fishing guide. For an extra fee, he will pack you into the mountains so you can fish away from the crowds. The Riglers also will share Insiders' tips on where to go and what to do. They offer three rooms and two shared baths on the first floor of their house. In addition to a large living room with a bar, refrigerator and range top, guests can walk right out the door and enjoy the view (Electric Peak will be staring you in the face). If you're in the mood to cook up a steak, there's a barbecue on the patio. There are also laundry facilities. Susan serves up a ranch breakfast garnished with Western hospitality. There are two private fishing ponds on the property.

The vaguely Scandinavian feel of this bed and breakfast's main living area is unusual in mostly log- and pine-paneled Jackson Hole.

Slip and Slide is open from mid-May to mid-September.

The Yellowstone Inn

$ • Main St. and U.S. Hwy. 89, Gardiner, Mont. • (406) 848-7000

In the heart of Gardiner, this turn-of-the-century stone bed and breakfast is clean and country, but not cutesy-country. It is the closest bed and breakfast inn to the park's North Entrance and the oldest operating inn in Gardiner. Nine spacious, simply decorated rooms, divided between two buildings, offer a multitude of choices. On the third floor is the Yellowstone Suite. With two bedrooms, a bath and a sitting room, it is private and big enough to accommodate a family. Or get together a gang and reserve four bedrooms on the second floor. You'll have to share the bathrooms, though.

Breakfast — usually a hot country dish with muffins, cereal or yogurt — is cooked up in a huge kitchen and served in a communal dining room. Ask about the two-story Stone Cottage, a converted chicken coop that sleeps four and has a kitchen. This bed and breakfast fills up fast with folks frequenting the park, so make your reservations well ahead of time.

INSIDERS' TIP

Need help planning your trip or making reservations? Call 1-800-CAPTIVE or (307) 587-9002 for PAN-O-RAMA WEST, Inc., a central reservation service in Cody, Wyoming. Or try (888) 468-6996 or (307) 587-0200 for Central Reservations, LLC, in Cody.

Yellowstone Suites Bed and Breakfast

$ • 506 Fourth St., Gardiner, Mont. • (406) 848-7937

The bottom is made of river rock, and the top half is made of rock left over from the construction of the Roosevelt Arch, Yellowstone National Park's first (and grandest) entrance, dedicated in 1903 by Theodore Roosevelt. Simple in design, this three-story home built in 1904 is a unique bed and breakfast. The second floor, which has two bedrooms with a shared bath and the dining room, opens at the back onto a porch and an "upstairs" yard. Owned by John and Anita Varley, both longtime park employees, this bed and breakfast makes the perfect place to stay while snooping about Yellowstone Country. John and Anita currently staff a manager during the week, but their son, Nathan, often makes an appearance. Nathan, a biologist, guides film crews, photographers and anyone else who's curious (and wants to pay the price) to Yellowstone's wolves. His clients often stay at the Yellowstone Suites. As a result, the Yellowstone Suites Bed and Breakfast is quickly becoming known as the wolf-watchers' B&B.

Bay windows, balconies, a veranda and a hot tub add to the airiness here. A third-floor suite offers privacy with a queen-size bed, private bath, window seat, nifty dormer, TV and kitchen. Another third-floor room with a queen-size bed has a private bath. Both the second and third-floor rooms rented together make good family accommodations. Breakfast is a quasi-continental serve-yourself setup in a charming upstairs dining room.

Bozeman, Montana

Lindley House Bed and Breakfast

$$$ • 202 Lindley Pl., Bozeman, Mont. • (406) 587-8403, (800) 787-8404

Goldilocks would have had a hard time choosing just which of the eight rooms she liked best in this historic Victorian bed and breakfast inn. No matter which bed she tried, she would have found a piece of candy on the pillow. She also would have found fresh flowers, a carafe of purified water and gingerbread cookies awaiting her in each of the rooms. Owner Stephanie Volz spent three years restoring this four-story brick mansion, literally from the rafters down. Mature trees, an English flower garden and private nooks and crannies all add to the Lindley House experience.

Afternoons, Volz offers her guests tea, coffee, wine or sherry in the parlor. And evenings, you'll find brandy and a snifter beside your bed. At breakfast you'll sit down to a three- or four-course meal with delicacies like fruit-stuffed French toast with chokecherry syrup, spinach and mushroom soufflé topped with freshly grated cheese, or sourdough crepes wrapped around plump blueberries — all served on fine china and polished silver. You'll recognize the Lindley House by the antique bed filled with flowers on the front lawn, and by the sign out front that tells all about it.

The Lindley House, two blocks south of Main Street, is on the National Historic Register. Volz offers a range of rooms that includes a penthouse suite. She also has a massage therapist on call for her guests. She requires a two-night minimum stay.

Torch and Toes Bed and Breakfast

$ • 309 S. Third Ave., Bozeman, Mont. • (406) 586-7285, (800) 446-2138

You'll find the Torch and Toes in Bozeman's historic Bon Ton District near downtown. Built in 1906, this two-story Queen Anne-style brick house has three guest rooms, a carriage house suite and 30 different mouse traps collected during the innkeepers' travels. While the traps are displayed in the breakfast nook, other objets d'art are scattered throughout the house, adding charm and fancy to the inn's eclectic decor. Downstairs features oak woodwork and maple floors. Upstairs you'll find carpet, cafe curtains across big windows, and a private bath in each room. The carriage house — a favorite among Torch and Toes guests — has a bedroom, bath and kitchen downstairs, with a sitting room, fireplace and futon sofa upstairs. It sleeps up to six people.

All guests will find facilities for badminton, horseshoes and a soak in the hot tub. There is also space for a game of English croquet. Breakfasts are complete with fresh fruit, homemade sweet breads and entrees such as coddled eggs or omelets with a breakfast meat.

Livingston, Montana, Area

The Island Bed and Breakfast

$, no credit cards • 77 Island Dr., Livingston, Mont.
• (406) 222-3788, (800) 438-3092

Location, location, location: It's secluded. It's five minutes from downtown Livingston. And it's on an island.

Owner Fran Eggar offers two bedrooms with a shared bath, three ponds with catch-and-release fishing and 60 acres with lots of deer and a shy moose. Guests have access to the living and dining rooms as well as a sun room with refrigerator. A patio with a barbecue (feel free to use it) is off the sun room. Fran encourages relaxing and wandering about the island.

She also has a three-bedroom, two-bath guest house at the end of the island road that rents for $1,000 weekly or $175 nightly.

The River Inn

$ • 4950 Hwy. 89 S., Livingston, Mont.
• (406) 222-2429

Owners Ursula Neese and Dee Dee Van Zyl restored and remodeled this 100-year-old farmhouse to create an airy, serene inn on the shores of the Yellowstone River south of Livingston. They succeeded. The three rooms in this sunny inn all have private baths and stupendous views of the Absaroka Mountains and the Yellowstone River below. All three are upstairs; two have French doors that open onto a private deck. One room has a double bed, another has a queen-size bed, and the Absaroka Room comes with a queen as well as a single futon couch.

The rooms at the River Inn are so comfortable and soothing that guests often want to linger in bed for a while. That's why there's a coffeepot in the upstairs hall. Breakfast is served outside on the patio when weather permits, otherwise you'll dine in the simple elegance of the dining room. For more privacy try Calamity Jane's, an airy cabin with a double bed, table, chairs, refrigerator and hot plate. Adjacent to the cabin is a composting toilet. Inside the farmhouse is your bathroom with a claw-foot tub. For the adventure of your life, try Dottie Spanger's, a turn-of the-century sheepherder's wagon in mint condition. The view from your bed (a double futon) is stupendous. The wagon is outfitted with a fine collection of books and an electric lamp.

Ursula, who owned a landscaping business in Bozeman for 20 years, is an avid skier, hiker, biker, canoeist, climber, guide and first responder. Dee is a professional actor from Portland, Oregon. For a fee, Ursula will guide you on a variety of trips including a mountain-bike trip to Chico Hot Springs or a mostly downhill ride from the mountains to the inn. She also guides a Yellowstone River canoe trip and day hikes.

Ennis, Montana

9T9 Guest Ranch

$ • 99 Gravelly Range Rd., Ennis, Mont.
• (406) 682-7659, (800) 484-5862, pin 7659

Owners Vaughan and Judy Herrick like to say they are "inconveniently located" 10 miles south of Ennis. Their place is worth the drive just for the view. They overlook building-free meadows, the Madison River — world-renowned for its trout fishing — and the towering Madison Mountain Range beyond. They have private access to the river, and Vaughan is a licensed fishing guide and a great casting instructor. He accommodates anglers with a place in the garage for them to hang waders and fly rods. Guests are welcome to use a fly-tying table in the living room or watch wildlife through his spotting scope.

If you aren't into fishing, the drive is worth it just to experience the gracious and genuine welcome of this vibrant retired couple. Judy, a bubbly blond involved in her church and the community, is such a good cook that locals began requesting that she begin a Saturday night "restaurant." She applied for the license

INSIDERS' TIP

Many bed and breakfast inns rent family suites or separate cottages with or without kitchens.

and now serves 12 people (by reservation only) at "Judy's Table" in her dining room during the winter months when local restaurants close. Her breakfasts will delight you. And their chuckwagon dinners, served from the chuckwagon around the fire, are out of this world.

Accommodations are simple, clean and country. A large living room downstairs (where the three bedrooms are located) is a comfortable refuge after a long day on the river. Judy also manages vacation homes. You'll find more about them in our Vacation Rentals chapter.

Red Lodge, Montana

Willows Inn

$ • 224 S. Platt, Red Lodge, Mont.
• (406) 446-3913

If you arrive at this charming Victorian inn after dark, you'll find proprietress Carolyn Boggio has left the lights on for you. The cheery white Christmas lights strung on the fence in front are just one of the thoughtful details she uses to make your stay at the Willows Inn unique. Beautifully restored inside and out, the Willows Inn says, "We care," from each perfectly appointed room to the English flower garden outside. Carolyn serves refreshments in the afternoon and offers a continental-plus breakfast that includes homemade Finnish pastries made by her mother-in-law, fresh fruit, hot and cold beverages and cheese.

The Willows Inn also offers two equally beautiful cottages year round. Adjacent to the inn, each cottage is bright, cozy and loaded with antiques. Equipped with kitchens and linens, these cottages each sleep six. They rent for $80 per night for two people (add $10 for each additional person and subtract 10 percent for stays of five days and longer).

Eastern Idaho

Teton Valley

Alta Lodge Bed & Breakfast

$ • 590 Targhee Town Rd., Alta, Wyo.
• (307) 353-2582

Teton climbing legend Paul Petzold once owned this property. The story goes that he traded climbing lessons for construction assistance, but the lodge he intended was never finished. When Bob and Judy Blair bought the place in 1989, they tore the half-built structure back down to its foundations and began again.

What the Blairs created was a four-guest-room inn, quiet and comfortable, with Teton views through the 25-foot-tall windows that are the house's eastern wall. The inn has the youthful landscaping of a new home in a spacious subdivision, but you won't care about that once you're inside.

The Blairs and daughter Susie offer quiet comfort, a hot tub and private baths in two of the four rooms. Downstairs in the basement is a big-screen satellite TV with VCR. The Blairs will join you in the living room for conversation. You can also make use of their well-stocked library.

Extra touches include a massive unpeeled lodgepole pine pillar that anchors the vaulted ceiling. One large guest room, called the Grand Room, has windows on three sides and white carpets and walls for an airy, spacious feel.

Rooms do not have TVs. The inn is 6 miles northeast of Driggs, Idaho, on a good dirt road that will barely slow your car.

Pines Motel-Guest Haus

$ • 105 S. Main St., Driggs, Idaho
• (208) 354-2774, (800) 354-2778

Bed and breakfast is an option at John and Nancy Nielson's friendly motel. Well, OK, it's not exactly a motel (but see our Hotels, Motels and Cabins chapter anyway). It's more like a . . . like a — OK, we give up. There's nothing quite like this delightful old building with its handmade matching quilts, lamp shades and curtains in each small, quaint room. Behind the motel you'll find almost an acre of tree-shaded lawn; in front is Driggs's character-packed Main Street with its shops and eateries.

Many of the breakfast offerings are one-of-a-kind, too: Pumpkin waffles get great reviews from guests, as does Blueberry Surprise (we won't ruin the surprise by telling you what it is, but we will say this may be your first chance to have ice cream for breakfast).

For Nancy, taking over the eight-room motel from her parents has meant coming home: She lived in one of the upstairs rooms as a teen. John, who used to run a dairy near here (not fun in Teton Valley's harsh winters, he'll tell you), does all the renovation on the little motel that, the Nielsons explain, has always been a work-in-progress.

Pines Motel-Guest Haus is a 20-minute drive from Grand Targhee, a ski area known for its outstanding powder and short lift lines.

The Refuge Bed and Breakfast

$, no credit cards • 867 S. 450 W., Victor, Idaho • (208) 787-2828

This simple log house, home of Drexel and Sarah Gibson, is the only bed and breakfast inn we know in Teton Valley that's not on the valley floor. It looks down onto the valley from the feet of the Big Hole Mountains. Two no-frills guest rooms share a bath and the upstairs sitting room, which has a computer and fax machine that guests may use. Three cats roam the house. When we were there, the warm smell of popovers filled the living areas downstairs. The Gibsons' home is not easy to find, so call before you head out there. The inn closes in winter, when access is a problem.

Teton Canyon Bed & Breakfast

$$ • Alta N. Rd., Alta, Wyo.
• (307) 353-2208

This massive older log home has four guest rooms with shared baths and a few fun surprises. Long porches run the length of the house, front and back. Neighbors are visible but at a pleasant distance. Massive knotty pine pillars support the high roof. A half-log mantel is suspended by thick rope over a lava rock fireplace. Play chess or Yahtzee downstairs in the living room, or pool or darts upstairs. There's a satellite TV with VCR (house movies are mostly ski flicks, so bring your own if you're looking for something with a plot). The stereo plays CDs, and again, you're welcome to bring your own. These features, as well as the open floor plan of the living and dining areas, makes this a great house for a large group to take over. The outdoor hot tub is open year round. Fresh fruit, juice, toast or bagels, cereal and yogurt are part of every breakfast, but beyond that the meal depends on your tastes. Offerings range from the standard pancakes and eggs to crepes and souffles.

Wilson Creekside Inn

$, no credit cards • Alta N. Rd., Alta, Wyo. • (307) 353-2409

We liked this inn before we even saw it: The drive toward the mouth of Teton Canyon and the Grand Teton, alongside Teton Creek is, well, Teton-ful. Then we saw the sprawling, 3-acre lawn surrounded by a white fence. A profusion of flowers marched around the sides of the house. A hot tub waited on the back deck.

It only got better inside. Each room is pleasantly and simply decorated to remind you of home. Bathrooms are shared. The upstairs rooms are particularly nice with high ceilings and small private balconies.

Surprises are around every corner: a barbed-wire collection, family photos dating back generations, family heirlooms and antiques and the gift shop, a tiny room stuffed with handmade collectibles and gifts. Most of the crafts people represented here are family members and friends.

Another nice surprise comes when you learn that Janice (say it Ja-NEESE) will, on request, cheerfully prepare your evening meal as well as the full breakfast she offers in the mornings.

Church groups and large families will love the largest guest room, a converted garage. It contains nine pull-down bunk beds with space left over.

Janice's inn is only 5 miles from Grand Targhee, just inside the Wyoming border. Janice says that during the busy summer season a month's notice will probably be necessary to secure a room.

INSIDERS' TIP

A great time to come to Jackson is off-season: spring or fall. Vacancies are affordable and easy to find, and restaurants aren't overflowing into the streets.

Island Park, Idaho

Meadow Creek Lodge

$, no credit cards • Big Springs Loop Rd., Island Park • (208) 351-2782 cellular

In winter, 5-year-old Meadow Creek Lodge is accessible only by snowmobile, snowshoes or cross-country skis. Situated north of Big Springs, the big log lodge looks across the snowy valley floor to where distant Sawtelle Mountain peeks through the trees. It's part of a ranch that's been in the Enget family for 100 years. Eight guest rooms are upstairs; they're clean and simple, with private baths and hand-made log beds. Walls are painted white in contrast with dark green carpeting. East-facing rooms look out at the forest and are quieter than west-facing rooms, which look at Henry's Lake Flats and the parking area.

An all-you-can-eat breakfast includes sourdough hotcakes, bacon, eggs and hash browns. Meadow Creek's first floor is open and spacious, with a lounge, bar and restaurant. This stopover is popular with snowmobilers, especially those headed up to Two Top Mountain. Except in emergencies, there is no telephone.

Ashton, Idaho

Jessen's R.V. Park and Bed & Breakfast

$, no credit cards • 1146 S. 3400 E., Ashton, Idaho • (208) 652-3356

Velvet upholstery on the chairs, lace edging on the comforters and matching pillows, floral patterns everywhere: Jessen's small guest rooms are literally crammed with nostalgic comfort. Both rooms have televisions. They share a bedroom-size bath outfitted with a claw-foot tub and an Exercycle.

The rest of the two-story farmhouse is filled with more velvet furniture, well-kept antiques and pictures of the Jessens' large family. It's like a visit to grandma's house.

Nieca and Jack Jessen, your hosts, have been here long enough to seem a part of the 10-acre property, with its wild rose bushes, fruit trees, white gazebo and massive black willow trees. The property also encompasses several guest cottages (breakfast is not included in this option) and an RV park and campground. These accommodations as well as the spacious grounds make Jessen's ideal for family reunions in which different members may prefer different levels of comfort. (See our Hotels, Motels and Cabins chapter and our Campgrounds and RV Parks chapter for more information.)

Stegelmeier Farmhouse Inn

$ • 1357 N. 4350 E., Ashton, Idaho • (208) 652-3363

If you'd like your bed and breakfast stay to include a healthy dose of local history, you are in the right place. Cathy Stegelmeier invites you into the 1912 farmhouse in which her father was born. Out the kitchen window you can see the spot where a sod cabin once stood. Her grandfather was born there. And she'd love to tell you how to find the remains of the dugout home built by her great-grandfather, a trapper and German immigrant named Otto Stegelmeier.

The two-story farmhouse was the first in the area to have an indoor bathroom: At that time it was a simple gravity feed to the tub.

Cathy and her family remodeled the old farmhouse in 1996-97 in order to open its doors to you, so while you'll enjoy her stories and the finely preserved family antiques, you won't lack for comfort or modern amenities. A large deck stretches behind the house, perfect for morning coffee. You'll eat breakfast in a pleasantly modern dining room connected to the kitchen by a bar. Each of the four small but comfortable rooms has its own bathroom (Grandma's room is especially fun with its claw-foot tub and suspended shower curtain).

St. Anthony, Idaho

Riverview B & B

$ • 155 E. Third S., St. Anthony, Idaho • (208) 624-4323

Across the Henry's Fork from the town swimming hole, facing a slow bend in the river, this lushly landscaped bed and breakfast inn has three guest rooms accessed by a back stairway so you don't have to pass through the house to reach your room. Each room has a large bathroom and a fireplace. Other extras include the canoe which guests occasionally

Photo: A Teton Tree House

The view from the window seat of this bed and breakfast room is of the Gros Ventres and a distant mountain that locals call the Sleeping Indian.

borrow, the grassy side yard begging to be picnicked on, the bird feeders here and there, and the second story deck and big main floor windows, both perfect for bird and critter watching. Innkeeper Donna Clark says that in the spring of 1998, 30 trumpeter swans spent about two weeks in the still water in front of the inn, and that a moose lives on the island just upstream. A typical breakfast includes bacon, eggs, toast, fruit and hash browns. The inn is generally closed in winter.

Rexburg, Idaho

Porter House Bed & Breakfast

$ • 4232 W. 1000 N., Rexburg, Idaho • (208) 356-6632

When we walked into Virginia and Craig Porter's home, the smell of fresh bread spread from the kitchen. Somehow, though, it seemed to stop at the door to a startlingly anomalous room. The step through that doorway transported us from a modern country farmhouse to a rustic hunting lodge.

The lodge room is festooned with bear skins and elk, deer and pronghorn antelope mounts. Log rafters span the high ceiling above a massive, river-rock fireplace. The room, in which you are encouraged to relax, is equipped with a TV, VCR and a small selection of movies.

Back in the very unlodge-like farmhouse, Virginia stenciled floral patterns on the guest room walls, most of which have private baths. One of the best features is that three guest rooms downstairs connect to create a wonderful three-bedroom, two-bath suite for families.

Also perfect for families is the expanse of landscaped lawn out front. The swing set and

INSIDERS' TIP

Many bed and breakfast inns are happy to accommodate special dietary needs.

trampoline out back belong to the Porters' kids, but you're welcome to join them.

The inn is close to Teton Lakes Golf Course and is only 10 minutes from U.S. Highway 20, near Rexburg.

Virginia would hate to have you drive out to her place and find it booked up, so she recommends reservations. However, unlike many bed and breakfast inns, Porter House requires no deposit and accepts drop-ins with ease.

Rigby, Idaho

Blacksmith Inn

$ • 227 N. 3900 E., Rigby, Idaho
• (208) 745-6208, (888) 745-6208

Ringed by huge cottonwoods, cedar-sided Blacksmith Inn presides over a swath of lawn and pretty flowerbeds. The building consists of two cylinders with low, conical roofs, connected by more conventional architecture. The nearby farm town of Rigby, Idaho, is about 20 minutes north and east of Idaho Falls.

Inside, a large breakfast room holds several oak tables, and the adjacent sitting room, outfitted with overstuffed couches and Western artist Bev Doolittle's prints, practically begs you to stretch out and relax after breakfast.

Two of six guest rooms have private entrances. Among the niceties are alarm clocks, generous storage areas recessed into the walls and access to the first-floor or second-floor deck. All have large private bathrooms. Beds wear handmade quilts; each room features a wall-sized Western mural by a local artist.

Northwestern Wyoming

Buffalo Valley

The Inn at Buffalo Fork

$$$$ • 18200 E. U.S. Hwy. 287, east of Moran, Wyo. • (307) 543-2010

The Buffalo Valley is a broad, flat expanse of sage, grasses and moose willow. It takes its name from the Buffalo Fork, which winds through it. Sandwiched between the Teton Wilderness to the north and Bridger-Teton National Forest to the south, both valley and river empty into Grand Teton National Park.

The 5-year-old Inn at Buffalo Fork sits on 5 acres of open valley, seemingly contemplating the distant granite masses of Mount Moran and the Grand Teton. In this remote valley with few inhabitants — and little traffic after the summer folks have come and gone — the inn is frequently visited by wildlife, especially moose. The Moran entrance to Grand Teton National Park is only 6 miles away.

Three of five guest rooms offer Teton views, as does the dining room, guest sitting room, the deck and its hot tub. One of the rooms is a suite; its private deck faces the Tetons as well. Flower beds and boxes enliven the exterior of the house.

Gene and Jeannie Ferrin are your innkeepers; he is a fly-fishing guide, and she is a former schoolteacher. Many of the inn's guests fish with Gene. He takes them floating down the Snake River as it slips past his grandfather's old homestead, now part of Grand Teton National Park. The inn is completely surrounded by an 800-acre working cattle ranch, the Hatchet Ranch. In winter guests can watch the hands plow through deep snow on horseback to feed cattle. The inn is near an easy access to the Continental Divide Snowmobile Trail.

Cody, Wyoming

Parson's Pillow

$$ • 1202 14th St., Cody, Wyo.
• (307) 587-2382, (800) 377-2348

Innkeepers Lee and Elly Larabee say, "It's OK to sleep in our church." But before you sleep, you'll want to peek in every little nook and cranny that this converted church hides. In the steeple, you'll find a bathroom decorated cowboy-style with an oak-framed prairie tub and telephone-style shower head. In the Garden Room, you'll find relaxation and roses,

INSIDERS' TIP

Your innkeeper probably knows a lot about must-do activities in the area and almost certainly can provide maps and brochures.

greens and lattice, and a vintage pedestal tub tucked into a cozy corner. In each of the four rooms is a delightful armoire.

Built in 1902 by Methodists (it was Cody's first church), the building has been completely restored and converted. The long, narrow church windows offer lots of light; lace adds a touch of grace. And the Larabees' thoughtful antique selection bespeaks style. A large parlor is always open to guests who want to lounge, read the morning paper, peruse the library shelves, play the piano or the fiddle or, if you must, watch the evening news.

Breakfasts are abundant and delicious.

Windchimes Cottage

$ • 1501 Beck Ave., Cody, Wyo. • (307) 527-5310

Windchimes aren't the only soothing sound at this charming bed and breakfast in a quiet residential neighborhood one block off Cody's Main Street. The wind rustling in the leaves of the giant elm trees and the birds singing in the secluded yard are just what your doctor would order after a day of sightseeing, rafting, hiking or shopping. A native-stone patio invites you to sit for a spell under the old apple tree and sip something cool and soothing to the soul. Owners Hardy and Sylvia Stucki have restored and remodeled this beautiful home using imagination and ingenuity. Each bedspread in the light, airy rooms is hand-quilted by Sylvia. The wallpaper and woodwork, combined with antiques and art, create a cheery space. Families will want to check on the new Jungle Bungalow, a suite in the Stucki's converted garage that is creatively and humorously conceived.

Meals are straight from the farm (read: fresh) and served with a touch of elegance.

Wapiti, Wyoming

Kinkade Guest Cabin

$ • 87 Green Creek Rd., Wapiti, Wyo. • (307) 587-5905

Guests at this off-the-beaten-path bed and breakfast like to linger . . . and often offer to buy the place from co-owner Becky Kinkade, who grew up here. You'll want to stay here just for the Kinkade Guest Cabin's location in the Wapiti Valley. The log cabin, which features open beams and skylights, sits next to Green Creek and is surrounded by a terraced lawn with rock walls. Becky lives in a basement apartment below the house. Upstairs, two bedrooms, each with a bath, are separated by a sun room with a player piano. Both rooms open into a dining/living area.

Becky gives guests the option of cooking their own breakfast or having her serve them. A native of Park County (her father was sheriff), Kinkade can clue you in to local lore and Insider information. Both rooms rented together cost $100. Becky also has a big barn with bunks and showers that she rents for $10 per person per night. And she rents a sheep wagon. Because she operates on reservations-only, Becky can be flexible enough to rent all or part of her accommodations for as long as you like.

INSIDERS' TIP

Some bed and breakfast inns serve afternoon snacks or even make dinner on request. These services can be particularly pleasant at more remote inns. Ask when you make your reservation.

To experience what is unique to Yellowstone country, stay in a resort or lodge. These places have made mountain surroundings and mountain recreation as integral to vacation lodging as the bathtub or the bed.

Resorts and Lodges

Early Yellowstone area settlers eked livelihoods from the wilderness. They trapped, farmed with irrigation water diverted from the mighty Snake and other rivers, grazed cattle in alpine meadows, mined the mountain's mineralized bones and harvested her trees. And from the earliest pioneering days, particularly around Yellowstone National Park, locals served tourists drawn by the presence of wilderness.

More recent imports also feel connected to mountains, no longer because they feed us — that's becoming less practical — but because we play in them. We ski, bike, hike, fish, climb, hunt, boat, snowmobile and golf. We still serve tourists, but today's visitors don't want simply to see mountains but also to recreate in them. So, although our region offers standard lodging options as well as more intimate bed and breakfast inns, that's not where you can experience what is unique to Yellowstone country. For that, try a resort or lodge. These are the places that have made mountain surroundings and mountain recreation as integral to vacation lodging as the bathtub or the bed.

Resorts and lodges offer both a roof and activities. At most, you'll pay for recreation separately, à la carte. We'll refer to these as European-plan resorts. American-plan resorts, less common and of course more expensive, charge a single lump fee for lodging, meals, and often activities as well. Establishments often specialize; we've listed fishing lodges, ski resorts and even, for the more civilized, golf and tennis resorts. Some lodges also offer a range of options, say horseback riding, mountain biking, rafting, volleyball and fishing. Many lodges and resorts are home to restaurants; others provide family-style meals at long, friendly tables. What ties these diverse establishments together is that they make playing in Yellowstone country easy.

To help you choose the resort or lodge best-suited to your tastes, we've provided a price code (see the gray box) derived from information supplied by the establishments. Codes represent the lowest high-season charge for a two-person, one-night stay. For most lodges, the high season is summer; for ski resorts, winter. Fishing lodges are generally busiest in late summer and fall. If à la carte prices are available (European plan), that's what we provide. In that case, the price we indicate represents your lodging cost only: Activities and meals are separate. If a resort's price includes meals and/or activities (American plan), they'll look very expensive, but may not be: Read our descriptions carefully to find what your dollars buy. Some American-plan resorts serve up all activities and meals for one charge; others supply only breakfast and snacks. If price is important to you, call and check for special packages or seasonal rates.

Price Code

$	$60 to $90
$$	$91 to $140
$$$	$141 to $200
$$$$	$201 and more

Grand Teton National Park

Grand Teton Lodge Company operates three lodge facilities in Grand Teton National Park: Jenny Lake Lodge, Colter Bay Village and Jackson Lake Lodge. The park's largest concessionaire also operates tour buses, a golf course and more. From any of its facilities you can book activities at any other. And don't worry about driving: The Grand Teton Lodge Company buses will get you where you need to go.

Jenny Lake Lodge

$$$$ (American plan) • Teton Park Rd. at Jenny Lake • (307) 733-4647, (800) 628-9988

The exquisite fine dining and 37 cabins of Jenny Lake Lodge constitute perhaps the only place on earth to which the words elegant and rustic both apply. The original six buildings date to 1922, when Tony Grace homesteaded 160 acres in what was not yet Grand Teton National Park.

Folks who know rave about Jenny Lake Lodge's culinary delights, which you'll definitely sample since your room rate includes both breakfast and dinner (see our Restaurants chapter). Others point out that Jenny Lake Lodge is the only luxury accommodation within Grand Teton that has managed to retain a secluded, rugged feel. It wasn't easy: When a steel support roof was added to reinforce the original lodge so it would safely hold winter snowloads, it had to be carefully concealed above the old log ceiling.

Your cabin has a private bath and distinctive handmade quilts on the bed. You'll enjoy other thoughtful touches, such as those two umbrellas in the corner of your cabin. The main lodge has a small store and tiny lending library. The concierge can set you up with golf or tennis, whitewater and flatwater float trips on the Snake River, guided fishing, cruises of Jackson Lake and more. Horseback riding and bicycling are included in your daily rate.

Despite the heavy price tag, Jenny Lake Lodge is wildly popular both for its accommodations and dining. Short-notice availability is rare; many make their reservations a year in advance. The return rate is around 60 percent. The lodge is open from the end of May to early October.

Jackson Lake Lodge

$$ (European plan) • U.S. Hwy. 89 at Jackson Lake Junction • (307) 543-2811, (800) 628-9988

This huge lodge complex sits on a bluff overlooking Jackson Lake. Some areas offer a fine view of Mount Moran, from this angle more spectacular than the Grand Teton herself. Nevertheless, staying here is not a wilderness experience. Thirty-six rooms occupy the blocky, mountainous main lodge building, which also contains various shops, two restaurants and a bar (see our Restaurants chapter).

The lounge, with its famous picture-window view of Moran, is built on a scale to rival the mountain itself. You could host a small wedding in each of the two massive fireplaces. Scattering out from the lodge are dozens of motel buildings — the "cottage" accommodations. Rooms are pleasantly shaded by spruce and fir, and many have log privacy walls at their entrances. In the evening, you can order a box lunch to carry with you on your adventures the next day.

Jackson Lake Lodge offers horseback riding, including breakfast and dinner rides (wranglers cook the meal over a fire) and trail rides of varying lengths. The lodge also hosts boat rides on Jackson Lake, Snake River float trips, bus tours of Grand Teton and Yellowstone parks and a lifeguarded swimming pool. Use of the pool is free to guests, but other activities are à la carte. Accommodations are available from mid-May to mid-October.

Colter Bay Village and Marina

$ (European plan) • U.S. Hwy. 89 on east shore of Jackson Lake • (307) 543-2811, (800) 628-9988

Calling itself a "family resort," Colter Bay offers accommodations of every imaginable sort. You may stay in the Park Service campground, the RV park or the refurbished older log cabins that lie along roads stacking up the hill to the most offbeat option: cabin tents. A cabin tent is canvas and log with a canvas roof and a concrete floor. Bunks pull out from the walls (you can rent sleeping bags and mattresses). Each has a covered outdoor cooking area for rainy-day dinners. The more conventional cabins are simply furnished, Western style. You also get use of a communal lounge cabin.

Many activities are available at Colter Bay, all at additional charge except for Park Service programs like the nightly campfire programs at the amphitheater in Colter Bay Campground. Colter Bay Village Corral offers breakfast and dinner rides as well as trail rides of varying lengths. Breakfast trout-fry and scenic cruises on Jackson Lake originate from the marina daily, as do evening steak-fry trips.

Other services at Colter Bay include a laundry, showers, snack bar, grocery store, gas station, fishing tackle, gift and clothing shops and two restaurants. Colter Bay opens near the end of May and closes the end of September.

Flagg Ranch Resort

$$ (European plan) • U.S. Hwy. 89 on John D. Rockefeller Jr. Memorial Pkwy. • (307) 543-2861, (800) 443-2311

Find Flagg Ranch on the map and it appears to be nothing in the middle of nowhere. Perhaps that's why it's so popular. Situated on a narrow, 9-mile-long gooseneck between Yellowstone and Grand Teton parks, Flagg Ranch is a bustling tourist center with RV park, cabin and motel accommodations and a tempting array of activities — in the middle of nowhere. Motel rooms look across a grassy river frontage to the Snake River. They're in three two-story buildings connected by wooden boardwalks with glass doors that open toward the river. Although rooms have no phones and no TVs, they are standard motel fare in every other way.

The nicest rooms here are in the duplex or four-plex cabins clustered into a cabin town. These newer log buildings have baseboard heat, full baths, coffee makers and phones. Their vaulted ceilings add to the impression of spaciousness. If you stay here, ask about the cabins that occupy a low ridge overlooking the Snake; they each have private decks with wooden rocking chairs and a bit more room.

Activities include short whitewater trips in Flagg Canyon and longer scenic floats lower on the Snake. You can also trail ride in summer and snowmobile or ride the resort snowcoach into Yellowstone in winter. All involve additional charge. Other reasons to come to Flagg Ranch include: a pleasant restaurant in the large, rustic-modern lodge building; a gift shop; and the entire Greater Yellowstone, in the middle of which this resort is uniquely and centrally located.

Signal Mountain Lodge

$ (European plan) • Teton Park Rd. on south shore of Jackson Lake
• (307) 543-2831

This is the only major lodge facility in Grand Teton Park not run by Grand Teton Lodge Company. The general feel is pleasant, a bit quieter than other communities in the park. You have several accommodations options. The least expensive are the simply furnished log cabins, some with fireplaces. You can also choose from motel rooms and lakefront apartments, some of which have fireplaces, too. The lakefront apartments are spacious and newer, opening onto decks that face Jackson Lake.

The main lodge building has big windows and a large deck facing the lake. A short walk from the lodge takes you to The Aspens dining room and the Cottonwood Café; between the two, you can get breakfast, lunch and dinner. The house specialty at Aspens Lounge is huckleberry Margaritas. We recommend you eat (or drink) on the deck if the weather is nice.

Also at Signal Mountain are a clothing store, gift shop, service station, convenience store and marina. The marina offers boat rentals, guest buoys and guided fishing trips. The lodge can also take you and your family on a 10-mile scenic float on the Snake River. These activities are all at additional charge. Signal Mountain Lodge is open from mid-May to mid-October.

Jackson Hole

Rusty Parrot Lodge

$$$$ (American plan) • 175 N. Jackson St., Jackson, Wyo.
• (307) 733-2000, (800) 458-2004

If we had to pick our three favorite upscale accommodations options in the Jackson/Grand Tetons area, they'd be Jenny Lake Lodge, the Wort Hotel and the Rusty Parrot. Jenny Lake Lodge made rusticness luxurious, the Wort is a classic with class, and Ron Harrison's Rusty Parrot just couldn't have been done any better. Perfect isn't a word to use lightly, so maybe we'd better explain. First, the lobby and dining room: Imagine white walls and hallways with adobe-style curved corners, accented with hand-turned log. Imagine emerald carpet and a river-rock fireplace where the flames never flicker out from October to May.

Upstairs in your room, imagine down comforters, handmade Mexican tile in the bathroom, woven willow screens on the closet doors and an outdoor hot tub on the tiled roof. A few rooms have in-room hot tubs; half are warmed by fireplaces (the staff lays the fire for you). If the word "rustic" came to mind when you imagined logs and fireplaces, kick it back out and let's talk breakfast. Chef Magnus Hansson serves up breakfasts like whole-grain wheatberry pancakes with seasonal fruits, raspberry-cinnamon maple syrup and apple-smoked bacon. Or scrambled eggs with pesto and prosciutto di Parma served with a croissant.

Last but not least, there's the staff. Ron

tells us that, besides being professional and friendly, there's almost no reasonable request they won't accommodate.

Snow King Resort

$$ (European plan) • 400 E. Snow King Ave., Jackson, Wyo. • (307) 733-5200, (800) 522-5464

This is Jackson's in-town ski hill and resort (see our Winter Sports chapter). The resort was built in 1976 and recently renovated. Accommodations include condominiums and a hotel at the base of Rafferty Chairlift. Furnishings are Western, accented with pine and log. Stay in one of the 204 rooms in the seven-story hotel building and you'll have use of the year-round outdoor heated pool, sauna, two whirlpools and exercise room.

Not included in your room price but worth stopping by are the ice-skating rink, gift shops, The Atrium Cafe and Shady Lady Saloon. Other activities available on the premises in summer include mountain biking, miniature golf and an alpine slide. You can also buy a ticket up the lift in summer to access Panorama House, a restaurant that serves up a spectacular view.

Spring Creek Ranch

$$$$ (European plan) • 1800 Spirit Dance Rd., Jackson, Wyo. • (307) 733-8833, (800) 443-6139

Head out of Jackson toward Wilson and Teton Pass, then turn off on Spring Gulch Road: You'll immediately begin winding up into sage-covered hills. It feels like you're headed for wilderness — until you roll over the top of East Gros Ventre Butte and see the condos, neat lawns and houses of Spring Creek Ranch.

This upscale resort sits on 1,000 acres of a wildlife preserve overlooking Jackson Hole 700 feet below. Enjoy the views on horseback. Swim in the pool, soak in the hot tubs and play tennis. In winter, ski the resort's groomed Nordic trails. The concierge will competently and cheerfully book you into a staggering variety of other activities in the area. In fact, "cheerful" seems to be the staff motto: It's hard to sneak past a Spring Creek employee without receiving a smile and a pleasant nod.

Accommodations range from hotel rooms and condos to suites and homes that accommodate up to eight people. Prices range clear up to $1,400 per night. All are luxurious in a Western sort of way and include fireplaces, refrigerators, remote-control cable TV and coffee makers. Some have fully equipped kitchens and washer/dryers. Even the houses get daily maid service. Convention facilities are available, as are various kinds of activities packages. Spring Creek is open year round.

Make sure you check out The Granary while you're here: The only thing better than the food and the wine list at this fine dining restaurant is the view (see our Restaurants chapter).

Lone Eagle Resort

$ (European plan) • U.S. Hwy. 89 near Hoback Junction, Wyo. • (307) 733-1090, (800) 321-3800

Drive under the totem pole arch and down a dirt road lined with buck-and-rail fence. Just after you cross the Hoback River on a narrow bridge, you'll enter civilization in the middle of wilderness: the RV and cabin resort of Lone Eagle. The grounds are immaculate, grassy and illuminated by electric lanterns at night. The resort has basketball and volleyball, an outdoor swimming pool, a laundry facility, hot tubs, a snack shop/convenience store, a gift shop and a casting pond. You could picnic on the sparkling clean floors of the tiled shower rooms.

Lone Eagle offers overnight visits and special rates on longer stays. Accommo-

INSIDERS' TIP

In Yellowstone country, the difference between a resort and a motel can be little more than the name. Check our Hotels, Motels and Cabins chapter for more lodging establishments, some of which help you find your fun in addition to supplying the roof over your head.

dations range from your own tent or RV, to simple, newer log cabins, to what Lone Eagle calls deluxe guest houses — the only accommodations option with private bathrooms. Meals are prepared by the staff at this à la carte resort. There's a barn dance with a live band every Saturday night. You can enjoy whitewater fun on the Snake River or zipping around Palisades Reservoir on a personal watercraft, plus two- and three-day guided adventures in the Wind Rivers on four-wheelers, foot, bike or horseback. The resort does not provide bikes or backpacks. Meals and activities cost extra, but use of facilities is included in your lodging price.

Teton Pines Resort

$$$ (European plan) • 3450 N. Clubhouse Dr., Jackson, Wyo.
• (307) 733-1005, (800) 238-2223

Smack in the middle of flamboyantly rustic, neon-Western Jackson Hole is an elegant little resort — only 22 guest rooms — with an Arnold Palmer-designed golf course, indoor and outdoor tennis, 14 kilometers of groomed cross-country ski trails in winter, spacious accommodations and aspen-dotted landscaping. In winter special rates can make this resort surprisingly affordable. Ask about winter value rates nearly two-thirds lower than the peak summer rate. Guests take advantage of the stocked casting pond below the clubhouse and engage the services of the Jack Dennis Fly Fishing School for a little brushing up or a brand-new hobby. Your room rate buys reduced greens fees and preferred golf starting times, access to tennis courts, the outdoor swimming pool, hot tub and Aspens Athletic Club's racquetball courts and workout equipment. Continental breakfast is served every morning in the clubhouse.

A full bar and fine-dining restaurant are also on the premises (for a tip on après ski at Teton Pines clubhouse, see our Nightlife chapter). Teton Pines Resort is closer to Teton Village than to the town of Jackson, so your location is perfect for winter skiing as well as summer golfing.

Jackson Hole Mountain Resort

Teton Village, Wyo. • (307) 733-2292

Jackson Hole Mountain Resort has no accommodations of its own. If you want to stay here, check our Hotels, Motels and Cabins and our Vacation Rentals chapters for options. What it does have in winter are two mountains' worth of skiing (more on this in our Winter Sports chapter) and dinner sleigh rides out to a remote cabin for a four-course meal. You can also enjoy the 17-kilometer Nordic track or take a guided cross-country trek into Grand Teton and Yellowstone parks. In summer, enjoy horseback riding, aerial tram rides and a lineup of great music festivals and other events. By the way, don't get confused when you hear the ski hill referred to as Jackson Hole, which is actually the name of the valley, or Teton Village, which is actually the name of a cluster of tourist facilities, of which Jackson Hole Mountain Resort is one.

Surrounding Areas

Southwestern Montana

The Bar N Ranch

$$$$ (American plan) • Targhee Pass Hwy., 5 miles west of West Yellowstone, Mont., off U.S. Hwy. 20
• (406) 646-7121, (800) BIGSKYS

Inside, the Bar N Ranch lodge oozes luxury. Giant Douglas fir beams, solid-brass fixtures, a wide, sweeping split-log staircase and deep, cushy couches in the high-ceilinged living room of this lodge, built in 1997, conjure up images of formal balls and black-tie dinners in days gone by.

INSIDERS' TIP

Many Greater Yellowstone attractions become extremely congested. If you want to enjoy these places under less-crowded conditions, come early in the day and avoid July and August. With the most popular destinations, your best bets are spring and fall weekdays.

Don't dress up, though, because outside you'll find a relaxed ranch atmosphere.

The Bar N occupies a square mile of land, including 5 miles of frontage on the South Fork of the Madison River and four fishing ponds. Owned by the Kephart family of Philadelphia since the turn of the century, the Bar N Ranch is just 5 miles from Yellowstone National Park. In 1997, the owners moved their guest quarters out of the old ranch house and into the 10,000-square-foot, three-story lodge. With eight rooms (including the Hound Dog Hideaway, a third-floor apartment that sleeps up to 15) and four cabins, this is the perfect place for a corporate retreat, honeymoon or a family vacation.

Each room, named and decorated in honor of family members and former ranch employees, is uniquely decorated with mostly Montana antiques and art. Most have Jacuzzis, some have private balconies, and all have fireplaces. Meals (country-style comfort food interspersed with an outside barbecue and weekly gourmet dining) are included in the room price.

Summer evenings, you might dine to piano music and sing along around the fireplace after dinner. Also included in the room price are minimal ranch activities such as the use of rowboats, a paddleboat, inner tubes and a small sailboat. Self-guided fishing on the nearby river or in the ponds is also free. During the winter, the Bar N offers unlimited cross-country skiing and short dogsled rides on the ranch. No snowmobile rentals are available; you can either bring your own or travel in the ranch's mini-snowcoach (dubbed "Miss Kitty") 5 miles to West Yellowstone.

Big Sky Ski and Summer Resort

$$$ (European plan) • Mountain Village, Big Sky, Mont. • (406) 995-5000, (800) 548-4486

Big Sky Resort owners like to say even a ski-buff couldn't tire of their trails in a week of solid skiing. And snowboarders can't help but like Big Sky's new state-of-the-art terrain park equipped all the essentials: piped-in music, snowmaking capabilities and a slopeside party deck. In celebration of Big Sky's 25th anniversary in 1999, resort owners have added runs, built more condominiums and opened more shops.

This snow-play mecca caters to families. For each adult who buys a ticket, two children 10 and younger can ski free. (Adult tickets cost $48.) Those who stay at the Big Sky condos can also take advantage of free evening entertainment. Big Sky has 850 rooms — 4,000 pillows nightly — and is owned by Boyne USA Resorts.

The dream of the late NBC news anchor Chet Huntley, Big Sky opened in March 1974. Today Big Sky offers quality, quantity, convenience and year-round recreation galore. In winter, it's skiing: 3,500 acres of terrain accessed by 15 lifts built to accommodate 18,000 skiers an hour. Snowmobilers will find groomed trails and off-trail opportunities. And nearby Lone Mountain Guest Ranch has 65 kilometers of groomed cross-country ski trails.

In summer, it's golf at an 18-hole, par 72 golf course, swimming at the Huntley Lodge and tennis club, rafting on the Gallatin River, hiking or biking in the backcountry, horseback riding, touring Yellowstone National Park (it's a 30-minute drive from Big Sky) and fishing blue-ribbon streams.

The Huntley Lodge and Shoshone Condominium Hotel, owned by the Big Sky Resort, have a combined 294 rooms. The Shoshone Condominiums feature loft and one-bedroom suites, while the adjoining lodge has 200 guest rooms. You can also choose from an assortment of condominiums. In the year 2000, Big Sky will have completed its latest accommodation addition: Summit Hotel, a 10-story luxury complex of suites, rooms, shops, and more.

INSIDERS' TIP

Whether you stay at Jackson Lake Lodge in Grand Teton or not, a stop at the main lodge building will not disappoint. The massive picture window view of Mount Moran is rightfully famous.

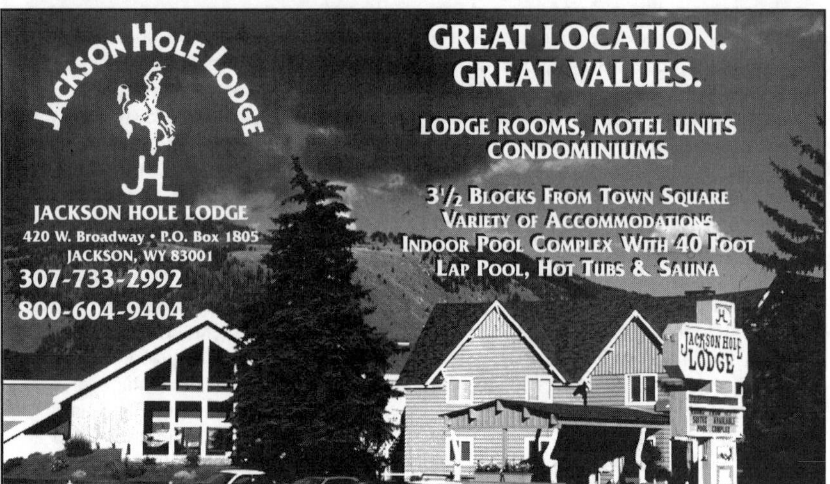

Chico Hot Springs Lodge

$ (European plan) • Pray, Mont.
• (406) 333-4933, (800) HOT-WADA

Tucked into a nook of the Paradise Valley 30 miles north of Yellowstone National Park, Chico Hot Springs has a reputation for excellence as far away as the East Coast and across the Atlantic. As famous as it is, Chico is an affordable paradise with accommodations options ranging from Victorian-themed rooms without baths to plush suites with custom-made hardwood furniture. Built at the turn of the century, Chico has been restored to its former glory and then some. Sweeping lawns and plump perennial gardens surround the sprawling Victorian-era hotel, which houses the Chico Inn (a world-famous restaurant featured in our Restaurants chapter), the hot spring pool, the Poolside Grill, a bar and an array of refurbished rooms in the Main Lodge.

The inn offers other accommodations (there are 90 in all) on the 150-acre property. The Lower Lodge, built in 1996, is home to 16 plush, spacious units with custom-made Mission-style oak furniture. Units in the Lower Lodge range from upscale standard rooms to two bedroom suites with kitchens. The Upper Lodge, a modern motel on a hill overlooking the Main Lodge, looks like any other motel you might stay in. Chico also offers five log cottages furnished with log furniture. Fully-equipped condos and houses sleep from two to 20 guests. There are no telephones or televisions in the rooms, but you will find an unusual landing strip if you want to fly in for a stay. After radioing ahead to the Lodge, pilots land on the secluded county road leading to Chico. Construction of a 300-person convention hall should be completed by the spring of 1999.

The Chico Inn is known for its exceptional food served in elegant Western style. The more casual Poolside Grille serves lunch and dinner. The Chico Saloon rocks with live bands on the weekends and is a comfortable place to hang out the rest of the week. The bar caters to the *Monday Night Football* crowd with two big-screen TVs.

Besides its 104-degree hot spring pool,

INSIDERS' TIP

All Grand Teton Lodge Company facilities (Jenny Lake Lodge, Jackson Lake Lodge, Colter Bay and others) close down for the winter, although around 30 year-round staff members winter at Jackson Lake Lodge, preparing for the spring season.

Chico features horseback riding, fishing at a private lake, hiking, mountain biking, river rafting, cross-country skiing (you can rent skis here), dogsled tours, and massage therapy — all for extra fees. Chico Hot Springs also has a children's activity program for kids ages 5 to 12. This program includes arts and crafts, gardening, noncompetitive sports, nature walks and educational games.

The Firehole Ranch

$$$$ (American plan) • 11500 Hebgen Lake Rd., West Yellowstone, Mont. • (406) 646-7294

In Yellowstone country, when you have to drive 14 miles on a dirt road to get to a lodge, you just know that at the end of the trail you're going to find someplace special. That's just what we found at The Firehole Ranch. Surrounded by National Forest lands and situated in a lush meadow that leads right to the banks of Hebgen Lake, The Firehole Ranch is an angler's dream. While guests can opt for horseback riding, mountain biking, hiking or canoeing, most prefer to fish all day every day on every blue-ribbon stream in Yellowstone.

After a hearty gourmet breakfast in Firehole's cozy 50-year-old lodge, you'll stroll to the lake — chances are you'll see a moose along the way — and ride a 30-foot pontoon boat to the other side where nine professional fishing guides wait to lead you to the fishing paradise of your choice. And, after a day of reeling 'em in, you can look forward to cocktail hour in the lodge followed by a gourmet dinner cooked up by chef Bruno Georgeton. Georgeton works for broadcasting magnate Ted Turner when he is not at the Firehole Ranch.

Firehole accommodates 20 guests in 10 spacious, updated cabins that come with carpet, plush upscale furniture, wood stoves, modern bathrooms and private decks. This dream ranch has a 100-percent occupancy rate and an 85-percent return rate. To secure reservations, it's best to call at least a year (and maybe more) ahead of time. Because prospective guests are required to pay a hefty deposit in January, you may be able to pick up someone else's cancellation for the coming season after New Year's. The Firehole Ranch, open from the first week in June until the end of September, has a minimum four-night-stay requirement, and stays must begin or end on a Saturday. Nightly rates include lodging, three meals, beverages, open bar and all ranch activities except guided fishing trips.

The Hibernation Station

$$$ • 212 Gray Wolf Ave., West Yellowstone, Mont. • (406) 646-4200, (800) 580-3557

Chances are you won't want to get out of bed once you sleep between the country-fresh sheets topped with a goose-down comforter at The Hibernation Station. They're so cozy and homey that, once you get out of bed, you may not want to leave your cabin. All 30 picture-perfect cabins, built with big, fire-killed Douglas fir logs, are unique — no cookie-cutter cabins here. Each has at least one tapestry-covered wall and hand-hewn log furniture. Each has some carpet accented with tile. Some have fireplaces, a few have kitchenettes and a few have spas and fireplaces. Most are one-room, one-bath units approximately 16-foot-by-22-foot. But there are also a few two-bedroom cabins with kitchens, as well as several king suites.

The Hibernation Station, which opened in 1993, is still evolving, which means you'll see signs of construction around the complex. The owners have so far built 10 cabins each year, and they plan to keep on going until they have 55 cabins and a huge lodge. Situated at the south edge of town, The Hibernation Station is within easy walking distance of the Grizzly Discovery Center and the Yellowstone IMAX Theater (see our Attractions chapter). Snowmobiles and clothing are available, and the place has easy access to Yellowstone's West Entrance and all other trails.

Rainbow Ranch Lodge

$$ (European plan) • 5 miles south of the Big Sky, Mont., entrance on U.S. Hwy. 191 • (406) 995-4132, (800) 937-4132

Known in the 1920s as the Halfway Inn — it's midway between Bozeman and

Yellowstone National Park — the newly renovated Rainbow Ranch Lodge offers travelers a taste of the New West with a twist of the Old. Twenty-one rooms, each with lodgepole beds, down comforters, heavy canvas curtains and deep, comfortable chairs and couches, have decks overlooking the Gallatin River below.

The lodge itself, which is surrounded by beautiful landscaping, has a custom-made bar, a comfortable lounge and gourmet dining so popular with locals and guests from other ranches you'd better call ahead for a reservation if you plan to arrive around dinner time. Meals are not included in the room rates. For breakfast and lunch you'll have to go elsewhere. The Corral across the highway serves great food at a reasonable price.

If you're interested in horseback riding — there are trails galore in the Gallatin Canyon — Diamond K Outfitters operate from corrals at the Rainbow Ranch Lodge. They offer two-hour, half-day or all-day rides. They also offer Western horsemanship lessons, evening dinner rides and daylong backcountry fishing trips. Diamond K also runs overnight to six-day, full-service tent-camping pack trips into Yellowstone National Park backcountry.

Rock Creek Resort

$ • U.S. Hwy 212 S., Red Lodge, Mont.
• (406) 446-1111, (800) 667-1119

The Beartooth Lodge lobby, with its massive river-rock fireplace, antler chandelier and grand arched windows, invites guests to relax at this elegant but reasonably priced resort on the banks of beautiful Rock Creek. This resort has been evolving since the 1970s when former Olympic skier Pepi Gramshammer began adding to the Piney Dell restaurant and cabins already existing. To house students at his international summer race camp, he first built the Grizzly Condos and Townhouses. The Rock Creek Resort has since grown into a favorite for family reunions, corporate retreats, seminars and weddings. It's also a favorite for those traveling to Yellowstone National Park or skiing at Red Lodge Mountain.

Gramshammer built an array of suites, condos, townhomes and standard rooms that can connect side to side or from floor to floor. That means the accommodations combinations are endless. Decor themes include Native American, Southwestern, Mexican and Guatemalan with Western thrown in. When you aren't relaxing, there's plenty to do here. Inside are a health club with a heated swimming pool, Jacuzzi, exercise room and sauna. Outdoors, you'll find tennis courts, a soccer field, playground, volleyball, horseshoes and a catch-and-release fishing pond. Winter, cross-country ski and snowshoe rentals are available. The Piney Dell Restaurant is well known for its fine food. And the Fine Gift Emporium in the Twin Elk Lodge promises to put a twitch in your check-writing fingers.

Yellowstone Valley Ranch

$$$$ (American plan) • U.S. Hwy. 89, south of Livingston, Mont.
• (406) 333-4787, (800) 626-3526

There is one thing that can tear an angler away from a hot blue-ribbon fly-fishing stream. That's the promise of a fabulous supper simmering on the stove in the ranch kitchen. Anglers will find both, and more, at the Yellowstone Valley Ranch south of Livingston. Don't think "ranch" as in old and rustic. Think "ranch" as in comfortable and quietly elegant.

World-class trout fishing on privately leased and fish-for-fee spring creeks is the calling card of this ranch overlooking the Yellowstone River and the Absaroka Mountains. In case you or your spouse are not into fishing, though, the

INSIDERS' TIP

The reason you can stay in guest ranches and lodges on private land within Grand Teton National Park is because of the piecemeal way park lands were acquired. Yellowstone National Park was created by one flourish of a pen, but much of Grand Teton was purchased over a period of years, mostly by John D. Rockefeller Jr., and then ceded back to the people.

Yellowstone Valley Ranch offers an alternative outdoor adventure package that includes horseback riding, mountain biking, naturalist-led hikes, guided tours of Yellowstone National Park and introductory lessons in kayaking and canoeing. No matter what you choose to do each day, at the end of it you'll find dinner waiting at the lodge.

Here you can choose when you want to eat (as long as it's between 6:30 and 9:30 PM) and you can select from three entrees (seafood, pasta or beef based) prepared by chef Dave Rees. Rees, who concocts new creations and old favorites depending on the season and his whim, came with the Yellowstone Valley Ranch when owners Steve and Taffy McGrath and John and Nancy Boisvert bought it in 1993.

The Yellowstone Valley Ranch has 10 rooms, each with two queen beds and a private patio overlooking the river. The Ranch offers six-night, five-day packages that begin on Saturday and end on Friday. Included in the price are transportation to and from the airport, meals, lodging and guided fishing trips or the adventure trips mentioned above. Options are available for shorter stays. For children's rates, we recommend the same since the owners will negotiate rates depending on their ages and lodging arrangements.

Eastern Idaho

Teton Valley

Grand Targhee Ski and Summer Resort

$$ (European plan) • Ski Hill Rd., Alta, Wyo. • (307) 353-2300, (800) 827-4433

The decor at this homegrown ski resort is Western and so is the hospitality. Choose from standard rooms at Targhee Lodge or open-loft condos in Sioux Loft Condominiums or the deluxe Teewinot Lodge. Grand Targhee has won awards for the cozy design of its ski village.

Summer activities include mountain biking (rentals are available). Take the ski lift to the top and let gravity do the work. You can also enjoy horseback riding (you can take Western- or English-style lessons), tennis, volleyball, horseshoes, Frisbee golf, swimming, hot tubbing, an adventure ropes course and the small fitness center. Massage and aromatherapy are available at the spa. In winter, Grand Targhee offers ski packages.

Several dining establishments are available, summer and winter. For locals, the biggest reasons to go to Targhee in summer are the two music festivals, both held in July (see our Annual Events chapter).

Except for use of the pool, exercise room and hot tubs, you'll pay extra for activities and meals. In winter, a variety of evening social activities are free, including ice skating if you have your own skates (you can rent if not). For a fee, winter activities such as snowshoe tours, dog sledding and sleigh-ride dinners are also available. (For more about skiing at Grand Targhee, see our Winter Sports chapter.)

Teton Valley Lodge

$$$$ (American plan) • 379 Adams Rd., Driggs, Idaho • (208) 354-2386

You won't be roughing it. This upscale fishing lodge charges top dollar with good reason: Prices cover meals, spacious cabin lodging, guide service, flies and leaders, transportation, soft drinks and beer. If you get back late from fishing and would like dinner served in your cabin, just ask. Cabins — they look more like houses — face the Teton River across a well-kept strip of lawn. Some are smaller and appropriate for couples. Others can accommodate up to three couples. All have four-poster beds and pine paneling. Most have living rooms, wet bars and wood stoves. All have covered porches from which to watch the river.

Dry-fly fishing specialist since 1938, Teton Valley Lodge attracts the serious angler. The Teton River, Henry's Fork and Snake's South Fork are well-suited for dry-fly fishing. Teton Valley Lodge guides float those rivers and can also show you great wading areas on the Teton, Fall River and Henry's Fork. With a total of 17 river sections to fish, you can use up all your vacation time and not fish the same spot twice. An average fishing day nets 60 fish per boat. The lodge record is 206.

The lodge is open May through October, with a special "Cast and Blast" option that starts with the opening of grouse season.

Teton Teepee Lodge

$$$$ (American plan) in winter, $ (European plan) in summer • Ski Hill Rd., Alta, Wyo.
• (307) 353-8176, (800) 353-8176

Fifteen minutes from powder heaven at Grand Targhee and 45 from the dramatic vertical rise of Jackson Hole Mountain Resort is the ultimate ski lodge. The Melehes brothers and their partner, Brent Palmer, promise to do everything for you but carve your turns. You pay a flat fee (a three-night minimum is requested), and your lift tickets, transportation, accommodations, all-you-can-eat breakfast, dinner and beverages are included. That makes what looks like a steep price extremely reasonable.

In the evenings, relax around the huge fireplace, watch videos on the big-screen TV or warm your bones in the hot tub. Kids enjoy the game room and the un-hotel-like freedom to wander around the lodge and play. Teton Teepee even takes care of your social life during your ski vacation: The lodge's 18 rooms all open into the huge, teepee-like interior of the lodge. You'll meet everyone there in no time. And don't worry if the music and merriment don't sound fun to you tonight: Your room is equipped with not one but two doors to block out the noise.

For a real social experience, rent the dormitories downstairs. Each bunk bed is equipped with locker space and shower access. School and Scout groups love it. In summer Teton Teepee operates much as a hotel, although it also hosts weddings, conferences and reunions. If you're visiting in summer, we recommend you take advantage of the lodge's bike rentals and maybe even participate in a guided bike trip. The staff will take care of your transportation and snacks and show you the prettiest rides (see our Other Recreation chapter).

Swan Valley

The Lodge at Palisades Creek

$$$$ (American plan) • 3720 Hwy. 26 east of Irwin, Idaho • (208) 483-2222

Anglers book their visits here a year in advance — and with good reason. Nowhere else in Swan Valley can you revel in such secluded, pleasantly upscale cabins or dine on delicacies like those that come from chef Elizabeth Olsen's ever-changing menu. The main lodge is a sunlit building where you can visit with other guests or enjoy a quiet drink. You'll float the adjacent South Fork of the Snake every day with the lodge's fishing guides, catching nearly as many big, beautiful trout as you dreamed about the night before. Other extra touches include nightly linen turndowns and a bottle of complimentary Idaho wine to celebrate your arrival.

A four-day minimum stay is requested between July 1 and September 1. The lodge's season runs from early June to mid-October. The base rate includes lodging, meals, your guide and his boat. For those in your party who don't fish, lower rates and scenic trips in the area can be arranged. If you like more room, be sure to ask about the two-bedroom A-frame house with deck over the river.

South Fork Lodge

$$$$ (American plan) • 40 Conant Valley Loop, Swan Valley, Idaho
• (208) 483-2112, (800) 483-2110

The Snake River, literally jumping with trophy-size native cutthroats, winds past South Fork Lodge through cottonwood flats. Fishing packages include motel-style lodging, meals and guided fishing. The 19 rooms also can be rented by the night on a walk-in basis during fishing season (when they're expensive) and are reservable without a fishing package outside of fishing season (when they're cheaper).

Spence Warner, whose family owned this lodge for decades, recently sold to Mark Rockefeller, son of Nelson Rockefeller. He's making big changes. Eight new suites and two motel rooms were added for the summer of 1999. All rooms have private baths, some have decks and most have river views, but among the things not decided at this writing are whether they will have TVs or not. Prices are still being reviewed as well and will almost certainly change in the next year or three. As of 1998, Spence continues to manage the lodge.

South Fork Lodge is a great option for a family with one or two anglers as well as members who'd rather eat a fly than cast one. The lodge arranges trail rides and

Photo: Meadow Creek Lodge

Meadow Creek Lodge on the snowmobile trail to Two Top Mountain offers meals and a warm bed to snowmobilers. The popular trail gets more than 80,000 visitors each winter.

cattle drives with nearby Granite Creek Guest Ranch (see our Guest Ranches chapter) and the property has plenty of run-around room for kids. Fishing parties should make guide and accommodations reservations well in advance. The office is open year round, although the restaurant and motel have traditionally closed for the winter.

Island Park, Idaho

Henry's Fork Lodge

$$$$ (American plan) • Off U.S. Hwy. 20, Island Park, Idaho • (208) 558-7953

Stroll across the back deck, a glass of complimentary wine in hand, and survey the Henry's Fork of the Snake below. Remember with pleasure the 30 or more fish that rose to your fly today; anticipate the fine dinner being created in the cedar-paneled lodge at your back. You'll choose from several entrees — the menu changes daily — ranging from veal piccata to roast duck breast to Chilean sea bass (see our Restaurants chapter).

Henry's Fork Lodge is a topnotch fishing lodge that has spared few expenses when it comes to comfort and aesthetics. The lodge was designed by architect Joseph Esherick and perches on the bank of the Henry's Fork. Local artist Mark Smith's fish imprints hang on the walls (yes, he really does make those lovely images by coating fish with paint and then pressing them onto paper), along with work by other outdoor and wildlife artists. The rough cedar paneling manages to look more warm than rustic.

All but four of the 14 simply decorated rooms has a fireplace bricked with warm, tan sandstone; a large window in each room looks down on the river. Several rooms in the main lodge have more dramatic river views. All have private baths. In the morning the lodge will pack you a gourmet picnic lunch to take along on another day of blue-ribbon fishing. In fact, the only amenities not in easy reach are phones and television. They're available on request, explain staff members, but most people find little need of them. The fishing's just too good.

The lodge offers lodging/meal packages as well as packages that include guided fishing. The guide service is provided by local outfitters up the road at Last Chance; you're welcome to arrange your own fishing guide if you prefer or to fish without a guide. Transportation from Idaho Falls or West Yellowstone is included in the base price. The lodge is open May 15 to October 15, depending on weather. You must stay a minimum of three nights.

Jacobs' Island Park Ranch

$ (European plan) • Off Kilgore Rd., Island Park, Idaho
• (208) 662-5567, (800) 230-9530

For an unstructured ranch vacation, it's hard to beat Jacobs'. Your accommodations are one of eight comfortable cabins, three of which perch on a forested ridge overlooking the main ranch buildings. Families and groups of up to 16 may elect to stay in the huge, two-story lodge with three bedrooms, a full kitchen, arched ceilings and two-story deck. Cabins and lodge are constructed of peeled logs and feature private baths, hot tubs, decks and wood stoves. The owners thoughtfully positioned several cabins out of view. One, .75 mile from the others, has only The Barn for company.

Friday and Saturday nights, you may choose to eat at The Barn, a massive structure that houses Jacobs' weekend barbecues (see our Nightlife chapter). There is no minimum stay at Jacobs' and no real schedule; the staff are happy to arrange trail rides, fishing excursions, boat tours, personal watercraft riding, hayrides, cattle drives and even babysitting, all at additional charge. Jacobs' is open winters, too, unlike most ranches. After the snow flies, guests cross-country ski or snowmobile on the 2,000-acre ranch.

Elk Creek Ranch

$$ (American plan), no credit cards
• 3906 Loop Rd., Island Park, Idaho
• (208) 558-7404

Eight rustic but comfortable cabins scatter around a 100-year-old lodge furnished with family antiques and mounts collected for a museum in England but never sent there. Access is surprisingly easy, considering you feel as if you're in your own private wilderness retreat. U.S. Highway 20 is out of sight in the trees but can be reached by a quick drive down a good dirt road.

Included in the accommodations price are meals (picnic lunches for anglers) and fishing (no license required) in the private pond. Wildlife viewing is also a popular pastime: Trumpeter swans are regular visitors, as are elk, moose, osprey and sandhill cranes.

The cabins vary in size and age. All are log, most have fireplaces and deer mounts on the walls, and all have bathrooms and living areas. Several offer pleasant views of the shallow lake beyond the lodge. Some have covered porches and rockers. The serious angler won't be disappointed. A 10-minute drive takes you to the renowned fly-fishing waters of the Henry's Fork of the Snake. Other nearby streams beckon, too: the Buffalo, Madison, Firehole, Gibbons and Gallatin rivers. Managers Gary and VeAnn Merrill know the area and its fishing opportunities well. VeAnn has spent her summers here since she was a child. The ranch has been in the family for almost a half-century. Elk Creek Ranch's cabins aren't winterized, so their season runs June through September.

Island Park Village Resort

$$ (European plan) • N. Big Springs Loop Rd., Island Park, Idaho
• (208) 558-7502, (800) 272-8824

It's like a mirage: Island Park Village Resort is a tennis and golf resort — in the middle of nowhere. Accommodations for nonowners consist of 66 condos, most pri-

INSIDERS' TIP

If you stay on what locals call the "outside road," U.S. Highway 26/89, you can drive through 28 miles of Grand Teton without paying the park's entrance fee.

vately owned and individually decorated in Western motifs, stacked about the manicured grounds. All condos have kitchens, woodburning fireplaces and cable TV. You can rent a VCR. At the clubhouse, guests have free access to the indoor pool, a sauna, two hot tubs, a racquetball court, tennis courts (clinics available) and, for a fee, the nine-hole golf course. Nearby are grocery and dining facilities. N. Big Springs Loop Road is off U.S. Highway 20.

Northwestern Wyoming

Elephant Head Lodge

$$ (American plan) • 1120 WP Yellowstone Hwy., Wapiti, Wyo.
• (307) 587-3980

Warning! The log cabins at this lodge 11 miles east of Yellowstone National Park are so cozy you may not want to do anything but sit and soak in pure priceless peace. Each of the 11 cabins, which owners Phil and Joan Lamb modernized without sacrificing their Old West charm, is decorated uniquely. All, though, have thick, old-fashioned quilts and screened windows you can throw open to enjoy the cool Rocky Mountain night air. One sleeps nine, another has a fireplace, and a few have kitchenettes.

No matter how comfy you are, sooner or later hunger will drive you to the dining room, another log building just a hop, skip and a jump from yours. There you'll find a Franklin stove, five tables decked with red-checked tablecloths and home-style meals served with fresh-baked bread and homemade desserts. At dinner, Phil will be outside grilling rib eyes, filets mignon and New York strip steaks. Joan will be in the kitchen cooking up a storm.

While the owners welcome overnight guests, most visitors stay three to five days to do some horseback riding and to use the lodge as a base for touring Yellowstone National Park and Cody. The Elephant Head also offers hiking, rock climbing, antler-hunting nature walks, nightly movies in the old lodge living room, a recreation area for children and a small lounge for Mom and Dad.

The Elephant Head offers a European Plan in which guests pay a flat rate for their cabin, then pay extra for meals and activities. The American Plan package is good for guests who want to do a lot of horseback riding. In addition to your cabin, the package includes three meals a day and up to four hours a day of riding.

Pahaska Tepee

$$ (European plan) • 183-B1 Yellowstone Hwy., Cody, Wyo.
• (307) 527-7701, (800) 628-7791

Situated just outside the east entrance to Yellowstone National Park on U.S. Highway 14-16-20, Pahaska Tepee is the site of Buffalo Bill Cody's hunting lodge. Pahaska, which has a gas station, a gift store, a restaurant and horseback riding (for an extra fee), houses guests in older A-frames and other buildings.

Now a buzzing burg for visitors going to and from the park, Pahaska is also known as a winter recreation mecca. It is the only resort open all year (it's closed when Yellowstone National Park is closed) serving snowmobilers and cross-country skiers. You can drive your snowmobile from your room and travel on groomed roads 110 miles through Yellowstone National Park to West Yellowstone, Montana. Pahaska has a fleet of snowmobiles for rent as well as suits and other equipment needed to brave the cold. Just a mile to the east, the Sleeping Giant Ski Area (see our Winter Sports chapter) offers 17 downhill trails. There are also several miles of groomed cross-country trails in the area.

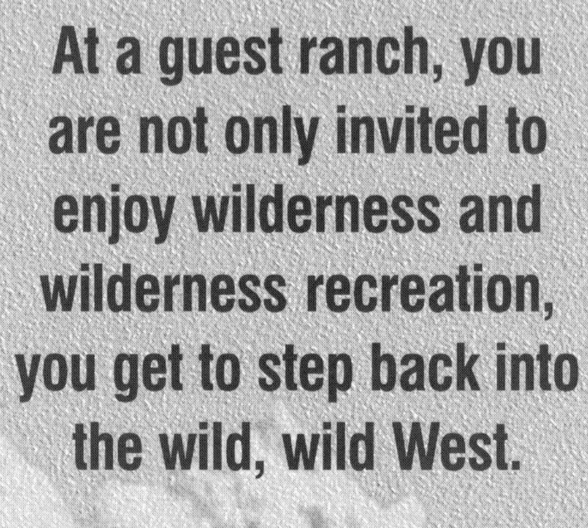
At a guest ranch, you
are not only invited to
enjoy wilderness and
wilderness recreation,
you get to step back into
the wild, wild West.

Guest Ranches

Hasn't every little kid wished to be a cowboy? Indulge that childhood whim where dude ranching is a time-honored tradition. At a guest ranch, you are not only invited to enjoy wilderness and wilderness recreation, you get to step back into the wild, wild West.

Guest ranches offer accommodations, meals and activities, generally for one lump price. At most guest ranches you'll trail ride, enjoy cookouts and barbecues, go fishing and perhaps float a nearby river. Other activities can include swimming, volleyball, horseshoes, barn dances, cattle driving, riding lessons and gymkhanas (a series of competitive horseback games). You may head into town to see a rodeo, shop or go dancing.

Guest ranches vary in how long they ask you to stay (usually at least three days), how many activities they offer for their blanket price and how flexible their schedule is.

Unlike resorts and lodges, guest ranches can be so isolated you can't just jump in your car and spend a day elsewhere. They also do more planning for you, so it's important that you like the plan. While reading these guest ranch descriptions, think first about what you want to do with your days, how comfortable you want to be (lodging can be luxurious or rustic, but don't expect in-room phones, alarm clocks, TVs or wall-to-wall carpet) and how many decisions you want made for you. If you have kids, do you expect help supervising them? Do you want riding lessons, or just someone to check the girth strap before you mount? Think about how secluded you'd like to be. Some guest ranches are practically in town. Others are accessed by a half-day's drive on dirt road.

Then make phone calls. Ask to see the schedule of activities: It may detail every hour of your vacation, or you may be told there isn't a schedule. Ask for names of satisfied customers you can call. Ask about the riding program. You'll probably spend part of every day on a horse, so this is perhaps the most important facet of the ranch operation to check on. Also ask if the ranch is a member of the Dude Ranchers' Association. Some very fine guest ranches aren't members, but association members do submit to periodic inspection and abide by certain rules likely to increase your vacation enjoyment.

The price code (see the gray box) is based on a two-person, one-week stay in peak season. If ranches offer a range of prices, we list the least expensive option. At most guest ranches, that rate includes all meals and most, if not all, activities. Most guest ranches and resorts also offer complimentary or inexpensive shuttles from the nearest airports, saving you the cost of a rental car.

Price Code

$	**$1,900 to $2,200**
$$	**$2,201 to $2,600**
$$$	**$2,601 to $3,250**
$$$$	**$3,251 to $5,100**

Grand Teton National Park

Lost Creek Ranch & Spa

$$$$ • U.S. Hwy. 89, 8 mi. north of Moose, Wyo. • (307) 733-3435

Western it may be, but rustic it ain't. Think along the lines of Club Med in Wyoming. From the nightly bed-linen turndowns (with mints, of course) to the bronze sculptures, antler chairs and antique-rifle collection in the main lodge, this guest ranch is topnotch. More than 30 staff members devote their time and attention to a maximum of 55 guests — ensuring personal, attentive service.

Cabins are plush, with views of the Tetons and the sage-covered valley that backs the ranch. Two cards are left on your pillow each evening next to those mints: One tells you what sort of weather to expect tomorrow, and the other contains a local historical tidbit.

Lost Creek prides itself on the wide range of activities included in its fee, so you can pretty much leave your checkbook at home. Just head to the ranch office and sign up for your float down the scenic Snake River, horseback riding or riding lessons, laundry service, a van tour of Yellowstone National Park, selections from the youth program and more. You'll pay for massages and facials, fishing trips, whitewater rafting trips and skeet shooting.

Lost Creek has been a guest ranch since the late 1960s, but it was originally homesteaded in the 1920s. It is completely enclosed by Grand Teton National Park. The ranch is open from early June to mid-October.

Triangle X Ranch

$, no credit cards • U.S. Hwy. 89, 12 mi. north of Moose, Wyo. • (307) 733-2183

Only 25 miles from Jackson, Wyoming, at the edge of Grand Teton National Park is the only dude ranch in this country under concession from the National Park Service. Other guest ranches in Grand Teton are actually on private lands called inholdings. Triangle X is sitting on your national park. The ranch is run by the Turner family; four generations ago they owned the ranch. Then they sold it to John D. Rockefeller Jr., who leased it back to them until the ground became national park. This makes Triangle X one of the oldest guest ranches in the area — it's been in operation since 1926. It's also one of the cheapest for groups of four or more, a fact which attracts many families.

Harold Turner says that Triangle X is a riding ranch. The ranch owns horses to suit all levels of riders; you'll ride the same horse every day, developing a relationship with your animal.

Included in your base price are meals (served family style in the lodge), rustic cabin lodging, horseback riding and other ranch activities. For an additional charge, you may enjoy wilderness pack trips, float trips, fishing and hunting trips and an inexpensive airport shuttle. If you call the Turners for more information, make sure you request that they send the fact- and photo-filled *Triangle X News*, a little annual newspaper for guests.

Buffalo Valley

Most of Buffalo Valley, through which U.S. Highway 26 and the Buffalo Fork River run, is not in Grand Teton. We've listed Buffalo Valley guest ranches with park listings in this chapter to show you how very close to one another they are. You get the same views and the same wildlife here as inside the east entrance gate at Moran a few miles away.

Heart 6 Guest Ranch

$$ • 16985 Buffalo Valley Rd., Moran, Wyo. • (307) 543-2477

The folks at Heart 6 have a lot of well-thought-out plans for you. This ranch is planted on a hill overlooking the Buffalo Fork River

INSIDERS' TIP

During the off-seasons, many guest ranches offer overnight accommodations to travelers for prices similar to a motel's fee.

and Buffalo Valley as it meanders toward the Tetons. Fishing is good on the Buffalo Fork; so is wildlife viewing along the willow flats.

The ranch is open year round. In summer the focus is on riding, rafting and fishing mixed into a pleasant schedule of social events such as slide shows and cookouts. In fall the business is hunting; the ranch maintains hunting camps 17 and 35 miles into the Teton wilderness. The upper camp is on the headwaters of the Yellowstone River. Starting in December, Heart 6 invites you snowmobiling: The ranch buys all new snowmobiles every year. The staff will guide you on dayrides out of the ranch or take you on longer adventures into Yellowstone National Park, Togwotee Pass and the Continental Divide Snowmobile Trail.

Amenities at Heart 6 include a hot tub, heated pool (in summer), a comfortable lodge building with two dining rooms and a main recreation area with an oversize fireplace and comfortable cabins and cabin/motel accommodations, each with a private bath and some with fireplaces or woodstoves. Cabins do not have phones or TVs. In summer, rates include meals, lodging, riding and other ranch activities. Float trips cost extra.

Minimum stays of three nights or six nights are the norm, but during fall, winter and spring, cabins may be rented by the night; in those seasons, no organized dude ranch activities are available.

Diamond D

$ • Buffalo Valley Rd., Moran, Wyo.
• (307) 543-2479

Rod Doty was raised in windy, snowbound South Dakota, where he made his living as a farmer. But after a stint in the military, Doty vowed to hunt and fish for the rest of his life. He has. Diamond D is a guest ranch in summer, runs pack and hunting trips into nearby mountains in fall and in winter offers bed and breakfast accommodations to snowmobilers and cross-country skiers.

The ranch is small and the staff friendly. Dude ranch employees tend to be wanderers, but many of Diamond D's staff have been coming back every year for five, 10 and even 18 years. The ranch can accommodate up to 36 guests at once, but Doty likes to keep the number around 20.

The lodge is a pleasant building with a sunken sitting area cradling a wood stove, and its tall windows practically invite the pretty valley surroundings in. From the kitchen wafts the aroma of fresh-baked bread, homemade cookies and other temptations. The newer duplex cabins are log or log-sided, with picnic tables on the lawn; many face the Tetons.

Rooms have refrigerators and fireplaces. Furnishings are simple but comfortable.

Included in the ranch price is an overnight pack trip, van tours of the area, guided horseback riding, Western riding lessons (Doty is particularly proud of his 4-H-style horse safety program for kids), and planned ranch activities such as hayrides, antique car rides, dogsled rides and photography outings.

Turpin Meadows Ranch

$ • East end, Buffalo Valley Rd.
• (307) 543-2496, (800) 743-2496

The staff are like family here, and after a couple of days, owner LaRae Castagno promises, so are you. LaRae and husband Dale's three sons and their wives all work here, too. Says LaRae, "Those boys love the outdoors. Put 'em in a building and they'd knock out the walls." But Dale says the friendly atmosphere, cozy, rustic accommodations and lovely scenery aren't the real reasons you come to Turpin Meadows: He says it's the food. It's Western-style home cooking, served up buffet style. Steaks and ribs get rave reviews.

Eight older cabins, furnished simply and equipped with heat and full baths, face out onto the lovely meadow that gave the ranch its name. One luxuriously large cabin with two huge bedrooms, a living room and two bathrooms, once was visited, so legend has it, by radio personality Arthur Godfrey. The ranch also has four motel-style rooms that are clean, modern and simple. Their big glass doors face the grassy clearing around which other ranch buildings cluster.

Included in the fee are lodging, meals, horses, scheduled ranch events such as the chuckwagon and a trip into Jackson to watch the rodeo, a Yellowstone National Park van tour and transportation to and from Jackson Hole Airport. Turpin Meadows is open year round. Fall hunting trips are available, as are snowmobile rentals in winter with or without guides (most folks prefer to be guided so they end up in the prettiest places).

Jackson Hole

Darwin Ranch

$, no credit cards • Gros Ventre Ranch near Darwin Peak, Wyo. • (307) 733-5588

The story — all hearsay — goes like this: Homesteader Fred Darwin, a Rough Rider friend of Teddy Roosevelt, fell in love with lush upper Gros Ventre Valley. So, by presidential decree, Teddy gave him 160 acres of it. True or not, Darwin Ranch sits on an original homestead completely surrounded by Teton National Forest, at an elevation of 8,200 feet. The nearest town, Pinedale, is 50 miles away over mostly dirt roads rough enough that you may want to charter a plane, hire a taxi or rent a car rather than put the wear and tear on your vehicle. The final 4-mile approach to the ranch is so rough that staff members drive out to meet you in a four-wheel-drive vehicle. If none of this has scared you off, you'd probably enjoy a stay in what may be the most remote guest ranch in Wyoming, so read on.

Rates cover everything but your transportation into and out of the ranch. You'll stay in rustic-looking but renovated cabins with private or shared bathrooms and electricity generated by nearby Kinky Creek or by propane. Meals are served family-style on a long table in the log dining room. You may take pack trips (usually very small and intimate; you'll help with the chores), fish on the Gros Ventre or trail ride.

A maximum of 20 guests are invited at any one time. Believe it or not, the ranch is open year round, although winter guests book their stays under several restrictions, including a commitment to bring a group large enough to utilize the entire ranch. Winter activities are cross-country skiing, snowshoeing and snowmobiling.

Gros Ventre River Ranch

$$ • 18 Gros Ventre River Rd., near Kelly, Wyo. • (307) 733-4138

Cowboy-hatted, blue-jeaned Tina Weber and her husband, Karl, bought this ranch in 1988. Back then it was only four cabins in an idyllic location. Gros Ventre River Ranch is still an idyllic location — just outside Grand Teton's southeast boundary on the banks of the rollicking Gros Ventre River. But now it has corrals, four more cabins and a lovely new lodge building. The lodge has a dining room, two decks overlooking the river, a bar, a game room, a living room and a long, covered porch.

Most of the cabins cluster around a grassy circle equipped with swing sets, hammocks and a fire ring. Older cabins are more rustic; the newest lodging is upscale. All have carpeting, electric heat, private baths and log furniture made by a local artisan. Some have private decks, brick-floor entryways, kitchenettes, washer/dryers and woodstoves.

Two favorite nights for guests are those evenings when a local expert drives out to teach fly fishing in the ranch's stocked pond and Wednesdays, when a local cowboy poet with handlebar moustache and guitar recites Robert Service poems and sings cowboy songs. The staff bring out the ranch's brand and heat it in the fire to brand guests' boots, belts and wallets.

The ranch can accommodate 34 guests. During the riding season, your rate includes lodging, meals, your horse and use of ranch facilities such as the game room with its big screen TV and VCR, Ping-Pong, pool tables and foosball. Although the guest ranch is open only May 1 through the end of October, the three housekeeping cabins are available year round. Cross-country skiers will enjoy coming home to warm, modern comfort at the end of a winter trek. Snowmobile trips can be arranged at additional charge.

Red Rock Ranch

$$, no credit cards • Gros Ventre River Rd. past Crystal Creek • (307) 733-6288

Yellowstone country hosts all kinds of guest ranches. This is the kind that makes you forget the world you came from. You'll stay for a minimum of six days at this small, family-owned ranch in the heart of the Gros Ventre Mountains. Navigating the road in is slow; once here you're likely to see nobody but the wranglers and the 29 other guests.

INSIDERS' TIP

Many guest ranches offer overnight pack trips into nearby wilderness at little or no additional cost. Don't miss this chance to feel very remote ... and saddle sore.

You stay in comfortable but rustic cabins; each has a private bath, a sitting room, a woodburning stove and a sun porch. Cabins are one to three bedrooms. Your daily rides into the Bridger-Teton National Forest and Gros Ventre Wilderness are included in the price, as are meals and all other ranch activities. Kids enjoy playing volleyball and pickleball. A counselor/wrangler arranges just-for-kids trail rides and even a kid version of an overnight camping trip into the mountains.

The ranch also has laundry facilities, a heated outdoor pool and hot tub, a casting pond and a pleasantly rustic lodge building. Although relatively schedule-free, this remote guest ranch offers something exciting every day. Red Rock Ranch is open only in summer; winter access is a bit of a problem.

R Lazy S Ranch

$ • 7800 N. Moose-Wilson Rd., near Teton Village, Wyo. • (307) 733-2655

Most cabins face the parklike lawn, and each backs into the aspens that ring the ranch. Porches and decks are equipped with flower boxes and hanging flower baskets. Cabins have private baths, fireplaces or woodstoves, coffee makers and carpeted floors with Indian-weave throw rugs.

When you arrive, you'll find a bowl of snacks and fruit waiting in your cabin; fresh-cut flowers brighten your temporary log home. One hundred yards from the four newest cabins is the buck-and-rail fence that separates the ranch from Grand Teton. A couple of hundred yards down a dirt trail is a child's dream: a small swimming hole, filled with chilly water from nearby Lake Creek, a rope swing and a wooden raft. Parents can take the plunge off the diving platform or bask in the sun on the deck. Manager Claire McConaughy likes to keep her 45 guests busy. On Wednesdays the staff will take you into Jackson to enjoy the rodeo. Thursday is cookout night. Friday night talent shows are a favorite for many guests.

Rates include lodging, meals, riding and instruction, scenic boat rides and water-skiing on Jackson Lake and fishing in the ranch's stocked pond. For an additional charge, you can take a guided fishing trip or a wilderness pack trip. The ranch is open mid-June through September.

Spotted Horse Ranch

$$ • 12355 S. U.S. Hwy. 191, near Hoback Junction, Wyo. • (307) 733-2097

Most folks reserve their spots here six months in advance. Some book their next adventure before heading home from their current one. You'll see why when you drop down to the Hoback River and find this cluster of cabins and corrals nestled on its bank. Spotted Horse Ranch has a unique combination of easy, paved-road access and a secluded atmosphere with rides originating right at the ranch.

The ranch has 10 guest cabins, all pleasantly close to the Hoback, most with river views from their porches; one guest room is in the lodge. All have private baths. A hot tub and sauna cabin sit a stone's throw from the river. Dining is family-style. Lodge amenities include laundry facilities, a big-screen TV, a video library and a recreation room. Activities include river floating, Western dance lessons, a steak cookout across the Hoback and excursions into nearby Jackson for the rodeo.

If you were looking for the perfect combination of dude ranch and fishing lodge, you may have found it here. Not only will guides take you to the best waters in the area, but especially in August, you can literally reel 'em in from your porch. The fishing pond was recently expanded and stocked; the ranch can arrange fly fishing lessons. Spotted Horse

INSIDERS' TIP

In Cody, some folks make a distinction between "dude" and "guest" ranches: They say dude ranches generally offer only weeklong stays, while guest ranches let you stay for a shorter time with guests coming and going at odd times.

Ranch is open June to October for three-night minimum stays.

Trail Creek Ranch

$$, no credit cards • Old Pass Rd., Wilson, Wyo. • (307) 733-2610

Five decades ago, former Olympic skier Elizabeth Woolsey skied through the 300-acre, forested valley that is now Trail Creek Ranch: It was love at first sight. Elizabeth's guest ranch began as a place where her many friends could get together and ride horses or ski. Although the ranch's famous owner died in 1996, this Western home away from home is alive and well.

Most of the fresh greens and herbs used in guests' meals are harvested from the ranch's garden, and the trout served on Friday nights once swam in the pond just behind the main ranch buildings. Kids enjoy the game room, with its bumper pool table and board games. Horseshoe pits are set up outside. For guests who are kids at heart, the ranch hosts a shindig (called a gymkhana) featuring horseback games and barrel racing. Besides the daily trail rides and riding instruction in the arena, fishing opportunities abound in Jackson Hole. Wranglers can arrange pack trips that loop past good fishing streams or set you up with a local fishing guide on the Snake, Teton or Green river. Canoes are available for guest use, as is a limited supply of fishing equipment. The ranch also has a heated swimming pool.

Trail Creek hosts as many as 25 guests in summer and 12 in winter. If you're considering a visit, Trail Creek Ranch will cheerfully provide references, but don't be surprised if you are asked for yours. With its 40-percent return rate and a long tradition of patronage by friends and family, the ranch works hard to protect its small, intimate style.

Surrounding Areas

Southwestern Montana

The Covered Wagon Ranch

$ • 34035 Gallatin Rd., Gallatin Gateway, Mont. • (406) 995-4237, (800) 995-4232

You won't find hot tubs or TVs at the Covered Wagon Ranch in the Gallatin Canyon. Established as a dude ranch in 1925 and owned until 1990 by the founding family, The Covered Wagon is one of the few remaining ranches where visitors can find the Old West alive and well. Families with toddlers will scoot their youngsters up to the table in the same high chair former owner Vic Benson used as a boy. And they'll stay in cabins that, except for the addition of bathrooms, have changed little since the old days. That's because guests who have returned to the ranch year after year (The Covered Wagon has a 65-percent return rate) insist on the same simple charm and the genuine Western hospitality they've come to count on through the years.

Hearty country meals are served family style — the ranch accommodates only 24 guests at a time — in a new lodge (until 1996, guests dined in two shifts in a smaller dining hall.) Evenings, children and adults alike gather 'round the campfire or in the game room, a separate building equipped with a piano, a foosball table, books, puzzles and board games. In summer, horseback riding is the mainstay of the Covered Wagon experience. Guests are assigned a horse for the week; everyone has a favorite, and some longtime guests even buy horses to keep on the ranch. With no more than six guests assigned to a wrangler, you can choose which trail you want to ride each day.

If your knees start creaking after too

INSIDERS' TIP

At some guest ranches you must load up in a vehicle and drive to the place you'll trail ride. Other ranches are lucky to be in locations that allow them to saddle up and ride from the ranch. If this convenience matters to you, ask when you call.

Photo: Moose Creek Ranch

Family-style dining is what you're likely to find at dude ranches and bed and breakfasts in Yellowstone country.

many days in the saddle, you can put on your city duds and head for Bozeman, slip on your fishing vest and cast your line into the nearby streams or break out your camera and drive into Yellowstone National Park, just a few miles away, for the day. Winters, the Covered Wagon is open for cross-country skiers and snowmobilers. The ranch is also close to Big Sky.

Lone Mountain Ranch

$$$$ • Lone Mountain Rd., Big Sky, Mont. • (406) 995-4644, (800) 514-4644

While Lone Mountain is busiest these days from June through August, this oasis of Western hospitality began in the 1970s as a cross-country ski center. Today, its 65 kilometers of meticulously groomed trails are legendary among skiers nationwide. Also legendary is Lone Mountain's food served in a Western log dining lodge lit by handmade antler chandeliers and warmed by a floor-to-ceiling stone fireplace. In addition to in-season wild game, fresh trout, local beef and lamb, you can expect to find vegetarian dishes and home-baked breads, pastries and desserts. In summer, Lone Mountain features weekly outdoor barbecues. During the winter, a weekly trail buffet is served on the snow, much to the delight of guests.

Another winter favorite is an evening sleigh ride to the North Fork cabin where the staff will serve you a prime rib dinner cooked up on an old-fashioned wood cookstove. (Breakfast and lunch are also open to nonguests, but you'll have to take your chances as a walk-in because reservations aren't accepted for these meals.)

Lone Mountain employs a staff of naturalist guides to lead hiking, biking, fishing, horseback riding and Yellowstone National Park tours in both summer and winter. Winter tours, which feature both snowcoach and cross-country skiing, are open to nonguests. The cost for these tours is extra for guests. During the summer, Lone Mountain specializes in family groups (the ranch can accommodate 115), with a kids' program from June 15 to August 30. Youth activities, which change depending on ages and interests, might include volleyball, adventure hikes, nature discovery hikes, llama hikes, horseback riding, overnight campouts and canoeing.

Lone Mountain has 23 cabins in varying sizes. None have TVs or telephones, and the ranch is smoke-free. Lone Mountain offers summer (and winter) fly-fishing vacations, a discovery package that includes horseback riding and many naturalist-guided trips, and a winter cross-country ski package. All packages are for seven-night stays and include meals, lodging and transportation to and from the airport.

Mountain Sky Guest Ranch

$$$$ • Emigrant, Mont.
• (406) 587-1244, (800) 548-3392

Tennis, anyone? A quick swim in the pool? The menu of options at Mountain Sky is enough to keep even the most easily bored occupied: Ping-Pong, volleyball, softball, horseshoes, hiking, fishing, riding, dining, dancing — or nothing at all. From its sweeping lawns and graciously appointed rustic cabins to its gourmet meals and thoughtful staff, Mountain Sky is pure luxury carved into the Western landscape. An optional children's program, run by trained staff, offers youngsters of all ages a diversity of activities, including crafts, nature walks, swimming, games and fishing in Mountain Sky's private trout pond.

Dining at Mountain Sky is an event all by itself. Whether it's poolside barbecues featuring steaks and chicken or seafood or an inside meal of gourmet continental cuisine, you won't want to be late. Breakfasts range from light to hearty, depending on your preference. Lunch, served outside buffet-style after the morning ride, may include homemade soups, pasta salads, pizza, enchiladas, stir-fries or a host of other Mountain Sky specialties.

For a special experience, Mountain Sky offers a rent-a-ranch program, in which your group can have Mountain Sky all to itself.

Nine Quarter Circle Ranch

$$, no credit cards • 5000 Taylor Fork Rd., Gallatin Gateway, Mont.
• (406) 995-4276

Gather up your young'uns and head for the Nine Quarter Circle Ranch, where the Kelsey family has perfected the fine art of treating young and old alike to the Western experience. Situated in a picture-perfect setting at 7,000 feet, the Nine Quarter Circle is surrounded by national forest filled with breathtaking views, mountain meadows and alpine lakes.

Yes, there's riding, and lots of it, with 120 ranch-raised horses (the Kelseys raise Appaloosas) from which to choose. Four or five rides head into the mountains daily, each taking a trail tailored to a different ability level. When you get there, you might want to kiss your kids good-bye for a week. Between the Kiddie Wrangler, the Baby Sitter and a herd of kids to play with, chances are you'll only catch a glimpse of them now and then. Saturday morning you and the rest of the parents will drape yourselves over the corral fence and watch the kids take their turns in a gymkhana. Later that night you'll swing with them at the square dance in the hayloft of the ranch's old barn.

During the week the ranch holds volleyball and softball games as well as an added-fee overnight pack trip. The log ranch buildings which stretch a half-mile from one end to the other were built with timber from the ranch. A big lodge with living and dining rooms plus a string of cabins built mostly for family groups accommodate guests. Come fall, when the families head back home for school, anglers fly in to the ranch's 4,000-foot-long airstrip, soak in the still autumn air and fish to their heart's content. Others just come to soak in the peace.

The Nine Quarter Circle has been written up in more than 40 national publications, so make your reservations a year ahead of time — it's popular.

320 Guest Ranch

$$$ • 205 Buffalo Horn Creek, Gallatin Gateway, Mont. • (406) 995-4283, (800) 243-0320

With 60 rooms, a dining room open to the public, a 200-person convention hall and a kaleidoscope of on-site activities, 320

INSIDERS' TIP

One way to learn more about individual dude ranches is to call the Dude Ranchers' Association. Its many members are voluntarily inspected. Call (970) 223-8440.

Guest Ranch offers plenty of variety year around for anyone seeking a corporate convention or a Western vacation near Yellowstone National Park. With so many people coming and going, the 320 isn't as personal as some folks like, but it offers an option many other ranches don't: You don't have to sign on for a whole week to get a taste. Many guest ranches require at least a three-night stay, but you can hang your hat at the 320 for a minimum of two nights. Rooms and cabins range from a one-room duplex log cabin to a three-bedroom log home with a full-size kitchen, two bathrooms, beds for eight adults and plenty of floor space for kids and sleeping bags. By the way, children 12 and younger stay free at the 320 Guest Ranch.

The 320 offers several winter and summer packages. Winter packages, like the two-day Get-A-Way or the seven-day Winter Dream, include extras like ski-lift passes at Big Sky Resort, Yellowstone snowmobile excursions and some meals. In summer, you can choose from a four-night mini-vacation or the seven-night Western Dream package that includes horseback riding, the Chuckwagon BBQ, an all-day horseback fishing trip to an alpine lake and two meals a day. Meals are served in a Western dining room. If you pay by the night, it'll cost you extra for meals and ranch activities such as the Chuckwagon Dinner and Breakfast rides, the Camera Safari, horseback riding or guided fishing trips.

Wild Trout Outfitters operates a fly shop and outfitting service from a tiny, old log cabin on the premises. Included with your room, though, are horseshoes, volleyball, evening bonfires and hayrides. The 320 also has a small playground for children and a guest laundry in one of the older log cabins.

A popular spot for snowmobilers, the 320 is just a few miles from the Buck Ridge snowmobile trail. The area also has plenty of groomed cross-country ski trails.

Eastern Idaho

Teton Valley

Moose Creek Ranch

$ • 215 E. Moose Creek Rd., Victor, Idaho • (208) 787-2784, (800) 676-0075

As you walk away from the 4,500-square-foot main lodge on the planked sidewalk, you pass under a sign that says "Hurry back." Take our word for it: You'll want to. If there's such a thing as the guest ranch that has everything for a family vacation, Kelly Van Orden's Moose Creek Ranch is it.

A kid counselor is always around to entertain young'uns. The ranch prides itself on the "Horse Sense" training program which teaches guests not only how to ride, but also how to care for and stay safe around horses. You'll ride and care for the same horse all week. The grassy grounds house a playground, a generous indoor pool, a sauna, a hot tub, a picnic area, Ping-Pong tables, horseshoe pits and volleyball courts. Moose Creek meanders across ranch property, so although more famous fishing rivers — the Snake, Teton and Henry's Fork — are a moderate drive away, you always have the option of getting your line wet a short stroll from your cabin. Van Orden has been riding since he was a kid. He remembers a time when guest ranches catered mostly to families. That's the kind of traditional experience he and his family work to provide on the land Van Orden's dad bought in 1964.

Moose Creek Ranch is not a working ranch, which means it's all about you. For a change of pace, every fall for several weeks, Moose Creek Ranch hosts adults only. In winter the ranch, situated on the Western slope of the Tetons barely a stone's throw from the Jedediah Smith Wilderness, offers very reasonably priced bed and breakfast accommodations to skiers and snow lovers.

Swan Valley

INSIDERS' TIP

Most guest ranches have minimum stays ranging from three days to a week.

Hansen-Silver Guest Ranch

$$ • 956 Rainey Creek Rd., Swan Valley, Idaho • (208) 483-2305, (800) 277-9041

You might come for the cooking: Ranch-style meals cooked in Dutch ovens and on the barbecue grill, served outside when weather permits. Breads and soups are homemade, as are pasta, pies and pastries. You might come because this working family ranch is real Idaho: The Hansen family emigrated to the state in the late 1800s. Que Hansen owns and manages the ranch.

You can trail ride and muse at the nightly campfire, sightsee in Yellowstone and shop in Jackson. Children appreciate the expanse of lawn, the stocked casting ponds and the TV room. And the nearby blue-ribbon waters of the South Fork beg to be fished — in fact about half the guest ranch's guests are anglers. The Hansens invite you to do as much or as little as you please in this unstructured setting. Unlike many guest ranches, there's no schedule of activities: The agenda is relaxation and fun, and the schedule is yours to create. There's no minimum stay requirement.

Accommodations are pleasantly upscale. The ranch has one duplex cabin with decks front and back, one white frame cottage and a barn. Our recommendation: Stay in the barn. It's 100 years old, renovated by Brett Hansen and his father-in-law, Calvin Collins. It features exposed beams from the original structure. The spacious rooms have pine furnishings, oddly undersize windows and extra nooks and crannies. In two of the bathrooms, Brett and Calvin sawed holes into old vanity dressers, mounting working sinks into them. All rooms have private baths and queen-size beds, but no phones. One room has a TV.

The guest ranch operates late May to mid-September, but when they have space, the Hansens offer overnight accommodations with or without reservations year round. Swan Valley has little in the way of accommodations, so this is a real find for anglers. Hansen-Silver Guest Ranch is only a 15-minute drive from the Spring Creek boat ramp in Swan Valley.

Idaho Falls, Idaho

Granite Creek Guest Ranch

$, no credit cards • Off Swan Valley Hwy., Ririe, Idaho • (208) 538-7140

Every guest ranch is different. That's why some vacationers sample a new one every year. But if you like things on the rustic side — small, informal and friendly — and if your idea of a ranch is a place where real cowboys live and work and where you can help them with their chores, you may decide to stop sampling here. Granite Creek's buildings were mostly built around the turn of the century with logs cut from ranch property. Electricity and plumbing (but no heat) have been added; your cabin will be rough but clean.

What we like best about Granite Creek is its cozy size. It has only four guest cabins, which can accommodate a total of 15 guests, so you'll get lots of personal attention and plenty of quiet. You also get to try your hand at activities most guest ranches can't provide: Learn to rope in the corral, help on a real cattle drive, feed the animals and help with other ranch chores. There's little in the way of a schedule here — another advantage of the small size. You decide what you want to experience, and the staff tries to make it happen.

The ranch likes to cater to families; kids canoe on the 5-acre, spring-fed pond. Everyone enjoys the homemade root beer. Meals are often cooked and served outside. No alcohol is allowed on the ranch, which is usually open from May to October, depending on weather.

Northwestern Wyoming

Allen's Diamond Four Ranch

$, no credit cards • Lander, Wyo. • (307) 332-2995

There are few ranches left, even in

INSIDERS' TIP

Gratuities are customary at guest ranches. Some ranches will add them to your bill. Others leave the tipping to you.

Yellowstone country, that are beyond electricity, television and neighbors. Allen's Diamond Four Ranch at the edge of the Popo Agie Wilderness in the Wind River Mountains is one of them. You won't find fancy fare here, just simple charm and log cabins with propane lights and woodstoves. At 9,200 feet, you may want to fire up that wood stove, sending a wisp of smoke winding through the dewy, damp woods, before heading to the lodge for breakfast. Fees pay for three meals a day, horseback riding, fishing, natural-history hikes and wildlife watching. Guests share a shower house. And, by the way, it's BYOB — Bring Your Own (sleeping) Bag. Children younger than 6 stay free.

Owners Jim and Mary Allen also offer an assortment of popular pack trips that leave from the ranch June through September. Guided pack trips ($175 per day per person) supply everything you need, including a camp cook. For half that much, you can outfit your own camp and let the Allens furnish the horses and the pack train in and out of remote areas. (Early reservations are highly recommended for these drop camp trips.) The Allens also outfit and guide custom trips including hiking with pack horses, wilderness seminars, cross-Continental Divide tours as well as an Oregon Trail wagon trip and cattle drives. Spring and fall, the Allens offer a working-ranch experience in which you can help with branding, roundup and general ranch work. They also have a hunting guide service in the fall.

Bill Cody Ranch

$$ • 2604 Yellowstone Hwy., Cody, Wyo. • (307) 587-6271

Drive into the Bill Cody Ranch on a Wednesday evening about 5:30 and you're liable to find guests moseying down to dine at the chuckwagon cookout. You'll see elderly couples holding hands and young adults dressed in cowboy duds draped over lodgepole rails on the log lodge porch. In the thick of it all, John and Jamie Parsons, Wyoming natives and owners of the Bill Cody Ranch since 1996, are natural-born hosts dishing out a generous portion of cheerful Western hospitality.

At the ranch, horseback riding is the specialty. The Parsons employ eight wranglers, and John keeps his string of 70 horses on a rotating schedule so that each one stays fresh with plenty of time off. He offers two-hour, half-day and all-day rides into the Shoshone National Forest. A horse hand himself, Parsons these days most often rides the "Blue Horse" — an all-terrain vehicle with a saddle for a seat — back and forth to the corrals and to the post office down the road at Wapiti.

The Bill Cody Ranch offers nightly and packaged vacation rates that include meals and horseback riding. The ranch also offers regular trips to the Bill Cody Nite Rodeo, and the Parsons can arrange for other services such as fishing guides. While you can probably get a room here at the last minute during the off season, we advise reservations during the summer months. The "No Vacancy" sign is becoming a regular sight each evening at the Bill Cody Ranch gate on the Yellowstone Highway.

The Bill Cody Ranch doesn't take credit cards for a reservation deposit, but they do accept credit cards once you're here.

Double Diamond X Ranch

$$$ • 3453 Southfork Rd., Cody, Wyo. • (307) 527-6276, (800) 833-RANCH

You may come as a guest to Double Diamond X, but you'll leave as a friend. Staffed by a crew of friendly wranglers, cooks and housekeepers, the Double Diamond X offers a regular menu of Western guest ranch options, including a children's program designed to educate and entertain. An indoor swimming pool and spa,

INSIDERS' TIP

Check our Resorts and Lodges Chapter for more guest-ranch type accommodations along with horseback riding.

History of the Dude Ranch

The impetus for the dude ranch didn't start here, in the acknowledged home of dude ranching: It began back East. By the late 1800s, stories of natural wonders and brawling pioneer adventure in the mountain West had the nation's attention. A new national park, the nation's first, had just been created in a remote corner of Wyoming. Particularly compelling was the image of the wandering cowboy on horseback — the perfect dream for a country that valued individuality and freedom, but whose urban centers had gotten short on elbow room.

A torrent of tourists headed West to see its wonders firsthand. They rode the recently completed transcontinental rails, so the journey was easy. But the frontier was just that — a frontier. The lodging these urban Easterners were accustomed to did not yet exist. So tourists in Yellowstone country often ended up staying in the only places available: ranches. Ranchers, isolated and hungry for news and new faces, were pleased to have company. Tourists in turn found their stay at the ranch as fine an experience as the mountains and wildlife they had come to see.

Nobody knows who first accepted money in exchange for ranch hospitality. Legend has it, though, that the sum in question was $10. Soon many ranches in Montana and

— continued on next page

Photo: Randy Hayes, Post Register

A wrangler watches a mare, colt and stallion inside the corral.

Wyoming hosted paying guests as part of their normal operations. "Dudes" stayed for weeks or months, participating in the day-to-day life of the ranch.

Another detail nobody knows is how the term "dude" became so firmly entrenched. Some say the word was coined by stagecoach drivers and packers who served tourists in Yellowstone National Park; they supposedly referred to any man from the East as a "dude," women as "dudines" and children as "dudettes."

When the automobile began to take a bite out of railroad travel in the 1920s, the Northern Pacific decided to fight back. It invited owners of 35 Yellowstone area dude ranches to meet in Bozeman, Montana. What was needed, thought the railroad, was more interest in tourism, especially the kind of tourism that required railroads. Out of that meeting came the Dude Ranchers' Association, an organization that has promoted and organized the industry ever since. A little healthy self-promotion can work wonders: By 1940, more than 300 dude ranches were operating in the United States and Canada.

The world, and the people running to catch up with it, don't take two-month vacations anymore. Nor do dude ranches offer them. The typical stay on a dude ranch is one week. Dude ranches — many owners prefer to call them guest ranches these days — have become more sophisticated, offering organized programs of entertainment, horseback riding, riding instruction and other ranch activities. Accommodations are often anything but rustic.

But contemporary dude ranches try not to be simply resorts with horses and saddle-sore guests. In the words of the Dude Ranchers' Association membership requirements, they attempt to "exemplify the Western ranch ideal of personal, homelike hospitality and atmosphere."

---

plus a recreation building and a cozy living room in the main lodge offer plenty of pleasant diversions. During the day, chances are you'll want to go for a horseback ride. Wranglers here work with guests young and old to make sure they're comfortable and capable before they head out of the arena and onto the trail.

Five log cabins and the Trail House Lodge offer comfortable accommodations. In addition to a family-style dining room, the main lodge houses a living room, library, kitchen, gift shop and offices. Ranch cuisine is varied and includes a cookout by the river as well as sack lunches for your day rides. If you catch a trout and want to eat it, the chef will oblige you. Besides riding, the Double Diamond X features a first-class children's program, fishing in the Shoshone River or the ranch's private pond, nightly entertainment and trips to Cody. Whitewater rafting and tours of Yellowstone National Park are easily arranged. Wildlife viewing, photography and hiking are also popular options. DDX offers overnight pack trips and hosts corporate retreats, workshops and seminars.

Rimrock Ranch

$ • 2728 Northfork Route, Cody, Wyo. • (307) 587-3970

Three generations of Fales will be your hosts at the Rimrock Ranch, tucked into the trees on Canyon Creek where views of the surrounding Absaroka Mountain Range will take your breath away. The nine cabins, rustic and weathered on the outside and just as charming on the interior, come in all sizes to accommodate both couples and families. Meals are served in the lodge or outside on the deck where guests like to gather and gab. The Rimrock takes only about 30 guests, all of whom will stay a week. That means you'll likely make some new lifelong friends.

Guests arrive Sunday afternoon and begin their week with a picnic. For the rest of the week, the Fales have a jam-packed schedule that includes several horseback rides geared to each person's skill level. Other scheduled events include a trip to the Cody Nite Rodeo, an evening campfire with a cowboy singer, an afternoon of river rafting, a day in Yellowstone National Park and a ranch gymkhana with lots of horseback games. Other favorites are the softball games in the sagebrush, fishing in the Rimrock's private pond, dips in the pool and a game of pool or Ping-Pong in the recreation room. The week is topped off with a talent show. Guests are free to bow out on any of the activities.

Ranch staff provide rides to Cody as well as airport shuttles. Rimrock also offers custom backcountry pack trips as well as two eight-day trips between Cody and Jackson, Wyoming. In the winter, they offer a variety of snowmobile trips into and through Yellowstone National Park.

UXU Ranch

$$ • 1710 Yellowstone Hwy., Wapiti, Wyo. • (307) 587-2143, (800) 373-9027

At the UXU, the attraction is the horses — and a lot more, such as water-skiing and windsurfing on Buffalo Bill Dam Reservoir, mountain biking or museum meandering in Cody, trap shooting in Cody or traveling to Yellowstone National Park just 17 miles to the West. Take your pick. And, if you want to stay on the ranch, there's still plenty to please you: a pool table, a piano, porch swings, a horseshoe pit and a well-stocked honor bar. Or you may just want to sit on the lodge deck watching the horses graze in the lush meadow below.

UXU has a resident fishing guide for those who want to cast their line in the North Fork of the Shoshone or any Yellowstone river. For those who long to see the wilds of the backcountry, the UXU provides pack trips. Guests stay in 11 one- to three-bedroom cabins equipped with carpeting, remodeled bathrooms, brand-new mattresses, down comforters and private porches. A few have fireplaces. Meals at the UXU are among the best we found. The chef prepares two gourmet entrees each evening, and meals are served in the main lodge dining room with wraparound windows overlooking the meadow. Come September, the UXU offers cooking, photography and painting workshops.

The UXU has a four-night minimum stay. The ranch is open from the end of May to October 1.

No matter what your pleasure, once you get to Yellowstone country, you'll find the camping spirit rising with the flames of an evening campfire and soaring with the osprey on their morning flights.

Campgrounds and RV Parks

Load up your gear, put the dog in the kennel, say goodbye to your neighbors, and breathe a sigh of relief. You're headed for camping country where the possibilities are almost limitless. Hook up your TV, plug into a phone jack, play video games or dive into a pool at some of the more modern privately owned RV parks. Or ditch the crowd and pitch your tent at a quiet little Forest Service campground outside the parks. Stake your claim to a site in one of Yellowstone National Park's reservation campgrounds. Or take your chances on finding a nook in the wildly popular Jenny Lake Campground. No matter what your pleasure, once you get to Yellowstone country, you'll find the camping spirit rising with the flames of an evening campfire and soaring with the osprey on their morning flights.

On your way, you'll come across RV parks and campgrounds that range from simple mom-and-pop stops in and out of town to high-tech, asphalt-covered parking lots with amenities galore. Inside the parks are big, busy campgrounds and smaller, cozy ones. Countless free and nondesignated campsites are scattered throughout the public lands, but you'll have to leave the highway and head into the mountains to get to them. We recommend you stop at a local ranger district office for advice and a map (see the Parks and Forests chapter for the names, addresses and phone numbers).

In this chapter, we've listed numerous public and private campgrounds that, for one reason or another, make them special places to stay inside and outside the parks. Some are reservation-only campgrounds while others on national forest lands have only a few reservable sites.

Generally, Forest Service and Bureau of Land Management campgrounds are less expensive than privately owned RV parks, but they also have fewer amenities. Forest Service campgrounds often have full-time hosts who can answer your questions or sell you firewood. To pay fees, though, you place your money in an envelope and then pop it into a locked box. Staff pick up the money each day.

Because the national parks are slightly different, we'll tell you what you'll find in each. And since you'll be in bear country whether you're in the parks or outside them, we'll first give you some special tips for camping with bruins. Finally, because none of us wants our backcountry (or front country) camping experience marred by the careless remains of others' campsites, we'll remind you of a few courtesies in the "Leave No Trace" land ethic.

Camping Information

Bear Safety

When you get off the plane at Cody's Yellowstone Regional Airport, you'll see your first bear sign — a giant grizzly paw print painted on the airport wall. Believe the signs and similar ones posted elsewhere in Yellowstone country campgrounds. Black bears range throughout all of Greater Yellowstone — not just inside the parks. Read and heed the rules about food storage. They're there for your own and the bears' protection. It takes only one sweet can of Pepsi or a bag of buns for a grizzly or a black bear to put a campground on his list of regular nightly food stops.

Bears that hang around campgrounds looking for a handout become dangerous and demanding very quickly. That's when park and Forest Service rangers have to step in. And they have only three options to take care of the problem bear. They can close the campground until the bear forgets about the reward (this may be years), they can trap and transport the bear to a location 100 miles away, or they can destroy the bear. Each year in Yellowstone National Park, at least one bear has to be destroyed. In Grand Teton, the average is lower. Outside the parks the number is much higher. In 1997, 19 grizzlies died in all of Greater Yellowstone. Ten deaths were caused by humans.

In the front country, store your food and other fragrant items like lip balm, sunscreen or shaving cream either in a bear-proof box or the trunk of your car. If you store your food inside your car, you may be surprised like one visitor to Cooke City who awoke to find a bear had broken into her convertible and tried to pull her back seat through the window. In the backcountry, where you don't have a car, officials recommend hanging food at least 10 feet high in a tree. Yellowstone National Park provides food storage poles at designated campsites, and Grand Teton offers detailed instructions about how to hang food from a branch.

Park and Forest Service rangers also advise campers to cook at least 100 yards from their tents, to keep clothes with food odors outside the tent and to thoroughly wash cooking utensils away from your tent. In both parks and some national forests, food storage regulations are strictly enforced by patrolling rangers. If you leave food out, they will confiscate it. At some campgrounds, you will find bear-proof storage boxes. Almost all campgrounds in and around the parks have bear-proof garbage cans.

For more information on bears, see the Close-up in our Hunting chapter.

Leave No Trace

The explosion in the number of campers and other recreation enthusiasts has brought heavy use to some parts of Greater Yellowstone. To minimize the effects and, let's face it, the damage, public land management agencies promote a Leave No Trace ethic. We have included some of their tips for loving the lands of Greater Yellowstone.

Use designated campsites whenever possible and camp at least 200 feet from streams, rivers, lakes, trails and meadows.

Pick a campsite where the drainage will be good. Digging ditches or trenches around tents causes erosion and leaves scars.

Use established campfire rings whenever possible. If you must build a campfire in a new site, dig out a divot of sod, build a small fire, then replace the sod before you leave. Build fires away from trees, shrubs, rocks and meadows. Fires built on top of a deep layer of pine needles can burn down into the rotting needles, smolder unnoticed for days, then erupt into a forest fire. Use only dead and down wood. When you're finished, make sure

INSIDERS' TIP

Tuck a bandanna or two into your pack. We've seen them used to cool hot necks, wash dirty faces, protect windblown hair, soak up sweaty brows, cradle injured arms, bandage lacerations and carry wild mushrooms. They can also dress up your grunges.

the fire is dead-out and scatter the ashes to naturalize the area.

Plan to filter or boil all drinking water.

Use a "cat-hole" to bury human waste. It should be at least 6 inches deep, 200 feet from your camp and at least 200 feet from any water source.

Never bury your trash! Pack it in. Pack it out.

Reservations

For Yellowstone National Park campsite reservations call AmFac Reservations at (307) 344-7311. For campground reservations in national forest campgrounds, contact the National Recreation Reservation System at (877) 444-6777. Grand Teton National Park has two concessionaire-run campgrounds: one at Colter Bay and the other at Flagg Ranch. The number to call for Colter Bay is (307) 543-2811 or (800) 628-9988. For Flagg Ranch, call (307) 543-2861 or (800) 443-2311.

Price Code

The following ranges of nightly rates, indicated by a dollar-sign code in each write-up, are intended as a guideline for pricing your stay in Greater Yellowstone campgrounds and RV parks. We based our information on the cost of a full hookup at RV parks. Generally, fewer dollar signs indicates a campground with limited amenities.

$	$4 to $9
$$	$10 to $16
$$$	$17 to $23
$$$$	$24 and more

Yellowstone National Park

Yellowstone National Park has 11 campgrounds and one RV park with a total of 2,145 campsites. Of the 12 sites, seven are operated on a first-come, first-served basis and require no reservations. The other five — Madison, Canyon Village, Grant Village, Bridge Bay and the Fishing Bridge RV Park — contain more than 1,700 spaces that may be reserved in advance by calling AmFac Parks and Resorts. See our Parks and Forests chapter for more information about AmFac, the concessionaire that runs most of the lodging and many of the activities in Yellowstone National Park. Fees can be paid to AmFac Resorts by either credit card or check.

You'll find at least minimal amenities such as tables, fire grills, drinking water and flush or pit toilets at all of the campgrounds. Amphitheaters or campfire circles where park naturalists give presentations each evening are also in many of the campgrounds. The reservation campgrounds generally have more amenities such as firewood for sale, showers and laundries. They are also often close to general stores, post offices, restaurants and gas stations.

You can learn more about any of the Yellowstone National Park campgrounds by calling AmFac Resorts at (307) 344-7311.

Madison Campground

$$ • West Entrance Rd., Yellowstone National Park

Only 14 miles east of West Yellowstone, the Madison Campground makes a good staging area for exploring Geyser country in Yellowstone National Park. Away from the hustle and bustle of areas such as Canyon or Grant Village, Madison provides a bit of that peaceful, woodsy feeling despite the fact that it has 280 campsites, all of which are filled almost nightly from Memorial Day to Labor Day. Below the campground is the very scenic and fishable Madison River. Each evening at the amphitheater, a naturalist presents programs on such topics as the bison, the mountains and rivers of the park, geology and hiking.

The Information Station, adjacent to the amphitheater, is a log and stone structure built in 1929 and 1930 as a ranger station. It later became one of the first roadside museums in Yellowstone National Park and now serves as a small information center that also sells educational books. Within easy biking or hiking distance is the turnoff for the one-way, 2-mile Firehole Canyon Drive where you'll see several cascades and waterfalls up close.

The average stay at Madison is three nights, just long enough to explore Geyser country at a leisurely pace. To the south are several geyser basins with self-guiding trails with interpretive signs that wind through them as well as other trails that lead into the hills. To the north is Norris Geyser Basin, with more trails. In between are several points of interest including the Artists' Paint Pots and Gibbon Falls.

Madison Campground offers firewood for sale. It also has flush toilets and an RV dump station. Madison is a reservation campground operated by AmFac Parks and Resorts. It is open from early May to late October.

Norris Campground

$$ • Mammoth-Norris Rd., Yellowstone National Park

Open mid-May to late October, the Norris Campground winds among the conifers bordering an open meadow that often sports elk. Just below the campground, at the edge of the meadow, is the Museum of the National Park Ranger. Take a stroll to this museum with your morning coffee. The large stone fireplace won't warm your bones, but a chat with the museum keeper is liable to warm the cockles of your heart and fire your imagination. Chances are you'll walk away from this old ranger station with a glimpse into the past, since it is staffed by a rotating crew of former Park Service employees who are full of historical anecdotes.

We recommend taking a short (or long) hike on one of two trails leading away from the Norris campground. To the north, you'll find open meadows and Whiterock Spring. To the east, follow Solfatara Creek through a burned area to a large meadow that is popular with elk during the summer months. From there, it's an uphill climb to Ice Lake. Norris Campground is also a good staging spot for forays into the Geyser, Mammoth and Canyon areas. Twenty-one miles to the north lie the Mammoth Hot Springs and Yellowstone National Park Headquarters. The Norris Geyser Basin is within walking or biking distance, and Norris is easy driving distance to the geyser basins south of Madison. The Grand Canyon of the Yellowstone is about 14 miles to the east. We suggest taking at least a day to see each of these areas. Evenings, a park naturalist gives presentations at the Norris Campfire Circle near the "C" Loop.

Norris has 116 campsites offered on a first-come, first-served basis. It is 12 miles to Canyon Village.

Indian Creek Campground

$ • Norris-Mammoth Rd., Yellowstone National Park

Hidden among the conifers at the edge of a large meadow, non-reservation Indian Creek Campground holds 75 spaces adjacent to the creek for which it is named. In a large meadow next to the campground you're apt to see wildlife such as elk and bison. Just 8 miles south of Mammoth, Indian Creek is a good staging spot for both Mammoth and Geyser Country. It is also one of the more popular campgrounds in the park and one of the few that allows you to look past the lodgepoles. To the north, within easy walking distance, is Sheepeater Cliff, once home of the Sheepeater band of the Shoshone Indians, Yellowstone National Park's only resident Native Americans. Indian Creek is open from early June until mid-September. Firewood is for sale at this campground.

Mammoth Campground

$$ • Mammoth Hot Springs, Yellowstone National Park

Squeezed into a hairpin curve on the Mammoth-Gardiner Road, the 85 well-used campsites at the Mammoth Campground are doled out on a first-come, first-served basis. With

INSIDERS' TIP

Bring and use sunscreen. High altitude means thinner air; thinner air allows more ultraviolet rays through to beat on your tender skin. Snow and water reflect those rays back up at you, further adding to the problem.

binoculars you might be able to see antelope, elk or bison grazing in the distance. An amphitheater tucked into a draw at the head of the campground offers nightly educational programs. Plenty of other tours begin just up the hill at the Albright Visitor Center in Mammoth. We recommend leaving your vehicle behind while you explore the many attractions of Mammoth Hot Springs. You can start by touring the Albright Visitor Center, which contains an educational bookstore, a historical display with early era photographs and an interesting 25-minute film on Yellowstone National Park. A new gray wolf display is upstairs. From there, you'll want to walk the Mammoth Terraces (see our Attractions chapter).

Mammoth is the only year-round campground in Yellowstone National Park.

Slough Creek Campground

$ • Northeast Entrance Rd., Yellowstone National Park

The smallest and the most beautiful of the Yellowstone National Park campgrounds, this one has 29 campsites that lie next to Slough Creek, renowned for its good trout fishing (see our Fishing and Watersports chapter). Eight miles northeast of the Tower-Roosevelt Junction and 1 mile north of the main road, this quiet area is only about a half-mile from the head of the Slough Creek Trail, which leads to the park's northern boundary. After a short climb through a Douglas fir forest, the trail follows Slough Creek into a beautiful meadow. Besides finding great fishing here, you are apt to run across moose in the spring, coyote, trumpeter swans and birds of prey in the summer and elk and bison in the fall. You may also catch sight of a wolf or two. Slough Creek is a good place to hole up and get away from the crowds for a while.

Slough Creek Campground, open from late May until early November, lies at the northern edge of Lamar Valley, where wildlife is abundant and tourist traffic is relatively sparse. It's first-come, first-served here.

Pebble Creek Campground

$ • Northeast Entrance Rd., Yellowstone National Park

Open mid-June to September, Pebble Creek is one of the smallest campgrounds in Yellowstone National Park. Situated next to — you guessed it — Pebble Creek, this 36-site campground has plenty of shade but not so many trees that you can't see out. Like Slough Creek Campground, Pebble Creek fills up fast during the summer. About 10 miles southwest of the Northeast Entrance at Silver Gate, Pebble Creek offers a quiet camp for those who want to hike or drive the park. The Pebble Creek Trail leaves the campground and heads up a series of switchbacks to a small meadow. From there it heads up into the mountains and connects with the Bliss Pass Trail, which heads to the west, or it continues on to the Warm Creek Picnic Area a few miles west of the Northeast Entrance. This is a non-reservation campground.

Photo: ?Steve Fischbach

Labor Day weekend in St. Anthony, Idaho, is a popular time to enjoy the dunes.

Tower Fall Campground

$ • Tower-Roosevelt-Canyon Rd., Yellowstone National Park

Hidden in the trees on a knoll 3 miles south of the Tower-Roosevelt Junction, Tower Fall is a popular campground with only 32 spaces. Right across the road from the campground is a Hamilton Store, and next to that is the trailhead to Tower Fall, a beautiful 100-foot waterfall that tumbles between towerlike rocks.

You'll find all kinds of hiking trails in this area. One of them, a 3.5-mile trail, leads from the campground to the Roosevelt Lodge where you can enjoy several different kinds of activities such as a stagecoach ride, horseback riding and a chuckwagon dinner (see our Attractions chapter). Another begins at the campground entrance and leads 3 miles up Tower Creek. Several more trails begin in the Tower-Roosevelt Junction area. One of them, the Yellowstone Picnic Area Trail, follows the Grand Canyon of the Yellowstone River for about 2 miles. For more information on these trails, we recommend contacting Yellowstone National Park's backcountry office, (307) 344-2160. This non-reservation campground is open only in the summer.

Canyon Village Campground

$$ • Canyon Village, Yellowstone National Park

This is a full-service reservation campground with 271 spaces. Open from early June to early September, Canyon Campground is hidden in the trees away from the rest of the village. While you won't be able to see the bustling hamlet from your campsite, you may be able to hear it, and you definitely can walk to Canyon Village, home to a few stores well-stocked with gifts, groceries and outdoor gear. In case you're tired of your own cooking, the Hamilton Store in Canyon has a big lunch counter, and the Canyon Lodge has a cafeteria, a fast-food counter and a full dining room. Canyon also has a visitor center where you can get information and ideas for mapping out your stay in the park. The most centrally located of all the campgrounds, Canyon makes a good staging area for anyone wanting one-stop camping (and shopping) in Yellowstone National Park. From here you can choose a different direction in which to go each day.

There's a laundry at the campground office. Also available are firewood for sale, an RV dump station and hot showers.

Bridge Bay Campground

$$ • West Thumb-Fishing Bridge Rd., Yellowstone National Park

The largest of Yellowstone National Park's 11 campgrounds, Bridge Bay is a sprawling reservations campground open from late May until late September. Don't be surprised if you wake up to an unexpected visitor here. Bison like to roam through the area. The main feature at this campground is Yellowstone Lake (see our Attractions chapter) and the marina adjacent to the campground. At the marina are a boat launch, scenic cruises and guided fishing trips on the lake. Also, a biking and hiking trail leads to a natural bridge. This campground is only 3 miles — an easy bike ride — south of Lake Village. Bridge Bay, a reservation campground, has 429 campsites.

Fishing Bridge RV Park

$$$$ • East Entrance Rd., Yellowstone National Park

This is the only campground in the park where tents and pop-up campers are not welcome. This reservations campground, open from mid-May to early October, accommodates only RVs — 341 of them. That's because it's in bear country. The RV park is just a mile from the Fishing Bridge junction and a short walk to a Hamilton Store as well as a visitor center and a gas station. The Fishing Bridge RV Park's central location makes it an ideal base camp for sightseeing in the lower portion of the park. It is also close to the Pelican Valley Trailhead which leads into beautiful hiking (and bear) country and connects to several of the more remote trails in Yellowstone National Park. You'll find showers and a laundry at this RV park. Call ahead for reservations.

INSIDERS' TIP

Need to get your clothes or body clean while camping in the Island Park area? Stop by Historic Ponds Lodge for a shower and use of the laundromat. You can get a bite to eat at the cafe while you wait for your clothes to dry.

Grant Village Campground

$$ • Grant Village, Yellowstone National Park

Campsites in this 425-unit reservation campground are strung out along the shore of Yellowstone Lake. While the sites are mostly in the trees, there are plenty of places where you can peek through the forest across the lake. You'll find showers, a laundry, Hamilton Store, gas station and post office at Grant Village. This campground is also within easy biking distance of the geyser basin at West Thumb. Grant Village is a good staging spot for daytrips into both Geyser and Lake countries.

Lewis Lake Campground

$ • South Entrance Rd., Yellowstone National Park

Located on the west side of South Entrance Road, the Lewis Lake campground has 85 campsites overlooking Lewis Lake, renowned for its trout fishing. Open from mid-June to early November on a first come, first-served basis, Lewis Lake is the first campground you'll encounter if you enter Yellowstone National Park from the south. It is a popular spot, so stake your claim to a site early. A boat launch adjacent to the campground provides access to Lewis Lake.

Grand Teton National Park

Grand Teton National Park contains five campgrounds operated by the Park Service and two concessionaire-operated trailer parks. Gros Ventre, Jenny Lake, Signal Mountain, Colter Bay and Lizard Creek do not accept reservations. In summer, most fill by midafternoon. The most popular campgrounds, Jenny Lake and Signal Mountain, generally fill before 10 AM. Reservations are allowed at Colter Bay and Flagg Ranch trailer villages. These two campgrounds are the only camping facilities with full hookups in Grand Teton National Park and the adjacent John D. Rockefeller Jr. Memorial Parkway.

Just as in Yellowstone National Park, all Park Service campgrounds supply basic amenities: water, trash disposal (in bear-proof dumpsters), picnic tables, grills and flush or pit toilets. All have outdoor amphitheaters to house the regular naturalist-ranger evening presentations. All but Gros Ventre and Lizard Creek are close to concessionaire services like stores and cafes. Tenters may find they prefer Jenny Lake, where no RVs are allowed (no RVs means no noisy generators), or Lizard Creek, where you'll find walk-in sites, which offer more privacy and seclusion than is typical in busy campgrounds. All charge the same fee, regardless of whether you're tent camping or in an RV. The two concessionaire-operated campgrounds have more amenities and charge more.

All campgrounds ask that you take seriously the bear-care restrictions explained previously. It's easy to make the mistake of feeling that wilderness is banished. After all, you're surrounded by satellite dishes on shiny RVs, running children and tents of every size, shape and color. But wilderness is just past your nose, and the animals do amble through, despite — and sometimes because of — the human zoo. For more information about Park Service campgrounds, call (307) 739-3300. To learn about the two concessionaire-operated campgrounds, call the numbers listed below with their descriptions.

Jenny Lake Campground

$$ • Jenny Lake Loop at Jenny Lake

Popular and small, this tent-only campground can fill by 8 AM in July and August. The 49 sites are scattered among mixed aspens and pine. Small hills, jumbled boulders and dense brush provide privacy. A few sites, designated for hikers and bikers who don't have secure vehicles for food storage, are equipped with bear boxes. The Jenny Lake area is frequently visited by bears. A campground host is on-site. Jenny Lake Campground is open by mid- to late May and closes in late September.

Lizard Creek Campground

$$ • U.S. Hwy. 89 at the top of Jackson Lake

Lizard Creek, with its 60 sites on Jackson Lake's north shore, is our favorite park campground. The lodgepole forest shelters both conventional campsites and walk-in sites.

Walk-in sites require that you park out on the road and then take a short trail (30 feet to 30 yards) to your secluded, private camp. Nearest services are about 10 miles south at Colter Bay or 8 miles north at Flagg Ranch. Lizard Creek opens in mid-June and closes in early September.

Signal Mountain Campground

$$ • Teton Park Rd. on south shore of Jackson Lake

Views of Jackson Lake make some of Signal Mountain's 86 sites particularly pleasant. Others, tucked into the more densely forested south end of the campground, feel pleasantly secluded. Or, if you like sunny and open, camp in the sites on the thinly treed hill stretching away from the lake. In short, Signal Mountain has a site to match almost every camper's tastes.

RVers may find sites a bit small. You have access to the services of adjacent Signal Mountain Lodge: a restaurant and bar, gift shop, gas station and convenience store. There is a trailer dumping station here. All this convenience makes the campground very popular: In the busy months of July and August, sites fill up as early as 10 AM. This campground opens in late May and closes in early October.

Colter Bay Campground

$$ • U.S. Hwy. 89 on east shore of Jackson Lake

Colter Bay is the busiest service area in the park. Part of the cause of all this traffic is the 310-site Park Service campground (second-largest in the park) combined with the 112-site, concessionaire-operated Colter Bay Trailer Village. Some sites in the Park Service campground are for hikers/bikers only. Some loops are designated tent-only, with no generator operation allowed.

Nearby Colter Village offers a gas station, showers, laundry facilities, trailer dumping and propane. The complex also includes a marina, two restaurants, a gauntlet of gift shops, a visitor center and a Grand Teton Lodge Company activity center to hook you up with horseback riding, lake cruises, raft trips and more. Much of the campground is so heavily forested that, even though 12,600-foot Mount Moran looms nearly at your shoulder, you only catch fragmented glimpses of it. Colter Bay Campground opens in late May and closes in late September.

Colter Bay Trailer Village

$$$$ • U.S. Hwy. 89 on east shore of Jackson Lake (307) 543-2811, (800) 628-9988

This concessionaire-operated RV park is the only campground actually inside Grand Teton National Park offering full hookups. Your alternative, at Flagg Ranch, is sandwiched between Yellowstone and Grand Teton parks. Expect to make your reservations up to a year in advance. All 112 sites have full hookups; no tents or open fires are allowed. Flush toilets are available in the campground, but you'll take your showers in the adjacent — and busy — service cluster for an additional $2. The best thing about this campground is its layout: Sites are clustered six to a loop so that you only have a few neighbors and a few cars driving by your site.

Everything's within walking distance at Colter Bay, including the gas station, showers, laundry facilities and a trailer dump. The park has a marina, two restaurants, gift shops, a visitor center and a Grand Teton Lodge Company activity center to entice you into horseback riding, lake cruises, raft trips and more. Security personnel drive through several times a night. Other occasional visitors include deer, moose and bison. Bears are seen here as well, but less often than in other park campgrounds. The RV park opens in late May and generally closes around the end of September.

Gros Ventre Campground

$$ • Gros Ventre River Rd. near Kelly, Wyo.

Sprawling through the cottonwoods in the riverbottom near the Gros Ventre River, this 360-site campground offers shady, spacious sites for RVers and tenters. It is also the National Park Service campground that opens earliest in the season (beginning of May), closes last (mid-October) and generally doesn't fill until evening, if then. Some campsites have gravel tent pads. Rangers say bears wander through the campground regularly, sometimes several times a week. Proper disposal and storage of food is important. A ranger staffs the tiny information center at the campground entrance.

Flagg Ranch Resort

$$$$ • U.S. Hwy. 89 (John D. Rockefeller Jr. Memorial Pkwy.) • (307) 543-2861, (800) 443-2311

Although tent camping is allowed here, most folks are in RVs. Sites are open and sunny; each has a picnic table and fire grate. Clumps of lodgepole pine provide occasional shade, but not privacy. All 77 sites have full hookups. The campground has two shower facilities and a 24-hour laundry. Three minutes' walk from your site is Flagg Ranch lodge, with its restaurant, bar, convenience store, gas station and gift shop. At the end of the lodge's long parking lot is a small Park Service information center. The ranger here can point you to great area hikes and points of interest. Flagg Ranch Resort offers a range of activities, including horseback riding and rafting. The campground opens in early June and closes at the end of September. The resort itself is open from June to mid-October and from late December to mid-March (see our Resorts and Lodges chapter).

Jackson Hole

Jackson Hole is a big valley, so we've grouped the campgrounds here according to their proximity to attractions and scenic sites you may be interested in spending time at.

Atherton Creek Campground

$ • Gros Ventre River Rd. at Lower Slide Lake • (307) 739-5400

This 13-site campground, choked with wild rose and sage and dotted with aspen and cottonwood, is often quiet when the nearby national parks are crammed. The campground has drinking water, pit toilets and dumpsters. Some sites have paved pads for trailers and RVs; several offer views of pretty Lower Slide Lake just below. Campground roads are paved, as is the boat ramp. The campground is open from early June until late October. No sites are reservable.

Red Hills and Crystal Creek Campgrounds

$ • Gros Ventre River Rd. at Crystal Creek • (307) 739-5400

Four and 5 miles, respectively, beyond Atherton Creek Campground lie these two. Together they have 11 sites. What your white-knuckled perseverance on that jouncing, rocky dirt road bought you was peace and quiet: You may have the campground to yourself. You certainly won't see a lot of traffic. Both campgrounds have drinking water, pit toilets and dumpsters. Trailers and RVs are not recommended, and no sites are reservable. The campgrounds are open from early June until the end of October, which makes them and the Atherton Creek facility popular with hunters. That late in the hunting season, other Jackson Ranger District campgrounds are closed.

Pacific Creek Campground

No charge • Pacific Creek Rd. at wilderness boundary • (307) 739-5400

Head out of Grand Teton National Park on a nondescript little road called Pacific Creek that winds toward the Teton Wilderness and you'll end up at this primitive little campground. Pacific Creek Campground is often used by horsepackers heading into the wilderness. It has only six sites, drinking water and dumpsters. Sites are not reservable, but we'd be surprised if you have a problem finding a tent spot. Bear boxes are provided, and it's

INSIDERS' TIP

For a small one-time fee, individuals 62 and older can purchase a Golden Age and Access permit that provides free lifetime entrance to Yellowstone and Grand Teton parks and a 50 percent discount on camping in federal campgrounds. These permits can be purchased at park entrances and most Forest Service ranger stations.

recommended you use them: You're definitely in the bears' backyard. Pacific Creek Campground is open from mid-June until late September.

Grand Teton Park RV Resort

$$$$ • U.S. Hwy. 26, Moran, Wyo. • (307) 733-1980, (800) 563-6469

Only 6 miles from Grand Teton National Park, sprawling through the willow bottoms around the Buffalo Fork River, this year-round campground offers a convenient alternative to national-park camping. Campsites in Grand Teton National Park can't be reserved — but these can. Most sites offer views of the Tetons. Amenities include a game room, outdoor hot tub, laundry, showers and a playground. Sites are generally open and sunny. Many are pull-throughs. All have picnic tables and grills. For those without tent or RV, the campground has 16 simple cabins (bring your own bedding) and five teepees with wooden sleeping platforms. The store sells gas, firewood, fishing tackle, ice and groceries; it also rents videos. Winter visitors can rent snowmobiles with which to explore Buffalo Fork Valley, Togwotee Pass and even Yellowstone National Park. In summer, staff can arrange whitewater and scenic Snake River floats or horseback trail rides.

Wagon Wheel RV Park

$$$$ • 435 Cache St., Jackson, Wyo. • (307) 733-4588

Part of the Wagon Wheel Village complex with its coin-operated laundry, restaurant, saloon and liquor store, gift shop and motel, the Wagon Wheel RV Park nevertheless offers an almost secluded feeling for an in-town facility. Flat Creek, wide and slow, meanders across the back of the grassy open campground (see our Kidstuff chapter for the goods on Flat Creek fishing). Busy Cache Street, which borders the complex, is not visible from most sites. The campground has 30 or so sites; a fourth of those are used by long-term residents and Wagon Wheel employees. The upshot is that you'll feel more like you've joined a small rural village than that you're smack in the middle of town. A bathhouse and campground manager are on-site.

Virginian RV Resort

$$$$ • 750 W. Broadway Ave., Jackson, Wyo. • (800) 321-6982 summer, (800) 262-4999 winter

This modern RV park offers 103 full-hookup sites with cable TV. Sixty-eight are pull-throughs. A bit of thoughtful landscaping has placed a small aspen, red plum or evergreen at nearly every site. Sites also have picnic tables and grills. A laundromat and bathhouse facility can be found at the center of the park; nearby Virginian Lodge allows campers to use its swimming pool and hot tub. This Good Sam- and AAA-approved park closes down sometime in October and reopens in early May. It does not allow tent camping.

Hoback Campground

$$ • U.S. Hwy. 189 near Hoback Junction, Wyo. • (307) 739-5400

The nicest of these 14 sites are near the Hoback River where the water's rush can muffle road sounds. The campground road is paved, as are parking pads; this makes Hoback unusual among area Forest Service campgrounds. Mosquitoes can be a problem in July. Among the amenities are bundled firewood for sale from the campground host, drinking water, dumpsters, picnic tables and grills. The campground opens in early June and closes in mid-September. Picnicking is pleasant here, but the host will charge non-campers $5. Sites are not reservable.

INSIDERS' TIP

August is yellow jacket season. Yellow jackets are aggressive bees attracted to bright colors, sweet smells and meat. If you want to avoid their company, keep food-preparation areas clean and wear a minimum of lotions and cosmetics.

Photo: Randy Hayes, Post Register

Winter camping can be fun — just know your limits.

Lone Eagle Resort

$$$$ • U.S. Hwy. 89 near Hoback Junction, Wyo. • (307) 733-1090, (800) 321-3800

Drive under the totem pole arch and down a dirt road lined with buck and rail fence. Just after you cross the Hoback River on a narrow bridge, you'll enter civilization in the middle of wilderness: an RV and cabin resort. The grounds are immaculate and illuminated by lantern at night. Amenities include basketball and volleyball courts, an outdoor swimming pool, hot tubs, snack shop and convenience store, gift shop and casting pond (they're pretty serious about catch-and-release here — keep your fish and you pay $15). You could picnic in the tiled shower rooms, they're so clean. Lone Eagle offers overnight visits and special three-day packages. The resort closes down in early October and reopens the first of May. See our Resorts and Lodges chapter for more about the resort's activities.

Granite Creek Campground

$$ • Granite Creek Rd. off U.S. Hwy. 191 • (307) 739-5400

A short drive from Granite Creek Hot Springs, this Forest Service campground in the Jackson Ranger District offers generously large sites in an open, sunny meadow and others tucked into groves of spruce and fir. Granite Creek bustles by the edge of the campground, nearly at the base of the dramatic pinnacle folks call The Open Door (it takes a bit of imagination to see the door). Vault and flush toilets, drinking water and garbage disposal are available. Some pull-through sites exist for RVers. Best of all, that 10 miles of jouncing road you drove down after you turned off U.S. Highway 191 keeps traffic down. Even on summer weekends, this campground often doesn't fill. However, all sites are reservable, and it's not a bad idea to be sure. The campground opens in early June and closes late in September.

Snake River Park KOA

$$$$ • 9705 S. U.S. Hwy. 89, Hoback Junction, Wyo. • (307) 733-7078, (800) 562-1878

The cabins watch the Snake River from the edge of the bench on which most of the campground is built. Willow, aspen and fir create pleasant shade. RV sites and most of the tent sites are also up on the bench, but several tent sites are along shady, rollicking Horse Creek and on the sandy bank of the Snake. Campground amenities include showers, a small convenience store with a breakfast bar, a lounge with a pool table and a TV, a laundry

Dutch-Oven Cooking

So, you and your family are camping in Yellowstone country and you want to rough it without sacrificing scrumptious, easy-to-make food such as brownies or pot roast, homemade bread or biscuits. That doesn't mean you have to buy a camper, a travel trailer or a fancy whatchamacallit with an oven. Instead, we recommend you pack a Dutch oven or two (one for the entree and one for dessert). The only hard thing about Dutch oven cooking is wondering if you can do it. Once you try this old-fashioned but easy form of cooking, we're betting you'll make a special place for Dutch oven cooking on your patio back home.

Anything you can bake in an oven (or cook in a crock pot) you can cook in a Dutch oven with just a little bit — a very little bit — of practice. To get you on your way, we've given you a couple of recipes for easy, delicious one-pot dishes. Feel free to bring along your own favorite recipes. (If you're like us, you'll carry them in your head.)

But first, let's go over the ways to control the heat on your Dutch oven so it cooks perfectly every time. Because you may not always be in a place where you can build a campfire, we'll tell you how to cook with charcoal briquets. Feel free, though, to use a wood fire wherever possible.

To bake in a 12-inch Dutch oven you will need:

At least one Dutch oven

A small shovel

A pair of channel-lock pliers to lift off the lid and to pick up the pot by its wire handle

A pair of gloves (some people like to use them as a buffer against the heat and to keep their hands clean)

Charcoal briquets

Briquet starter

All you need to do is fire up those briquets — about 30 of them — then sit back and relax. Some folks like to cook slowly and carefully, and that's probably a good idea for a beginner. We like to go for the gusto. If you'd rather cook slowly, cut back the number of briquets to about 20.

For the best results, you should find a way to heat the Dutch oven lid over the briquets while they're on their way to becoming red hot. If your environment prohibits this, don't worry. Once the briquets are hot, just spread them over your Dutch oven's lid and let it heat up. When the lid is hot, take about one-third of the coals from the top of your oven and evenly distribute them on the ground within the circumference of your Dutch oven. Place the Dutch oven over the coals and redistribute the remaining coals evenly on the lid. Depending on what you're cooking and how close it is to the lid, you'll need to check your dish from time to time, especially after the first 15 minutes. If you sense it is getting too hot, lift your Dutch oven up off the coals and adjust them accordingly. Do the same with the coals on the lid (you're less apt to burn dishes from the top because heat rises).

Timing your cooking is fairly easy — just follow your nose. When you can smell it, it's done or close to it. Adjust the number of briquets up or down according to the size of your Dutch oven. Also, if you're using more than one Dutch oven, stack them one on top of the other, using fewer coals for the lids of the bottom ovens.

— continued on next page

Photo: Candace Burns

Dutch-oven cooking is a great way to enjoy hearty, one-pot meals while camping.

Birthday Casserole

This meal is hard to beat for a no-mess, no-fuss, plate-licking-good dinner. You'll need:

1 small cutting board
A paring knife
4 large potatoes
5 large carrots
1 large onion
1½ pounds hamburger
1 large can tomatoes
Salt and pepper
1 12-inch greased Dutch oven

Slice and stack vegetables and meat in the order listed. Salt and pepper to taste. Bake about 1 hour in medium-hot oven.

Peach Cobbler

OK, so this is too easy to be good, you say. If you're traveling light and don't want to cart along all the fixings for a real cobbler crust, this peach cobbler will do in a pinch, especially if you have a batch of hungry kids. You will need:

2 boxes of yellow or white cake mix
2 large cans of peaches

Pour peaches and cake mixes into a greased Dutch oven and stir if you like. Bake at medium heat for about 1 hour.

Kitchen Sink Breakfast Casserole

Also known as: Gladys's Breakfast Casserole

For those mornings when everyone feels like eating a real meal instead of munching on granola or bagels and cream cheese, this great-tasting casserole fits the bill. It's deliciously filling and is prepared the night before. If you're like us, you'll use this recipe as a good start and make your own creation using the leftovers that have been cluttering your cooler.

At least eight slices of bread (preferably French), cubed
½-pound grated cheese (your choice)
3 cups milk
6 eggs, beaten
¾-teaspoon dry mustard, a small squirt of regular mustard or a half-cup of salsa
1 teaspoon salt
½-pound sausage or other cooked meat.

The night before: Mix eggs and milk in bowl. Brown sausage, then put the meat into egg mixture. Add grated cheese and the rest of the ingredients to the egg mixture. Put the bread on the bottom of the Dutch oven, cover with the egg mixture, place the lid on the Dutch oven, put it into the car away from bears and let set overnight. Bake at medium heat about 45 minutes. Serves four.

room and a playground. The campground even has its own whitewater rafting company; both operations close in winter.

Cabin Creek Campground

$$ • U.S. Hwy. 89 between Hoback Junction and Alpine, Wyo. • (307) 739-5400

It costs $5 to stop here and picnic. Facilities include pit toilets, barbecue grills and picnic tables at each site. No water is available. U.S. Highway 89 runs through a steep-sided, narrow river canyon here, so this campground and the next two are close to the highway, but heavy forest screens the road from sight. Cabin Creek Campground is on a high bench overlooking the river. Sites are large, shady and private. The best ones sit right at the edge of the bench, with views of the Snake River. Some of the 10 non-reservable sites in this Jackson Ranger District campground are pull-throughs. The campground opens in late May and closes in mid-September. Like Station Creek and East Table, this campground will be periodically noisy or even closed due to major construction on U.S. 89. The project to widen and improve the highway will continue at least into 2002.

East Table Creek Campground

$$ • U.S. Hwy. 89 between Hoback Junction and Alpine, Wyo. • (307) 739-5400

Of the three campgrounds in this area, East Table is our favorite. It's also favored by rafters, so if you find an empty spot here on a summer weekend, be very, very glad. Each of the campground's 18 sites have picnic tables and grills. Sites are spacious, with some privacy. Drinking water, dumpsters and vault toilets are available. The campground stretches away from the road on a wide bench with a short access road, so the sites are farther from the highway than others in this canyon. East Table Creek winds across the bench. When funding is available, the small amphitheater hosts evening programs during summer weekends. Programs in 1997-98 often involved river management issues, as Jackson Ranger District was working with boaters to develop use plans for the heavily floated upper Snake. The campground opens in early June and closes in mid-September. Sites are not reservable. Like Station Creek and Cabin Creek campgrounds, East Table may occasionally be unpleasantly noisy or even closed due to major construction on U.S. 89. The highway project will continue at least into 2002.

Station Creek Campground

$$ • U.S. Hwy. 89 between Hoback Junction and Alpine, Wyo. • (307) 739-5400

In the narrow, steep upper Snake River canyon, it's hard to get far from U.S. Highway 89 — there's nowhere to go. But Station Creek Campground is almost far enough. You can still hear the traffic vaguely, but you can't see it. The bench on which the 12 sites are scattered is wide and heavily forested. Sites are generous and well-shaded; some have tent pads. Other amenities include picnic tables, vault toilets, dumpsters and grills. A campground host is on-site. Station Creek opens in mid-June and closes in mid-September. Sites are not reservable, but almost across the road at Little Cottonwood is reservable group space. Like East Table and Cabin Creek campgrounds, Station Creek will be noisy or even closed sometimes due to major construction on U.S. 89. The highway project will continue at least into 2002.

Teton Village KOA

$$$$ • 2780 N. Moose-Wilson Rd., Wilson, Wyo. • (307) 733-5354, (800) 562-9043 reservations only

This campground couldn't be in a more convenient spot. The Village Road (a.k.a. Moose-Wilson Road) shoots straight up through the ski mecca of Teton Village and into Grand Teton National Park in 20 minutes, bypassing Jackson. (However, no RVs are allowed into the park on this narrow road.) Several restaurants serve great meals within a few miles in either direction (see our Restaurants chapter). Jackson is 6 miles away. Willows and shrubs splash cool shadows onto the lawn in almost every one of the 160-odd sites. And the long, thin shape of the campground means that most sites are so far from the busy road that campers can forget it's there. Laundry facilities and a game room are available for guests, who would be wise in summer to make a reservation, especially if looking for an RV hookup or a cabin. The campground is open May through mid-October.

Surrounding Areas

Southwestern Montana

West Yellowstone, Montana

Baker's Hole Campground

$$ • U.S. Hwy. 191, West Yellowstone, Mont. • (406) 646-7369

Because this full-service campground is frequented by black bears (and an occasional grizzly), no tents are allowed at Baker's Hole. (For more information about camping with bears, see our section on bear safety earlier in this chapter.) Otherwise this campground would be filled early each summer day with overflow campers from Yellowstone National Park. Just 3 miles north of West Yellowstone, Baker's Hole has 72 sites, shaded by lodgepole pines, strung out along the Madison River, which provides ample fishing opportunities. A trail to streamside fishing platforms (they protect the vegetation) leads from the campground just north of Unit 1. All facilities, including the fishing platforms, are wheelchair-accessible. Units 61 and 62 are situated closest to the river.

Besides bears, you might see mule deer and osprey while camping here. The Forest Service has 19 reservation sites at Baker's Hole. See this chapter's introduction for more information about reserving campsites in U.S. Forest Service campgrounds. Baker's Hole is open from Memorial Day to mid-September.

Beaver Creek Campground

$$ • U.S. Hwy. 287, Quake Lake, Mont. • (406) 646-7369

This quiet Forest Service campground overlooks the Madison River and Quake Lake (see our Attractions chapter). Moose, deer, elk, osprey, black bear and bald eagles frequent Beaver Creek campground, which is tucked into a wooded aspen and pine forest next to Beaver Creek. Open from June 10 until Labor Day, this campground has 64 sites with picnic tables and fire rings. Eighteen of the sites can be reserved through the National Recreation Reservations System (see "Reservations" earlier in the chapter). Site No. 13 in Loop C is wheelchair-accessible and has a toilet. The rest are available on a first-come, first-served basis. You'll find drinking water here as well as vault toilets and paved loops, but no hookups. The campground is near popular hiking trails and is a mile from the Quake Lake boat ramp. The campground has a 32-foot RV limit.

Cherry Creek Campground

No charge • Hebgen Lake Rd., West Yellowstone, Mont. • (406) 646-7369

At dawn, sip a cup of java and watch the rising sun splash daylight across the smooth waters of Hebgen Lake. If you must, hurry a bit to beat the crowds in Yellowstone National Park. We recommend taking a break, though. Lounge in the shade and read a good book or break out your float tube and fish on the lake. Whatever you do, bring your own drinking water, because you won't find well water here. Eight miles west of West Yellowstone and 6 miles north on the Hebgen Lake Road, Cherry Creek Campground is a free Forest Service campground with dispersed camping for about eight parties. It has a few fire rings, picnic tables and vault toilets. It has neither RV hookups nor wheelchair access.

INSIDERS' TIP

Having a problem with your RV? If you're near West Yellowstone, Repairs by O'B, a mobile RV repair service, will come to your rescue. If you break down within 20 miles of West Yellowstone, you pay no service-call charge. Outside the 20-mile radius, O'B charges $1 per mile. In West Yellowstone, call (406) 646-9084. Outside West, call (888) 646-9084.

Lionshead Resort

$$$$ • U.S. Hwy. 20, 7 mi. west of West Yellowstone, Mont. • (406) 646-9584, summer (406) 646-7662

In summer, this hopping, happening RV park 8 miles west of Yellowstone National Park turns into a mini-town. Set up to serve Yellowstone visitors, this little burg has 153 RV spaces, 18 tent sites and enough amenities so that you can get out of your car and forget about errands at the end of the day.

Alice's Restaurant and Lounge, right in the middle of it all, serves breakfast, lunch and dinner. A Super 8 Motel at the edge of the RV Park has 44 guest rooms for those in your party who might prefer a motel room to camping. The Lionshead has a volleyball net, a playground, horseshoe pits and a pavilion for large groups. The Lionshead also has a gift store, a gas station, a grocery store and a guest laundry.

Lonesomehurst Campground

$$ • Hebgen Lake Rd., West Yellowstone, Mont. • (406) 646-7369

If it's lake fishing you're after, Lonesomehurst offers a great camping and angling combo with a boat launch adjacent to the campground. On the banks of Hebgen Lake, Lonesomehurst is 8 miles west of West Yellowstone on U.S. Highway 20 and 4 miles north on the Hebgen Lake Road. The closest to West Yellowstone of several Forest Service campgrounds on the west side of Hebgen Lake, Lonesomehurst has 26 sites. Five can be reserved through National Recreation Reservations System (see "Reservations" earlier in the chapter), and one is wheelchair-accessible. You'll find shade, water, fire-ring grills, picnic tables, trash cans and vault toilets. And you can call home from the pay telephone. Lonesomehurst is open from Memorial Day to mid-September.

Madison Arm Resort

$$$$ • Madison Arm Rd., West Yellowstone, Mont. • (406) 646-9328

This campground on the south shore of Hebgen Lake is a favorite with anglers. The Madison Arm Resort has 90 campsites with picnic tables, a shower house, laundry, marina and convenience store. It also has three new housekeeping cabins, two of which have lofts and sleep six people. The cost for these cabins is $85 for the first two people. This resort is open from May 15 to October 1.

Rainbow Point Campground

$$ • Forest Rd. 6954, West Yellowstone, Mont. • (406) 646-7369

Tales of a 1983 incident in which a grizzly bear dragged a camper from his tent before killing (and eating) him may be why this campground remains under-used to this day. Since then, only "hard-sided camping" has been allowed here — no tents and no pop-ups. Rainbow Point Campground is near Hebgen Lake about 10 miles northwest of West Yellowstone.

A quiet, wooded campground that features occasional visits by moose, deer, osprey and grizzly bears, Rainbow Point offers swimming, water-skiing, fishing and boating on Hebgen Lake. A beach and a boat ramp are adjacent to the campground. Open from Memorial Day to mid-September, the campground provides water, fire rings, grills, picnic tables, trash cans, vault toilets and paved loops. You won't find any RV hookups, though, and Rainbow Point has a 32-foot RV limit. Site 13 in loop C has a wheelchair-accessible toilet. There's also a pay phone at this campground.

Spring Creek Campground

No charge • Hebgen Lake Rd., West Yellowstone, Mont. • (406) 646-7369

When you get on a dirt road in Yellowstone country, you can be pretty sure you'll be leav-

INSIDERS' TIP

Traveling through the backcountry? Carry a plastic bag or coffee can to receive used toilet paper. That way your family won't leave behind the little white clumps some call "mountain blossoms."

ing the crowds behind. Try this one: Drive 8 miles west of West Yellowstone on U.S. Highway 20, then 8 miles north on Hebgen Lake Road (it's a gravel road) to Spring Creek Campground on the west side of Hebgen Lake (see our Fishing and Watersports chapter). You'll find wild grass and casual camping spots where you can bask in the sun or beat the heat in the shade on the shores of the lake. There are a few fire rings, picnic tables and vault toilets. The campground has neither drinking water nor hookups.

Wagon Wheel Campground and Cabins

$$$, no credit cards • 408 Gibbon Ave., West Yellowstone, Mont. • (406) 646-7872

Spic and span and neat as a pin! What this RV park and campground lacks in space it makes up for in charm and attention to detail. RV spaces, interspersed among mature conifers, are clustered near the (sparkling clean) restrooms, laundry and a game room. Tent sites, designated by numbered wagon wheels in the nooks and crannies of their own special yard, are equally snug. Older, well-maintained log cabins range from a heavenly honeymoon cabin to a three-bedroom, two-story cabin with a fireplace and Western decor. The owners also rent a heated sheep wagon by the night. The Wagon Wheel is open only during summer.

Yellowstone Grizzly RV Park

$$$$ • 210 S. Electric St., West Yellowstone, Mont. • (406) 646-4466

Mapped out, laid out, lined up — this 1996 state-of-the-art RV park makes up for its lack of mature trees (the owners have planted 80 young conifers and deciduous trees) with carpetlike grass and an impressive array of amenities. The Grizzly RV Park, rimmed by a jackleg fence at the south edge of town, offers cable TV hookups, a convenience store, game room, groceries and gift shop, squeaky-clean showers, a laundry, dump station and even telephone hookups at some sites. The park also has a playground and a volleyball net. Tenters will find soft sleeping on the lush lawn, and large groups, like Scout troops or families here for reunions, can cluster on one large island of grass. Asphalt roads lead to the 152 RV sites. Grizzly RV has 30 pull-through spaces and 16 individual tent sites.

Gardiner, Montana

Bear Creek Campground

No charge • Jardine Rd., Gardiner, Mont. • (406) 848-7375

Step out of your camper and fall into Bear Creek from one of five or six informal spaces next to the creek in this little campground northeast of Gardiner on the Jardine Road. We're exaggerating, of course, but several camping spaces are close to the creek. Hidden in a forest of spruce, Douglas fir and lodgepole, Bear Creek campground is 6 miles northeast of Jardine and offers only scenic wonders and fair brook-trout fishing in Bear Creek. You'll find enough room here for about 10 parties to squeeze in, but the RV limit is shorter than most at 28 feet.

Canyon Campground

No charge • U.S. Hwy. 89, Gardiner, Mont. • (406) 848-7375

East of U.S. Highway 89 about 18 miles north of Gardiner, cute little Canyon Campground has 12 units hidden behind big boulders and juniper trees at the base of a hill in Yankee Jim Canyon, named after Jim George, who operated the first toll road into Yellowstone National Park. Across the highway is the Yellowstone River. Despite the steep banks and poor access, quite a few people fish here. On the other side of the Yellowstone River you can see traces of the old toll road as well as the old railroad bed and the Yellowstone Trail, the first automobile route into the park. Other than two toilets (one is handicapped-accessible), there are no services at this year-round campground. The vehicle length limit is 48 feet.

Eagle Creek Campground

$ • Jardine Rd., Gardiner, Mont. • (406) 848-7375

If a day in the park or on the road has you yearning for the soothing sound of a creek and the sweet smell of wild grass, head straight for the "CAMP" sign of the Rocky Mountain RV Camp, but don't turn in. Instead, bear to the left past the RV Camp entrance and drive north about 1.5 miles (the road leads to Jardine, a tiny mining town about 5 miles north of Gardiner) until you see a Forest Service sign on the left that reads, "Eagle Creek Campground." Turn left, slow down and cruise through this campground from top to bottom before choosing your home for the night. At the top, you'll find tent spaces tucked into the trees. At the bottom you'll find open spaces with mowed grass. To the east are a corral and plenty of room to pull through with a fifth-wheeler. The place has no designated campsites and no campground host. And don't be surprised if an elk or two join you for breakfast. Bring your own water, pack out your garbage and don't count on finding firewood here. There are two toilets; one is handicapped-accessible.

Rocky Mountain RV Camp

$$$ • 14 Jardine Rd., Gardiner, Mont. • (406) 848-7251

If you're hot, tired and dusty, the neon "CAMP" sign of the Rocky Mountain RV Camp will look mighty welcome. Perched on a bluff overlooking Gardiner and Yellowstone National Park, this campground features 50 RV sites and 21 tent spaces with grass. This is a good spot for an overnight rest or for a base camp while you explore the park. If it's a shower you're after, get up early to beat the crowd. You'll find the ladies' restroom packed with women showering themselves and their children, drying their hair and applying makeup at the sinks. Rocky Mountain has a coin-operated laundry (it's open to the public) and a store that carries an assortment of food and camping supplies. This RV park has a dump station, and you can unload your garbage (just toss it into the back of the 1948 Dodge dump truck parked by the office). There is an after-hours registration box by the office door so latecomers can slip into the campground in the wee hours of the night. Rocky Mountain RV Camp is open May 1 to November 1.

Timber Camp Campground

No charge • Jardine Rd., Gardiner, Mont. • (406) 848-7375

An open meadow splashed with wildflowers, a little creek, a lodgepole and Douglas fir forest and isolation — what more could you want? Open from June 15 through December 1, Timber Creek campground is about 9 miles northeast of Gardiner and 4 miles north of Jardine. You won't find water here so bring your own. The RV limit at Timber Creek is 48 feet.

Cooke City, Montana

Colter Campground

$ • U.S. Hwy. 212, Cooke City, Mont. • (406) 848-7375

This is one of the few campgrounds you'll find in this neck of the woods that has a scenic view. Burned in the 1988 Yellowstone Fire (see the Close-up in our History chapter), the Colter Campground is thick with wildflowers and new young trees growing up through the rubble left by the fire. Open from mid-July until mid-September, the 23 sites in this campground fill quickly each summer day with overflow campers from Yellowstone National Park 3 miles to the west. While you'll find few trees to screen your view of other campers at Colter, you will find there's plenty of space between each campsite. The campground has several toilets, drinking water and trash cans. The RV length limit is 48 feet.

Soda Butte Campground

$ • U.S. Hwy. 212, Cooke City, Mont. • (406) 848-7375

Big bear-paw signs warn visitors they're in grizzly country at Soda Butte, a popular staging campground for visitors to the park. It is also the first campground to fill with overflow campers from Yellowstone National Park's northeast entrance. At this campground, hidden among the conifers, dawn breaks slowly and night comes quickly. The cold nights (don't be sur-

INSIDERS' TIP

The Yellowstone Grizzly RV Park has the only RV dump station in West Yellowstone.

prised if it snows on July 4 or August 1) and the forest canopy make Soda Butte a good place to catch up on sleep. But, oh, it's hard to get up to the usually cold mornings here. You'll find water and trash pickup here. The RV limit is 48 feet, and the campground has 21 sites.

Bozeman, Montana

Sunrise Campground

$$ • 31842 E. Frontage Rd., Bozeman, Mont. • (406) 587-4797, (888) 704-7966, pin 8162

If you're one of those people who has to check out the bathrooms before you check into an RV park, then take your peek and park your vehicle at the Sunrise Campground. Maryjo and Marty Stanek, owners since 1996, pride themselves on their glistening bathrooms. The Sunrise, on the eastern edge of Bozeman, is easy to reach from Interstate 90. Just take Exit 309, then turn left off the ramp onto Frontage Road. The Sunrise Campground is the second business on the right. About half this campground is shaded by mature trees planted 25 years ago when the RV park was first built. It has 52 RV spaces (all but three are full hookup) and a wide expanse of lawn where tent campers can pick their own spots to pitch their tents. Besides sparkling bathrooms, you'll find laundry facilities, a TV room and small playground. During the summer, it's a good idea to call ahead for reservations.

Bozeman Hot Springs KOA

$$$$ • 81123 Gallatin Rd., U.S. Hwy. 191, Bozeman, Mont. • (406) 587-3030

Location, location, location. Park your RV, hit the hay and sleep into the cool dawn. Then slip out of bed, grab your towel and your swimsuit and pick up the well-worn trail that leads from the KOA, through a hedge, to the Bozeman Hot Springs. Ahhh. Now, you have a choice. Do you want to swim in the giant blue indoor pool? Or do you want to soak outside under Montana's big, blue sky? Besides their neighbors with the hot springs, this KOA has plenty of amenities including a playground, laundry, showers, a convenience store, game room and miniature golf course. Located about 8 miles southwest of Bozeman, the Bozeman Hot Springs KOA has 130 RV spaces and 14 camp cabins.

Big Sky, Montana, Area

Red Cliff Campground

$ • U.S. Hwy. 191, Gallatin Gateway, Mont. • (406) 587-6920

Forty-eight miles south of Bozeman on U.S. Highway 191, this Forest Service campground at the base of a red (of course) cliff has 68 campsites. Across the Gallatin River from the highway, it offers shade and seclusion. You'll find toilets, water, trash pickup and firewood. This campground offers fishing on the Gallatin River as well as hiking. It is easily accessible to Big Sky Ski and Summer Resort to the north and to Yellowstone National Park to the south.

Spire Rock Campground

No charge • Squaw Creek Rd., Gallatin Gateway, Mont. • (406) 587-6920

There's no water, no garbage and no fee at this little campground which offers hiking and fishing. To get to Spire Rock, drive 26 miles south of Bozeman on U.S. Highway 191, then turn east on the Squaw Creek Road. Spire Rock is about 2 miles up the creek, which runs happily beside the campsites. If you take the road up the creek a ways, you'll find a trail that leads to Rat Lake and good fishing. You'll probably find better fishing, though, down the road in the Gallatin River. This campground has 10 campsites and an outhouse and can accommodate a 50-foot-long vehicle.

Swan Creek Campground

$ • Swan Creek Rd., Gallatin Gateway, Mont. • (406) 587-6920

This nifty little 11-unit Forest Service campground is tucked into the trees and brush beside Swan Creek. You'll find water, outhouses, trash pickup and firewood here. You'll also have access to Forest Service Trail #186 at the top of the campground. It leads to the ridge above, where you can view the Gallatin Canyon. If you want to keep on hiking, this trail also leads into the Paradise Valley. Down the road, you'll find fishing in the Gallatin River. The campground has a 45-foot RV limit.

Livingston, Montana

Paradise Valley KOA Kampground

$$$ • U.S. Hwy. 89, 8 miles south of Livingston, Mont. • (406) 222-0992

"Don't get the gumps. It's only a few more bumps to KOA," reads a sign posted along the way to the Paradise Valley KOA. This campground has it all: huge cottonwood, Douglas fir and quaking aspen trees and lush green brush to separate campsites, camp cabins, an indoor swimming pool, cheerful restrooms, a laundry, gift shop and the standard KOA kiddie bikes. In the mornings, you'll find free coffee and a simple, inexpensive breakfast (a limited dinner menu is available, too). Sundays, you can attend a worship service at the campground chapel. The Paradise Valley KOA is on the banks of the Yellowstone River, about 1.5 miles east of U.S. Highway 89. It has 47 RV sites, 23 tent sites and 23 cabins.

Ennis, Montana, Area

Lake Shore Lodge and Campground

$$ • McAllister Rd., McAllister, Mont. • (406) 682-4424

Lake swimming and blue-ribbon fishing come with the RV and tent spaces at this summer and fall favorite on Ennis Lake, created when Montana Power dammed the Madison River. Besides the 20 RV spaces, Lake Shore Lodge has five fully equipped housekeeping cabins ranging in style from older studio log cabins, each with a queen-size bed, to two-bedroom, two-bath newer cabins overlooking the lake. Campers can use the showers, restrooms and a laundry, and they can pick up supplies at the store and tackle shop. Boat rentals are available at the Lodge's small marina. Children will like the campground's playground. Lake Shore Lodge keeps its older cabins open May 1 through October 1. The newer, larger cabins are open until December. See our Vacation Rentals chapter for information about the owners' four-bedroom, four-bath vacation home.

Madison River Cabins and RV

$$$ • 1403 U.S. Hwy. 287 N., Cameron, Mont. • (406) 682-4890

This small RV park has a great view and lots of amenities. For more information, please refer to our Hotels, Motels and Cabins chapter.

Ruby Creek Campground

$ • U.S. Hwy. 287, Cameron, Mont. • (406) 683-2337

Just 3 miles off U.S. Highway 287 on a paved road pocked with potholes, the Ruby Creek Campground is smack-dab in the middle of a boulder field. The rocks offer no screen from the sight of other campers, but neither do they interrupt the view of the nearby Madison River and the Madison Mountains to the east or the Gravelly Range to the west. If you have a vanload of restless children, we suggest you pull out their bikes or skateboards (we hope you brought some along) and turn them loose on the paved road that weaves through the boulders. While anglers cast their lines into the waters of the Madison River (world-renowned for trout fishing), the family chef can cook up burgers and watch the setting sun play on the Madison Range. Later, climb into bed and let the river lull you to sleep. This under-used Bureau of Land Management campground has 28 spaces.

Virginia City Campground and RV Park

$$$ • U.S. Hwy. 287, Virginia City, Mont. • (406) 843-5493

The only private campground in town, the Virginia City Campground and RV Park has 18 RV sites and 26 tent sites. It sits on the east edge of town, against the base of a hill where several campers and tents can squeeze into the shade near Daylight Creek. Along with hot showers, you'll find clean restrooms, a minia-

INSIDERS' TIP

Gathering wood for campfires is generally allowed as long as the wood is dead and downed.

ture golf course and horseshoe pits. There is an active cricket choir at the Virginia City Campground. And, in case you don't like cricket music, the campground is just around the corner from Virginia City, a restored and preserved historic mining town that offers other entertainment (see our Attractions chapter).

West Fork Cabin Camp

$$ • U.S. Hwy. 287, Cameron, Mont. • (406) 682-4802

This hopping place on the banks of the Madison River has 24 full-hookup RV sites and an array of other amenities including raft rentals, guided fly fishing and a fly shop. For more information about the West Fork Cabin Camp, please refer to our Hotels, Motels and Cabins chapter.

Red Lodge, Montana, Area

Parkside Campground

$ • Rock Creek Rd. #421, Red Lodge, Mont. • (406) 446-2103

Next to Rock Creek on the west side of U.S. Highway 212 about 12 miles south of Red Lodge, Parkside Campground is the largest of three Forest Service campgrounds in the Red Lodge Ranger District of the Custer National Forest. You'll find conifers, grass, wildflowers and cool mornings. (The elevation here is 7,200 feet.) The access roads are paved, and sites have back-in spurs. The RV limit is 40 feet. Of the 26 sites at Parkside, 15 can be reserved through the National Recreation Reservation System.

Perry's RV Park and Campgrounds

$$ • U.S. Hwy. 212, Red Lodge, Mont. • (406) 446-2722

If you like cozy, comfortable and a just little bit wild with all the amenities, you'll feel like you've come home or at least found your own little corner of the world when you stay at Perry's RV Park and Campground. Situated 2 miles south of Red Lodge on the banks of Rock Creek, this RV Park has plenty of cottonwoods and aspens for shade. Below the brow of a hill, it is also shielded from the highway. The only sounds you'll hear at Perry's are the creek, the chattering aspen leaves and the muffled voices of campers. You'll also find showers, electrical and water hookups, laundry facilities, a convenience store and dump station at Perry's. There are picnic areas and barbecue grills for guests. Perry's has 20 RV units and space for 10 tent camps.

Sheridan Campground

$ • East Side Rd. #389, Red Lodge, Mont. • (406) 446-2103

Just 5 miles from Red Lodge, this little Forest Service campground is best suited for tents and campers. At Sheridan, situated beside Rock Creek about a mile off U.S. Highway 212 on a dirt road, you'll encounter grass, a few trees and the comforting sights and sounds of the creek. Despite the fact that this campground is close to some small subdivisions, you'll feel as if you're in the wilds. Sheridan Campground has a hand pump for drinking water and eight camping spaces. The campground has five reservation sites. For more information about the campground call the Red Lodge Ranger District office at the above number.

Beartooth Pass

Beartooth Pass, between Red Lodge and Cooke City, is dotted with campgrounds from top to bottom. Our campgrounds are listed just that way: from the top, heading west down the pass toward Cooke City.

Island Lake Recreation Area

$$ • U.S. Hwy. 212 • (307) 754-7207

Camp on top of the world (elevation 9,600 feet) at Island Lake Recreation Area in the Clarks Fork District of the Shoshone National Forest. Sites in this beautiful and well-used

INSIDERS' TIP

Forest Service campgrounds are still owned by all of us, but the days when they were run by your friendly local ranger are gone. Most campgrounds in national forests are run by private concessionaires trying to make a profit.

campground are scattered among big round boulders, behind conifers, below and above the winding road and back in the trees. Adjacent to the campground you'll find a boat launch leading into the icy waters of — you guessed it — Island Lake, a popular float-tubing lake full of pan-size brook trout. (You'll need a Wyoming fishing license here.) Trail #620 is a popular trailhead leading across alpine meadows to scads of lakes in the Absaroka-Beartooth Wilderness.

Island Lake has 20 campsites. Generally, this campground and others on the Beartooth Highway are open from June 1 until September 15, depending on snow conditions. Expect snow and ice in September, though. The Beartooth Highway is closed during the winter.

Beartooth Lake Campground

$ • U.S. Hwy. 212 • (307) 754-7207

Situated on the shores of Beartooth Lake, the 21 units in this sparsely timbered campground are 9,000 feet up. That means cool mornings (and evenings). Beartooth Lake provides good brook trout fishing (you'll need a Wyoming license) and a spectacular reflection of Beartooth Butte, which looms above the lake. Two trails take off from this spot: Trail #621 leaves from the campground, while Trail #619 heads about a half-mile up Beartooth Lake at the inlet. Both trails lead to myriad other lakes and spectacular views (see our Hiking and Backpacking chapter). This campground is open only during the summer and early fall, until about October 15. There are no firm opening and closing dates because they depend on the weather conditions, which can change in hours.

Crazy Creek Campground

$$ • U.S. Hwy. 212 • (307) 754-7207

When you pull into the Crazy Creek Campground 6 miles south of the U.S. Highway 212 junction, you're apt to think you've traded the wilds of Wyoming (the campground is just inside the Wyoming border) for a picture-perfect park. Tucked into the lush grass, lupine and lodgepole are 19 camping spaces with a 32-foot RV limit. A trail, which begins in the campground, leads to some tumbling falls on Crazy Creek.

Chief Joseph Group Campground

$ • U.S. Hwy. 212 • (406) 848-7375

Reserve this six-unit campground for your next family reunion or any other group outing. Four miles east of Cooke City, the Chief Joseph Campground is a favorite for groups, but if you happen along and don't see a cluster of tents here, help yourself. If you plan to stay for a while, check with the Gardiner Ranger District (the number is listed above) to see if it has been reserved.

Chief Joseph Highway

Wyo. Highway 296, also known as Chief Joseph Highway, offers several camping possibilities, including the following campground.

Hunter Peak Campground

$ • Wyo. Hwy. 296 (Chief Joseph Hwy.) (307) 754-7207

Away from the highway and hidden in heavy timber, this small Forest Service campground makes a good stopover if you're traveling between Cooke City and Cody. Right next to the Clarks Fork River, this nine-unit campground promises good fishing. It also offers the possibility of at least seeing grizzly signs because the bears regularly cruise the river for food. You'll find full Forest Service amenities here, including water. This campground, popular with hunters, stays open until the snow closes it.

INSIDERS' TIP

National Forest managers distribute a wide range of free brochures that can tell you everything from how to survive a bear attack to how to stay on the right side of local fishing regulations. Stop by any ranger station or national park visitor center.

Eastern Idaho

Teton Valley

These campgrounds are grouped as if you encountered them driving into Teton Valley from Idaho Falls on Idaho Hwy. 31, then headed toward Jackson over Teton Pass, but then changed your mind, headed back down toward Driggs on Idaho Hwy. 33 and turned east again, this time toward Alta, Wyoming, and Grand Targhee Ski and Summer Resort.

Pine Creek Campground

$ • Idaho Hwy. 31 at Pine Creek Pass, Idaho • (208) 354-2312

This is the cheapest Forest Service campground in the area, mostly because it has no safe drinking water. Four dollars rents your space just below the summit of Pine Creek Pass. Some of the 11 sites are carved into dense underbrush and are very private. Most are shaded; a few are almost buried under heavy forest cover. A couple are reachable by small footbridges crossing Little Pine Creek, a tiny tributary to the Teton River. Some sites are closer to the road than we'd like. All have picnic tables and grills. Pit toilets are on-site; there is no campground host. The campground opens in early June and closes in late September.

Teton Valley Campground

$$$ • 128 Idaho Hwy. 31, Victor, Idaho • (208) 787-2647

Green, grassy and equipped with 32 pull-through RV sites, this 74-site campground is better suited to RVs than tents. Long-term visitors will appreciate several sites with phone hookups. Teton Valley Campground is equipped with a heated outdoor pool (summer only), showers and a recreation room. For those without RVs or tents, there are four heated sleeper cabins. Best of all, it's open year-round as sort of an experiment on the part of new owners, Ruth and Gary Ellis. Nearly all area campgrounds shut down in September or October.

Mike Harris Campground

$ • Idaho Hwy. 33 at Teton Pass, Idaho • (208) 354-2312

This national forest campground in the Teton Basin Ranger District is barely a mile off heavily traveled Idaho Highway 33, but the dirt road to the campground crosses Trail Creek, then winds around a hill and into a lodgepole pine forest. You'd never know there was a road near. Your fee gets you a spacious site in lodgepole forest dotted with wild geranium. Water and pit toilets are available; reservable sites are not. Despite its attractiveness, convenient location barely 20 miles from Jackson and small size — only 11 sites are available — the campground is often quiet and empty, especially during the week. The campground has a trailhead to the Mike Harris trail, which is steep, rocky and, of course, lovely. The facility opens in early June and closes in late September.

Trail Creek Campground

$ • Idaho Hwy. 33 at Teton Pass, Idaho • (208) 354-2312

As Idaho Highway 33 begins the serious climb up and over Teton Pass, this little campground hides, almost out of sight, on Trail Creek below the highway. Don't miss it. Once you top the pass and drop over into Jackson Hole, you'll pay twice as much for Forest Service campgrounds. Trail Creek's 11 sites are not reservable. Each has a picnic table and a grill; most enjoy shade. Pit toilets and drinking water are on-site. There is no campground host. The campground opens in early June and closes in late September.

Teton Canyon Campground

$ • Forest Rd. 009, off Ski Hill Rd. near Alta, Wyo. • (208) 354-2312

Some of the best hiking in the area leaves from this campground, 4 miles out of Alta on a

INSIDERS' TIP

To reserve your national forest campsite, call the National Recreation Reservation System at (877) 444-6777, or find them on the Internet at www.ReserveUSA.com.

dirt road. The Alaska Basin and Table Mountain trails both wind toward heaven from here (see our Hiking and Backpacking chapter). The campground has several sites in deep forest. Shade keeps the undergrowth down for an oddly parklike feel. Other sites scatter about a sunny meadow ringed with aspen and dotted with wildflowers. Campers will appreciate raised gravel pads, picnic tables and fire rings, water and access to pit toilets. Some sites are equipped with the most intricate-looking grill systems we've ever seen, on which you can hang pots or swing either of two grates over or away from the fire. Because of the hiking, Teton Canyon also offers trailhead parking and horse corrals. A campground host lives here, but not for much of the year: The campground is open only from early August to late September.

Swan Valley, Idaho

Palisades Creek Campground

$ • Palisades Creek Rd., Irwin, Idaho • (208) 523-1412

Swan Valley's most scenic little campground isn't easy to find, but it's worth the hunt. Eight generously large sites cling to the bank of Palisades Creek, 2 miles from U.S. Highway 26 on a well-maintained gravel road. The drive to the campground is pretty, but remember to watch out for horseback riders. The area is popular for trail riding. Pit toilets, running water and bundled wood for a nominal fee are the only amenities, but if you like to feel as if you're in the backcountry even though you've just stepped from your camper, this is your place. Walk from your campsite to the trailhead for one of the nicest hikes in the area: up Palisades Creek to upper and lower Palisades Lakes (see our Hiking chapter). The first several miles of the hike are on wide, level trail, perfect for trail runners and horseback riders. This campground opens in late June and closes in early September. No sites are reservable.

Palisades RV Park

$$ • 3804 Swan Valley Hwy., Palisades, Idaho • (208) 483-4485

This is a smaller, older, backyard-style RV park, the kind that tends to attract long-term visitors (about one-fourth of the 16 sites are occupied by folks staying for a big chunk of the season). All sites have full hookups. There's a small laundry room, bathroom and shower. Two older, fully furnished pine-paneled cabins are also available. At Palisades, you're close to the recreational possibilities of the reservoir and to the world-class trout fishing of the South Fork of the Snake.

Timberwolf Resort

$$ • 3781 Swan Valley Hwy., Palisades, Idaho • (208) 483-3581

All sites at this small RV park have full hookups. The 15 grassy sites are a smidge larger and more pleasant. If you're here to fish the South Fork or to boat on Palisades Reservoir, the location is ideal and the price excellent. Huskey's also includes a gas station, a convenience store, guest laundry and showers, and a fishing supply shop. The RV park closes in mid-October and reopens in May.

Island Park, Idaho

These campgrounds are generally listed as you'd encounter them heading north on U.S. Highway 20.

Historic Ponds Lodge

$$ • 3757 N. U.S. Hwy. 20, Ponds Lodge in Island Park, Idaho • (208) 558-7221

Most of the private RV parks in the area are large and busy, but Ponds Lodge offers an alternative. An easy walk from the lodge's grocery store, gift shop, cafe and bar, the 50 RV-only sites are scat-

INSIDERS' TIP

We've said it before, but this is important: A fed bear is a dead bear. Please treat bears and other wild creatures with respect by not allowing them to learn that they like human food. Your safety and theirs depend on it.

tered among stands of pine and clusters of wildflowers. They are refreshingly unimproved — no concrete pads, no pavement — and spread out more than most. Guests who come here to fish will appreciate being a stone's throw from the Buffalo River and five minutes from both Island Park Reservoir and the famous fly-fishing waters of the Henry's Fork. All sites have full hookups. Showers and a public laundry are on-site. Weekly, monthly and seasonal rates are also available. The RV park closes in winter, but cabins are available year-round (see our Hotels, Motels and Cabins chapter). The lodge itself was built in 1935 by Charles and Myna Ponds; it's a massive log structure with vaulted ceilings. The solemn faces of its builders peer down from one wall.

West End Dispersed Campground

No charge • Forest Rd. 167 at Island Park Reservoir • (208) 558-7301

"Dispersed" means you can pitch your tent or park your trailer under the tree of your choice. West End is an open area by a bend of Island Park Reservoir. The Forest Service charges nothing, but it provides vault toilets and a boat dock for your convenience. There are also some sites with picnic tables for those who like life to be a bit more organized. You must pack out your trash and haul your water from the pump about a half-mile from the main camping area. (To find the water pump, look for the tiny wooden corral. Sometimes there's also a sign.) Boaters love the freedom and seclusion enough to drive in 9 miles over a slow, winding dirt road to get here. So while you won't see any passing traffic, you will have plenty of company in the summer boating and fishing months. This campground opens in late May and closes in mid-September.

McCrea's Bridge Campground

$ • Yale/Kilgore Rd. off U.S. Hwy. 20 near Island Park, Idaho • (208) 558-7301

The 25-site campground is situated on a thinly wooded hillside slipping down to Island Park Reservoir. U.S. Highway 20 with its traffic noise is nearly 3 miles away. Each site has a picnic table and fire pit. Vault toilets and running water are provided, as is a campground host. As with nearly all Forest Service campgrounds in the area, bear-proof dumpsters are available. Just across the water, visible from your campsite, is a small cafe and bar. The nearest gas station and convenience store are 2 miles away. Reservations can be made for about half of the sites in this campground, and it, like all Island Park Ranger District campgrounds, opens in late May and closes in mid-September.

Coffee Pot Campground

$ • U.S. Hwy. 20 near Mack's Inn in Island Park, Idaho • (208) 558-7301

Perhaps because it's 1.5 miles off U.S. Highway 20 on a dirt road, this small Forest Service campground tends to be quieter than others in the area. The setting is idyllic; most sites are within rock-skipping distance of the clear, dimpled Henry's Fork. Picnic tables, fire pits, drinking water, new vault toilets and bear-proof dumpsters are provided. There are only 14 sites, none reservable. You won't find much turnaround room for a large camper vehicle or RV. Anglers and tent campers will love it, though. Trails leave from here to travel both up and down river. Hike down to look at Upper Coffee Pot Rapid, one of the few spots where the Henry's Fork gets to make noise. A ranger-guided nature walk leaves from here every Saturday morning in summer. This campground opens in late May and closes in early October.

Flatrock Campground

$ • U.S. Hwy. 20, Mack's Inn in Island Park, Idaho • (208) 558-7301

This Forest Service campground is conveniently located just off U.S. Highway 20, moments from Mack's Inn with its restaurants, boat ramp, convenience store and gas station. Many campsites have views of the placid, trout-filled Henry's Fork. More private sites are farther from the river on a wooded hillside. Running water and pit and flush toilets are available. Sixteen sites are reservable; however, none of these have river views. A campground host lives on-site. Convenience tends to make this a busy, busy campground, so we don't recommend it in midsummer. Like all

Island Park Ranger District campgrounds, this one opens in late May and closes in mid-September.

Mack's Inn Resort

$$$ • U.S. Hwy. 20 at Mack's Inn in Island Park, Idaho • (208) 558-7272

This 69-unit RV park is attached to busy Mack's Inn Resort with its store, boat rental, playground, dinner theater, laundromat and recently remodeled coin-operated shower facility. All sites have full hookups. Recreational features include sand volleyball, horseshoes and an outdoor basketball court. None of this stuff is up at the RV park, however, which gives you the best of both worlds: access to the bustle without having to sleep next to it. You can walk or drive down to the main resort complex in a minute or so.

Mack's Inn is popular because of its location: right on the bank of the Henry's Fork of the Snake, 10 minutes' drive from lovely (and very fishable) Henry's Lake. It also sits at the junction of Big Springs Road, which shoots away from civilization toward the valley's most interesting scenic attraction, Big Springs, where a whole river pours up out of the ground. Tent sites were $10 in 1998.

Grand Mountain Studio & RV Park

$$$ • 50 N. Big Springs Rd., Island Park, Idaho • (208) 558-7863 in summer, (208) 354-2329 in winter

Carl Nelson's RV park is our favorite kind: small with a residential feel. In fact, most of his guests are there for the summer. He keeps a few available for short timers, though. Park amenities include 20-foot-long cement pads next to RV spaces. Blue spruce, mountain ash, aspen and brush wall in each site. There's a coin-operated laundry across the street. No showers or toilet facilities are available, so you must be self-contained to stay here. RV sites have full hookups. The last benefit of Carl's park is location: Unlike almost every other commercial RV park in Island Park, this one is away from the main road while still being very easy to reach. It's a few minutes' walk from the valley's golf course and a few minutes' drive from great fishing on the Henry's Fork. Grand Mountain is open May through October. Be sure you make a reservation. And don't forget to check out Carl's jewelry shop on the premises. He works in gold and elk ivory, among other materials.

Big Springs Campground

$ • Big Springs Rd. off U.S. Hwy. 20 near Island Park, Idaho • (208) 558-7301

Adjacent to two of the area's most interesting attractions, Big Springs and the Johnny Sack Cabin, is this small, wooded campground. It has 17 sites, each with tables and fire pits. You'll have access to running water and bear-proof dumpsters, new vault toilets and group picnic areas. In June, you'll be attacked by voracious mosquitos, so come prepared. The nearest gas station is nearly 5 miles distant, at Mack's Inn. West Yellowstone is 25 miles away. You'll enjoy pleasant hiking and great wildlife viewing in the immediate area. A mile west is the Big Springs boat ramp, which marks the beginning of a lovely float along the nation's first wilderness water trail. And, of course, you must feed the fish at Big Springs (fish food, healthier than bread or corn, is available from a vending machine on the bridge). This campground opens in late May and closes in mid-September. None of its sites are reservable. No fishing is allowed near the campground.

Henry's Lake State Park

$$$ • Off U.S. Hwy. 20, north of Island Park, Idaho • (208) 558-7532

Parklike and open, this busy campground with a boat ramp has recently gone to an all-reservation system for its sites. Sites are

INSIDERS' TIP

If weather permits, make sure you sleep outside your tent or RV at least one night: Our high-altitude, low-humidity air makes fine star watching, particularly in August when meteors streak across the sky every few minutes. (You'll probably wake up damp in the morning from dewfall.)

planted with young trees; each has a gravel pad, a fire circle and a picnic table. The nicest sites are spacious and nearly at the water's edge. Showers are available to campers and, for a fee, to day-users. Attendants are available during business hours to answer your questions and keep an eye on things. The campground is open from early June to late September.

Ashton, Idaho

The campgrounds around Ashton are generally arranged as you'd encounter them heading north toward Island Park and West Yellowstone.

Jessen's RV Park

$$$, no credit cards • 1146 S. 3400 E., Ashton, Idaho • (208) 652-3356

Nieca and Jack Jessen have created the kind of RV park that ends up serving more seasonal residents than passers-through. If you ask them, they'll probably say that guests are drawn to the "home away from home" atmosphere. We think there are a few more reasons. Convenient at U.S. Highway 20 near Ashton, the Jessens' park has 16 sites with shade, pull-throughs and full hookups as well as a scattering of others with water and electricity. Many of these abut the irrigation canal that winds through the property. Even in the intense, high-altitude sunshine of Ashton, the massive willow trees keep things cool and shaded. Fruit trees and flower beds are scattered across the 10-acre property. A white gazebo, a big patio and a fire circle encourage campers to leave their RVs and tents and visit. Amenities include shower and laundry facilities and a pop machine. Tent campers set up on the lawn festival-style without specifically designated sites. Firewood is provided. Propane is available.

Other accommodations options on the property include two bed and breakfast guest rooms in the old farmhouse and several small cottages at one end of the RV park. (Please see our Bed and Breakfast Inns and our Hotels, Motels and Cabins chapters.) The campground is open from May to November, depending on weather. Reservations are recommended.

Photo: Dave Sipe

These works are prime examples of woodsculpting in Jackson Hole.

Aspen Acres Campground

$$$, no credit cards • 4179 E. 1100 N., Ashton, Idaho • (208) 652-3524

Imagine 18 holes of golf on an aspen-dotted course rolling across low hills. Grouse chuckle from the shelter of the trees; at one point you think you see a bear pad silently out of view. Finish your game, hop in your golf cart and drive to your campsite nestled into a large aspen grove tangled with wildflowers. Heaven? No, Aspen Acres. Most campers are here to golf, and most have RVs, although Aspen Acres is happy to accommodate tent campers, too. The campground offers show-

INSIDERS' TIP

Our streams and rivers are lovely and clear, but don't be tempted to drink from them without treating or boiling the water. Giardia, a nasty microorganism that likes to set up housekeeping in your intestines, is not uncommon.

ers, laundry facilities and firewood to its guests. The 40 sites are semiprivate, tucked into the trees and underbrush.

Many visitors stay for quite a while, so Aspen Acres offers weekly and monthly as well as daily rates. Mosquitoes can be a problem, particularly down in the campground, so bring your repellent. Campers and golfers are welcome from early May through late October. A small pro shop and snack bar is on premises. Golf carts are available for rent (see our Other Recreation chapter for more on the golf course).

Warm River Campground

$$ • Fish Creek Rd. off Mesa Falls Scenic Byway • (208) 558-7301

This pretty little campground is the most parklike of the national forest campgrounds in the area. Sites are tucked among the willows on a grassy bench along the Warm River. There are nine tent-only sites and 10 RV sites, plus a few day-use picnic sites. Not all are available for reservation, so although this campground is very popular with local anglers and tourists-in-the-know, there still may be sites available if it's not too late on a weekend afternoon. Warm River Campground is equipped with vault toilets and potable water. A campground host lives on premises and can sell you bundled firewood. The shallow, crystal-clear river running by the campground is stocked at least every two weeks through the summer with rainbow trout.

Riverside Campground

$ • Off U.S. Hwy. 20 near Ashton, Idaho • (208) 558-7301

This Forest Service campground, located on the blue-ribbon fishing waters of the Henry's Fork, is extremely popular with the fly-fishing set. Most of the desirable riverside sites are reservable; the rest are first-come, first-served. Sites not near the river are tucked into lodgepole forest. The campground has 55 overnight sites arranged in three loops and a day-use parking area for anglers at a small fee. Campsites have picnic tables and fire pits. The campground is also equipped with new vault toilets. A new well was in the works during the winter of 1998, so there should be potable water; call and check. A campground host lives on the premises. Bundled firewood is available for sale.

Cave Falls Campground

$ • Cave Falls Rd. at Bechler, Idaho • (208) 652-7442

This campground has 23 sites — none can be reserved — tucked along the banks of the Fall River, which runs fast and deep in its steep banks. During the wildflower season (June and July, usually) both the long road in and the campground itself are spangled with color. No RV hookups are available. You can almost throw a rock from your campsite into Yellowstone National Park. Although you can drive about 2 miles past the campground into Yellowstone in order to view Cave Falls, a giant, river-wide step in the Fall River, access to the park beyond the falls is restricted to nonmotorized traffic only. This makes the Bechler entrance to Yellowstone the quietest, most secluded of them all. Until a couple of years ago, the National Park Service didn't even charge admission to those who entered Yellowstone here. All Cave Falls Campground's sites have picnic tables and fire pits, access to water, vault toilets and bear-proof storage boxes. The campground is in grizzly habitat, so pay attention to how you handle food and pleasant-smelling objects.

Rexburg, Idaho, Area

Rainbow Lake & Campground

$$ • 2245 S. 2000 W., Rexburg, Idaho • (208) 356-3681

What makes Rainbow Lake a pleasant stop is not its convenience, although the man-made

INSIDERS' TIP

June and July are the mosquito months throughout most of Yellowstone country. Read labels: The most effective repellents contain the most DEET, up to 100 percent.

lake with the 60-site campground on its treeless shore sits immediately adjacent to U.S. Highway 20, 1.5 miles from Rexburg. It's the fishing. The main lake is stocked.

You can rent paddleboats and canoes to get farther out on the lake. A few rods are available for rent. A smaller pond is perfect for kids and casting practice. No Idaho fishing license is required to fish either lake. The campground is equipped with recently renovated restrooms and shower facilities. Sites are open and sunny, but offer no privacy.

Idaho Falls, Idaho, Area

Idaho Falls KOA Kampground

$$$$ • 1440 Lindsay Blvd., Idaho Falls, Idaho • (208) 523-3362

This pleasant RV park was well designed to screen Idaho Falls from view with walls of trees. You won't know you're in town; you probably will have a shaded site. About one-third of the more than 170 sites have full hookups; some have picnic tables and grills. Special features include a seasonally open swimming pool, miniature golf course and outdoor hot tub, showers, a playground, game room and store. In summer you can enjoy nightly (except Sundays) outdoor movies and barbecues, with all-you-can-eat ice cream for dessert. Six mornings a week wake up to a big pancake breakfast. The campground is open year-round, a rarity around here.

Juniper Campground

$$ • 226 Meadowcreek Rd. at Ririe Reservoir, Ririe, Idaho • (208) 538-7443

This pretty little campground was a well-kept secret until recently, but its popularity is rising. Use has risen more than 400 percent in the last few years. Nevertheless, you can usually drive in and find a site. Even at its busiest, Juniper still manages to seem quiet and peaceful. Sites are scattered among low, brushy juniper trees, some right at the edge of a cliff overlooking Ririe Reservoir.

Increased use has probably been spurred by recent improvements to the 22-year-old campground. Grass and junipers are watered so they're green and inviting. Most of the 49 sites were recently upgraded to full hookups. There are showers, flush toilets and a new pavilion. Horseshoe pits, volleyball courts and a playground are planned. Juniper is managed by Bonneville County (it was built and once was operated by the Bureau of Reclamation).

Months of operation are April through September, depending on weather. Golden Eagle Pass holders receive a discount.

Jefferson County Lake Recreation Area

$ • U.S. Hwy. 20 near Rigby, Idaho • (208) 745-7756

Rumor has it that highway builders originally created Jefferson County Lake by accident. Gravel mined to build roads eventually created a hole so deep it started to fill from below. The recreation area includes a 1.25-mile path around the lake, shaded picnic and camping areas, picnic tables (scattered about but not in campsites), drinking water, showers and flush toilets. The charm of the campground is not in its amenities, though, but in that clear cool water and those tangled trees. When you call the number listed above, you're reaching not the campground but Jefferson County Clerk and Recorder's Office. The staff can take your reservation after January 1 for the current year. The campground opens in April and closes early in October, depending on weather.

Northwestern Wyoming

Cody, Wyoming, Area

Camp Cody Campground

$$$ • 415 Yellowstone Ave., Cody, Wyo. • (307) 587-9730, (888) 231-CAMP

Just look for the state flags — all 50 of them — flying in front of this campground on the north side of U.S. Highway 20 west of Cody. The new owners of Camp Cody Campground (they took ownership in June of 1997) were busy planting grass and trees and building cabins to make their RV park more inviting. Until those trees grow big enough to make shade, you can refresh yourself in Camp Cody's heated pool. This RV park has 60 RV spaces, 15 cabins, 15 tent spaces, free cable TV, a laundry and clean restrooms.

Gateway Motel and Campground

$$ • 203 Yellowstone Ave., Cody, Wyo. • (307) 587-2561

The lush lawn, mature trees and plentiful shade at the Gateway Motel and Campground will soothe your nerves and cool your cranky kids. About a mile west of downtown Cody, the Gateway is within easy walking distance of the Cody Nite Rodeo grounds and Old Trail Town (see our Attractions chapter). It's also right across the highway from Cassie's Supper Club, which features fine food and fantastic dancing (see our Restaurants chapter).

Next to the campground, owner Lura Showman's father offers horseback riding (see our Other Recreation chapter to learn more about the Gateway Ranch). Tucked behind the office and a row of motel rooms, the campground is quiet and countrified. A comfortable yard behind the office accommodates 87 tenters and is popular with large groups.

The Gateway has 29 electric hookups and 13 full-hookup sites. You'll find a laundry, clean showers and restrooms, a pay phone, UHF television reception and free coffee in the morning. The motel rooms and cabins, cute and clean, are older but adequate. Most have kitchenettes but no refrigeration. The motel rooms and cabins begin at $30. The Gateway is open from May 1 until October 1.

KOA Kampground of Cody

$$$ • 5561 Greybull Hwy., Cody, Wyo. • (307) 587-2369

East of Cody on U.S. Highway 14/16/20, this place is the first franchised KOA campground in the nation. Built in 1969, it is a couple of miles east of town. The Cody KOA makes up for its distance from town by providing on-site amenities such as a swimming pool, hot tub, playground, showers and a laundry. Each morning during the summer, the staff serves a pancake breakfast under an awning. Monday through Saturday evenings they serve a chuckwagon dinner enlivened with entertainment by the Diamond C Chuckwagon crew. The campground also offers a free shuttle to the Cody Nite Rodeo and is a pickup point for Powder River tours (see our Getting Around chapter). You'll find plenty of grass, a few mature trees and a measure of peace and quiet here.

Ponderosa Campground

$$$ • 1815 B St., Cody, Wyo. • (307) 587-9203

What the Ponderosa Campground lacks in vegetation it makes up for with location. Just three blocks west of the Buffalo Bill Historical Center (see our Attractions chapter) and within easy walking distance of downtown, the Ponderosa Campground is a popular RV park and camping complex that's generally jam-packed. Besides its proximity to restaurants, shopping and museums, the Ponderosa has an array of amenities including a large gift store, video arcade, laundry and playground. In addition to 133 spaces with full hookups, the Ponderosa has 72-foot pull-throughs, several cabins, six teepees and special spots for tenters. The Ponderosa is open from May 1 to mid-October.

U.S. Highway 20

The following campgrounds are west of Cody, Wyoming.

Eagle Creek Campground

$ • U.S. Hwy. 14/16/20, Cody, Wyo. • (307) 527-6921

With paved spurs and shaded by conifers, this Forest Service campground has a pressurized water system with spigots throughout. You'll find 20 units next to the North Fork of the Shoshone River. Remember — the signs here won't let you forget — this is bear country, and the Wapiti Ranger District has stepped up its efforts to avert human-bear conflict. You'll find good fishing in the North Fork. A trailhead and horse corrals are just a half-mile away. The trailer limit is 22 feet.

Newton Creek Campground

$ • U.S. Hwy. 14/16/20, Cody, Wyo. • (307) 527-6921

You'll find several campsites right next to the North Fork of the Shoshone River here and bear signs to remind you to lock your food up. The Forest Service has made it easy by installing new, user-friendly bear boxes in which to lock up your food at night. The boxes are about waist-high, and the lids, hinged with chains, fold down to make a working surface adequate for a Coleman stove. This campground closes for a while each spring when the bears come out of hibernation and wander the riverbanks looking for food. Newton Creek has 31 campsites.

Three Mile Campground

$ • U.S. Hwy. 14/16/20, Cody, Wyo. • (307) 527-6921

Three miles east of the East Entrance to Yellowstone National Park, this Forest Service campground is a popular staging spot for visitors to the park. Of the 33 campsites, four are isolated from the others on the banks of the North Fork of the Shoshone River and are reserved for day-use only. The area is a favorite corridor for grizzly bears during the night, especially in the spring and fall. The Forest Service had plans to install new bear-proof food boxes here by 1998. Because of bear problems, only hard-sided campers are allowed in this campground.

Yellowstone Valley Inn

$$$ • 3324 Yellowstone National Park Hwy., Cody, Wyo. • (307) 587-3961, (888) 705-7703

In addition to 100 RV sites and ample tent spaces with grass, shade, barbecues and picnic tables, the Yellowstone Valley Inn has a restaurant, lounge and motel for those in your party who aren't into roughing it. Twenty-five of the RV spaces are full hookup, while 75 are water and electric. There is also a dump station and free use of the bathhouse. For more information on the Yellowstone Valley Inn midway between the park and Cody, see our Hotels, Motels and Cabins chapter.

Most cabins, condos and houses exist in clusters on the valley floors where homesteading ranchers once grazed their cattle. These accommodations look toward the magnificent mountains, but they're not in them.

Vacation Rentals

The Yellowstone region encompasses everything from potato fields and 13,000-foot granite peaks to mysterious steaming holes filled with what looks like bubbling gray paint; its vacation rental options are varied, too. In general, you're choosing between condos, cabins and houses. The surroundings can be aspen grove or rangeland-turned-subdivision, a busy resort or an isolated, lodgepole-bristled mountainside. All require minimum stays, but sometimes these can be waived or are for short periods like three or four nights. Minimum stays tend to vary with seasons, with longer stays required at busiest times. Monthly stays are sometimes required for houses. Rexburg's wonderful seniors program requests (but does not require) that participants stay the entire summer.

In a week's stay, you can buzz through the most well-known spots in the region — from Yellowstone National Park to the Tetons to St. Anthony Dunes to the Henry's Fork — from nearly any home base within Greater Yellowstone. So don't limit your geographic choices too quickly as you read these rental options. Also note that more cabins are described in the Hotels, Motels and Cabins chapter, particularly those that rent by the night.

You won't find vacation rentals within the parks themselves. Yellowstone National Park is public property, and although Grand Teton National Park enfolds private "inholdings," none that we know of are available for short-term rental. If you want to lodge within the parks, you'll camp, stay at guest ranches or resorts, or in hotels, motels or cabins. 'Nuff said.

Jackson Hole, Wyoming, and Big Sky, Montana, have lots of condos, usually in resort complexes which may also offer transportation and use of spas, golf courses, tennis courts and swimming pools. These upscale areas are also home to large, luxurious houses, but the right to call them yours for a while doesn't come cheap. Houses also might not be as close to ski hills and businesses, as their locations were often chosen for aesthetics more than for convenience.

In Teton Valley and Island Park, Idaho, and the broad valleys of southwestern Montana, most of your choices are best called cabins. Many are rustic; most are log. Often they lack amenities you may consider basic, like phones and televisions. However, much of the construction in our region has taken place in recent years, so just because a cabin is rustic doesn't mean it isn't fairly new. And an older cabin is often charming enough to offset any minor hassles such as driving out to make a phone call or do laundry.

Greater Yellowstone consists largely of public land, and much of the terrain is steep. This means that the secluded cabin in the pines you may have in mind is practically

INSIDERS' TIP

Planning a family reunion? Larger cabins and houses can be ideal gathering places for the entire clan.

nonexistent. Most cabins, condos and houses exist in clusters on the valley floors where homesteading ranchers once grazed their cattle. These accommodations look toward the magnificent mountains, but they're not in them. And if a property manager tells you a cabin or house is secluded, that doesn't necessarily mean you can't see other cabins and houses nearby. Our mountains are heavily wooded, but the valleys are broad swaths of sage, willow, grasses and wildflowers. Unless you're positioned along the cottonwood trees that line most of our rivers, you can usually see for miles. Availability is particularly slim in communities adjoining Yellowstone National Park because the towns are squeezed between the park and national forest. With private land so hard to come by, most folks are living on theirs.

You can save a bundle by coming in the fall when the trees flame and the mosquitoes are gone. Or try late spring, when early wildflowers are just beginning to bloom. Summer is high season for most of Yellowstone country, but near ski resorts (Jackson Hole, Teton Valley, Big Sky and Red Lodge) and snowmobiling meccas (Island Park, Togwotee Pass, West Yellowstone, Cooke City and Pahaska Teepee), winter can be pricey, too.

The subsequent listings are mostly property management companies and realties. The list is not inclusive, but it does point you at larger companies with wide selections of rentals. Some areas, particularly Island Park, Swan Valley and Teton Valley in Idaho, are not yet well represented by property management firms; there, homeowners may try to find their own renters. Phone books and chambers of commerce can sometimes help you hook up with these folks, as can classified ads in local papers and Internet classified ads. (Chambers of commerce are listed in our Resources chapter; local and regional newspapers are discussed in our Media chapter.)

When you call, be sure to ask about policies on smoking, pets and children if these policies concern you. Many properties do not allow smoking; most frown on pets. Unless noted, these companies will accept your credit card or check.

If you're planning a winter visit, also inquire about ski storage and firewood. Most properties provide firewood if they have fireplaces. Outdoor ski storage lockers will make your life easier.

Jackson Hole

Alpine Vacation Rentals

Teton Village, Wyo. • (307) 734-1161, (800) 876-3968

This property management company merged with the 15-year-old Jackson Hole Racquet Club Resort, and then was purchased by Jackson Hole Mountain Resort, adding even more vacation rental options for you. Choose from more than 175 properties ranging from condos to six-bedroom homes; rates range, too, between $90 and $1,400 per day. Most rentals are in the pleasantly upscale West Bank, which means they're away from the traffic snarls of Jackson; or they're in Teton Village near the ski resort, a convenient drive to the back route into Grand Teton National Park. All rentals are fully furnished.

Black Diamond Vacation Rentals

Jackson, Wyo. • (307) 733-6170, (800) 325-8605

These folks have condos, town houses

INSIDERS' TIP

If you're heading from Idaho Falls to your vacation rental in Island Park, take the Mesa Falls Scenic Byway outside Ashton, but allow plenty of time. The road is narrow and a bit bumpy, and you're going to want to stop and look at Upper and Lower Mesa Falls. This road is closed in winter.

www.insiders.com
See this and
many other
Insiders' Guide®
destinations online.
Visit us today!

and family homes available in several locations, including the town of Jackson and Teton Village. Prices range from $75 to $280 for condos and vary even more widely for houses — from $3,000 to $8,000 per month. Minimum stays vary from property to property, anywhere from two days for some condos to 30 for houses. Black Diamond condos and houses have fully equipped kitchens, washer/dryer, fireplaces, color TV with cable hookup, telephone, linens and towels. Some properties also have hot tubs and garages.

First Cabin Rentals (Prime Properties of Jackson Hole)

1230 Ida Ln., Wilson, Wyo.
• (307) 739-9145, (800) 989-9145

Like the personal touch? A few of First Cabin's properties are condos, but what they specialize in are private homes, scattered through the valley but mostly in the desirable West Bank outside Jackson. A few of these houses are secluded enough that you can look through any window and not see another home. All are fully furnished. Most properties rent on a per-month basis — for $1,100 to $12,000 — but a few are available nightly. First Cabin represents approximately 40 properties, but the company promises that if it doesn't have what you're looking for, it'll look for someone who does.

Jackson Hole Central Reservations

Jackson, Wyo. • (307) 733-4005,
(800) 443-6931

The Hole's largest and oldest reservation service is hooked in almost everywhere; they book for 33 hotels, bed and breakfast inns, and property management companies. These folks charge a small fee for making your life easy, but especially if you're calling during the busy ski or summer seasons, you'll enjoy the convenience of one phone call instead of many. Jackson Hole Central Reservations specializes in complete and money-saving vacation packages, which include airfare, car rentals and lift tickets for Teton Village, Snow King and nearby Grand Targhee. (See our Winter Sports chapter.) Most accommodations are subject to minimum-stay requirements, which vary by season and property.

Mountain Property Management

175 S. King St., Jackson, Wyo.
• (307) 733-1684, (800) 992-9948

Mountain Property Management handles about 14 houses and 28 condos. Some condos are at Teton Shadows, 7 miles north of town near Jackson Hole Golf and Ten-

Photo: Post Register Photo Archive

A vacation rental can put you right where the best access to Yellowstone's variety of activities is.

nis Club; this course is open to the public. Other condos are at The Aspens, also known as Jackson Hole Racquet Club Resort. Costs range from $90 per night to $600, generally with a five-night minimum. The houses have two to five bedrooms and rent for a monthly charge of $4,000 to $14,000. All are fully furnished; all have cable TV and VCRs, washer/dryers and fireplaces with firewood provided. Some have hot tubs.

Jackson Hole Reservation Center

Park City, Utah • (800) 255-6451

With one phone call to Jackson Hole Reservation Center, a subsidiary of Reservations Network Inc., you can book everything you need for a ski vacation here. The Utah-based company, in business since June 1990, will hook you up with hotel rooms, condos and any of about 50 private homes scattered through the valley.

Most condos have hot tub access, some have private hot tubs, many have fireplaces, and nearly all include laundry facilities. They range from $100 to $900 per night, generally with three-night minimums (peak travel weekends will have greater minimum stays). Homes rent from $300 to $1,500 per night, with varying minimum stays. All homes and condos are fully furnished and offer fully equipped kitchens.

Resnet and the Jackson Hole Reservation Center are not only convenient, they can save you money. They charge no booking fee, and on short notice, especially in the off-season, they've been known to offer discounts of up to 50 percent to folks with flexible travel plans. Call within 30 days of

INSIDERS' TIP

If you're coming in June or July, bring your mosquito repellent and citronella candles. Your vacation rental probably has a deck that you'll enjoy more if you can subdue the 'skeeters.

your arrival to try for these deals. Resnet is also hooked into bulk airfare rates and discount car rentals.

Surrounding Areas

Southwestern Montana

West Yellowstone, Montana

The Cabin

West Yellowstone, Mont.
• (406) 646-7784

One block from downtown West Yellowstone and 250 feet from the Yellowstone National Park boundary, this 70-year-old log cabin is a favorite among winter snowmobilers and summer sightseers. The Cabin, which has been modernized, comes complete with a dishwasher, microwave and coffee maker. Furnished with a combination of antiques and comfortable Western decor, it holds a maximum of eight people. In the summer, guests can enjoy a backyard barbecue. In winter, you can rent snowmobiles right down the block. A bargain at $130 per night for the first six people, this cabin usually is booked months ahead of time. (Add $5 for each additional person.) Owner Pat Henrie has a three-night minimum.

Sportsman's High Vacation Rentals

750 Deer St., West Yellowstone, Mont.
• (406) 646-7865

Wow! What a duo. He builds them. She decorates them. And are they beautiful. Together, Gary and Diana Baxter have created five rental homes that will accommodate from six to 12 people each. They also manage a neighbor's house adjacent to their property. All are 8 miles from the hustle and bustle of West Yellowstone in a country setting surrounded by aspen groves and wildflowers and bordered by national forest. These homes, each designed and furnished with a different theme, rent from $125 to $305 per night, depending on the duration of your stay, the house and the time of year. There is a three-night minimum.

Yellowstone Village Rental Condominiums

West Yellowstone, Mont.
• (406) 646-7335, (800) 276-7335

Nine miles from the west entrance to Yellowstone National Park, these quiet, clean one-, two- and three-bedroom units are near Hebgen Lake. Guests at these 20 year-round condos need only to bring groceries and clothing. Everything else will be there: linens, dishes, firewood, laundry detergent, and dishwasher and hand soap. Guests have access to an outdoor pool and two tennis courts. In winter you can snowmobile straight into the park or onto hundreds of miles of national forest lands. Because vacation rentals are scarce in the West Yellowstone area, these condos fill up fast. Rent ranges from $99.50 to $159 per night. There's a two-night minimum.

Gardiner, Montana

Slip and Slide Ranch and Outfitters

No credit cards • U.S. Hwy. 89, 11 mi. north of Gardiner, Mont.
• (406) 848-7648

You'll need a four-wheel-drive vehicle to get to this 7-year-old log cabin furnished with antiques and pine furniture. Two miles above the Slip and Slide ranch house, this cabin is surrounded by national forest and has a great view. The cabin, which has an upstairs loft with six beds, has electricity but is heated with a pellet stove. The kitchen is stocked with dishes and food staples. The cabin goes for $150 a night for groups of six, and there is a three-night minimum. For more than six people, the cost is $200. The owners take personal checks. Slip and Slide also offers bed and breakfast rooms as well as horseback riding, private fishing ponds and guided hunting trips.

Mountain Retreat

No credit cards • U.S. Hwy. 89, 10 mi. north of Gardiner, Mont.
• (406) 848-7272, (800) 727-0798

Mountain Retreat offers two homes 10 miles north of Gardiner and .75 miles east of Mont. Highway 89 on Cedar Creek. Built in the 1950s, this home accommodates six people and rents for $150 per night. The house is ready to live in but has no dishwasher or washer/dryer. A smaller 700-square-foot cabin built in the 1890s offers a taste of the Old West with a root cellar, smokehouse and a two-hole outhouse out back. It rents for $100 a night. The owners accept personal checks.

Bozeman, Montana

Mountain Home — Montana Vacation Rentals

Bozeman, Mont. • (406) 586-4589

Owner Suzy Hall is more of a concierge than a property manager. She has combed southwestern Montana for the very best rentals. Her criteria: well-maintained homes with character and a great view in the middle of a big chunk of private property. Once you make a reservation, she will send you an arrival packet telling where to stock up on supplies and how to find fun things to do. Her 25 homes range from an $800-a-week, 500-square-foot honeymoon cabin to a luxurious Big Sky home that rents for $5,000 a week. On the average, her homes will cost you from $1,500 to $2,000 per week. Each has a fully equipped kitchen and is stocked with necessities such as linens, laundry detergent, dish and hand soap, toilet paper and paper towels.

Bridger Pines Property Management

15792 Bridger Canyon Rd., Bozeman, Mont. • (406) 587-3096

Bridger Pines manages four homes and one condo near Bridger Bowl ski area. Depending upon the size, rental prices range from $500 to $2,500 per week. Some of the homes are equipped with amenities such as hot tubs, steam showers and fax machines. These rentals are popular with anglers in the summer months and skiers during the winter. Bridger Pines does not accept credit cards.

Intermountain Property Management

611 W. Main St., Bozeman, Mont. • (406) 586-1503, (888) 871-7856

Intermountain Property handles cabins, condos, cottages and country homes throughout Yellowstone country. While most are within a 25-mile radius south of Bozeman, a few are very close to Yellowstone National Park. Among those closer to the park are a split-level, six-guest condo overlooking a golf course and with access to a swimming pool 6 miles from the Big Sky ski area. Intermountain also offers a new home overlooking Hebgen Lake, 15 miles from the park, as well as the three-bedroom Rainbow Point Log Cabin with a bunkhouse on Hebgen Lake. All rentals have a one-week-minimum policy. Rates range from $400 to $3,500 per week.

Big Sky, Montana

Big Sky Chalet Rentals

Big Sky, Mont. • (406) 995-2665, (800) 845-4428

Jim and Kern Popkin manage about 45 condos and homes in the Meadows and Mountain villages at Big Sky. While they mostly cater to large groups, they do have rentals for singles. Their rentals run the gamut from studio apartments to six-bedroom homes. Demand for their rentals is increasing each year, so if you're hoping to rent one for next winter, you'd better call by midsummer. Homes are rented during the Christmas holidays, sometimes a year in advance. Summer is an easier time to find a rental.

INSIDERS' TIP

Some property management firms can help you figure out not only where you'll stay while you're here, but also what you might want to do.

Golden Eagle Condominium Rentals

Little Coyote Rd., Meadow Village, Big Sky, Mont. • (406) 995-4800, (800) 548-4488
Black Eagle Rd., Mountain Village, Big Sky, Mont.

Golden Eagle manages about 180 condos year round in Big Sky. Condo prices vary dramatically depending on their size, amenities and how close they are to the ski hill. Minimum stays range from three to six nights. Rental prices begin at $110 per night.

Livingston, Montana

The Innskeeper

119 S. Main St., Livingston, Mont. • (406) 222-5456, (800) 590-5456

The Innskeeper is a central reservation service that handles private accommodations of all kinds, including vacation rentals, mostly in the Yellowstone Valley. Homes range from secluded rustic log cabins to the Lazy Heart Lodge, a remodeled farmhouse in the Paradise Valley. The Innskeeper also handles The Centennial, a beautifully appointed railroad car (now offered as lodging) that traveled to New York in 1963 for Montana's territorial centennial celebration. Now sitting on 16 acres next to the Yellowstone River, it once stood in Gardiner where it housed the chamber of commerce. These homes rent for an average of $125 per night, with discounts for longer stays.

Ennis, Montana

9T9 Rental Houses

99 Gravelly Range Rd., Ennis, Mont. • (406) 682-7659

Judy Herrick, co-owner of the 9T9 Guest Ranch Bed and Breakfast, manages 11 vacation homes including a historical stone power house on 50 acres, the Old Grand Daddy Retreat, and a two bedroom log cabin with a loft. The houses, all in the Ennis area, sleep from four to 14 people and rent for $400 to $1,200 per week. They're very popular with anglers.

Photo: Robert Bower, Post Register

A Canada goose airs out after being swept over the falls in Idaho Falls

Red Lodge

Red Lodging

16½ N. Broadway Ave., Red Lodge, Mont. • (406) 446-1272, (800) 6-RED LODGE

The folks at Red Lodging manage 38 properties including cottages, condos,

INSIDERS' TIP

Know how to tell whether that distant speck of soaring raptor is an eagle or vulture? Vultures soar with a distinct wobble and sharply upturned wings that form a wide V. Eagles' wings form nearly a straight line and don't wobble markedly in flight.

creekside cabins and Victorian town houses. Rates range from $125 to $225 per night with a two-night minimum year round except during the Christmas holidays when the minimum stay increases to three nights. Most of their rentals are upscale, many with hot tubs and fireplaces. Some overlook a creek or river, while others have a front row view of Red Lodge's golf course. Rentals sleep from 4 to 10 people, and some allow pets.

Willows Inn

224 S. Platt Ave., Red Lodge, Mont. • (406) 446-3913

The Willows Inn is a bed and breakfast in Red Lodge, and proprietress Carolyn Boggio has two storybook cottages she rents for a minimum of two nights and generally by the week. See our Bed and Breakfast Inns chapter for further information.

The Cedar Guest House

3450 Barley Cir., Billings, Mont. • (406) 656-5747, (888) 626-5747

You've been there: You're in a log home just made for playing house, but when you open the cupboard doors they resemble Mother Hubbard's. Owner Sharon Cobetto has been there, too. That's why you'll find spices and herbs, sugar, salt, pepper, flour, coffee and tea to get you started. She also sees that you have one package of pancake mix, and either pancake syrup or sparkling cider. The cider, by the way, is for you to enjoy while dipping in the hot tub on the multilevel deck.

This sunny cedar home in Red Lodge has vaulted ceilings and lots of windows to enjoy the beautiful views everywhere you turn. The dining room table seats eight, and Sharon caters to families, providing a high chair and a playpen. The Cedar Guest House is close to a golf course and a ski hill and is 65 miles from Yellowstone National Park via the Beartooth Highway. While Sharon mostly rents her house by the week, she will let it go nightly for a rate that amounts to about $33 per person. Longer stays bring reduced rates.

Eastern Idaho

Teton Valley

Grand Valley Lodging

Driggs, Idaho • (208) 354-8890, (800) 746-5518

This valley, although not yet a tourist destination of Jackson's scale, is just as pretty and perhaps a bit more, well . . . real. The cowboy hats are worn by cowboys, and the cracked leather cowboy boots weren't purchased that way. This broad, flat valley is lined on one side by the Big Holes and on the other by the Tetons. Liz Pitcher has about 15 cabins, condos and homes to entice you into the valley. Most are newer log homes on the valley floor; some are more secluded. Each is privately owned and fully furnished. Most have color TVs, VCRs, microwaves and coffee pots, laundry facilities and wood stoves or fireplaces w/ wood. Rates range from $120 to $400 per night, with weekly and monthly rates available. Most have minimum stays of at least three nights. Several have great Teton views, hot tubs or creek access. One, with an indoor sauna and outdoor hot tub, can sleep up to 18.

Island Park, Idaho

The Henry's Fork Realtors of Island Park, Idaho

3404 Idaho Hwy. 20, Last Chance in Island Park, Idaho • (208) 558-7354, (888) 558-7354

Choose from several cabins scattered through Island Park. These are people's vacation homes, but you're invited to make use of them when their owners can't, summer or winter. They rent nightly for $125 to $250 and weekly from $700 to $1,100. All are fully furnished; you bring only yourself and something to eat. Small cabins accommodate four people; the largest will hold 20. Some are on exclusive Bills Island, a limited-access tract of land surrounded by the waters of Island Park Reservoir.

Rainbow Realty

3376 Idaho Hwy. 20, Last Chance in Island Park, Idaho • (208) 558-7116

This real estate office rents eight fully furnished cabins for between $700 and $1,200 per week. One is on Island Park Village Resort Golf Course; three perch north of Henry's Lake with lake views. One is a secluded fishing cabin near the Henry's Fork. Several are available year round. The folks at Rainbow are happy to serve as an emergency answering service for people staying in cabins unequipped with phones.

Rexburg, Idaho, Area

Sunbird Program/Rexburg Chamber of Commerce

420 W. Fourth S., Rexburg, Idaho • (208) 356-5700

Back in 1978, some bright Rexburgian noticed that hundreds of off-campus student apartments sat empty when Ricks College students went home for the summer. Now in its 20th year, the Sunbird Program offers affordable summer accommodations to retired Southerners who want to escape to cool northern air. Approximately 2,000 senior citizens participate every year. The Rexburg Chamber of Commerce runs the program; the apartment building owners charge between $950 and $1,900 for the summer. The minimum stay is one month, but most folks come for the whole three months. Many sunbirds have migrated here annually since the program started.

Accommodations are apartments; most have two to four bedrooms. Some have access to pleasant extras like hot tubs, swimming pools, computer rooms and pool tables; some have TVs and telephones. None provide linens or dishes. None have air conditioning, but it's unlikely you'll miss it.

Northwestern Wyoming

Cody Guest Houses

1401 Rumsey Ave., Cody, Wyo. • (307) 587-6000, (800) 587-6560

These eight guest houses aren't just places to stay — they're an experience. Take the Victorian House, with its graceful grounds and beautifully appointed interior. Romance is written in every detail. From the hardwood floors to the formal dining room, it is decorated with antiques, art and historical artifacts. The four-bedroom Western Lodge, where guests can indulge in barbecues and billiards, is different only in its theme — the best of Old West charm. The Country Cottage and two others, the Annie Oakley and the Buffalo Bill, are smaller but not shy on charm. Or choose from two air-conditioned suites equipped with laundry and kitchen facilities, a carport and a beautiful yard with a gazebo.

One block from Main Street in a historic residential neighborhood, all eight rentals are within walking distance of the Buffalo Bill Historical Center, intriguing shopping possibilities and fine dining. Single-night double occupancies range from $95 to $405 per night. The Victorian House, the queen of the collection, can be rented either as a house or by the room (there are three of them). The Mayor's Inn, Cody's first mansion and the king of the collection, was rescued from destruction then transported to its current location near owner Kathy Singer's photography studio. Like the Victorian House, the Mayor's Inn oozes luxury, from its down comforters and pillows to its terry-cloth robes, in-room spas and heated floors.

Friday evenings Singer hosts an evening of hors d'oeurves and a no-host bar at the Mayor's Inn. Situated either on the same street or within blocks of each other, these homes, rented collectively, offer a moderately priced — and priceless — opportunity for family reunions and conferences.

In many Greater Yellowstone communities, fine dining often means meat — but not the kind you buy at the supermarket. Buffalo, elk, venison, duck, pheasant, ostrich and emu are standards, garnished with wild mushrooms, berries, nuts and leeks.

Restaurants

Picture Yellowstone National Park as the sun and Yellowstone country communities as tiny planets whipping around it. Without our sun, most communities in this region would loll in economic emptiness. Only a few larger towns, like Idaho Falls, don't seem to be shaped primarily by Yellowstone and its tourist dollars.

Local dining options reflect how heavily a town relies upon Yellowstone sunlight and in what direction it has grown under that light. In some towns, tourist services have bloomed into extravagance. Each in its small-town way surprisingly cosmopolitan, these towns are Jackson, Cody, Bozeman, Big Sky and Livingston. Treat yourself to Thai, Chinese or classical Italian food: It's all here. In these communities, fine dining often means meat — but not the kind you buy at the supermarket. Buffalo, elk, venison, duck, pheasant, ostrich and emu are standards, garnished with wild mushrooms, berries, nuts and leeks.

Another staple you're almost sure to find on the menu is trout. Even in the classiest restaurants, it may be pan-fried. You'll pay dearly for the trendy food in these towns, but you'll also get what you pay for: Topnotch chefs abound.

Elsewhere in Yellowstone country, menus tend to follow a single trend. A lot of folks call it home cookin' because even inexpensive restaurants in this region pride themselves on avoiding pre-prepared food and microwave cooking. It's a Western self-sufficiency perhaps born of a time when home cookin' was the only cookin' to be had. These folks bake their own breads and pies, make their own sauces, jams and breaded items. Some cut their own french fries. This may mean that service is friendlier than it is fast. It also means that when your plate comes out, you'll be happy to have waited. In these restaurants, meat and potatoes are king, and "good" means plentiful but cheap. Idaho potatoes are famous, so the menu may proudly point out that the spuds served up fried, mashed, baked or diced into hearty salads or soups are local. The meat? Nearly every restaurant serves burgers and steaks; prime rib or barbecue is every cook's specialty. Chicken and seafood options add variety.

We've tried to pick for you an entertaining range of dining options. It wasn't easy, and we left out plenty of good ones. Most of our picks have been around for years. In this volatile, tourist-driven market, restaurants can appear and disappear in a year. The restaurants that last almost invariably enjoy strong local support, which gets them through the slow times. We've also left off the extensive collection of chain restaurants that crowd shopping areas, particularly in Idaho Falls, Bozeman and Cody. We figure you know what they're serving.

Price Code

Each restaurant write-up includes a price code to help you plan your dining experience. Categories are based on an average-price dinner for two, without appetizers, dessert, alcoholic beverages, tax or tip. At some restaurants, this includes salad and/or soup with your entree. At others, entrees stand alone. If an establishment doesn't serve dinner, we looked at its most expensive meal, usually lunch.

$	**$10 to $19**
$$	**$20 to $27**
$$$	**$28 to $35**
$$$$	**$36 and more**

Most establishments accept credit cards. If they don't, we let you know. Most of those that don't will accept personal checks no matter where you live. We note for you the establishments that accept or recommend reservations. We've also let you know what alcoholic beverages you can order with your meal. Nearly all of Yellowstone country's restaurants welcome children, and many offer children's menus to accommodate smaller stomachs and pickier palates. It never hurts to check when you make your reservation, however. Remember that in summer the fine dining restaurants with the highest reputations may book popular dining times days in advance. Make plans early if you want to enjoy justly famous meals at places such as Jenny Lake Lodge in Grand Teton National Park, the Snake River Grill, The Range or Stiegler's in Jackson Hole, or Franca's in Cody.

One last tip that might help you pack for your trip: Fine dining around here does not mean fancy dress. If it entertains you to put on a jacket and tie or a nice dress and heels, by all means do so. But you'd be hard-pressed in Yellowstone country to find a restaurant that would flinch at jeans, hiking boots and a T-shirt.

Happy eating!

Yellowstone National Park

In this chapter, we don't include information about franchise fast food options, but even inside Yellowstone National Park there's a pretty good assortment of them. All are operated by park concessionaires. Many Hamilton Stores also have lunch counters.

Lake Hotel

$$$ • Lake Village, Yellowstone National Park • (307) 344-7901

Supper will be served at 6 o'clock sharp, *mesdames et messieurs* — supper for two, just your sweetheart and you. It's not required, but we recommend that you dress for the occasion. The dining room, the lake and the hotel will make a dinner here special enough. But why not do it up big? Lounge in the sun room, sip a little gin, tap your toe to the piano music then float into the Lake Hotel dining room. We recommend the Blackened Prime Rib, an item that remains on the menu year after year.

The menu changes each season. Last year, you might have tried the quail with spinach, walnut and goat cheese stuffing, or breast of duck or scallops with sun-dried tomatoes. Open from May until the first week in October, the Lake Hotel is for the romantic and — let's face it — the hungry. Lake has a full bar and a long wine list. Reservations are accepted here.

Mammoth Hotel Dining Room

$$ • Mammoth Hot Springs, Yellowstone National Park • (307) 344-7901

It's big, grand, spacious and historic. There's something for everybody at the Mammoth Hotel Dining Room, from the all-American hamburger and orange roughy to tenderloins of turkey. The mix of diners here is as varied — but probably not so colorful — as tourists during the stagecoach days who began and ended their park stays at Mammoth. This is a popular supper spot in the park. Complement your meal with wine and mixed drinks, if you like.

The Mammoth Hotel and Dining Room are open from the first week in May until mid-October. They reopen for the winter season about December 20 and remain open until the first week in March. Reservations are accepted.

Old Faithful Inn

$$$ • Old Faithful, Yellowstone National Park • (307) 344-7901

At the turn of the century, when the Old Faithful Inn was built, ladies were required to dress — we mean *dress* in long silk dresses with sweeping hoops — for dinner. Anyone who was late for supper had to eat outside in a tent. After supper, diners removed themselves to the lobby where they danced until the wee hours. The band played from the Crow's Nest high above.

Times have changed at the Old Faithful Inn, but the dining room still says "Western" and still rings of the frontier. The menu is a bit more contemporary. It includes entrees such as honey lemon chicken; fettuccine with mushrooms, artichoke hearts and olives; and Rocky Mountain trout. Take your time dining here; the pioneers did. Old Faithful has a full bar and a healthy wine list.

Strictly a summer hotel, the Old Faithful Inn is open from about May 1 until mid-October. Reservations are welcome.

Old Faithful Snow Lodge

$$ • Old Faithful, Yellowstone National Park • (307) 344-7901

Traditional meals like meat loaf, chicken-fried steak and fried chicken are served family style. That means that, except for your entree, the meal — it might be a bowl of beans or mashed potatoes, salad and rolls — is set on the table in big bowls with serving spoons. With cathedral ceilings, picture windows and pine chairs adorned with wildlife carvings, this log building is a fine newcomer to the Yellowstone National Park lodge dining facilities. The Old Faithful Snow Lodge opens and closes with the park. Liquor and wine are served here. Reservations are not accepted.

Roosevelt Lodge

$$ • Roosevelt-Tower Falls Junction, Yellowstone National Park • (307) 344-7901

Hang your hat and pull up your chair at Yellowstone National Park's most comfortable Western dining room where the fare is simple and the atmosphere like a dude ranch. This turn-of-the-century log dining room is reminiscent of the days when Teddy Roosevelt and his Rough Riders might have stood on the stoop smoking cigars and sipping whiskey before heading in for supper. The menu has changed somewhat since the early days. In addition to prime rib and rib-eye steaks, Cajun catfish, linguine with artichoke hearts, mushrooms and garlic, Cobb salad and the All-American burger will tempt your taste buds. Wine is also on the menu.

The Roosevelt is open only during the summer, mid-June until the first week in September. Reservations are not accepted.

Grand Teton National Park

Jenny Lake Lodge

$$$$ • Inner Loop Rd. at Jenny Lake • (307) 733-4647, (800) 628-9988

It may be the only restaurant for hundreds of miles that has a dress requirement — men are asked to wear jackets at dinner if possible — but with the food so well-coiffed, you won't mind. Garnishes and sauces include ginger chutney, wild mushrooms, cognac-laced jus, baby leeks and warm caviar vinaigrette. Entrees can be exotic: buffalo, ostrich, antelope, venison and rabbit. Food aside, we suspect that so many people choose this restaurant for the rustic old log dining room, bright throw rugs on wood floors, white curtains and matching white linen tablecloths, fresh flowers and the whimsical cowhide upholstered seats.

Jenny Lake Lodge serves breakfast, lunch and dinner from early June to mid October. Reservations are required. There are two bracketed seatings per night, both of which book solid.

Dornan's Chuckwagon

$$ • Teton Park Rd. at Moose Junction • (307) 733-2415

Dornan's has been serving outdoor chuckwagon meals here in summer since 1948. Eat on the lawn when the weather's nice (believe us, the view couldn't be better), sit at the long picnic tables, or pile into one of two big teepees if it's raining. The specialties here

INSIDERS' TIP

If you're in the Big Sky area, a dinner reservation at the Lone Mountain Ranch may just lead to the best meal of your vacation. The 320 Guest Ranch also has a dining room that welcomes drop-ins.

are barbecued short ribs, roast beef and Dutch-oven fixin's, all you can eat.

The Chuckwagon closes in winter, but even after all the other park concessions close, you can always find a meal at Dornan's. Across the parking lot from the Chuckwagon, Dornan's Pizza and Pasta Company serves calzones, gourmet pizzas and pasta dishes for lunch and dinner year round. The adjoining well-stocked grocery store offers a third option with its deli and bakery goods.

The Mural Room at Jackson Lake Lodge

$$$$ • U.S. Hwy. 89 at Jackson Lake Junction • (307) 543-2811, (800) 628-9988

The Mural Room in massive Jackson Lake Lodge looks across distant Jackson Lake to Mount Moran and the Teton range. Other walls display murals of early fur traders, trappers and hunters. (The well-known creator of these murals, Carl Roters, became so enamored of his Western subjects' home that he moved to Jackson in 1968.)

The Mural Room serves breakfast, lunch and dinner. Dinner options include a scattering of Teton specialties such as prime rib of buffalo (no, these aren't Yellowstone bison) or skillet-seared Idaho trout, as well as more traditional items. Reservations are recommended for dinner.

Other dining opportunities in Jackson Lake Lodge are the Blue Heron, a bar with the same stunning mountain views as the Mural Room and an extended bar menu, and The Pioneer Grill, a cafe in which you trade in the views (The Pioneer looks out the back of the lodge into lodgepole forest) for more affordable prices. Jackson Lake Lodge is open in summer only.

Signal Mountain Lodge

$$$ • Teton Park Rd. on south shore of Jackson Lake • (307) 543-2831

You spent the morning touring Jackson Lake and now you're hungry. It's time to participate in a Teton tradition: nachos and Margaritas (blackberry, preferably) on the deck at Signal Mountain Lodge. The breeze off the lake provides perfect seasoning. You can also order soups, salads, sandwiches and burgers from the Cottonwood Cafe menu, and enjoy them in the bar, on the deck, or — before 2:30 PM — in the main dining room looking out on Jackson Lake.

In addition to its cafe, Signal Mountain Lodge also offers evening fine dining at Aspens Restaurant. Enjoy lake views as you sample daily trout and salmon specials prepared differently each night. A tempting array of pasta dishes is also available, along with entree options ranging from Italian to Chinese. Enjoy your meal with a gourmet coffee beverage or a drink from the fully equipped bar. Both Aspens Restaurant and Cottonwood Cafe offer children's menus. No reservations are accepted.

Also at Signal Mountain are a clothing store, gift shop, service station, convenience store and marina. The marina offers scenic floats, boat rentals, guest buoys and guided fishing trips. Signal Mountain Lodge opens in mid-May and closes in mid-October.

Jackson Hole

Jackson, Wyoming

Bubba's Barbecue

$ • 515 W. Broadway Ave., Jackson, Wyo. • (307) 733-2288

Big servings of affordable food have made Bubba's a popular choice in Jackson. Ribs — baby back or spare — are the house specialty. You can't make reservations, but the timing usually works out about right if you sign onto the waiting list, wander across the street to the grocery store for a six pack of beer (no alcohol is served at Bubba's, but you can bring it in) and wander back. In the off-season, you'll find the dining room busiest at breakfast. Even President Clinton enjoyed a generously sized Bubba's country breakfast on a Jackson visit. Bubba's serves breakfast, lunch and dinner seven days a week.

The Bunnery

$ • 130 N. Cache St., Jackson, Wyo. • (307) 733-5474

Locals know The Bunnery as a great breakfast shop and the home of OSM — Oatmeal

Sunflower Millet bread. Other local favorites include chocolate cheesecake and flaky, nut-encrusted sticky buns. Lunch (and in summer, dinner) includes gourmet burgers, hot and cold sandwiches, salads, soups and omelets. With your meal enjoy fresh-squeezed juice, gourmet coffee beverages, soft drinks, beer or wine. From June through September, expect to wait in line during breakfast and lunch rushes.

Make sure you grab a loaf of OSM on your way out. You can even get OSM pancake mix or The Bunnery cookbook, which includes the OSM recipe for your bread machine.

Calico

$$ • Teton Village Rd., near Teton Village, Wyo. • (307) 733-2460

The menu at this family favorite ranges from macaroni and cheese to pizza to rotisserie-prepared whole chickens or prime rib, so a variety of palates and pocketbooks can be satisfied. Dining is casual. And the long deck is a perfect spot to sip wine and watch your kids play on the large lawn well off the road. Calico even provides the toy box. Before it was transported here, the tiny attached bar was a schoolhouse and later a church in nearby Kelly. Calico serves dinner seven nights a week. No reservations are necessary.

Camp Creek Inn

$$ • U.S. Hwy. 189, near Hoback Junction, Wyo. • (307) 733-3099

U.S. Highway 189 winds out to Pinedale with little but trees on the sides of the road. This location makes the relaxed fine dining offered by Camp Creek Inn, just 4 miles out of Hoback Junction, even more delicious. Flowered linen tablecloths under glass contrast with woven rawhide and peeled-pine chairs. You'll peruse a menu that features locally renowned prime rib (order by the inch), while in the exposed rafters overhead, a stuffed cougar crouches in such a lifelike pose that you expect his dangling tail to twitch. Camp Creek Inn offers a children's menu with kid-sized portions. The inn serves breakfast, lunch and dinner in summer and winter, lunch and dinner only in fall and spring.

Gouloff's

$$$ • 3600 N. Teton Village Rd., near Teton Village, Wyo. • (307) 733-1886

We were charmed by the little restaurant's backyard. It's fragrant with raised beds of sage, chives, oregano, rosemary, cilantro, red romaine lettuce, three kinds of mint, thyme, tarragon and dill, all destined for your plate. Owner Vicky Gouloff even cultivates edible flowers for garnishes.

Vicky calls her food "Teton Cuisine," and the dining experience here, "a casual, affordable sort of fine dining." This means wild game, creatively prepared with lots of berries and nuts in an atmosphere as casual as dinner at your neighbor's house. Locals recommend the corn ginger soup and the pistachio nut chicken. Gouloff's serves dinner only, Tuesday through Saturday. The two dining rooms are small, so reservations are a good idea. The restaurant generally closes for several weeks in spring and fall.

The Granary at Spring Creek

$$$$ • 1800 Spirit Dance Rd., Jackson, Wyo. • (307) 733-8833

Some swear the best fine dining in the valley isn't in the valley. It's at Spring Creek Resort on East Gros Ventre Butte, almost 1,000 feet above Jackson Hole. The Granary is open for breakfast, lunch and dinner, serving what it calls American cuisine.

You'll have trouble paying attention to the food, creative and complex though it is, because the huge windows seem to hang you off the cliff edge. Hawks soar below you and granite peaks saw off the horizon. But if you order an elk dish (the elk is from New Zealand, not the Elk Refuge) or trout (this is local) from the ever-changing menu, you'll probably find you can tear your eyes off the windows after a

INSIDERS' TIP

Most guest ranches between Cody and the east entrance to Yellowstone National Park serve mouthwatering food and welcome drop-in dinner guests.

couple of bites. A good bet for lunch is the Portobello mushroom sandwich with watercress and caramelized onion or the elk flank fajitas. And don't skip the wine list: In 1998, The Granary won an award of excellence from *Wine Spectator*. Reservations are advised.

Horse Creek Station

$$ • 9800 S. U.S. Hwy. 89 near Hoback Junction, Wyo. • (307) 733-0810

Eleven miles south of Jackson and perfectly located for anglers and whitewater rafters is Horse Creek Station. Barbecue tops the menu: Locals love the baby back ribs, barbecued shrimp and barbecued pork chops. But prawns come dressed at least four different ways here; our personal favorite is the crab-stuffed shrimp. The on-premises sports bar offers an extensive selection of beers, plus wine, mixed drinks and a finger-food menu. The restaurant serves lunch and dinner only; in warm weather, enjoy your meal on the deck.

During football season, make this your Monday night stop. Every Monday night a drawing determines which lucky patron gets to enjoy the game from the plush recliner, drinking and eating gratis (even the chair is given away — at halftime during the Super Bowl). Although the restaurant doesn't serve breakfast any other time, Sunday mornings during football season you can come in for a steak and egg breakfast served with a Bloody Mary from the Bloody Mary bar.

Jedediah's Original House of Sourdough

$ • 135 E. Broadway Ave., Jackson, Wyo. • (307) 733-5671

Named for Jedediah Smith, early 1800s wanderer in these parts, this breakfast hot spot serves sourdough made from a culture born in that wilder century. Seventeen years ago when Mike Gieran and his partners opened this restaurant, they asked locals to bring in family sourdough cultures. Some of the sourdough starters were more than 100 years old. Mixed together and cultured in 60 gallon crocks in the basement, the bubbly result becomes biscuits and pancakes and other goodies every morning. Some summer days, the little log cabin restaurant goes through 30 pungent gallons of the stuff.

Jedediah's serves breakfast, lunch and, in summer, dinner. Reservations can be made for dinner. While you're in, check out the sign-up sheet for Jedediah's catalogue: You can order house jams and sourdough culture for your friends.

SilverDollar Grille at The Wort Hotel

$$$ • Corner of Glenwood St. and Broadway Ave., Jackson, Wyo. • (307) 733-2190, (800) 322-2727

The Wort is a Jackson landmark. Inside the historic old hotel, decorated with black and white photographs from Jackson's wilder days, the SilverDollar Grille serves what it likes to call "New West Cuisine," in a family restaurant atmosphere. The main attraction is the main course: meat. Whether it's lamb, pork, duck, buffalo or elk you've got a taste for tonight, you'll find it. The SilverDollar Grille boasts that it serves the best prime rib in town, a tall claim in beef-happy Jackson. There are also seafood and vegetarian options. The restaurant serves breakfast, lunch and dinner; dinner reservations are recommended.

The Lame Duck Chinese Restaurant

$$ • 680 E. Broadway Ave., Jackson, Wyo. • (307) 733-4311

So here you are in cowboy country, land of beef, beef and more beef, and what will you enjoy for dinner? May we suggest sushi? Sylvia and Joe Diprisco have been serving up their authentic Oriental dishes (mostly Chinese — Joe studied Oriental cuisine in Hong Kong) to Jackson Insiders for 17 years.

If you're planning a get-together at your condo or motel, consider ordering up a big sushi platter. Or call and reserve one of three private rooms. Each is separated from the main dining area by rice-paper screens. Two feature Western-style seating; one is traditional, its low table equipped with a floor pit into which you extend your legs for comfort. Each private room seats from four to 12. You can also enjoy counter seating or, on warm evenings, eat alfresco on the small, screened deck.

The Lame Duck has a full bar, including, of course, sake. The drink menu is almost as fun as the food menu, featuring such concoc-

Photo: Robert Bower, Post Register

The dining room of the Old Faithful Lodge is probably what your hometown steakhouse modeled itself after.

tions as Disaster and Chinese Firedrill (sorry, you'll have to see for yourself what's in 'em). The restaurant serves dinner only. Reservations are accepted for the private tea rooms.

Nani's Genuine Pasta House

$$$ • 240 N. Glenwood St., Jackson, Wyo. • (307) 733-3888

Sicilian Carol Mortillaro Parker, padrona of this little restaurant, serves only authentic Italian cuisine. Olive oil, balsamic vinegar and other key ingredients are imported from Italy. Fresh herbs are harvested from the restaurant's garden. The regular menu is classic Italian, but every month dishes from a different region of Italy are featured. Wine selections complement the region's style.

The restaurant is small and intimate; reservations are recommended, although a room added in 1998 creates a bit more seating. Deck seating is available in summer. Dinner is served seven nights, except in spring and fall when the restaurant cuts back its hours.

Nora's Fish Creek Inn

$$ • 5600 W. Wyo. Hwy. 22, Wilson, Wyo. • (307) 733-8288

If you're looking for the place locals love to love, you've found it. Nora's serves a breakfast so popular you'll probably stand in line for it on weekends (sorry, no breakfast reservations). But when you lay your fork into those huevos rancheros or blueberry pancakes, you won't mind the wait. Nora's serves breakfast, lunch and dinner seven days a week; the bar draws crowds in the evenings. Classic country music plays through the speakers day and night.

In April of 1982, owner Nora Tygum took over what was once a dance studio and before that Wilson's general store and post office. The peeled logs of the 1930s building have been left exposed. Fresh flowers decorate the tables every day, 12 months a year. Pretty Fish Creek flows almost right past the door.

On the dinner menu, black Angus beef gets rave reviews from locals. The fresh — that's right, fresh — salmon and trout are the biggest sellers among tourists. Folks who live near the sea and ought to know say Nora's charbroiled salmon or pine nut crusted halibut taste about as good as you could want. Dinner reservations are accepted.

Pearl Street Bagels

$ • 145 W. Pearl Ave., Jackson, Wyo. • (307) 739-1218
$ • 1230 Ida Ln., Wilson, Wyo. • (307) 739-1261

The original shop opened in Jackson in 1990 and quickly became a locals' coffee-sipping hangout. Recently, owner Maggie Gibson decided to bring her tasty fare to little Wilson at the base of Teton Pass. Both locations feature old-fashioned boiled and baked bagels — none of that steam-oven shortcutting. Fancy cream cheeses top the fresh, fragrant bagels, making a fine breakfast or lunch. You can even get bagels and lox. These folks also serve a variety of premium coffees and teas, including Chai ice tea. Stop by mornings for a bag of discounted day-olds while they last.

The Range

$$$$ • 225 N. Cache St., Jackson, Wyo. • (307) 733-5481

Chef Arthur says that the designer who gave The Range its unique look was striving for "metropolitan prairie." You'll have to judge for yourself, but what's certain is that with that open-style kitchen, light jazz in the background, cherry wainscoting and an unobtrusive street entrance, you won't confuse The Range with any other Jackson restaurant.

The award-winning wine list contains 120 to 130 selections that range from American to French to Italian to Australian. The menu shows Chef Arthur's desire to "take the usual and make it unusual." Nightly specials include an appetizer, salad and a meat or fish entree. Nightly trout specials mean The Range has offered more than 200 trout preparations since it opened in 1988.

The Range is open for dinner seven nights a week, except for one-month closures in the spring and fall. A full bar is on premises. Reservations are recommended.

Shades Cafe

$$, no credit cards • 75 S. King St., Jackson, Wyo. • (307) 733-2015

They used to call it the Vuarnet Cafe, but Vuarnet, the snazzy sunglasses manufacturer with first claim to that name, apparently didn't much like that idea. Ten-year-old Shades is a coffeehouse and restaurant with more seating space on its shaded deck than inside its dining room. In summer on that deck, look for the Smoothie Bar, serving up fruit smoothies and java frosties, a perfect treat while strolling around town. Breakfasts are bakery goodies, Belgian waffles, eggs Benedict and more, washed down with a gourmet coffee. Lunches are focaccia sandwiches, burritos, soups and salads. Dinner is a bit more surprising: It's Thai. Served Wednesday through Sunday in summer and shorter hours other seasons, the Thai menu is as authentic as these folks can make it.

This locals' favorite tends to fill fast for dinners, so reservations are strongly recommended. Shades currently serves no alcohol, but is hoping to obtain a license. For now, you may bring your own beer and wine. Expect a small corkage fee for wine.

Snake River Brewing Co.

$$ • 265 S. Millward St., Jackson, Wyo. • (307) 739-2337

There are no logs here. No cowboy art and no elk mounts. Instead you'll see patterned concrete floors, cable bannisters and high ceilings crisscrossed by a profusion of shiny white steel beams. The bar is a huge black S curve. Blocks of light stream through tall, square-paneled windows.

In typical Jackson style, the food is also a new take on an old thing: The menu features pizza baked in a wood-fired oven, but these pizzas are, well, different. For instance, there's the mozzarella and fontina pizza topped with duck sausage and fresh sage. Or the smoked chicken and sun-dried tomato pizza. You can also get pastas, salads and soups, plus a few eclectic surprises. Make sure you have the bartender pour you a pint of one of the pub's award-winning brews to go with your meal (we recommend the Zonker Stout).

Snake River Brewing Co. serves lunch and dinner seven days a week. The kitchen stays open late for the party crowd (see our Nightlife chapter).

Snake River Grill

$$$$ • 84 E. Broadway Ave., Jackson, Wyo. • (307) 733-0557

Rumor has it that Harrison Ford owns this upscale restaurant. Actually he just eats here. President and Mrs. Clinton have, too. Winters, it's full of chummy, red-faced skiers. This is Jackson-style elegance, with log walls, wrought-iron accents and a moss rock fireplace. The food is simple but artfully combined and presented; mashed potatoes, asparagus and mustard sauce might complement your seared salmon, or spicy cole slaw your rainbow trout with pecan-butter. Snake River Grill has a full bar and award-winning wine list. It serves dinner only, seven nights a week. Reservations are recommended but not required; in summer, it's a good idea to make them well in advance. The restaurant closes November and April.

Stagecoach Bar and Patty Cake West

$, no credit cards • 5755 W. Wyo. Hwy. 22, Wilson, Wyo. • (307) 733-7225

Strange things happen — and sometimes they end up strangely right. One such event occurred in November 1996, when upscale deli Patty Cake Patisserie (now renamed Patty Cake West) moved into Wilson's popular locals' country-and-western hangout (see our Nightlife chapter). Now you can play pool, listen to country music and sip a local microbrew while enjoying fine pastries, homemade bread or soup and tasty pasta salads. Long lines queue up at lunch for such favorites as the grilled-chicken sandwiches or the made-to-order burgers. Don't forget to grab dessert, too: big chocolate chip cookies or pastries made fresh that morning. If you're not moseying over to the bar for a cocktail, add an espresso to wash it all down. You can also grab breakfast and dinner here. In summer, enjoy the deck or the new sand volleyball court (Patty Cake West provides the ball). Reservations are not necessary.

Steak Pub

$$ • 4125 S. U.S. Hwy. 89, near Jackson, Wyo. • (307) 734-8070

The Steak Pub turns its back on U.S. Highway 89, facing its windows and cottonwood-shaded deck toward the distant Snake River. When the little roadhouse that is now Steak Pub's dining room was built back in 1938, the road was in front of the building. It was later moved. You'll enjoy the views and breezes on the deck, screened from U.S. 89 by additions to the old log building in the '60s, '80s and in 1997.

We heard that Steak Pub's fully equipped bar, which has its own sandwich and finger-food menu, is the best place in town for hot wings. The dining room features beef but doesn't forget about chicken, shrimp, salmon and pasta. "Outstanding," is how bartender Eric Weber describes the prime rib, in half-pound and 1-pound servings. After dinner, enjoy a decadent homemade eclair — flaky and drizzled with chocolate, they're the size of a small loaf of bread. Dinner reservations are recommended.

INSIDERS' TIP

Occasionally, a menu will offer Rocky Mountain oysters as an appetizer or entree. These are bull calf testicles, normally removed each spring when the bulls are branded and castrated. When they come from young animals, Rocky Mountain oysters are very tender and tasty. Be sure to ask your waitress, though, about the source of the "oysters" listed on the menu. These days we've seen people cooking up slices of full-grown bull testicles and calling them Rocky Mountain oysters. What they most resemble are leather boot tongues.

Stiegler's Restaurant and Bar

$$$$ • Teton Village Rd. at Jackson Hole Racquet Club • (307) 733-1071

Some will tell you this restaurant offers the best fine dining in town. Austrian Peter Stiegler serves continental delicacies in a plushly carpeted, lace-curtained dining room. The tiny adjoining bar is warmed by a river-rock fireplace; the bar itself is topped with beaten copper.

Peter is both head chef and maitre d' in this classy little restaurant with its own house china service and fresh flowers on every table. Some menu items are, as Peter says, "as Austrian as it gets." Like the Bauern Schmaus, a two-person platter of roast pork tenderloin, smoked pork, bratwurst, dumplings, sauerkraut and red cabbage. Or the Schlipfkrapfen, a stuffed-ravioli appetizer from Peter's home province. Portions are exquisitely presented rather than large. Reservations are requested. Stiegler's serves dinner nightly except Mondays; it closes for a few weeks in spring and fall.

Vista Grande

$$ • 2550 Teton Village Rd., near Teton Village, Wyo. • (307) 733-6964

In 1978, newlyweds Becky and Tom Schnell decided to build a restaurant. It became a family endeavor: Tom was his own contractor, the couple's mothers sewed the waitresses' dresses, and their fathers made the tabletops.

They still spend much of their time at the restaurant they began their marriage with. Go there often and you'll find yourself greeted by name. The restaurant now seats 160. A recent addition is the covered deck that wraps around the west and north sides of the building overlooking a spacious grassy area big enough for kickball or Frisbee (which is what you're likely to find your kids doing while you sip that Margarita). A second, glassed-in patio allows the next-best thing to outdoor dining in winter. The menu is extensive, but Becky says customers are particularly partial to the fajitas (made with skirt steak, the traditional cut) and the chimichangas. A full bar is on premises; Vista Grande serves dinner seven nights per week.

Surrounding Areas

Southwestern Montana

West Yellowstone, Montana

Bullwinkle's Saloon and Eatery

$ • 19 Madison Ave., West Yellowstone, Mont. • (406) 646-7974

Besides homestyle food, good humor and easy camaraderie are the regular fare at Bullwinkle's Saloon and Eatery, which also happens to be West Yellowstone's resident sports bar. Jackie and Dennis LaFever have surrounded themselves and their customers with mementos from their hometown in Sheboygan, Wisconsin: The walls in Bullwinkle's are lined with Green Bay Packers memorabilia.

Noted for their baby-back pork ribs, their Sicilian-style tenderloins and their Snowmobiler (a 20-ounce T-bone steak), Bullwinkle's serves an array of burgers, a few pasta dishes, frog legs and at least one wild-game entree, depending on the season. What Jackie really specializes in, though, is soup and appetizers. Expect to find soups like Grandma used to make: chicken dumpling soup, split pea, navy bean and ham. And her appetizers are legendary. They include Tater Skins smothered with cheese and topped with bacon bits, homemade Hay Stack Onion Rings, Winkle's Hot Wings and Nacho Supreme, piled high with fresh-cooked beans, beef, cheese, tomatoes, onions and olives — enough to make a meal for two. Reservations are recommended. (See our Nightlife chapter for more about Bullwinkle's.)

INSIDERS' TIP

Many Greater Yellowstone bars not listed in this chapter serve inexpensive meals including juicy burgers.

Cappy's Bistro and Coffee Bar

$ • 104 Canyon St., West Yellowstone, Mont. • (406) 646-9537

If eggs, bacon and a short stack sound like too much too soon for breakfast, try washing Cappy's plump, moist muffins down with a smooth, steaming latte. Aaah. Cappy's, located in the rear of the Book Peddler, also serves an assortment of breakfast pastries along with rich, strong coffee in a casual atmosphere that includes a collection of regional newspapers — so you can read, sip and nibble at the same time. Lunches feature gourmet soups and sandwiches.

The Coachman

$$$ • 209 Madison Ave., West Yellowstone, Mont. • (406) 646-7381

If it's meat and potatoes you're after, you'll find it at The Coachman in the Stage Coach Inn. But it's the seafood, especially the fresh salmon, that folks often favor here. Chef Jack Cole, who has been serving up consistently good meals at the Coachman since 1989, changes the menu according to the season and the situation. In summer, you might find a selection of steaks, homestyle pot roast or pesto chicken primavera. From mid-November through early December you'll find a menu designed for hard-working U.S. cross-country ski teams in training. On holidays — the Coachman is open seven days a week year round — Cole turns out traditional fare with a flair. Don't let the fresh flowers (when they're available) or the linen service scare you. It's strictly come as you are, breakfast, lunch and dinner. The dinner menu includes a long wine list. And you can order drinks from the hotel bar. Reservations are accepted.

Coyote Junction

$ • 17 Madison Ave., West Yellowstone, Mont. • (406) 646-7921

This is the picnic lunch place. Order your sandwich and deli salad on the spot, or pay $5 to have the Coyote crew make up a sack lunch for you. Europeans favor this grocery and deli because its cooler carries more than 20 Wisconsin cheeses and a good selection of foreign cheeses. Coyote Junction also sells home-baked bread and a growing selection of bratwurst from Wisconsin.

Doris's Cantina

$ • West Yellowstone Airport, West Yellowstone, Mont. • (406) 646-9533

Open seven days a week, June 1 through September 30, Doris's Cantina features fresh Tex-Mex cuisine in a small corner of the West Yellowstone Airport. The 2-mile drive from town doesn't deter locals bent on biting into Doris Barton's Pancho Villa chile relleno dinner, the hottest — read: most popular — item on her dinner menu. Tuesday is traditionally 50¢ Taco Day. Doris, who hires extra waitresses to help her with the Tuesday crowd that shows up for the bargain lunch, says she sometimes sells more than 500 tacos in a couple of short hours.

In addition to standard breakfasts, Doris serves huevos rancheros and chorizo con huevos. Lunches include tacos, burritos, hot sandwiches and burgers served at the counter or at a table overlooking the airport runway. Doris closes her Cantina from 2 to 5 PM each summer afternoon. Dinner reservations are accepted.

Eino's Bar

$, no credit cards • 8955 Gallatin Rd., West Yellowstone, Mont. • (406) 646-9344

The price is right, and the juicy burgers and big steaks are cooked to your exact order. That's because you are your own chef at Eino's, where customers get to grill their own steaks or burgers. Nine miles north of West Yellowstone on U.S. Highway 191, Eino's sign is so small you could easily miss it, so watch

INSIDERS' TIP

Many restaurants in Jackson deliver to your motel room or use a delivery service which will. Look for a delivery brochure in your room with participating restaurant menus, or ask at the motel desk.

for it at the junction of U.S. Highways 191 and 287. Cook up your steak — they offer only T-bones and top sirloin — in the grill room. Sip a beer, then devour that steak while you gaze across the open landscape through Eino's giant picture windows. Or head downstairs with a pitcher of beer and try your hand at pool. Winters, Eino's is a popular dinner spot for snowmobilers: Groomed trails lead from West Yellowstone to Eino's.

Eino's is closed for about three weeks between Thanksgiving and Christmas. During the summer, it opens about noon. When snowmobilers are on the loose, though, the place opens at 9 AM. Eino's has a full bar and a friendly staff. Reservations are not accepted.

The Gusher

$ • Madison Ave. and Dunraven St., West Yellowstone, Mont. • (406) 646-9050

Relaxed and comfortable, The Gusher is the sort of place where you can sink into a padded chair and stare after a long day in the park or on the road. Read a newspaper or peruse a guidebook. Or sip a Guinness served Dublin style at 46 degrees. (The Gusher has a good selection of beer.) In addition to pizzas (they deliver), The Gusher boasts the biggest burgers in town as well as some seafood, sandwiches and a dinner steak. Lunch and dinner are served here from May 1 until mid-October, and from December 1 until mid-March.

Happy Hour Bar

$ • 15400 Hebgen Lake Rd., West Yellowstone, Mont. • (406) 646-7281

Situated on the shores of Hebgen Lake about 10 miles northwest of West Yellowstone, the Happy Hour Bar is a local favorite. Besides juicy garlic burgers on French bread and an array of steaks, locals come here to eat steak and shrimp kabobs, scampi dinners, and shrimp served on ice. The folks at the Happy Hour know how to have a good time. Like other businesses in the area, the Happy Hour closes during the shoulder seasons. Reservations aren't accepted. For more information see our Nightlife chapter.

Nancy P's Baking Co.

$ • 29 Canyon St., West Yellowstone, Mont. • (406) 646-9737

Nancy Pfeiffer, owner of Nancy P's, doesn't do donuts. She does do huckleberry buckle, strawberry rhubarb bars, morning-glory carrot muffins and big bad brownies. And she serves a great cup of coffee — Torrefazione Italia (coffee lovers may recognize the brand) — in her cheery little bakery. Her showcase is loaded with so many goodies (three kinds of sweet rolls, too) that you may forget to look up and around.

Nancy P's usually has an assortment of European specialty breads and almost always has fine focaccia bread. If you get there early, look for a basket full of lunch-sized pizzas — they're just right for two — atop her showcase. These are perfect for a picnic. So are her ham and cheese croissants, her Mediterranean rollups and humongous to-go sandwiches made on focaccia bread. Nancy P's is open from May through September. She opens early for the breakfast crowd and closes midafternoon. No need for a reservation.

Oregon Short Line

$$$ • 315 Yellowstone Ave., West Yellowstone, Mont. • (406) 646-7365

This popular restaurant is tucked into a nifty nook adjacent to the 1903 Oregon Short Line Railroad Car (see our Attractions chapter for more information about this railroad car, the anchor around which the West Yellowstone Conference Hotel was built). The Oregon Short Line combines consistently good food with comfort and convenience, especially if you're staying at the Conference Hotel. Feel free to start your dinner hour at the Iron Horse Saloon next door (you can take your drink to the dining room). Be forewarned, though: You'll be sharing the room with a few wild animals — like a mounted pheasant, a bobcat, an antelope and a black bear.

The menu here is pleasantly varied with entrees ranging from chicken pesto linguine to prime rib to broiled lamb chops. We recommend you try the Steak Durango, a grain-fed beefalo top sirloin steak. Top it off with a glass of wine. Reservations are accepted.

Pete's Rocky Mountain Pizza Company

$$ • 104 Canyon St., West Yellowstone, Mont. • (406) 646-7820

Just try walking by Pete's Rocky Mountain Pizza on a summer's evening with the smell of an Incredible Edible pizza wafting out the door. This popular pizzeria makes as many as 180 Italian pies a day at the peak of their season. Pete's also serves steaks, an assortment of chicken dishes and pastas with homemade sauces (the lasagna is delicious) as well as lunches during the summer. If you can't stand confinement on a summer's evening, try one of the tables on the sidewalk patio. Or, if you like, kick back in your motel room and order out. Pete's, closed during the shoulder seasons, delivers.

Running Bear Pancake House

$ • 538 Madison Ave., West Yellowstone, Mont. • (406) 646-7703

Ask Insiders who serves the best breakfast in town and chances are they'll say, "The Running Bear Pancake House." This place is such a popular breakfast spot that some summer mornings latecomers willingly wait their turn for their morning meal. Lunch favorites include real turkey sandwiches and half-pound, extra-lean, hand-shaped hamburgers. Owners Dixie and Mike Klostrich also serve breakfast for lunch.

This restaurant, which seats 75, closes from October 31 through December 25, and from March 31 through May 1. It opens at 7 AM and closes at 2 PM. The owners don't accept reservations.

Rustler's Roost

$$ • 234 Firehole Ave., West Yellowstone, Mont. • (406) 646-7622, (800) 646-7622

Upstairs next to the Big Western Pine Motel, the Rustler's Roost is a local favorite with families and couples. While you dine on wild game or standard pasta, seafood or steak fare, big picture windows let you take in the town below and the mountains beyond. Downstairs is a cozy lounge. Upstairs cushy couches invite you to wait in comfort for a table or your friends. A piano is also provided for guests who want to play some tunes before or after their meals. Reservations are accepted.

Three Bear Restaurant

$$$ • 205 Yellowstone Ave., West Yellowstone, Mont. • (406) 646-7811

Come as you are and come when you can, says manager Tom Schaap. If you aren't the bashful sort, you'll want to wander about looking at the historic photos that line the Three Bear Restaurant's walls. You may have to peer over other peoples' tables, though.

This is a popular place. The food here is consistently good. And the decor, a rustic blend of giant log pillars and soothing green carpet and wallpaper, is comfortable. It's just right for dining on the Three Bears' hand-cut steaks or slow-roasted prime rib. (We dare you to tackle the 16-ounce Cattleman's Cut. If you aren't into dares, we suggest the 8-ounce Petite Cut.) Besides a good assortment of steaks, the Three Bear menu includes chicken and seafood, pork and pasta.

The Three Bear closes from October 18 to December 15 and from March 1 to May 1. It serves breakfast, lunch and dinner. There is a lounge adjacent to the dining room. Feel free to bring your drink to the table. Reservations are accepted for large groups.

Gardiner, Montana

Bear Country Restaurant

$$ • 232 Park St., Gardiner, Mont. • (406) 848-7188

After a day in Yellowstone National Park drive straight to the Bear Country Restaurant. Have a piece of apple pie or chicken pot pie, lasagna or stir-fry shrimp. Everything here is homemade. Sometimes hopping until 11 o'clock on a summer's night, this place is casual. You may just feel like you're at Aunt Sue's potlucking with your long-lost relatives. The Bear Country serves breakfast, lunch and dinner, and is open year round. Reservations are not accepted here.

Corral Drive Inn

$, no credit cards • U.S. Hwy. 89, Gardiner, Mont. • (406) 848-7627

If you're a burger lover, chances are you've heard about this place. If you haven't, don't pass through Gardiner without stopping at the Corral Drive Inn. The burgers here, served up for 37 years by Helen Gould (the Corral is the oldest single-owner business in Gardiner) are legendary half-pound, handmade whoppers. Besides an assortment of regular hamburgers, Helen does a fine buffalo burger and an array of hot burger-type sandwiches.

Summers, you may like to eat on the patio outside. Otherwise there are a few strictly functional tables inside. More than a juicy hamburger, Helen dishes up a serving of old-fashioned straightforward local color. Dining here is an experience. Don't try to make reservations.

Sawtooth Restaurant and Deli

$$ • 222 W. Park St., Gardiner, Mont. • (406) 848-7600

We defy you to walk past the Sawtooth Restaurant and Deli around mealtime. Aromatic fumes waft out the door from the kitchen of this small restaurant which turns out mouthwatering pasta dishes, steaks, barbecued ribs and dinner specials that might include a giant, thick grilled pork chop with mashed potatoes, Caesar salad, fresh bread and perfectly done veggies. Summers, the garden deck overlooking Yellowstone National Park's north entrance is alive with folks feeding on ribs from "The Pit" and sipping microbrews from the cooler. The lunch menu includes hot and cold submarine sandwiches, grilled sandwiches, burgers, and an assortment of fresh salads. The Sawtooth packs sack and box lunches, caters and makes up party platters. The Sawtooth Restaurant and Deli is open from June 1 through October 31, Monday through Saturday. Reservations are not recommended.

Silver Gate and Cooke City, Montana

Joan and Bill's Family Restaurant

$$ • U.S. Hwy 212, Cooke City, Mont. • (406) 838-2280

Known by locals as "the pie place," Joan and Bill's Family Restaurant offers an impressive array of delicious homemade pies and other baked goods. Comfortable, with a casual rustic atmosphere à la Cooke City, Joan and Bill's is the kind of place where you might find yourself doubling up at a table with a stranger (the management would never ask you to do it, and you won't be strangers for long) to make room for a larger crowd. At your service, you'll find the second, third and fourth generations of Cooke City restaurateurs (Grandma's dad began the restaurant on Cooke Pass just after World War II). The menu offers pretty typical Western fare, and chicken-fried steak is their best seller. Joan and Bill's serves breakfast, lunch and dinner spring through fall. Most years they reopen for winter snowmobilers. Reservations aren't necessary.

The Prospector

$$$ • U.S. Hwy. 212, Cooke City, Mont. • (406) 838-2251, (800) 527-6462

The Prospector is the only restaurant in Silver Gate/Cooke City that consistently stays open all year. While The Prospector is renowned for its great chili (it goes through 15 gallons every other day no matter what the season), there are plenty of other entrees on the menu. For breakfast we recommend the Sunrise Breakfast Special: two eggs, two pancakes, two pieces of bacon for $3.50. If you're a bit hungrier, try the steak and eggs. Prime rib and Chicken Mediterranean (chicken breast cooked in white wine, shallots and garlic with marinara sauce) are the dinner favorites. You'll also find an assortment of pasta dishes, three

INSIDERS' TIP

In Idaho Falls, find many familiar fast-food restaurants on 17th Street near Grand Teton Mall, or on the part of Yellowstone Highway locals call the Northgate Mile.

Photo: Randy Hayes, Post Register

Idaho's famous russet potatoes sit out on the ground exposed to the sun for a very short time before being loaded into a truck and placed in a climate-controlled cellar.

kinds of steaks, Mexican food and shrimp scampi. This busy place is open from early morning until pretty late at night during the high season. Reservations aren't necessary.

Bozeman, Montana

The Crystal Beer Garden

$, no credit cards • 123 E. Main St., Bozeman, Mont. • (406) 587-2888

During fair weather, you can rise above it all at the Crystal Beer Garden, a rooftop cafe that serves beer and burgers. Enter from the outside via a wooden staircase that leads from the rear parking lot. Or treat yourself to a peek into Montana — not the dressed-up tourist version — by strolling through the Crystal Bar door on Bozeman's Main Street. The burgers are juicy. The beer is cold.

John Bozeman's Bistro

$$$ • 242 E. Main St., Bozeman, Mont. • (406) 587-4100

Since its owners opened John Bozeman's Bistro in 1983 in the land of cowboys, this place has been on the cutting edge of fine food in the West. For example, when Chef Perry Wenzel creates a dish, he not only thinks about doing a delicious ballet on your taste buds, but he also envisions delivery, style, form. Just listen to him talk about a new dish and chances are you'll hear him wax eloquent about things like verticality and elevation.

On a given night, Wenzel might serve French, Italian and Cajun cuisine. The Bistro is known for its fresh — very fresh — seafood. While he changes the menu often (on a given night you might find seven or eight seafood entrees on the menu), Wenzel offers a few house specialties, including the macadamia nut-crusted fresh catch served with mango sauce, black beans, fried bananas and a tiny pile of greens. The wine list here is phenomenal. So is the food. Reservations are recommended.

MacKenzie River Pizza Co.

$ • 232 E. Main St., Bozeman, Mont. • (406) 587-0055
$ • 409 Main St., Belgrade, Mont. • (406) 388-0016

Livingston residents drive 26 miles to Bozeman just to get a taste of a MacKenzie River Pizza. This mom-and-pop-comfortable gourmet pizzeria has 23 different kinds of pizza, ranging from the Vegetarian to the Pesto Fajita to the Meat Lovers. The Rancher (a combo) and the pepperoni-packed Good Old Boy are still the all-time favorites with customers. On a Friday night you might find the place packed and a friendly crew cranking out as many as 500 Italian pies. You'll also find music and an assortment of sandwiches. MacKenzie River is open for lunch and dinner. It doesn't accept reservations.

Gallatin Gateway, Montana

Gallatin Gateway Inn

$$$$ • 76405 Gallatin Rd., Gallatin Gateway, Mont. • (406) 763-4672

You know the scene. The chef tastes the sauce, pinches all five finger tips together, kisses them just so, closes his eyes and listens to the delicate symphony playing on his taste buds. Chef Scotty Burton at the Gallatin Gateway Inn uses only the very best ingredients then combines them in ways that defy the normal imagination. The Inn's award-winning food might include entrees such as grilled Boston cod with Pernod-creamed red lentils, or Chinese-steamed king salmon or five-peppercorn seared certified Angus tenderloin.

The dining room, set with linen and fresh flowers, is ringed with tall windows reminiscent of the early railroad days when tourists stopped over on their way to Yellowstone National Park. Burton changes his menu often and offers an extensive wine list to complement it. The Gallatin has a full service bar. Reservations are recommended.

The Gourmet Gas Station

$ • 76250 Gallatin Rd., Gallatin Gateway, Mont. • (406) 763-4564

If you aren't careful, you'll zoom right by this unlikely place for fine food between Bozeman and Big Sky on U.S. Highway 191. The most prominent sign says "Gateway Market, Grill and Casino." Another one above the café entrance reads. "Good Food." And it is. Dinner entrees at The Gourmet Gas Station are a mix of Mexican and traditional entrees such as steaks and shrimp cooked in a beer batter or Mexican style. Prime rib is added to the menu on Fridays and Saturdays. Wednesday through Saturday (the only days you'll find dinner here) the chef cooks up weekly specials. The menu also includes an assortment of juicy burgers and hot sandwiches. Diners sit in several booths and at a counter. Breakfast and lunch menus also include Mexican meals. No need for reservations. Beer and wine are available.

Big Sky, Montana

Buck's T-4 Lodge

$$$$ • U.S. Hwy. 191, 1 mile south of Big Sky, Mont. • (406) 995-4111

If it's a taste of wild game you have a hankering for, Buck's T-4 has it. The menu here includes ranch-raised bison, New Zealand red deer, South Texas antelope and a wild game meat loaf that combines all of the above. Buck's also serves wild game stew in a burgundy sauce and wild game pâté, a combination of buffalo, wild boar, venison and caribou layered with fresh herbs and pistachio nuts.

INSIDERS' TIP

The "wild game" on many restaurant menus isn't really wild. It is harvested from game farms. It's illegal to kill wild game and sell the meat.

Here's your chance to sample it all. (In case you're traveling with someone who can't stomach wild game, Buck's has plenty of other standards including steak, chicken, seafood and pasta.) You'll find a full bar and a decent wine list at this laid-back place. Buck's T-4 is a favorite with locals. During the high season, it's best to make a reservation.

The Corral Cafe and Steakhouse

$$$ • U.S. Hwy. 191, Big Sky, Mont. • (406) 995-4249, (888) 995-4249

It's Western. It's comfortable. And it's reasonably priced. The Corral turns out juicy steaks and burgers in a casual atmosphere, making it the hot spot for Gallatin Canyon residents and visitors alike. We recommend you try the 25-ounce porterhouse . . . if you dare. A full Western bar and a pleasant mixture of locals and visitors make The Corral a good place to begin or end the day. You'll also find a friendly, welcoming staff and a taste of the Old West. Beer, wine and mixed drinks are available. Reservations are accepted only for extremely large groups.

Rainbow Ranch Lodge

$$$$ • U.S. Hwy. 191, Big Sky, Mont. • (406) 995-4132

Resurrected, refurbished and revived in 1995, the Rainbow Ranch Lodge offers fine dining on the Gallatin River. Chef Phillip Scott Boswell changes the menu twice a year to keep himself on his creative toes. Favorites on last winter's menu included roasted rack of lamb with a truffle-scented morel-veal reduction, and mesquite-smoked-then-roasted breast of chicken with spinach and toasted pine nut risotto with a port wine reduction. Potato-crusted rainbow trout with grilled Portobello cornbread pudding and a lemon-chive butter also ranks high among diners at the Lodge.

A spacious lounge with deep chairs, sofas and a fireplace is a good place to begin or end your meal. If the weather's fair, you can dine on the deck. The wine list here is extensive. The Rainbow Ranch Lodge closes from November 1 to November 15, and from April 15 to May 15. This is a very popular place so play it safe and make a reservation.

Livingston, Montana

Chatham's Livingston Bar and Grille

$$$$ • 130 N. Main St., Livingston, Mont. • (406) 222-7909

Simply elegant sums up Livingston artist Russell Chatham's first venture into haute cuisine. The San Francisco-born artist, writer, and-now restaurateur brings his creative talents to the kitchen and the dining room with its high ceilings and walls like blank canvases. (Here and there, of course, one of Chatham's paintings fits into the space.) The menu changes often, but you may find a dinner salad of mixed baby field greens or a Thai charred-beef entree salad. Fall entrees might include something like duckling with wild rice and turnips or grilled squab grown in Great Falls, Montana, or wild king salmon baked in a mashed potato crust. The Livingston Bar and Grille, which serves only dinner, has a fully restored hardwood bar and an impressive wine selection. Reservations are recommended.

Mark's In & Out

$, no credit cards • Park and Eighth Sts., Livingston, Mont. • (406) 222-7744

Carhops on Rollerblades? Who can resist? Mark's In & Out has been serving burgers and fries, malts and shakes, since 1954. Home of the Super Cheese — two patties with two slices of cheese and your choice of toppings for less than $2 — this cute little drive-in is a must for nostalgia nuts and families alike. Mark's is open from March 1 to November 1 depending on the weather. Check it out.

Martin's Café

$ • 108 W. Park St., Livingston, Mont. • (406) 222-2110

From the outside Martin's looks like it has seen better days — and it has. You can experience those better days once you step inside this high-ceilinged local favorite. Historic railroad photos line the walls, while about 30 trains per day rumble right past on the tracks just outside the building. Martin's menu, which bears a few surprises, is noted for its standard Western coffee shop fare: steaks, chops, roast beef and pork, and chicken-fried steak. Some folks come to Martin's especially for their chicken liver and liver-and-onion entrees. You can order Chinese pork noodles for breakfast or pancakes and eggs for supper. No need for reservations. Martin's is open year round.

The Sport

$$ • 144 S. Main St., Livingston, Mont. • (406) 222-3533

Little jeans, big jeans — we mean big jeans, like jeans with a 76-inch waist and a 45-inch inseam — old newspapers and cowboy memorabilia line the walls of this historic restaurant. Heck, the decor and a chance to hobnob with history are half the reason folks like Robert Redford and Peter Fonda pack into the old Sport.

Owned since 1983 by Livingston resident Suzanne Schneider, The Sport began as the Beer Hall in the late 1800s. Within the now-tame walls of this eating and drinking establishment, fortunes have been won and lost in poker games, and whole paychecks have been spent on a round for "the boys" (women weren't allowed in The Sport until the 1940s).

The food at The Sport is reasonably priced with a menu that features the famous Sport Burger (some folks say it's the best in Livingston), Sport Bar-B-Q Baby Back Pork Ribs, several Mexican dishes, seafood and hot sandwiches. The Sport, open for lunch and dinner, serves Montana-grown steaks and veal and has a full bar. Reservations may be wise on weekends.

The Stockman Bar

$$, no credit cards • 118 N. Main St., Livingston, Mont. • (406) 222-8455

Wear your spurs, chaps and cowboy hat if you like. The Stockman is Montana as it used to be with a steakhouse stuck in the back of a cowboy bar. Juicy steaks and giant stacks of homemade fries are served at prices even a family can afford. Burgers, one of The Stockman's top sellers, are big and super juicy. Prime rib is a weekend special. The Stockman serves supper seven days a week and lunch every day except Sunday. Carry your drink from the bar to the table or order it on the spot. No reservations.

Uncle Looie's Ristorante

$$$ • 119 W. Park St., Livingston, Mont. • (406) 222-7177

"If you find yourself a quart low on olive oil, Uncle Looie's Ristorante offers some of the best Italian dishes this side of New York's Little Italy," wrote David Lyons in the May 1997 issue of *Northwest Airlines Magazine*. Now Uncle Looie's owners tout Lyons' description in their advertisements. Although the image may not appeal to weight watchers, if you're going to indulge, this is the place to do it. At Uncle Looie's, you may feel like you're walking into a cozy New York restaurant minus that Eastern formality. Menu favorites include chicken scarpiello (a half-chicken sauteed in oil with Italian sausage, pepperoncini, capers, kalamata olives, onions and white wine) and veal del giorno (tender veal prepared in a different way each day). Uncle Looie's also features pastas of the day. Lunches include sandwiches, pasta and pizza. The wine list is extensive.

Lunch is served Monday through Friday, dinner seven days a week. Reservations are suggested.

Winchester Cafe and Grill

$$$ • 201 W. Park St., Livingston, Mont. • (406) 222-2708

The only things missing from a dining experience at the Winchester are the old cowpokes and Wall Street financiers who once lounged in the Murray Hotel lobby before taking supper at the Winchester. The spruced-up Winchester still echoes the understated elegance of its heyday as the hotel restaurant across the street from the Northern Pacific train depot.

Spacious and airy with high ceilings, this

INSIDERS' TIP

Many restaurants and cafes in and out of the parks will fix you a sack lunch for a fee. Ask around to find out who makes lunches in the area you're visiting.

popular place combines the new and the old with dinner entrees ranging from a porterhouse steak (cooked the way you like it) to a shrimp cashew stir-fry and vegetarian dishes. The Winchester has an extensive wine list and a full-service bar. Open year round, the Winchester serves breakfast, lunch and dinner. Reservations are accepted.

Emigrant, Montana

The Livery Stable

$$$ • U.S. Hwy. 89, Emigrant, Mont. • (406) 333-4688

Montanans love their steak. Half rare or medium well-done, it doesn't matter. (If you order it well-done, though, the chef warns customers he's not responsible if you don't like it.) The Livery Stable, housed in what was once the Old Saloon, Pool Hall and Hotel, serves up steaks, prime rib and an array of chicken and seafood in fine Western tradition. Charbroiled steaks are the calling card here. The Livery Stable, adjacent to the Old Saloon, serves drinks and wine. This is a popular place, so play it safe and make a reservation.

Old Saloon

$ • U.S. Hwy. 89, Emigrant, Mont. • (406) 333-4482

The Old Saloon serves up a taste of the West for breakfast and lunch at old-fashioned prices. No matter that you'll be eating in a bar, where cowboys and other local residents may be sipping something other than coffee for breakfast. This is Montana, where movie stars and welders, cowboys and counts drop their titles at the drop of a hat.

The menu at the Saloon is simple: burgers, toasted sandwiches and saloon dogs for lunch. No need for reservations.

Pray, Montana

Chico Inn

$$$ • Pray, Mont. • (406) 333-4933

Bon Apetit, *Gourmet*, *The New York Times*. They've all written about the food at the Chico Inn, the dining room at Chico Hot Springs. But words won't tell the story. "Fresh" means the rainbow assortment of lettuce in your salad came straight from the Chico garden. It also means fresh seafood is flown in daily, and the poultry dishes are made with free-range chickens raised by Montana Hutterites. Depending on the season, you might find sauces made with wild mushrooms, huckleberries, cherries, raspberries or other natural bounty from the area.

The entrees — beef Wellington and rosemary crusted rack of lamb are among the favorites — are nationally renowned. And the desserts are legendary, especially the orange flambe: A hollowed Valencia orange, lined with chocolate, is filled with Grand Marnier ice cream, topped with meringue then flamed at the table with Baccardi 151 rum.

Chef Jack Hall has a crew of 25 to help him during the summer months. Expect an elegant wine list and drinks from the in-house bar. (For more information about Chico, refer to our Resorts and Lodges chapter.)

MacAllister, Montana

Bear Claw Bar and Grill

$$ • U.S. Hwy. 287, MacAllister, Mont. • (406) 682-4619

Built in 1923, the original part of this added-onto rustic relic from the past is now the main part of the bar. In back is the dining room, a funky sort of addition used as living quarters by one of the past owners.

Owner Bob Miller serves up a mouthwatering array of steaks, crab, shrimp (two ways), chicken and swordfish or salmon. Comfortable and Western country verging on chic, the Bear Claw doesn't attract many cowboys during the summer. But as soon as tourists leave, the ranchers and other locals take over and turn the place into a sort of community center. The Bear Claw Bar and Grill is open 364 days a year (the bar, but not the kitchen, is open Christmas Day). Lunch and dinner are served here. During the high season it's best to make a reservation.

Ennis, Montana

Scotty's Long Branch Supper Club

$$$ • 125 E. Main, Ennis, Mont. • (406) 682-5300

Some folks just don't like having to stroll through a bar to find a meal. If you want to eat at Scotty's Long Branch Supper Club, though, you'll have to bite the bullet and take that hike. The folks who frequent the Long Branch Saloon are friendly locals, and Scot Davidson's food, consistently good, is well worth the walk.

Davidson doesn't do burgers and fries. He does do fresh seafood, an assortment of veal dishes, chicken, pork chops and steaks. His menu is small, but it changes often and includes weekly specials. Davidson's French onion soup is legendary, and his desserts are all homemade. Hours vary according to the season. We recommend calling ahead to check his schedule. Reservations are also a good idea, especially in the summer.

Cameron, Montana

Grizzly Bar and Grill

$$$ • 1409 U.S. Hwy. 287, Cameron, Mont. • (406) 682-7118

You know the food is good when a restaurant that's in the middle of nowhere regularly has a crowd of cars parked outside. The Grizzly Bar and Grill, owned for more than 20 years by Eric Smith, is near the West Fork of the Madison River, about 20 miles south of Ennis.

The menu is simple. The food is great. And the steaks, cooked over an aspen-fired grill, are out of this world. Ask Chef Nikolai Fleeson about the filet mignon du jour or have the house favorite, filet mignon Churasco. In addition to the regular steak menu, you'll find pasta, shrimp and chicken entrees as well as juicy burgers. Fleeson features two specials each night. The Grizzly Bar and Grill is open from April through November. Reservations are discouraged.

Red Lodge, Montana

Bogart's

$ • 11 S. Broadway Ave., Red Lodge, Mont. • (406) 446-1784

Bogart's has great pizza and magnificent Margaritas. In fact, when the doors open at 11:30 AM, Bogart's staff is prepared with a 15-gallon batch of Margarita mix. Years ago, owners Tom Leatherberry and Judy and Jodie Christensen enlisted friends to help them taste-test experimental recipes of the mix. It will soon be sold commercially along with Bogart's canned salsa, Ruggie's Rocky Mountain Salsa, and their fajita marinade.

Bogart's is a big brick building filled with old photos of Humphrey Bogart, mounted game animals and an abundance of antiques. Bogart's sells atmosphere (it's comfortable and Western) and good food. We recommend any of the pizzas, the sour cream enchiladas and the Margaritas. Reservations are not accepted.

Greenlee's at the Pollard

$$$$ • 2 N. Broadway Ave., Red Lodge, Mont. • (406) 446-0001

Walking into Greenlee's at the Pollard in Red Lodge feels a little like entering the dining room of an exclusive Eastern or Midwestern club minus the high-priced tab. Crisp linen tablecloths, fresh flowers, abundant oak woodwork, plush drapes, excellent service and delicious food accent the award-winning menu at this renowned restaurant.

Chef Scot Greenlee, who has been with the Pollard since it opened in 1994, keeps the menu interesting and himself interested by changing it often — like twice-a-week often. Among Greenlee's most popular dishes are sage-smoked chicken, risotto with wild mushrooms and huckleberry duck breasts. Other

INSIDERS' TIP

Livingston is the home of Wilcoxson's Ice Cream, a homemade-tasting brand sold since 1912. Watch for Wilcoxson's ice cream when you're in Livingston, West Yellowstone and Yellowstone National Park.

signature foods include Greenlee's French bread and his creme caramel, a baked custard with caramel sauce. The wine list is tip-top. Dinner reservations are recommended.

The Round Barn

$$ • U.S. Hwy. 212, Red Lodge, Mont. • (406) 446-1197

You'd never know this homey, old round brick building was once a dairy barn. Owner Marcee Farrar has fixed it up as a restaurant and dinner theater. Dinner is served buffet style with four entrees (a range of meats and fish), homemade mashed potatoes, a fresh vegetable such as steamed snow peas and dessert. A 15-foot salad bar features fresh salads, homemade soups and bread just out of the oven. For information about the theater upstairs in the hayloft (you don't have to eat dinner to get into the theater, but we recommend it), see our Nightlife chapter. The schedule changes here depending on the season, so it's best to call ahead.

Bearcreek, Montana

Bear Creek Saloon

$$ • 108 Main St., Bearcreek, Mont. • (406) 446-3481

You get to eat top-notch steak and watch pig races in the middle of nowhere. Located 7 miles from Red Lodge in Bearcreek, population 57, this lively place is open Friday, Saturday and Sunday from Memorial Day to Labor Day and from Christmas until Easter. Owners Lynn and Pits DeArmond follow their meals with free family entertainment: pig races. Reservations are recommended. For more information about the Bear Creek Saloon, see our Nightlife chapter.

Eastern Idaho

Teton Valley

Breakfast Shoppe

$ • 95 Main St., Driggs, Idaho • (208) 354-8294

Pay a little attention here, and you'll notice the special little touches: The eggs Benedict are topped with a hollandaise sauce made daily from scratch. The French toast is made with challa, a rich egg-batter bread. The green sauce, served on huevos rancheros and other dishes, won an award for owners Tricia and Allen Davis in 1996. This ma-and-pa shop serves breakfast and lunch daily.

Knotty Pine Bar and Restaurant

$$$ • 27 E. Main St., Victor, Idaho • (208) 787-2866

One of the interesting tidbits about the Knotty Pine is that none of its many owners over the years (Knotty Pine received the second liquor license in Teton Valley) has been a valley native. Knotty Pine serves lunch and dinner seven days a week and breakfast Tuesday through Sunday. The dinner menu is heavily slanted toward beef, but baby-back ribs prepared with homemade barbecue sauce are the house specialty. A bar menu is also available.

Lost Horizon Dinner Club

$$$$, no credit cards • Mile 6, Ski Hill Rd., Alta, Wyo. • (307) 353-8226

It's not dinner, it's a dining adventure. Locally famous Lost Horizon is a tiny, intimate restaurant serving a single seating of 12 people every Friday, Saturday and Sunday night. The meal consists of 10 leisurely courses of Japanese and Chinese delicacies. You'll spend about four hours here, eating your hot and sour soup, tempura, tori katsu, chicken and cashews and other courses and relaxing around the circular hooded fireplace between courses. And after all that, we'll be surprised if you flinch at the bill.

Owners Chuck and Shigeko Irwin know Oriental food. Shigeko is Japanese; Chuck spent a decade in Asia as a career serviceman. They named their restaurant after the book by James Hilton about a mythical Shangri-la, an Eden-like place where people never aged. Lost Horizon is open year round except in May and October. As you no doubt guessed, reservations are required.

Mike's Eats

$, no credit cards • 10 N. Main St., Driggs, Idaho • (208) 354-2797

You'll pass the jukebox on your way in. The linoleum is blocked out in black, green, blue and red. Red upholstery highlights chromed bar stools and booths. A bar runs the length of the long, skinny dining room beneath an ornate silver ceiling. In short, Mike's is a flamboyant 1950s-style diner, smack in the middle of cowboy country.

Folks come here for the buffalo: buffalo chili, buffalo hot dogs, buffalo polish sausages, meat loaf and burgers. Probably they're not thinking of the health benefits of that choice, but they could be; buffalo meat is significantly lower in cholesterol, fat and calories than either beef or chicken. So you might as well order a shake or a root beer float to go with that burger, eh? Mike's Eats serves breakfast, lunch and dinner seven days a week in summer. Winters it closes.

Otto Brothers' Brew Pub

$ • 430 Old Jackson Hwy., Victor, Idaho • (208) 787-9000

Nothing fancy about this place; what you're here for is the good local beer, brewed in big tanks behind you. In summer, enjoy your pizza, sandwich, salad or nachos outside, facing Teton Pass. If you're tired of mountain views, big windows allow you to see the brew tanks from the small bar/restaurant area. When the pub is really busy, you might get seated in the brewery itself, instead of in the small dining area. Stop on your way home from skiing at Grand Targhee. You can even get a "growler," a refillable jug of Otto Brothers' best, to go. This microbrewery boasts that it uses Idaho barley and American hops in its beers. We're big fans of the Moose Juice Stout, but ale, porter and wheat beers are generally available as well. The restaurant is open seven days.

Tony's Pizza & Pasta

$$ • 364 N. Main St., Driggs, Idaho • (208) 354-8829

The cooks at Tony's make the sauces from scratch with fresh tomatoes, fresh garlic, whole leaf basil and oregano. They grate their own Parmesan cheese and buy their mozzarella in old-fashioned 50-pound wheels. The menu is pizza (with red, white or pesto sauce), pasta and sandwiches. Wash your meal down with one of 40 brands of imported and micro-brewed beer. The dining room is casual, bright and high-ceilinged with rough wood flooring. Some outdoor seating is available. So is takeout and delivery. If you want to sample house specialties, owner Glenn Gresly is particularly proud of his white lasagna and his baked-to-order rosemary chicken with whole garlic cloves and whole sun-dried tomatoes.

Victor Emporium

$ • 45 N. Main St., Victor, Idaho • (208) 787-2221

You could come here for fishing hooks, flies, guide books, camping gear, plastic worms, hats, ice or beer. Or you could be after lunch: homemade shredded beef burritos, green chile chicken burritos or the wildly popular fish tacos (be flexible — daily specials vary and can sell out quickly). If you're like Ronald Reagan, Supreme Court Justice Sandra Day O'Connor and about 12,000 locals and tourists each summer though, you're here for a huckleberry shake. Made from real ice cream and handpicked local huckleberries, served up in a tall glass with the creamy left-overs waiting their turn in a chrome mixing cup, Victor Emporium's huckleberry shakes are famous in these parts. As they should be.

Bob and Marilyn Meyer serve lunch only. They're open from 8 AM to 7 PM most days, and between meals you can catch a cup of coffee, a cherry phosphate or a fresh lime freeze. Or a huckleberry milk

INSIDERS' TIP

Occasionally, you'll see a dish that uses "beefalo," low-fat, low-cholesterol meat that results from crossbreeding bison and cattle. Beefalo, developed 40 years ago by Montana rancher Jim Burnett, is 37 percent beef and 63 percent buffalo.

shake. (You can also take home a souvenir T-shirt, commemorating your shake experience.)

Star Valley, Wyoming, and Swan Valley, Idaho

Bette's Coffee Shop

$ • S. U.S. Hwy. 89 at Alpine, Wyo. • (307) 654-7536

Bette says, "I wouldn't want to see anybody go away hungry." Not only are her portions generous, but almost everything, from the breads to the soups to the cinnamon rolls, is made right here. Bette's serves breakfast, lunch and dinner seven days a week. The standard cafe menu is jazzed up a bit: You can order not just hot cakes but strawberry hot cakes, banana-nut hot cakes and cinnamon and spice hot cakes. Or choose from 12 different kinds of burgers. Bette's little coffee shop on the northwest shore of Palisades Reservoir has been serving up meals for locals and travelers for 15 years.

Brenthoven's Restaurant

$$$ • U.S. Hwy. 26 at U.S. Hwy. 89, Alpine, Wyo. • (307) 654-7556

He once played Carnegie Hall. Now he performs seven days a week, breakfast and dinner, in the kitchen. Pianist and chef Brent Johnston's little restaurant has six tables, each adorned with fresh flowers. Entrees include chicken Brenthoven, featuring the chef's special plum sauce, and cod Parmesan, Norwegian cod fillet stuffed with crab and baked with a Parmesan topping. It's hard to say which is more pleasant, the food or the intimate dining room.

The bar next door is also tiny and intimate; it offers a full range of alcoholic beverages. Brenthoven's closes in mid-October and reopens in June. If you start wondering whether he plays as beautifully as he cooks, you can pick up one of Johnston's CDs in the adjoining gift shop. You can also purchase a bottle of his plum sauce or the house poppy-seed dressing.

The Last Cast

$ • 40 Conant Valley Loop, Swan Valley, Idaho • (208) 483-2229

Moose and elk mounts watch you from the walls while you watch the Snake River slide past the cottonwoods below your window. If it's a Friday or Saturday night, you're probably enjoying the locally famous prime rib. Folks from as far away as Idaho Falls make a regular pilgrimage to Swan Valley for this South Fork Lodge feast. But perhaps the friendly staff and comfortable, casual lodge setting have got you craving a more down-home dinner. No problem: The lodge can serve up a generous chicken-fried steak or a plate of liver and onions. Reservations are not required. Weekends during fishing season can be busy. South Fork Lodge has recently been sold to a new owner, so changes could be in the works here.

Sandy-Mite Fly Shop and Cafe

$$ • 3333 Swan Valley Hwy., Irwin, Idaho • (208) 483-2609

Since 1986 the Sandy-Mite has been serving up fresh breads and bakery goods, fluffy omelets (served all day), burgers and sandwiches. Dinner offerings include steak and various chicken dishes. These folks will even box up a river lunch for you. If you're an angler, take a quick look at the fly selection after you order your meal: All of Sandy-Mite's flies are tied locally.

Island Park, Idaho

Henry's Fork Landing

$ • 4238 U.S. Hwy. 20, Mack's Inn at Island Park, Idaho • (208) 558-7672

It's simple home-style food that you can enjoy while staring out the window onto the Henry's Fork of the Snake River, barely 5 miles from where it bubbles, clear and cold, out of the ground. The game room upstairs and a little ice cream parlor in the other room make this a good family stop.

The restaurant is open year round, except for about six weeks in the spring and fall when things are slow.

Henry's Fork Lodge

$$$$ • Off U.S. Hwy. 20, Island Park, Idaho • (208) 558-7953

The dining room is hung with authentic woven Indian blankets; each heavy oak table is graced with fresh flowers. Outside, a wildflower-covered slope steepens into the Henry's Fork canyon. Dine on the patio if you'd like to watch trout dimple the river's surface.

Henry's Fork Lodge is a quietly luxurious fishing lodge just south of Last Chance. And from 6 to 9 PM seven nights a week, it opens its dining room doors to the general public. The menu changes nightly, but we bet your mouth will water with one example: Imagine sautéed salmon medallions topped with a Dijon mustard sauce, green peppercorns, bay shrimp and scallions. The chefs prepare all desserts and breads from scratch.

Reservations are highly recommended for this fine dining experience, but fancy dress is not. The restaurant, like the lodge, is open mid-May to mid-October.

Chalet Restaurant

$ • Last Chance in Island Park • (208) 558-9953

Breakfast is the popular meal at this simple, family-owned restaurant. Portions are generous, the sausage, bacon and ham are top-quality, and the hash browns and scones are homemade. Even the earliest-rising fishermen will probably find that the Caldwells already have coffee on. You can also enjoy burgers and sandwiches, homemade soups and salads for lunch (the french fries are cut by hand). Dinners are steak, chicken and fish dishes. No alcoholic beverages are available and the dinner hours are short: The restaurant closes at 7 PM.

Island Park Lodge

$$ • N. Big Springs Loop Rd., off U.S. Hwy. 20 at Island Park, Idaho • (208) 558-7281

Ask for a nice place to eat in Island Park and you're liable to get steered here, especially if you like pasta with homemade Alfredo sauce or tender, juicy ribs. Lighter meals like soups, salads and sandwiches are also available. The lodge serves lunch and dinner in a low-ceilinged log building dating to the 1940s. Enjoy your meal with beer, wine or a cocktail from the adjoining saloon. Island Park Lodge is open summer and winter, with a six-week hiatus in spring and fall.

Ashton, Idaho

Big Jud's Country Diner

$ • 265 S. U.S. Hwy. 20, Ashton, Idaho • (208) 652-7806

When Jud Niederer set out to open a restaurant, he thought big. Four years later Idaho supports four Big Jud's. The Ashton restaurant was his second. The original is about 6 miles south of Rexburg.

What was Jud's big idea? Well, basically — bigness. There's the Big Jud, a 1-pound burger housed in a specially made bun 8 inches across. Finish it and you'll get your picture on the wall with all those who've managed the same feat. Pound down a double and your photo will grace a much smaller board (how many people do you know who can eat 2 pounds of beef in one sitting?). Another big favorite at Jud's is the Hungry Heifer, a literal mountain of ice cream — 15 scoops — crowned with as many as five different toppings. Jud's serves lunch and dinner Monday through Saturday.

St. Anthony

The Relay Station

$$ • U.S. Hwy. 20, 2 mi. N. of St. Anthony, Idaho • (208) 624-4640

Owners Lynn Klein and Wanda Harshbarger named their restaurant — situated in rolling farmland between St. Anthony and Ashton — after the old travelers' way stations on railroad lines. But they're more of a locals' joint than a travelers' stopover. Maybe it's the cozy log building, with its pine paneling and lodgepole pine rafters. Maybe it's the sunny deck where you can enjoy your meal on nice days. But more likely it's the food — home cooking, right down the line. Lots of folks like the generous steaks, but Lynn is most

INSIDERS' TIP

On a tight budget but want to sample some fine area cuisine? Many high-end restaurants serve a very affordable lunch.

proud of her shrimp. It's the biggest she can find, peeled, cleaned and breaded right here.

The Relay Station serves breakfast, lunch and dinner every day but Tuesday. Beer and wine are available. It's a good idea to call in your reservation if you're planning on coming during the busy weekend evenings. The restaurant stays open year round.

Chiz's

$, no credit cards • 246 N. 2 W., St. Anthony, Idaho • (208) 624-7633

Scott Kamachi is a fanatic about fresh. His family opened this restaurant in 1968; they're pros at giving you lots of fresh food at great prices. Almost nothing comes out of a can. The gravies start out as meat on the bone. The steaks are aged in-store and then hand-cut. The menu is Chinese and American. Entrees include shrimp, seafood, steak and nightly specials. The food may be on its best behavior, but you don't have to dress up: Seating consists of 20 stools at a wraparound counter.

The restaurant serves lunch on Mondays and lunch and early dinner Tuesday through Saturday. No alcohol is available. Watch when you're at grocery stores in Idaho Falls, Rexburg, St. Anthony and Rigby for Chiz's homestyle, hand-packed salad dressings. The obsession with fresh goes double here: Chiz's dressings contain no preservatives. Scott travels to each grocery store that carries his product once a week and replaces the stock.

Idaho Falls, Idaho

The largest town in Greater Yellowstone, Idaho Falls has more than 120 eating establishments. A striking number are major chains or fast food joints, though, so the odds of finding a culinary surprise aren't as high as you might think. The trend in recent years has been for new chains to locate on 17th Street near the mall, so if you want familiar food you can either grab a local phone book or just hop in your car and head toward Grand Teton Mall. (Broadway and the Northgate Mile also host their share of franchises.) Idaho Falls' originals are scattered about town. The following is a too-short list of longtime local institutions and other interesting alternatives to the national franchise scene.

The BBQ Pit

$ • 775 N. Yellowstone Hwy., Idaho Falls, Idaho • (208) 523-0255

Nearly 20 years ago, Rachanee Lengyel from Thailand met Floyd Oberg, a butcher from Montana. Out of that meeting grew this Idaho Falls favorite, a restaurant serving authentic Thai food — and barbecue. The portions are big, the prices reasonable. The restaurant serves lunch and dinner every day but Sunday. Reservations are recommended for dinner. Beer and wine are available.

Brownstone Restaurant and Brewhouse

$$$ • 455 River Pkwy., Idaho Falls, Idaho • (208) 535-0310

This attractive newer brewpub and restaurant has brick walls, high ceilings and beers that seem to keep getting better as the brewery matures. Brewmaster Michael Storms produces selections such as India pale, amber and nut brown ale. The kitchen supplies pastas, pizzas with homemade crusts, sandwiches and entree items such as steak and salmon. A full bar is on-premises. Brownstone serves lunch and dinner; reservations are accepted for dinner. It closes on Sundays.

Hawg Smoke Cafe

$$$, no credit cards • 4330 N. Yellowstone Hwy., Idaho Falls, Idaho • (208) 523-4804

Grab a beer from the cooler. Order off a menu written on paper with felt-tip pen and hung on the wall. Sit down, chat with your companions and prepare for a fine dining experience. This eight-table restaurant in what looks like a shack specializes in the kind of high quality food and creative dishes most often associated with jacket-and-tie joints. For instance, there's the popular Steak Watsonville, a petite filet served with large succulent Mexican shrimp. On the side are artichoke hearts and leaves, drizzled with a gorgonzola cheese sauce. Or there's the house mole/curry, which spices up tenderloin or chicken breast.

One word of warning: There are no quick meals here. Plan to spend an evening, enjoying good friends and original, exquisite food. Hawg Smoke is open Tuesday through Saturday for dinner only. Beer and wine are available, but mixed drinks aren't. Reservations are recommended.

La Yaquesita

$ • 110 Science Center Dr., Idaho Falls, Idaho • (208) 523-1779

Ask a local where to go for Mexican food, and they're likely to say, "La Yaq." The Mendez family, from Sonora, Mexico, opened this old-fashioned Mexican restaurant 11 years ago. It serves dynamite chile relleno, chile verde, carne asada and chimichangas. Other items on the extensive menu are just as authentic and just as reasonably priced. Enjoy your meal with a cold Dos Equis, Tecate, Negro Modelo, Pacifico or Carta Blanca, or a wine cooler or Margarita. La Yaq serves lunch and dinner Monday through Saturday. A private banquet room upstairs accommodates up to 50 people.

Mongolian Grill Authentic Stir Fry

$ • 2153 E. 17th St., Idaho Falls, Idaho • (208) 524-7768

How about fast, inexpensive food that's good for you? Here you order one of three sizes of bowls and heap it full of 21 different kinds of vegetables and meats. Ladle any combination of 12 different sauces over the top, from sweet and sour to ginger sauce, and hand your meal-to-be to the chef. It'll be stir-fried right in front of you on the restaurant's big round grill in about two minutes. This restaurant is particularly popular at lunch, but it also serves dinner every day but Sunday.

North Hi-Way Cafe

$ • 460 Northgate Mile, Idaho Falls, Idaho • (208) 522-6212

North Hi-Way Cafe is across the street from Idaho Falls' stockyards. Open since 1947, it may be the oldest restaurant in town. Stockmen eat here when they're in town for Wednesday cattle auctions or on alternate Mondays when sheep auctions take place. You won't pay a lot of money for your rare beef sandwich (like a French dip only cooked up rarer), your prime rib sandwich (think slab, not slice, of meat inside the bun) or your Triple Crown burger with pastrami and Swiss, but you will get a lot of food. Two people could make a meal of some of those sandwiches. The cafe serves breakfast, lunch and dinner.

Rutabaga's

$$$ • 415 River Pkwy., Idaho Falls, Idaho • (208) 529-3990

The intimate dining room feels like a very upscale coffeehouse, so you won't be surprised by the full espresso bar. What may surprise is the first bite of your meal: Owner and self-taught chef Wes Beard calls his menu international. We call it fun. Portions are attractively presented without being tiny, and even traditional items like fillet of beef get dressed up, perhaps with gorgonzola cheese and cabernet-sautéed mushrooms. Pasta dishes are a house specialty. The restaurant serves beer and wine from an extensive domestic wine list. Specials change weekly, and the entire menu gets a face lift about every two months. In summer enjoy sidewalk dining. Large groups will find plenty of space in an adjoining banquet room. Dinner reservations are recommended.

Sandpiper Restaurant

$$ • 750 Lindsay Blvd., Idaho Falls, Idaho • (208) 524-3344

Prime rib has been the house specialty for 25 years — these folks slow-roast and serve a minimum of 276 pounds of certified Black An-

INSIDERS' TIP

A culinary delight peculiar to this area is "fry sauce," a pale pink blend of mayo and ketchup for french fry dipping.

gus every week. You can also choose from fresh halibut, chicken and pork dishes as well as a selection of pasta meals. A children's menu is available. Sandpiper serves only Idaho potatoes and it has the most extensive wine list in town. Dine near the solarium windows, or in nice weather, enjoy your meal on one of two decks overlooking the Snake River and the greenbelt.

This restaurant has a full bar and serves lunch and dinner daily except weekends, when no lunch is served. Banquet facilities are available for up to 100 people. The Sandpiper is locally owned and operated by longtime residents Ron and Rose Anne Obendorf. Reservations are accepted.

Smitty's Pancake and Steak House

$ • 645 Broadway Ave., Idaho Falls, Idaho • (208) 523-6450

Smitty's is an Idaho Falls institution serving breakfast, lunch and dinner daily. Breakfast is probably the most popular meal here, although the relatively inexpensive rib eye, filet mignon and other dinners draw folks, too. Because soup, salad and dessert are included in your dinner price, Smitty's is a down-home good value. If you come for a weekend breakfast, you'll probably wait in line for your chance at specialty pancakes such as potato, baby Dutchman, banana, pecan and German. Smitty's has had only two owners in its 29-year history. In Idaho Falls' volatile restaurant market, that ought to earn these folks a prize.

The Snake Bite

$$ • 425 River Pkwy., Idaho Falls, Idaho • (208) 525-2522

Think of it as a yuppie burger joint. The Snake Bite was voted Idaho Falls' best lunch spot in 1997. It serves microbrews, premium wines from the West and Northwest, pasta dishes, gourmet burgers (made with ground sirloin) and steak. The fresh king salmon sandwich with creamy dill sauce is worth a visit all by itself. The Snake Bite serves lunch and dinner most days. The restaurant is small and personable, with a Southwestern feel that matches the jazzed up, spiced-up food.

Northwestern Wyoming

Cody, Wyoming

Cassie's Supper Club

$$$ • 214 Yellowstone Ave., Cody, Wyo. • (307) 527-5500

Owned in the 1920s by Cassie Waters, the renowned madame of a Cody sportin' house, Cassie's Supper Club has been recently resurrected by owners Steve and Melody Singer. Steve, who plays nightly in the house band, grew up down the street from Cassie's. As a boy, he frequented the place, playing piano tunes for the bar regulars. Since buying the place (Singer sang on the road for 20 years before buying Cassie's), Singer has become an enthusiastic collector of Cassie memorabilia. Look for her fur lap robe displayed in the entry way and the parrots above the bar.

At Cassie's, known these days for its steaks, prime rib and seafood, the house specialty is the 14-ounce prime rib. Singer serves only Choice USDA grade beef, along with homemade soups and breads. Lunches include a variety of sandwiches as well as a small rib-eye steak and prime rib. Cassie's is open seven days a week year round. Dinner reservations are recommended.

For more about Cassie's, read our Nightlife chapter.

Cody Coffee Company and Eatery

$ • 1702 Sheridan Ave., Cody, Wyo. • (307) 527-7879

The food at the Cody Coffee Company is great — and it's a fun place to eat. Owners Paul and Beth are the nice-guy versions of Sonny and Cher. Instead of putting each other down, they build each other up. Their enthusiasm and good cheer is contagious, which is partly why you'll find a comfortable crowd eager to fill the few tables here. Mornings, they serve a variety of plump, moist muffins and rolls. At noon, they serve a limited but tasty menu of gourmet sandwiches, soups and salad. The Cody Coffee Company and Eatery is open from 7 AM until 4 PM, so you can polish off the last of the muffins for your midafternoon coffee break. Their espresso drinks are tops. Try lunch reservations, but be there on time.

The Irma

$$ • 1192 Sheridan Ave., Cody, Wyo. • (307) 587-4221

The reason you'll want to come here is for the experience. The Irma, built by Buffalo Bill Cody at the turn of the century, oozes Old West ambiance. The high, pressed-tin ceiling, the very long cherrywood bar (a gift to Bill Cody from the Queen of England) and the old photographs on the wall will take you back in time. Many locals come to The Irma for the prime rib dinner. The menu also features an array of chicken dishes, baby-back ribs and chicken-fried steak. Steak, trout, shrimp and halibut entrees are also featured. The Irma serves breakfast, lunch and dinner. You can order alcoholic beverages from the Silver Saddle Bar adjacent to the dining room. It's okay to make reservations for dinner in the winter, but summers it's first-come, first-served.

Franca's

$$$$, no credit cards • 1421 Rumsey Ave., Cody, Wyo. • (307) 587-5354

Plan to spend the whole (romantic) evening at Franca's, a small Italian restaurant (it seats 24 people) on the main floor of a 1920s French colonial Cody house. Leave your watch at home. Bring your heart and a healthy appetite. Franca Franchetti — yes, she's Italian, accent and all — cooks all day then shucks her apron and dons her big-hearted hostess persona. Pasta specials and homemade focaccine (an Italian specialty bread) are among her signature foods, and the house special is Tortelloni Verdi al Mascarpone (spinach pasta stuffed with an Italian cream cheese). Franca also serves daily specials like sausage and spinach ravioli, followed by salad and bread, or baked pork loin with rhubarb sauce (in the summer) with stuffed peppers.

Since Italians believe wine is married to the food, Franca provides endless marital combinations with a voluminous, award-winning wine list including more than 100 selections. Three dining rooms (one is a converted sun porch and another has a fireplace) are joined by arched openings. Each table is set with linen, its own antique china pattern, real silverware and antique crystal. The walls display art by Franca's husband, Joseph.

Franca's is open Wednesday through Sunday May 15 through January 15. Reservations are a must.

La Comida

$ • 1385 Sheridan Ave., Cody, Wyo. • (307) 587-9556

The honey locust trees and patio outside this reasonably priced restaurant say "Mexican," and so does the menu, which features award-winning food. (Articles from *Bon Apetit* and *Gourmet* magazines are posted as proof on the wall.) Spinach enchiladas, fajitas and pechuga de rey (chicken breast over rice) are among the house favorites. In addition to their fine Mexican fare, the desserts at La Comida are legendary.

La Comida serves lunch and dinner seven days a week year round. During summer, dine outside under the stars on the patio. Inside, choose between the East and the West rooms — they're like night and day. Summer dinner reservations are advised.

Maxwell's

$ • 937 Sheridan Ave., Cody, Wyo. • (307) 527-7749

A favorite with locals and tourists alike, Maxwell's may be best known for its pasta and its outstanding specialty breads. Maxwell's also serves fine soups and salads as well as an array of mouthwatering standard fare. Occupying a historic home moved to town then turned into a restaurant, Maxwell's has an airy and comfortable atmosphere, especially during the summer on the patio ringed with prolific flower planters. Maxwell's serves lunch and dinner.

A coffee shop and bakery next door

INSIDERS' TIP

Fine dining in Yellowstone country doesn't mean you have to dress up. Dress is casual almost everywhere.

serves espresso, gourmet coffee, muffins, scones, sweet rolls and European breads. It's a wonderful place to eat while reading the morning paper.

Our Place

$, no credit cards • 148 W. Yellowstone Ave., Cody, Wyo. • (307) 527-4420

Folks pack into Our Place for more than the 25¢ coffee. Waitresses here serve up hearty, low-priced meals with Western coffee shop flair — a few "honeys" and "how ya doin's" mixed with casual bustling service. Our Place serves three squares a day. We recommend the Rustler, Wrangler, Cowhand or the huevos rancheros for breakfast. (You can order breakfast from dawn 'til dark.) At lunch and dinner you'll find typical Western coffee shop fare at prices you can afford. (Try the prime rib on Friday and Saturday nights for $8.95.) Our Place is open year round seven days a week.

The Proud Cut Saloon

$$ • 1227 Sheridan Ave., Cody, Wyo. • (307) 527-6905

The carved wood sandwich sign outside this Western chic bar and restaurant advertises "Kickass Cowboy Cuisine." Whatever you call it, you'll find a long list of juicy steaks and shrimp at The Proud Cut, where the walls are lined with old photos and cowboy memorabilia.

Comfortable and crowded on weekend nights, The Proud Cut produces several choices that are popular among customers, such as the tenderloin and the 14-ounce prime rib. It also offers a 22-ounce porterhouse steak and Rocky Mountain oysters (breaded bull calf testicles). By the way, if you think Proud Cut refers to the steaks this saloon serves, ask an Insider. They'll tell you "Proud Cut" is the term used for castrated stallions that can't quit acting like studs because the castration was botched. Just enough of their male equipment is intact to make them act almost-but-not-quite like a stallion.

This restaurant is for adults only. Reservations are recommended for both lunch and dinner during the high season.

Stefan's

$$ • 1367 Sheridan Ave., Cody, Wyo. • (307) 587-8511

He (Stefan Bennett) is the chef, and she (Nina Bennett) is the hostess at Stefan's, a softly lit restaurant that serves contemporary American food. That means that when Stefan cooks up untraditional traditional meat loaf or chicken pot pie, he adds a kiss of mysteriously mixed herbs and sauces that leaves the palate wishing for just one more taste. Everything, we repeat, everything, is made from scratch, much like the restaurant itself. Produce is locally grown in season, and the restaurant is smoke-free.

Stefan and Nina worked and slept in the building for three weeks while they transformed it from Queen Bee Fashions to an upscale restaurant with a Southwestern look. The walls (three layers of paint that make them look like they're covered with terra cotta-colored suede), ficus trees strung with white Christmas lights, a dark green ceiling and carpet, and the fountain at the front create a scene soothing to the soul.

We recommend you start with the seafood Delmar or the stuffed filet mignon. Stefan's serves breakfast, lunch, and dinner. Dinner reservations are recommended.

Zapata's

$ • 325 W. Yellowstone Ave., Cody, Wyo. • (307) 527-7181

Simply decorated in a Southwestern motif, Zapata's combines good service with great New Mexico-style Mexican food. The menu is simple and the same for both lunch and dinner. It includes the basics: burritos, tacos, tostadas, enchiladas, chile rellenos, chimichangas and flautas for starters. The food is light and as hot as you like. Wash it down with beer or Margaritas. Reservations are accepted for six or more people.

In winter, the après-ski bars jam to their maximum nearly every afternoon, but most of them clear out before dinner as tired skiers head for the hot tub and bed.

Nightlife

Night falls in Yellowstone country, and a new realm unfolds. Diamond-edged stars wink into place and, even in July, a chill touches your face. Four-legged residents who spent the day curled out of sight wander out into evening, into their time. What had begun to seem familiar — towering Douglas fir, misty steam rising from a hot spring, the jagged outline of the Tetons — becomes mysterious again. This is no time for sleeping.

You're likely to find yourself a ways from the nearest bar, but closer at hand is another style of nightlife. It often starts with a campfire. Campfires seem to turn people in, toward each other and the flickering flames. Sometimes they take you into yourself: Maybe you'll remember old campfire songs you thought you'd forgotten, or how to construct a s'more. Or you'll remember the scary ghost stories you learned when you were a little kid. Perhaps you'll spit-cook the trout you caught today: clean it, leaving the head on (no need to scale or skin trout), spit it on a stout green willow stick, sprinkle with butter, salt and pepper, tie the body shut and roast it, belly up, above the coals until the eyes turn white. Eat with your fingers.

Perhaps you'd like to skip the fire and instead turn your attention outward. In this clear air, a full moon sheds enough pale light for strolling flat trails (note this is not a recommended activity in bear country) or for cross-country skiing with a bota bag of wine on your hip. Some even snowmobile, tree and hill shadows skating away before their headlights.

On August evenings, meteors put on a dramatic show. If you keep your eyes tipped up it's hard not to see at least one streaking meteor every minute or two. And any time of year you can watch satellites spin across the night sky, learn constellations or locate the North Star (sky charts are available at many outdoor shops and most bookstores). You can even turn good binoculars onto the face of the moon to see its cratered, rough skin.

An eerie fall treat that lasts into November is the nightly concert of rutting elk. Bull elk bugle in long whispery whistles, hollow grunts and screaming sobs. You'll listen in awe as first one, then another of these massive animals lifts that thin, unworldly call into the darkness. It's hard not to think you're experiencing the voice of Wilderness itself. Bugling elk can be heard through much of Yellowstone country around sundown and again around sunrise. A few particularly good places to experience this are the Jenny Lake area and the Oxbow in Grand Teton National Park, Harriman State Park near Island Park, and near Mammoth Hot Springs, Hayden Valley and Madison Junction in Yellowstone National Park.

One of Yellowstone country's summer bonuses is nearly endless daylight. Full, pitch darkness falls after 10:30 on a June night, so summer sunsets are a late-evening attraction. Of course, the flip side is that winter sunsets precede dinner. Summer and winter, sunset watching is a popular evening activity. If you happen to find yourself in one of our towns at sunset, try wandering a greenbelt. Jackson, Idaho Falls, Teton Valley and Bozeman all have pleasant, parklike walkways on which folks can stroll and exercise. Idaho Falls' greenbelt affords a particularly nice sunset show, since it runs on both sides of the Snake River through town. Two of the town's most popular photo opportunities, the falls themselves and the monolithic Mormon temple, are along your route and look particularly fine around sunset, especially from the west side of the river.

A magical sunset spot in the Madison Valley is Sphinx Mountain. A quirk in the Gravelly Range to the west provides a notch through which the setting sun spotlights the Sphinx while her sisters stand in shadow. You can see the Sphinx from almost anywhere in the Madison Valley near Ennis.

Mountains in general look stunning in evening light. Part of the cause is a phenomenon called alpenglow. On clear evenings the mountains seem to pull a soft pastel light from the air and into their snow-covered slopes. It can make for the most beautiful photographs you'll take on your trip. (Early morning light is even sweeter, but it's hard to crawl out of bed at 5 o'clock on a summer morning to take photos.)

But sometimes nothing hits the spot like jostling, laughing crowds and music that makes your toes tap. You may notice that in summer the evening action starts late, although summer tourist towns like Jackson hop all evening and nearly every night of the week, June through September. Bozeman, partly because it's a college town, has a lively nightlife scene, too. In winter, the après-ski bars jam to their maximum nearly every afternoon, but most of them clear out before dinner as tired skiers head for the hot tub and bed.

In smaller or quieter communities, more focused on going about their business than on tourists, nightlife can be a bit sparse. For instance, in West Yellowstone, where families are the main summer visitors, you'll find little nightlife except on special occasions such as the Fourth of July. Most people leave the park with only enough time for dinner, a bit of shopping and then bed. West Yellowstone in winter is a bit livelier as snowmobilers replace families as the primary visitors. Only a little, though: Like skiers, snowmobilers mostly want to eat and hit the hay after a day's ride.

But even if you can't find a band to listen to or a show to watch — a likely scenario outside the tourist hotspots — belly up to the bar at a local pub. You'll probably find yourself next to somebody who'll be happy to tell you a story or three about Yellowstone country. We've included here a selection of the more popular bars, particularly those that frequently host live music. We've also listed a few choice alternatives to the bar scene. You can, for instance, ski the night slopes at Snow King or attend a dinner show.

Another place to find evening diversions is our Annual Events chapter. Many Yellowstone communities are better at putting on periodic great parties (usually in summer) than maintaining a dynamic week-to-week, season-to-season night scene. Maybe it's because a relatively small segment of Yellowstone country residents frequent bars and nightclubs. Remember that nearly all eastern Idaho communities as well as many in western Wyoming and southern Montana are home to large Mormon populations that, for the most part, have little truck with the party scene. And many of the rest of us would rather grab our weekends and run — straight into the mountains.

Unless noted, the establishments described in this chapter charge no admission and are open all year. Don't assume, though: Bars and playhouses in Yellowstone country live with a seasonal ebb and flow that can mean unexpected changes to door policies and even last-second fall or spring vacations for the entire staff. Credit card policies vary. Some folks will let you pay your tab with plastic, but not your door charge. If you plan to leave your cash in the motel room, call your intended party spot first.

Drinking laws vary in Yellowstone country. Wyoming defines intoxicated driving as a blood-alcohol level greater than .10. In Idaho the law's a bit tougher; you're considered intoxicated over .08. But all three states take drunk driving seriously. In Wyoming, in fact, if you refuse a breath test, you automatically lose your driver's license for 180 days, whether you're a resident or a visitor. In Idaho, state police policy says there is no tolerance for intoxicated drivers and the absolute minimum penalty is a 90-day suspended license.

Bars in Wyoming and Montana are generally open until 2 AM. Idaho bars are required by state law to close at 1 AM, but individual counties may choose to allow their bars to stay open until 2 AM. No Idaho counties within Greater Yellowstone have, however.

Wyoming and Idaho both allow people younger than 21 to enter bars that are also restaurants, but in Montana kids can walk into any bar. They can't drink, but they can be there. Generally in Idaho and Wyoming, if a place has a bar area separate from the food-service area, kids won't be allowed in the bar.

Idaho, Yellowstone and Grand Teton parks and many Wyoming counties have open-container laws that make it illegal for you to drive with an open bottle containing an alcoholic beverage. Teton County Wyoming allows no open containers on the streets, either, so if Jackson's town square looks like a perfect place for a bottle of wine, it isn't. Alcohol can be carried on the streets during some events; check with the local police or ask event hosts if you're uncertain. Wyoming also has an odd law called an "intoxicated pedestrian law." It allows enforcement officers to remove an intoxicated person from a public way, like a parking lot, a sidewalk or the side of a road.

The prices listed in this chapter are generally based on the 1998 season, and they're subject to change without notice.

Grand Teton National Park

Blue Heron at Jackson Lake Lodge
U.S. Hwy. 89 at Jackson Lake Junction • (307) 543-2811, (800) 628-9988

Contemplate massive Mount Moran as you sip a mixed drink or a glass of wine. The Blue Heron is a complete bar with big picture windows pointed in exactly the right direction. Snacks are available off the extended bar menu. Sunset is the perfect time to drop in. Find this bar upstairs from the lobby in Jackson Lake Lodge, open in summer only.

Dornan's Bar
Teton Park Rd. at Moose Junction • (307) 733-2415, Ext. 200

Dornan's Bar hosts concerts from time to time, so give them a call if you'll be staying in or near Grand Teton National Park and want to enjoy a little live music. Concert tickets cost around $10. The thought of cold beer in the warm sun draws many patrons to the bar's second-floor deck.

Signal Mountain Lodge
Teton Park Rd. on south shore of Jackson Lake • (307) 733-5470

Some nights when the crowd gets rowdy, it's hard to remember that you're buried in lodgepole forest at the base of some of the wildest looking mountains you've ever seen, and that you'll soon be headed through dark mountain chill to your tent or cabin. No better reason exists to order another Margarita and perhaps a mountainous plate of nachos. Signal Mountain Lodge is open from mid-May to mid-October. Two restaurants are on-site.

Jackson Hole

Jackson, Wyoming

Bar-J Chuckwagon Suppers & Original Western Show
Teton Village Rd., Wilson, Wyo. • (307) 733-3370

Fortlike, the Bar-J buildings box a spacious patio and lawn. Paths lead across it to a memorabilia hall, a gift shop, and of course the giant dining room that seats up to 750 every night in summer. You'll enjoy barbecued beef, chicken or rib-eye steak, baked potatoes, beans, homemade biscuits and more. The rest of the evening is given to traditional Western music, tall tales and cowboy poetry from the Bar-J Wranglers. The charge for adults is $14 to $18, meal and all. The Bar-J puts on its supper shows from Memorial Day to the end of September. The ranch sits in a grove of cottonwoods about a 10-minute drive from Jackson.

Cadillac Grill
55 N. Cache St., Jackson, Wyo. • (307) 733-3279

Besides serving an interesting selection of what the menu calls "new American cuisine,"

INSIDERS' TIP

You'll find music festivals listed in the Annual Events chapter.

Cadillac Grill often puts on a fine late-night happy hour. Abstract paintings hang on the walls, black napkins rest on white tablecloths and oldies play through the speakers. Cadillac Grill is right on town square, an easy walk from other local nightspots. If you're coming early for dinner, it's best to make a reservation. Cadillac Grill sometimes closes in November.

The Clubhouse at Teton Pines Resort

3450 N. Clubhouse Dr., Jackson, Wyo. • (307) 733-1005, (800) 238-2223

In summer, The Clubhouse is 22,000 elegantly appointed square feet of golf clubhouse, with a fine dining restaurant, pro shop, bar and lounge. In winter, the cathedral-ceilinged second floor, with its 35-foot-long leather couch and massive fireplace, becomes a busy après-ski sushi bar. Stop by on your way back to Jackson from the ski hill at Teton Village or after your cross-country ski tour of the golf course's 14-K groomed track.

Grand Teton Mainstage Theatre

50 W. Broadway Ave., Jackson, Wyo. • (307) 733-3670

If you happen to be passing the Pink Garter Plaza any night but Sunday and hear singing and laughing and a gathering crowd, you're probably witnessing the pre-show antics of Grand Teton Mainstage Theatre. In a few minutes the actors and their new fans will tromp up to the 340-seat theater that comprises the shopping center's third floor, hold a sing-along and then get down to the serious business of comedy. Summer shows feature professional actors, are often musicals and always lighthearted, and are available every night but Sunday all summer long. Tickets cost around $15, and although reservations are a good idea, same-day tickets aren't usually a problem.

In fall, winter and spring, the theater takes on a different persona. Look for films, dance concerts, live music and community theater. Some events are free. To learn what's going on in those quieter seasons, call the information line (listed above).

Jackson Hole Playhouse

145 W. Deloney Ave., Jackson, Wyo. • (307) 733-6994

This playhouse exudes historical charm. It's the oldest theater in Wyoming, the oldest frame building in Jackson, a former livery stable, a former Western Union office and a former bowling alley. In the 1950s it was made over into the Pink Garter Theatre. In 1969 a newer theater was built across the street. The old theater's name jumped the road, but the theater stayed.

What you'll see at the former Pink Garter is Western musical theater, mostly old Broadway musicals like *Seven Brides for Seven Brothers*, *Oklahoma!*, *Shenandoah* and *Paint Your Wagon*. Performances are staged by a 12- to 25-member cast Monday through Saturday evenings, Memorial Day to Labor Day. Although the Playhouse has not historically done winter shows, it's considering it, so give them a call if you're in the area in January-March. Tickets are around $13.

Mangy Moose Saloon

3825 W. McCollister Dr., Teton Village • (307) 733-4913

An entire antique shop is stapled to the ceiling. Through the chaos above your head, a moose with dangling legs pulls a dangling sleigh. The house beer is — you guessed it — Moose Brew. Blues Traveler and Widespread Panic have played here. So have Leo Kottke and Five Fingers of Funk. Arlo Guthrie wows the crowds a couple times a year. Did we say crowds? Oh, yeah. You can ski from the lifts at Teton Village to the door, so the Mangy Moose is, from 3 to 7 PM in winter, wall-to-wall skiers. In fact, *Snow Country's* reader poll has named the Mangy Moose the best ski bar in the country three years running.

INSIDERS' TIP

In Idaho Falls, the best source for fun entertainment is the "Let's Go" section in the Friday Post Register.

You'll pay a cover for some of these acts, but they're generally worth it. Entertainment is scheduled most nights in winter and most weekends in summer. Mangy Moose is open seven nights a week. It closes in April.

Million Dollar Cowboy Bar
25 N. Cache St., Jackson, Wyo. • (307) 733-2207

This famous Jackson institution must be seen to be believed — from the glossy log-slab tables to the knobby pine pillars, railing and ceiling trim, and from the saddle bar stools (yes, they really are saddles) to the huge grizzly mount supposedly dispatched in a battle to the death with a weaponless man. For a moderate cover charge (usually $3 to $5) you can play pool or dance to live Western music Monday through Saturday nights, sipping on the beer or cocktail of your choice.

Stop by the gift shop out front for a T-shirt, mug, sheriff's badge or pair of Million Dollar Cowboy Bar panties. You can pick up a good steak dinner in the restaurant downstairs. The bar closes for a week or two in the spring and again in the fall. It may also close Sundays and Mondays in those slow months.

Rancher Spirits and Billiards
20 E. Broadway Ave., Jackson, Wyo. • (307) 733-3886

The huge, mirrored hall is lined with rows of pool tables; the second floor deck looks over the hullabaloo in town square. Rock music plays over the speaker system. Folks come here to play pool, because that's what you do at the Rancher.

SilverDollar Bar at The Wort Hotel
Corner of Glenwood and Broadway, Jackson, Wyo. • (307) 733-2190, (800) 322-2727

The long bar was designed in 1950 by a German cabinetmaker who embedded 2,032 uncirculated silver dollars into its surface. Why? In rough and tumble Wyoming, gambling, though illegal, was tolerated. The Wort Hotel had an active casino operation from the time it opened until a raid in the late 1950s, and apparently the shiny silver dollars celebrated that fact. The designs burned into the wooden bar tables commemorate another piece of Western color: They are brands from working ranches across Montana, Idaho and Wyoming.

SilverDollar Bar serves a busy lunch. Tuesday through Saturday you can enjoy live music here with no cover charge. There's no room to dance, but the music is generally quite good, ranging from bluegrass and folk to country.

Snake River Brewing Co.
265 S. Millward St., Jackson, Wyo. • (307) 739-2337

This pub's award-winning beers are brewed in big shiny tanks behind the S-shaped bar.

Winter nights, you can sit by the fireplace and watch the lit ski runs at nearby Snow King through tall windows. Snake River Brewing Co. is also a restaurant, serving lunch and dinner seven days a week. The kitchen stays open late for the party crowd (see our Restaurants chapter).

Snow King Center's Hootenanny
400 Snow King Ave., Jackson, Wyo. • (307) 733-5200

Hootenanny (n): A gathering of folk singers, typically with participation by the audience.

Don't take the American Heritage Dictionary folks at their word: Come see a hootenanny for yourself Monday nights year round. Hear old-time folk, cowboy songs and bluegrass performed by local talent and others who wander in with a song and an instrument. You'll pay a $2 door charge

INSIDERS' TIP

If you find yourself hungry after midnight in West Yellowstone, try Daley's Pub next to The Gusher. It serves pizza and sandwiches until 1 AM.

for the early evening event. Food and drink are available.

Snow King Resort

400 E. Snow King Ave., Jackson, Wyo. • (307) 733-5200, (800) 522-5464

Snow King looms at the edge of Jackson, so the best part of night skiing its 110 acres of lit slope is the sight of town lights glowing below you. Night skiing is available from 4 to 8 PM, Tuesday through Saturday, weather permitting. Adult tickets are $14 for the evening, or $8 for one hour's skiing. The mountain generally opens Thanksgiving weekend and closes in late March.

Stagecoach Bar

5755 W. Hwy. 22, Wilson, Wyo. • (307) 733-4407

It's a classic local hangout: pool tables, dart board, a juke box on one wall. The building dates to the 1940s; it has a settled-in look that makes a beer go down just fine. The music is country-and-western; the full bar has three tap handles, two of which are generally microbrews.

The food is a bit surprising. In November 1996, Patty Cake Patisserie, an upscale deli, changed its name to Patty Cake West and moved into the building. Now the folks tossing darts are also munching fresh pastries or pasta salads.

You won't see many tourists here except on Sunday nights when the Stagecoach Band performs. These boys are a piece of Jackson Hole history. Local legend has it that the band's founder, Bill Briggs, was the first guy to ski the Grand Teton. His country band has performed for fans at the Stagecoach on Sunday nights since 1969.

Surrounding Areas

West Yellowstone, Montana

Bullwinkle's Saloon and Eatery

19 Madison Ave., West Yellowstone, Mont. • (406) 646-7974

Monday nights and Sundays Bullwinkle's is packed with folks watching ball games, hockey, you name it, on the six TVs. Is it the food or the TVs that attracts sports fans to this bar? We think it's both. Decorated with Green Bay Packer uniforms, pennants and other memorabilia (the owners moved from Sheboygan, Wisconsin), Bullwinkle's offers a menu of appetizers that would please folks even without a ball game to watch. Among the treats that owner Jackie LaFever cooks up are smoked trout, shrimp cocktail, bratwurst with sauerkraut, a homemade haystack of onion rings and her enticingly good Nachos Supreme — so homemade she even makes the nacho chips. LaFever, who serves lunch and dinner, also has her soup pot filled with concoctions similar to those that Grandmother used to make on her wood cookstove. During the summer, and snowmobile season, Bullwinkle's is open from 11AM until 11PM. Shoulder seasons it closes closer to 9 PM except on football nights. For more information about Bullwinkle's, see our Restaurants chapter.

INSIDERS' TIP

Marcellar's Vintage Wines and Brews, 431 Park Avenue in Idaho Falls, is the town's own personal wine merchant. The selection isn't bad, but the best thing about Marcellar's is that the Spruills are happy to make recommendations and special orders. Call (208) 523-0503.

Visitors to Greater Yellowstone should keep an eye peeled for one of the two dozen brewpubs and microbreweries in the region.

Eino's Bar

8955 Gallatin Rd., West Yellowstone, Mont. • (406) 646-9344

Comfortable and casual are the bywords at this lonely outpost 8 miles north of West Yellowstone on U.S. Highway 191. During the winter, this full-service bar is packed with snowmobilers who have driven their sleds right up to the door. From West Yellowstone, it's an easy jaunt by car or snowmobile (we recommend the latter for a special night out). Customers cook their own steaks and burgers on a communal grill. Open and spacious, Eino's overlooks meadows leading to Hebgen Lake. Downstairs you'll find a pool table. See our Restaurants chapter for more information.

Happy Hour Bar

15400 Hebgen Lake Rd., West Yellowstone, Mont. • (406) 646-7281

If you see a bumper sticker that reads, "I was honked at the Happy Hour Bar," you'll know the folks in the car have been to this spot on the shores of Hebgen Lake. You won't find any happy-hour discounts here, but owners Bud and Karen Klungervik were born to run a bar that exudes happy-hour hilarity. Housed in an old A-frame originally intended as a home, the Happy Hour has huge windows that frame the lake below and the mountains beyond. During winter, snowmobilers and ice anglers dot the ice-and-snow-covered lake. A deck shaped like the bow of a boat juts toward the lake. From this vantage point, the owners and customers honk an airhorn at passersby. They also launch water balloons with a giant slingshot that propels the bombs up to 200 yards.

The Happy Hour marina with its four docks invites boaters to stop in at the bar for a meal or a quick drink — Margaritas are their specialty. The Happy Hour, which seats about 50, serves lunch and dinner, including juicy half-pound hamburgers and an assortment of steaks. For more information about the Happy Hour, see our Restaurants chapter.

Iron Horse Saloon

315 Yellowstone Ave., West Yellowstone, Mont. • (406) 646-7365

Located in the West Yellowstone Conference Hotel, the Iron Horse hosts open-mike nights on Tuesdays and a dance band on some winter and summer weekends. The saloon itself doesn't have much of a dance floor, but a sliding door opens onto a banquet hall big enough to accommodate hundreds. When things are slow in town, you generally won't find a band here, so it's best to check ahead to see what's happening.

Playmill Theater

29 Madison Ave., West Yellowstone, Mont. • (406) 646-7757

People regularly drive from as far away as Pocatello, Idaho, and Belgrade, Montana, just to watch a performance at the Playmill Theater. The 272-seat theater celebrated its 35th anniversary in 1998 with three shows: *Oklahoma*, *Love Rides the Rails* (a melodrama back by popular demand) and *Joseph and the Amazing Technicolor Dreamcoat*. Owner John Bidwell, who teaches theater and related subjects at Ricks College in Rexburg, first acted at the little theater as a student in 1973. He bought the playhouse in 1989 and now hires about 20 players (mostly college students) each summer. Bidwell also has a regular steady staff that includes a director, a choreographer and costume maker. Students are provided with lodging and given a $2,500 stipend for the season.

From Memorial Day through Labor Day, the Playmill runs two shows each night at 6 and 8:30 PM Monday through Saturday. Tickets cost $10 for adults, $8 for children and $9 for seniors. Groups of 25 or more get a $1 discount on individual ticket prices.

Stage Coach Inn

209 Madison Ave., West Yellowstone, Mont. • (406) 646-7381

You'll have to wait for winter to dance here. On winter and summer weekends, the bar upstairs often has a piano player or some other light musical entertainment. During snowmobile season, though, you can find rompin', stompin' dance music downstairs in the Barrel Bar. This place packs 'em in so fast that people often head downstairs hours ahead of time just to reserve a table. If you're into live poker, the Stage Coach is the only place for miles around that deals real cards. The friendly dealers are good about teaching newcomers the ins and outs of poker.

Gardiner, Montana

Blue Goose Saloon

206 W. Park, Gardiner, Mont. • (406) 848-7434

Named the Blue Goose back in the 1940s, this local hangout has been serving beer and drinks since the 1920s. Now a favorite hangout for park employees and locals alike, the Blue Goose has brought together its share of park employees who later married.

The Blue Goose has two pool tables (you can play pool for free on Sundays), a large-screen TV, 12 brands of beer on tap and an impressive array of mounted game.

Silver Gate and Cooke City, Montana

Miner's Saloon

U.S. Hwy. 212, Cooke City, Mont. • (406) 838-2214

Local color lives at the Miner's Saloon. And there's a mini-museum hanging mostly from the walls and ceiling. The Miner's Saloon imports an occasional band. Otherwise, it's the juke box, conversation or the game room in back, which features pool tables, air hockey, those poker gambling machines and an impressive collection of pin-up posters tacked to the ceiling.

The Ore House Saloon

U.S. Hwy. 212, Cooke City, Mont. • (406) 838-2251, (800) 527-6462

Located in the Soda Butte Lodge, the Ore

INSIDERS' TIP

Dornan's in Grand Teton National Park near Moose has a wine shop with a startlingly fine selection. Their beer selection isn't bad, either.

House Saloon is a sprawling bar overlooking the Clarks Fork River and a regular thoroughfare for bears. The Ore House is another one of those popular *Monday Night Football* hangouts. It has three TVs, one of them a big-screen. There are gambling machines here, but no pool table.

Range Rider's Lodge
U.S. Hwy. 212, Silver Gate, Mont.
• (406) 838-2359

During the summer, this comfortable old log lodge comes to life when the sun goes down. On weekends June through August you can count on live music that'll set your toes to twitching. A rock fireplace, a pine bar and locals with a down-home hospitality will make you feel right at home here. If you're the sort who prefers to sit and watch others dance, there's plenty of space around the dance floor with tables for folks just like you. If you're a dancer with a hankering to step into the rhythm of the West, Range Rider's Lodge is a must. The Lodge is open only during the summer.

Bearcreek, Montana

Bear Creek Saloon and Bearcreek Downs
108 Main St., Bearcreek, Mont.
• (406) 446-3481

The bell rings, the trumpet sounds, the gate opens, and the pigs race around a track to the finish line where a trough of food awaits. This could be the cheapest — and most memorable — entertainment you'll find anyplace in Yellowstone country: A reasonably priced steak dinner followed by pig races. Economic desperation led owners Lynn and Pits DeArmond to come up with this outlandish idea for attracting crowds to their out-of-the-way saloon 7 miles east of Red Lodge. It worked. Friday through Sunday the pigs at Bearcreek Downs do their thing for crowds of up to 300 people.

In addition, the DeArmonds hold a pig-racing Calcutta (they had to get a special "pig racing bill" passed by the Montana legislature). Since the races began in 1989, proceeds from the Calcutta have generated $39,000 for local scholarships. Weaner pigs race outside during the summer. The owners have dropped their popular baby-pig winter races held in a glass-enclosed track.

The Bearcreek Saloon and Downs are open from Memorial Day through Labor Day, and from Christmas through Easter.

Bozeman, Montana

Cat's Paw
721 N. Seventh Ave., Bozeman, Mont.
• (406) 586-3542

The Cat's Paw is the cat's meow when it comes to good times and big crowds. It's a mostly blue-collar bar that attracts a healthy mix of clientele including college students, lawyers in suits, cowboys, teachers and even a 96-year-old regular who plays poker and dances when he can. The Cat's Paw features live music Thursday through Saturday and well-known bands that play during the week several times a month.

The Cat's Paw seats nearly 400, including 60 patrons at the bar, which extends the length of the room. Happy hour runs from 4 PM until 8 PM daily. Thursday is free-beer night from 9:30 PM until 12:30 AM (there's a $6 cover charge), while Wednesday is $1-a-pint night. The Cat's Paw has 20 brands of beer on tap.

Livingston, Montana

Firehouse 5 Playhouse
U.S. Hwy. 89 S., Livingston, Mont.
• (406) 222-1420, (800) SLAPSTICK

The Firehouse 5 Playhouse presents cabaret-style musicals and vaudeville shows year round. Using casts comprised almost entirely of community members, Playhouse owner Bill Conch changes the marquee once a month.

INSIDERS' TIP

Snake River Brewing Co. in Jackson is a smoke-free bar.

In 1998, Firehouse Five's performances included *Oliver*, *Cinderella* and *Grease*.

Summer performances are Thursday through Sunday, while winter presentations are Friday through Sunday. The Sunday shows are matinees. Tickets cost $9 for adults and $8 for senior citizens. Children 12 and younger get in for $6.

Murray Lounge and Grill

201 W. Park Ave., Livingston, Mont.
• (406) 222-1350

Anything attached to the Murray Hotel, Livingston's oldest and most Western hotel, manages to mix the slightly upscale with the definitely down-to-earth. Belly up to the oval bar, play pool or dance to the band of the week. The Murray features music to match its clientele — eclectic, eccentric, egalitarian. Even the walls reflect the sometimes-crazy combos. One sports brands from the movie *Keep the Change*. The others display art by Livingston artists Parks Reese and Michael Simon.

Depending on the night — and the mood — you may find rock 'n' roll, country-and-western, blues or reggae music most weekends. (During the winter, bands play on Thursday and Friday. The Murray adds Saturday nights to the summer schedule.)

Big Sky, Montana

Chet's

Mountain Village, Big Sky, Mont.
• (406) 995-5000

From 4:30 to 6 PM each day, more than 150 people — about a third of which are kids — pack into Chet's, a lounge named after Big Sky's founder, former newscaster Chet Huntley. The crowd comes to see what the Crazy Austrians are going to do next. This duo, which is practically an institution in Big Sky, has the audience singing along, doing the polka and playing nearly 100 funky musical instruments including kazoos. Once the Crazy Austrians get your children up on stage to do silly things, they'll send them back out to drag you up there. Anyone hauled in front of the audience might end up in a funny little outfit or buffalo skull masks or weird hats. Before you know it, they'll have everybody in Chet's doing the Chicken Dance.

After 6 PM things calm down. From 9:45 PM until 1 AM, an acoustical guitar player makes background music.

Half Moon Saloon

U.S. Hwy. 212, Big Sky, Mont.
• (406) 995-4533

This is the biggest bar in Big Sky (it seats 238), and it sells the most reasonably priced drinks. It also has a pleasant mix of locals and tourists. Huge bay windows overlook the Gallatin River on one side and the Madison Mountain Range on the other. The Half Moon imports a band most Saturday nights, and during the busier summer months it adds to that by a night or two each week. When they aren't using the dance floor, the owners cover part of it with a Ping-Pong table and a foosball table. The Half Moon also has three pool tables, shuffleboard, dart games and a few poker and keno machines.

The Half Moon serves lunch and dinner from 11 AM to 9 PM in the winter and from 11 AM until 10 PM in summer. Locals say this place serves the best burgers in the area.

INSIDERS' TIP

Keep your eyes peeled for local musical talent such as Kip Attaway. He's a Wyoming native known for his outrageously funny country-and-western songs. You're equally likely to find him performing at a bar or simply camped out in the Hawg Smoke Café in Idaho Falls, playing for his friends and a lucky group of patrons.

Milkie's Pizza and Pub

Westfork Meadows, Big Sky, Mont.
• (406) 995-2900

Milkie's is the local after-work bar. Since many employees work in restaurants and don't get off 'til after the dinner dishes are done, things don't really get going here until 9 or 10 PM. During dinner, though, you'll find families dining on Milkie's pizza, which, by the way, can be delivered. The walls are a regular museum, displaying photos and sports memorabilia such as old golf clubs, fishing gear, ice skates and fishing creels. Enhancing Milkie's casual atmosphere are a pool table, dart board, poker machines and a jukebox with an amazing selection of oldies.

The Round Barn Restaurant and Dinner Theater

U.S. Hwy 212 N., Red Lodge, Mont.
• (406) 446-1197

The atmosphere here is worth the meal alone. And the food would be worth the drive (it's only a couple of miles from town) without the round red-brick barn built as a dairy by the Kent family in 1941. Owner Marcee Farrar has converted this beautiful barn into a restaurant on the ground floor and a theater in the loft. June through September Farrar books professional actors, singers, musicians and comedians to perform in her "theater in the round."

The rest of the year performances are not so regularly scheduled so it's best to call ahead. Dinner, served buffet style, includes four kinds of meat, potatoes (often real mashed potatoes), a very fresh salad, vegetables, bread, soup and a dessert. The curtain rises at 9 PM. The rates are reasonable. The Round Barn is usually closed during January and February.

Scissorbill's Bar and Grill

Mountain Village, Big Sky, Mont.
• (406) 995-4933

We think Scissorbill's has the best happy hour in Big Sky. From 4 to 6 PM seven days a week, you can slurp reduced-price specialty beers and Margaritas. Another late-night happy hour begins at 10 PM and ends at midnight. Too small for a dance band (it holds 80 customers), Scissorbill's does feature live music from 4 to 6:30 each Saturday afternoon. Thursday nights, stop in for open-mike night. For the slow times, you'll find dartboards and a few poker machines. This ski-in bar is open November through April.

Pray, Montana

Chico Saloon

Old Chico Rd., Pray, Mont.
• (406) 333-4933

Located about 25 miles south of Livingston, the Chico Saloon at the Chico Hot Springs Lodge hires a different kind of band every Friday and Saturday night. Depending on the band, folks drive for miles to mingle with a mixed crowd of locals and visitors that might range from stove-up old cowboys to duded-up movie stars. Just off the dance floor is the Chico Hot Springs pool where you can either start or finish the night. The Saloon offers a special menu for patrons, and for those evenings when there's nothing much else going on, you'll find the standards: a couple of TVs, a pool table, darts and gambling machines.

Gallatin Gateway, Montana

Stacey's

300 Mill St., Gallatin Gateway, Mont.
• (406) 763-4425

If it's cowboy kitsch you crave, don't go to Stacey's. This comfortable cowboy bar is the real McCoy. It hosts a country-and-western band every Friday and Saturday night, and it boasts a huge collection of rodeo photos given to owner Stacey Crosby by his cowboy friends. Don't expect anything fancy at Stacey's (the sign will say the "Old Faithful.") Do expect a homey horseshoe-shaped bar with a fireplace and pool table on one side and a dance floor on the other.

Eastern Idaho

Teton Valley

Knotty Pine Bar and Restaurant

27 E. Main St., Victor, Idaho
• (208) 787-2866

In the 1920s it was a service station. Then it was a six-stool bar. Now it's got three TVs, a fireplace, a pool table, a dining room (see our Restaurants chapter) and a deck outside. On occasional Friday or Saturday nights the old log walls of the somewhat renovated, much-expanded Knotty Pine vibrate with the sounds of rock 'n' roll, country-and-western or pop music from local dance bands. There is no cover charge. Thursday night is open mike night.

Pierre's Playhouse

27 N. Main St., Victor, Idaho
• (208) 787-2249 summers only

What goes perfectly with the laughs and delightful overacting of an old-fashioned melodrama? How about an all-you-can-eat Dutch-oven dinner of chicken, potatoes, salad and homemade scones? Enjoy the show alone ($8) or take our suggestion and have dinner as well ($15) Wednesday through Saturday, mid-June through August. Two shows play on alternate days, each with a cast of six to eight players.

This is a family operation, so owner Peggy Egbert's son plays the villain, as did her husband before him. A daughter also acts in Playhouse productions. Two other daughters work behind the scenes. Pierre's Playhouse celebrates 36 years of fun and good food in the summer of 1999.

Spud Drive-in Theater

231 S. Idaho Hwy. 33, Driggs, Idaho
• (208) 354-2727, (800) 799-SPUD

The giant potato on the old flatbed truck is a local landmark, and an outdoor movie at the Spud Drive-in is a local tradition. The summer of 1998 marked the venerable old drive-in's 45th year. Unlike many drive-ins, the theater shows only one movie per night. Most of the audience are families, and with summer darkness falling around 10 PM, a one-movie evening doesn't end until midnight.

The regular admission price is comparable to local indoor theaters, but the Spud runs specials like Family Night and Cheap Date Night that are worth checking for. The season runs from mid-April to early October.

Trap Bar and Grille

Grand Targhee at Ski Hill Rd., Alta, Wyo.
• (307) 353-2300, (800) TARGHEE

Ski to the stairs and climb out of the cold into Trap Bar, which serves snacks, lunch and dinner. You can also enjoy live music almost every night except when there's a football game. There is never a cover, even for acts as fine as Peter Rowan, Sam Lee's All Star Band, and U.S. Blues. Music is eclectic here at Trap Bar. It ranges from blues to bluegrass and Motown R&B to reggae, plus the uncategorizable, such as String Cheese Incident. What it mostly is, is danceable.

Bands start playing around 4:15 PM during ski season. They break from 6:30 to 8 PM and then play until around 10 PM, when all good skiers go to their beds to dream the next day's turns. Trap Bar closes in spring and fall.

INSIDERS' TIP

The IMAX Theater and the Grizzly Discovery Center in West Yellowstone qualify for evening family entertainment. For more information refer to our Attractions chapter.

Swan Valley

Covered Wagon Saloon

No credit cards • Swan Valley Hwy. at Irwin, Idaho • (208) 483-2027

Bob Jackson retired, got bored and opened this saloon more than a decade ago. Judged by the fact that the bar hasn't closed a day since, he's not bored now. He can seat about 100, and on the summer Saturdays and holidays when he brings a country-and-western or soft-rock band to town (no cover), those 100 seats are often taken.

Other nights, Covered Wagon Saloon is quieter. Locals and visiting anglers drink at the bar and play pool or shuffleboard.

Island Park, Idaho

Jacobs' Island Park Ranch

Off Kilgore Rd., Island Park, Idaho • (208) 662-5567, (800) 230-9530

Get ready for an evening of Western entertainment. You begin around 5:30 PM with a ride in an authentic antique English-style carriage behind a Clydesdale or Belgian horse. Your driver delivers you to The Barn for an evening of Dutch-oven treats and barbecued meats. All this is followed by a Western variety show with comedy acts, singing and dancing.

While at The Barn, you'll be interested to know that the massive structure was actually built as a barn. But when it was finished, the Jacobs realized it was far too pretty to simply house carriages and horses, so they decorated with the Indian rugs you see before you, added the stage and — ta-da!

Jacobs' Island Park Ranch hosts these reservation-only evenings every Friday and Saturday night in summer. The cost is $20 per person. The ranch also offers pleasant cabin accommodations and horseback riding (see our Resorts and Guest Ranches chapter).

Mack's Inn Dinner Theater

4111 Big Springs Rd., Mack's Inn at Island Park, Idaho • (208) 558-7871

All-you-can-eat home-cooking — that would draw most of us from our campsites and fishing holes. Now add live drama in a casual dining atmosphere that welcomes your dusty jeans and hiking boots.

Needless to say, summer weekends are busy, and reservations are recommended. Shows and dinner run Monday through Saturday all summer.

Idaho Falls, Idaho, Area

Alive After 5

498 A St., Idaho Falls, Idaho • (208) 535-0399

Listen to music outside early Wednesday evenings June through August. Each week the town blocks off A Street from Capital to Park avenues. Local musical groups perform, and a different local restaurant each week is invited to sell its specialty to the après work crowd. Beer and wine are available. Street merchants get into the act with specials and sidewalk tables of merchandise. Between 300 and 500 attend. Attendance is free, but food and beer are not.

DB's Steak and Brew House

216 First St., Idaho Falls, Idaho • (208) 529-4070

Some of the better dance bands this town hears play this bar on Friday and Saturday nights. The music is usually classic rock 'n' roll or blues. DB's can seat nearly 300 people; when a good band comes in, it often does. Bands have included Commander Cody and the Lost Planet Airmen, Black Oak Arkansas and Norm Buffalo. If Rebecca Scott is playing, don't pass it up. Her brand of energetic contemporary folk has made her an Idaho Falls favorite.

The door charge for local acts is usually about $2. Special shows sometimes cost as much as $5.

A popular Friday stop for locals is DB's Power Hour from 5 PM to 7 PM. You pay $6 for all the beer you can drink. All three bartenders spend those two hours pouring as fast as they can. DB's attracts a mixed crowd of partiers, mostly younger folks.

Dust Lounge

700 Lindsay Blvd., Idaho Falls, Idaho • (208) 523-1865

Locals say this upscale country bar in the Stardust Motor Lodge is probably the friendliest place in town to kick up your cowboy boots and two-step the night away. Rodeo pictures line the walls, and cowhide lines the barstools, but this isn't where folks go to get wild. Dust Lounge hosts country-and-western bands every Friday and Saturday night. There is no cover. In the past they've offered free line and two-step dance lessons from 6 to 8 PM to get you ready for the action. They may not continue, but if you'd like to learn, it's worth a phone call.

Ford's Bar

444 A St., Idaho Falls, Idaho
• (208) 523-4840

Come here because play at the five pool tables is free, just like in the old days. Or come for the live country music, or for that unassuming, smoky atmosphere that every neighborhood bar used to have — or to check out the scrolled and intricate antique back bar. It was brought here by wagon in the late 1800s and installed as the building was constructed. Ford's has been around for nearly a century. Tourists don't come here much, but if you want a peek into the past, make this one of your evening stops. There is never a cover charge for the Friday and Saturday night bands.

Heise Hot Springs

5116 E. Heise Rd., Ririe, Idaho
• (208) 538-7312

Mineral-laden hot water bubbles out of the ground at 123 degrees at the Snake River's edge. The water fills a large mineral hot pool maintained at a pleasant soaking temperature of 105 degrees. Through heat exchangers, it also warms a freshwater pool that's kept at about 94 degrees. Both pools are outdoors and open until 10 PM, making for a pleasant evening diversion — especially in winter when you can watch the snowflakes melt on your steam-warmed arms. The cost is $5 for adults. The pools are open year round except for three weeks in November when they close for maintenance. Both are chlorinated.

There's a lot more going on at Heise than hot water. See our Attractions chapter to learn about the golf course, summer pool and other features.

Mountain River Ranch

98 N. 5050 E. Ririe, Idaho
• (208) 538-7337

In summer, watch the Old West shoot-out, then hop onto big Percheron-drawn wagons for a 15-minute ride out to the ranch's dinner theater for chicken or steak dinner and an Old West variety show. Adults pay around $20 for the show, ride and a meal of potato salad, baked beans, corn on the cob, sourdough garlic bread and Italian ice. Sodas, beer and wine are available at additional charge. The evening's entertainment takes a little over three hours and runs June through September, Thursday through Saturday.

In winter, the festivities become more holiday-oriented. You ride a sleigh with carolers aboard, and dinner features Cornish game hen or prime rib. Lights sparkle off the snow. Winter shows start the Saturday after Thanksgiving and run into February. In December, you can hop on the sleigh almost every night. Winter shows cost a bit more. Reservations are required.

Peppertree Lounge

888 N. Holmes Ave., Idaho Falls, Idaho
• (208) 523-5993

Thursday is the best night to come to the Peppertree: That's comedy night, when two comedians take the stage for the evening. Tickets are $5. There is no admission charge other nights.

Some weeknights the bar makes available that most modern opportunity for embarrassment: karaoke. On weekends the lounge hosts a DJ. The Peppertree has a full bar, multiple TV sets, pool and darts.

Northwestern Wyoming

Cody, Wyoming

Angie's Silver Dollar Bar and Grill

1313 Sheridan Ave., Cody, Wyo.
• (307) 587-3554

You'll recognize this place by the big burger painted on the front window. The Silver Dollar, which hires a band nearly every Friday and Saturday year round, is a favorite local hangout that attracts revelers of all kinds and ages, as well as businessmen for lunch. (Some locals say this place serves the best burgers in town. The menu features seven varieties.) In front is the regular old Silver Dollar, and Angie's, a new addition with another bar, is where the band plays and the customers dance. When summer comes, proprietors open their doors onto a tent-covered patio that borders the sidewalk.

Weeknights from 5 to 7 PM, the Silver Dollar has a 50¢-off happy hour. The Silver Dollar has five pool tables and three TVs to absorb your time.

Cassie's Supper Club

214 Yellowstone Ave., Cody, Wyo.
• (307) 527-5500

If it's dancing you're up to, this is the place to go in Cody. Owned by musician Steve Singer, a Cody native who played music on the road for 20 years before returning home, Cassie's is a classic country-and-western dancing bar. Cassie's features live music here seven nights a week through the summer — Singer plays them all. The rest of the year, you can generally find dancing music Wednesday through Saturday nights, plus two Sundays per month. Weeknights, you won't have to share the dance floor with quite so many others. Expect a jam on summer evenings. (Singer opens up the back bar and another whole room to make space for the crowds.)

Cody Nite Rodeo

421 W. Yellowstone Ave., Cody, Wyo.
• (307) 587-2992

Among visitors, the Cody Nite Rodeo has to be the town's No. 1 summertime nighttime entertainment for young and old alike. Nearly 90,000 people attend this fast-moving nightly rodeo each summer from Memorial Day until Labor Day. For more information about the Cody Nite Rodeo, see the Close-up in our Rodeo chapter.

Gib's Sports Pub

1901 Mountain View Rd., Cody, Wyo.
• (307) 527-5253

Mondays and Sundays during football season, this place is packed with folks drinking beer and watching the ball games on the seven screens in the bar. Attached to the verging-on-upscale Black Sheep restaurant, Gib's offers comfortable chairs and eight kinds of beer, including Guinness and Moose Drool, on tap. The bar, which is carpeted in plush burgundy, has no dance floor, but the Black Sheep does, though dances here are sporadic. Drinks are reasonably priced — even better at the 50¢-off happy hour from 5 to 7 each evening.

Skate Away

3534 Bighorn Ave., Cody, Wyo.
• (307) 587-6556

Skate away the day and evening at the 12,000-square-foot Skate Away roller rink. Or just turn the kids loose while you sit back and watch. Skating here costs from $3.25 to $3.50 depending on the time of day. For most sessions, the admission price includes roller-skate rental. (In-line skates cost extra.) The hours of operation here change with the season, but generally it's open Fridays through Sundays during the winter and only Fridays and Saturdays during the summer. It's best to call ahead for the times since the hours seem to change often.

Shopping

In the early days, visitors hacked away at geyser cones and petrified trees, bagged up the pieces and took them home to keep as souvenirs from Wonderland, an early nickname for Yellowstone National Park. Today, visitors still like to bring home something from the towns surrounding the wild lands they've visited. Throughout Greater Yellowstone, and especially in towns such as Jackson and Cody, you'll find myriad shops displaying man-made creations wrought from and inspired by the area's natural resources.

Maybe you'll find a particularly pleasing painting of a familiar landscape or simply a pair of cowboy boots and a hat to match. Maybe it will be a chandelier made of antlers or a set of mugs made of local clay. Whatever it is you're looking for, chances are you'll stumble upon it if you spend some time in our shops. And, if you're not in the mood for buying, it's fun just to look and marvel at the inventive ways artisans have used local materials to create functional works of art.

In this chapter we've included plenty of the frivolous. And we've also listed a good representation of absolutely essential sources such as sporting goods and fly shops to outfit your recreational pursuits. And, of course, we've listed sources for the Greater Yellowstone fashion look.

Because we think you'll likely want to learn more about Greater Yellowstone, we've listed bookstores where you will find enlightening information (see our Resources chapter for suggested reading). We've also included a healthy menu of places where you can trade in your tenny-runners for a pair of shiny new cowboy boots. You'll find a few furniture stores under functional art, simply because they feature nifty Western-style creations like gnarly pine four-poster beds or intricate antler coat racks. And we've told you about a few extraordinary antique stores.

Our list of stores is not all-inclusive by any means. For your convenience, we have listed stores first by geographic area, then according to category. If, in your meanderings through Yellowstone country, you come across a shop you think absolutely needs a write-up, we encourage you to let us know about it.

Yellowstone National Park

Sporting Goods

Hamilton Stores

Various locations throughout the park

Hamilton Stores, operated by the park's oldest existing concessionaire, are located throughout the park. (For more information, refer to the Close-up on Hamilton Stores in this chapter.) In some locations such as Tower Fall and Lake, you'll find a comparatively limited menu of food, supplies and gifts. At other stores, such as the one in Canyon, you'll find everything you could imagine you might need for camping, cooking, traveling and more. Several locations also have lunch counters, especially the older ones, such as those at Fishing Bridge and Old Faithful.

At Mammoth and Canyon, Hamilton operates separate "nature" shops. In addition, the stores at Fishing Bridge, Old Faithful and the Canyon Nature Shop all have on-site one-hour photo processing. You'll notice that most Hamilton Stores employees are senior citizens. Hamilton Store at the Fishing Bridge is a beautiful old place with a huge stone fireplace. At one time, a couple of big sofas in front of the hearth used to be favorite conversation spots for locals. Merchandise has replaced the couches.

Hamilton Stores Inc. has offered its *Yellowstone On-Line Catalog* since June 1997. In addition to such items as Yellowstone souvenirs and apparel, gifts, recreation products, jewelry and Native American handicrafts, you'll find information about road conditions, weather, fishing updates, campgrounds, hotels and employment. Hamilton Stores Inc. also has a web site: http://www.hamiltonstores.com.

Bookstores

Yellowstone Association

100 Chittenden House, Mammoth, Yellowstone National Park
• (307) 344-2293

The Yellowstone Association sells a hefty selection of park- and nature-related books through all park visitor centers. You'll find books on birds, animals, hiking, fishing, geology, geysers and lots of other topics. Proceeds from book sales go toward the Yellowstone Association, a nonprofit group that helps Yellowstone National Park with funding, research and interpretive projects.

Jackson Hole

Sporting Goods

Gear Revival

854 W. Broadway Ave., Jackson, Wyo.
• (307) 739-8699

If you're looking for a deal, stop on by Gear Revival's consignment section. Consignment items generally include kayaks, skis, snowboards, ski boots, outerwear, tents and sleeping bags. The retail section, which is stocked with outerwear, backpacking accessories and mountaineering equipment, aims to have the lowest prices in town. The sales staff includes experienced telemark skiers, as well as mountaineering and ice climbers. In winter, Gear Revival closes Sundays.

High Country Flies

185 N. Center St., Jackson, Wyo.
• (307) 733-7210

Shop owner James Jones grew up fishing in Pennsylvania; he worked as a guide for High Country Flies before he bought the place in 1984. Jim carries Patagonia brand clothing; his is the only fly shop in town in which the guy behind the counter is likely to be the owner.

The shelves are stocked with all the supplies an angler needs: rods, flies, clothing, books on fishing and odd gifts for the angler who has everything. Jim's shop is open seven days a week in summer but closes Sundays in slow winter months. See our Fishing and Watersports chapter to learn about High Country Flies' guiding services.

Jack Dennis Sports

50 E. Broadway Ave., Jackson, Wyo.
• (307) 733-3270

This is the granddaddy of Jackson fishing shops. Fishing celebrity Jack Dennis Jr. opened his fly shop and guide service here in 1967. Seven years later he expanded into a full-blown sporting-goods store. Now the business even includes a gallery hung with wildlife and landscape art. But most important, Jack Dennis Sports carries the area's largest selection of fishing and fly equipment, including fly-tying supplies you may be accustomed to finding only in catalogs. Look for equipment and accessories by Sage, Scott, Winston and Loomis.

This shop is also home to one of the better known fishing guide services in town (see our Fishing and Watersports chapter).

Moosely Seconds

Dornan's at Moose, Wyo.
• (307) 739-1801
150 E. Broadway Ave., Jackson, Wyo.
• (307) 733-7176

Both Moosely locations are owned by Skinny Skis; think of them as the sporting-goods alternative for the wallet-conscious. Moosely carries less-expensive brands as well as discounted seconds and closeouts from makers such as Gramicci, Mountain Hardware, Marmot, Lowe Alpine and Moonstone.

The Moose location focuses on climbing equipment, although it also has a good selection of sportswear and high-performance outerwear. The shop rents plastic boots, climbing and approach shoes, crampons and ice axes. The Jackson location focuses more on soft goods: clothing, accessories and outerwear. The Moose store closes from early October through April.

Rendezvous River Sports/Jackson Hole Kayak School

1035 W. Broadway Ave., Jackson, Wyo. • (307) 733-2471

Rendezvous was Jackson's first all-paddle shop. Owner Aaron Pruzan says he stocks the best selection of paddle sports equipment in the area. A prospective kayaker can get completely outfitted here, from a helmet, paddle and pile sweater to wetsocks, kayak and nose plugs. Rendezvous carries boats by Dagger, Riot, Perception, Prijon, Wilderness Systems and Wave Sport.

Rendezvous is open every day from March 15 to October 15 and by appointment through the winter. To learn about the associated Jackson Hole Kayak School, see our Fishing and Watersports chapter.

Skinny Skis

65 W. Deloney Ave., Jackson, Wyo. • (307) 733-6093

Patagonia, Marmot, Mountain Hardware, Rossignol, Arcteryx, Dana, Lowe Alpine — if you're into outdoor gear, you're in the right place. The 24-year-old Skinny Skis is Jackson's snowshoe, nordic and skate ski headquarters in winter and a camping, climbing and jogging store in summer. The sportswear selection is worth stopping in for even if the most strenuous activity you're planning is a walk in the park.

The staff tends to be practitioners of the sports for which they sell and rent equipment.

Teton Aquatic Supply/Snake River Kayak and Canoe School

155 W. Gill Ave., Jackson Wyo. • (307) 733-3127

Think of this shop as two stores in one: It houses diving gear, air and a five-star PADI training facility with certified instructors who can teach you to breathe underwater; it also stocks paddle-sports gear and offers kayak and canoe instruction for those who'd rather remain on the surface. You can buy whitewater kayaks, sea kayaks and whitewater and lake canoes. Complementary gear fills the store's shelves.

In summer, the shop is open seven days a week. In fall, winter and spring, hours are more variable, but you can always call for an appointment. To learn about the Snake River Kayak and Canoe School or the PADI dive facility, check out our Fishing and Watersports chapter.

Teton Mountaineering

170 N. Cache St., Jackson, Wyo. • (307) 733-3595, (800) 850-3595

Although Teton Mountaineering carries gear, from hiking books to camp chairs, for the casual outdoorsperson and the weekend camper, the specialty here is mountaineering and backcountry travel. The store carries the town's best selection of climbing gear and outdoor books and videos, and it stocks all the topographic maps of Greater Yellowstone and plenty of touring, camping, hiking and climbing guides to the area.

The staff tends to be knowledgeable and ready to help plan your routes and campsites. Teton Mountaineering rents gear, too. In winter, it's ski gear; in summer, almost everything for your backpacking or mountaineering trip is available. Fees are reasonable: $3 per day for self-inflating sleeping pads and $5 per day for backpacks.

Westbank Anglers

3670 N. Moose-Wilson Rd., Teton Village. Wyo. • (307) 733-6483

This fly shop carries outdoor clothing, reels and waders for your fishing adventure. About the only fishing supplies this shop doesn't sell, in fact, are fly-tying materials, but if you're a fly-tier, you can order anything you might want from their catalogs.

In summer the shop is open seven days from around 7:30 AM. In winter it closes Sundays. To learn more about Westbank's guiding services, see our Fishing and Watersports chapter.

Western Wear

Baggit Men's and Ladies Western Boutique

35 W. Broadway Ave., Jackson, Wyo. • (307) 733-1234

What's with that name? Well, 20-odd years ago, Baggit was a bag store. If you wanted a bag, in canvas or leather, you came here. Baggit also carried a small selection of pretty women's clothing that other stores in the area didn't have. This corner of the store became so popular that it eventually took over. Now Baggit is the place to shop for a feminine, Victorian Western look as well as for non-Western men's and women's dressier clothes. You can buy a Western wedding dress here or a versatile Linda Lundstrom coat, creamy wool with a detachable shell and detachable fur ruffs at collar and hood.

The store carries a selection of midpriced clothing among its more upscale offerings. Customers like the more low-key Western look of Baggit's clothing — much of Jackson's other Western wear offerings are splendidly, unabashedly ornate.

Beaver Creek Hat and Leather Company

36 E. Broadway Ave., Jackson, Wyo.
• (307) 733-1999, (800) 533-4522

Felt hats in almost every imaginable shape line the walls. Floor space is filled with leather vests; wool, leather and canvas jackets; belts and belt buckles and, of course, hatbands. John Bickner Sr. makes his hats by hand on equipment dating to 1904. He also makes the hatbands.

Hat prices range from $50 to $350, depending on the style and felt quality you choose. A favorite style among customers is the Old Timer hat, which John shapes and treats to make it look like it's been on a few cattle drives.

While you're shopping for your custom-shaped hat, make sure you wander toward the back of the store where two Bickner sons have set up shop. John Jr. runs Elkhorn Industries, which sells antler chandeliers, cutlery, cribbage boards and lamps. Elkhorn also carries mountain-man hats in silver fox, coyote, bobcat and beaver. Rick's enterprise is called Moo's Gourmet Ice Cream; the all-natural, all-organic ice cream is made by hand right here.

Corral West Ranchwear

840 W. Broadway Ave., Jackson, Wyo.
• (307) 733-0247

Working cowboys and Jackson locals shop here because the prices are moderate and the clothing ranges from Wranglers to fancy leather vests and Western dresses. Shop the large selection of Western jeans, shirts, boots, belts, jackets, vests and cowboy hats. Pick up a straw hat for as little as $10. Wool felt hats start around $30, fur felt around $80. There's even a kids' corner where you can outfit your little buckaroo.

While you're here, step back to the video corner and ask to see the hat video, which proves that anything can be fascinating, even the making of cowboy hats. These folks stay open until midnight Wednesdays and Saturdays during the summer so the post-rodeo crowd can shop.

Corral West has stores in Bozeman and Livingston, Montana, and Cody, Wyoming. Read about those locations in sections that follow.

Jackson Hole Clothiers

45 E. Deloney Ave., Jackson, Wyo.
• (307) 733-7211

Check out Western glamour wear from DD Ranchwear, Hairston Roberson, Clarissa Cassandra, Stubbs, Manuel and others. You'll find clothing for women, men and children, as well as jewelry, bedding and gloves, at this boutique.

Jackson Hole Hat Company

255 N. Glenwood St., Jackson, Wyo.
• (307) 733-7687

Marilyn and Paul Hartman are that rare breed: self-taught craftspeople. They build, service and restore fur felt hats (cheaper felt hats are made from wool). They can also sell

INSIDERS' TIP

In Montana, check antique stores for *Antiques in the Heart of Montana*, a guide to more than 30 antique shops from Dillon to Billings.

you the braided-horsehair hatbands and Western shirts and vests to go with your new hat. The price for a custom hat is surprisingly reasonable, starting at around $100.

Bookstores

Grand Teton Natural History Association

Grand Teton National Park, Moose, Wyo.
• (307) 739-3403

This nonprofit organization supports the educational, interpretive and research efforts of the National Park Service, Forest Service and U.S. Fish and Wildlife. Funding comes from book sales at visitor centers in Grand Teton National Park, ranger stations in Targhee and Bridger-Teton national forests, in Jackson, and at the National Elk Refuge and the Eastern Idaho Visitor Information Center in Idaho Falls, Idaho.

The association carries approximately 900 book titles and more than 3,000 items if you include maps, posters and other interpretive items. In the park, you can browse the shelves at Moose, Colter Bay, Flagg Ranch, Menor's Ferry or Jenny Lake. You can also call to order materials or request a catalogue of selected titles. This is money well-spent no matter how you add it up, because your purchases support programs and educational efforts that would otherwise go unfunded.

Teton Bookshop

25 S. Glenwood St., Jackson, Wyo.
• (307) 733-9220

You could shop here for the books, of course, particularly the selection of Western and local titles. Or you could check out the posters and maps. You could be a collector here to peruse the tall bookshelf of old and rare books. But Jackson locals stop in to talk to owner Gene Downer as much as to shop.

Teton Bookshop was established in 1972. Hours vary depending on time of year, so if it's not summer, call before you stop by.

Valley Bookstore

125 N. Cache St., Jackson, Wyo.
• (307) 733-4533, (800) 647-4111

Jackson holds about 6,000 people; its biggest bookstore boasts 40,000 titles. Valley Bookstore is known for its extensive collection of regional titles, especially in Western history. Also noteworthy is the "staff picks" shelf, where the avid readers who work here place recent discoveries, and "shelf talkers," cards containing book synopses and recommendations from staff members. Shelf talkers let you browse through the store feeling as if a well-read clerk is hovering at your shoulder whispering suggestions.

Functional Art

Barlow's

164 E. Deloney Ave., Jackson, Wyo.
• (307) 733-1649

We can almost guarantee you won't find anything you've seen before on the shelves at Barlow's. Innovative jewelry, pottery, art glass, candleholders, fountains and dinnerware make up most of the inventory. The shop also has educational and interactive toys. Barlow's closes on Sundays.

Beads Unlimited

87 W. Deloney Ave., Jackson, Wyo.
• (307) 733-0761

Folk art, mostly by Wyoming artists, adorns the walls along with samples of the main business here: custom-made bead jewelry. Beads — porcelain, stone, amber, wood, bone, copper and sterling silver — fill the display cases.

You can buy the beads, but what Beads Unlimited is really about is creating from the masses of beads in inventory the exact necklace, bracelet or earrings you envision. For a custom necklace, you can spend from $20 to $2,000. You choose the price by choosing the materials, and these folks create your masterpiece.

Ingrid Weber's shop is open seven days a week in summer, Monday through Saturday in winter and shorter hours in spring and fall.

Crazy Horse Authentic Indian Jewelry

133 N. Cache St., Jackson, Wyo.
• (307) 733-4028

This small shop sparkles with polished sterling silver — jewelry, hair clips, bolos and belt buckles — from Southwestern Native American artists. Also available here is one of our favorite inexpensive gift choices, sterling-silver button covers to dress up your shirts. You can also find local beadwork in Crazy Horse's display cases.

Dan Shelley Jewelers

Gaslight Alley, Jackson, Wyo.
• (307) 733-2259

There's plenty to ooh and ahh over even if you're not buying: one-of-a-kind gemstones cut by award-winning gem cutters, museum-quality fossil specimens including massive stone panels practically swarming with the tiny fossilized fishes called kneightia, and original jewelry designs in 14- or 18-karat gold. Dan Harrison and Shelley Elser, both jewelers, own the store.

Elkhorn Designs

165 N. Center St., Jackson, Wyo.
• (307) 733-4655

This is a great place to pick up well-crafted antler art of various kinds. You can get antler candleholders, chandeliers, tables and chairs. A large Elkhorn Designs chandelier might weigh 180 pounds and cost $10,000. The store also carries a selection of Western furniture, silver jewelry set with turquoise, lapis, hematite and other semiprecious stones. Walls are hung with moose, bison and elk mounts, as well as deer, bear, cougar and bison hides.

High Country Accents

265 W. Pearl Ave., Jackson, Wyo.
• (307) 734-1301, (800) 736-1301

From the sublime to the silly, from the reasonable to the wildly expensive, this store has it all. High Country Accents is a Western-style home-furnishings shop in which lovely bird's-eye maple chairs, elegantly simple of design, sit beside vases made from old cowboy boots. You can buy an $8,500 twisted-juniper leather club chair on which a stuffed cougar lounges alertly, or perhaps a wolf-hide wall hanging. The selection also includes $10 accessories such as leather light-switch covers, drawer pulls, lamp finials and cabinet handles to add that Western touch to a home that isn't quite ready for a stuffed cougar. High Country Accents closes Sundays.

Jackson Moore Ltd.

130 E. Broadway Ave., Jackson, Wyo.
• (307) 734-2425, (800) 667-4616

Who knows what you'll find to admire when you stop in, but we liked a bed. It was outfitted with a supple buckskin bedspread with a matching buckskin bedskirt and pillowcases, all rough-edged and hand laced. Three floors of such surprises await you in this upscale Western-furniture store. Nothing here is cheap, but we can almost guarantee you'll never again have this much fun looking at furniture.

Knife Shop

160 N. Cache St., Jackson, Wyo.
• (307) 733-7289

Ken and Meri Wientjes' little shop houses the expected selection of better known knife brands, like Schrade, Buck and Spyderco. Meri likes to say that the store doesn't stock junk. But the best reason to come here is the chance to appreciate regional craftsmen such as George Walker, a knife maker from Alpine, Wyoming, who works with handfolded Damascus steel, or Hal Solum from Georgetown, Idaho, whose knife handles are of exotic woods.

Mursell's Pottery

#14 Gaslight Alley, Jackson, Wyo.
• (307) 733-7542

Our favorite Jackson souvenir is sold here: Mursell McLaughlin's ceramic oil lamps. She's been making them for more than 20 years, and they're still inexpensive (tiny ones start at $3.50) and attractive. Mursell's Mountain Pottery is also popular, as are her handmade

INSIDERS' TIP

In Idaho Falls, you can buy Grand Teton Mall gift certificates for your favorite shopper. They're good, dollar-for-dollar, at all mall stores and restaurants, including those on the parking lot but not in the main mall building. Pick them up at the customer service booth in Center Court.

Photo: Jackson Hole Chamber of Commerce

Arches made of elk antlers stand at the entrances of the square in Jackson Hole.

chocolates and fudge. The store is generally open seven days a week.

Sweaters etc. International
95 W. Deloney St., Jackson, Wyo.
• (307) 733-6444

Jackson's crisp summer evenings and icy winters make this little store a perfect shopping stop. Sweaters etc. carries men's and women's fine wool and cotton sweaters from around the world. Shop for cozy wool warmth from Canada, Norway, Nepal, China, Bolivia, Peru and Scotland. Cotton sweaters are mostly American-made. Prices range from around $50 for a light cotton sweater to $200 for a bulky machine-knit Norwegian wool. Accessories include wool hats, vests, throws and scarves.

This shop closes Sundays in winter except during the Christmas season.

Warbonnet Indian Art and Jewelry
60 E. Broadway Ave., Jackson, Wyo.
• (307) 733-6158, (800) 950-0154

This shop carries an impressive range of Native American folk art, jewelry, pottery and weaving. Jewelry comes mostly from the Navajo, Zuni, Hopi and Santa Domingo tribes of the Southwest. Prices range from pocket change to serious investment. One nice feature of this shop is that it sizes jewelry to fit, at no charge, while you wait.

Antiques

The Jackson antique scene isn't for the timid-of-pocketbook. If that disclaimer doesn't scare you off, the town's high-quality antiques will provide hours of happy hunting. Ask the owners of the shops in this section to steer you toward the several local dealers not listed.

Beyond Necessity
335 S. Millward St., Jackson, Wyo.
• (307) 733-7492

Look here for a broad range of contemporary American folk art, antique furniture and collectibles. These folks also offer restoration services. We were told that local antique dealers frequently get their restoration work done here. The shop is closed on Sundays year round.

Cayuse Western Americana
255 N. Glenwood St., Jackson, Wyo.
• (307) 739-1940

This is the cowboy and Indian antique shop, carrying vintage photos, Navajo rugs, chaps, spurs, national park collectibles and more. The inventory is attractively presented but not extensive. The store closes on winter Sundays and sometimes for part of the slow month of November.

Fighting Bear Antiques

35 E. Simpson Ave., Jackson, Wyo.
• (307) 733-2669

If your brand of sweet tooth considers antique Western furniture tasty, this is your candy store. Terry and Sandy Winchell have been in business in Jackson since 1981; they handle no reproductions. Their specialty is the work of a whimsical Western furniture maker — sort of the Andy Warhol of Western design — named Thomas Molesworth. Trained at the Chicago Art Institute, Molesworth worked mostly in leather and fir. These days his work brings anywhere from $800 for a simple brass-tacked leather armchair to $15,000 for a club chair of burled fir and leather with matching Native American woven upholstery patterns.

Shop here Monday through Saturday and Sundays by appointment. Fighting Bear usually closes for a bit in early spring and late fall.

Miscellaneous

Crystal Falcon Rock Shop

50 W. Broadway Ave., Jackson, Wyo.
• (307) 733-9158

Two cases of collectors' specimens brighten one wall — minerals such as rich, blue crystalline cavansite, root beer-colored wulfenite and a rare crystal form of the blushing pink mineral rhodochrosite. The rest of the store is full of polished, carved or cut pieces of such materials as geode, petrified wood and rainbow obsidian. You can even find a little jewelry. Look for the shop's selection of regional fossils. Under the display cases are cabinets holding more surprises.

Manager Scott Allison has been collecting minerals for more than 15 years, but he runs his shop so we noncollectors will feel at home (and find things to buy). Crystal Falcon is closed on Mondays and Tuesdays in winter.

Jolly Jumbuck Leathers and Sheepskin

Gaslight Alley, Jackson, Wyo.
• (307) 733-6562

Jolly Jumbuck is an old Australian term for a young sheep. At Jolly Jumbuck, most of the high-end, custom-made outerwear you see has something to do with sheep. The shop carries handcrafted wool coats, lamb suede and sheepskin items. Other materials include deerskin and hand-knitted beaver. Looking for a gift that's a bit . . . odd? How about a designer dog collar studded with silver-plated conchos?

These folks are closed part of April and may be closed Sundays in November.

Wyoming Buffalo Company

80 W. Broadway Ave., Jackson, Wyo.
• (307) 733-0636, (800) 453-0636

What's lower in fat than chicken and higher in protein than beef? It's buffalo, and it's available in a variety of forms right here. Try a smoked buffalo roast or buffalo summer sausage, salami or jerky. Buffalo meat isn't cheap, though, mostly because compared to cattle, buffalo are difficult to raise. They'll walk right through an electrified fence that would put a horse on its knees, and they have a tendency to get a bit surly around humans.

If you'd rather wait 'til you get home to purchase these and other regional treats, no problem: You can order by phone. The store may be closed on fall and spring Sundays.

Wyoming Wear

20 W. Broadway Ave., Jackson, Wyo.
• (307) 733-2889

Frannie Huff came here in 1969 after finishing high school. She started a company called Wyoming Woolens in 1981. Now the store, which sells a variety of fleece accessories and jackets, pants, high-tech outerwear and other items, has grown to four. Wyoming Wear products, made in Afton, Wyoming, are also available through the mail and in dozens

INSIDERS' TIP

If you're looking for an unusual gift, try some of the galleries in our Arts chapter.

of stores throughout the country.

The Jackson flagship store carries Woolrich and other clothing brands, in addition to its own Wyoming Wear products.

Yippy I-O Candy Company

84 E. Broadway Ave., Jackson, Wyo. • (307) 739-3020

Barrels, baskets and jars full of candy fill this store — every color and flavor you can imagine plus a few that will surprise. These folks have more than 500 different kinds of sweet morsels, including hand-dipped chocolates, sugar-free candies, saltwater taffy and various kinds of huckleberry treats. The cream and butter fudge is made fresh in the store. So are the brownies.

Surrounding Areas

Southwestern Montana

West Yellowstone, Montana

Sporting Goods

Arrick's Fishing Flies

125 Madison Ave., West Yellowstone, Mont. • (406) 646-7290, (800) 646-7290

If you've never tied a fly before, you'll want to after walking into this small shop jam-packed with fly-tying paraphernalia. If owner Arrick Swanson isn't out guiding an angler on a nearby river, chances are he'll be tying flies behind the counter. If it's fishing information and esoteric fly-tying goodies you're after, this is the place to stop.

Bud Lilly's Trout Shop

39 Madison Ave., West Yellowstone, Mont. • (406) 646-7801

It's trout and fly everything in this world-famous trout fishing shop. Even Trico, the shop dog, is named after a fly. Trico, a coal-black cocker spaniel, has a tip of white, just like her namesake. Besides a huge rod, reel and fly assortment, you'll find clothing, accessories and everything you'd want for a Yellowstone fishing expedition. Plan to spend some extra time looking at the photos of successful anglers. Lilly's features a ton of snapshots of local and visiting folks with the big ones that didn't get away.

Eagle's Store

3 Canyon St., West Yellowstone, Mont. • (406) 646-9300

The selection of Western wear, outdoor clothing, fishing gear, cameras and gifts here is not the largest you'll see. But you will find a taste of the olden days that begins with the tiled counter of the soda fountain — and an old-fashioned chocolate soda. Parts of this store date back to 1910, but most of it was built from 1927 to 1930 to serve tourists. (The shop once had cabins attached to it.) Eagle's Store was one of the three original projects granted special-use permits by the Forest Service in 1908 when the Oregon Short Line of the Union Pacific Railroad reached the west entrance of Yellowstone National Park.

Bookstores

The Book Peddler

106 Canyon St., West Yellowstone, Mont. • (406) 646-9358

Walk into this homey, hopping place and you'll get the message: read. Selections include travel and guide books, books about the West with a special section for women, and a healthy array of children's books. Besides having a great selection of books, the Book Peddler is stocked with travel games, spotting scopes and binoculars. Your nose will tell you there's a coffee bar somewhere in the house. Stroll straight to the back and you'll find the source of the aroma. Order a cup of java, pull your new book out of its bag, plop down at one of the tables and read on.

The Bookworm

14 Canyon St., West Yellowstone, Mont. • (406) 646-9736

Don't be fooled by the small exterior of this year-round store. West Yellowstone's long winters were made for reading, and the bookworms that own and run this store have packed the long, tall walls with everything from classics to contemporary poetry, from travel to hard-to-find out-of-print editions, from fly-fishing titles to romances. This store has such a reputation that folks come from other towns because they know they're apt to find the unusual.

Functional Art

Homeroom

121 Madison Ave., West Yellowstone, Mont. • (406) 646-4338

A woman shouted to her husband as he headed into Arrick's Fly Shop in West Yellowstone, "I'll be in that store with the bathtub full of white balls." That would be Homeroom, a unique store filled with mostly art and functional furniture. Take the handpainted antique trunk converted to a coffee table, or a lamp made of antlers. Besides a fascinating collection of handpainted shelves, cupboards, chests and mirrors, you're apt to see a selection of William Herrick's "waterflow wood carvings." Herrick creates glass-topped tables that feature his beautiful wood carvings of stream life beneath the surface.

Seldom Seen Knives

22 Canyon Ave., West Yellowstone, Mont. • (406) 646-4116

While you watch, Steve Hulett makes knives from start to finish in his little hole-in-the-wall shop. Colorful in dress and language, Hulett not only shares the inner workings of a nearly lost art, he also displays his own array of gleaming knives as well as those of several fellow knife makers. Don't miss the show — and the irresistible knives — at this shop.

Silver Heels Jewelry

115 Yellowstone Ave., West Yellowstone, Mont. • (406) 646-7796, (805) 256-4010

If you have a set of elk ivories you want made into earrings for your sweetheart, the folks at Silver Heels can do it. They have a knack for working jewelry magic. Owners Greg and Beverly Huth make and repair jewelry on the spot. By the end of the summer, they're so swamped with orders they have to shut down and make jewelry (which they'll later ship to you).

The bulletin board at this custom-jewelry store is cluttered with thank-you notes from pleased customers around the world. A wall-to-wall case displays the owners' jewelry as well as the fine collection of gems they use in crafting bracelets, necklaces, earrings — you name it.

Gardiner, Montana

Sporting Goods

Parks' Fly Shop

U.S. Hwy. 89, Gardiner, Mont. • (406) 848-7314

Like the town of Gardiner, this fly shop is simple compared to some. Still, you can find what you need here and plenty of Insider information on area fishing. This shop has been around for decades, and the owners offer a wealth of information.

Western Wear

Kellem's Montana Saddlery

U.S. Hwy. 89, Gardiner, Mont. • (406) 848-7776

Oh, Mama. Take your honey into this shop and buy him some cowboy duds. While you're at it, ask him to buy you a pair of those smooth, red fringed leather gloves. This saddlery, owned for more than a dozen years by Les and Carol Kellem, has a relatively small selection of Western wear. What you find, though, will be unique. In addition to clothes, belts, buckles and bridles you'll find a rack full of horseshoes.

Les makes saddles in the back room. Kellem's saddles are so popular that he doesn't have to advertise. They cost anywhere from

INSIDERS' TIP

See our recreation chapters for other stores that sell specialized sporting goods.

$1,700 to $10,000 depending on the detail. His customers live as far away as Europe. Carol makes beautiful chaps (pronounced "shaps").

Functional Art

Off the Wall Creations

226 W. Park St., Gardiner, Mont.
• (406) 848-7775

For more than 20 years, folks in Yellowstone country have been returning to Off the Wall Creations for yet another piece of unique custom-made jewelry. Michael Furtney and Chris McIntosh handcraft everything in the store — from the customized elk-ivory rings to the silver bracelets set with Montana sapphires to finely spun silver earrings. You'll also find unusual versions of antler art and furniture.

Off the Wall is open from May through October. During the winter months, McIntosh and Furtney open the store by appointment. They also take orders by phone.

Bozeman, Montana

Sporting Goods

Northern Lights Trading Co.

1716 W. Babcock St., Bozeman
• (406) 586-2225
Meadow Center, Big Sky
• (406) 995-2220

Now Montana's largest outdoor store specializing in paddle sports, backpacking, climbing and Nordic ski equipment, Northern Lights is one of those great American success stories. Owner Mike Garcia began selling rafting equipment out of his garage in the early 1980s because nobody else in town was selling it. Before he knew it, Garcia had moved into a small store and had expanded his inventory to include other sports.

Northern Lights sells and rents rafting, backpacking and ski equipment. You'll also find a good selection of casual outdoor wear and name brands that include Marmot, Mountain Hardwear, Royal Robbins and Ex Officio. Northern Lights carries the only complete line of Patagonia clothing in Bozeman. The staff here are outdoor sports enthusiasts who know the area well. They're also friendly, knowledgeable and very helpful.

The Powder Horn

35 E. Main St., Bozeman, Mont.
• (406) 587-7373

Even if you don't want to buy one thing, The Powder Horn on Bozeman's Main Street is a store worth gawking at. One side looks like an old Yellowstone lodge, with pine and stone floors and a 30-foot-high rock fireplace set into a log wall. It's the new side. Except for the giant log archway that joins the two rooms, the original half looks pretty much as it did when Ivan Dieruf's dad opened the store more than a half-century ago. Today, two carved, fish-bearing grizzlies hold up the arch, the gateway between the new and the old.

Dieruf, a Bozeman boy who ended up as a designer in New York City, paid big bucks to have masons create special effects with their rockwork. (You'll have to see it for yourself.) Besides soft lighting and a dreamy atmosphere, you'll find plenty of other surprises at The Powder Horn. By the way, Dieruf's father believed that "only rich men could afford to

INSIDERS' TIP

Want to buy a Western hat while you're here? Check out these hat facts: Cowboy hats are made from straw, wool felt or fur felt. Straw is cheapest, wool felt a bit more and fur felt the most expensive. Fur-felt hats are made from beaver or from some combination of beaver and, say, rabbit. Beaver felt is prized because it's said to be more waterproof and better able to hold its shape than wool felt or other fur mixes. Straw hats can be had for $20; a high-end custom beaver felt hat can cost you $200 or more.

Yellowstone Style

People who like to adopt the clothing styles of a region fly home from Hawaii wearing floral shirts and surfer shorts. They return from Japan with kimonos. Greater Yellowstone, with its many takes on what it means to be Western, offers three looks worth playing with: faux-sport, couture cowboy or gen-yeww-ahn cowboy.

Faux-Sport

A funny thing happened on the way to the sporting goods store: The functional high-tech fabrics and clothing designs of outdoor athletes and adventurers became Greater Yellowstone high fashion. For instance, there's fleece, which is light and able to retain warmth even when it's wet. It can be a lifesaver in the backcountry, but it's purchased more for town wear, in sweaters, jackets and tunics. Gore-tex, a fabric that repels rain but lets sweat evaporate, is equally important in the backcountry, and equally common in the grocery checkout line.

In summer, finish the ensemble with canvas, cotton or nylon shorts — long, baggy ones, please. Grab a mesh and nylon, high-tech version of the old-fashioned ball cap. Fit your feet into sport sandals like Tevas or Chacos, or leather sandals like Birkenstocks. In winter, substitute jeans, sport tights or nylon pants. Add Sorel snow packs, the ones with the fur strip around the top. Don't tie the laces.

Brand names, which in faux-sport fashion are plainly visible on the outside of your clothes, are important. Look for Patagonia, Gramicci, Kavu, Sorel, Teva, Marmot, North Face or any item of clothing that you can't wear to a fancy dinner party but costs more than a tux.

One last tip: Remember not to match colors. It's the beginner's most common mistake and will immediately mark you as a wannabe faux-sport fashion plate, instead of a genuine faux-sport fashion plate.

Couture Cowboy

Now, perhaps you don't care to adopt the look made cool by frostbitten Everest climbers and unbathed river guides. Another option is cowboy couture, available at trendy stores in Jackson, Wyoming. With this look, you most certainly match, from your silver-tipped, sharkskin boots and your handtooled belt to your satin-appliqued, silk-embroidered, pearl-snap Western shirt (for which you will have paid a cool $150). Shrug into a fringed calf or deerskin jacket (kept short in women's styles to show off that belt). And don't forget the cowboy hat, which will be fur felt (consider nothing but beaver, please) with a handtooled hatband that makes liberal use of horsehair or antique trade beads. Women, your arms should drip with turquoise-encrusted silver bracelets. Men, you can go with bracelets, too, but don't miss out on a bolo tie, perhaps on a rattlesnake theme with an embedded bear claw or pair of elk ivories. Note: Couture cowboys don't wear shorts, even in summer. They also don't sweat. We're not quite sure how they manage that.

Cowboy couture is pricey but fun — as fun to shop for as to wear. But keep in mind

— continued on next page

as you hunt for your costume that that's just what it is. Cowboys don't wear this stuff. They'd swallow their Skoal at the thought. And you'll probably find that the look does not become part of your fashion riff. Like that lime-green plastic miniskirt you bought when retro-'60s reared its ugly head a couple years ago, this costume will be fun a few times — then it'll be relegated to the back of the closet.

The Real Cowboy

Option number three is the authentic cowboy look. For that, head straight for the Wrangler jeans. Any color will do, but buy boot cut. Tapered-leg jeans look like stuffed sausages when pulled down over boot tops. And after a session of sitting in the stands, they'll slide up your boot, pucker at the knee, and stay there when you stand.

Every cool cowhand goes for the casual comfort of Ariat's lace-up ropers and dress boots. Built like tennis shoes — flexible and easy to break in — Ariats mark you as a man or woman in the know. Justins or Tony Lamas will do in a pinch. See that you don't apply that pinch to your toes, though. Old-timers who grew up with pointy-toed boots and high, underslung heels can get away with wearing them still. The rest of us look like we missed the point.

Any color belt, with or without silver, will pass as long it matches your hat and boots. You can't go wrong with a smallish Montana Silversmith buckle. Stay away from the giant plate-size buckles. Unless you won it at the National Finals Rodeo, that silver plate across your belly button will mark you as a shining wannabe.

Now buy a long-sleeved, button-up shirt by Wrangler, Adobe Rose, Rocky Mountain Blaze or Mo' Betta. Don't be tempted by the bright, wild Brush Popper shirt.

Top your authentic look off with a black, gray or cream hat by Stetson or Resistol. Buy a Montana Silversmith watch and all the jewelry you can (big earrings are in). For those cool evenings, throw a double-breasted, military style jacket over your shoulder.

---

buy junk." For that reason, you'll only find top-of-the-line fishing, hunting, and backpacking gear at The Powder Horn.

Western Wear

Corral West Ranchwear

1527 Main St., Bozeman, Mont.
• (406) 586-8671
1106 W. Park St., Livingston, Mont.
• (406) 222-7473

If there's a Corral West that can meet your every Western clothing need, the Bozeman store is most likely the one. One of the biggest and oldest Corral West stores in the country, it serves a wide variety of customers from ranchers in the outlying areas to Montana State University students. The Livingston location, a smaller version of Bozeman's, has fewer choices when it comes to fashion, but it has a collection of wildlife mounts worth seeing. This incredibly successful chain is headquartered in Cheyenne, Wyoming, and has stores all over the country. For information about other Corral West locations in the region, read the entries under Jackson and Cody, Wyoming.

Bookstores

Country Bookshelf

28 W. Main, Bozeman, Mont.
• (406) 587-0166, (800) 621-7977

When this bookstore opened its doors in 1957, it was a tiny shop around the corner from its current location. Today, the Country Bookshelf has 75,000 titles housed in a 7,000-square-foot, two-story building. Owner Mary Jane DiSanti stocks a wide variety of books including a large Montana and Western history section, a travel section and a large children's section. She also has frequent book signings and readings. Be sure to look for the special shelf of autographed books by Montana authors.

Hastings Books, Music and Video

1601 W. Main, Bozeman, Mont.
• (406) 587-8024

This big bookstore has 90,000 book titles, 31,000 CD titles, 1,900 magazine titles and 3,000 video titles (for rent and for sale). In addition, the store stocks 1,850 different software titles for home and office. You can browse through numerous subject areas, including a New Age boutique and an extensive children's section.

Museum of the Rockies Museum Store

600 W. Kagy, Bozeman, Mont.
• (406) 994-2252

Stacked among the children's games, the Native American crafts, T-shirts and general gifts at the Museum of the Rockies Museum Store is a healthy supply of books — about 5,000 titles worth. This store has an array of books on geology, history, natural science and travel. (For more information about the Museum of the Rockies, see our Attractions chapter.)

Phillips Bookstore Inc.

111 E. Main St., Bozeman, Mont.
• (406) 587-3195

Established in 1897 and still in its original building, Phillips was once the biggest bookstore between St. Paul, Minnesota, and Seattle, Washington. Today, the store stocks 4,000 volumes, including a nice selection on Montana and the West in general. You'll also find art supplies, gifts, greeting cards, maps and computer software.

Poor Richard's News

33 W. Main St., Bozeman, Mont.
• (406) 587-9041

In business on Bozeman's Main Street since 1957, Poor Richard's has a selection of more than 2,000 magazine titles. It's also a first-rate tobacconist, with four dozen tobacco blends and a fine selection of imported cigarettes. Poor Richard's cigar selection is tough to beat. The shop also carries a selection of pipes ranging from a $1.95 corncob pipe to a $375 English-made Dunhill. Poor Richard's is open seven days a week.

Sax and Fryer

109 W. Callender, Livingston, Mont.
• (406) 222-1421

Established in 1883, one year after the Northern Pacific Railroad laid its tracks and rolled into town, Sax and Fryer became an all-purpose store that sold books, musical instruments, stationery, sleds and bikes. It also had a soda fountain. Today, Sax and Fryer, owned by John Fryer, has a complete collection of hard-to-find books about Montana and Western history. If you can't find it at the library, chances are Fryer has it.

Vargo's Books

1 E. Main St., Bozeman, Mont.
• (406) 587-5383

You'll want to drop into this place just to banter with the lively owner, book nut Francis Vargo. Besides carrying 30,000 titles, Vargo has a collection of first-edition, out-of-print, old and rare books for sale. He'll also hunt up hard-to-find books for you.

Vargo's also has a nice selection of jazz CDs. Chances are when you enter his domain,

INSIDERS' TIP

High-tech outdoor clothing maker Patagonia usually allows one or two vendors to sell its products in a town. Jackson, Wyoming, has several, a nod to the importance of outdoor sports in the area and the huge market for high-performance outdoor clothing. Patagonia products are available at Skinny Skis, Teton Mountaineering and High Country Flies, all listed in this chapter. There's even talk of letting Westbank Anglers, located just outside of Jackson, sell Patagonia products.

Vargo will be playing one of the lighter selections of his jazz collection.

Functional Art

Quest Gallery/Oberon

122 E. Main St., Bozeman, Mont.
• (406) 586-0611

This combination art gallery and gift shop is worth checking into if you're looking for something unique to take home. Quest Gallery/Oberon carries work by local artisans that includes jewelry, wood carvings, artistic woodworking, pottery and a few antiques. The gallery, tucked into a nook on Bozeman's Main Street, is a refreshing change from other more cluttered shops in the area. You'll also find dried flower arrangements here.

Thomas McGuane Co.

121 E. Main St., Bozeman, Mont.
• (406) 522-9739

Displayed like the finest jewelry on black velvet, the gleaming knives at Thomas McGuane are handcrafted and top quality. McGuane, a knife maker since 1987, crafts his knives from handmelted or pattern-welded Damascus steel, and he has traveled to Japan to meet the men who still mine the ore and smelt the steel. He makes folding knives, hunting knives, chef's knives, Bowies and Japanese blades. Stop in and see for yourself.

Antiques

Country Mall Antiques

8350 Huffine Ln., Bozeman, Mont.
• (406) 587-7688

If you're headed from the Bozeman airport to Yellowstone National Park via Big Sky, make this 2-mile detour when you get to Four Corners about 8 miles south of the airport on U.S. Highway 191. Sixty vendors display their antique wares in this giant mall. Each has a slightly different selection artfully displayed in an individual section.

My Home's In Montana

26 E. Main St., Belgrade, Mont.
• (406) 388-9751

"My Home's in Montana, I wear a bandanna,

My spurs are of silver, My pony is gray.

When riding the ranges, My luck never changes.

Foot in the stirrup, I gallop away."

Two Montana girls grew up singing that song in grade school. Now they own a 10,000-square-foot antique store called, "My Home's in Montana." Inside, you'll find things you'd never expect, like an old smokehouse cabin and an outhouse, for starters. This antique store is so huge and so full of surprising antiques that we recommend bringing a picnic lunch so you can stay all day. (Owners Sandy and Mary Lou keep the coffeepot going.)

Miscellaneous

Earth's Treasures

8695 Huffine Ln., Bozeman, Mont.
• (406) 586-3451

Take a trip around the world with rocks, stone and crystals in this little shop on the western edge of Bozeman. Fossils, agates, crystals, stone kitchenware and rainbow obsidian are among the natural wonders displayed and sold at Earth's Treasures. You'll also find books, jewelry, rock tumblers and gold pans among other things.

Quilting in the Country

5100 S. 19th Rd., Bozeman, Mont.
• (406) 587-8216

Open Tuesday through Saturday from 11 AM to 4 PM, Quilting in the Country is 3 miles south of downtown on an old farm. This place is so popular with quilters that the shop has moved from the farmhouse to the bunkhouse and now to a bigger outbuilding. Quilting in the Country has about 1,000 bolts of fabric, many of them in flannel and wool. They also have a long list of very popular quilting classes.

INSIDERS' TIP

Many Jackson, Wyoming, shops close for part of November and part of April.

Livingston, Montana

Sporting Goods

Dan Bailey's Fly Shop

209 W. Park St., Livingston, Mont.
• (406) 222-1673, (800) 356-4052

Nostalgia may be enough to pull you through the door of Dan Bailey's Fly Shop in Livingston. Looking much the same as it did when legendary fly-fisherman Dan Bailey owned the place, this fly shop in the heart of fly-fishing country carries a full line of fishing gear: flies, ties, rods, reels, shorts and shirts. The Wall of Fame, as legendary as Dan Bailey himself, consists of three walls filled with wooden plaques bearing the penned outlines of 4-pound-plus trout caught in Yellowstone country since the 1940s.

The shop has a mail-order catalog jam-packed with absolutely everything for the fly-fishing fanatic. To get a catalog, write Dan Bailey's Fly Shop, P.O. Box 1019, Livingston, MT 59047, or call.

Functional Art

FishTales

124 N. Main St., Livingston, Mont.
• (406) 222-0844

This living gallery is loaded with functional art you'll want to take home and put to use in your house. Try the ceramic-and-stone-mosaic birdbath or the uniquely beautiful quilts with hidden figures, designed and made by gallery owner Carol Baker. More than 30 regional artists display work here, featuring everything from folk art, clay, metalworks, photography, and furniture made of twigs and logs. Also look for jewelry, leatherworks and a host of other surprises.

Mordam Art

109 S. Main St., Livingston, Mont.
• (406) 222-0321

He paints traditional oil landscapes while she crafts handmade glass beads and jewelry before your eyes. Stop in and check out Bonnie Goodman's Bonnified Designs — she has a whole case of baubles from which to choose.

Antiques

The Cowboy Connection

108 Second St., Livingston, Mont.
• (406) 222-0272

Long before they knew each other, Vangie and Jerry Lee fell in love with Montana. Then they fell in love with each other. They married and collected cowboy memorabilia. Now, they've turned their passion for the West into a booming business. The couple moved to Livingston from northern California to open The Cowboy Connection in 1994.

Among the cowboy collectibles and antiques in their shop in 1997 you would have found Jesse James' Smith and Wesson, sold in 1903 by his mother (she got $60 for it). The original bill of sale comes with the purchase of the gun. Or you might have seen an 1840s California mission saddle or a heavy silver parade saddle. The Lees also carry such items as an old wheel of fortune, bits, spurs, chaps and black-powder antique firearms.

Miscellaneous

White Buffalo Lodges

522 E. Park St., Livingston, Mont.
• (406) 222-7390

Plains Indians once lived in them. Now Don Ellis makes them for people around the world. They are teepees, and Ellis makes four types: the Sioux, the Cheyenne, the Crow and the

INSIDERS' TIP

You can purchase great souvenirs at some Jackson restaurants. For instance, Jedediah's House of Sourdough sells recipe books, its own homemade jams and dry sourdough starter. The Bunnery sells a book of recipes, OSM (oatmeal, sunflower and millet) mixes for breads and pancakes and other souvenir items.

Blackfoot. The Sioux, though, is the most popular. Teepee sizes and prices range from $330 for a 9-foot children's teepee without poles to $2,073 for a 24-foot teepee with poles.

Inside White Buffalo Lodges, about five blocks east of downtown, you'll also find a gift shop featuring an assortment of Native American work including jewelry, drums, dresses, rugs and small bags.

Big Sky, Montana

Bookstores

Moose Rack Books

Big Horn Center, U.S. Hwy. 191, Big Sky, Mont. • (406) 995-4521
Mountain Village, Big Sky, Mont. • (406) 995-2551

Moose Rack specializes in hard-to-find, out-of-print books, but they also have a good selection of cards, cassettes, gifts and new books, including a special children's corner. The main store in the Big Horn Mall on U.S. Highway 191, also has an espresso bar.

Antiques

Dancing Waters/Cabin Fever

15 Skywood Rd., Big Sky, Mont. • (406) 995-4223

Buffets, hutches, beds, benches. Whatever antique you need to outfit your cabin may be waiting for you at Dancing Waters/Cabin Fever next to the Hungry Moose Market. And while you're at it, you'll want to buy a handmade quilt or two to drape across your new antique bed or chest. In addition to antiques, this shop has other furnishings as well as unique gift items, all designed to beautify your cabin in the woods.

Miscellaneous

Paparazzi Fur and Leather Boutique

Huntley Lodge, Mountain Village, Big Sky, Mont. • (406) 995-4705, (406) 995-4605

Paparazzi boasts the most unusual and unique collection of designer furs, wearable art, and leather fashions in Montana. Besides an unusual collection of jewelry and women's clothing in the leather boutique, there are about 250 handmade coats of beaver, fox, sable, mink, coyote and other furs. Long coats, short jackets, swing coats — it doesn't matter, Paparazzi probably carries the one you want. Coat prices range from $500 to $80,000, with the average being about $15,000. Mink is still the fur of choice among Paparazzi shoppers.

Red Lodge, Montana

Sporting Goods

Sylvan Peak

9 S. Broadway, Red Lodge, Mont. • (406) 446-1770, (800) 425-0076

Besides manufacturing Polartec clothing in-house, Sylvan Peak also sells a wide range of generally outdoor clothing on the main floor. Downstairs is the mountain shop, which during the summer months is a full backpacking store. Come winter, the mountain shop turns into a ski shop where you can buy or rent almost any kind of snow gear you might want.

Owner Mary Ellen Mangus started Sylvan Peak in 1980 after years of making and designing custom outdoor and sports clothing for family and friends. She decided to either quit sewing altogether or to move someplace she liked and start a business. That's how she and Sylvan Peak ended up in Red Lodge.

Miscellaneous

Montana Candy Emporium

7 S. Broadway, Red Lodge, Mont. • (406) 446-1119

Willie Wonka, eat your heart out. While the Montana Candy Emporium makes 22 kinds of fudge as you watch, this store's real claim to fame is the volume of confections packed inside its turn-of-the-century walls. The Montana Candy Emporium has 2,300 kinds of sweets, including more than four tons of hard candy contained in bushel baskets. Even if you aren't a candy lover, we recommend you stroll the aisles of this store on Red Lodge's main street just to experience the mind-boggling and mouthwatering sight of so many goodies.

While you're here, you might want to try the killer fudge or huckleberry bark.

Ennis, Montana

Functional Art

Antler Designs
119 E. Main St., Ennis, Mont.
• (406) 682-4999, (800) 522-0999

Among the slew of handcrafted furniture and gift shops in Greater Yellowstone, Antler Designs is a standout. Besides elk-antler chandeliers and mirrors ringed with deer horns, Antler Designs features a line of dreamy aspen furniture that captures the eye and lifts the spirit. High-backed bar stools sit on a snarl of elk antlers, and a perfectly balanced lodgepole coatrack wears a crown of deer antlers, each prong a coat hook. A display case holds exquisite and reasonably priced jewelry as well as handcrafted antler-handled knives. Antler Designs closes from November through April so the owner can scour the Rockies for the next year's wares.

Antiques

The Blue Heron
101 Main St., Ennis, Mont.
• (406) 682-7171, (888) BLHERON

Besides a selection of antique desks, hutches and dressers, you'll find some surprising things in The Blue Heron: antique fishing reels, snowshoes, dishes, picture frames and used cowboy boots. You also might find a silver-studded saddle or a hard-to-find bolt cabinet. The Blue Heron has an espresso bar and an impressive selection of Western books.

Eastern Idaho

Teton Valley, Idaho

Sporting Goods

Mountaineering Outfitters
62 N. Main St., Driggs, Idaho
• (208) 354-2222, (800) 359-2410

This is the grandpa of area sporting-goods stores. Part army surplus, part discount shop and part retail store carrying brands such as Kelty, Jansport, Carhartt and Patagonia, Mountaineering Outfitters crams its shelves to the ceiling with performance outdoor clothing and outerwear. Some of its best surplus gear are the European army surplus wool pants and coats. You can also pick up backpacking food, some camping equipment and Driggs' best souvenir: a T-shirt that proclaims the little town the "Cultural Hub of the Universe."

Mountaineering Outfitters is open Monday through Saturday year round.

Peaked Sports
70 E. Little Ave., Driggs, Idaho
• (208) 354-2354, (800) 705-2354

The valley's alpine ski and snowboard shop in winter is its Schwinn bike headquarters in summer. Scott Prindle, who runs the shop, skied pro for seven years and currently

INSIDERS' TIP

Crazy Creek Products, a company that makes padded camp chairs for backpackers, is headquartered in Red Lodge, Montana. Owner Robert Hart, an outdoor enthusiast and former Outward Bound instructor, spent a year perfecting a prototype. He planned to go on the road selling them from his van, but the chairs were instantly so popular among his friends that he did nothing but sew for three months (he could sew 34 a day). Now the bulk of Hart's chairs are made in China, and they're sold by more than 2,000 stores. Employees still do custom orders at the Red Lodge office on U.S. Highway 212, but Hart says you'll get a better deal on the chairs from local retailers than through the Red Lodge office.

Photo: Cody Rodeo Company

No. he's not alive, but it darn sure looks that way.

coaches the local ski team. He likes to share his expertise with competitive skiers. If you're not a competitive skier, you may feel like one by the time you walk out the door with your newly tuned mind and skis .

The shop rents ski equipment in winter and mountain bikes in summer. Bike rental includes a helmet, an extra tube, a seat pack, a pump, a patch kit, bottle cages and advice about where to go.

Peaked is closed on Sundays in summer, but the shop is open seven days a week during the busy winter season.

R.U. Outside

455 S. Main St., Driggs, Idaho
• (208) 354-3455, (800) 279-7123

The newest sporting goods store in Driggs was born between the pages of a catalog. The retail location, like the catalog, carries outerwear and gear for snowmobilers and other outdoor enthusiasts. Particularly successful has been the line of orthopedic devices that address snowmobilers' aches and pains: back, knee and thumb supports (thumbing that throttle lever gets uncomfortable after a while).

If you're a "what's new?" type of gear lover, stop in: The store is a test ground for items the company may want to include in its catalog. R.U. Outside is open every day but Sunday. During the winter ski season, it may open seven days a week.

Yöstmark Mountain Equipment

12 E. Little Ave., Driggs, Idaho
• (208) 354-2828

Think of it as one-stop shopping for your backcountry adventure. Clair Yöst owns this shop, which in winter specializes in telemark, cross-country and snowboard equipment for the backcountry. In summer Yöstmark becomes an Orvis fly shop and a hiking/backpacking store.

Look for Clair's own wide-shoveled and blunt-nosed telemark ski designs, named the Classic Noodle and the Mountain Noodle. Both are popular around here.

Yöstmark also rents snowshoes, snowboards and touring, telemark and skate skis in winter. In summer it rents inflatable kayaks, an inflatable drift boat, fishing rods and reels, life jackets, wetsuits and other water gear, and camping and backpacking equipment such as sleeping bags and stoves.

Bookstores

Dark Horse Books

55 N. Main St., Driggs, Idaho
• (208) 354-8882

This bookstore is small — only 4,500 volumes in stock. Still, it offers a surprisingly eclectic selection of books and magazines and a comfortable sitting area where you can examine potential treasures. Pick up CDs and tapes by local musicians here, too. The store often hosts literary readings and workshops, film and slide shows, lectures and debates.

The staff is happy to special order any book in print. It's open Monday through Friday, year round.

Functional Art

The Quilt House

No credit cards • 200 N. Main St., Victor, Idaho • (208) 787-2220

The little robin's-egg-blue building houses the work of at least 12 area quilters, as well as 83-year-old native Bertha Gillette's biography, *Homesteading with the Elk*. Both are worth the stop. Bertha has been selling quilts and quilting supplies since 1945. These days, you can buy a machine-sewn quilt from her for $450 to $600. Handsewn quilts cost more: $600 to $1,600.

Bertha closes up sometimes in winter when the snowplows push big hills of snow in front of her shop's door. Other seasons, she's generally open six days a week. The Quilt House is always closed on Sundays.

Miscellaneous

Fin and Feather

946 S. Idaho Hwy. 31, Victor, Idaho
• (208) 787-2771

Taxidermist Keith Davis displays and sells a broad range of mounted upland game birds and waterfowl, including exotic species like African Crowned Crane and Golden Pheasant. He will also custom mount your bird. His specialty is diorama-style coffee tables, with birds and other creatures under glass in lifelike poses. Mounts start at less than $100; the showroom is closed Sundays. (For more, see our Attractions chapter.)

Teton Jade and Gem at Driggs Plumbing and Heating Supply

140 N. Main St., Driggs, Idaho
• (208) 354-2562, (208) 787-2483

Teton Jade and Gem is a real old-fashioned rock shop. Much of the material was gathered on family vacations by shop owners/collectors David, Janeane, Jack and Neta Driggs. These folks know the area and its rockhounding possibilities, but they sell material from all over the country. The selections of Wyoming jade and Idaho opal are particularly nice. Local Bitch Creek jade, a pale to nearly blackish-green mineral, is available both polished and rough. You can also find glass-clear quartz crystals, collected near Dillon, Montana. The shop carries some jewelry and can provide basic jewelry repair services.

Teton Jade and Gem is open weekdays in winter; in summer the shop is also open Saturday mornings.

Rexburg, Idaho

Antiques

Main Street Antique Mall

52 E. Main St., Rexburg, Idaho
• (208) 356-5002

A range of merchandise and good display makes this two-story antique shop a pleasant stop. Among the items here are furniture, pottery and military collectibles. You can also sell or consign your treasures to Ray and Shirley Park, the managers. Most merchandise is dis-

INSIDERS' TIP

Were you about to hit the trail and found you forgot to pack the stove, or the tent, or your sleeping bag? Many area sporting-goods stores rent these items and more (see our Sporting Goods sections in this chapter).

played in well-lit cases; everything is price-tagged.

The shop is open Monday through Saturday.

Idaho Falls, Idaho

Sporting Goods

Canyon Whitewater Supply

450 S. Yellowstone Hwy., Idaho Falls, Idaho • (208) 522-3932

Dave's little shop in the old gas station has been a touchstone for area floaters for as long as we can remember. Dave sells rafts, kayaks and accessories. His inventory is small, but if he doesn't have it, he's happy to order it in.

Dave also custom builds catarafts, stable whitewater craft that have become popular for their maneuverability and willingness to stay upright . The shop is a one-man operation, so hours can vary, especially in winter. In summer, Dave stays open every day but Sunday. Call before you stop by. You can also call for river-flow information.

Idaho Mountain Trading

474 Shoup Ave., Idaho Falls, Idaho • (208) 523-6679

In summer you can purchase backpacking, climbing and mountain-biking gear and accessories. In winter the emphasis is on skiing, ski-touring and snowboarding. The rental and repair shop has ski mechanics on duty in winter and bike and in-line skate mechanics in summer. Idaho Mountain Trading rents toys ranging from telemark skis to backpacks, and in-line skates to mountain bikes.

The store, which has been here since 1977, is closed Sundays.

Jimmy's All Seasons Angler

275 A St., Idaho Falls, Idaho • (208) 524-7160

You'll find everything a fisherman needs here, from rods by Sage and Winston, to waders, to small watercraft, to the fishing license. The store stocks what is probably the largest selection of fly-tying materials in Eastern Idaho. The father-son operation also prides itself on staying up on local water flows and hatches. The store is conveniently located just off Yellowstone Highway in downtown Idaho Falls; it's closed on Sundays so everyone can go fishing.

Sports Korner Inc.

660 Northgate Mile, Idaho Falls, Idaho • (208) 528-7222

Stop by to talk about rivers and kayaks, or to look at the latest designs from Dagger, Necky, Riot and Wave Sport. You can also rent rafting and kayaking gear, or get a kayaking lesson or three. In winter, this is a ski shop which sells and rents both skis and snowboards and prides itself on a good custom tune. Ski technicians here say they customize your base and bevels to the conditions you generally ski and to your level of expertise. The shop is closed Sundays.

Western Wear

Hunters' Creek Saddlery

629 W. Sunnyside Rd., Idaho Falls, Idaho • (208) 529-4349, (800) 560-4349

This little shop is the only English riding apparel and tack store between Jackson and Salt Lake City. It also sells Western saddles and tack, but little in the way of Western apparel. You can check out the used equipment, which owner Kathryn Curl takes on consignment.

Also expect to find veterinary supplies, including the Professional's Choice line of sports-medicine boots for horses and humans, Ariat Western and English riding boots, Breyer model horses and other horse-related gift items. Riding videos and horse books are also available. Hunters' Creek is closed Sundays.

Vicker's Western Store

3855 N. 5th E., Idaho Falls, Idaho • (208) 522-5030

Vicker's sells Justin, Tony Lama, Nocona and other brands and everything from jeans to boots to buckles. They also carry Whites, which may be the best laceup work boots you can buy. Handmade and custom fit, a pair of Whites will run you around $325. This store is part of a small chain of Idaho Western wear stores; it's closed on Sunday.

Bookstores

Barnes & Noble Booksellers

2385 E. 17th St., Idaho Falls, Idaho • (208) 522-1010

These folks are the nation's largest bookseller, with more than 470 stores (not counting their smaller B. Dalton shops). The Idaho Falls location carries around 100,000 titles and, like other Barnes & Nobles, scatters comfy chairs around the store, encouraging its patrons to indulge in library-esque browsing sprees. It also has a coffee shop that serves Starbucks coffee and treats from a local bakery. By the way, you are welcome to take books you haven't yet bought into the coffee shop or wander the stacks with latte in hand.

This is a store that prides itself on carrying not only front-list titles, but also those by more obscure authors and small presses, as well as lesser-known works by popular authors. Barnes & Noble also sponsors regular events with a literary tilt, such as their weekly Story Time, book signings and occasional concerts. Pick up the monthly calendar while you're here if you want to learn more (or check out our Kidstuff chapter to find out about Story Time).

B. Dalton Bookseller

2300 E. 17th St., Grand Teton Mall, Idaho Falls, Idaho • (208) 528-6401

These folks devote one whole bay — six shelves — to their regional book collection. B. Dalton also prides itself on its complete stock of bestsellers and on the ordering system that helps the store keep major titles, even very popular ones, reliably in stock. The small staff of about six employees has good product knowledge because each works a lot of hours; they're here enough to see what sells and what ships in.

Deseret Book Company

2300 E. 17th St., Grand Teton Mall, Idaho Falls, Idaho • (208) 523-5061

Owned by the Church of Jesus Christ of Latter-day Saints, this bookstore is part of a 35-store chain scattered throughout the Midwest and West. The chain's original shop opened in Salt Lake City in 1866. Although Deseret is a full-line bookstore, carrying national bestsellers and a range of both fiction and nonfiction, it is very family-oriented, and its titles reflect that. Make sure you check out the extensive children's section.

Other services offered by Deseret Book include mounting and framing of standard-size art. These folks can also emboss with gold lettering the books you purchase; they're closed Sundays.

Functional Art

Wild Country Creations

609 E. First St., Idaho Falls, Idaho • (208) 529-0207

This is our favorite place to shop for Western-themed gifts. Wild Country Creations stocks Native American jewelry, including beadwork and sterling silver. Some polished, shaped mineral art is available; so are antler art, custom knives, dream catchers and more. The store closes on Sundays.

Antiques

The antique business is booming in Idaho Falls, with new shops opening all the time. These are the biggest and our personal favorites, but be sure to ask about others in town. There are plenty.

Antique Gallery

341 W. Broadway Ave., Idaho Falls, Idaho • (208) 523-3906

The area's largest antique mall sprawls over nearly 8,000 square feet of floor space, but still feels cluttered with treasures. More than 20 dealers display antiques and collectibles ranging from vintage clothing and tools to costume jewelry and furniture.

Country Store Boutique

4523 Ririe Hwy., Idaho Falls, Idaho • (208) 522-8450

This old building north of Idaho Falls houses a wide selection of antique and refurbished furniture. Restoration services are available on site. One whole room is devoted to oak dining sets; another contains mostly dressers, bookshelves and chests. The front room is crowded with smaller antiques, oddities and collectibles. The store closes Sundays.

Park Avenue Antique Mall

393 Park Ave., Idaho Falls, Idaho • (208) 528-0472

One of the words on owner/manager Jeanne Cooper's business card is "affordable." You gotta love truth in advertising. Jeanne and husband Jim fill 5,000 square feet with pieces from 30 dealers, they allow layaway, and prices are reasonable. You'll find lots of smaller items, from glass to vintage clothing, as well as some furniture. The store keeps a "wanted" file: You can leave a description of what you're looking for, and the Coopers will try to find it for you at the shows and auctions they attend.

Miscellaneous

Growers' Market of Idaho Falls

501 W. Broadway Ave., Idaho Falls, Idaho • (208) 522-7336

Now in its 11th year, this farmers' market opens in May with about 15 vendors and swells to more than 30 vendors by August. The market runs through October. You'll find bedding plants, berries, exotic mushrooms, emu meat and craft items. The market is also a good source of fresh herbs, cut flowers, honey, seafood and more kinds of potatoes than you might have known existed.

Various food vendors supply the walking-around munchies. For a small fee and the time it takes to preregister, you can even set up a booth of your own for the weekend or the season. Hours are Saturday mornings and Wednesday afternoons. The location is the Key Bank parking lot adjacent to the Snake River.

Made in Idaho or U.S.A. Inc.

2300 E. 17th St., Grand Teton Mall, Idaho Falls, Idaho • (208) 529-5118

If you haven't found the right souvenirs for your friends back home yet, you might want to drop by the Made In Idaho store. One of three such stores in the state (there's also one in Twin Falls and another in the state capital of Boise), its merchandise is mostly made in Idaho or somehow relates to Idaho. Bestsellers are the huckleberry candies, syrups and other specialty foods. Anything on the potato theme is available here, including such products as potato hand lotion, potato bath salts, baked-potato sprinkles and potato refrigerator magnets.

Malls

Grand Teton Mall

2300 E. 17th, Idaho Falls, Idaho • (208) 525-8300

Eastern Idaho's largest mall, and perhaps its largest conglomerate of retail stores, turns 15 in 1999. The mall's anchor stores are the Bon Marché, JCPenney, Sears and ZCMI. All told, you have more than 80 shopping options here, with about 10 dining options in the Food Court. Plans for expansion include new stores within the mall, new restaurants nearby and a movie theater. What makes Grand Teton Mall so dynamic and attractive to retailers is its regional draw: Shoppers flock here from as far away as Salmon, Idaho, and Dillon, Montana. Most mall stores are open seven days a week, with shortened hours on Sundays.

Northwestern Wyoming

Cody, Wyoming

Sporting Goods

Foote's Mountaineering

1280 Sheridan Ave., Cody, Wyo. • (307) 527-9937

Foote's Mountaineering is the new kid on the block when it comes to a specialty outdoor store. Don Foote, who opened his store in 1997, moved in January 1998 from a 550-square-foot location into a new 2,100-square-foot building down the street. For a buck a

INSIDERS' TIP

Interested in buying telemark skis designed specifically for local powder conditions? Stop by Yöstmark in Driggs, Idaho, and take a look at the Mountain Noodles.

climb, you can scale the 32-foot climbing wall outside Foote's from June through August. The wall is equipped with ropes and harnesses, and an employee is on hand to help. In addition to rock- and ice-climbing gear, Foote's carries all the equipment you'll need for heading into the backcountry, including tents, sleeping bags and backpacks. Foote also guides rock- and ice-climbing expeditions as well as snowshoeing trips.

Rocky Mountain Sports

1820 17th St., Cody, Wyo.
• (307) 527-6071

If it has to do with hunting, fishing or camping, and it's not too trendy, chances are Rocky Mountain Sports carries the item. This 9,000-square-foot store is loaded with clothes and toys to tantalize sports enthusiasts, including nearly 500 firearms, 1,000 pairs of gloves, gun safes, spotting scopes, binoculars, ammunition and reloading equipment. Rocky Mountain Sports also carries a large selection of outdoor clothing that includes an array of wool garments by Woolrich and Johnson, as well as boots by LaCrosse and Field and Stream. You'll also find a virtual museum of more than 35 mounted wildlife heads.

Sunlight Sports

1251 Sheridan Ave., Cody, Wyo.
• (307) 587-9517

This hometown sporting goods store, which features a huge antique handmade cabinet from a Fort Laramie hardware store, has been serving Cody residents for 29 years. Inside you'll find outdoor gear for backpacking, climbing, skiing, snowboarding, snowshoeing and rock and ice climbing.

During the winter, Sunlight has a ski shop complete with rentals (Cody residents ski at Red Lodge). Sunlight is well-stocked with pepper spray. This repellent, packaged in large-size cans, is carried for self-defense in case of a bear attack. Sunlight sells about four cans per day during the summer. (For more information about pepper spray, see the Close-up on bear safety in the Hunting chapter.)

Tim Wade's North Fork Anglers

1438 Sheridan Ave., Cody, Wyo.
• (307) 527-7274

This serious fly-fisher shop carries everything from hooks to books, including polarized sunglasses so you can spot those trout under the water. In fact, the people at North Fork Anglers are so bent on pleasing that they'll arrange to have your prescription glasses polarized. Besides carrying the largest fly-tying selection in the Bighorn Basin, North Fork Anglers sells more than 1,000 kinds of locally tied flies. North Fork Anglers is a pro shop selling an impressive list of name brands including Sage, Winston, Diamondback, Bucks Bags, Simms (for waders) and Glacier (for gloves). The store's biggest asset, though, is the enthusiastic and courteous staff who spend every free moment fishing. For information about Tim Wade's guided fishing trips, see our Fishing and Watersports chapter.

Western Wear

Cody Rodeo Company

1291 Sheridan Ave., Cody, Wyo.
• (307) 587-5913

We've listed the Cody Rodeo Company under shopping, but this store is so unique it ought to be included in the Attractions chapter. For starters, you'll want to have your photo taken on Buford, the bucking Brahma bull. (He's stuffed.) Make that your family photo, because Buford is big and strong enough for the whole family to ride at the same time. Second, you'll want to wander around and take in all the cowboy humor — like the VW bug clown car (it

INSIDERS' TIP

If you like upscale clothing bargains, make sure you swing by Coldwater Creek's basement. There you'll find sale-priced women's clothing, jewelry and other items from the store's catalog and store. The best prices are on seconds, which may be flawless catalog returns. Coldwater Creek is located at 10 E. Broadway Avenue in Jackson, Wyoming.

came from the wrecking yard) with mannequins sprawled around inside and legs sticking out from underneath. Then there's the cowboy taking a bath in the livestock watering trough. Windmill power circulates the water in the "tub." (There's more, but we'll let you discover it for yourselves.)

The Cody Rodeo Company sells cowboy clothes, furniture, housewares and accessories. The most popular place in this store, though, is Stetson country, where the cowboy hats live.

Owners Susan and Ev Diehl also have a shop at the Cody Nite Rodeo. (Refer to our Rodeo chapter for more information.) And they have a mail-order catalog featuring the best of their stock.

Corral West Ranchwear

1202 Sheridan Ave., Cody, Wyo.
• (307) 587-2122
1625 Stampede Ave., Cody, Wyo.
• (307) 587-4493

Corral West, a chain of stores nearly synonymous with Western wear, finds its roots in Cody where a Red Lodge, Montana, businessman opened the Cody Corral in 1953. That's why you'll find two Corral West Ranchwear stores in Cody. What the smaller downtown store doesn't have, the bigger store on the hill does. Clothes and accessories here are reasonably priced, and the stores are thoroughly stocked with everything the well-dressed cowboy or cowgirl might need.

The bigger store on Stampede Avenue has a great collection of mounted animals including two bears — a Kodiak and an Alaskan grizzly — wolverines, caribou, moose and even a walrus. Corral West is a family-owned business headquartered in Cheyenne, Wyoming. In 1997, Corral West had 55 stores in 13 Western states. Be sure to check other geographic locations in this chapter for Corral West Ranchwear stores.

Wind River Hat Company

144 W. Yellowstone Hwy., Cody, Wyo.,
• (307) 527-5939, (800) 899-5939

Step into master hatter Gary Anderson's shop and chances are pretty darn good you'll buy yourself a hat. Anderson, a reformed cowboy, horse shoer and cowboy poet, makes cowboy hats on site. Western singers Tanya Tucker and Ray Price, among others, cover their heads with Anderson's hats, which cost from $125 to $1,200 depending on the amount of braiding, burning and beading. Anderson shows his hats each year at Cody's Western Design Show.

Antiques

Olde' General Store

1323 Sheridan Ave., Cody, Wyo.
• (307) 587-5500

At first glance, it looks like a regular upscale gift shop crammed full of cards, candles, crafts and every typical and atypical gift or home accessory you might imagine. Underneath it all are the display cases: antique bookcases, cupboards, tables, chests and chairs. Downstairs more mouthwatering antiques await. Plan to stay a while if you really want to take in all there is.

Traditions West Antique Mall and More

1131 Sheridan Ave., Cody, Wyo.
• (307) 587-7434

Barber chairs, books and buffets. Dressers, dolls and doilies. China, chairs and chests of drawers. Tables, tablecloths and aprons. Cowboy collectibles. Doll furniture. Everything

INSIDERS' TIP

During the summer in Red Lodge, you'll see beautiful flower planters up and down Main Street. These planters are provided and maintained by Francie Marble, owner of the Mother Earth Greenhouse. She and her partner fill a tank truck from the chlorine-free water at the Red Lodge Chamber of Commerce, then they drive around town early in the morning to water the plants and pinch off dead blossoms.

including the in-house coffee bar is delightfully displayed in the spacious mall.

Bookstores

Cody Newsstand

1121 13th St., Cody, Wyo.
• (307) 587-2843

The Cody Newsstand offers 20,000 book titles, 4,000 magazine titles and a fine collection of cigars. In Cody since 1988, this bookstore carries a wide range of books for all ages. It also has a large children's section.

Museum Selections, Buffalo Bill Historical Center

720 Sheridan Ave., Cody, Wyo.
• (307) 587-3243, (800) 533-3838

Located in the Buffalo Bill Historical Center, this store has a small selection of books aimed at art and Western history. You'll also find an array of gifts, posters and reproductions. The store has a coffee bar. Authors frequently make appearances here.

Antiques

Olde' General Store

1323 Sheridan Ave., Cody, Wyo.
• (307) 587-5500

At first glance, it looks like a regular upscale gift shop crammed full of cards, candles, crafts and every typical and atypical gift or home accessory you might imagine. Underneath it all are the display cases: antique bookcases, cupboards, tables, chests and chairs. Downstairs more mouthwatering antiques await. Plan to stay a while if you really want to take in all there is.

Traditions West Antique Mall and More

1131 Sheridan Ave., Cody, Wyo.
• (307) 587-7434

Barber chairs, books and buffets. Dressers, dolls and doilies. China, chairs and chests of drawers. Tables, tablecloths and aprons. Cowboy collectibles. Doll furniture. Everything including the in-house coffee bar is delightfully displayed in the spacious mall.

Functional Art

Timbercreek Interiors Furniture and Design

1371 Sheridan Ave., Cody, Wyo.
• (307) 587-4246

Maybe it's the cushy denim sofas or the antler chandeliers. Or is it the selection of Mexican candles and Western-style dining tables? Aha, it must be the fountain and the fireplace. Whatever it is, walking into Timbercreek is like coming home. Arranged like a house with all its rooms, Timbercreek carries a wide selection of generally Western, casually sophisticated furniture and household accessories.

Even if you aren't in the market for new furniture, a tour through Timbercreek is like stepping into a stronghold of gracious Western hospitality.

Miscellaneous

The Crafty Quilter

1262 Sheridan Ave., Cody, Wyo.
• (307) 527-6305

Listed in *The Quilters' Travel Companion*, The Crafty Quilter is on the list of must-see stops for quilters on the go. This store carries more than 2,000 bolts of fabric displayed like a rainbow around the walls. Many visitors who have never sewn a stitch before, buy fabric hoping to take it home and fashion a quilt full of vacation memories. They also buy unusual Western fabrics as gifts for that hard-to-buy-for family member who just happens to quilt.

Diamond 88

1304 Sheridan Ave., Cody, Wyo.
• (307) 587-3222

Dick and Peg Bryan, buffalo ranchers in the Big Horn Basin, sell buffalo-related products through their Cody store each summer. Among other items, they have skulls, hides, furniture, mounts and meat. Hides and meat (they ship it frozen next-day mail) are their top sellers.

Morning Star Indian Gallery

1236 Sheridan Ave., Cody, Wyo.
• (307) 587-6577, (888) BEADS-WY

The most prominent sign above the door says, "Tandy Leather." Inside, though, is a selection of neat things for kids (young and old) to do: woodburning and woodcarving kits, watercolor kits, model car kits, travel games, books, beads and tapes. This store is loaded with unusual and useful gifts and games.

Prairie Rose Northern Plains Indian Gallery

1356 Sheridan Ave., Cody, Wyo.
• (307) 587-8181

Besides handmade Indian art hanging on the walls, the Prairie Rose has an extensive selection of "things" used in making Native American jewelry and clothing: seed beads, eye beads, trade beads, coyote knuckles, wolf knuckles, bear claws, porcupine quills, elk hide, moose hair and feathers, to name a very few. Prairie Rose also carries books about the Native American culture, as well as music, jewelry and some pretty spectacular clothing.

Wyoming Buffalo Company

1276 Sheridan Ave., Cody, Wyo.
• (307) 587-8708

So, you've been wanting a taste of buffalo ever since you hit Yellowstone country. If you step inside the Wyoming Buffalo Company, someone will treat you to a tiny taste of bison jerky for starters. Once you're inside, you won't believe all of the different buffalo-meat concoctions and prepackaged cute cowboy foods. Step right in.

Opened in 1997, this store is owned by the same Wyoming Buffalo Company featured earlier in the Jackson section of this chapter.

Stepping into the circle of celebration, whether it's a New Year's Eve ball, a gun show or a music festival, is a good way to get an Insider's look at life in Greater Yellowstone.

Annual Events

Throughout Greater Yellowstone you'll find events that are a celebration of our Western myths. Indian powwows, mountain-man rendezvous, frontier days, rodeos and shootouts are examples of events that have grown out of Westerners' fascination with "the way it was." For visitors, these events can be both fascinating and educational. For locals, they are also social events, or excuses to head for the hills until the crowd has moved on and the dust has settled.

You'll find celebrations of the arts throughout the region. In some cases, we've listed purely community celebrations such as the New Year's Eve Ball at the Gallatin Gateway Inn near Bozeman, Montana. Affairs like this are reminiscent of the frontier days when families would drive miles in a team-pulled wagon to dance with their neighbors. Sometimes they met at the local grange or one-room schoolhouse, as a few of the very small communities in Greater Yellowstone still do. Other times, a family with a "big" house (small by today's standards), would push back the furniture, roll back the rugs, tune the fiddles and throw their doors open to friends and neighbors.

Other events have been driven by our climate. Carnivals and snowmobile expos take place in winter in such places as Red Lodge and West Yellowstone, Montana, and Jackson, Wyoming. And you'll find a few other surprising events like skijoring and dogsled racing.

We invite you to join us in our festivities, whether it's a New Year's Eve ball, a gun show or a music festival. Stepping into the circle of celebration is a good way to get an Insider's look at life in Greater Yellowstone.

We organized this chapter as a calendar of events covering the Greater Yellowstone region. If you see an event that appeals to you, consult a map to determine the location. As you will note in our entries, the dates of these annual events are not always the same each year. Generally, they fall on weekends, and often they fall on the same weekend year after year. But, as each community adds more and more events to their attractions list, the dates of even well-established events occasionally are changed. We urge you to call the information numbers we provide or contact local chambers of commerce to get more particulars on events that interest you. Addresses and phone numbers of area chambers are listed in our Resources chapter.

Admission prices are often, but not always, based on 1998 events. These, too, are subject to change.

January

New Year's Eve Ball
Gallatin Gateway Inn, Bozeman, Mont.
• (406) 763-4672

Each New Year's Eve, several hundred people from the area push back the furniture and dance into the New Year at the Gallatin Gateway Inn (see our Hotels, Motels and Cabins chapter). Dress ranges from casual to formal. A swing band usually provides the music. The Gallatin Gateway Inn offers a package for those who want to spend the night, dance and eat breakfast on New Year's Day. Admission to the ball is around $15, while a dinner and dance ticket costs about $50 per person. Make dinner reservations well in advance.

New Year's Eve Dinner Dance

Mammoth Hotel, Yellowstone National Park, Wyo. • (307) 344-7311

Dinner and dancing at the Mammoth Hotel have become a popular New Year's Eve event — so popular that AmFac Parks and Resorts already has a waiting list for those wanting to ring in the new millennium in the park. Dinner and the dance costs around $50.

International Rocky Mountain Stage Stop Sled Dog Race

Various locations in the Jackson Hole area • (307) 734-1163

This 11-day race draws world-famous mushers and topnotch sled teams. The race begins and ends in Jackson Hole, with other start and finish lines scattered about Wyoming. The first stage is best watched from Jackson's town square. The final push, another good show, brings contestants barreling into Teton Village.

Jackson Hole Powder 8's

Jackson Hole Mountain Resort, Teton Village, Wyo. • (307) 733-2292

This early January event requires two alpine skiers to link their turns into figure 8's. Judging is based on form and synchronization; tracks are judged on symmetry and roundness. Watching is fun and free.

Telemark Powder 8's

Jackson Hole Mountain Resort, Teton Village, Wyo. • (307) 739-2710

Two telemark skiers match their linked turns to create the most perfect figure 8's possible. The skiers and the tracks they leave behind are both judged. Watching is fun and free.

February

Jackson Hole Shrine Club Cutter Races

Off U.S. Hwy. 26, 5 miles south of Jackson, Wyo. • (307) 733-3316

Cutters are sleighs pulled by horse teams, but you won't see any at this race. Instead you'll cheer two teams of two horses each as they thunder wheeled chariots across the finish line. At least 20 races are staged each day. Food and beverages are available. So is Calcutta betting, where tickets representing the two teams are auctioned to the highest bidder. The holder of the winning team's ticket also wins. Contestants come from all over the Intermountain West. Spectators come from across the country. The event is held every Presidents' Weekend, usually the second weekend of February. Tickets cost around $5 per day. Make sure you bundle up: You'll be sitting outside. The popular event raises money for Shriners' programs and hospitals.

Cowboy Ski Challenge

Jackson Hole Mountain Resort, Teton Village, Wyo. • (307) 733-2292

The Old West and the new meet in mid-February for a Western music concert, novelty ski races, a rodeo, a Dutch-oven cookoff, cowboy poetry and more. Ski activities on the mountain are the focus on day one. Day two, centered around the outdoor snow arena, is devoted to snow-rodeo events such as skijoring, in which two-person teams race, one on horseback pulling the other on skis. You can watch most events at no charge; a chance to compete costs around $30 per person.

Valentine's Day Dinner

Old Faithful Snow Lodge and Mammoth Hotel, Yellowstone National Park • (307) 344-7311

Snow and scenery surrounding park hotels make Valentine's Day in the park high on our list of romantic getaways. Hotel chefs add to the occasion by cooking up a special supper for sweethearts seeking romance in the park.

Ashton American Dog Derby

Main St., Ashton, Idaho • (208) 652-3377

Sled dogs waiting to pull bark excitedly and nonstop. So during the third week of February every year, Ashton fills with the energetic yipping of up to 46 six- and 10-dog teams. During the two-day derby, six-dog teams will clock around 80 miles, and 10-dog teams more than 120. Hundreds and sometimes thousands

Photo: Jackson Hole Chamber of Commerce

A dog sled racer makes his way along the trail during the annual 10-day, 350-plus-mile Rocky Mountain Stage Stop Dog Race neld near Jackson, Wyoming.

show up to watch the start and finish-line excitement on Main Street. Others come for the silliness of the Mutt Races one block off Main. One year two Chihuahuas participated in this short race, one of them pulling a tiny sled driven by a Barbie doll. Other events include weight pulls and junior dogsled races.

Buffalo Bill Birthday Ball
Cody Auditorium, Cody, Wyo.
• (307) 587-2777

In Cody, it's Buffalo Bill everything — even in winter long after the tourists have gone home. If you happen to be in town on the Saturday before Buffalo Bill's February 26 birthday, dress up for his Birthday Ball. Check with the Cody Country Chamber for the date in 2000, when February 26 lands on a Saturday. It's the locals' celebration of the frontiersman's birth. By day, residents cover the front of the Cody Auditorium with a Western façade of old barn wood. A sign on the front reads "Wolfville Hall." By night, 500 folks don their turn-of-the-century attire, dance until the wee hours and howl 'til the hens come home. In 1998, the ball began with a roast buffalo dinner. Admission is around $13 per person.

March

Celebrity Winter Extravaganza
Locations in Jackson Hole
• (307) 734-2878

This fund-raiser includes skiing and tennis events, evening entertainment and celeb-watching. It is scheduled for two days in mid-March. Connie Stevens usually hosts. The event benefits programs for adults with disabilities.

Nordic Fest
Grand Targhee, Alta, Wyo.
• (307) 354-2823

Free-heel skiers compete in parallel, telemark, advanced combined and a fun class on a slalom course. This event is about costumes, food, refreshments and $5,000 to $8,000 in prizes drawn out of a hat more than it's about winning. Participants pay about $20 for the day's events. In 1998, which marked its 19th year, Nordic Fest drew 150 racers. Call race host Yöstmark at the number listed above.

Anheuser Busch Spring Snow Games

Grand Targhee, Alta, Wyo.
• (307) 353-8148, (800) 827-4433

This is a weekend of ski hill activities for all ages and skill levels. Kids participate in races, a scavenger hunt and more; adults compete in NASTAR-type slalom races or an obstacle race. Prizes include mountain bikes, snowboards and Targhee season and day passes. At Trap Bar, enjoy great live music and the Bud Girl competition, where the girls aren't girls. Costumed men compete in a beauty contest complete with talent and interview components. The audience selects the winning Bud "Girl."

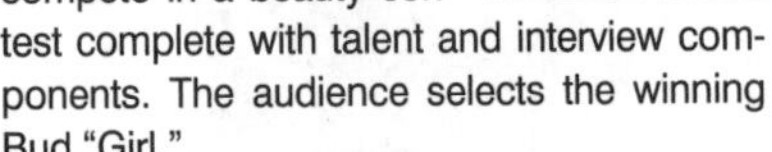

World Snowmobile Expo

Various locations in West Yellowstone, Mont. • (406) 646-7701

Thirteen thousand people showed up in 1997 for the World Snowmobile Expo, a kaleidoscopic event held in conjunction with the World Championship Snowmobile Races in West Yellowstone. In addition to the four major snow-machine manufacturers that display next year's models, about 70 vendors set up booths and tempt the crowds with their wares. If it's related to snowmobiling, you'll find it at this show: helmets, hats, coats, boots, goggles, mufflers, tracks, skis — you name it. Even if you only go to watch the people, this end-of-the-season hurrah is worth watching.

Usually a weekend in mid-March or later is set aside for the expo, which charges an admission fee ranging from $8 to $15. Highlighting the weekend are the SnoWest SnoCross and the ISOC Cross Country Snowmobile Races. At the SnoWest SnoCross Races the huge jumps and high-flying sleds separate the pros from the Sunday drivers. This race is one of the top-10 snowmobile races in the snowbelt and is the last of the season. The ISOC sponsors a 100-mile cross-country race that is less spectacular only because there's no way to watch it except at the beginning and end.

World Championship Snowmobile Hillclimb

Snow King Ave., Jackson, Wyo.
• (307) 734-9653

This snowmobile event draws enough spectators to fill every motel in Jackson to its roof. Professional and amateur riders compete in what is perhaps the nation's best-known hillclimb competition, a four-day event at the end of March. Jackson Hole Snow Devils, a nonprofit snowmobile club, sponsors the event, which attracts more than 200 contestants every year. You can buy a lift ride up the mountain to your viewing spot, but if you're willing to hike up you'll only pay a small entrance fee. When you have seen enough roaring, racing snowmobiles, check out the circus-like camp of vendors at the bottom of the mountain. Each evening, you can participate in Calcutta-style gambling for the next day's winners. Sunday is arguably the wildest day, since that's when the finals are run, and only about 30 percent of each class qualifies to participate.

Yellowstone Rendezvous Nordic Ski Race

Rendezvous Ski Trails, West Yellowstone
• (406) 646-7701

One of the highlights of the American Ski Marathon Series, this 50-kilometer marathon race attracts more than 600 entrants and several thousand spectators each year. It is held on the finely-groomed Rendezvous Ski Trails at the edge of town.

National Finals Skijoring

Red Lodge Rodeo Grounds, Red Lodge, Mont. • (406) 446-1718

They used to do it out in the snow-covered hayfields. Now, horse, cowboy and skier hook up the second weekend every March to compete in a crazy competition that pulls skiers around a 250-yard-long course marked by 16 to 24 gates and several jumps. In 1998, more than 100 teams from across the country showed up for the competition held at the Red Lodge Rodeo grounds. In order to place, competitors must be upright with at least one ski on the ground when crossing the finish line. Admission is about $3.

Red Lodge Winter Carnival
Various locations in Red Lodge, Mont. • (406) 446-1718

While this carnival sometimes features snow sculpting (depending on the snowfall), the highlight of the entire weekend festival is the Cardboard Classic Race down Red Lodge Mountain. Costumed racers ride the hill in their glued-together cardboard "vehicles," waving to fans and family. Another favorite is the Firehose Race featuring teams of firemen from as far away as Minnesota. Dressed in firemen's garb, the skiers race down the hill in teams holding a 50-foot section of firehose. Other fun events include a Friday-night parade and a costume contest, as well as obstacle races and treasure hunts for children. The festival, well-attended by regional residents, ends with a torchlight parade down Red Lodge Mountain. Admission prices vary by event.

April

Cowboy Songs and Range Ballads
Buffalo Bill Historical Center, Cody, Wyo. • (307) 587-4771

Each spring, cowboys duded up in Brush Popper shirts, leather vests and Wrangler jeans ride into Cody to yodel, croon and boom tunes learned at home on the range. One of the oldest in the country — 1998 was its 16th season — this gathering of cowboy songsters and balladeers catches them fresh out of their winter cabins where most have had time to pen a few new poems and practice some old tunes. The old favorites can stand the retelling and the re-singing. Dates vary from year to year, and admission prices range from free to $7.50 depending on the show.

Pole Pedal Paddle
Various locations in Jackson Hole • (307) 733-6433

Cabin fever can produce some strange ideas, like the one someone had 24 years ago that grew into this race. Hundreds of teams and individuals alpine ski, cross-country ski, bike and kayak or canoe from Teton Village to Astoria Hot Springs below Hoback Junction, a combined distance of more than 39 miles. All skill levels are welcome. Weird costumes are encouraged for the untimed fun class. Participation will cost you between $25 and $35. Watching is free but kind of tough: This race moves fast. Pole Pedal Paddle is held the last weekend Jackson Hole Mountain Resort's ski lifts run — usually mid-April.

Lakeside Bike Ride
West Yellowstone Chamber of Commerce, West Yellowstone, Mont. • (406) 646-7701

Set up to complement off-season bike riding in Yellowstone National Park, the Lakeside Bike Ride, held in mid-April, heads north from West Yellowstone on U.S. Highway 191 before turning west past Hebgen and Quake lakes on U.S. Highway 287. Cyclists pedal past Henry's Lake after climbing over Raynolds Pass on U.S. Highway 87. To get back to West Yellowstone, they have to climb another hill: Targhee Pass on U.S Highway 20. This ride offers van support and costs about $25 to participate.

8 Ball Pool Tournament
West Yellowstone Conference Hotel, West Yellowstone • (406) 586-9526

Forty pool tables set up in the West Yellowstone Conference Hotel banquet room make an impressive playing field for this Montana state tournament held the last weekend of April. More than 470 players and their spouses showed up in April 1998 for this popular three-day event.

May

Elk Antler Auction
Town Square, Jackson, Wyo. • (307) 733-5353, 733-4467

Local Boy Scouts gather some 3 tons of shed antlers from the nearby National Elk Refuge every year. Antlers are auctioned off to the public the third Saturday in May in the world's largest public antler auction. Private

Photo: Scott Caraway, Post Register

At West Yellowstone, thousands of professional and amateur racers gather every spring for the World Snowmobile Expo.

sales (of shed antlers only) are conducted simultaneously on a neighboring street. Much of the product, sold in lots that range from two matched antlers to 40-pound bundles, ends up in Asian markets where ground antler is believed to have aphrodisiacal properties. In this country, elk antler decorates homes, becomes furniture and chandeliers, or is carved into belt buckles and bolo ties. The average price has hovered around $10 per pound. Jackson Hole Historical Society cooks up meals in the town square so you can nibble as you watch or bid.

Old West Days
Various locations in Jackson, Wyo.
• (307) 733-3316

Jackson celebrates the Old West with parades, a rodeo, street dancers, an amateur Western swing contest, stagecoach rides, Native American dancers, shooting matches, plays, movies, concerts and — whew! — more. Up in Teton Village outside Jackson, a Mountain Man Rendezvous keeps the mood of the weekend with muzzleloader shoots and tomahawk throws. This Memorial Day weekend celebration, Wyoming's second-largest festival, draws crowds from all over the region. Contact the Jackson Hole Chamber of Commerce at the number above for more information.

Free Fisherman's Breakfast
Keefer Park, St. Anthony, Idaho
• (208) 624-3540

More than 40 years ago, a group of St. Anthony business people decided to provide coffee and donuts to anglers traveling to favorite waters for Memorial Day weekend's Saturday season opening. That nice idea gradually escalated into the full-scale event it is today. Every Friday before Memorial Day weekend, 1,200 pounds of pancake mix and 500 pounds of sausages feed more than 5,000 folks — for free. The meal is courtesy of the community and in honor of the opening of fishing season. Speakers include local politicians, representatives from the Forest Service and Idaho Fish and Game. Local musicians perform.

June

Cody Nite Rodeo
Stampede Park, Cody, Wyo.
• (307) 587-5155

Memorial Day marks the beginning of the nightly Cody Nite Rodeo, sanctioned by the Professional Rodeo Cowboys Association. Admission in 1998 cost $10 for adults. See our Rodeo chapter for more information.

Cody Gunslingers

Irma Hotel, Cody, Wyo. • (307) 587-4221

Each evening Monday through Saturday from Memorial Day until Labor Day, 13 "gunslingers" slink from the shadows for a shootout on the steps of Buffalo Bill Cody's historic Irma Hotel. Researching and representing authentic Wild West characters such as Bill Hickok, Flatnose George and Jaded Jean, the players do a bang-up job of presenting Western skits. There's no admission charge.

Mountain Brewers Beer Festival

McDermott Field, Idaho Falls, Idaho • (208) 523-1010

Started in 1994, this event draws around 70 breweries and a couple hundred beers for your sampling pleasure. Festival organizers also provide an inexpensive designated-driver rate for those who aren't planning to sample brewers' wares. The rest of us pay around $15 for entry and sampling rights, with all profits going to charity. While you sip, you can listen to live music, check your fast ball with Idaho Falls Braves' radar gun, participate in a silent auction and more. The one-day event is held the first Saturday in June.

Plains Indian Powwow

Robbie Powwow Garden, Buffalo Bill Historical Center, Cody, Wyo. • (307) 587-4771

Beads, feathers, buckskin and leather fly to the rhythm of the Northern Plains Indian powwow drums each mid-June in Cody. Sponsored by the Buffalo Bill Historical Center (see our Attractions chapter), the Plains Indian Powwow has been held for the past 17 summers. Adults and children alike will be mesmerized by the movement and color as dancers compete for prize money. Admission is $3 for adults and $2 for kids ages 6 to 18. Children younger than 6 attend free.

Town Square Shootout

Town Square, Jackson, Wyo. • (307) 733-3316

Experience six-gun justice. From Memorial Day to Labor Day, every night but Sunday, watch the longest-running shootout in the country (it's 40 years old). The Jackson Hole Shootout Gang supplies five to 12 "gunslingers" at a typical show.

J.H. Rodeo

Fairgrounds on Snow King Ave., Jackson, Wyo. • (307) 733-2805

Good old-fashioned cowboy competitions rollick across the arena every Wednesday and Saturday, Memorial Day to Labor Day. (See our Rodeo chapter for more.)

Idaho Falls Braves Baseball

McDermott Field, 568 W. Elva, Idaho Falls, Idaho • (208) 522-8363

It's professional baseball with an old-fashioned, kick-back-and-enjoy-a-summer-evening flavor. Braves games don't often sell out, but more than 62,000 fans attended 38 home games last year. In 1998, the Braves brought home their league championship for the first time since 1974. A farm team for the San Diego Padres, the Braves have 400 season-seat holders, 150 corporate sponsors and 300 to 500 members of the Junior Braves Club. The season opens in mid-June and ends around Labor Day weekend. Better seats are $6; general admission is $4.50. A variety of contests and mascots enliven the evening including a chipping contest in which fans try to hit a golf ball into a regulation-size hole from 20 yards. Last year one man came within a few inches, but so far nobody has won the prize: a $10,000 car.

Idaho Falls Centennial Rodeo

Sandy Downs, 6855 S. 15 E., Idaho Falls, Idaho • (208) 522-5030

One of the region's first rodeos every year is the Centennial Rodeo, which draws big crowds and plenty of cowboys and cowgirls. The rodeo is usually scheduled for early June. (For more, see our Rodeo chapter.)

Snake River Summer Concerts

Snake River greenbelt off Memorial Dr., Idaho Falls, Idaho • (208) 522-0471

At noon on summer Thursdays, spice up your lunch with free live music by the Snake River. The folk, country, blues and choir concerts are brought to you by the Idaho Falls Arts Council. They start about mid-June.

Free Fishing Day

All of Idaho • (208) 525-7290

One Saturday, usually in June, Idaho Fish and Game invites you to pick up a rod without picking up a license. Drop a line into some of the world's best fishing waters — free. This goes for non-Idaho residents and locals alike.

Downtown Idaho Falls Street Festival

Various locations in downtown Idaho Falls, Idaho • (208) 535-0399

Around 75 retail and food vendors unpack their goodies into carts and booths for this one-day event. Five streets in the core downtown area are blocked off from vehicle traffic for the 10,000 to 15,000 festival-goers to wander on. Two stages host music and other entertainment. The festival normally takes place the third Saturday in June.

Virginia City Players

Virginia City, Mont. • (406) 443-2081

From the second Saturday in June through Labor Day, the Virginia City Players perform turn-of-the-century style melodramas and vaudeville Tuesday through Saturday. The longest continuously-running summer theater west of the Mississippi River, The Virginia City Players will celebrate their 50th anniversary in 1999. Memorial Day marks the opening of both Virginia City and Nevada City, including historic buildings, saloons, cafes, hotels and narrow-gauge railroad. Admission to the Players is $12.50 for adults. Children 12 and younger pay $7.50.

July

Mountain Man Rendezvous

Locations vary in Red Lodge, Mont. • (406) 446-1718

Pitching their tents and teepees the first weekend in July, mountain-man enthusiasts set up camp and display their wares, which include wrought-iron goods, jewelry, trade beads, beadwork, black-powder rifles and pistols, knives, clothing and a kaleidoscope of other goods. Stroll through their camp and ask questions. Buy if you must. Afternoons and evenings you'll find a variety of events for adults and children, as well as black-powder shootouts and lectures on the era. Admission is $3 for adults, $1 for kids ages 6 to 12 and free for kids younger than 6. Persons dressed in fur-trade-era costumes are admitted free. Contact the Red Lodge Chamber of Commerce (the number is above) to find out the 1999 location for the rendezvous.

Fourth of July Celebration

Snow King Resort, Snow King Ave., Jackson, Wyo. • (307) 733-3316

Jackson hosts a parade, a rodeo and a barbecue for the nation's birthday, but the best part is the culminating event: Snow King Mountain's spectacular dusk fireworks show.

Music in the Hole

1855 High School Rd., Jackson, Wyo. • (307) 733-1128

This Fourth of July event starts in midafternoon with food concessions and regional musicians playing outside at Jackson Hole High School's Alpine Field. It culminates in a free performance of the renowned Grand Teton Music Festival orchestra, featuring the *1812 Overture*. Appropriate crashing sounds are provided by the howitzers of the Wyoming Military Department's 300th Field Artillery Battalion. Thousands attend. The concert is scheduled early so you don't miss the fireworks show on Snow King Mountain.

Teton Valley Balloon Festival

Various locations in Teton Valley, Idaho • (208) 354-2500

Crayola-bright hot-air balloons hover above the green valley floor; mountains frame every photo you attempt. This is the weekend to be in Teton Valley, with a 30- to 40-contestant hot-air balloon race, an arts festival and other fun events. The festival always falls on Fourth of July weekend.

Fourth of July Fireworks

Greenbelt, Idaho Falls, Idaho • (208) 523-1010

Thousands crowd the greenbelt on both sides of the Snake River for an impressive fireworks display that begins right after dark (around 10 PM) every Fourth of July. Come early if you want a comfortable patch of grass. Viewing is good from both sides of the river between Broadway and Science Center Drive at Freeman Park. If you want to do as the locals do, bring blankets, chairs, ice chests and a radio you can tune into KLCE, the station that broadcasts the accompanying music.

Cody Old West Show and Auction

Cody Auditorium, Cody, Wyo.
• (307) 587-9014

You'll wish you had a fat wallet full of money if you attend this growing annual event at which dealers show, trade, buy and sell cowboy memorabilia. Firearms, chaps and spurs with a history along with unusual decorator pieces, beadwork, saddles and more are among the collectibles displayed. Admission is $5 for the show on Friday and Saturday. There's no charge for the auction.

Livingston Roundup Rodeo

Park County Fairgrounds, Livingston, Mont. • (406) 222-4185

The Livingston Roundup Rodeo is one of three "Gateway Rodeos" (Livingston, Red Lodge and Cody) held over the Fourth of July. Admission is $12 for reserved seats, $8 for general admission and $4 for children ages 6 to 12. For more information see our Rodeo chapter.

Home of Champions Rodeo

Red Lodge Rodeo Grounds, Red Lodge, Mont. • (406) 446-0850

This rodeo is one of three followed each Fourth of July by some of the top rodeo hands on the circuit. Admission ranges from $8 to $16. For more information, refer to our Rodeo chapter.

Stampede Rodeo

Stampede Park Rodeo Grounds west of Cody, Wyo. • (307) 587-5155

This is the richest Fourth of July rodeo in the country in terms of prize money. Admission is $14 July 1 to 3 and $15 on July 4. For more information, see our Rodeo chapter.

Yellowstone Jazz Festival

Locations vary in Cody, Wyo.
• (307) 587-3898

This two-day event in mid-July treats music lovers in Cody and Powell, Wyoming, to swing, big band, blues and more beginning with a performance by Yellowstone Jazz Camp students in Powell at Washington Park. The 1998 roster of performers included the Yellowstone Big Band; Bozeman, Montana, singer and pianist Eric Funk; Ralph Sappington; and Eric Thorin. Freeman Lacy and the T-Bones played at Cassie's Supper Club. (See our Nightlife chapter for more information.) Admission prices vary from $10 to $18 depending on the performance.

Frontier Festival

Buffalo Bill Historical Center, Cody, Wyo.
• (307) 587-4771

This two-day event in mid-July is a celebration of frontier life and culture. It features outdoor activities and demonstrations of the skills people needed to survive way back when. Watch for the pack-horse race in which contestants pack one horse, then hop onto another horse and lead the packed animal on a merry gallop around the track. The first rider who crosses the finish line with the pack still intact wins. The festival also features a campfire cooking contest in which cooks are each given a uniform set of ingredients with which to concoct a culinary delight. Judges taste them all. Kids will find plenty to do: gold panning, rope making, cattle roping and a petting zoo. Admission is $2 for adults and $1 for children.

Rockin' the Tetons Festival

Ski Hill Rd., Alta, Wyo. • (307) 353-2300, (800) 827-4433

Grand Targhee Resort's music festivals bring crowds from around the region, and this one is no exception. Enjoy rock, blues and reggae music, a street breakfast and chairlift rides. Regional microbreweries' beers are available for sampling in the sun. Previous years have featured bands such as Poco, the Marshal Tucker Band and Jefferson Starship. Tickets for this three-day event, held the second weekend in July, are around $20 per day. For an additional $10 per person, your group can set up camp for the weekend within walking distance of the party. Generally 4,000 to 5,000 attend.

Winchester Gun Show

Sweitzer Gym, Cody, Wyo.
• (307) 587-2777

Since 1976 collectors have been converging on Cody in mid-July to sell, buy, try or simply drool over the guns on display at the Winchester Gun Show. Whether you're a collector or not, the numbers and varieties of old guns — 90 percent of them are Winchesters — will astound you. Admission is $4 (free for kids 12 and younger).

Idaho Falls Braves Baseball

McDermott Field, 568 W. Elva, Idaho Falls, Idaho • (208) 522-8363

Play continues in July for this farm team for the San Diego Padres. The season begins in mid-June and finishes around Labor Day weekend. Better seats are $6; general admission is $4.50. For more, see our description under June events in this chapter.

Grand Teton Music Festival

Walk Festival Hall, Teton Village, Wyo. • (307) 733-1128

The 1999 season marks the 38th year for this composite orchestra made up of 175 talented musicians. Performances are highlighted by special appearances of world-class guest conductors, soloists and artists. Concerts begin in late June and end in late August. Some events are free, but most run between $15 and $30 per seat. (For more, see our Arts chapter.)

Cody Nite Rodeo

Stampede Park, Cody, Wyo. • (307) 587-5155

This rodeo, described under the June header in this chapter, continues to run nightly through July.

Snake River Summer Concerts

Snake River greenbelt off Memorial Dr., Idaho Falls, Idaho • (208) 522-0471

At noon on summer Thursdays, enjoy free live music on the grass. The folk, country, blues and choir concerts are brought to you by the Idaho Falls Arts Council.

Mountain Artists' Rendezvous Art Show

Jackson, Wyo. • (307) 733-8792

This nationally-recognized, juried fine arts and crafts fair is too fun to happen just once a year, so it runs two weekends each summer: once in mid-July and again in mid-August. There is space for 120 artists, but hundreds apply every year. Most, if accepted, will exhibit in both shows. You'll enjoy browsing through the displays, shopping, munching goodies and taking in the schedule of live entertainment. The 1999 show marks its 34th year. Admission is $1.

Madison Valley Cutting Horse Competition

Ennis Rodeo Grounds, Ennis, Mont. • (406) 682-5039

If you've never seen a cutting horse at work, it's poetry in motion. This growing three-day weekend event in mid-July attracts top riders and outstanding horses from across the country. Ducking and diving, these highly trained, livestock-smart horses are tops in demonstrating how horse and rider work cattle on the ranch. This event is free.

Teton Village Summer Festival Event: Antique Show and Sale

Teton Village, Wyo. • (307) 733-2292

This three-day event is said to be Wyoming's biggest antique show and sale. More than 40 vendors bring out their best treasures for display in tents and under the sun throughout this mid-July weekend.

Teton Village Summer Festival Event: Indian Art Show and Dance

Teton Village, Wyo. • (307) 733-2292

About 500 people per day wander through the exhibits of Native American arts and crafts on this late-July weekend. Enjoy Native American dancing, singing and foods. Many of the approximately 35 exhibitors are nationally recognized artists.

Teton County Fair

Snow King Ave., Jackson, Wyo. • (307) 733-5289

Listen to live music and watch clowns and other acts. Wander the food booths or peruse exhibits representing dozens of contests, from cut flowers to cut hay. You can also enjoy canine-obedience competitions and horseback events. Evening events such as bull riding, a rodeo, pig wrestling and the demolition derby cost around $8. Most events are free, however. The event runs for a week at the end of July.

Eagle Rock Art Guild Sidewalk Art Show

Greenbelt at Memorial Dr., Idaho Falls, Idaho • (208) 522-4409

Up to 100 exhibitors from states as distant as Oklahoma and California display their best at this juried show: painting, jewelry, pottery, woodworking, photography and more. This event is more than 40 years old, but it got a big boost in 1990 when it moved from a local park to a more visible and pleasant location — the greenbelt that runs through town alongside the Snake River. Organizers estimate some 8,000 people wander through the event, held every year the fourth weekend in July.

Big Sky Arts Festival

Meadow Village Pavilion, Big Sky, Mont. • (406) 995-2742, (877) 995-2742

From July through August, the Big Sky Association for the Arts sponsors a series of weekend performances on the lawn at the Meadow Village Pavilion. In 1998, events included performances by the Brubeck Brothers Jazz Quartet, the Bozeman Symphony Pops Concert and the Nitty Gritty Dirt Band. For specific dates and times for this season's events, we suggest you call the above number. Admission prices vary.

Montana State Cowboy Mounted Shooting Championship

Ennis Rodeo Grounds, Ennis, Mont. • (406) 642-3040

Wearing period Old West clothes and mounted on old-style saddles, cowboys carry two .45-caliber single action revolvers with five rounds each of special blank ammunition. From their horses they compete in a variety of shooting events. From the stands, you can watch it all for $4. Children can watch for $2.

Photo: Steve Fischbach, Post Register

The Pole Pedal Paddle race is an annual rite of spring in the Jackson Hole area.

Taste of Bozeman

Main St., Bozeman, Mont. • (406) 586-5421

Belly up to a block-long table that stretches up and down Main Street. City officials block off the road for the occasion, allowing diners to enjoy their suppers purchased from and served by a number of Main Street restaurants. Diners who want a taste of Bozeman must purchase tickets ahead of time from the restaurant of their choice. While the crowd at the table dines, residents milling on the outskirts can indulge in a "Bite of Bozeman" by paying for sam-

INSIDERS' TIP

If you're passing through Swan Valley on Memorial Day, Fourth of July or Labor Day weekends, check out the small arts and crafts fair sponsored by the Bear Hug Gallery in Palisades. In past years, the fair has attracted about 20 vendors. On the Fourth of July, the neighboring RV park, called Timberwolf Resort, sweetens the deal with a dusk fireworks.

plings offered at sidewalk stands. Ticket prices vary depending on the restaurant you choose. The taste fest is always held the Wednesday before the Sweet Pea Festival (see our August listings).

August

War Bonnet Roundup

Sandy Downs, 6855 S. 15 E., Idaho Falls, Idaho • (208) 523-1010

The state's oldest rodeo is held the first weekend in August. Sponsored by American Legion Bonneville Post 56, the rodeo raises money for Legion projects and charities (for more, see our Rodeo chapter).

Island Park Wild Horse Stampede

Idaho Hwy. 67, north side of Henry's Lake at Island Park, Idaho • (208) 754-4271

The first weekend of August at Crystal Brothers Ranch Arena overlooking Henry's Lake, all hell busts loose. This three-day rodeo attracts around 7,000 spectators. (For more, see our Rodeo chapter.)

Idaho International Folk Dance Festival

Various locations in Rexburg, Idaho • (208) 356-5700

During this nine-day festival the first week of August, little Rexburg throws open its doors to more than 300 dancers and musicians from around the world, as well as to the thousands who come to enjoy the dancers' art. In previous years, teams have come from Malaysia, New Zealand, Denmark, Sweden, Israel, China, Russia and other nations. Free events include a parade and a street dance, Youth Culture Day at Ricks College and a community picnic and band concert. You'll pay between $5 and $12.50 for seats at the evening indoor performances and matinees. Western traditions are honored with a rodeo one night during the festival.

Sweet Pea Festival of the Arts

Locations vary in Bozeman, Mont. • (406) 586-4003

Art, music, dance and flowers mark this festival of the arts held at locations throughout town. Listen to bluegrass music or learn to country dance in Lindley Park. Decorate Main Street sidewalks at Chalk on the Walk, race in the Sweet Pea Run, compete on your bike, watch Shakespeare in the Parks or listen to a big-name band. This three-day festival the first full weekend in August regularly attracts 18,000 people. Join the fun and get lost in the crowd. The cost of a Sweet Pea Button, allowing access to all events, ranges from $5 to $7.

Festival of Nations

Locations vary in Red Lodge, Mont. • (406) 446-1718

Begun in 1949 as a community celebration of the town's rich cultural diversity, the Festival of Nations has become Red Lodge's biggest tourist event. The weeklong celebration, held the first week of August each year, will take you back to the days when Red Lodge was a mining town with tight-knit neighborhoods of German, Scandinavian, Finnish, Italian, Slavic, Scottish, Irish, English and Welsh families. During the event, festival-goers celebrate the food, clothing, arts, crafts and dancing of each nationality. It's all yours for the sampling. Admission is free.

National Cutting Horse Show

Jacobs' Island Park Ranch off Kilgore Rd., Island Park, Idaho • (208) 662-5567, (800) 230-9530

Cutting horses are cow ponies, bred and trained to be fast and smart. At the National Cutting Horse Show at Jacobs'

INSIDERS' TIP

For a romantic holiday evening, consider Mountain River Ranch's sleigh-ride and dinner theater, featuring cornish hen or prime rib. The evening's entertainment takes a little more than three hours. See our Nightlife chapter. Mountain River Ranch is near Idaho Falls, Idaho, along the Snake River.

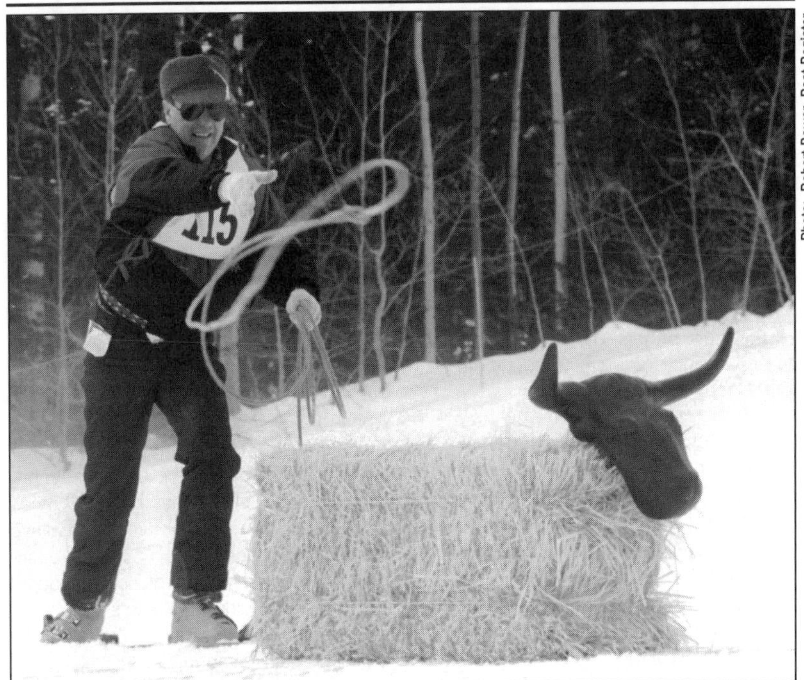

Photo: Robert Bower, Post Register

The cowboy ski race is held at Jackson Hole Mountain Resort every spring.

intimate outdoor arena, you can see just how fast and how smart horses can be. The event, free to spectators, takes place the second weekend in August. (See our Rodeo chapter for information on rodeos and other Western events hosted by the Jacobs family on their 2,000-acre Island Park ranch.)

Grand Targhee Bluegrass Music Festival

Ski Hill Rd., Alta, Wyo. • (307) 353-2300, (800) 827-4433

Imagine three days of live bluegrass under the crisp blue skies of the Tetons. You'll also find crafts and food booths. This event, which marks its 12th year in 1999, attracts first-class musical talent and festive crowds. Previous years' performers include String Cheese Incident, the David Grisman Quintet, Vassar Clements and Peter Rowan. The festival falls on the second weekend in August. Tickets are about $20.

Wild West Balloon Fest

Mentock Park on Blackburn Ave., Cody, Wyo. • (307) 587-2692

There is no admission charge to see the colorful balloons that light up Cody's early morning skies each year at the mid-August Balloon Fest. In 1998, nearly 20 balloonists showed up for the growing two-day event which includes races and other competitions among the balloonists.

Mountain Artists' Rendezvous Art Show

Jackson, Wyo. • (307) 733-8792

This nationally recognized arts and crafts show is held one weekend in mid-July and again in mid-August. Please see the show's listing under July events.

Buffalo Bill Celebrity Shootout

Cody Shooting Complex, Cody, Wyo. • (307) 587-2777

In a town that houses the largest collection of American firearms in the world, it seems natural to have a celebrity shootout. Naturally, in Cody, that shootout would be named after Buffalo Bill. This bang-up event at the end of August attracts celebrities who compete with amateurs and professionals in a series of shooting events. There's no better place to watch the big boys shoot. Admission is free.

Grand Teton Music Festival
Walk Festival Hall, Teton Village, Wyo. • (307) 733-1128

For more on this 175-member orchestra and its summer performances, see the July listing.

Idaho Falls Braves Baseball
McDermott Field, 568 W. Elva, Idaho Falls, Idaho • (208) 522-8363

This farm team for the San Diego Padres opens its season in mid-June and finishes around Labor Day weekend. See our description under June events in this chapter.

Cody Nite Rodeo
Stampede Park, Cody, Wyo. • (307) 587-5155

The Cody Nite Rodeo, sanctioned by the Professional Rodeo Cowboys Association, begins each Memorial Day and runs through Labor Day. See our description under June events in this chapter.

Snake River Summer Concerts
Snake River greenbelt off Memorial Dr., Idaho Falls, Idaho • (208) 522-0471

At noon on summer Thursdays, enjoy free live music on the grass. The folk, country, blues and choir concerts are brought to you by the Idaho Falls Arts Council.

Buffalo Days
Downtown Gardiner, Mont. • (406) 848-7971

A combination end-of-the-season celebration and fund-raiser for the Gardiner Ambulance Service, Buffalo Days is one of those typical small town weather-dependent affairs where officials rope off Main Street for dancing and dining. Wear your old jeans, though. And prepare to dine on burgers, cole slaw, potato salad and an array of other delights. The music starts at noon, and the celebration continues into the wee hours. Children will hoot and holler at events just for them, and everyone will enjoy the dunking booth where, if your

Photo: Post Register Photo Archive

At the Mountain Man Rendezvous near Chester, Idaho, latter-day mountain men demonstrate primitive woods skills, including musketry, leather crafts, cooking and teepee camping.

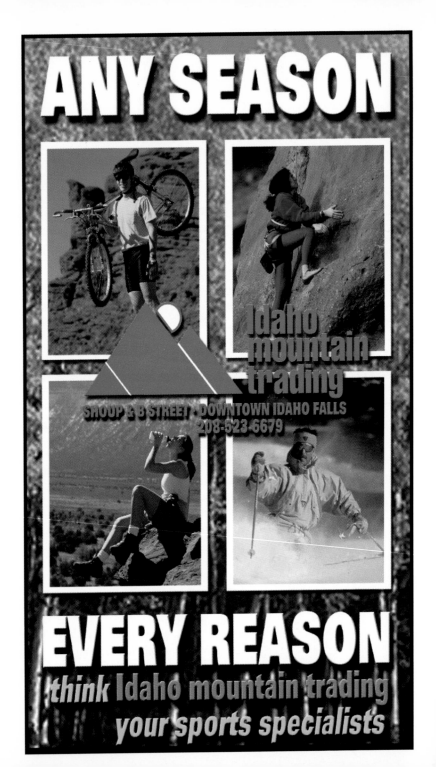

aim is good, you can dunk local celebrities. Buffalo Days is held the Saturday of Labor Day weekend. The admission price varies.

Wild West Vette Fest

West Yellowstone, Mont.
• (208) 524-3087

The Corvettes of Southeast Idaho club hosts this get-together the third or fourth weekend of each August. In 1998, the event's third year, more than 100 Corvettes came from as far away as Kentucky to this growing event. The club rents a whole hotel or motel where the Vettes can be displayed in the parking lot. Among the events are a parade, poker runs and scavenger hunts. Entrance fees cost from $50 to $75.

September

Jackson Hole Fall Arts Festival

Various locations in Jackson Hole, Wyo.
• (307) 733-3316

Every year from mid-September to mid-October, Jackson, Wyoming, hauls out its best arguments for naming the town Wyoming's arts center. Most major galleries — Jackson has more than 30 — feature special exhibits. Arts for the Parks, an international competition in which artists celebrate the United States' national parks and monuments, juries thousands of entries and selects the top 100 for local display. You can also enjoy concerts, poster signings, fiber-arts exhibits, workshops and more.

Miniature Show at the National Museum of Wildlife Art

2820 Rungius Rd. off U.S. Hwy. 26 near Jackson, Wyo. • (307) 733-5771

Part of the Jackson Hole Arts Festival, this event begins with a one-week show featuring the work of 100 artists from around the world whose work is 9 by 12 inches or smaller. Then on the third Thursday night in September, the museum hosts a popular Wild West Preview Party, which many of the artists attend. The next morning features free seminars by gallery owners and artists. This is followed by a sale-by-drawing of the exhibited art. Miniatures can be attractive to art collectors with limited wall space or budgets. See the exhibit for the museum's regular entrance fee, or on Thursday night and Friday, pay about $50 for the party, $30 to be present at and participate in the drawing, or $75 for both.

Western Design Conference

Cody Auditorium, Cody, Wyo.
• (307) 587-2777, (888) 685-0574

Furniture, fashion and accessories with a Western flair are the heart of this high-energy conference held in Cody at the end of September each year. In 1998, more than 50 artisans displayed their work gallery-style at the Cody Auditorium. Admission to exhibits is $5 per day; tickets to the fashion show held at the BBHC cost $17. The Sunday morning awards banquet costs $20, and entrance into each of six seminars offered at the conference costs $25. A $200 registration fee for exhibitors entitles them to attend all events.

Buffalo Bill Art Show, Sale and Quick Draw

Buffalo Bill Historical Center, Cody, Wyo. • (307) 587-2777

Held in conjunction with the Western Design Conference, this art show and sale with both live and silent auctions raised $72,000 for the BBHC in 1998. (See our Attractions chapter.) The show features regional and national Western artists. Tickets for Friday's live auction cost $60. The Saturday lunch and Quick Draw in which about 25 artists work in different mediums, costs $20. A ticket for both events costs $75.

Patron's Ball

Buffalo Bill Historical Center, Cody, Wyo. • (307) 587-2777

A black-tie dinner and dance is held in the very grand BBHC museum. Attended by about 650 people in 1998, this gala event held Saturday night during the Western Design Conference is another fund-raiser for BBHC. Patrons pay $175 each for tickets. For others the tickets cost $200 each.

Eastern Idaho State Fair

97 Park St., Blackfoot, Idaho
• (208) 785-2480

Beginning every Labor Day Saturday and

running through the following Saturday, exhibitors and contestants from 16 Eastern Idaho counties and nearby states park their pickups in Blackfoot. This fair, which began in 1925, attracts some 250 commercial exhibitors, 65 food concessionaires and around 30 carnival rides. More than 200,000 visitors wander through exhibits and sample events such as a rodeo, a demolition derby, a tractor pull, horseracing and concerts with acts that have included REO Speedwagon and Alabama. Agriculture is important in Eastern Idaho, and the fair doesn't forget this: You can view more than 2,000 animals of different types, most entered for competitive judging. Food booths feature the usual country fair fare. Adults pay around $3 to enter.

October

Yellowstone/Old Faithful Fall Cycle Tour

West Yellowstone Chamber of Commerce, West Yellowstone, Mont. • (406) 646-7701

Almost 70 people showed up in 1998 for this new bike ride from West Yellowstone to Old Faithful. This ride has sag wagons. Riders carry their sack lunches with them. The fee is $25.

Hunter's Feed

Main St., Ennis, Mont. • (406) 682- 4263

Local business owners kick off the hunting season and clean out their freezers by cooking up culinary delights using wild game. Residents get to hike up and down Main Street tasting all of the dishes, then vote on the winners of several categories. Past dishes have included wild pheasant with dill sauce, deer fudge, moose meatballs and elk chili. If you happen to be in Ennis about the third Saturday of October, step in line and help yourself. It's free.

November

Jackson Town Square Lighting Ceremony

Town Square, Jackson, Wyo. • (307) 733-3316

Santa Claus shows up to help light up the square; elves provide homemade cookies, hot cider and coffee. The Jackson Hole Community Band and Chorale play the songs of the holiday. Garlands bedeck the boardwalks and lights twinkle in the trees and antler arches of Jackson's town square. This event is always scheduled right after Thanksgiving to get folks focused on the next holiday in line.

Festival of Trees

640 E. Elva, Idaho Falls, Idaho • (208) 524-1550

Get in the Christmas spirit early and help raise money for disabled Idahoans. Festival of Trees, held each year at the Idaho Falls Elks Lodge, starts in mid-November and runs four days. Purchase a decorated tree (or donate one), visit 30 to 40 holiday booths and enjoy live entertainment ranging from elementary-school choirs to cloggers and other dance groups. You'll pay about $10 at the door for your family. Meals are available for purchase: soup, bagels, bread, baked potatoes and more.

Fall Camp Rendezvous

Ski Trails, West Yellowstone, Mont. • (406) 646-7701

As soon as there's enough snow on the 40 kilometers of Rendezvous Ski Trails, the word gets out and international nordic ski teams head for West Yellowstone to ski the finely groomed trails. Fall Camp ends with the weeklong ski clinic during Thanksgiving week. That same week, college, community and high school ski teams from across the nation come to West Yellowstone to get a head start on their winter training. For more information on the Ski Clinic, see the next entry.

Fall Clinic Rendezvous

Ski Trails, West Yellowstone, Mont. • (406) 646-7701

In the late 1970s locals began hosting a ski clinic that would attract cross-country skiers to their winter wonderland. The first year only a handful of people came. These days, though, the 160 slots in the Thanksgiving-week clinic are filled, with a long waiting list. The clinic includes several multi-day workshops and is tailored to meet individual needs. Participants can ski the snow-covered streets from their hotels right to the trails. The clinic ends with a couple of races. Entry fees differ depending on the length of the workshop.

December

Community Visual Arts Association Christmas Bazaar

Snow King Center, Snow King Ave., Jackson, Wyo. • (307) 733-8792

On the first Saturday of December, usually the day the ski lifts at Jackson Hole Mountain Resort open, locals have a tough decision to make. Should they head for the mountain or the jam-packed craft show at Snow King? Historically a locals'-only event, recent years have seen more visitors from nearby communities as the word gets out that this is a primo Christmas-shopping opportunity. Admission is a dollar.

Cowboy Christmas Ball

Buck's T-4 on U.S. Hwy. 191, Big Sky, Mont. • (406) 995-4111

Held at Buck's T-4 (see our Hotels, Motels and Cabins chapter) the first Saturday of December, this gala event brings skiers and snowmobilers out in their blue jeans and black ties. Admission for the dinner and dance costs $15 ahead of time and $20 at the door.

Island Park Snowcross

Henry's Lake Flats, U.S. Hwy. 20 at mile marker 396, Mack's Inn at Island Park

Imagine a moto-cross race on snow and ice, with low-slung snowmobiles executing those jumps and whipping turns. That's snowcross. Sanctioned by the Rocky Mountain Cross Country Racing Circuit, this race is now in its fifth year and growing fast. The first weekend of December can find as many as 200 racers in Island Park competing in categories that range from junior novice to pro. Spectators pay around $5 per day for a standing-area view of the action on the track.

Torchlight Parades

Jackson Hole, Snow King and Grand Targhee Ski Resorts • Jackson Hole (307) 733-2292, Snow King (307) 733-5200, Grand Targhee (208) 353-8148

A torchlit parade of skiers snakes down the dark mountain, surrounded by their own spreading glow. This visual treat is available at Grand Targhee and Jackson Hole on December 25. All three resorts sponsor a parade on New Year's Eve. Starting times depend on the weather.

Christmas Dinner and Dance

Locations vary in West Yellowstone, Wyo. • (307) 646-7701

Locals kick off the winter season with a dinner and dance held at the Yellowstone Conference Hotel Holiday Inn. For a peek into the world of those who serve tourists and keep the town going, and for a chance to dance away the night, step inside and trip the light fantastic with West's best. It's held the first or second weekend in December. Admission is less than $20.

Bozeman Christmas Stroll

Main St., Bozeman, Mont. • (406) 586-5421

On the first Saturday in December, from 4 to 7 PM, Bozeman's Main Street turns into a Christmas wonderland with sparkling lights, carolers, sleigh rides, food booths, arts and crafts and a gingerbread-house decorating contest for children. Admission is free.

From pig wrestling contests at the Park County Fair in Livingston to kids-only parades in Cody and Bozeman, families will find plenty to keep the younger set entertained.

Kidstuff

Skip rocks across a slow stretch of river. Or see how far you can throw them. Build yourself a fire and roast a hot dog. Better yet, roast marshmallows or make s'mores. Tell tall tales or play "Telephone" and laugh at how your secret has changed. Climb a tree. Walk a log. Hop from rock to rock. Play tic-tac-toe with a stick in the dirt. Carve yourself a walking stick. There are plenty of things for kids — and families — to do in Yellowstone country.

Besides all the fun you may discover on your own along the way, this book is chock-full of organized activities for kids and the young-at-heart to seek out — like horseback riding, dog sledding or riding in an old stagecoach. (See our various recreation chapters and our Attractions chapter to learn more about these things.)

Just to top it off, this chapter is a kaleidoscopic alphabet of just-for-kids stuff. We've tried to include the unusual, such as pig wrestling contests at the Park County Fair in Livingston or kids-only parades in Cody and Bozeman. As you will quickly see, this chapter is not arranged geographically, but we have listed the phone numbers and addresses for each entry to help you on your way.

Parents, you'll be happy to know that many kidstuff events listed in this chapter are either free or very inexpensive. And some are unusual enough that you may just want to veer off your planned course to be where the kid action is.

A

is for adventures in art, like drawing chalk pictures on Bozeman's downtown sidewalks during the **Sweet Pea Festival** each August. Or check out the **Emerson Cultural Center** and **Beall Park Art Center**, (406) 587-9797, 111 S. Grand Avenue in Bozeman, Montana, where you'll find a rainbow of art activities for kids after school and on Saturdays. Each year, these art and cultural centers offer classes in such activities as clay sculpture, dance, singing, painting and weaving.

B

is for the **Buffalo Bill Fast Draw Championship** at the Buffalo Bill Festival on a weekend in mid-August each year in Cody, Wyoming. Besides the Fast Draw Championship, which is held both days, there's a special festival just for you. At this same event in past years, kids participated in a bike rodeo, practiced roping and fly fishing, rode on a fire engine, had their faces painted and went for carriage rides for starters. To learn more about the Buffalo Bill Festival, call the Cody Chamber of Commerce at (307) 587-2777.

C

is for cowboy hats. Grab Mom or Dad by the hand and don't let go until they've bought you a cowboy hat. For a good selection at prices Mom might be willing to pay, go straight to a **Corral West Ranchwear**. These stores are in Cody, Wyoming, at two locations: 1202 Sheridan Avenue, (307) 587-2122; and 1625 Stampede Avenue, (307) 587-4493. In Bozeman, Montana, Corral West is at 1527 W. Main, (406) 586-8671, and in Livingston, Montana, Corral West is at 1106 W. Park Street. In Jackson, Wyoming, you'll find one of these jam-packed cowboy stores at 840 W. Broadway Avenue, (307) 733-0247. In Idaho Falls, go to Corral West at Grand Teton Mall, (208) 535-0326. Or try **Teton Kids**, 130 E. Broadway Avenue, Jackson, (307) 739-2176. They can outfit even the tiniest buckaroos. Or just keep your eyes open. There are ranch supply stores and even old-style dry goods mercantiles that sell hats in every town in Greater Yellowstone.

D

is for diving into a commercial hot-springs pool. This country is full of them. No matter where you go, look for the cool pool, too. Nothing's better than going back and forth between the two extremes. The Bozeman Hot Springs is great for this — the lip between the pools is curved and smooth so you can sort of slither back and forth (see below).

Try **Bozeman Hot Springs**, 81123 Gallatin Road, Bozeman, (406) 586-6492. Located right next to the Bozeman Hot Springs KOA, this hot spring features a small pool outside under the big sky or a big blue pool inside. In the Paradise Valley near Livingston, Montana, you can dip into the **Chico Hot Springs**, (406) 333-4933, at Pray, Montana. If Mom and Dad aren't in the mood for swimming, they'll love sitting poolside sipping lemonade while they watch you dive. Near Jackson, Wyoming, try **Granite Creek Hot Springs**, way out in the woods with shaded picnic spots on nearby Granite Creek. It's on Granite Creek Road, 10 miles off U.S. Highway 191, (307) 739-5400. More convenient is **Astoria Hot Springs**, also near Jackson. Located on U.S. Highway 89 outside Hoback Junction, (307) 733-2659, Astoria has camping, a snack bar and lots of grass to run and play on when you get tired of the water. It also has a nice patio overlooking the pools for parents whose idea of a good time is a long, slow soak in the sun. Near Idaho Falls, Idaho, check out **Heise Hot Springs** at 5116 E. Heise Road, Ririe, Idaho, (208) 538-7312. At the foot of bluffs that box the Snake River Canyon, Heise has a soaking pool and two play pools, along with camping and picnicking. Best of all is the big waterslide. South of Idaho Falls, try **Lava Hot Springs Inn and Spa**, 94 E. Portneuf Avenue, Lava Hot Springs, Idaho, (208) 776-5830 or (800) 527-5830. It has three pools that range in temperature from about 90 degrees to more than 106.

is for elk bugles. Buy one at a sporting goods store almost anyplace in Yellowstone country and drive your parents crazy while you learn to produce the whistling call of a real elk bugling. Cow calls are cheaper and easier to use than the bull elk bugles, by the way. Don't bugle in the parks, though, because it's illegal.

F

is for fishing in easy-to-catch-a-fish ponds. If you throw your line into the **Bozeman Pond** on the west end of town next to the Main Mall, 2825 W. Main Street, chances are good that you'll hook onto a rainbow, brook or brown trout. String your fish on a stick, Tom Sawyer-style, pick a piece of grass to hold in your mouth like a giant toothpick, then take your fish home and ask Ma to cook them up for dinner. (If you aren't a fish eater, ask her, "pretty please," if she'll cook you up a hot dog — then watch her eat the fish you caught.) Teton Valley, Idaho, and Jackson, Wyoming, both have kids-only fishing spots. In Jackson it's **Flat Creek**, which meanders sedately across town and is reserved just for kids within city limits. In Teton Valley, it's the **Trail Creek**

INSIDERS' TIP

Tell mom to look up Blast Off in the Attractions chapter if you end up with some extra time for fun in Idaho Falls. It's like an indoor playground, only better. Big kids (and kids-at-heart) can play laser tag or video games. Little kids get their own play areas and toys.

Pond at the base of Teton Pass, fenced safely away from Idaho Highway 33, surrounded by blooming yellow mules' ears and bright green picnic tables. Wherever you are, call a local fishing shop. The folks there will know where to send you.

Photo: Steve Fischbach, Post Register

A young buckaroo hangs on for dear life.

G

is for golf — miniature golf, that is. In Cody, Wyoming, the lush **Cody Mini Golf Course**, (307) 587-3685, is right across from the Chamber of Commerce on Sheridan Avenue. Owned by the city, this golf course is open from Memorial Day until Labor Day. In summertime in Jackson, Wyoming, you can play miniature golf at the base of **Snow King Mountain**. Call (307) 733-5200. In Idaho Falls, Idaho, the indoor **Land of Enchantment** is open year round at the Plaza Lanes Building, 1811 N. Yellowstone Highway, (208) 523-3985.

If you like miniature golf and your folks are looking for a place to camp in Idaho Falls, tell them to check out the **Idaho Falls KOA Kampground** at 1440 Lindsay Boulevard, (208) 523-3362. This place has its own private course for patrons. One really fun course in Idaho Falls is at **Tautphaus Park Funland**, 395 Sunken Diamond Drive, (208) 525-9814. Shoo your little brother toward the merry-go-round and try your hand at 18 challenging holes. Putt into a fiberglass rabbit, through four revolving barrels or up a ramp to jump a sticky obstacle. Some longer holes have multiple obstacles. No two are alike.

H

is for horseback riding. Put on that new cowboy hat, boots and belt, look that wrangler square in the eye and tell him, "Pardner, I've got a hankerin' to ride one of your hosses." You'll find horses waiting for you at **The Bill Cody Ranch**, 2604 Yellowstone Highway, Cody, (307) 587-6271. The wranglers here will take you for a ride right into the mountains where the elk roam. After the ride, you and your parents can eat a delicious dinner in the log lodge or outside chuckwagon style, depending on what day you go. In West Yellowstone, Montana, try out the horses at the **Parade Rest Guest Ranch**, 7979 Grayling Road, (406) 646-7217, about 9 miles north of town. (See our Other Recreation chapter for more on these ranches.)

Other good bets are at **Flagg Ranch**

INSIDERS' TIP

Allen's Diamond Four Ranch, P.O. Box 243, Lander, WY 82520, (307) 332-2995, offers 14-day classes to teach kids ages 9 through 15 wilderness skills like camping, horsemanship, riflery, fishing, axemanship, orienteering, map reading, cooking, safety and first aid. You get to ride a section of the Oregon Trail with camping gear pulled in a horse-drawn chuckwagon. Write for a catalog.

near Yellowstone's south entrance, (307) 543-2861; at **Snow King Resort** in Jackson, Wyoming, (307) 733-5781; at **Jackson Lake Lodge** within **Grand Teton National Park**, (307) 543-2811; and with **Jackson Hole Trail Rides** in Teton Village, (307) 733-6992. In Island Park, Idaho, there's great riding within **Harriman State Park**, (208) 558-7077. A short drive from Idaho Falls can find you near Ririe at **Granite Creek Guest Ranch**, a real working cattle ranch that also rents horses for short rides. Call (208) 538-7140.

I

is for "I scream, you scream, we all scream for ice cream!" If you've got that ice-cream-screaming urge, look in any **Hamilton Store** in Yellowstone National Park for **Wilcoxson's Ice Cream**, made in Livingston, Montana, at 314 S. Main Street, (406) 222-2370. This old-fashioned creamy ice cream comes in 50 flavors and has been made in Livingston since 1912. Try the Peanut Butter Chip, Huckleberry, Cookies and Cream or Pecan Praline. Look for Wilcoxson's outside the park, in West Yellowstone and other Montana towns.

In Swan Valley, Idaho, the I-scream stop is at the **Swan Valley Commissary**, locally famous for its hand-dipped, square ice creams. Look for the Commissary at the intersection of U.S. Highway 26 and Idaho Highway 31, (208) 483-2151. Teton Valley may be the Huckleberry Shake capital of the world, so make sure you stop at the **Victor Emporium** for an old-fashioned treat made with handpicked local huckleberries and lots of smooth, rich ice cream. Victor Emporium is at 45 N. Main Street in Victor, Idaho, (208) 787-2221. Around Ashton, you can get a fine milk shake served by a former real carhop. This'll be a blast from the past for your parents, so be sure you make them stop at the **Frostop Drive-in**, 26 N. U.S. Highway 20, Ashton, Idaho. The tater tots aren't bad, either.

J

is for jumping into the **Firehole River Swimming Hole** in Yellowstone National Park. Pack a picnic and steer your parents toward Firehole Canyon Drive (you'll see it on the Yellowstone National Park map they give you at the entrance gate). The road is just south of Madison Junction on the west side of the Madison-Old Faithful Road. Keep on going until you come to the Firehole River Swimming Hole. You can't miss it unless you have your eyes closed. Wear your life jacket and float in the water from one end of the hole to the next. Or stick to the swimming hole off the tiny beach.

If the weather's not right for outdoor swimming, do your jumping at the **Teton County/ Jackson Parks and Recreation Center**. Summer and winter, you can play on the two-story water slide, hide behind the waterfall, swirl in the whirlpool or giggle on the geyser. Find this watery playground at 155 W. Gill Street in Jackson, Wyoming; call (307) 739-9025. For a real small-town, old-fashioned swimming hole, stop at St. Anthony near Rexburg, Idaho for a dip in a slow bend of the **Snake River**. There's a diving board, a valiant attempt at a beach (they trucked the sand in), a waterslide made from irrigation pipe and often a volunteer lifeguard. Find the swimming hole across from the city park, but be aware that it's best-suited for competent, confident swimmers: The water is cold, and just downstream is a concrete diversion pour-over that big kids play with and parents watch closely.

INSIDERS' TIP

If your parents are driving through Idaho Falls and need to stop for a bunch of groceries, ask them to shop at Fred Meyer. It's got a supervised little-kid play area where you can drop off your irritating baby brother. The store's at 1555 Northgate Mile, (208) 535-2520.

K

is for kids-only parades. Dress your dog like a clown, put him in your little red wagon, don your most outrageous gypsy outfit and head for Main Street with all the other kooky kids in town. Cody, Wyoming has a kids-only parade every July 2 during its **Stampede Rodeo**. Bozeman, Montana, has a kids-only parade the first Saturday of December when the town holds their Christmas stroll. We suggest you check with the Cody Chamber of Commerce, (307) 587-2777, 836 Sheridan Avenue, and the Bozeman Chamber of Commerce, (406) 586-5421 or (800) 228-4224, 1205 E. Main Street, to learn the exact times and starting points for these parades.

L

is for learning more about the ins and outs of Greater Yellowstone. In Cody, Wyoming, you can catch hands-on, kids-only workshops at the **Buffalo Bill Historical Center**, 720 Sheridan Avenue, (307) 587-4771. If your family is planning to be in Cody for a while, check into multi-day workshops offered July through August. Each year, kids learn to paint with Western artists and write songs with cowboy songsters. In the past, they've also learned to powwow dance with Native Americans and tool leather with a saddlemaker.

Both **Teton Science School** and **Snake River Institute** offer classes for kids, too, mostly in summer (Teton Science School also has great winter programs for area schools and school groups). Teton Science School, within Grand Teton National Park, is all about nature: Lucky students spend as much as six weeks learning hands-on about ecology and the natural world while they live in cabins within the park. Nonresidential programs are also available for kids and adults. Call (307) 733-4765 or see our Education chapter.

Last but not least, Yellowstone and Grand Teton parks are home to **ranger-naturalist programs** that can teach you about elk, bears and bison, geysers and forest fires and how the mountains were formed. In Yellowstone National Park, check the Yellowstone Today newspaper that the ranger will give you at the entrance gate; Grand Teton's newspaper, available at all visitors centers and park entrances, is called *Teewinot*. Inside you'll find descriptions of available programs. You can also check the bulletin board at your campground for a schedule of evening campfire talks. Often the evening programs are geared for children and adults.

M

is for museums. Hold on a minute. Before you say "Yuck," "Yawn" and "Do we have to?", we know of a couple of museums that are pretty darn fun for kids. The **Museum of the Rockies**, 600 W. Kagy Boulevard, Bozeman, Montana, (406) 994-2251, is home to T-Rex, one giant dinosaur skeleton (he takes up a whole big room) pieced together from bones found near Jordan, Montana. In the rest of the museum, you'll find lots of buttons to push and handles to pull. Upstairs may be the best part, though. The Martin Discovery Room, equipped with puzzles, puppets and other activities, is made especially for kids. A half-hour east of the Museum of the Rockies, T-Rex's relatives hang out in **The Natural History Exhibit Hall**, 120 E. Park Street, Livingston, Montana (406) 222-5335. Except for some neat small displays such as frog and dragonfly fossils, you may be the smallest critter here. The skeletons of giant mastodons, prehistoric elephants and pigs, and a dozen dinosaurs dug up in China, stand together to dismay your mind.

Or get your parents to bring you to the

INSIDERS' TIP

Fish hatcheries are great places to learn more about trout. Some hatcheries also have feeding ponds where you can purchase a handful of fish food and attract trout as long as your arm.

Photo: Robert Bower, Post Register

Young entrants in the Pioneer Days parade in St. Anthony.

National Museum of Wildlife Art north of Jackson, Wyoming. The children's gallery lets you interact with art; for instance, you get to redesign famous wildlife art masterpieces just the way you like them — all the paintings' parts have been cut apart and made into magnets. You're the artist! The museum is at 2820 Rungius Road off U.S. Highway 26, (307) 733-5771.

The **Bonneville Museum**, 200 N. Eastern Avenue, Idaho Falls, (208) 522-1400, is worth the visit just for the Main Street Eagle Rock display downstairs, where a series of storefronts chock-full of cool old stuff recreate the town of yesteryear. The museum features hands-on displays — most recently, a chance to run the kind of remote control grippers used to move nuclear waste from behind thick glass walls. Admission is $2 for adults. The museum is open Monday through Friday, and Saturday afternoon. See our Attractions chapter for more about the Bonneville Museum.

In Cody, be sure to go to the **Old West Miniature Village and Museum**, 142 W. Yellowstone Highway, (307) 587-5362. The owner began carving and painting animals and people for this miniature depiction of Western history at age 14. There's more about this museum in our Attractions chapter. Kids can see it for $1.

N

is for navigating the **Children's Fire Trail** near Mammoth Hot Springs in Yellowstone National Park. This trail is only a half-mile (that's about six city blocks). It winds through forest that was burned in 1988. Signs along the way tell you about the fire and invite you to get down on your hands and knees to look for new life sprouting up through the burn. If you get tired of looking at the signs, you can always race your parents or your brothers and sisters back to the car.

O

is for ordering dinner at Jackson,

INSIDERS' TIP

In Yellowstone National Park, fishing permits are required for children older than 11.

Wyoming's, **Calico** or **Vista Grande**, at **Choices** in Idaho Falls, Idaho, or at **Dornan's Chuckwagon** in Grand Teton National Park. All four are extremely kid-friendly. Calico, Vista Grande and Dornan's offer outdoor seating (in season) and run-and-play space. Calico and Vista Grande face each other across a huge lawn safely away from the road. Kids eating at either restaurant are welcome to use the contents of the toy box on Calico's deck. Find Calico, which serves Italian food, on Teton Village Road near Teton Village, (307) 733-2460. Vista Grande, a Mexican restaurant, is next door, (307) 733-6964. Dornan's Chuckwagon, open in summertime only, serves up its selection of barbecued sandwiches and treats at 10 Moose Street off the Teton Park Road at Moose Junction, (307) 733-2415. Choices has no grassy lawn to play on, but it does serve the most varied, family-favorites menu you're likely to find: burgers, pizza, prime rib and steak. Find them at 1869 N. Yellowstone Highway in Idaho Falls, or call (208) 523-2131.

P

is for pig races at the **Bear Creek Saloon**, 108 W. Main Street, (406) 446-3481, in Bearcreek near Red Lodge, Montana. People drive from all over to this tiny town so they can eat a steak dinner (kids may prefer their juicy burgers) then watch the pig races outside. The pigs run from their cages to the other end of the track where a trough of food is waiting.

P is also for pig wrestling contests at the **Park County Fair** in Livingston, Montana. On Friday of fair weekend (it's either the last weekend in July or the first weekend in August, depending on when the fair board can schedule a carnival) 40 four-person teams wrestle muddy pigs into a 55-gallon drum. The teams jump into the very muddy pen with a 150-pound pig, then have 30 seconds to get it into the barrel and stand the barrel upright. It's a hoot to watch.

Q

is for quiet time with books from stores that feature a strong selection of kids' favorite reading material. Some of our favorites are **Valley Bookstore** in Jackson, Wyoming, 125 N. Cache Street, (307) 733-4533; **Deseret Book Company** in Idaho Falls, Idaho, at the Grand Teton Mall, 2300 E. 17th Street, (208) 523-5061; or Idaho Falls' **Barnes & Noble Booksellers**, 2385 E. 17th Street, (208) 522-1010.

In addition to selling great books, Barnes & Noble hosts a year-round Saturday morning Story Time for kids. A staff member shares a favorite children's book every Saturday morning at 11 o'clock. A scattering of other literary activities for kids is available as well. Call Barnes & Noble for a calendar or stop by.

Visitor centers in both Yellowstone and Grand Teton parks sell an enticing array of kids' books that can teach you about wildlife and park wonders.

R

is for rodeo — for kids. Nearly all area rodeos offer a kids' event. Sometimes it's mutton busting, where participants try to ride a sheep. Sometimes it's calf riding. Sheep bolt and calves buck, so it's hard to say which is more fun to watch or harder to do. You usually have to sign up in advance if you want to rodeo, but in Cody, Wyoming, at the **Cody Nite Rodeo**, 421 W. Yellowstone Avenue, (307) 587-2992, announcers invite kids out of the stands to join in the rodeo fun. In the calf scramble, a calf with dollar bills stuck to it (sometimes it's someone's pet milk cow) is turned loose in the arena. A herd of kids chases the calf around the arena trying to grab the bills off the calf. Be forewarned: Wooly sheep and darting calves have hard hooves and heads, which means these events aren't for the fainthearted. Kids occasionally do get injured, sometimes just from colliding with each other.

At Jackson Hole's twice-weekly **J.H. Rodeo**, two unlucky calves have ribbons tied to their tails. Fifty to 100 kids ages 4 to 11 try to capture the ribbons to win. J.H. Rodeo is held at the fairgrounds on Snow King Avenue in Jackson, Wyoming, (307) 733-2805, from Memorial Day to Labor Day. Check our Rodeo chapter for other rodeo times and locations.

S

is for skating on ice. In Bozeman, Montana, there are three free ice-skating rinks. At **Southside Park** on West College Avenue at S. Seventh Avenue, you can play hockey or just skate. **Beall Park** at Villard and Black streets offers broomball on certain days of the week and recreational skating the rest of the time. Or play hockey at **Bogert Park** at 325 S. Church Avenue. West Yellowstone, Montana, makes a skating rink each winter on Electric Street, and there's a nifty skating rink at the **Mammoth Hotel** in Yellowstone National Park. (In case you forgot to bring skates, the Mammoth Hotel will rent skates to you and your whole family.)

In Jackson, Wyoming, you can pay a few bucks to skate at the indoor **Snow King Center Ice Rink** at 100 E. Snow King Avenue, (307) 733-5200. Dad and Mom can relax with a hot chocolate or a snack while you skim across the ice. The rink is open from August to mid-April. Call first, though, because the rink hosts a range of events and isn't always available for public use.

You can also ice skate at the **Tautphaus** (say it TOFF-us) **Park** hockey rink in Idaho Falls, Idaho, (208) 529-0941. Hours can vary, but usually there's public skate time every day, winter only. And at **Grand Targhee** in Alta, Wyoming, you can ice skate for free (if you have your own skates) outside in the tennis courts. The ski resort floods the court and rents skates to those who just don't feel like skiing right now. Call Grand Targhee at (800) 827-4433 or (307) 353-2300, or drive on up Ski Hill Road out of Driggs, Idaho.

U

is for utterly confusing your parents on **Uncle Tom's Trail**. Make them (or your siblings) count the steps leading down into the Grand Canyon on Uncle Tom's Trail in Yellowstone National Park. Can you count past 300? (To find the Grand Canyon of the Yellowstone River, look at that map you'll get at the park's entrance.) Turn east off the Canyon-Lake road onto South Rim Drive. Stop at Uncle Tom's parking lot, pile out of the car and look for the signs telling where to go. We must warn you, this is a very strenuous walk, so if anybody in your family has a health problem, you'd better skip this one.

V

is for **Virginia City**, Montana. This is one great old mining town with plenty for kids to do. Play the nickelodeons in the Bale of Hay Saloon. Go to a melodrama (you get to hoot, boo and hiss with the rest of the crowd) at the Virginia City Players. Fish in the kids-only fishing pond at Nevada City. Go to Boot Hill and check out the headstones of the Plummer Gang. Or ride the narrow-gauge railroad from Virginia City to Nevada City 3 miles away.

X

is for x-ing off the pictures of each animal on page eight of your Yellowstone National Park Junior Ranger Activity Paper for kids 8 to 12 years old. (They have one for younger kids, too.) At the end of your park visit, you can turn your activity paper in. If you've done everything required, you become a Junior Ranger

INSIDERS' TIP

Allen's Diamond Four Ranch, P.O. Box 243, Lander, WY 82520, (307) 332-2995, offers 14-day classes to teach kids ages 9 through 15 wilderness skills like camping, horsemanship, riflery, fishing, axemanship, orienteering, map reading, cooking, safety and first aid. You get to ride a section of the Oregon Trail with camping gear pulled in a horse-drawn chuckwagon. Write for a catalog.

and get a patch to prove it. In order to qualify, you must attend at least one ranger-naturalist program, view a visitor center or roadside exhibit and tell about it, take a walk on a park trail, read and understand the Junior Ranger pledge and understand six basic park rules. You must also do a certain number of pages of your activity paper. For $2 you can buy one of these at any one of the visitor centers in Yellowstone National Park.

Y

is for yummy candy. The **Montana Candy Emporium**, 7 S. Broadway Avenue, Red Lodge, Montana, (406) 446-1119, has 2,300 kinds of candy. While you're drooling over the other candy, you can watch the owners make Killer Fudge or Gooseberry Bark right in the store.

In Jackson, Wyoming, don't miss the **Yippy I-O Candy Co.** at 84 E. Broadway Ave., (307) 739-3020. This shop is lined with barrels, baskets and jars full of candy — every color and flavor you can imagine plus a few that will surprise — including hand-dipped chocolates, sugar-free candies, saltwater taffy and various kinds of huckleberry treats. The cream and butter fudge is made fresh in the store.

In Idaho Falls, stop by **Sarah's Candy Cottage** near Grand Teton Mall at 1503 E. 17th Street, (208) 528-0499. These folks carry truffles, hard candies, chocolate roses, Jelly Bellies and yummy imported treats from around the world. They even deliver!

Z

is for **Tautphaus Park Zoo**, 2725 Carnival Way, (208) 529-1470, and **Tautphaus Park Funland**, 395 Sunken Diamond Drive, (208) 525-9814, in Idaho Falls, Idaho. The zoo houses more than 250 critters, including endangered snow leopards, Siberian tigers and ring-tailed and red-ruffed lemurs. In the Children's Zoo, you can feed goats and sheep and pet the donkey. Funland is more than 50 years old. Its first ride, still operating today, was a merry-go-round with 30 leaping horses and two chariots. Now it has four more rides and an 18-hole miniature golf course (see "G" for golf, above). You pay by the ride; it's free to walk about the amusement park or wander to the concession stand to buy a sandwich or a snack. Both zoo and Funland are open seven days a week in spring and summer, and many weekends through the fall. Both close for the winter.

Nurtured by the students and staff of Montana State University, the arts community in Bozeman has grown to include several dance and acting groups, a couple of orchestras, the Emerson Cultural Center and a rich menu of arts workshops and presentations each year.

The Arts

In 1982, Joel Jahnke, artistic director of Bozeman's Montana Shakespeare in the Parks, was setting up for a production of Moliere's *Imaginary Invalid* atop Poker Jim Butte in eastern Montana. Next to the stage were the Poker Jim Fire Lookout, a small campground and a one-holer outhouse. The closest town was Birney, Montana, population 23. Jahnke looked at his cohorts, shook his head and said, "This is crazy. Nobody's going to come here." About an hour before show time, from every direction far below the butte, tiny plumes of dust shot up behind pickup trucks full of ranchers speeding to Poker Jim Butte. By show time, there were nearly 200 people perched on lawn chairs and sprawled on picnic blankets, awaiting a taste of culture under Montana's big sky.

While Birney is a stretch outside Greater Yellowstone (it's just south of the Northern Cheyenne Indian Reservation in eastern Montana), the thirst for culture is not. In Montana alone, there are more than 200 nonprofit arts organizations, more than 200 art galleries and more than 130 museums. In Southwestern Montana, and in Greater Yellowstone, Bozeman is a center for the arts. Nurtured by the students and staff of Montana State University, the arts community has grown (mostly in the last 25 years) to include several dance and acting groups, a couple of orchestras, the Emerson Cultural Center (see its write-up in this chapter) and a rich menu of arts workshops and presentations each year.

Even in the most rural areas of Greater Yellowstone, you'll find a few towns with tiny, volunteer-driven arts councils and organizations working hard to bring artists, musicians, actors, dancers and entertainers to their communities. In some communities, you'll find people making their own music through chamber orchestras, old-time fiddler groups, community plays, dance groups, choirs, cowboy poetry gatherings, artist workshops and music camps. At county fairs you'll see a sampling of artistic endeavors in booths where locals have entered their work for judging. In many cases, the art grows out of the local lifestyle and the pursuit of personal passions. Flower arranging, photography, watercolor and oil paintings, quilting and even canning and baking entries display skills honed to artistic achievement.

Bozeman's not the only cultural hot spot. At the southern end of Greater Yellowstone is Jackson, Wyoming, a town that prides itself on its art galleries (there are more than 30). Clustered around town square, these galleries represent both undiscovered and nationally known artists working in every medium imaginable. To the north in Montana, art galleries have sprung up in Livingston, longtime home to a growing enclave of writers and artists. Galleries are also starting to bud in Red Lodge to the east; and the number of galleries in Cody is also growing. In large part, gallery owners in Jackson (and elsewhere in Greater Yellowstone) are promoting and selling the same thing: a piece of the West in general, and Greater Yellowstone in particular.

In many places, the arts scene isn't as readily visible as in Jackson or Bozeman. If you dig, though, you'll find a budding (and sometimes struggling) cultural renaissance all over Greater Yellowstone. Inside the parks, there are few organized artistic programs. However, endless opportunities to study the artistry of nature exist everywhere in Yellowstone country.

In this chapter, we'll tell you, by region, where to find dance, music and other artists who practice and perform in Greater Yellowstone. We'll also tell you about some of the art galleries along the way. Our list of galleries is by no means all-inclusive. Because so many rise and fall within a few years of opening, we have first chosen to list those that have been in business the longest. We have also included galleries that Insiders appreciate for their unique artwork. We suggest that as you tour Greater Yellowstone, you keep your eyes peeled for art that suits you. It is often hanging quietly in restaurants, office buildings, banks, gift shops and furniture stores. Finally, we have featured a few of the organizations that support the arts in Greater Yellowstone.

www.insiders.com
See this and many other
Insiders' Guide
destinations online.
Visit us today!

Jackson Hole

Jackson, Wyoming, Area

Art Organizations

The Art Association
260 W. Pearl Ave., Jackson, Wyo.
• (307) 733-6379

The Art Association showcases experimental juried non-Western art, attracting talented artists from around the country. One popular annual show exhibits the top entries from the Arts for the Parks contest. This international competition draws thousands of entries depicting scenes from the nation's national parks and national monuments. The top 200 tour the country with stopovers at Jackson Lake Lodge and at the Ranch Inn, then move on to the Art Association. The top five become postage stamps. At least four additional shows are oriented toward the local art community each year.

The Art Association also sponsors art outreach into local schools and open studio sessions in which you can draw, paint or sculpt from a nude or clothed model for a small fee ($6 in 1998). An associated art school offers short courses in photography, darkroom technique, watercolor and oil painting and more. Classes for kids are available, as is a computer for public Internet access.

Performing Arts

Grand Teton Music Festival
Walk Festival Hall, Teton Village, Wyo.
• (307) 733-1128

Now in its 38th season, the Grand Teton Music Festival is a composite orchestra made up of talented musicians from all over. The 175-member company spends most of July and August playing traditional and contemporary music in the shadow of the Tetons. Appearances by world-class guest conductors, soloists and artists ice an already sweet cake. Last year Minnesota Orchestra's Eiji Oue (a former protégé of Leonard Bernstein) debuted as music director. Full orchestra, spotlight and chamber music concerts alternate days, Tuesday through Saturday. In addition to concerts, you may attend pre-concert talks with composers, post-concert talks with the music director, open orchestra rehearsals, Fourth of July celebration and two young people's concerts. Ticket prices range from around $15 for chamber music concerts to almost $30 for full-orchestra concerts.

Museums

National Museum of Wildlife Art
2820 Rungius Rd. off U.S. Hwy. 26 near Jackson, Wyo. • (307) 733-5771

This museum building, with its startling, award-winning design, will remind you of a crumbling pueblo or an ancient castle. It opened in the fall of 1997. It has been completely funded by donations from more than 600 individuals, foundations and corporations. The museum is next to the National Elk Refuge, as if to place the art as close to its inspiration as possible. Twelve exhibit rooms house special shows and a permanent collection that includes the work of greats such as John Clymer, C.M. Russell, Frederic Remington, Titian Ramsey Peale and Albert Bierstadt. The auditorium hosts films, symposiums and lectures, some of them free. Past events have included the Wildlife Film Festival, the weeklong Photography at the Summit workshop, a lecture and slide show on saddlemaking and another on the history of Navajo textiles (ask for a calendar at the desk).

The museum is open seven days a week, summer and winter. In spring and fall, Sunday hours are shortened. The adult admission fee is $6. The on-premises Rising Sage Cafe serves light meals during museum hours.

Galleries

Jackson prides itself on its art galleries, most focusing on high-quality Western and wildlife art. There are more than 30 galleries in the Hole, with new ones opening nearly every year. Most of our picks were recommended by gallery owners and artists; nearly all are an easy walk from each other and town square, so park your car and spend an afternoon enjoying the Jackson art scene.

Caswell Gallery of Jackson Hole
145 E. Broadway Ave., Jackson, Wyo.
• (307) 734-2660

Sculptor Rip Caswell has filled his large gallery with both representational bronze wildlife studies and more whimsical ones. Many of the pieces are his work. The gallery features a small outdoor sculpture garden where life-size statues of children, deer and other creatures are guarded by a startlingly huge grizzly bear. Because Rip owns his own foundry he maintains more control over his art, unlike most bronze sculptors, who contract out one or more steps in the sculpting process. Rip is also a former award-winning taxidermist: His familiarity with the animals he sculpts is apparent. The gallery may close Sundays during spring and fall, but the outdoor sculpture garden is always accessible.

Center Street Gallery
110 Center St., Jackson, Wyo.
• (307) 733-1115

Its sculptures are of wildlife, all right, but they're slant-lined, elongated and shaped from poly-resin, stone and steel as well as the traditional bronze. When Beth Overcast opened Center Street in 1987, no local gallery focused on abstract expressionism, bold colors or startling shapes. She decided to do something about that. Much of the work Overcast displays is one-of-a-kind. She selects pieces that seem to her stimulating, alive and active. Two of her more popular artists are Taos-based painter

Malcolm Furlow, who renders traditional Western subjects in startling colors and simple lines, and Colorado-based Mary Jane Schmidt, who paints large, boldly colored abstracts and florals. Also popular (and affordable) are Idaho resident Jane Wooster Scott's Americana depictions of Jackson. Center Street closes on Sundays during the spring and fall.

Shippen Sculpture Studio

No credit cards • 185 N. Center St., Jackson, Wyo. • (307) 733-6171

Shippen's little gallery isn't easy to find unless you know it's on the second floor of the Home Ranch building, accessed through a sort of back door. You're not stopping here to take in an extensive collection of painting and sculpture. What you'll see is Shippen's work and that of a few friends and select acquaintances — and you'll probably meet Shippen himself. He creates much of his bronze sculpture in the little studio attached to this little gallery. Shippen's subjects are both human and animal, slightly stylized and intricately detailed.

This Wyoming native, whose work is in private collections and museums around the world, has been sculpting Western figures since 1975. When he's not working in one of his two studios, he often goes out into nearby mountains and works on location. Shippen conducts summer art workshops for those with a hankering to become artists. The gallery is open Monday through Saturday in summer, and Tuesday through Saturday with abbreviated hours in winter, fall and spring. You may also call for an appointment.

Images of Nature

170 N. Cache St., Jackson, Wyo. • (307) 733-9752

Thomas Mangelsen's wildlife photography is internationally famous and locally beloved. Of his 12 galleries in six states, the Jackson location was first. Mangelsen sells limited edition prints of his striking wildlife images. If your budget is tight, you can shop the gallery for his cards, books and posters. Upstairs you may view videos about Mangelsen and his photography. The large Jackson gallery is open seven days a week, year-round.

The Legacy Gallery

150 Center St., Jackson, Wyo. • (307) 733-2353

Like many Jackson galleries, The Legacy specializes in traditional, representational Western art. Wildlife, landscape, Native American and cowboy subjects abound, as does sporting art featuring anglers and hunters. You'll find Teton scenes here as well. Showcased on a table with legs made from the arcing horns of Texas Longhorns, the work of several award-winning jewelers is represented in silver and gold, turquoise and other semiprecious gems. Jewelry ranges in price from $80 to $10,500. The Legacy prides itself on catering not only to the experienced art collector, but also to the novice: Staff members help you educate yourself about specific artists and the collecting world. The Legacy closes on winter Sundays.

Light Reflections Gallery

35 E. Deloney Ave., Jackson, Wyo. • (307) 733-4016, (800) 346-5223

One of three photo galleries we recommend in Jackson, Light Reflections showcases the work of landscape photographer Frederic Joy. Not only has Joy done breathtaking work with the local breathtaking scenery, but his photos of seascape, desert and sandstone turn the contours of land, water, sky and rock into abstract compositions of shape and color. Joy hand

INSIDERS' TIP

If you enjoy the art gallery scene, come for the Jackson Hole Fall Arts Festival in September. Activities range from a banquet to a "quick-draw" competition for artists, and every gallery puts on its best show. For more information, call the Jackson Hole Chamber of Commerce at (307) 733-3316.

Photo: Buffalo Bill Historical Center

The Whitney Gallery of Western Art shows the work of artists who captured the West's mythical beauty.

prints all of his work, so what you see on the wall is exactly what the artist envisioned. Another good reason to stop by Light Reflections is affordability. Small matted prints of Joy's work, full-size posters of his and other fine Western photography, even greeting cards and books, can satisfy your desire to own lovely art without paying gallery prices. Light Reflections generally closes Sundays in spring and fall.

Martin-Harris Gallery

60 E. Broadway Ave., Jackson, Wyo. • (307) 733-0350, (800) 366-7814

This 7,000-square-foot gallery hosts contemporary Western art at its most striking and whimsical. There's nothing here without surprise capability, but the most fun pieces aren't the paintings or the sculptures. They're furniture. As many as 30 furniture artisans showcase work here — leather, wood and forged steel pieces ranging from fanciful to stolid. Every piece is unique. Many of these artisans will also work with you, creating your offbeat dream couch, chair or armoire. Among the more than 40 artists represented here are John Nieto, Nelson Boren, Bill Schenk, Donna Howell-Sickles and Anne Coe. The gallery closes Sundays in spring and fall.

Mountain Trails Gallery

172 Center St., Jackson, Wyo. • (307) 734-8150

This gallery belongs to bronze sculptor Vic Payne. His work and that of other bronze artists is well represented here. So are works by the very collectible Russian artist Oleg Stavrowsky, whose oil paintings Payne displays by special arrangement. Although themes and subjects tend toward traditional Western, some treatments are more impressionistic than representational. Mountain Trails also showcases the work of emerging young sculptors. Sometimes you'll find them working on their pieces in the gallery. When we were there, 20-year-old Chris Schiller was putting the finishing touches on the clay version of a rioting elk sculpture. Mountain Trails may close Sundays in winter.

Trailside Galleries

105 N. Center St., Jackson, Wyo. • (307) 733-3186

This is one of the oldest galleries in Jackson and one of the largest Western galleries in the country. Trailside specializes in representational treatments of Western scenes, wildlife, mountain landscapes and Native Americans. More than 60 artists, many of them members of the Cowboy Artists of America, have pieces displayed here. Some of these artists are very collectible: Clyde Aspevig, a landscape painter of increasing renown, and G. Harvey, whose busy but somehow cozy 19th-century city scenes are a pleasant contrast to cowboys, elk and mountains, are both represented. You can also view many smaller table sculptures. The showcased sculptors work in monumental scale as well.

Two Grey Hills Indian Arts & Jewelry

Corner of Broadway and King, Jackson, Wyo. • (307) 733-2677

Two Grey Hills names both an area in New Mexico and the fine Navajo weavings produced there. It's a perfect moniker for this high-end gallery, now in its 22nd year, which specializes in one-of-a-kind Native American art. Pottery, weavings and jewelry, much of it museum quality, cram the little shop. You'll find jewelry you can easily afford and pieces you'll want to keep in your safety deposit box; you'll find weavings ranging between $100 and $16,000. Two Grey Hills closes some Sundays in winter.

Wilcox Gallery

1975 N. U.S. Hwy. 89, Jackson, Wyo. • (307) 733-6450

If you're wondering why we'd send you clear out of town, nearly to the Wildlife Art Museum, you won't after you've wandered through the work featured here. First, it's not all Western. If you've been to other galleries in town, you're probably ready for paintings from two popular Chinese artists, or wooden bowls so finely carved they're translucent, or unique wooden boxes whose only decoration is the scalloped live edge, sometimes with bark still attached, wavering across the front of the lid. But the biggest reason to come out here is Jim Wilcox, local landscape painter, whose work is showcased here and whose son manages the gallery. Wilcox's work has received seven awards from the Arts for the Parks competition, where artists from around the world celebrate this nation's national parks and monuments. One piece is part of the permanent collection at the Cowboy Hall of Fame in Oklahoma. If you're looking for an inexpensive souvenir rather than fine art, check out the Jim Wilcox T-shirts and posters.

Wilcox first came here in 1959 for the series of summer jobs that put him through college. He fell in love with Jackson then, and when the time came to open his own gallery in 1969, he opened it here. Wilcox Gallery is open Monday through Saturday year round, with shorter hours in winter.

Wild by Nature Gallery

95 W. Deloney Ave., Jackson Wyo. • (307) 733-8877

Henry Holdsworth is a wildlife/nature photographer whose work has appeared in such publications as *National Geographic World*, *Audubon*, *Nature Conservancy* and others. Enjoy his vision of the natural world in this small gallery, which sells limited edition prints of Holdsworth's work, as well as cards, calendars and books. Don't expect bland cameo critter closeups: Holdsworth's eye is apparently caught by the distinctive, the lovely and the quirky. The artist is often on premises. Wild by Nature closes Sundays in winter.

Southwestern Montana

Bozeman, Montana

Arts Centers and Organizations

Emerson Cultural Center

111 S. Grand Ave., Bozeman, Mont. • (406) 587-9797

This cultural mecca housed in an old Bozeman school building is home to not only 30 studios, but also about 10 galleries. On any given day, the halls ring with the sound of

INSIDERS' TIP

Interested in touring the galleries of Greater Yellowstone? Bob Richard of Grubsteak Expeditions, (303) 527-6316, designs custom gallery trips for groups of any size, including busloads.

Thomas Mangelsen, Nature Photographer

Thomas Mangelsen learned to love wildlife as a boy, hunting and fishing along the Platte River in his native Nebraska. That love led to undergraduate and graduate work in biology and zoology and later to jobs shooting educational wildlife films. He first saw Jackson Hole in 1978. Its rugged beauty and plentiful wildlife stuck in his mind.

Even while he worked in films, Mangelsen pursued his first love, still photography. By 1981 he had a sizable collection of prints under his belt; he decided it was time to open a gallery in Jackson Hole. Most photographers who manage to make a living at all do it by selling their work to magazines, books and calendar companies. "I had this idea that maybe you could sell limited-edition photographs," Mangelsen told a reporter for the *Jackson Hole Guide*. At first it wasn't easy. Mangelsen house-sat in winters and spent his summers living alternately in a shack in Black Canyon, a barn in Ditch Creek and a garage room in Wilson, Wyoming. None of these havens had running water, and a couple had no electricity. For nearly a decade Mangelsen supported his work more than it supported him.

But the man produced beautiful images. Maybe, as one writer put it, it was his commitment to "capture creatures on film while they are immersed in the arduous business of survival." His images record polar bears, backs to a wind that whips snow into icy tongues around their feet; an Alaskan brown bear at the top of a waterfall, jaws extended to snap shut on a huge leaping salmon; a bald eagle, soaring against an ominous sky. "I'm not interested in the cutesy wildlife image," Mangelsen says.

Photo: Thomas Mangelsen

Nature photographer Thomas Mangelsen captures compelling images of everyday events in the natural world.

The days of unheated housing with no running water are past. Now Mangelsen has 12 galleries, including one in Hong Kong. Probably his most famous work has been with polar bears, but the prolific photographer has also created spectacular images of bald eagles, grizzly bears, trumpeter swans, cheetahs, Teton landscapes and more. In fact, with a half-million slides in his photo library, there's probably not much Mangelsen hasn't photographed — except captive animals. According to Mangelsen, many wildlife photos and most shots of wary predators like wolves and cougars are taken at game farms. Mangelsen says that 99 percent of the mountain lion photos you see in magazines were not shot in the wild. Despite the fact that a morning at a game farm could produce a year's worth of marketable images, Mangelsen shoots all of his photos in natural, wild settings.

For more on Mangelsen's Jackson, Wyoming, gallery, called Images of Nature, see the listing in this chapter.

music from musicians in their upstairs studios teaching piano, string and horn instrument workshops. A hub of art, music, dance and design studios rented by local artists, Emerson Cultural Center is a living, changing gallery of the artists' work. A dozen or so shops and galleries, including the Indian Uprising Gallery, Botannica Fine Art, A Thread Runs Through It and the Tibetan Trader, offer the wares of local artists. In addition, the Emerson Cultural Center has an auditorium that hosts regular theatrical events. Café International offers continental cuisine for lunch and dinner.

Montana Arts

321 E. Main St., Bozeman, Mont.
• (406) 585-9551

Founded in 1948 as the Montana Institute of the Arts, this nonprofit organization acts as an umbrella bookkeeper, grant administrator and conference organizer for several arts organizations. In the 1960s, Montana Arts was instrumental in bringing arts groups together and was set up to accept money from the National Endowment for the Arts for the state of Montana. The organization served in this role until the Montana Arts Council came into being.

Each year Montana Arts organizes an artist showcase for the Montana Performing Arts Consortium. Montana Arts also acts as a nonprofit umbrella for emerging arts organizations, and it sponsors special projects including artist exchange programs with Russia. An offshoot of this exchange program is an exhibit from the Brodsky Museum in St. Petersburg, Russia, that was displayed in the fall of 1998 at the Yellowstone Art Museum in Billings, Montana. Montana Arts also sponsors the Mary Brennan Clapp Memorial Poetry Contest for Montana poets.

The Montana Arts Council

316 N. Park Ave., Helena, Mont.
• (406) 444-6430

This state agency is charged with promoting and expanding the role of arts and culture in Montana. The Arts Council administers grants and other programs that benefit all arts endeavors in Montana.

Performing Arts

Big Sky Dance Center

2304 N. Seventh Ave., Bozeman, Mont.
• (406) 586-1880

Operated by Jeff and Cathy Giese, the Big Sky Dance Center offers ballet, modern and tap classes to dancers of all ages. The Gieses also operate the Dance Alliance, a nonprofit organization designed to enhance education of area dancers by offering top-quality dance workshops with nationally known instructors, as well as scholarship and performing opportunities.

Bozeman Symphony Orchestra and Symphonic Choir

104 E. Main St., Bozeman, Mont.
• (406) 585-9774

Concerts presented by the Bozeman Symphony Orchestra have become so popular in the past few years that it's best to buy tickets well ahead of time. Celebrating its 32nd season in 1999, the Bozeman Symphony is a nonprofit orchestra that began in the Montana State University School of Music, then crept into the community. Each year, the 80-member symphony presents five season concerts. In addition, the symphony offers a family concert that costs only $10 per household, a gala fund-raising event and a free concert for 4th graders. An 80-member choir also performs — sometimes with the symphony and sometimes alone.

INSIDERS' TIP

The Buffalo Bill Art Show, Sale and Quick Draw, held each September in Cody, Wyoming, features regional and national Western art sold through both live and silent auctions. This sale, a must for Western art aficionados, raised $72,000 for the Buffalo Bill Historical Center in 1998. (See our Attractions chapter.) For information call the BBHC in Cody at (307) 587-2777.

The Vigilante Theatre Company showcases popular performances, such as this production of *Sherlock Is That You*?

The Bozeman Symphony mostly performs in the Willson auditorium, 404 W. Main Street. Except for an annual gala performance, which is more costly, tickets generally cost from $10 to $22 and can be purchased by stopping by or calling the office. Tickets for the family performance cost $3 for adults and $2 for children. Student tickets are discounted.

Montana Ballet Company
221 E. Main St., Bozeman, Mont.
• (406) 587-7192

Montana Ballet Company, formed in 1983, presents several top-quality performances each year featuring ethnic dance as well as traditional ballet in Bozeman and Butte, Montana. Montana Ballet Company also offers classes to rural schools and a private school and gives two summer workshops at Montana State University. A theater dance workshop called Headed for Broadway is designed for young adults interested in acting, voice and dance. The New York Connection, a workshop for intermediate and advanced ballet dancers, brings teachers from the New York City Ballet and draws from among the nation's best ballet dancers to give students a taste of the professional dancer's schedule and experience. Montana Ballet School offers a full range of dance classes for children and adults of all ages.

Montana Shakespeare in the Parks
MSU Sub Rm. 354, Bozeman, Mont.
• (406) 994-5885

Since 1974, Montana Shakespeare in the Parks has performed in the parks and on the prairies of Montana. A part of Montana State University's College of Arts and Architecture, this troupe of a dozen or so professional actors plays in communities across the state from Polson to Miles City, from Libby to Livingston. Their performances are free to the public.

In addition to about 50 tour dates scheduled for 1998 in small Montana towns, Shakespeare in the Parks presented *A Midsummer Night's Dream* and *The Winter's Tale* at several Bozeman locations throughout the summer and fall. For information about the tour schedule, call (406) 994-3901.

Vigilante Theatre Company

111 S. Grand Ave., Bozeman, Mont.
• (406) 586-3897

For 19 years, four actors calling themselves the Vigilante Theatre have toured Montana and the Northwest with original productions indigenous to the Northwest. While only two of the four founding actors are still with the company, the style is the same. They bring it all — lights, sets, costumes, props — presenting unique productions like *Who Shot the Sheriff*, the story of a 100-year-old shooting, and *Wuf!*, the satirical story of wolf reintroduction in Yellowstone Park. Since this company tours a lot, and often does private performances, it's best to call Joanne Eaton at the above number to find out how you can catch its act.

Galleries

Artifacts

308 E. Main St., Bozeman, Mont.
• (406) 586-3755, (888) 586-3755

One of the first craft galleries in the area, Artifacts still features finely crafted art more than 20 years after Patricia Bloom opened its doors in Bozeman. Sandwiched between John Bozeman's Bistro and O'Brien's, a restaurant serving fine continental cuisine, Artifacts takes advantage of the dinner crowd through an arrangement made between Bloom and a former owner of O'Brien's. Diners can mosey over, with wine in hand, from O'Brien's to Artifacts and browse through the gallery items while waiting for their dinner. Current owners Jim and Linda Brown are the second owners of Artifacts since Bloom sold it in the mid-1980s. At Artifacts, open seven days a week, you might find one-of-a-kind jewelry, ceramics or wood work.

Emerson Cultural Center

11 S. Grand Ave., Bozeman, Mont.
• (406) 587-9797

There are about a dozen galleries and shops in the Emerson Cultural Center that feature a range of art media by local artists. For more information, see the previous entry under Arts Centers and Organizations.

Frame Work Designs

119 E. Main, Bozeman, Mont.
• (406) 586-3626, (800) 533-9396

Owned for nearly 15 years by founder Skip Tubbs, Frame Work Designs on Bozeman's Main Street features Western wildlife and landscapes by mostly Montana and Bozeman artists. In addition to original oil and watercolor paintings, Tubbs carries sculptures with a Western theme and limited edition prints by Bev Doolittle and other Western artists. Frame Work Designs is a dealer for three print publishing companies: Greenwich Workshop, Mill Pond Press and Hadley House. These days, it's the original oil landscapes and the etchings that are hot at this gallery, open year-round from 10 AM until 5:30 PM, Monday through Friday, and from 10 AM until 4 PM on Saturdays.

Grey Fox

23 W. Main St., Bozeman, Mont.
• (406) 587-9778

If it's local landscapes or nostalgic Western scenes and buildings you're looking for, chances are you'll find it at the Grey Fox way out West on Bozeman's Main Street. When

INSIDERS' TIP

At noon on summer Thursdays in Idaho Falls, enjoy lunch on the grass by the Snake River and free live music. The concerts are brought to you by the Idaho Falls Arts Council. For more information, call (208) 522-0471.

owners Pam and Dean Coleman bought this gallery in 1995, it was called La Petite, a gallery that sold only miniatures. The Grey Fox now specializes in local, original art and is open year-round, generally from 9:30 AM until 5:30 PM.

Old Main Gallery and Framing

246 E. Main St., Bozeman, Mont. • (406) 587-8860, (888) 587-8860

The oldest gallery in Bozeman — it's been here since 1964 — the Old Main is both a gallery and a booming framing shop with five full-time certified picture framers, more than any other gallery in Montana. In addition to the framing, the Old Main handles mostly two-dimensional Western, wildlife, Native American and fishing art as well as antique paper art, with a wide range of prices in both prints and originals. Among the artists handled by Old Main are Native American artist Kevin Red Star, Daryl Poulin and Gary Carter. You'll also find prints by wildlife artist Nancy Glazier and originals as well as prints by fish artist Michael Stidham. The Old Main is open seven days a week from 9 AM to 7 PM Monday through Friday, and from 9 AM until 5 PM on Saturday and Sunday.

Livingston, Montana

Performing Arts

Blue Slipper Theater

113 E. Callender St., Livingston, Mont. • (406) 222-7720

Since 1964, this nonprofit volunteer community theater has been presenting three plays per year — mysteries, dramas and comedies — to the residents of Livingston. Supported by patrons and housed in a turn-of-the-century sandstone building in downtown Livingston, the Blue Slipper Theater seats 85. Make reservations by calling the above number. Tickets cost $7.

Yellowstone Ballet Company

109 S. B St., Livingston, Mont. • (406) 222-0430

Owned by Rick Pittendop and Kathleen Rakela, both former professional dancers, Yellowstone Ballet Company bills itself as Montana's only professional ballet company specializing in classical ballet training and performance. In addition to instructing about 50 local Livingston dancers September through May, Yellowstone Ballet produces several classics each year from Christmas through spring. In June 1999, the company will host an international premiere of *Romeo and Juliet of the Rockies*, featuring principal dancers from the Joffrey, Sacramento, Bolshoi and Kirov ballets.

Galleries

Burl Jones RocheJaune Galerie

5237 U.S. Hwy. 89 S. #1, Livingston, Mont. • (406) 222-8719

You'll recognize the Burl Jones RocheJaune Galerie by the bronze eagle on the front of the building. Jones, a Livingston dentist who retired in 1991 to devote full time to sculpting, is just one of the artists featured in the RocheJaune (which, by the way, is French for "yellow stone"). In addition to Jones' sculptures, you will find oil paintings and limited edition prints with a — you guessed it — Western and wildlife theme. The RocheJaune is open seven days a week from 9 AM to 5 PM Monday through Saturday, and from 10 AM to 3 PM on Sundays. To get to this gallery from Interstate 90, take Exit 333, turning south on U.S. Highway 89. The bronze eagle flies about a half-mile south on the west side of the highway.

Chatham Fine Art

120 N. Main St., Livingston, Mont. • (406) 222-1566

You've heard of the one-man band. Russell Chatham, internationally known Western impressionist painter, plays just about every artistic instrument around. In addition to his sweeping, out-of-the-mist oils, expect to find original lithographs, books, posters, drawings and his video, *Winter Above Deep Creek*, in Chatham's Fine Art gallery. If none of the pieces from Chatham's palette tempts you, try pleasing your palate a few doors down the street at the Livingston Bar and Grille, owned and honed by none other than Russell Chatham himself. (See our Restaurants chapter.)

Danforth Gallery
106 N. Main St., Livingston, Mont.
• (406) 222-6510

Operated by the Park County Friends of the Arts, the Danforth is Livingston's oldest gallery and its only nonprofit art gallery. From June through December, the Danforth features more than 100 artists ranging from the internationally acclaimed to well-known regional to the obscure. All proceeds from its sales go back into the arts program, which includes a two-month film festival each winter and the Main Street Theater, a series of winter variety shows. During its summer season, the Danforth is open from 10 AM until 6 PM seven days a week.

FishTales
124 N. Main St., Livingston, Mont.
• (406) 222-0844

We've also listed this gallery in the Shopping chapter. That's because almost everything in FishTales falls into the category of functional art — art you'll want to take home and use. FishTales, which carries work by more than 30 regional artists, moved in 1998 from its former hole-in-the-wall location to a more visible spot on Main Street. Look for a kaleidoscopic display of eclectic art that includes folkart, clay, twig and log furnishings, batik, quilts, leatherworks, jewelry and floorcloths for starters. For more information about FishTales, see our Shopping chapter.

Mordam Art
109 S. Main St., Livingston, Mont.
• (406) 222-0321

Husband-and-wife team Parke and Bonnie Goodman have their studios in this gallery. Parke paints traditional oil landscapes in the back room while Bonnie fashions handmade glass beads and jewelry in the front room. The gallery walls are lined with Parke's work. Bonnie's beads and baubles fill a room-length display case. For more about Mordam Art, see our Shopping chapter.

Visions West Gallery
108 S. Main, Livingston, Mont.
• (406) 222-0337

Open since 1991, Visions West features Western wildlife and sporting art, including original paintings, photography, sculpture, ceramics or pottery and gifts. In 1997, owner Evelyn Walinchus had several shows including the work of Montana ranch photographer Barbara Van Cleve and a set of 50 original watercolors of fish painted by Evenlyn's husband, artist/guide/author Rod Walinchus. In 1998, she featured the work of Mike Mahoney, a Billings artist who does impressionistic landscapes in oil. Winters, Visions West is open from 10 AM until 5:30 PM, Monday through Saturday. Summer hours are flexible, but generally extended to seven days a week.

The Wade Gallery
116 N. Main St., Livingston, Mont.
• (406) 222-0404

Established in 1986 and open year round, the Wade Gallery features fine art by regional artists and has Montana's most complete selection of photographs and photogravures from *The North American Indian* by Edward Sheriff Curtis. Owner Kelly Wade, who has built a reputation for offering top-quality work by local artisans, also features a selection of pottery, weavings and jewelry. Wade provides a complete framing service and is open seven days a week during the summer months. The rest of the year, she recommends calling to find out seasonal hours, as store hours during slow times can be subject to the weather and other mercurial factors.

Ennis, Montana

Galleries

Hole in the Wall Gallery
123 Main St., Ennis, Mont.
• (406) 682-7235, (800) 992-9981
Mountain Mall, Mountain Village, Big Sky, Mont. • (406) 995-4988

Hole in the Wall is aptly named. From the outside, this gallery looks deceptively small. Inside, though, the gallery stretches deep into the back of the lot, which means visitors find themselves following the long walls from one mind-teasing piece of art to the next. No matter what your taste, we're betting you'll find something in the eclectic artistic mix at Hole in the Wall that tempts you to max at least one credit card. Hole in the Wall displays work by regional artists that includes three-dimensional sculptures in wood, bronze and stone; handmade baskets, pottery and knives; and an array of oil and watercolors by well-known artists. The year-round Ennis gallery is open Tuesday through Saturday from November 1 through June 1, and every day from June to November. The Big Sky gallery is open only from December 1 to April 15, seven days a week. Gallery hours for both locations are 10 am to 7 pm.

Virginia City, Montana

Performing Arts

Virginia City Players

Virginia City Playhouse on Main Street, Virginia City, Mont. • (406) 843-5569

In 1999 the Virginia City Players, billed as the longest continuously running summer stock theater west of the Mississippi River, celebrates its 50th anniversary. Specializing in melodramas and vaudeville, the Virginia City Players begin their season each year about mid-June and run until Labor Day. Tickets are $12.50 for adults and $7.50 for kids 12 and younger.

Red Lodge, Montana

Performing Arts

Red Lodge Chamber Orchestra

(406) 446-3419

This group, which performs monthly winter concerts in groups ranging from small ensembles to a 14-member orchestra (depending on the composer), mushroomed after one individual decided he wanted to get together with others to make music. The orchestra plays in various locations including Red Lodge's Roman Theater, the Carbon County Arts Guild and a local resort. The orchestra also performs with a local chorus. An offshoot of the Red Lodge Chamber Orchestra is a Glendsiddle group — just picture a bunch of semi-burly Montana guys walking around in kilts playing pretty music. They also perform at weddings.

Galleries

Carbon County Arts Guild

11 W. Eighth St., Red Lodge, Mont. • (406) 446-1370

This nonprofit arts organization and gallery is housed in the old railroad depot where it operates an art gallery featuring the work of members. The guild also exhibits monthly shows by well-known area artists. The Carbon County Arts Guild also sponsors workshops for both adults and children.

Coleman Gallery and Studio

223 S. Broadway Ave., Red Lodge, Mont. • (406) 446-1228, (800) 726-2228

In a land so filled with powerful natural images, it's a wonder there aren't more galleries displaying photographs capturing Greater Yellowstone. Merv Coleman's stunning landscape and nature photographs grace walls at work and at home across the country. Pattern, place, texture and time are captured in Coleman's limited- and open-edition photos. If you want a really special memento, have Coleman photograph you somewhere in the Beartooth Mountains.

Kevin Red Star Gallery

15 S. Broadway Ave., Red Lodge, Mont. • (406) 446-1322

This gallery displays the bold works of oil artist Kevin Red Star, a Native American who

INSIDERS' TIP

Check with chambers of commerce in Red Lodge, Montana and Cody, Wyoming, for area music festivals that feature summer workshops for teenagers, as well as performances by their instructors, who are topnotch university instructors and orchestra members. Look for student performances too. See our Resources chapter for chamber numbers.

grew up in Lodge Grass on the Crow Reservation in Montana. Using a masterful style with depth that has earned his work a place in many a museum, Red Star's work does not aim for realism. A medicine man, for example, might be portrayed as part human and part animal. This gallery is open year-round, Monday through Saturday, 10 AM to 6 PM.

Eastern Idaho

Idaho Falls, Idaho

Arts Centers and Organizations

Eagle Rock Art Guild
(208) 522-4409

The guild's primary events are its three annual art shows. The juried summer Eagle Rock Art Guild Sidewalk Art Show is the biggest (see our Annual Events chapter for more); the fall show is also juried for non guild members; and the spring show is dedicated to work by members only. The guild has about 100 members. Most, but not all, are artists. In addition to their art shows, the guild sponsors scholarships and art contests for kids.

Idaho Falls Arts Council
498 A St., Idaho Falls, Idaho • (208) 522-0471

If you want to learn about the local arts scene, start here. The Arts Council can hook you into more than 15 local performing and visual arts groups, including the American Guild of Organists, the Eastern Idaho Photographic Society, the Snake River Woodcarvers, the Weavers and Spinners of Idaho Falls and the Idaho Falls Opera Theatre.

Idaho Falls Arts Council has three other important roles in town. First, it maintains a 2,000-square-foot art gallery, the only public showcase of its kind in town, with parquet floors, stained-glass windows and high ceilings.

Second, the council operates the Colonial Theater, a 953-seat house dating to 1919. Once home to vaudeville and silent film performances, the recently rescued and refurbished Colonial Theater is located, along with the art gallery, in the Willard Arts Center. More than $4 million was raised recently to reopen the facility. The theater is home to musicals, dramatic performances including children's plays, Broadway shows and lectures.

Third, the council sponsors art classes, mostly for elementary schoolchildren, to support the limited art programs available in area schools. Professional artists and art educators teach the classes. Some drama classes for kids and adult art classes are also available. Tuition is nominal.

Performing Arts

Actors' Repertory Theater of Idaho Inc.
(208) 535-2585

This active volunteer theater group schedules four shows a year, usually classics by playwrights such as Neil Simon, Oscar Wilde or Ira Levin. You can catch a performance at the Stardust (around $20 for dinner and the show or $10 just for the show) at 680 Lindsay Boulevard, Idaho Falls, Idaho. Even more fun is the Sunday champagne brunch for about $15. Opening night at the Stardust is popular because it often coincides with a wine tasting. ARTI occasionally does one-acts for holiday parties. If you're moving to town, remember that these folks can always use help; they'd love to tap your acting, set building, writing or management skills. Call ARTI for show schedules and locations.

Idaho Falls Opera Theatre
(208) 522-0471

Greater Yellowstone residents are willing

INSIDERS' TIP

In Livingston, Montana, you can sip wine and walk between several downtown galleries during three summer gallery walks scheduled each June, July and August. For more information call the Livingston Chamber of Commerce at (406) 222-0850.

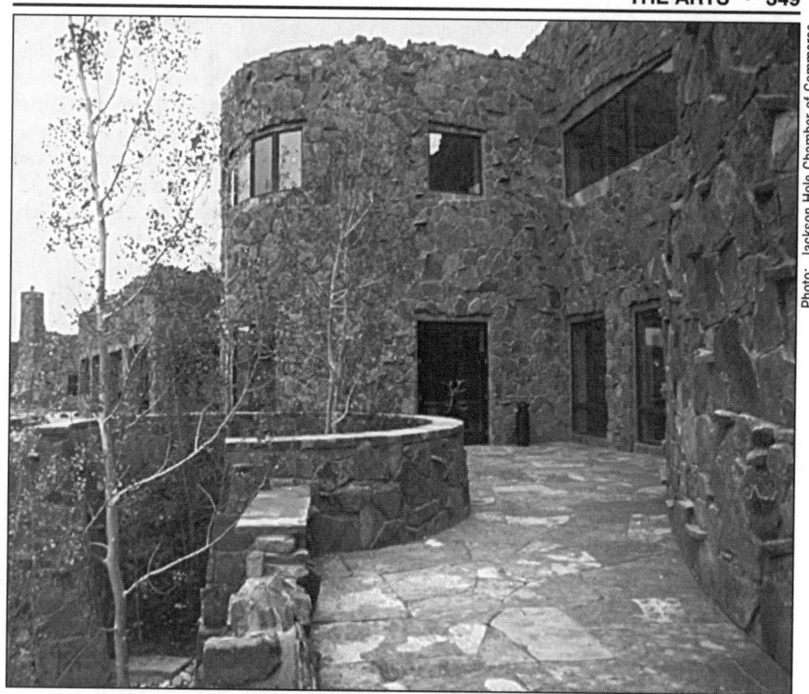
Photo: Jackson Hole Chamber of Commerce

The National Wildlife Art Museum north of Jackson , Wyoming.

to drive for their dose of culture: Idaho Falls community opera theater draws more than one-fourth of its audiences from out of town for the twice-annual shows. Audience members are from Montana, Wyoming and Utah, as well as from down the street. The company's spring productions tend to be light operettas or musicals; fall shows are heavier opera selections. One of the things this group prides itself on is a reservoir of singers talented enough that lead roles are generally performed by local amateurs, not guest professionals. Most Idaho Falls Opera Theatre shows involve about 30 performers and 120 orchestra members, set builders, costumers, etc. The company also hosts one Broadway show per year, usually in January or February. Reserved seats for operas run around $15; general admission is around $8. Seat prices for the Broadway shows vary according to the acting company involved. Shows are generally held at the Civic Auditorium, 501 S. Holmes Avenue, Idaho Falls, Idaho.

The Idaho Falls Symphony
498 A St., Idaho Falls, Idaho
• (208) 529-1080

This volunteer symphony began in 1949. In 1991 a chorale was added, expanding the symphony's range. The Idaho Falls Symphony plays a five-concert season, including one Pops concert. Guest artists are often world-class; they've included names such as violinists Daniel Heifetz and Nadja Salerno-

INSIDERS' TIP

According to the 1990 census, one out of every 83 Montana residents is a working artist.

Sonnenberg and pianists Misha Dicter and Alexander Toradze. Adult tickets range from $3 to $20. Season tickets range from $40 to $75 . Concerts are held at the Civic Auditorium, 501 S. Holmes Avenue, Idaho Falls, Idaho, except for the Pops concert, which is held at the Shilo Inn, 780 Lindsay Boulevard, Idaho Falls, Idaho.

Snake River Chamber Orchestra

335 E. 19th St., Idaho Falls, Idaho • (208) 542-0577

This pleasant recent addition to the Idaho Falls performing arts scene is the brainchild of conductor David Rutherford, who moved here from Afton, Wyoming, and noticed that Idaho Falls lacked a chamber orchestra. Chamber orchestras range in size from two to 20 musicians; Rutherford's group consists of about 25 volunteers who, he promises, will have paid positions within a year. The more delicate, intimate performances of a chamber group have been well received here. The versatile orchestra has backed up Craig Schulman, a Broadway singer probably best known as the Phantom in *Phantom of the Opera*, as well as popular singer Kenny Rogers.

The group has a five-show season from September to May, with a special January show that combines silent films and vaudeville with the chamber orchestra as musical accompaniment, a combination Rutherford says is authentic early 20th-century film presentation. Tickets for adults are $7 in advance and $8 at the door. Concerts are at the Willard Arts Center.

Galleries

Willowtree Gallery

210 Cliff St., Idaho Falls, Idaho • (208) 524-4464

This gallery is a dealer for limited edition prints, so it carries work by well-known painters such as Bev Doolittle, Braldt Bralds and James Christensen. It also features originals, mostly by local artists such as Ar. B Loosle, Gloria Miller Allen and Marilyn Hansen. Unlike many in the region, this is not a Western art gallery; rather, the displayed art represents an eclectic mix of subjects. The gallery also provides archival framing services. It's closed Sundays and Mondays.

Northwestern Wyoming

Cody, Wyoming

Galleries

Big Horn Galleries

1167 and 1414 Sheridan Ave., Cody, Wyo. • (307) 527-7587

At one time Bob and Nancy Brown's Big Horn Gallery was the only art gallery in Cody. Now one of a dozen or so, the Big Horn has split into two galleries on Sheridan Avenue, Cody's main street. The Big Horn Galleries feature fine art and limited edition prints with Western and wildlife themes. These shops are two of the few places in the country where collectors can buy James Bama's work. Bama, a nationally known Western artist from Cody, used to display his work exclusively at a gallery in New York City. The Browns have owned and managed several galleries in the Greater Yellowstone area. The Big Horn is open year round from 9:30 AM to 5:30 PM.

Jordan Gallery

1349 Sheridan Ave., Cody, Wyo. • (307) 587-6689

Known as "the guy with the good eye," Jerry Jordan features four types of art in his gallery: turn-of-the-century Indian artifacts, rare Western books and historic ephemera, Dan Begg sculptures and historic Navajo rugs.

INSIDERS' TIP

Greater Yellowstone in summer is home to several small acting troupes performing melodramas, dinner theater and other shows aimed mostly at visitors. Turn to our Nightlife chapter to learn about performances in Island Park, Teton Valley and Ririe, Idaho, and West Yellowstone and Jackson, Wyoming.

Begg is a multi-award-winning Canadian sculptor whose work is reasonably priced. Jordan Gallery, open since 1992, is one of only two galleries in the United States that carries Begg's work. For serious collectors, Jordan will dig until he comes up with that hard-to-find piece you've been hunting for. The gallery is open 9 AM to 9 PM June though September, and 9 AM to 5 PM the rest of the year. Jordan closes on Sundays.

Simpson Gallagher

1115 13th St., Cody, Wyo.
• (307) 587-4022

Owner Sue Simpson Gallagher returned several years ago to her hometown of Cody, then opened a gallery. She features the work of her "gang of friends," who happen to be nationally known artists from across the country. Featured work includes the oil paintings of pleine-air artist Clyde Aspevig and watercolors by cowboy artist William Matthews. She also carries sculptures by Walter Matia. The gallery specialty, though, is a collection of etchings with traditional sporting, wildlife, cowboy and landscape themes. The Simpson Gallagher stays open all year. Winter hours are 10 AM to 6 PM Tuesday through Saturday. Summer hours are the same, with the addition of being open Monday.

Whitney Gallery of Western Art

Buffalo Bill Historical Center, 720 Sheridan Ave., Cody, Wyo.
• (307) 587-4771

If you are into Western art, The Whitney Gallery of Western Art is a must-see. This gallery has one of the most extensive collections of Western art anyplace. A separate wing houses a collection featuring Frederic Remington, where the artist comes to life in his replicated New Rochelle, New York, studio. Charles M. Russell, turn-of-the-century "cowboy artist," also rates his own wing in the Whitney. Other names you may recognize include early 19th-century painter George Catlin; William Tylee Ranney, a self-taught artist determined to capture the Native American culture in oil; and Thomas Moran, a 19th-century artist who traveled with the 1871 Hayden Expedition and whose sketches helped convince Congress to establish Yellowstone National Park. Recently, the Whitney has begun aggressively collecting contemporary Western art as well.

A two-day admission ticket to the Buffalo Bill Historical Center costs $8 for adults, $6.50 for senior citizens, $4 for students 13 and older, $2 for children ages 6 through 12 and free for kids 5 and younger.

As you drive through Greater Yellowstone, we urge you to answer the call to explore the unexpected. We're betting that you'll gain the same sense of wonder that made early tourists dub this wild place "wonderland."

Attractions

"A thousand Yellowstone wonders are calling, 'Look up and down and round about you!'"

— John Muir, *Our National Parks*, 1909

Who can resist stopping to watch the clear waters of mountain streams cascading down a boulder-strewn gorge? Or the sun setting on snow-frosted peaks? Or a bull elk, his antlers in velvet, basking in the morning sun? For that matter, who but the most hurried wouldn't be attracted to a grassy spot by a river winding through a meadow? Everywhere we turn in Yellowstone country, the landscape beckons us, demanding attention and investigation.

Oddly, it's the determination to see the "Attractions" that drives so many people so fast past those smaller, unannounced attractions. As you drive through Greater Yellowstone, we urge you to answer the call to explore the unexpected. We're betting that you'll gain the same sense of wonder that made early tourists dub this wild place "wonderland."

In this chapter we have lifted the veil only slightly on some of the natural mysteries of Greater Yellowstone, such as geysers and mountain ranges. We've also listed some of the region's human-created attractions like museums, commercial hot springs and winter sleigh rides. As you will see, for your convenience we have chosen mostly roadside attractions. They're our favorites, but they're not all that's out there waiting for you. Explore. Enjoy.

Yellowstone National Park

General information about park admission fees, services and more can be found in the Parks and Forests chapter. Highlighted attractions are listed below.

Geothermal Features

Geothermal features are what first attracted expeditions to this wild country. And, with the exception of a stray bear, it's the brewing, bubbling bowls and cones that still attract most visitors today. That's why we've devoted a little extra attention to geothermal features in this chapter. We've provided the highlights, and leave you to decide which basins you want to visit. Before you tour the basins, we recommend you read our Natural World chapter for a brief explanation of what's happening below the surface.

We haven't told you how to get to these places because they're well-marked on the map you'll get as you enter the park and on road signs. Generally, though, the most accessible geyser basins are along the western edge of the park.

Mammoth Hot Springs

Mammoth Hot Springs is a mysteriously beautiful steaming, growing, living sculpture made of travertine (calcium carbonate). These springs, emanating from a hillside above park headquarters, discharge about 500 gallons of hot water per minute. The water deposits about 2 tons of travertine limestone per day, which means that these incredibly beautiful terraced formations grow. Unfortunately, they don't always grow where park managers want them. East of the Mammoth Road, for example, you'll see the very white Opal Terrace near a house. This terrace, which grows at a rate of a foot per year, took over a tennis court in 1947 and now threatens a historic home built in 1908 and designed by famous park architect Robert Reamer.

Minerva Terrace, the centerpiece of the Lower Terraces, includes a rainbow of bright colors and ornate travertine formations. Several other terraces and springs cover the hillside and provide a landscape that records the changing flow of the springs' waters. Boardwalks wind around the terraces, and a one-way road loops around the Upper Terraces.

Norris Geyser Basin

The water in the Norris Geyser Basin is much hotter than in many other basins (a drill hole in this basin came upon 459-degree water only 1,087 feet below the surface), and the geyser activity more violent. For some reason, during late summer, all of the Norris springs and geysers become simultaneously muddy.

The Porcelain Basin in the northern half is full of very active, constantly changing geysers. More than 40 geysers dot this basin; some are inactive, others suddenly rear their heads. The 1-mile trail through this area is well-signed and explains the various thermal features.

The Back Basin on the southern end of Norris contains more than 60 geysers interspersed among the trees. One of the most interesting is Steamboat Geyser, which didn't become active until 1878. Then it exploded with such force it blew huge rocks into the air killing nearby trees and plants with its burning mud. Steamboat behaved itself until 1911, when it rocked the area again in a series of violent eruptions. For the next 50 years, the geyser was again docile. Then from 1961 until 1969, Steamboat erupted 90 times, often very vigorously. Steamboat has been relatively inactive since 1985, but since 1969, some eruptions — no one can ever predict when this monster will go off — have been so violent that the geyser has shot as high as 380 feet into the air, more than three times as high as Old Faithful. The roar during its eruption is so loud people nearby cannot even shout at each other and make themselves heard. Legend has it that one winter eruption could be heard 14 miles away at Madison Junction.

Echinus Geyser is a favorite for several reasons. It is large and beautiful, spouting as high as 80 feet. It also erupts often and fairly regularly — every 20 to 80 minutes. Also, you can get very close to it.

The Veteran Geyser is a teaser that often keeps people watching it expectantly because it always looks like it's about to erupt. If you watch long enough, you won't be disappointed. This geyser erupts at irregular intervals from 20 minutes to three hours and reaches a height of 40 feet.

Lower Geyser Basin

The Lower Geyser Basin is the largest in Yellowstone National Park and contains a dozen geyser groups including the Fountain Paint Pots, so called because they contain creamy mud that resembles thick latex paint.

This basin has a number of interesting geysers. Among them is the Great Fountain Geyser, first geyser to greet the Cook-Folsom-

Photo: Robert Bower, Post Register

A larger-than-life bronze cougar peers down across the lobby at the National Wildlife Art Museum near Jackson, Wyoming.

Peterson Party (see our History chapter to learn more about these explorers). Great Fountain erupted just as they came upon it. Journals from the expedition indicate that to a man, they whooped and threw their hats in the air. Just down the road is White Dome, a geyser so old the cone is about 20 feet high while the spout has been nearly sealed off by mineral deposits.

Farther down the road is the Pink Cone Group containing Bead Geyser, one of the most regular erupters in the park. In the Firehole Lake Group you'll see Firehole Lake, the largest and hottest of several pools with a total water output of about 3,500 gallons per minute. Below it is a larger hot pool, Hot Lake, which actually contains the runoff of Firehole Lake and has a much lower temperature than its upstream neighbor.

The Fountain Group is the largest in the Lower Basin, and the activity here increased dramatically after the 1959 earthquake. The activity at this spot indicates that these geysers are all interrelated underground because their eruptions are dependent on those of their neighbors.

Midway Geyser Basin

There is one main attraction here: Grand Prismatic Spring, an expanse of amazingly beautiful water that comprises the largest hot spring in the park and the third-largest in the world. In addition, you'll see Excelsior Geyser, once the most impressive in Yellowstone National Park. Excelsior discharges 4,000 gallons of hot water a minute. Now relatively inactive, from 1882 to 1888 it sprayed as high as 300 feet and had a 300-foot-wide base. Excelsior, which in those days erupted every 20 to 120 minutes, rumbled and roared so violently beneath the ground that those who camped nearby couldn't sleep. Scientists theorize that Excelsior blew its plumbing apart in the 1800s and can no longer build the pressure it needs to explode.

Upper Geyser Basin

With 300 geysers clustered in a square mile, the Upper Geyser Basin has the highest concentration of geysers anywhere in the world. It is also the home of Old Faithful and a number of other spectacular geysers. If you want to take in the entire Upper Basin, you'll have to spend two or three days to see all the majors erupt. As of 1998, more than 150,000 Old Faithful eruptions had been recorded with an average interval of 81 minutes. (Intervals have varied between 33 and 120 minutes.)

Eruption heights average about 135 feet with a duration of 1½ to 5 minutes.

A loop trail will take you around nearby Geyser Hill where nearly 40 geysers are clustered. Among them you'll find Beehive Geyser, which has a beautifully shaped cone with a narrow vent that spews hot water up to 150 feet in the air like a fire-hose nozzle. Historical information about Solitary Geyser is conflicting. One version says it was nearly used as a swimming pool in the 1920s, but shortly after permission was granted to use it as a pool, the geyser erupted 25 feet into the air. Another version says water from Solitary was piped to an indoor pool northwest of Old Faithful Inn. You'll be lucky to see this beaut spout.

Until January of 1998, when an earthquake interrupted its activity, The Giantess was a hummer, constantly bubbling and boiling until, without warning, it blasted 200 feet into the air. Giantess' eruptions last up to two days and occur two or three times a year. They also have a visible effect on nearby geysers. For several months prior to the quake, Giantess increased her activity. Park rangers report that minutes after the 1998 quake, though, Giantess displayed an aborted eruption and has since been silent. Another mysterious event occurred that night. Nearby Cascade Geyser, which had erupted only a few times in the last century, came to life minutes after Giantess lost power. At first Cascade erupted almost constantly with only three-minute intervals. By the end of the summer in 1998, though, Cascade was erupting only about once a day. No one knows for sure how long Giantess will be silent, but they do know that this historical geyser reacted the same way to a 1983 earthquake. Members of the Washburn Expedition of 1870 described the eruption of Giantess as one of the grandest experiences of their visit to Yellowstone country.

The neighboring Giant Geyser came to life in 1997 after decades of relative dormancy and erupted regularly until the spring of 1998 when it again became quiet. Rangers reported one eruption in the fall of 1998.

Castle Geyser is very old, as evidenced by its 12-foot-high cone that resembles a castle tower. Over the years every geyser changes, and Castle is no exception. These days Castle erupts with a 20-minute display up to 80 feet high. This water eruption is followed by an impressive 40 minute roaring steam phase.

The Castle-Grand Group includes more than 20 geysers and is the best place to catch a multitude of major geyser eruptions. Some folks think Grand Geyser is the most impressive in the world. Grand erupts in a series of bursts, each about 150 feet tall. The first burst lasts about nine minutes and gradually subsides, only to be replaced by another spectacular eruption.

Lone Star Geyser Basin

Lone Star's regular eruptions (every three hours) last 30 minutes. But we think the nicest thing about Lone Star is you have to walk 2.5 miles away from the crowds to get there. The trail (an old road) begins on the highway near the Kepler Cascades of the Firehole River.

Besides Lone Star geyser, there are a few little hot pools visible along the trail.

West Thumb Geyser Basin

In the West Thumb Geyser Basin (named for a thumb-shaped bay on the southwestern end of Yellowstone Lake) you'll find the famous and well-photographed Fishing Cone, an odd little gray structure filled with boiling

INSIDERS' TIP

The Cody Murals Visitors Center, Wyoming Avenue and 17th Street, Cody, Wyoming, (307) 587-3290, features a spectacular mural depicting the story of the Latter-day Saints' colonization of Wyoming's Big Horn Basin. (To read more about the LDS colonization, refer to our Worship chapter.) The 18-foot-high mural spans the 36-foot-wide dome of Cody's Church of Jesus Christ of Latter-day Saints. Viewing the Cody Murals, open from June 1 to September 15, is free.

water in the lake's shallows. Historians claim early explorers and visitors caught fish in the lake, then dipped them into the cone to cook in the boiling water. Visitors even donned aprons and cook's hats for photos at the Fishing Cone. Apparently, the Fishing Cone used to erupt fairly regularly to heights of up to 40 feet earlier in the century. Cooking fish in the cone isn't allowed these days.

Near the Fishing Cone you'll find a series of hot springs including Abyss Pool and Black Pool, both beautiful blue-green pools as alluring as any in the park.

Other Park Attractions

Yellowstone Lake

Cradled atop the Yellowstone Plateau at 7,333 feet are the pure, frigid waters of Yellowstone Lake — 20 miles long and 14 miles wide. Amazingly, warm water rises out of fissures in the bottom of the lake, creating champagne-like bubbles. Despite these thermal features, the ice and snow that blanket the lake during the long winter months keep this lake so cold — the average temperature is 41 degrees — that swimming in it even in summer is discouraged.

Fishing is encouraged, however. Yellowstone Lake is home to the largest inland population of wild cutthroat trout in North America. Unfortunately, it also contains a growing population of lake trout, a non-native species that may threaten cutthroat populations in the lake.

For most people, the allure of Yellowstone Lake is its pristine beauty. On a clear day, the lake presents a huge expanse of glittering ripples with snow-capped peaks in the background. On other days the wind whips the lake's waters into churning, ocean-like waves. On the northern shores, you may see bison grazing around the Lake Hotel or soaring bald eagles searching the waters for trout.

Near West Thumb, a steaming pocket of thermal springs, mud pots and geysers on the western lake shore, you might see river otter playing in the water.

You have several options for viewing Yellowstone Lake. Some like to just sit inside the Lake Hotel sunroom and gaze out from the comfort of their wicker chairs. On pleasant summer days, some folks picnic on the lakeshore. If you happen to stop at the Fishing Bridge visitor center, you'll discover a nice little beach out the lakeside door and a handy bench where you can read, gaze at the scenery or have a bite to eat. At Bridge Bay Marina regularly scheduled scenic cruises depart throughout the day from June through September. From mid-June through mid-September at the marina, you also can rent outboard motorboats and canoes or take a guided fishing trip on the lake (see our Watersports chapter). Private outfitters also offer guided fishing, kayaking, canoeing, horsepacking and backpacking trips on or around Yellowstone Lake. You'll also find a fine selection of campgrounds, especially along the eastern shore of the lake.

On the Molly Islands in the southeast arm of Yellowstone Lake is a white pelican rookery, one of only seven such breeding areas in North America. Motorized boats are prohibited near it, and landing on the Molly Islands with any kind of boat is prohibited. Feel free to use your binoculars, though.

Old Faithful Inn

While Old Faithful, the geyser, is the No. 1 attraction in Yellowstone National Park, we urge you to spend time exploring the Inn. You can take one of the regularly scheduled tours of the place, during which your guide will give you a colorful and fascinating account of its

INSIDERS' TIP

A growing attraction in Yellowstone National Park is wolf-watching in the Lamar Valley. The best times to go are at dawn and dusk. Take binoculars or a spotting scope, and keep your eyes peeled for wolves or packs of wolf-watchers gathered in pullouts. Word spreads fast about wolf-whereabouts.

Photo: Buffalo Bill Historical Center

The Cody Firearms Museum claims the largest collection of American firearms in the world.

construction and early use by tourists. Designed by Seattle architect Robert Reamer, Old Faithful Inn is sometimes referred to as the only building that looks like it grew up in the park. It was built in 1904 using giant logs, with a massive four-sided stone chimney in the center of the lobby. Two railed balconies overlook the lobby. Old Faithful Inn survived the 1959 earthquake and the fires of 1988 and is still open to overnight guests as well as diners during the summer months. (See our Hotels, Motels and Cabins chapter.)

Up in the rafters of the 92-foot ceiling webbed with a log framework is a crow's nest where musicians once played for the after-dinner dancers twirling in black ties and ball gowns below. Equipped with running water and electricity, the inn even had a spotlight on the roof, which was used to illuminate night-time eruptions, bears raiding the garbage and "rotten loggers" stealing a few kisses in the shadows.

The Inn is so close to Old Faithful Geyser that visitors can watch the eruptions from a second floor veranda.

Fishing Bridge

Old-timers say they didn't dare drive across this bridge in a convertible for fear of being snagged by the flying hook of some angler casting from its side. In the early days, especially in June when the cutthroat trout were spawning, each side of this bridge was edged with elbow-to-elbow fishermen. These days, fishing is prohibited from the bridge. If you stop by in June and look into the waters of the Yellowstone River that pass beneath it, you'll see why: It's a major spawning bed for native cutthroat trout.

Lamar Valley

This valley, which generally lies in the Lamar Creek drainage in the Northeast corner of the park, is called the Serengeti of North America. It's also wolf country, especially in the winter when the range is teeming with elk and the wolves stand out against the white snow. The wolves, reintroduced into the park in 1995, can often be seen from the road and are a growing attraction. Even without its wildlife, Lamar is a beautiful open valley with a couple of campgrounds, including those at Slough Creek and Pebble Creek (see our Campground and RV Parks chapter). Slough Creek, a world-famous trout stream, also runs into the valley.

Several miles from the northeast entrance, you'll find the Buffalo Ranch on the north side of the road. It was here that early buffalo keepers brought bison populations from the brink of extinction by breeding and feeding bison as if they were cattle.

Mount Washburn

If the promise of an astounding view isn't enough to make you climb this mountain, then maybe the pay telephone on top will tempt you. Call your mom or a friend from the top of Mount Washburn — plenty of other people do. The park's best-known mountain rises 10,243 feet above the west edge of Yellowstone's Grand Canyon. Named after Gen. Henry Dana Washburn, a teacher, lawyer and auditor who led the 1870 expedition to Yellowstone country, the mountain is a popular hiking spot. Once you reach the summit and see the view, you'll know why. Along this 3-mile hike (no matter which of the two trails you take) you'll see fields of wildflowers and possibly bighorn sheep. On top there's a fire lookout. You can get out of the wind in a shelter on the bottom floor of the tower.

Grand Canyon of the Yellowstone River

This canyon — 24 miles long and 4,000 feet wide in places — left many an early explorer speechless with its yawning walls colored in hues of red, brown, white and orange. (Add pink and salmon to that at sunset.) The Yellowstone River rushes through the Grand Canyon 800 to 1,200 feet below. The elements of nature have exposed seven geologic layers, including those formed by volcanic ash, sediments formed by an inland sea and glacial gouging — a treasure-trove of geologic history for the educated eye.

You can view the Grand Canyon from several vantage points. The most famous of these is Artist Point on the south rim. Bring a camera, watercolors or a pen and paper to Artist Point. Take a photo, paint a picture, pen a poem. We defy you to capture the breathtaking beauty of the Grand Canyon and the Lower Falls. Inspiration Point on the north rim probably offers the best display of colors, especially at sunset. Nearby, a hiking trail leads to Seven Mile Hole, where you'll find a couple of camping sites. It takes a day to hike in and another to hike out, which means you'll have to spend the night. If you think you want to attempt this hike, you'll have to get a permit from the backcountry office (see our Hiking and Backpacking chapter). Lookout Point also offers a spectacular view into the canyon from the north rim.

Lower Falls, the highest waterfall in the park, plunges 308 feet into the Grand Canyon. It is a pounding, roaring monster during spring runoff in June. By August, it is still awesome, but tame compared to its June glory. You can view the Lower Falls from a variety of

INSIDERS' TIP

In 1989, Yellowstone National Park managers closed the Fishing Bridge Campground and removed the cabins to minimize conflict between humans and grizzlies. The area is a favorite haunt of grizzlies, especially in June when cutthroat trout spawn at the mouth of the Yellowstone River.

spots. If you want to see it up close, take the Brink-of-the-Falls Trail, which switchbacks down the hill from the southernmost parking lot on the North Rim Road to the lip of the falls. Uncle Tom's Trail (just follow the signs on the South Rim Road) leads down more than 300 metal steps to the foot of the Falls. (Warning: The walk back up is very strenuous. Folks with health problems should be cautious.)

The 109-foot Upper Falls tumble into a quiet pool above the Lower Falls. You can reach these with a quarter-mile round-trip hike from the Upper Falls parking lot.

The area is laced with all kinds of hiking trails and a number of well-used cross-country ski trails. Depending on the time of year, the trails may be closed because of ice and snow. Park officials warn visitors not to leave the paths, not to throw things into the canyon and to remember that the canyon is bear country.

Specimen Ridge

Near Tower Junction, Specimen Ridge is as mysterious a place as any in the park. Here scientists have discovered as many as 27 separate petrified forests, one on top the other. Some of the trees are still standing and indicate that at one time the climate was much warmer. Among the identified species are redwood, pine, magnolia, dogwood, oak, maple, hickory and walnut. The best way to see Specimen Ridge is through a tour led by one of the park's naturalist-guide rangers. Check at any visitor center to find out when you can catch one of these tours.

Firehole Canyon Road

This 2-mile side trip south of Madison Junction takes you along a stretch of the old road. Among other sites, you'll see Firehole Falls and Firehole Cascade. You'll also come across the Firehole River Swimming Hole, a delightful stop any day, but especially on a hot day — and there aren't many of those in the park.

Stagecoach Rides and Chuckwagon Dinners

Headquartered out of Roosevelt and run by AmFac Parks and Resorts, these stagecoach rides and chuckwagon dinners have been among the favorite attractions in the park for decades. The colorful stagecoaches will give you a taste of what the earliest tourists endured on their bumpy, dusty rides through the park. The chuckwagon dinners, which are regular feasts served from an outfitted chuckwagon pulled by a team of horses, make a really special night out. See our Other Recreation chapter for details.

Museum of the National Park Ranger

Situated on the edge of a meadow below

the Norris Campground, this old log ranger station was once an outpost for Fort Yellowstone soldiers guarding the park and later became a ranger station. (See our History chapter.) This museum is staffed by a volunteer who knows the park well and can tell you tales about the area.

Grand Teton National Park

General information about park admission fees, services and more can be found in the Parks and Forests chapter. Highlight attractions are listed below.

The Tetons

The Tetons are some of the youngest mountains on the continent. The range owes its sharp-edged silhouette and wall-like eastern front to that fact, as well as to the geologic fault that lifted this mountain range so high from its valley floor only a few million years ago. Vigorous carving by recent ice ages finished the sculpting. The Tetons include seven peaks more than 12,000 feet above sea level and a handful of others more than 11,000. The resulting skyline, viewed from a valley floor 7,000 feet above sea level, is awesome.

Most visitors are content to stare at or photograph the Tetons, or perhaps hike around their bases and ascend a little ways into the wild, rugged canyons at their feet (see our Hiking chapter). But almost from explorers' first encounters with these harsh peaks, some visitors respond to the mountains' awesome spectacle by wanting to attain the top. The first unsuccessful attempt to summit the Grand Teton, the range's highest mountain, may date to 1843. If so, more failed attempts followed.

The first successful ascent was in either 1872 or 1898, depending on which story you believe. Most accept the 1898 date and credit the first ascent to William Owen, Franklin Spalding and two other men. The reason these men get the credit is because three of them returned to the summit several days later, built a rock cairn and chiseled their names into the summit boulder while Owen took photographs from below. The 1872 attempt — by 14 members of the Hayden Expedition as it explored the Yellowstone region — had no such proof, only the word of the two men who said they reached the summit.

If you look at the Grand and dream of conquest, you're certainly not alone, but your dream is not one to be acted upon lightly. Climbing this mountain, or any peak in the Tetons, is a serious endeavor. The Tetons have claimed more than a few unfortunate or ill-prepared victims. Appropriate equipment and skill, as well as good physical condition, are musts for Teton climbers. Many believe that, without previous Teton experience, even knowledgeable, competent climbers should hire a professional guide. (To learn about the Tetons' two park-approved climbing services, see our Other Recreation chapter.)

Some mountain ranges are so well known that individual mountains within the range grow their own individual fame. This is true of the Tetons. Names like Grand Teton, Mount Moran and the Cathedral Group have genuine star appeal around here.

The Grand Teton

The Grand Teton's dramatic, craggy head rises to 13,770 feet. Often draped in clouds, always at least partly dressed in snow, the mountain is visible from the Idaho (western) side of the range from Teton Valley, from Grand Targhee Ski and Summer Resort on the Wyoming (eastern) side and from Jackson Hole.

The Grand is home to year-round ice fields called glaciers. The best known can be viewed

INSIDERS' TIP

If you're staying in Jackson, be sure to take the two obligatory photos: you standing under the elk antler arches in the town square, and you sitting on the saddle bar stools at the Million Dollar Cowboy Bar.

Photo: Buffalo Bill Historical Center

Teepees give visitors a taste of what's to come at the Buffalo Bill Historical Center.

from a road turnout south of Jenny Lake; it's called the Teton Glacier. Glaciers are ice accumulations so thick and heavy that they behave more like liquids than solids, flowing in ultra-slow motion downhill. Ice in the middle of Teton Glacier moves downslope at a rate of more than 30 feet per year, but surface melting keeps the glacier in roughly the same position — although not the same size. All of the Teton range's glaciers were larger 100 years ago than they are today. Photos taken by William Owen in 1898 seem to show a Teton Glacier about 200 feet thicker and 500 feet longer than the present version. Teton Glacier is a smaller cousin of the vast glacier fields that carved out the signature shapes of the Tetons, as well as partially shaping the valley floor you're driving on.

The Grand has a distinctive shape sometimes referred to as a horn. Another famous mountain of similar shape is Switzerland's Matterhorn. Both were carved into their sheer, dramatic lines by multiple glaciers simultaneously chewing on their flanks. Height and the abrupt drama of the Grand draw climbers from around the world: 2,000 or more summit the mountain each summer. Almost as many will attempt the climb but turn back before the summit. A few more serious adventurers challenge the Grand at its most forbidding, in winter. Climbers have explored and named more than 90 routes and variations on this mountain.

The South and the Middle Tetons, both immediately south of the Grand, along with the Grand itself, make up the famous Trois Tetons (three breasts), the peaks from which early French trappers borrowed the entire range's name.

Mount Moran

From most angles, the Grand Teton towers above other peaks of the Teton range, but if you approach the Tetons from the north or northeast, 12,605-foot Mount Moran takes over the skyline. From the famous picture windows of Jackson Lake Lodge's hotel viewing lobby, bar and dining room, it's Moran, not the Grand, that takes your breath away.

Mount Moran is named for landscape artist Thomas Moran, who accompanied the 1872 Hayden Expedition through the Yellowstone region. Together with the photographs of expedition member William Jackson, Moran's paintings of Greater Yellowstone wonders helped sway President Grant to sign into existence the nation's first national park.

Moran is unique among the Tetons in having a massive, flat summit. It measures about 600 feet by 1,600 and covers more than 15 acres. The mountain also has five active glaciers, the most famous of which, Skillet Glacier, is readily visible from Jackson Hole. It's called that because some people (we don't know any) think the glacier looks like a skillet with its handle pointing up. Another unique feature of this mountain is the readily visible dark band that runs vertically through its east face. This intrusion of darker rock, called a dike, measures 125 feet across and runs nearly 7 miles west through the mountain.

First summited in 1919, Moran was once one of the most frequently climbed mountains in the Teton range, but that was when a road still ran to the north end of Leigh Lake, ending almost at the mountain's foot. The road was closed in 1953 to protect wilderness values; the easiest way to approach Mount Moran now is to paddle a canoe about 3 miles across Leigh and String lakes, with a 200-yard portage.

The Cathedral Group

If you're driving along Teton Park Road (the Inner Road) near Jenny and Leigh lakes, look south and west at the biggest peaks you can see. You're looking at what is often called the Cathedral Group, which includes the Grand, Mount Owen and Teewinot, all higher than 12,000 feet. From this angle, the three stack together, framed by Nez Perce Peak and the Middle and South Tetons into a breathtaking and much photographed vista. This is also a good vantage to look for the Teton fault, the line along which the Teton range lifted to tower over the valley floor. Look a few hundred feet up the lower slopes.

Wildlife Viewing

The best times to see wildlife are at dawn and dusk. Spring, winter and fall tend to be better than summer, partly because of the decreased human traffic and partly because, in summer, food, water and adequate cover are more easily obtained away from the valley floor. Plus most animals are more visible against a background of snow.

Binoculars and a telephoto lens on your camera will come in handy, because if you're close enough to see and photograph wildlife well without magnification, you're probably too close. Park officials say if you make an animal move, you're too close to that animal. That goes double in the winter, when the difference between life and death for a creature may be the energy it expends getting away from well-meaning visitors.

According to helpful folks at the Jackson Hole Chamber of Commerce, the following are some of your best wildlife viewing bets.

Antelope Flats

Drive out Antelope Flats Road from the main park road, turn south toward Kelly and loop back in on the Gros Ventre River Road. Elk and bison migrate through this area in spring and fall. In winter and early spring, you may see moose feeding on grasses.

Sawmill Ponds

Just south of Moose on the Moose-Wilson Road, the park's back entrance, are a series of small ponds. Moose feed year round on the willows and alders that grow at the water's edge. In spring and in fall before the ponds ice over, this is a popular hangout for waterfowl. You're likely to see elk on hillsides west of here during spring and fall, feeding on grasses.

Buffalo Fork Meadows

The Buffalo Fork River, which flows into Grand Teton National Park from the east, meanders through a broad valley choked in spots with willow. Moose, which love to eat willow, often graze along the river near Moran in fall, winter and spring.

Oxbow Bend

You have two options for enjoying this wild-

INSIDERS' TIP

Near all major park attractions, keep your eyes open for a roving ranger-naturalist who can answer your questions.

life-rich area. One is to simply pull into the large parking area about halfway between Jackson Lake Lodge and Moran Junction, where the Snake River slows and swings a wide turn. Or you can rent a canoe and paddle out into the still waters of the Oxbow, which will bring you much closer to the plentiful waterfowl and the river otters fishing for their next meal. Watch for the moose that may be munching willow on the side of the river, the elk that may be browsing on grasses during spring and fall in the nearby meadows or the bald eagles carving circles overhead. Expect to see great blue herons standing as if frozen into long grayish statues on the river's edge. In the fall, the Oxbow is a great place to hear bull elk bugling at dawn and dusk.

Willow Flats

East of Jackson Lake Dam is an area of beaver-engineered ponds and freshwater marsh. Beaver ponds are often home to a wide range of wildlife, and this area is no exception. Waterfowl congregate here in spring and fall. Moose munch on the tangled willows year round. And, of course, there are the beavers. The Park Service closes the Willow Flats area to humans in winter to protect wildlife.

Gros Ventre River near Lower Slide Lake

In the early morning hours of fall, winter and spring, drive up the Gros Ventre River Road to just outside Grand Teton National Park, watching the ridgetops and south-facing hillsides. You may see Rocky Mountain bighorn sheep grazing. Males carry a heavy, curled rack of horn. Females and young males have goatlike spikes on their heads. Any time of year, watch for mule deer and, among the cottonwoods and willow near the riverbank, moose. Black bears are regular visitors to the Gros Ventre Campground (see our Camping and RV Parks chapter).

Other Attractions

Jackson Lake and Jackson Lake Dam

Seventeen-mile-long Jackson Lake was not created by its dams; the dams merely enlarged its water storage capacity to the benefit of irrigators downstream in Idaho. The first Jackson Lake Dam was a log structure that washed out in 1910. The earthen dam that replaced it was gradually heightened over the years to increase the reservoir's storage capacity. These days, the maximum depth of Jackson Lake is more than 400 feet.

Marinas at Colter Bay and Signal Mountain Lodge offer a variety of ways to enjoy this huge body of water. You can rent canoes, fishing boats and cruisers. You can sign up for scenic cruises of the lake at Colter Bay, including breakfast tours and steak-fry cruises. Both marinas provide guided fishing, and both, with tiny Leek's Marina, provide services and supplies to boaters. Colter Bay has a particularly well-equipped marina store (see our Fishing and Watersports chapter).

Fishing is generally good on Jackson Lake. Another place to drop a line is immediately below Jackson Lake Dam on the Snake River. You'll often find yourself in the company of osprey, also fishing. A boat launch and picnic area hide below Jackson Lake Dam. On the south shore overlooking the dam are interpretive signs worth checking out.

Jenny Lake

This glacier-formed lake at the foot of Mount Teewinot was named for the Shoshone wife of Beaver Dick Leigh, guide for the Hayden Expedition of 1872. In 1876, Jenny and her six children died of smallpox after the family took in a sick traveler. Nearby Leigh Lake is named for old Beaver Dick himself.

Recreation opportunities abound in this area. Teton Boating Company (see our Fishing and Watersports chapter) has a dock on Jenny Lake. The company rents fishing boats and provides regular shuttles across the lake, as well as scenic cruises. Hikers and climbers take advantage of the inexpensive ferry across the lake, cutting miles off their journey into the wild country behind Jenny Lake.

One popular short hike accessed from the ferry drop-off (see our Hiking and Backpacking chapter) is the Hidden Falls/Inspiration Point hike, which is less than 2 miles roundtrip from the ferry landing. See our Hiking chapter for more.

Jenny Lake is also known for its excellent

fishing. Lake trout weighing up to 40 pounds have been pulled from these clear waters.

Leigh and String Lakes

Also created by glaciers, these linked lakes provide pleasant hiking, canoeing and picnicking, as well as lovely photo opportunities. Try photos in the morning when the lakes are still and Mount Moran, Rockchuck Peak and the Grand Teton are reflected on their calm surfaces.

You can launch canoes, available for rent at several locations in the park, into shallow String Lake (see our Fishing and Watersports chapter). Your course then takes you for a half-hour paddle to the clearly marked portage that leads to much larger Leigh Lake. Or hike from the String Lake Trailhead north of Jenny Lake Lodge; you can go completely around String Lake, or skirt the south shores of both String and Leigh lakes to tiny Bearpaw Lake, and return as you came. (For more Teton hikes, see our Hiking and Backpacking chapter.)

Gros Ventre Slide and Lower Slide Lake

Mountains and rivers are always changing, but usually they do it so slowly we can't see it. In 1925, though, Sheep Mountain and the Gros Ventre River remodeled themselves, literally overnight, when the whole side of the mountain fell into the river's channel. The resulting dam rose 180 feet above the natural streambed, creating a lake about a half-mile wide and 4 miles long. The lake contained about 65 thousand acre feet of water (an acre foot would cover an acre of land with 1 foot of water). The lake came to be called Lower Slide Lake, because a similar but much smaller slide had years before created a tiny lake upstream of the new impoundment. Today you can still observe the fresh-looking 2,225-foot-long slide scar on Sheep Mountain south of the Gros Ventre River and drop your boat in Lower Slide Lake.

Two years after the Sheep Mountain slide, much of the natural dam disintegrated. The resulting flood wiped out homesteads and little towns in its path, killing six people and leaving more than 100 homeless. Interpretive signs on the Gros Ventre River Road tell the story.

Signal Mountain

A couple of miles south of the Jackson Lake Junction on the Teton Park Road, a narrow, paved side road takes off to the east and then gradually climbs flat-topped Signal Mountain. The road is 5 miles long; no trailers are allowed.

The drive up affords great views of Jackson Lake; at the top are picnic sites and two viewing areas. One viewing area, at the very pinnacle of Signal Mountain, faces down into the Hole to show you the winding Snake and the distant Gros Ventre and Hoback mountain ranges. The other, lower viewing area is at the end of a short ridgeline hike. From it, you stare massive, blocky Mount Moran right in the face — or perhaps the belly button. Interpretive signage at both viewpoints is worth stopping to read.

Menor's Ferry

In Grand Teton National Park, near Moose, Wyo. • (307) 739-3300

In 1894, Bill Menor, who lived on the eastern shore of the Snake River near what is now Moose, built a ferry for crossing the swift channel, then a formidable obstacle. His was the only dry crossing place for 40 miles, so he was able to charge passengers up to a dollar for the ride. The ferry was made obsolete by a bridge built near Moose in 1926. Bill's old cabin was later refurbished and outfitted with antiques and exhibits as an interpretive attraction. The trail through Bill's old property is less than a half-mile long; in summer, you can take a free ride on a replica of his ferry. Replica and period products are available for sale, courtesy of the Grand Teton Natural History Association.

Colter Bay Indian Arts Museum

In Grand Teton National Park, Colter Bay, Wyo. • (307) 739-3300

Part of the National Park Service visitor center in Colter Bay Village, the Indian Arts Museum contains artistically displayed examples of art and artifacts by Native American tribes from around the country. Some of the well-preserved, carefully crafted items — moccasins, bags, boomerangs, hide paintings and more — date to the 19th century, when local

Native American cultures were still largely intact.

The bottom floor houses one or more guest artists, Native American craftspeople who will show you their work and answer your questions. The museum is open in summer only. There is no admission charge.

Jackson Hole

The valley of Jackson Hole, encompassing much of Grand Teton National Park as well as the towns of Jackson, Wilson and Teton Village, is packed with both natural and man-made attractions. Those inside the park are covered above. Most of our other picks are in or near the town of Jackson. For more on the valley called Jackson Hole, see our Area Overview chapter.

Town Square

Jackson, Wyo. • No phone

Before Jackson was hip, this little park was surrounded by locally owned souvenir shops and restaurants. Then booming tourism caused town square shops to become the most expensive commercial properties in a very expensive town. Now the square is home to factory outlets for major chains such as Coldwater Creek, Ralph Lauren and Eddie Bauer, as well as upscale art galleries and fine dining establishments. Town square dates to 1932. Its official name, commemorating the birth of our nation's first president, is George Washington Memorial Park — though even locals don't recall that.

In summer, the square is home to one of the town's longest-running attractions, the Town Square Shootout. For more than 40 years, the Jackson Hole Shootout Gang has put on its show. The action starts around 6:30 every night but Sunday, barring torrential rains. Shows last about 20 minutes. When the dust clears, five to 12 gunslingers are sprawled in the streets. After they come back to life, performers shake hands and sign autographs. Big crowds are typical, so arrive early if you want to see the action up close. The closer you are to the intersection of Center Street and Broadway Avenue, the better.

The antler arches that bracket each of the park's four sidewalk entrances are attractions in themselves. They were built between 1953 and 1969 by the local Rotary Club. Nobody could think what else to do with antlers, which in those days were plentiful and valueless. Every late winter or early spring, bull elk drop the antlers they have sharpened and wielded in battles with other bulls. Thousands of antlers lie like dead branches across the National Elk Refuge just outside of town. Since the refuge's grasslands are tended to produce maximum browse for the wintering herds, the antlers must be removed. These days elk antlers are extremely valuable, but back then nobody wanted them, so they were warehoused. For a while in the 1920s, antlers were handed to tourists as free souvenirs of their visit to Jackson Hole. The arches were another solution to a sticky problem.

The southwest arch consists of approximately 500 antlers. The number has to be approximate because the southwest arch, like the other three, gradually becomes smaller over the course of the summer as tourists steal a chunk here and a bit there. Every year the Rotary Club replaces the missing bulk with new antlers salvaged from the refuge. Antlers not used for this purpose are sold at auction by the Rotary Club and the Boy Scouts (see our Annual Events chapter).

The Jackson Chamber of Commerce annually receives letters of protest from folks who believe the town killed hundreds of animals to create this tourist attraction.

National Museum of Wildlife Art

2820 Rungius Rd. off U.S. Hwy. 26 near Jackson, Wyo. • (307) 733-5771

Brooding 100 feet above the National Elk Refuge like a medieval castle overlooking its kingdom, the National Museum of Wildlife Art is worth stopping for even if you're not a wildlife art lover. We can guarantee you've never seen a structure like this before. The roughly fitted stone slabs of the exterior walls still host living lichen. Rooflines are rough and uneven, following the uncut shapes of the stones. Inside, the sandstone floor is imprinted with animal tracks, as though deer had wandered through just minutes ahead of you. A massive 700-pound bronze cougar, sculpted by Colorado artist Ken Bunn, crouches above the wide entrance stairway. One wall of the lobby area is formed by a huge window facing toward the National Elk Refuge, where thousands of elk congregate in late fall and through the winter.

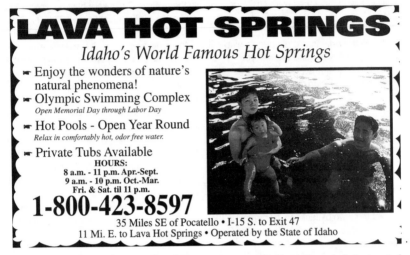

Fanning out from this lobby are 12 exhibit rooms, a gift shop, a 200-seat auditorium and The Rising Sage Cafe, which serves light meals during museum hours. The exhibit rooms house special shows and a permanent collection that includes greats such as John Clymer, C.M. Russell, Frederic Remington, Titian Ramsey Peale, Albert Bierstadt, Karl Bodmer, and Carl Rungius. The auditorium is home to an enticing array of films, symposia and lectures, some of them free (ask for a calendar at the desk).

The museum is open seven days a week, summer and winter. In spring and fall, Sunday hours are shortened. You pay the $6 entry fee only if you're going into the exhibit rooms; wandering the foyer or visiting the cafe are free.

National Elk Refuge and Elk Refuge Sleigh Rides

U.S. Hwy. 89 north of Jackson, Wyo. • (307) 733-5386

Created in 1912 to resolve winter conflicts between ranchers and starving elk, the nearly 25,000-acre National Elk Refuge provides a winter home to elk herds that once had the entire valley floor for forage. Most of the best winter range in the area is now inhabited by humans, so for about 10 weeks in the heart of winter, the 7,000 to 12,000 elk that find a winter home here are fed pelleted alfalfa; for the rest of their stay, the huge herds eat the native grasses and shrubbery as they once did all across Jackson Hole.

October to April, view the elk from turnouts along U.S. Highway 89 or in comfort and style from the lobby of the National Museum of Wildlife Art (see separate write-up).

Better yet, try the popular sleigh rides, which depart from the National Museum of Wildlife Art every 20 minutes between 10 AM and 4 PM from mid-December through mid-April. Purchase your ticket from the museum desk and head for the waiting room to see slide shows and ask refuge staff your questions. The sleigh rides, provided by Bar T 5 Ranch, take about an hour and cost $12 for adults. A combo ticket costs $3 more and buys you a sleighride and entry into the National Museum of Wildlife Art. Your 20-passenger wagon is drawn by two horses; it will circle the herd, coming sometimes as close as 25 or 30 yards. Best times are late in the winter, when the elk are accustomed to humans and sleighs and allow closer approach, and early in the day, when the alfalfa pellets put out at 8 AM are still being consumed. Early morning may also be the best time to view wolves stalking the elk or feeding on those they've already killed. Transplanted into Yellowstone National Park in 1995 and 1996, some of the wolves and their offspring showed up at the Elk Refuge in January 1999.

On your way back into town, make sure you stop at the visitor center just north of Jackson. It's a multi-agency effort to make your life easy. Under this roof, find services and information from the Grand Teton Natural History Association, the Jackson Chamber of Commerce, the National Elk Refuge, the Rocky Mountain Elk Foundation, Wyoming Game and Fish, and the U.S. Forest Service. Visitors center personnel tend to be very knowledgeable people.

Other times of year you won't see elk on the refuge, but trumpeter swans often frequent ponds at the southern tip of the refuge near the visitor center.

Jackson National Fish Hatchery

1500 Fish Hatchery Rd., Jackson, Wyo. • (307) 733-2510

One of about 70 federal hatcheries in the country, this facility stocks local waters with cutthroat and lake trout and ships some 200,000 cutthroat eggs across the country. Cutthroat spawn from March to June, making a visit during those months particularly interesting. Trout at this facility are hand-spawned alive, not killed for their eggs and sperm. Other times, enjoy the interpretive displays, the outdoor and indoor runways full of fry, fingerlings and 8- to 10-inch-long fish. The facility is 4 miles north of Jackson on U.S. Highway 26/89/191. It's open daily. Your visit is free.

Wyoming Balloon Company

335 N. Cache St., Jackson, Wyo. • (307) 739-0900

If you're in Teton Village and you look up to see a hot air balloon floating against blue sky, a silhouette of the Teton range stenciled on its canopy, you're looking at something you could be doing. Wyoming Balloon Company has a four-balloon fleet. The largest, 10 stories tall, will lift 12 people not including the pilot. The smallest takes two. You can be picked up anywhere in Jackson or Teton Village. You get to observe the cold-air inflation of the balloon and then the heating process that lifts the inflated balloon off the ground. Your flight will begin as the morning sun slips down the face of the Teton Range toward the valley floor.

Rates in summer run about $195 for a one-hour flight topped off by a continental breakfast and champagne on the ground afterward. The company offers shorter winter flights as well.

Summer and winter, the flight corridor is about 4,000 acres, which is an area about 2 miles wide and 4 to 5 miles long. This area reaches the south border of Grand Teton National Park and allows the balloon to overfly the Snake River.

Rainbow Balloon Flights

Jackson, Wyo. • (307) 733-0470, (800) 378-0470

Hot-air balloon flights in Teton Valley, just on the other side of the ragged wall of the Teton Range, give you the opportunity to find out where you stand on the old Idaho-versus-Wyoming controversy: Which side of the Tetons is prettier? Rainbow will drive you from Jackson Hole to Teton Valley and back, so you also get the scenic trip over Teton Pass before and after your flight. Get more information on this attraction in the Teton Valley listing in this chapter.

Peak Paragliding and Two Can Fly

Teton Valley, Idaho, and Teton Village, Wyo. • (307) 733-7712

Experience paragliding safely with a trained pilot. Soar from the top of Fred's Mountain at Grand Targhee (with Peak Paragliding) or from the top of the tram at Teton Village (with Two Can Fly). You'll spend between 20 minutes and an hour in the air for a cost of $125 to $175. Get more information on this attraction in the Teton Valley listings in this chapter.

Teton Rock Gym

1116 Maple Way, Jackson, Wyo. • (307) 733-0707

Maybe you've been wondering what rock climbing is all about, but you'd like to try it under controlled conditions. Or maybe you're an experienced climber itching to get your hands on some rock, but it's winter, so you'll just have to wait, right? Wrong. Teton Rock Gym is a pleasant newer facility with room for more than a dozen climbers at a time to navigate its artificial holds and vertical and overhung walls. Climbing walls surround an open, gravel-floored area. Climbing holds are arranged into new routes every few weeks.

Ropes and some other equipment are provided or are available for rent. There's also a small weight room and a shower facility on premises. Novice climbers must take a quick, free lesson before they can climb. More formal lessons range from $30 to $45 and include the $11 entry and rental charges. Teton Rock Gym is open afternoons and evenings.

Ripley's Believe It or Not!

140 N. Cache St., Jackson, Wyo.
• (307) 734-0000

Robert Ripley opened his first "Odditorium" at the Chicago World's Fair in 1933. The Jackson museum, one of 26 descendants around the world, opened in 1997. It's stuffed with "pranks of nature" like the bunny with two heads and 10 legs, whimsical displays like the 5,500-pound ball of barbed wire, real fossilized dinosaur eggs and a shrunken head (actually, one of the few things every Ripley's museum has is a shrunken head). The museum even has a few fun pranks to play on you. Up to half of the displays are changed every year. Ripley's is open seven days a week, except in April and November, when it scales back to mostly weekends. Adults pay around $7.

Jackson Hole Museum

105 N. Glenwood St., Jackson, Wyo.
• (307) 733-2414 (summer only)

Jackson Hole Historical Society

105 Mercill Ave., Jackson, Wyo.
• (307) 733-9605

Jackson Hole Museum, which opened in 1958, displays items of local historical interest dating from prehistoric times through the days of the fur traders and mountain men and into modern ranching times. Jackson Hole's history is even more colorful than its current incarnation, so expect to be entertained.

The museum is open in summer only. Admission is $3.

The affiliated Jackson Hole Historical Society is a Western researcher's dream. On display in this historic log cabin are artifacts, maps, old newspapers and photos. In the stacks are shelves of archival volumes, recorded oral histories from locals and thousands more photographs. Some of these photos depict a 19th-century Jackson, a rough-and-tumble town with a reputation for harboring horse thieves, gamblers and no-goods. Staff are happy to assist serious researchers or the merely curious. The Historical Center is open weekdays year round. There is no admission charge.

Alpine Slide

Snow King Resort, Jackson, Wyo.
• (307) 733-7680

The Alpine Slide snakes 2,500 feet from the top of Rafferty Chairlift to the resort hotel below, dipping into and out of the trees and slipping past wildflower meadows. You'll ride the lift up and pilot your own brakeable toboggan down the cement channel. Choose your speed: Your trip down can be as sedate or as exhilarating as you like. Adults ride for $7. Kids 6 and younger must ride with an adult.

Red Velvet Swing Old Time Photos

36 E. Broadway Ave., Jackson, Wyo.
• (307) 733-6467

David Dunn's place, tucked into the basement of Cache Creek Square, will bring out the exhibitionist in you. He has more than 50 complete, hat-to-shoes costumes. You can pose in the clawfoot bathtub, behind the saloon doors, in the saddle or against the wagon wheel. The walls, lined with photos of other sudden exhibitionists, will help you decide who you want to be.

Photos can be developed and framed while you wait. Dunn says he creates around 100 old-time photos a day in summer and about five a day after the snow flies.

Red Velvet Swing closes on Tuesdays and Wednesdays between Labor Day and Memorial Day.

Granite Creek Hot Springs

End of Granite Creek Rd., off U.S. Hwy. 189, near Hoback Junction, Wyo.
• (307) 734-7400

Granite Creek Road ends at a parking area. From there, pack your towel, your favorite pool toys and an ice chest loaded with drinks and lunch down the hill. Cross crystal-clear Granite Creek on a footbridge and walk up the short trail to heaven in the wilderness: a pool full of warm, clear water enclosed by a wooden deck and spectacular scenery.

About 50 feet in diameter and 8 feet deep at its deepest, Granite Creek Hot Springs is a great place for adults to relax and kids to play. Above you towers 10,808-foot-high Pinnacle Peak. Just outside the fence are picnic areas and a bathhouse with pit toilets. Down by the creek are more picnic sites. The pool was constructed in 1933 by the Civilian Conservation Corps and is operated by a Forest Service concessionaire. Summer temperatures dip down to around 93 degrees as snowmelt percolates into the ground somewhere above the hot springs pool to cool the naturally hot water. In winter, when up to 400 inches of snow accumulates on the ground, pool temperatures can be higher than 110 degrees, hot enough to make steam rise from your arms and legs and make rolling around in the snow feel good.

Pool attendants say that winter use often exceeds that of summer, as snowmobile, dog sled and sleigh tours all take the 10-mile trek in from Highway 189 to bask in the steamy heat. Ironically, the gravel-and-dirt Granite Creek Road, which slows cars down in the summer, makes for faster winter travel — the trail is not plowed, but rather groomed for snowmobilers. Despite its isolation, Granite Creek Hot Springs is not a quiet place; it sees an average of 120 visitors every day in summer.

The adult admission for a one-day pass is around $5.50.

Astoria Hot Springs

U.S. Hwy. 89, near Hoback Junction, Wyo. • (307) 733-2659

The Snake flows by, clear and cold, but the equally clear water of the concrete-lined swimming pool is warm, around 95 degrees. This is thanks to a natural hot spring that bubbles out of the ground here. It flows into and through two pools, creating warm, clean fun. The large pool is about 40 feet wide and 80 feet long. The smaller, triangular kiddy pool is about a foot deep. Astoria Hot Springs provides lifeguards, dressing rooms with hot showers, lockers and even swimming suit and towel rentals.

Don't come here looking for solitude. The pool, adjacent picnic grounds and camping area are busy in summer. Both pool and campground close in September and reopen in May. The adult charge is $5 to use the pools for the day.

Surrounding Areas

Southwestern Montana

West Yellowstone, Montana

Grizzly Discovery Center

201 S. Canyon St., West Yellowstone, Mont. • (406) 646-7001, (800) 257-2570

Before Yellowstone National Park officials began closing dumps and retraining bears to fend for themselves in the wild, bears were one of the main attractions in the park. They would hang out by the roadside and beg food from passing motorists. Today, if you want to be sure of seeing a bear, you'll have to go to the Grizzly Discovery Center, a zoo-like facility that offers visitors a chance to watch bears (and wolves) in an outdoors setting 365 days a year.

Eight bears (six adults and two cubs) take turns two at a time, roaming about in the outside 1.8-acre habitat easily visible by the public. Managers help keep the bears' behavior interesting by hiding food under rocks and in logs. And they supply young trees secured in subsurface tree stands for Toby, a Kodiak bear that loves to topple trees. (He has torn down all but one of the original trees in the pen.) A

INSIDERS' TIP

Read bulletin boards and local papers to learn what the natives are doing. Sometimes you can catch a dance at the local grange or a one-room schoolhouse. One of these potluck affairs is a good way to step into the local culture.

biologist is on hand to answer questions. Across from the bears, a pack of 10 wolves lives in a separate 1-acre pen. Vasectomized and spayed to minimize conflict and to prevent a population explosion, the wolves still exhibit classic pack behavior fascinating to watch. The bears, mostly adults orphaned as cubs, would otherwise have died or been destroyed. The center stresses bear and wolf education through exhibits, live presentations, signs and videos shown daily in a 50-seat theater.

Admission to the Grizzly Discovery Center is $7.50 for adults, $6.50 for seniors 62 and older, $3 for children ages 5 to 16 and free for children younger than 5. The Center offers an annual family rate of $48 and an individual annual rate of $28. The Discovery Center opens at 8:30 AM and closes at twilight, about 5:30 PM in midwinter and 8:30 PM in midsummer.

National Geographic Yellowstone IMAX Theater

101 S. Canyon St., West Yellowstone, Mont. • (406) 646-4100

Seeing the movie *Yellowstone* on The National Geographic Theater's 54-foot-high by 76-foot-wide screen makes geysers, waterfalls and bears look and sound so spectacular that you're liable to be disappointed when you see these wonders in real life. Watching a movie here is a total experience in movie technology. The IMAX theater has one of the largest movie screens in the world with a six-channel sound system surrounding the 350-seat theater. (The film for the movie weighs between 350 and 400 pounds.) Shown hourly 365 days a year, *Yellowstone* not only depicts the history but also captures the natural world in living color that some folks say is bigger than life. The movie was written and directed by Academy Award-winner Keith Merrill, who is known for other works about the American West.

Two other movies, *Everest* and *Special Effects*, a film that shows how the other movies were made, also showed during the summer of 1998. *Yellowstone* shows several times daily winter and summer. Each November, theater managers add other feature movies such as *Titanic* to their menu. Admission is $7.50 for adults and $5.50 for children ages 3 through 12. It's best to call ahead for showtimes.

Oregon Short Line 1903 Executive Rail Car

West Yellowstone Conference Hotel, 315 Yellowstone Ave., West Yellowstone, Mont. • (406) 646-7365

This beautifully appointed executive suite on rails is the centerpiece of the West Yellowstone Conference Hotel. When it rolled out of the shop at a cost of $16,424, the Oregon Short Line was the pride and joy of Union Pacific Railroad officials. For the next 32 years, the car traveled back and forth across the country carrying Union Pacific bigwigs and other dignitaries. In 1935, after the car's last trip to West Yellowstone, the Oregon Shortline 1903 was retired and set on a concrete foundation three blocks from where it now sits. The old railroad car changed hands many times before ending up in the care of Clyde Seely, one of the owners of today's Yellowstone Conference Hotel. To get to this museum on wheels, you must go inside the hotel. Admission is free.

Quake Lake Visitors Center

U.S. Hwy. 287, 8 miles north of West Yellowstone, Mont. • (406) 646-7369

August 17, 1959: It was the night the earth shook and the mountain fell into the path of the Madison River. Hebgen Lake tilted north, houses and chunks of highway dropped into the river. Cars were washed away, and so were unsuspecting campers asleep in their beds. Twenty-eight men, women and children died that night, and many others were trapped between the slide that blocked the rising river and the missing sections of road behind them. Rescuers worked through the day to save the stranded survivors. Today the scene at Quake Lake, formed when the mountain slid, is calm, but the scars remain. For a $2 charge, you can learn more about the 1959 earthquake by stopping at the Quake Lake Visitors Center. Besides a collection of old photos and interpretive maps and signs, the center shows a movie about the earthquake. Quake Lake Visitors Center is open from Memorial Day through the end of September.

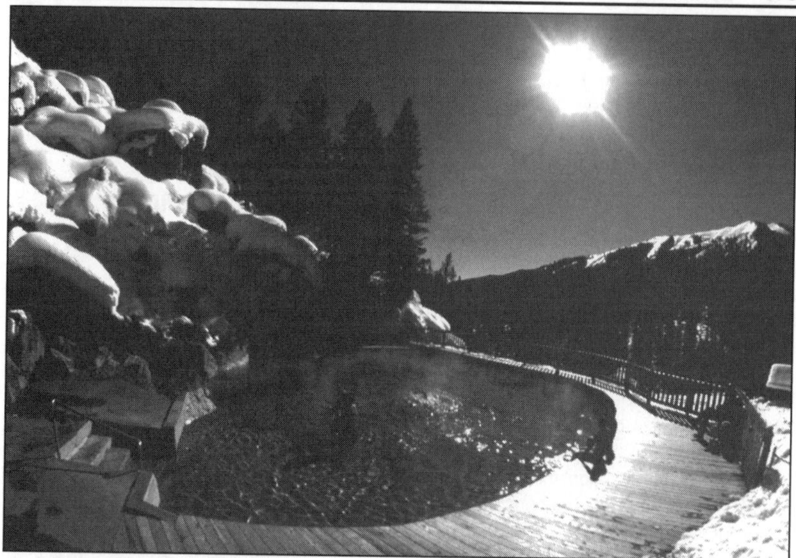
Photo: Robert Bower

Granite Creek Hot Springs near Hoback Junction, Wyoming, is a popular spot to soak your weary bones.

Gardiner, Montana

Roosevelt Arch

North Entrance, Yellowstone National Park, Gardiner, Mont.

Busloads of visitors to Yellowstone National Park pile out to have their pictures taken in front of this 50-foot-high basaltic stone arch. Designed by park architect Robert Reamer, the arch has a 20-foot-wide, 30-foot-high opening, with 12-foot-high wing walls extending 50 feet on either side. Built in 1903, it was designed to make up for the unspectacular terrain greeting tourists as they entered the park. The arch was dedicated that same year by President Theodore Roosevelt before a crowd of thousands. Inscribed on the arch are the words: "For the benefit and enjoyment of the people."

Bozeman, Montana

Museum of the Rockies

600 W. Nagy Blvd., Bozeman, Mont. • (406) 994-2251

At the heart of the Montana State University's Museum of the Rockies is a T. Rex dinosaur skeleton unearthed in 1990 near Jordan, Montana. Jack Horner, the curator of paleontology at the museum, was the scientific adviser for the movie *The Lost World*, the sequel to *Jurassic Park*. He is also author of *Dinosaur Lives: An Evolutionary Saga*. Horner and his staff have collected more than 15,000 fossil specimens from the badlands of Montana.

In other wings of this museum, enriched by its university connections, you'll find interactive exhibits on geology as well as the Taylor Planetarium and the Tinsley Homestead, a living-history farm. The focal point of the farm is the two-story log farmhouse built in 1921 by Oliver and Annie May Beiring. Now edged by newer subdivisions, a 12.5-acre piece of the family farm was purchased by the museum in 1995. The Living History Farm, open daily from 9 AM to 4 PM, Memorial Day through Labor Day, employs costumed interpreters who carry on 19th-century living at the farm. You might find them cooking on a woodburning stove, forging iron in the blacksmith shop, gathering eggs or plowing with a team of horses.

The Museum of the Rockies is open year round and offers a multitude of classes, workshops and educational tours. Admission to the Museum of the Rockies is $6 for adults and $4 for children ages 5 to 18. Children 4 and younger are admitted free. Memorial through Labor Day, the museum is open from 8 AM to 8 PM seven days a week. The rest of the year, it operates 9 AM to 5 PM Monday through Saturday, and 12:30 to 5 PM Sunday. The Taylor Planetarium regularly shows films with such titles as *The Dinosaur Chronicles*, *Rocky Mountain Skies* and *Laser's Southern Cooking*. It also features children's programs on Saturday mornings. The cost is $2.50 per person.

American Computer Museum
234 E. Babcock, Bozeman, Mont.
• (406) 587-7545

In this 6,000-square-foot museum, you can ponder the dinosaurs of the computer world in a program that takes you back 4,000 years. You'll see everything from calculating devices from ancient Babylonian and Egyptian times to a 1950 electronic calculator that weighs in at a ton and has more than 18,000 vacuum tubes.

This museum, open all year, could enlighten even the most computer-apathetic in your family. There's no doubt it will interest cyber-tech nuts. June 1 through August 31, the museum is open seven days a week from 10 AM until 4 PM. September through May, it's open Tuesday, Wednesday, Friday and Saturday from noon until 4 PM. Admission to the museum costs $3 for adults and $2 for children ages 6 through 12. Children younger than 6 are admitted free of charge. Ask about group rates.

Gallatin County Pioneer Museum
317 W. Main St., Bozeman, Mont.
• (406) 582-3195

Housed in a historic jail, this museum tells the story of the Bozeman area before, during and after its settlement. Besides a model of Fort Ellis, built along the Bozeman Trail to protect travelers from attacks by Native Americans, the Gallatin County Pioneer Museum contains a wealth of historic artifacts and is staffed by people who knew Bozeman when it was less civilized. A resource library available to the public contains rare family histories and books, as well as more than 8,000 photographs. In summer, the museum is open Monday through Friday 10 AM to 4:30 PM and Saturday from 1 to 4 PM. October through May the Gallatin County Pioneer Museum is open Tuesday through Friday, 11 AM to 4 PM. Admission is free.

Livingston, Montana

Montana Natural History Exhibit Hall
120 E. Park St., Livingston, Mont.
• (406) 222-5335

The name belies the treasures inside this old bottling plant. In 1998, a world-class exhibit of prehistoric mounted mammal skeletons from China dominated this nonprofit exhibit hall. Waiting in stacks of boxes is the next display — an exhibit of mounted dinosaur skeletons — both real and cast. Just when the exhibit will change is hard to say because it will be shipped to another museum when the crew finds one willing to rent the entire show. Plans are in the works for future displays from Argentina. Admission costs $3.

Park County Museum
118 W. Chinook St., Livingston, Mont.
• (406) 222-4184

Park County collected relics for 10 years before opening its museum in an old school building. Open Memorial through Labor Day, the Park County Museum features two replicated archeological digs, the Native Cultures room with an extensive arrowhead collection, a Yellowstone National Park collection, fire engines, an 1889 caboose and a blacksmith shop.

The museum is open from June 1 until Labor Day, and managers plan to operate from noon until 5 PM. During the off season, the curator will open the museum by special appointment. Admission is $3 for adults, $2 for juniors ages 12 to 17 and $1 for children younger than 12. This museum is not very wheelchair accessible.

Livingston Depot Center
200 W. Park Ave., Livingston, Mont.
• (406) 222-2300

Livingston was founded in 1882 as a base for Northern Pacific Railroad workers who ran the railways and maintained the shops in the region. Later, the town became the jumping-off point for Yellowstone travelers. To accommodate them, the railroad built a three-building brick complex for its depot. Today it has been restored and is the home of the Livingston Depot Center, a combination museum, meeting hall and convention and cultural center. On permanent display is "Rails Across the Rockies," an extensive exhibit on railroading. The depot is also a destination for the Montana Rockies Railroad, which originates in Sandpoint, Idaho, stays the night in Livingston and buses guests to Yellowstone National Park for the day.

Lewis and Clark Caverns State Park

Mont. Hwy. 2 between Cardwell and Three Forks, Mont. • (406) 287-3541

Guided trips through more than 2 miles of a limestone labyrinth will lead you down 600 steps from one cavernous "room" to the next. Along the way are stalactites and stalagmites created by the slow drip of mineral-bearing water. You'll also see and learn about bats that make their home in the caverns and whose routines have been interrupted by the lights now used during tours. Once under the care of the National Park Service and Yellowstone National Park, the Lewis and Clark Caverns were so forgotten that a local man named Dan Morrison built 2,000 steps into the caverns then charged for tours. Each summer he would break the Park Service lock and replace it with his own. Authorities at Yellowstone National Park were too busy and too far from the caverns to do anything about it. In 1937, the Caverns became Montana's first state park.

A trip to these caverns is worth a drive way out of the way. To get to them from West Yellowstone you must drive about 100 miles north on U.S. Highway 287. A tour of the caverns costs $7 for adults and teenagers and $3 for children ages 6 to 11. Group rates are available for parties of 15 or more that make reservations at least two weeks ahead. The caverns are open from Memorial Day through Labor Day. A 40-space campground with several camp cabins is on site.

Virginia City, Montana

U.S. Hwy. 287, Virginia City, Mont. • (406) 443-2081

Once a booming mining town with tens of thousands of residents, Virginia City was the Montana territorial capital in 1865. By 1870, though, the gold had played out and most of the people had left. In 1890, the town could boast only 125 full-time residents, and the buildings that lined Main Street were frozen in time. In the 1940s, Charles and Sue Bovey began buying the old buildings one by one, while importing other gold-rush structures to Nevada City, a mile down the road. The couple also collected mining and pioneer artifacts from around the state.

Each summer for many years, the Boveys — and later, their son, Ford — opened Virginia City to the public. In addition to the displays in each old building, the "town" was home to the Wells Fargo Cafe, the Bale of Hay Saloon with old nickelodeons, the Virginia City Playhouse, a museum and the Fairweather Inn, all connected by boardwalks. Above the town is Boot Hill, where the notorious Plummer Gang lies buried after being chased down and hanged by local vigilantes. The Plummer Gang, led by Virginia City's own sheriff, had been caught robbing and murdering miners.

In 1997, the state of Montana bought the Boveys' portion of Virginia City. The attraction is being managed through the Montana Heritage Commission. In 1998, concessionaires took over operation of the historic town. Plan to spend one long day meandering through this old mining town. Main Street is lined with buildings filled with artifacts, and a narrow-gauge train runs from Virginia City to Nevada City, where there is another hotel, a cafe and several other attractions to intrigue you. While local residents remain for the winter, the tourist parts of the two towns are open only from Memorial Day through September. Many of the displays are free, but entrance to the museum will cost $5 for adults, $4 for youth ages 13 to 18 and $3 for children ages 4 to 12. Rides on the narrow-gauge railroad running between Virginia City and Nevada City are priced the same. Ask about the reduced-price combination ticket if you want to do both. For information about tickets to see melodramas and vaudeville by the Virginia City Players, or adult cabaret at the Brewery Follies, see our Arts chapter.

Red Lodge, Montana

Carbon County Museum

Broadway Ave. and Eighth St., Red Lodge, Mont. • (406) 446-1920

This hometown museum had plans to move by the 1999 season from its former home in a very old log cabin into the Labor Temple Building, the abandoned home of the local miners' union. Started in the 1950s by rodeo personality Alice Greenough, the museum was taken over by Carbon County in 1980. Exhibits in the museum include the Greenough collection, old bootlegging stills, a rodeo collection, the town's first telephone switchboard, a general store, an old printing press and a grand piano used in the Pollard Hotel. The museum board also has plans for a simulated coal mine in the museum's basement.

The Carbon County Museum is open daily from 10 AM until 6 PM, Memorial Day until Labor Day. Admission is $4 for adults.

Beartooth Highway

U.S. Hwy. 212 between Red Lodge and Cooke City, Mont.

Throughout this book you'll see references to the Beartooth Highway, which has made many a tourist quiver with its narrow, winding ascents and descents. Charles Kuralt called this the most beautiful drive in America. Built in the 1930s, this road seems to crawl to the top of the world, where rocky crags jut out of lush alpine meadows in summer. At once rugged and fragile, this wild terrain is ruled by the stormy whims of winter. In summer, snow clings to north-facing slopes. Diehard skiers and snowboarders pack their snow-sliding toys to headwalls and bomb down vertical snowfields on the Fourth of July. Trails etched into the grassy meadows lead everywhere into the wilderness. And campgrounds invite travelers to stay for a spell.

At the summit, you'll find the Top of the World Store, open only in summer. The owners, former schoolteachers, return each June to dig their store out. In 1997, when they reached the store in mid-June, it was buried under a 23-foot snowdrift. Depending on the time and amount of snowfall, this road is open from mid-May until mid-October. It can snow any month of the year here.

Eastern Idaho

Teton Valley, Idaho

Teton Aviation Center

675 Airport Rd., Driggs, Idaho • (208) 354-3100, (800) 472-6382

On blue-sky days, summer or winter, you can get the bird's-eye view of the Tetons from a glider plane. Teton Aviation flies daily, weather permitting. Gliders have no engines of their own — they are pulled into the air by a tow plane. Once the tow plane detaches from your glider at 11,700 feet, you share the sky only with your pilot, the Tetons and the whispering wind. In summer, the glider pilot seeks out and uses thermal air masses to lift the kite-like plane high above Teton Valley. In winter, there are no thermals; instead pilots catch what they call "ridge lift," a gentle breeze in the valley deflected upward by a foothill or ridge; wave soaring won't usually carry you as high as summer thermals can.

Flights last up to an hour, stay within a 25-mile radius of the airport and cost $140 per person. Hour-long scenic airplane rides are also available.

Peak Paragliding and Two Can Fly

INSIDERS' TIP

Springtime is branding time in cattle country. Since brandings are generally a local affair, you'll be lucky to be invited to one. Still, keep your ears open in cafes or haunt local hardware stores or feed stores if you're bent on attending a branding. There's nothing like it.

Teton Valley, Idaho, and Teton Village, Wyo. • (307) 733-7712

Ever wonder how it feels to be a bald eagle, soaring upward on a thermal mass or cruising effortlessly along a ridgeline? Find out. Summer and winter, you can experience paragliding safely with a trained pilot. "Paragliding is one of the most relaxed adrenaline sports there is: You're sitting comfortable and secure, and yet there's plenty to be excited about," says Peak Paragliding's Tom Bartlett. Rides are available on windless and light-wind days on both sides of the Tetons. Soar from the top of Fred's Mountain at Grand Targhee (with Peak Paragliding) or from the top of the tram at Teton Village (with Two Can Fly). You'll spend between 20 minutes and an hour in the air, for a cost of $125 to $175. If the winds are right, your pilot may be able to lift the two of you above the ragged summits of the Teton range.

Rainbow Balloon Flights

Jackson, Wyo. • (307) 733-0470, (800) 378-0470

Rainbow launches its balloons from Driggs' fairgrounds seven fair-weather days a week. Balloons are nine stories tall and 90 feet in diameter, striped in rainbow shades. Flights are peaceful and silent; the balloon has no choice but to move with the speed and direction of the winds. The one-hour rides can take you as high as 3,000 feet, or, in cooperative wind conditions, as low as necessary to check out a fox, deer or moose.

Balloons hold seven adults plus the pilot, but generally the pilot takes a maximum of six passengers. The pilot may be able to bring you down nearly at your starting point, or the company's chase vehicle may have to come pick you up as many as 20 miles away. Flights begin at sunrise, when air is most stable.

Rainbow will pick you up in Jackson or meet you in Teton Valley. By balloonist tradition, flights always end with a champagne toast. The season runs June to September; the rate is $175 per person.

Moon Mountain Ranch Dog Sled Tours

Grand Targhee Ski and Summer Resort at Ski Hill Rd., Alta, Wyo. • (800) 827-4433

Make reservations early, preferably at least a week in advance, for your half-day or moonlight dog-sled tour in Targhee National Forest. You sit on the sled, cocooned in blankets, while the eight- or 10-dog team runs ahead through the snow. You can also try guiding the sled from the musher's spot on the back runners. Tours stop at the Trapper's Teepee where snacks and hot drinks are served. Larger groups (four or more) can arrange to have a full barbecue cookout at the Teepee. The dogs rest while you eat, then carry you back to your starting point.

Moonlight tours are magical, but require a clear night sky within a few days of the full moon. This means you need to be willing to reschedule or even get cancelled. These three-hour rides cost $260 for two adults with one sled. Each sled can carry 350 pounds. Daytime rides cost $200 for two people, if they can share a sled. Rides are available, weather permitting, from December through April.

Martin's Sleighride Dinners

Grand Targhee Ski and Summer Resort, Ski Hill Rd., Alta, Wyo. • (800) 827-4433

Here's an attraction and dinner rolled into one. The big horse-drawn, flat-bed sleigh, loaded with hay bales and warm blankets, carries you and 19 other guests to a toasty-warm, canvas-and-wood tent called a yurt. The ride takes about 15 minutes. Dinner is cooked for you on one of the yurt's two stoves (the other is for warming hands). You'll eat steak, chicken or a vegetarian entree with fixings and dessert. Hot tea, cider, coffee and water are provided. You're invited to bring your own alcoholic beverages.

There are two seatings per night, Tuesday through Saturday. Special arrangements can be made for large groups on Sundays and Mondays. Dinner runs $30 per adult.

Fin and Feather

946 S. Idaho Hwy. 31, Victor, Idaho • (208) 787-2771

A taxidermist since 1960, Keith Davis usually displays about 250 mounts of at least 50 species of upland game bird and waterfowl. He's good at what he does: his birds seem ready to fly from the walls of his in-home studio. Many displayed birds are surprising or rare: Blyth's Tragapan Pheasant is a blue-bibbed, gray-spotted bird with what look like blue horns sprouting from its head. The Gray Peacock Pheasant wears iridescent spots on its fan-spread tailfeathers. Baby ostrich are covered with wiry twists of feather, looking more like a kitchen scrubber with a head than an infant bird. The showroom is closed Sundays; yes, most of the mounts are for sale (see our Shopping chapter for more).

Island Park, Idaho

Big Springs

Big Springs Rd., Island Park, Idaho
• (208) 558-7301

It's a river's birthplace. One hundred and twenty million gallons of pure water a day — enough to meet the water needs of a million people — surge out of the ground here. A short distance from the glassy pool is a bridge. Toss bread crumbs into the water from it, and you'll see that constant flow (at a year-round temperature of 52 degrees) and the clean gravel bottom make for perfect trout habitat. Big Springs' trout get BIG. Leave your fishing pole in the car, though: No fishing is allowed until below the outlet to Henry's Lake, several miles away.

Take the short walking trail around the pond to reach Johnny Sack's cabin. Johnny was a German immigrant who built his cozy cabin and its furnishings by hand out of local trees. He also built a water wheel turned by spring water tumbling out of the hillside. The wheel provided electricity and brought water uphill to the cabin. Johnny's old place is now a visitor center and an attraction in its own right.

Your other Big Springs alternative is to rent a boat from Mack's Inn and float the gentle Henry's Fork's 5-mile-long National Water Trail. For more on the Big Springs National Water Trail, see the Close-up in the Fishing and Watersports chapter.

Harriman State Park Railroad Ranch

U.S. Hwy. 20 near Island Park, Idaho
• (208) 558-7368

Harriman State Park contains 15,000 acres of prime habitat for moose, bear, deer, trumpeter swans and more. The Henry's Fork of the Snake, a world-class fly-fishing river, runs through the park. An additional 10,000 acres of neighboring national forest lands are managed as a wildlife refuge, so game is plentiful.

Railroad Ranch is the park's main tourist attraction. Railroad Ranch was born in 1902 as a working ranch whose main objective was not profit, but recreation for the ranch's owners, who were mostly railroad management from the Union Pacific. In 1977, the Harriman family deeded the ranch and its property to the state of Idaho. Most of the buildings still stand, and the ranch still hosts an active cattle operation.

You can take a self-guided tour of the ranch any time; just pick up one of the detailed brochures from the visitor center. They'll describe the 28 buildings and building sites and explain their purposes. Guided tours are also available. Park entrance fees are $3 per vehicle. Learn more about Harriman in our Parks and Forests chapter. Also check out the park's cross-country ski trails, the area's best, in our Winter Sports chapter. A riding stable rents

INSIDERS' TIP

Jackson town square's four antler arches may seem huge, and they are: More than 1,700 elk antlers were used in their construction. A single antler can weigh up to 20 pounds, so the four arches together weigh well in excess of 10 tons. But there's a bigger arch in Afton, Wyoming — the biggest in the world. It spans U.S. Highway 89, stands 18 feet high and consists of more than 3,000 antlers.

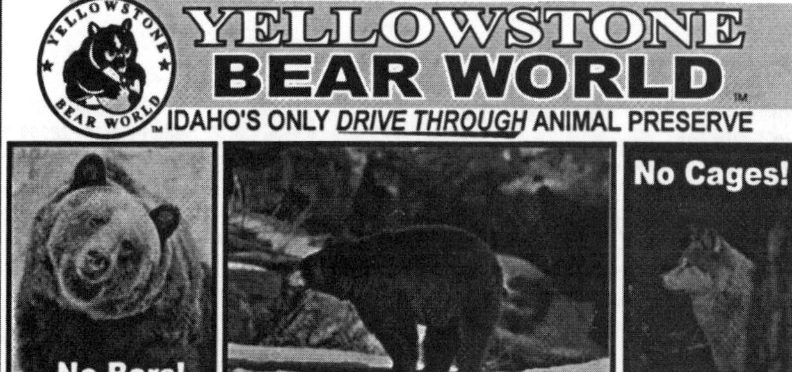

horses in summer (check out our Other Recreation chapter.)

Ashton, Idaho

Hess Heritage Museum

3409 E. 1200 N., Ashton, Idaho
• (208) 356-5674

This 17-year-old local history and lifestyle museum is open by appointment and, when the gate is open, for drop-ins. Find it a mile south of Ashton on Fish Hatchery Road (a.k.a. 1200 N.). Pioneer descendants Dan and Mary Hess are the curators of this remarkable, homegrown collection. Mary's grandfather was personal secretary to the 19th-century founder of the Mormon church, Joseph Smith. Her grandmother traveled from St. Louis to Salt Lake City in 1852, pushing her possessions in a hand cart. Dan's parents homesteaded what are now the museum grounds in 1909, moving into an old dirt-floored, sod-roofed cabin that had been built on this land in the 1890s. This cabin is now part of the main farmhouse; in summer it's the coolest room in the house.

Enjoy the museum's collections of old wagons, the reproduction one-room schoolhouse, the period clothing, antique furniture, old farm equipment, historical photos and more. But what you won't be able to tear yourself away from are Mary's stories. She's the real repository for the past she doesn't want forgotten. When Mary or Dan can't guide you around, they usually have volunteer curators on-site, also local, also full of stories.

You can make an appointment most days except Tuesday and Sunday from mid-April to mid-October. Entry costs $3 for adults. If you happen to be in the neighborhood on the Fourth of July, don't call — just stop on by the Hess Museum for the annual Pioneer Country Fair. You can learn about local history and pioneer skills like rope plaiting, listen to cowboy poets and hear stories from around 30 docents, some of whom are as old as the exhibits themselves.

Ashton Fish Hatchery

3330 E. 1200 N., Ashton, Idaho
• (208) 652-3579

Run by Idaho Fish and Game, this hatchery was constructed in 1920 to take advantage of a bubbling spring that flows out of the ground at a steady (and very fish-friendly) 50 degrees year round. Wandering through the facility's fish runs, which produce 50,000 pounds of grayling and trout per year, will take only a few minutes. You may find yourself down at the feeding pond for an hour or more, however. Buy special fish food from a pond-side dispenser for a dime; trout weighing up to 14 pounds swirl into view when the first pellet hits the water.

Fish stocked from this hatchery into the

Buffalo River, Warm River and the Henry's Fork are generally much smaller than these display fish. Idaho Fish and Game charges no fee for entering the facility. A staff member who can answer your questions is generally about.

Upper and Lower Mesa Falls and Big Falls Inn

Idaho Hwy. 47 (Mesa Falls Scenic Byway) • (208) 558-7301

Upper and Lower Mesa Falls on the Henry's Fork of the Snake River are the two best reasons to drive Idaho Highway 47, the Mesa Falls Scenic Byway. This long shortcut between Ashton and Island Park is dirt-over-pavement for part of its length, skirting the sheer edge of the Snake River gorge through lodgepole forest. Improvements in that road should give it a new, 24 foot-wide roadbed for its entire length and new pavement, hopefully by fall of 1999. Before completion of the project, of course, you may run into road crews. Camping and canyon-rim hiking are available along the byway. Be sure to stop and view Lower Mesa Falls, 65 feet high, and the upper falls, which are more than 100. As you view the lower falls from Grandview Campground, the almost-visible Upper Mesa Falls kicks mist into the air like distant smoke.

At Upper Mesa Falls, stop by Big Falls Inn, a historic old roadhouse built around 1907. Acquired by the Forest Service in 1986, the old building is being renovated at this writing. Project participants, which include the Forest Service and Idaho Department of Parks and Recreation, hope to stage a grand opening in July 1999. The building will feature interpretive displays that focus on local history, forest history and the state of Idaho. Books will be available for sale, and staff will answer questions and lead short hikes.

The upper falls also has a paved loop trail and viewing area that takes you right to the smooth, glassy lip of the cascade and into the mist rising from the narrow canyon. The falls' big voice rises from the canyon like a physical force. You could almost imagine that the force that destroyed the bridge spanning the river here at the turn of the century was the river's roar (really it was a winter flood).

St. Anthony, Idaho

St. Anthony Sand Dunes

North of St. Anthony, Idaho • (208) 524-7500

St. Anthony Sand Dunes are a startling anomaly among the fertile fields and sage-covered hills of the St. Anthony area. These quartz sand dunes range from 10 to 600 feet high, rolling one after another along an area 35 miles long and 1 to 5 miles wide. No services are available at the dunes besides parking and restrooms. Off-road vehicles, dirt bikers, hikers and picnickers frequent this surreal sea of sand.

To find the dunes, follow the signs from U.S. Highway 20 near Rexburg for about 15 miles. The Bureau of Land Management asks that you stay on the open sands; damage to the vegetation that stabilizes some dunes could force the closure of this sandy playground. You are also asked to use a safety flag if you plan to drive your dune rail or ATV here; please leave your glass containers back at the car.

A portion of the area is closed from December through March every year to protect wildlife. Before you come, it's a good idea to call the number listed above and ask the BLM about other regulations you should be aware of.

Rexburg, Idaho

Teton Dam Site

Off Idaho Hwy. 33 between Rexburg and Tetonia, Idaho • No phone

Teton Flood Museum

51 N. Center St., Rexburg, Idaho • (208) 356-9101

People in Rexburg, Sugar City and other nearby communities divide their histories like this: Before the Flood and After the Flood. They're talking about the day — June 5, 1976 — the brand-new Teton Dam failed. When Bureau of Reclamation engineers noticed clear springs of water spurting from canyon walls below their recently filled dam, it was already too late to divert disaster: 17 miles of the Teton River had become a reservoir containing 85 million gallons of water. Then cracks formed in the face of the dam itself. Desperate attempts to plug them with earth were unsuccessful: First the bulldozers were engulfed, and then the dam disintegrated like soggy cardboard. The towns of Wilford, Sugar City, Roberts and Rexburg were inundated first, but floodwaters eventually reached as far south as American Falls more than 120 miles away. In the aftermath, 11 were dead, hundreds injured, 25,000 homeless and the repair bill sat at about $400 million.

You can visit the Teton Dam site and stare at what remains of the earth-and-rock structure. Then look down into the river channel from the canyon edge (you can also hike down into the canyon) and see the effects of the tremendous flood. What was once a cottonwood-shaded river with a swift, riffly channel is now a series of stagnant pools and sharp drops. In some places the new river channel is yards from where the old one was. Experts say it'll be 10,000 years before the river returns to anything like its former state. Fishing, although still interesting, is not what it used to be.

When you finish thinking about the forces of nature unleashed upon man by himself, drive back to Rexburg and stop by the Teton Flood Museum. The first thing you'll see as you walk in the door is a flood-line on the wall to your right, showing how high the waters rose that day. Downstairs, along with all the cluttered mysteries of a small-town historical museum, are interpretive materials and personal recollections from the flood. The museum is open Monday through Saturday in summer, and Monday through Friday the rest of the year. You'll pay a small donation to enter.

Ricks College Horticultural Research and Demonstration Garden

525 S. Center St., Rexburg, Idaho • (208) 356-2018

Located on the campus of Ricks College behind the Ezra Taft Benson Building is gardeners' paradise. This botanical garden was created and is maintained by the students of Ricks College. Improvements are made every year. In the annual flower display area you can enjoy some 800 varieties of annual flowers and 200 varieties of perennials. The garden contains test areas where new annual and perennial flowers and vegetables grow. You'll also see a texture garden, which showcases the ornamental qualities of vegetables and herbs, and a dry river bed garden, which features wildflowers, ornamental grasses and hardy local perennials. Enjoy acres of additional surprises, all at no admission charge.

Yellowstone Bear World

6010 S. 4300 W., Rexburg, Idaho • (208) 359-9688, (208) 356-2011

If you want to be sure you'll see bears in Yellowstone country, stop here. Wild bears are generally elusive, but the bears at Bear World ramble alongside the road, sleep in corrugated pipe "caves" and wallow in artificial pools. New in 1998, this attraction allows you to drive through and past a series of fenced compounds in your car or RV. You'll see elk, reindeer and fallow deer, black bears and grizzlies. Pull-outs on the sides of the road allow you to stop and observe to your heart's content. Despite the fact that you'll be as close to these animals as if you were at a traditional zoo, we suggest you bring binoculars for a real "Discovery Channel" view. In 1998, Bear World had 21 black, grizzly and Kodiak bears wandering about. View the bears from mid-May to mid-October. Admission is $8.50 for adults. Children ages 6 to 12 pay $5.50; kids younger than 5 enter free. You also have the option of paying $40 for your carload, up to 14, if that's cheaper for you.

Idaho Falls, Idaho, Area

Stonewalls

751 S. Capital Ave., Idaho Falls, Idaho • (208) 528-8610

This indoor climbing gym draws folks looking for a good workout, curious adventure seekers who want a safe way to learn about rock climbing and serious climbers honing their muscles and skills. Rock gyms used to be where climbers went when weather wouldn't permit access to real rock, but these days indoor climbing is almost a sport in itself.

Stonewalls can rent you all necessary gear. It also provides ropes and basic instruction. Routes are up to 30 feet high; many are overhung and difficult, but there's something for every skill level here. Stonewalls is open Monday through Saturday evenings and Sunday afternoons. A one-day pass will cost you about $7. If you need to rent a harness and climbing shoes, expect to pay an additional $4.

Heise Hot Springs

5116 E. Heise Rd., Ririe, Idaho • (208) 538-7312

Choose your water temperature: The soaking pool is kept at 105 degrees, the small swimming pool runs about 94 degrees in summer and 98 in winter. The 10-foot-deep summer pool with its 350-foot water slide stays around 75 degrees. Adults pay $5 to use all of these outdoor facilities. Kids younger than 12 pay $3.50. You can even make a day of it, picnicking on the banks of the Snake River and then playing a round of golf at Heise's little nine-hole course. You'll pay a greens fee at the golf course.

The two warm pools are open year round until 10 PM except for three weeks in November. The golf course and summer pool close in fall and reopen in spring.

Idaho Falls Greenbelt and Falls

Snake River near Broadway Bridge, Idaho Falls, Idaho • No phone

The little town of Eagle Rock changed its name to Idaho Falls in 1891 on the advice of Eastern developers, who thought the new moniker more marketable. At that time, the Snake River flowed smooth and swift through the center of town — without a single splash. Decades later, a 1,500-foot-wide falls was built to generate municipal power and, coincidentally, create a namesake for the town.

In winter the falls are festooned with icicles; spring and fall find rows of Canada geese perched at the quiet lip over the maelstrom. Early summer, when the river runs high, the falls roar, foam and spit mist into the air.

Situated on either side of the river is the town's greenbelt. The walk, less than 2.5 miles from the Broadway bridge to the U.S. Highway 20 bridge and back, will take you along the river's grassy bank, past picnickers, in-line skaters, bicycle riders, joggers, and of course, the falls. You can also catch a stunning view of the local Mormon Temple, blocky and grand, topped with a golden statue of the angel Moroni. (If you're curious about the Mormon faith or just want to see the pretty grounds, guided tours are available through the visitor center. Only Mormons can walk into the temple itself. The visitor center is located at 1000 Memorial Drive, (208) 523-4504, right along your Greenbelt walk.)

Blast Off

1980 N. Yellowstone Hwy., Idaho Falls, Idaho • (208) 535-0500

It's an indoor playground, and not just for kids. Five kinds of diversions await you here, depending on your age. Little kids play in the Land of Make Believe, driving plastic cars, playing dress-up, etc. Galactic Galaxy is a mesh-defined, 3,800-square-foot world of plastic tunnels, slides and corridors. Little rooms are full of big huge balls and bigger rooms full of tiny balls. Children and adults can play here, as well as on the nine-hole miniature golf course, the Laser Tag area and the arcade. Laser Tag is played in a darkened maze of narrow passageways and low walls, splashed with neon paint and lit by black lights. You wear a vest with six sensors attached, and carry a gun that talks to you, telling you important things like when you've been hit by another player's gun, when you've hit another player, and when you're out of ammunition and need to re-energize your gun. Games last about 15 minutes. Kids younger than 6 aren't encouraged to play. Players are often teenagers, but adults and younger kids (who aren't afraid of the dark) also get in on the action.

Blast Off is generally quiet in the summer, but in the long, cold winter months, the place can be packed. It costs kids around $5 to play, depending on their age. Adults accompanying children get to play free. Laser Tag costs $6.25 per person per game.

Bonneville Museum

200 N. Eastern Ave., Idaho Falls, Idaho • (208) 522-1400

This historical museum tries to depict Bonneville County from prehistoric times up to the Atomic Age. Permanent displays focus on pioneer living, agriculture and natural history. Because the nearby Idaho National Engineering and Environmental Laboratory was home to the first nuclear reactor, a detailed exhibit traces the development of nuclear en-

Photo: Jackson Hole Chamber of Commerce

Every Presidents' Day Weekend, the Jackson Hole Shrine Club sponsors cutter races on snow at a track south of Jackson.

ergy. Researchers can make use of the reference room's wealth of historic documents, some quite rare and fascinating.

Museum admission is $2 for adults. The museum is open Monday through Friday, and Saturday afternoon.

Idaho Potato Expo

130 N.W. Main St., Blackfoot, Idaho • (208) 785-2517

If, for some reason, you wanted to encircle the world in french fries, how many would you need? These and other pressing potato issues are addressed at this fun stop just off I-15 in Blackfoot. Learn everything you ever wanted to know about Idaho potatoes; buy surprising products like potato lotion, potato soap, Darth 'Tater T-shirts and more. Then wander over to the kitchen to pick up your complimentary baked potato with butter and sour cream. Or buy potato fudge, potato cinnamon rolls and cookies.

The Expo is located, appropriately, south of Idaho Falls in Bingham County, the county that grows one-third of the nation's potatoes. While you're here, don't miss the world's largest potato chip. Even better, commune with the Dan Quayle potato, personally signed by the former U.S. vice president who is famous in Idaho for his inability to spell the name of that all-important tuber. This attraction is open May through September, seven days a week. Admission was $2 for adults in 1998.

Lava Hot Springs Inn and Spa

94 E. Portneuf Ave., Lava Hot Springs, Idaho • (208) 776-5830, (800) 527-5830

These hot springs on the Portneuf River near Soda Springs, Idaho — some 80 miles south of the area covered in this book, but we couldn't resist — carry 22 dissolved minerals. The water was once believed to have medicinal properties; people with arthritis, tuberculosis and other maladies came for lengthy treatments. Right now the facility maintains three pools that range in temperature from about 90 degrees to more than 106. The cold plunge pool cools you down after a long soak.

Nine Jacuzzi rooms, a cottage and 23 standard rooms are available for those too relaxed to drive after soaking. The Jacuzzis don't use the hot mineral water, because it corrodes pipes.

Expect to pay $5 for an all-day pass and between $60 and $165 for rooms. Lava Hot Springs Inn and Spa is open year round, seven days a week. Lava Hot Springs is a tiny town with all amenities and services, including motels and camping.

Northwestern Wyoming

Buffalo Bill Historical Center
720 Sheridan Ave., Cody, Wyo.
• (307) 587-4771

For anyone fascinated or even a little bit interested in the Old West, this world-class museum is a must-see. There is so much to do and see in the Buffalo Bill Historical Center that it could easily take you more than a day to work your way through it. Don't worry or hurry: Your BBHC ticket is good for two consecutive days. By the time you emerge from this 237,000-square-foot four-wing museum, you will have been steeped in Western history. Along the way you will likely find films, gallery presentations or tours for you and your children. Stop and enjoy them — especially the hands-on demonstrations scattered throughout the center.

The original Buffalo Bill Museum, housed in a log building similar to Cody's ranch house, opened in 1927. Today's version has wide, sweeping halls and houses four separate museums. The Whitney Gallery of Western Art features an extensive collection by artists who have documented and interpreted the West since the 19th century. The Buffalo Bill Museum contains the frontiersman's memorabilia. The Plains Indian Museum captures the past and present of the natives to the land, and the Cody Firearms Museum, the complex's newest wing, has the largest collection of American firearms in the world.

Also included in the Center is the Harold McCracken Research Library, which contains nearly 15,000 books and manuscripts as well as 250,000 photographs.

A full-time staff of 70 and a part-time staff of 125 work to not only run the museum, but also plan cultural events and educational workshops for all ages. The BBHC also has a special educational program designed for local schools.

The Buffalo Bill Historical Center is open year round, but the hours vary dramatically depending on the time of year. We suggest you call ahead to find out for yourself. Admission is $8 for adults, $6.50 for senior citizens, $4 for youth ages 13 to 21 and $2 for children ages 6 to 12. Children younger than 6 are admitted free.

Cody Nite Rodeo
421 W. Yellowstone, Cody, Wyo.
• (307) 587-2992

Started in the 1930s to entice travelers to spend a night (and some of their money) in Cody, the Cody Nite Rodeo is one big attraction that runs nightly from Memorial Day through Labor Day. For more information on the Cody Nite Rodeo, see our Rodeo chapter.

Heart Three Carriage Service
1701 Sheridan Ave., Cody, Wyo.
• (307) 754-0120, (307) 899-1485

Step back in time and leave the driving to Ken Larrew and his crew as they carry you through Cody in a carriage. You'll find Heart 3 Carriage Service on Sheridan Avenue (Cody's main street) somewhere near the Irma Hotel or at the Holiday Inn up the street during the summer only. (If you don't spot him right away, listen for the clip clop of his horses' hooves on the pavement.) For $35 per carriage, Larrew will take you on a half-hour historical tour of Cody June through mid-September.

If a historical tour isn't your bag, Larrew will take you most anyplace you want to go. Each year 15 to 30 wedding parties ride to and from the church in his carriages. And around the holidays, locals book Larrew to take them on a one-hour Christmas lights tour. Larrew also carries Santa Claus to the Buffalo Bill Historical Center each Christmas. Larrew runs carriages Monday through Saturday from 3 PM until the sidewalks are empty.

Old Trail Town
Yellowstone Hwy. west of Cody, Wyo.
• (307) 587-5302

This may be the most reasonably priced attraction and the most interesting in all of Greater Yellowstone. For sure, it's a labor of love.

Situated on either side of an old wagon road are 26 pre-1900 cabins, 100 horse-drawn vehicles and an extensive collection of frontier memorabilia. Behind the town you'll find the graves of frontiersmen such as Jeremiah "Liver-Eatin'" Johnston and Phillip Vetter, a trapper killed by a grizzly. The bones of these notables were exhumed and moved to the Old Trail Town graves.

Husband-and-wife team Bob and Terry Edgar began collecting cabins in 1967. Bob, an archaeologist, historian and Western artist, disassembled and reassembled old cabins in the townsite. Meanwhile, he and Terry lived in one of the cabins without electricity or running water. Admission to Old Trail Town is $3 for adults and free for children younger than 6.

Spirit Mountain Aviation

3227 Duggleby Dr., Cody, Wyo.
• (307) 587-6732

For a change of scenery, get above it all with Spirit Mountain Aviation, a charter flight service that offers scenic air tours over Yellowstone National Park. From the air, you can see how Yellowstone country fits together, how the Grand Canyon is tied to Yellowstone Lake by a ribbon of river and how Yellowstone National Park is protected by massive mountain ranges. From above, the changing colors of the park's hot springs come more into focus. Joe Siligato will also fly you anyplace else you want to see from a bird's-eye view. A flight over Yellowstone will cost you $240 per flight. That means if you bring some friends along you'll save money.

Tecumseh's Miniature Village and Museum

142 W. Yellowstone Hwy., Cody, Wyo.
• (307) 587-5362

When owner Jerry Fick was 14, he began building the miniature forts and leather tepees now included in Tecumseh's Miniature Village and Museum, a 30-foot-by-75-foot diorama depicting 200 years' worth of Western history beginning in 1800. The miniature museum is incorporated into Ficks' family-owned and operated Native American clothing store. (Jerry and Sherry Fick, along with their son, Michael, design and make the clothing themselves.) It includes four operating trains as well as hundreds of miniature figures — some of them hand-carved by Fick and others saved from childhood. Nearly all of the figures, including bison, horses and other animals, have been handpainted. Surrounding the miniature museum is Fick's private collection of Native American and frontier artifacts. The Ficks also have a good collection of Indian souvenirs like headdresses and drums for children. There was no admission in 1998, but the owners plan to charge a $2 admission fee for adults and $1 for children in 1999. Ask about group rates.

Buffalo Bill Dam Visitor Center

4804 North Fork Hwy., Cody, Wyo.
• (307) 527-6076

The Buffalo Bill Dam blocked the conjunction of the south and north forks of the Shoshone River, giving life to the dry lands of the Bighorn Basin. One of the first three major dams built by the newly formed Bureau of Reclamation, the Buffalo Bill Dam was the highest in the nation (328 feet) when it was built in 1910. It was raised to 353 feet in 1992.

Six miles west of Cody, the little visitor center/rest area depicts the story of the dam's construction. Standing on the walkway above the dam, you get spectacular views of the canyon and lake; you also get a sense of how dramatically it changed the river. This visitor center is open from May through September. There is no admission charge.

In today's rodeo riding events, competitors climb astride animals born to buck. They have to ride the critter for eight seconds. And they have to look good doing it.

Rodeo

Rodeo and the endangered cowboy culture it glorifies have penetrated the psyches of folks around the world since the 19th century when Buffalo Bill Cody took his Wild West Show East. An offshoot of the early days when cowboys tested their skills on broncs in ranch corrals, rodeo has grown into a high-profile sport that glorifies the skills once depended upon and now seldom used in cattle ranching. Bucking, grunting horses, snot-blowing bulls, finely tuned ropin' and doggin' horses, and flashy cowboys dressed for the part combine to create a show that tops the list of Yellowstone country attractions for many a visitor. Rodeos are broken into two kinds of events: riding and timed.

The riding events are remnants of the days when cowboys replenished their remudas (strings of saddle horses) with wild horses fresh off the range. Cowboys wasted no time breaking their horses. They just jumped on and rode — and hit the dirt plenty often before they had a bronc lined out. Those who could ride a high-pitching horse quickly built reputations repeated around the lonely campfires of the range. In today's rodeo riding events — bareback, saddle bronc and bull riding — competitors climb astride animals born to buck. They have to ride the critter for eight seconds. And they have to look good doing it. The better they look and the harder the animal bucks, the higher the score.

Even the best horseman wasn't worth a hoot if he couldn't throw a lariat. On the range and in the corral, cowboys depended on their lariats to rope, brand and doctor calves, yearlings, cows and even bulls. Today's calf-roping events, in which both calf and rider break at full speed out of their respective chutes, requires a fast, reliable horse and consistently good roping. (We've seen team ropers practicing in airports while waiting to catch a plane to their next rodeo.) The slower team-roping event is a timed event in which one rider ropes the head and the other ropes the hind feet of a steer. Each "takes a dally" (wraps the rope around the saddle horn) before stretching the animal out on the ground. On the range, a few cowboys still use these skills to doctor livestock. Steer wrestling, also known as bull doggin', is a crazy timed event in which the rider leans off his galloping horse, grabs a running steer by the horns, slides off his horse, then wrestles the steer to the ground. In barrel racing — the major event for women — riders race around three barrels then back to the finish line, trying to beat the clock.

At some rodeos, you'll see calf scrambles and mutton busting during a break in the regular action. In a calf scramble, a 150-pound calf (or even somebody's milk cow) is turned loose in the arena with dollar bills glued to it. A herd of kids chases after the animal, trying to grab the money. Each rodeo committee varies the details on the same theme. In mutton busting, kids try to ride bucking sheep. Other halftime events may include wild cow milking or a wild-horse race. Each can be plenty dangerous. The wild-horse race, though, may be the worst. Six teams are each assigned to a wild horse, which they must saddle, then ride.

In some smaller towns of Greater Yellowstone, like Gardiner and Ennis, you'll find less polished amateur rodeos with an earthy hometown flavor. For locals, these rodeos are an annual celebration. Clubs, businesses, kids, firemen, bands and cheerleaders dress up and parade down Main Street. The rest of the town watches them. At the smaller rodeos, you're apt to see hometown boys and girls entering events. You'll also eat a bit more dust — we said they were down to earth — and be exposed to whatever the weather brings. Afterward, chances are good you'll get swept into post-rodeo celebrations on local barroom dance floors.

At professional rodeos — especially the bigger ones like those in Red Lodge,

Livingston, and Cody, all held on the Fourth of July — the bucking stock is better and the cowboys are tops in the national rodeo circuit. Most of the hands who compete in these rodeos are working up to a dozen rodeos in a six-day period around the holiday. They'll fly into a rodeo (Red Lodge has an airstrip adjacent to the grounds) just in time to ride, then fly away again as soon as they've ridden. Cowboys following the timed events that require well-trained saddle horses borrow top horses brought by other cowboys. If a cowboy wins prize money on someone else's horse, he'll give the owner a share of his winnings.

Most rodeos are annual events, and, as we said, many in Greater Yellowstone happen on the Fourth of July. For more frequently scheduled rodeo shows, you can go to Cody and Jackson. In Cody, the self-proclaimed Rodeo Capital of the World, you can see a show every night from Memorial Day through Labor Day. Each summer up to 90,000 spectators crowd into the Cody Nite Rodeo, a show that has dominated the Cody tourist scene for 60 years. In Jackson, you'll find a twice-weekly rodeo during the summer months.

While every rodeo has the same basic events, each has its own distinct flavor. We've tried to capture the differences in this chapter. Most admission prices listed in the rodeo descriptions are based on the 1998 season.

Jackson Hole

Jackson, Wyoming

J.H. Rodeo

Fairgrounds on Snow King Ave., Jackson, Wyo. • (307) 733-2805

Most rodeos run once a year; this one goes twice a week, Memorial Day to Labor Day. Practice makes perfect: J.H. Rodeo runs snappy, with little hang time between events. All events except steer wrestling are represented. The rodeo owns its own stock: roughly 30 bulls, 70 horses, 30 roping steers and 25 calves. The audience-participation event is a calf scramble for kids ages 4 to 12. Two calves with ribbons tied to their tails are set loose among 50 to 100 kids from the audience. Winners snag the ribbons. Reserved seats cost around $10. Festival seating tickets purchased at the door cost a bit less.

Surrounding Areas

Southwestern Montana

Ennis Rodeo

Ennis Rodeo Grounds, Ennis, Mont. • (406) 682-4388

You're in the heart of ranching country here. Don't expect the high-powered, polished bucking stock of bigger rodeos. Do expect the unexpected and a much more homey feeling than at the bigger pro rodeos. And remember that many of the riders you'll see at this amateur rodeo have come right off the ranch. Like the horses, they're a little less sophisticated. Besides the rodeo, there's lots to see behind the scenes and in the stands. Unlike at some of the bigger rodeo grounds that make it difficult for you to connect with locals, at the Ennis Rodeo you can wander about among the pickup trucks and trailers catching glimpses of contestants caring for their horses, gear and families.

The Ennis Rodeo is always held on July 3 and 4. On July 3, the performance begins at 8 PM; on July 4, the show is at 2 PM. The weather

INSIDERS' TIP

Because so many big pro rodeos are held across the nation during Fourth of July week, July 4 is known as "Cowboy Christmas."

at this rodeo is pretty consistent — it either rains or snows, or it's hotter than blazes. Tickets cost $8 for reserved seating. General admission is $6.

Home of Champions Rodeo

Red Lodge Rodeo Grounds, Red Lodge, Mont. • (406) 446-1718

Red Lodge is the small town with the big rodeo. Marking its 70th season in 1998, the Home of Champions Rodeo has been so called because of the hometown boys and girls who have made good on the rodeo circuit. Most notable are the Greenoughs and the Lindermans. Sisters Alice and Marge Greenough, raised on a ranch outside Red Lodge, were champion bronc riders who went clear to Madison Square Garden in New York. Their brother, Turk, and Alice rode into fame from the 1920s clear into the 1950s. In the early days of the Red Lodge rodeo, the Crow Indians used to come from the reservation, set up their teepees and hold races on the track that then circled the rodeo grounds.

These days, you'll see a crew of champion riders emerging from a Lear jet that's just landed on the runway adjacent to the rodeo grounds. If you pay close attention, you'll note that they arrive just in time to compete before flying off to another rodeo. Besides the usual menu of events, Red Lodge features a wild-horse race and a calf scramble for kids. In Red Lodge, the rodeo doesn't begin or end in the arena. The parade is legendary, and the saloons are packed after showtime.

Admission ranges from $8 to $16. The rodeo is held July 2 through 4.

Livingston Roundup

Rodeo Park County Fairgrounds, Livingston, Mont. • (406) 222-0850,

This fast-paced rodeo features Kesler Rodeo Stock. Insiders know that means top-of-the-line bucking horses and bulls. (Kesler ranks among the top three stock contractors used at the National Finals Rodeo each year.) They also know that good stock attracts top hands. Combine those two ingredients with a crew that knows how to keep the action rolling and an award-winning announcer and you have one of the best little pro rodeos in the West. The Roundup, held July 2 through 4, is one of the three Gateway Rodeos held over the Fourth of July each year in Yellowstone Country. That means professional cowboys travel back and forth between Livingston, Red Lodge and Cody, riding at each place to increase the odds of winning prize money. (The purse at Livingston totaled $65,000 in 1998.) In addition to the traditional rodeo contests, the event features skydivers who land in the middle of the arena. Fireworks are also launched each night at the end of the rodeo events. Admission is $12 for reserved seats, $8 for general admission and $4 for children ages 6 to 12.

Upper Yellowstone Roundup

Gardiner Rodeo Grounds, Gardiner, Mont. • (406) 848-7971

This amateur rodeo, sanctioned by the Northern Rodeo Association and held on Father's Day weekend, is one of those hometown rodeos that's a little more like Montana used to be. Folks inside and outside the arena are more casual and a little less dressed up. Instead of featuring high-powered professionals who may have grown up east of the Mississippi, you'll be watching mostly homegrown cowboys and diehard grandpas who rodeo close to home because they just have to — rodeoing is in their blood. Besides its small town ambiance, the Upper Yellowstone Roundup is known for its long lineup of bull riders — 30 to 60 of them per rodeo — and its long, interminably long, slack time during which extra contestants compete after the rodeo. The stands are exposed to the elements.

INSIDERS' TIP

Idaho's biggest rodeo takes place every March in Pocatello, Idaho, about 50 miles south of Idaho Falls. More than $400,000 is up for grabs, making the Dodge National Circuit Finals Rodeo one of the most lucrative sponsored by the Pro Rodeo Cowboy Association. Area motels and grandstand seats fill fast for this five-day event. Call Pocatello's Holt Arena at (208) 236-2831.

Cody Nite Rodeo

In 1938 a group of Cody, Wyoming, businessmen started the Cody Nite Rodeo hoping the event would entice Yellowstone National Park visitors to spend the night — and some money — in their town. The idea grew, and the town has put on a nightly rodeo from Memorial Day through Labor Day each summer since. Rodeo, often the only English word clearly spoken by foreign visitors, has become Cody's hallmark.

Rodeo contractors Jim and Cathy Ivory make it easy for folks to get to their rodeo. First they make sure everyone knows about it. Each summer they hire a young cowboy to cruise main street for 10 hours a day, seven days a week, in a gold 1978 Cadillac. Draped across the hood of the slow-moving cruiser is a set of 5-foot-wide longhorns. Perched on top of the Cadillac is a loudspeaker blaring cowboy music interrupted by frequent announcements from the driver. Each evening the Ivorys send a bus to Cody motels and campgrounds to pick up fans.

Behind the chutes at the rodeo grounds west of town are the animals, the cowboys and the contractors — that would be the Ivorys — who keep the show rolling night after night. By day, Jim cares for his stock as carefully as if they were a football team in training. Their care doesn't end with feeding. Jim says he is so attuned to his horses — 150 of them, each with a different disposition — that he notices immediately if one of them is feeling out of sorts. Jim bucks them according to their age and personality. Some horses like to buck once a week, while others do better bucking every other week. Some horses perform better when they're packing a bit of extra weight, and others do better when they're slim and trim. It's Ivory's job to know which is which. Some

— continued on next page

Photo: Cathy Ivory

Bull-riding and other rodeo events at the The Cody Nite Rodeo attract about 90,000 spectators each summer.

are older horses that have been to the National Finals Rodeo but are too old to withstand the stress of traveling weekly in a semi-truck with a stock contractor who follows the regular rodeo circuit. Other horses are young ones just learning to buck.

That's right, there's an art to bucking. Like an athlete, horses develop their own techniques over time to best buck off those pesky riders. Just watch them in the arena after they've succeeded. They'll gallop or trot around the arena, head high, tail up, looking proud as can be. Often, a rancher will bring in a horse that nobody can ride and ask Jim to try him out in the rodeo. Ivory only has to watch the horse buck one time to learn whether or not it has potential.

Once horses have passed the born-to-buck test, Ivory looks for other qualities, such as straightforward "pretty" bucking that makes both horse and rider look good. (Some horses are dirty duckers, divers and whirlers. They look bad, they're hard to ride, and they can hurt the rider.) Next, he looks for a horse that will give a cowboy a soft landing. Some horses have a knack for throwing their riders high in the air. Ivory cares for his bulls the same way. And he looks for bulls that look good bucking and won't hurt the riders.

Ironically, Ivory's string of regular cowboys match his stock string: They're mainly either young and improving or older and staying close to home. Some of them are college kids bent on improving their riding and roping skills so they can follow the Professional Rodeo Cowboys Association rodeo circuit. While some of them work regular jobs by day, others simply rodeo each night and live on their winnings. A few PRCA riders rodeo in Cody during the week and at PRCA rodeos on the weekends. Like the older horses in Ivory's string, some of the riders are older family men who don't want to travel but can't get rodeo out of their blood.

Each day during the summer, Ivory and his crew work and draw stock for the night's rodeo. The announcer simultaneously encourages the budding young riders and educates newcomers in the audience. Two clowns fight bulls and fill in the gaps. Because following the pro rodeo circuit means kissing your family good-bye for most of the year, the Cody Nite Rodeo clowns are like many of their cowboys — great performers who like to stay close to home.

A tight-knit brotherhood, the rodeo hands hang out at the grounds by day, hauling hay, talking horses and helping out with the stock. For many, the rodeo grounds are home — so much so that they hold their own weekly church services there. Behind the scenes, Jim and Cathy Ivory are busy doing what they do best: rounding up visitors, stock and cowboys for 90 straight days of the Cody Nite Rodeo.

June weather in Gardiner is unpredictable. That means you could be going sleeveless, or bundled up or both. Bring a blanket, a cooler and sunscreen. And bring your friends. Admission is around $10.

Eastern Idaho

Island Park

Island Park Wild Horse Stampede
Idaho Hwy. 67, east shore of Henry's Lake at Island Park, Idaho
• (208) 754-4271

It all started 53 years ago, when actress Jane Russell, in Island Park to make a movie, told local rancher Vern Crystal she'd love to see a rodeo. He and other area ranchers obliged; it was so much fun they've been doing it ever since. Crystal Bros. Ranch hosts this three-day professional rodeo the first weekend of August in an arena overlooking the clear waters of Henry's Lake. It begins with bull wars on Friday, fine excitement since bull riders are arguably the smallest contenders in rodeo and bulls are the largest critters. Eight regular timed and rough stock rodeo events make up the action on Saturday and Sunday. Other events include calf riding for kids (Crystal Bros. provides the bicycle helmets) and wild-cow milking and wild-horse racing for adults. Wild-horse racing is particularly wild, because as many three-person teams as enter (usually around six) are in the arena at the same time catching, saddling and then riding the same number of unbroken horses. About 7,000 people attend the Stampede at a cost of around $7 per person.

Jacobs' Island Park Ranch Events

Off Kilgore Rd., Island Park, Idaho • (208) 662-5567, (800) 230-9530

Jacobs' intimate outdoor arena, 6 miles from U.S. Highway 20 on a 2,000-acre working ranch, hosts several Western events every summer. Some of these are bull wars, in which bull riders attempt to stay seated on huge animals 10 times their weight. Others include rodeos featuring a variety of other rough stock as well as timed events. Best of all is the National Cutting Horse Show in which highly trained cow ponies and their riders get to show their stuff. Watching a bronc rider or calf roper at Jacobs' is fun because the grandstands are small and close to the action: You won't need your binoculars here. Admission for rodeos and bull wars is around $7. The National Cutting Horse Show, which takes place the second weekend in August, is free to spectators. Call for other dates and times.

Idaho Falls, Idaho

Idaho Falls Centennial Rodeo

Sandy Downs, 6855 S. 15 E., Idaho Falls, Idaho • (208) 523-1010

In 1997 this Intermountain Professional Rodeo Association rodeo was voted best of the year by Association cowboys. It drew more than 500 competitors and 6,000 spectators. And although most spectators came to see the eight timed and rough stock events, from bronc riding to barrel racing, the calf riding probably got the most laughs: 5- to 11-year-old kids trying to ride skittish 150-pound calves. The calf-riding winner each night is awarded a trophy that often stands higher than the kid's cowboy hat. Tickets for this rodeo, held in early June, are around $7.

War Bonnet Roundup

Sandy Downs, 6855 S. 15 E., Idaho Falls, Idaho • (208) 523-1010

One of only four professional rodeos in eastern Idaho, the PRCA-sanctioned War Bonnet is also the state's oldest: The bucking chutes first blew open here in 1911. More than 250 contestants compete in seven events for prize money and the rodeo's trademark award: Winchester .30-.30s for each event's high score or best time. Around 7,500 spectators usually catch one or more of the three days' show. For kids, the best show is the mutton busting: Ten kids each night climb aboard a sheep, lace their fingers into woolly coats and, when the gate flies open, try to stay on. The rodeo's best mutton buster is awarded a BB gun. The event is held the first weekend in August. Tickets are around $7 for adult advance seats and $8 at the door. The rodeo is sponsored by American Legion Bonneville Post 56, and proceeds fund Legion projects and charities.

Northwestern Wyoming

Cody Nite Rodeo

Stampede Park Rodeo Grounds, Cody, Wyo. • (307) 587-2992

Pack into the Cody Nite Rodeo just once and you'll know why this town is called the Rodeo Capital of the World. Every summer night for the past 60 years, fans have sat on the edges of their seats watching bucking stock twist, twirl, buck and duck under the cowboys who dare to ride them. Geared for tourists, many of whom don't speak English, the announcer at this rodeo colors his com-

INSIDERS' TIP

Because every rodeo producer wants to keep the show short and interesting, many of the contestants — mostly calf and team ropers, barrel racers and steer wrestlers — ride during the "slack" after, before and between scheduled rodeos. Watching the slack competition can get you closer to the cowboys and lead you to Insiders' secrets.

ments with educational tidbits that only Insiders know. Contractors Jim and Cathy Ivory, who own the stock and run the show, produce more than a nightly tourist attraction. Behind the scenes, they're helping young rodeo hands hone their skills. And they're cultivating cayuses that are born to buck. (Some of them have been to or are headed for the National Finals Rodeo.) Besides bareback and saddle bronc riding, the nightly show includes calf roping, team roping, bull dogging, barrel racing for cowgirls and steer riding for the younger cowboys. Kids in the stands are also invited to join in a calf scramble and stick-horse races. The Ivorys make getting to the rodeo easy: A rodeo bus will pick you up at your campground or motel.

Grandstand seating for adults costs $10 ($4 for children). Seats in the Buzzard's Roost above the chutes cost $12 for adults and $6 for kids. Tickets for the 8:30 PM show can be purchased at the gate after 7 PM, at the ticket booth wagon in City Park, at many Cody businesses and at the chamber of commerce office (see the Resources chapter). Except for a couple of post-season specials, the rodeos begin June 1 and end August 31.

Stampede Rodeo

Stampede Park Rodeo Grounds, Cody, Wyo. • (307) 587-5155

Let's face it. Cody folks just like to be the best. And when it comes to rodeo, you'd be hard-pressed to find one better than the Cody Stampede, held July 1 through July 4. Celebrating its 80th consecutive season in 1999, Cody's four-day Stampede is the richest Fourth of July rodeo in the world. A $300,000 purse in 1998 drew 730 contestants. Among them were most of the top hands on the national circuit. Attracting the best cowboys doesn't stop with the purse. At the grounds, the Stampede Board provides a hospitality room for riders where they can lounge in comfort, eat homecooked meals and watch the rodeo on closed-circuit TV. The board also chauffeurs cowboys flying in and out of Cody's Yellowstone Regional Airport. You'll find a horseback-riding announcer, a top rodeo stock contractor and a state-of-the-art sound system. What you won't notice is how the chutes, gates and working corrals are set up to make the whole show run smoothly. This topnotch rodeo is a fast-moving show with world-class stock. Besides the usual events, Cody features a wild-horse race described in the introduction to this chapter. In addition to the rodeo itself, the Stampede features two parades (one just for kids) and music in the City Park. Admission is $14 for the July 1 to July 3 shows and $15 for the July 4 show.

INSIDERS' TIP

Both saddle bronc and bareback riders must "mark out" their horse. This means the cowboy's heels must touch the animal above the point of its shoulders as it makes its first jump out of the chute. The point is to force the rider to begin the contest in a compromised position, giving the bronc the advantage.

Comparatively unaffected by pollution and serious habitat degradation, Yellowstone's fisheries are in better shape than almost anyplace in the country.

Fishing and Watersports

Shimmering, shifting, splashing water — Greater Yelowstone has more than its share. There's blue-ribbon fishing streams, exciting whitewater and huge, water-skiable lakes. To help you match your destination to your favorite water-based activity, we've selected a few of the region's more popular fishing waters, as well as its best boating spots, whether your craft is powered by gas or muscle. For each lake, river section or stream listed in this chapter, we'll describe the watersports it's well-suited for. If it's good fishing water, we'll tell you a bit about that. If it's whitewater, we'll provide a thumbnail sketch of typical water conditions. If motorized craft favor it, we'll tell you where to find boat ramps and other necessaries. After each region's descriptions, look for sections on fishing guides, floatboat outfitters, powerboat tours and equipment rental centers. Consider our listings only a starting point: Once here, you'll discover additional interesting water and other reputable outfitters.

Remember that rivers and lakes change constantly. Old obstacles wash away and new ones are created as trees wash downstream or boulders slip from their earthen sockets and tumble into the river. Afternoon winds funnel through a notch in the mountains and peel 4-foot-high white-capped waves from what was a placid mirror at breakfast time. So even if you've seen a river or lake before, you should collect current information before you launch. Use previous experience and the information we include in this chapter as general guidelines only.

For more up-to-date info, call area sporting goods stores, paddling schools and outfitters. Fishing shops (see listings in this chapter, as well as those in our Shopping chapter) are often happy to clue you in on what's biting where. Park rangers, the Bureau of Reclamation and the Forest Service can provide water-level and other information to make your trip safer and more convenient. Find Forest Service contact numbers in our Parks and Forests chapter and other useful numbers in our Resource section. Where possible, our descriptions include phone numbers to help you do your homework.

Many of the campgrounds mentioned in this chapter are described in detail in our Campgrounds and RV Parks chapter.

Why You Should Pack Your Fishing Rod

Comparatively unaffected by pollution and serious habitat degradation, Yellowstone's fisheries are in better shape than almost anyplace in the country. Partly this is because Yellowstone National Park, starting point for many of the region's rivers, lacks irrigation diversions. Rivers aren't dewatered or warmed in farmers' fields, and the fish aren't diverted onto croplands. Also, underwater hot springs not only bring up nutrients from within the earth, they also warm river and lake waters through the winter. The warmer winter water raises fish body temperatures and metabolic rate. The warm water also supports aquatic vegetation in which many fish feed and find shelter. The upshot? Yellowstone trout grow fast. Finally, the region's heavy snows act as reservoirs, not only keeping water levels up during the hot summer months, but also keeping the water temperatures down during late summer. (Trout cannot survive in water that is too warm.)

Within Yellowstone National Park and through much of the region, anglers encounter seven varieties of game fish: cutthroat, rainbow, brown and lake trout as well as grayling and mountain whitefish. Cutthroat, the only native species, are so named for the red slash under their throats. The other species were introduced mostly by government agencies beginning in 1890. A few, such as the chub, sucker and shiner, were planted inadvertently by bait fishermen dumping unused minnows into rivers and lakes.

Montana, Idaho and Wyoming each have different regulations related to fishing and the purchase of licenses. Generally, the regulations are voluminous and require a bit of study. You'll find regulations and licenses at any sporting goods store that sells fishing equipment.

Many books have been written about fishing in Greater Yellowstone. A few of them are suggested in our Resources section at the end of this book.

Fishing Outfitters

Hiring a fishing outfitter can solve several problems for visiting anglers. Local guides have the local expertise that makes record catches more likely. They know where the fish have been biting and what they've been biting on. They know the regulations, so you won't accidentally end up on the wrong side of the law. Plus most guide services supply transportation to and from the fishing area, a boat, meals and drinks, and sometimes even equipment. If equipment isn't available to loan, it's generally available for sale at the outfitter's shop. One day of guided fishing in Greater Yellowstone will cost between $200 and $300 per person. Package deals that combine lodging or breaks for additional people are common.

River Outfitters

Boating with an outfitter offers many advantages. The outfitter provides most of the gear — usually you show up with the clothes you'll wear, plus sunscreen, sunglasses and perhaps a camera. Outfitters also supply the food, transportation and local expertise. You can generally count on boats and other gear to be reliable and the guides to be trained and familiar with the river. Many companies pride themselves on their guides' knowledge of local history, flora and fauna. Rates vary depending on length of trip, length of shuttle and other factors, but generally you can expect to spend $70 to $100 per person for what outfitters call a one-day float trip, which generally means three to five hours on the water, plus lunch. Shorter trips can cost as little as $35 per person.

Rating Rivers

When describing rivers, we'll refer to the international rating scale (see the gray box), which provides a general idea of a river section's difficulty. Ratings can change with water flows. The difficulty of a section is also tied to the craft you choose and your proficiency with that craft, so the information provided by this scale should be used with caution. Wading fly fishermen can use this scale also; it gives an idea of water turbulence and gradient. A class IV, V or VI river will be mostly or completely turbulent. It is likely to be very steep. Most of the region's best fishing rivers are rated I to III.

River Rating Scale

Class I (practiced beginner): Easy moving water with small or no waves.

Class II (beginner-intermediate): Regular waves, fast current, unobstructed rapids; may require some maneuvering.

Class III (advanced-intermediate): Large waves and obstacles, maneuvering required; clear route exists, but may not be obvious.

Class IV (expert): Large, chaotic waves, maneuvering difficult but required; route often not obvious; clear route may not exist; scouting recommended.

Class V (expert with previous class IV experience): No beginners on board; scouting strongly recommended; most people choose to portage.

Class VI (expert with previous class V experience): No beginners or intermediates on board; extremely dangerous; most people choose to portage.

In the sections that follow, you'll read about lakes, rivers and streams that offer prime fishing, floatboating or powerboating. For each body of water, we offer a brief description, then tell you about the activities that it's best known for. So just because we don't mention fishing as an activity for, say, Idaho's Fall River doesn't mean you can't or shouldn't fish there. It simply means that's not what the river is best known for. We also point you in the direction of fishing guide services, raft trips, powerboat tours and boat rentals to help you get started on the water adventure of your choice. At the end of the chapter, you'll find sections for paddling schools, scuba schools and some handy addresses and phone numbers.

Lakes, Rivers and Streams

Yellowstone National Park

To fish in Yellowstone National Park, you need to pick up a set of regulations and a permit. You can get a copy of the regulations at almost any fly shop or sporting goods store in towns surrounding the park. Anglers 16 and older must buy a fishing permit. Ten bucks will buy you a 10-day permit. For $20, you can buy a season permit. Permits are available at ranger stations, visitor centers and Hamilton Stores.

Generally, the park's fishing season begins on the Saturday of Memorial Day weekend and continues through the first Sunday of November. On Yellowstone Lake, the season opens June 1, while the lake's tributary streams open July 15. For complete information on park fishing, we suggest you pick up a set of the regulations. For more information you can write the Chief Ranger's Office, P.O. Box 168, Yellowstone National Park, WY 82190, or call (307) 344-2107.

Before you get out your rafts or your motorboats, be advised that, with the exception of the Lewis River channel between Lewis and Shoshone lakes, there's no boating on Yellowstone National Park rivers, and limited motorized boating is permitted on the park's lakes. Motorized boats are allowed on

INSIDERS' TIP

Anglers, remember: You're in bear country, so don't set up camp near spawning streams. Gut your catch away from camping areas and, after puncturing the air bladder, throw entrails into the water. Wash hands thoroughly after handling fish. Pack out or burn completely other fish remains. Don't leave them lying around camp, and don't bury them.

Yellowstone and Lewis lakes. Nonmotorized vessels, including float tubes, are allowed on all lakes except Sylvan, Eleanor and Twin lakes as well as Beach Springs Lagoon.

All vessels, including float tubes, require permits with a sticker displayed. You can buy boat permits at several places. For motorized-boat permits stop at the south entrance, the Lewis Lake Campground, Grant Visitor Center, Bridge Bay Marina and the Lake Ranger Station. For nonmotorized-boat permits, you'll have to go to the Bechler Ranger Station, the west entrance, the northeast entrance or the backcountry offices at Canyon and Mammoth visitor centers. In 1998, an annual motorized permit cost $20, while a 10-day permit cost $10. An annual nonmotorized permit cost $10, and a 10-day permit cost $5. For information about boat or slip rentals, call the Bridge Bay Marina from the first week in June until the end of September, at (307) 242-3876. The rest of the year, call (307) 344-7901.

Yellowstone Lake

This lake, described in greater detail in our Attractions chapter, is 20 miles long and 14 miles wide. Even on a day in August, the waters of this lake are so cold that Yellowstone National Park officials discourage any kind of watersport that involves being in the water (even with a wet suit). Hypothermia can set in after only 20 minutes in its 41-degree depths. They also discourage crossing the lake in smaller watercraft. In the blink of an eye, gale force winds can descend on Yellowstone Lake and whip its waters into a frothy monster. Nearly every year, at least one boat capsizes and the lake swallows its unwary occupants.

Fishing

About 50,000 anglers (nearly half of all those who fish in the park) cast their lines into the icy waters of the 136-square-mile Yellowstone Lake each year. Those who fish from boats are slightly more successful — they catch about 1.4 fish per hour — than shore anglers, whose average is .8 fish per hour. Those who fish from boats, though, should keep in mind that winds come out of nowhere and can turn Yellowstone Lake into a small sea with dangerous waves. Home to the famed Yellowstone cutthroat trout (and the illegally introduced lake trout), this lake is the gauge for fishery health in all of Greater Yellowstone. Despite more than a century of heavy fishing, and scandalously high egg collection rates by early fish hatcheries, Yellowstone Lake still has a pretty high cutthroat population for today.

Most anglers fish from shore between Sedge Bay and Grant Village. In June, when the ice is still melting, lake trout hug the slightly warmer waters along shore. Cutthroat hang out in shallower waters near sandbars and inlets.

Floatboating

Canoeists and kayakers should hug the shoreline. However, if you want to kayak or canoe the "other side of the lake," you can hire an AmFac shuttle boat (for $60 per hour) to cart you, your friends and your gear across the lake or to its southern arms. An abundance of primitive campsites can provide you with base camps so you can explore the area by water.

Powerboats

Yellowstone Lake has two boat launches: one at **Grant Village** near the campground and another that's operated by AmFac at **Bridge Bay Marina**, (307) 242-3876. Most people seem to opt for either riding with AmFac or renting one of its boats. Each summer AmFac hosts nearly 5,000 anglers on guided lake trips and another 15,000 who tour the lake on one of their hourlong scenic cruises. These cruises, which cost $8.50 for adults and $4.50 for children ages 2 to 11 in 1998, run five to seven times each day from the first week

INSIDERS' TIP

Headed this way on a fishing trip? Be sure you check our Resorts and Guest Ranches chapter for information on fishing lodges in the area. Many of these lodges are willing to supply guides to non-lodge guests.

Photo: Chip Rizotto, High Country Outfitters

Brown trout are the mainstay of southwestern Montana's fishing water, as they are in many of Greater Yellowstone's blue-ribbon streams.

of June until the last week in September. AmFac's guided fishing trips cost $50 or $65 per hour depending on the size of the boat. AmFac also rents rowboats for $5.75 per hour and outboards (with 40-horsepower, electric-start motors) for $26 an hour.

At Bridge Bay, you'll find 110 dock slips for rent. Rentals start at $9 per night for boats 16 feet and less. The marina sells fuel.

Lewis Lake

Twelve miles from the south entrance, Lewis is the only lake in the park besides Yellowstone that allows motorboats. At the southeast end is a campground and boat launch. At the opposite end is the mouth of the Lewis Channel, which leads from Shoshone Lake.

Fishing

Lewis Lake, which has a campground and a boat launch, has large lake trout and browns, with a few brookies and cutthroat. High winds and wavy water on this 2,000-plus-acre lake can make it dangerous to canoe, but fishing is fine from the shores. If you're canoeing, float tubing or kayaking, hug the shoreline even if you're headed up the Lewis River Channel to Shoshone Lake.

Floatboating

If you're into quiet water, paddling this lake in early morning or late evening will satisfy your longing for peaceful surroundings. From the lake, you can catch the pinks, peaches and grays of sunrise and sunset, as well as the faint smell of smoke rising from the campfires in nearby Lewis Lake campground.

Shoshone Lake

Shoshone is the second-largest lake in Yellowstone National Park (its surface covers more than 8,000 acres), and the largest lake in the Continental United States that can't be reached by road. Its remote location makes it a good fishing bet. And 26 campsites on its shores make it a popular backcountry camping site.

Fishing

Shoshone is home to lake, brown and brook trout. Fishing is best in mid-June just after the ice goes out, and in fall when the weather turns cooler. During the summer, fish hang out in deeper water and are harder to catch. You can keep two lake trout and two browns. In the Lewis River below Lewis Falls, however, it's catch-and-release only for brown trout. Browns spawn in this area.

Floatboating

Reachable only by trail or by a 4-mile channel from Lewis Lake, Shoshone Lake is still popular with canoeists, kayakers and float tubers. From the launch site near the Lewis Lake campground, you'll have to paddle about 4 miles just to get to the mouth of the Lewis channel. The upstream climb from Lewis to Shoshone ends with a swift shallow stretch that requires getting out and pulling your craft the rest of the way. If you want to relish your arduous journey to Yellowstone's second-largest lake, reserve ahead of time one of the 26 campsites on the lake's shore.

Firehole River

Beginning at Madison Lake south of Old Faithful on the north side of the Continental Divide, this 35-mile river wanders like a curious spectator through the Upper and Midway geyser basins before tumbling through the canyon leading to the Madison Junction.

Fishing

Ken Retallic, author of *Greater Yellowstone Flyfisher's Stream Guide*, says the fish in the Firehole River are smart and require "tiny flies for scholarly fish." It's fly fishing only on the Firehole. You can't keep rainbow, but you're allowed two browns smaller than 13 inches as well as five brookies. There is no fishing at all from Old Faithful to Biscuit Basin. Where the road leaves the river near Fountain Paint Pots, you'll find a side road leading west to Goose Lake. Trails lead from Goose Lake to the Firehole. In spring, though, this area may be reserved for grizzlies.

Gibbon River

This capricious 38-mile river begins as a small ribbon leading from Grebe Lake, home to some large rainbow as well as the feisty grayling. The Gibbon splashes down Virginia Cascade, wanders through the Norris Geyser Basin, winds through Elk Park and Gibbon Meadows, shoots through a narrow canyon, then plunges over Gibbon Falls. (The pool below this waterfall sometimes holds big rainbows and browns.) The Madison-Norris Road parallels much of this river.

Fishing

A 5-mile stretch that winds through Gibbon Meadows will take you away from the road where you'll find good-size rainbows and brook trout. The water here can be deceptively deep. Bigger browns and rainbows live below the falls, while smaller brookies and rainbows hang out closer to the source in the vicinity of Virginia Meadows.

Only fly fishing is allowed below Gibbon Falls: catch-and-release for rainbows and a two-fish limit for browns (they must be 13 inches and smaller), five for brook trout. Above the falls, though, you can keep two rainbow. At Grebe Lake, a 3.5 mile hike from the trailhead on the Canyon-Norris Road, you can't keep grayling, but you can keep two rainbow.

Slough Creek and Lamar River

Give a fly-fishing fanatic only one stream to dip a line into in Yellowstone National Park and chances are it'll be Slough Creek. Trails from the Slough Creek Campground Road lead to a series of three meadows through which Slough Creek slowly slithers before tumbling down to the next lazy crawl. Hidden in the pools, glides, riffles and side channels of this world-famous stream are plenty of large cutthroat (up to 24 inches).

The Lamar River, into which the Slough flows, falls from the east out of the Absaroka Mountains. Fifty-five miles long, it dumps into

INSIDERS' TIP

Altitude sickness is a serious condition, but feeling short of breath does not mean you are suffering from altitude sickness. Most altitude sickness occurs above 10,000 feet. Common symptoms of mild altitude sickness are nausea, vomiting and severe headache. The treatment is simple and effective: Head for lower elevations right now.

the Yellowstone River near Tower Junction after rushing through the canyon. Upriver in the Lamar Valley, where transplanted wolves were released in 1995, the river not only offers great fishing in its winding channels, but also a wonderful view and a chance to see wildlife.

Fishing

Both streams are home to good-size rainbows and have easy access to meadow fishing. The fishing season is from Memorial Day weekend through October 31. Cutthroat are catch-and-release, but anglers can keep two rainbow and five brook trout.

Grand Teton National Park

To fish in Grand Teton National Park, you'll need to be familiar with park fishing regulations, which you can pick up at the Moose Village Store, Signal Mountain Lodge, Colter Bay Marina, Flagg Ranch Village and many locations outside the park. Unlike Yellowstone, Grand Teton National Park does not require its own fishing permit. In general, fishing rules are the rules of Wyoming, with a few special restrictions. A one-day nonresident Wyoming fishing license costs about $6. Nonresident children younger than 14 may fish without a license, as long as they're accompanied by an adult with a valid Wyoming fishing license.

You will need a permit to float your boat in the park's lakes and rivers. You can buy craft permits at Moose Visitor Center year-round; in summer you can get them at visitor information centers at Colter Bay and Flagg Ranch, and at Buffalo and Signal Mountain ranger stations. A one-week nonmotorized permit costs about $5. A season permit costs about $10. Motorized permits cost about $10 for one week and $20 for the year. Motorized craft larger than 5 horsepower must also wear a state registration. Grand Teton National Park honors Yellowstone National Park's permits and vice versa; Yellowstone requires that craft with a Grand Teton National Park permit check in at a ranger station before launch.

No real whitewater exists within the park, but plenty of scenic paddling awaits. Canoes and kayaks are quiet craft and may allow you to observe wildlife that might otherwise startle away. The park's lakes and waterways also allow you to leave busy roads and experience a bit of Teton backcountry without a pack on your back.

Leigh and String Lakes

String Lake is extremely shallow along much of its meandering length. An offshoot of the Teton Park Road runs along some of its east side; a partially paved trail encircles it. Leigh Lake, like Jenny Lake, is big and deep and snugged up against a mountain's foot, in this case, block-topped Moran. There is no road access to Leigh. Boaters reach it by paddling up String Lake and portaging on a good, short trail over a hilly tongue of land. Shore anglers reach the lake by a short hike. The trail into Leigh Lake continues about halfway around its perimeter. Several attractive backcountry campsites perch on the lakeshore along the trail, providing great lunch stops when not in use by campers.

Fishing

Leigh Lake's deeper, colder water provides better fishing than shallow String. As in Jackson and Jenny lakes, resident fish are mostly the exotic and potentially huge lake trout, along with a few brook and brown trout. Stocked cutthroats are also caught. Leigh Lake, more difficult to reach, generally sees less fishing and boating traffic than the park's other lakes. In winter, ice-fishing groups tend to head for more easily reachable water at Jenny and Jackson lakes. The lake is open to anglers all year. The limit is six fish per day. Other regulations, including size limits, may apply.

Floatboating

Motorized craft are prohibited on these two lakes. In fact, Leigh Lake isn't even reachable by road. Visitors get to Leigh Lake on foot or by dropping a canoe or kayak into shallow String Lake at either of two parking areas on the southeast shore. Paddlers head up the lake until reaching a boulder-clogged inlet. A short portage on a well-maintained trail leads to much larger Leigh Lake. One of the more popular canoe trips on Leigh Lake takes you from the put-in and past two fine backcountry campsites — if unoccupied, stop and enjoy the beach — to the base of Mount Moran, a trip of about 2.5 miles one way. Climbers who wish to scale Moran generally canoe, although a foot trail leads to the mountain's base as well. Unlike placid String Lake, Leigh is deep and large enough to kick up respectable waves. Many canoeists choose to stay close to shore, especially when the wind's up.

Jackson Lake

Grand Teton National Park's largest water body at 31 square miles, Jackson Lake was not always this large: A dam at its southern end impounds additional water for irrigators downstream in Idaho. The lake offers miles of unroaded shoreline and several islands to explore. Several backcountry campsites along the lakeshore are available for reservation.

Fishing

The lake yields mostly lake trout, some of which can grow to 30 pounds and more. You may also catch cutthroat grown at the federal fish hatchery south of the park. Fish from shore at any of several access points or from any of the three marinas. Shore fishing is best in spring and fall; fish move into deeper waters in summer. Ice fishing is increasingly popular. The limit is six fish per day. The lake is closed to fishing in October. Other regulations, including size limits, may apply.

Floatboating

Most paddlers hug the shores out of concern for winds that frequently kick up intimidating waves. Access to the lake is good, so you have many options for paddling trips. One popular trip begins at the Spalding Bay access and takes you to Moran Bay, on the secluded, unroaded side of the lake. Hikers like to paddle across the northern arm of the lake from Lizard Creek Campground to access backcountry trails not easily reached from a road. Paddling this lake, huge though it is, is unlikely to feel like a wilderness experience. Powerboats are thick on sunny weekend days in summer, and water-skiers, personal watercraft, sailboats and windsurfers are allowed nowhere else in Grand Teton National Park.

Power Boating

Jackson Lake has three marinas. All services, including buoy rentals, boat rentals, guided fishing excursions, gasoline and groceries, are available at both **Signal Mountain**, (307) 543-2831, and **Colter Bay**, (307) 543-2811. **Leek's Marina**, (307) 543-2494, offers some services. Of the other lakes in Grand Teton National Park, only Phelps allows motorized traffic. Only Jackson Lake allows sailboats, water-skiers and personal watercraft.

Jenny Lake

This mountain lake, 2 miles square, would seem large if it weren't dwarfed by the watery sprawl of Jackson Lake. A pleasant trail completely bracelets it. Tucked up to the foot of Teewinot peak, it is arguably the most scenic lake in the park.

Fishing

Shore anglers use the trail that circles the lake. The Teton Park Road runs along its east shore, providing easy access to that side. As at Jackson Lake, the most common catch is lake trout, although there are cutthroats and brook and brown trout as well. Jenny Lake has several potential launch points for small fishing craft, including a marina at its southeast end. Motor craft exceeding 7.5 horsepower are prohibited. Ice fishing is popular in winter. The lake is open to anglers all year. The limit is six fish per day. Other regulations, including size limits, may apply.

Floatboating

The best launching point is at the lake's East End boat dock at South Jenny Lake. Since Jenny Lake is completely ringed by trail, your canoe will take you nowhere that hikers aren't. However, your destination can be the West End boat dock if you'd rather paddle over to Hidden Falls than take the ferry or walk around. (Read about Hidden Falls in our Hiking and Backpacking chapter.) You may find, though, that the most pleasant boat trip on Jenny Lake is out to the middle, where you can relax and enjoy the sight of the Tetons reaching more than a vertical mile above the mirrored surface on which you float. Mountain lakes are often perfectly still in early morning, so that's when we'd recommend a trip, with camera, to the center of Jenny Lake.

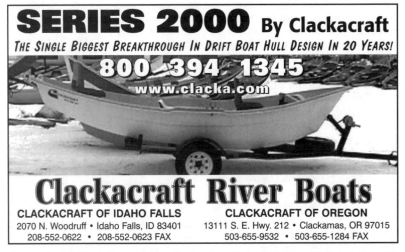

Power Boating

Jenny Lake allows motorized traffic, but motors must be less than 8 horsepower. No personal watercraft, sailboats or windsurfers are allowed. Besides Jenny and Jackson lakes, the only other park lake that allows motors is Phelps (not described here) near the southern park boundary.

Snake River in Grand Teton National Park and Lower Jackson Hole

The Upper Snake flows into, then out of, Jackson Lake, braiding its way south through the long valley of Jackson Hole. About 25 miles of Class I-II water later, it exits the park at Moose. It passes the town of Jackson and eventually flows into massive Palisades Reservoir at Alpine, Wyoming.

Fishing

Loaded with big cutthroats, this river is fishable by boat, with waders or from shore. Most commonly fished areas include stretches just above Jackson Lake and just below Jackson Lake Dam, the Oxbow area and the stretch between Wilson Bridge and West Table (the latter commonly fished by boat). Fish this river from April 1 to October 31. Only baitless fishing is allowed in Grand Teton National Park, and the entire section is subject to a three-fish limit. Other regulations may apply, including size limits. Read below for more detailed description of the river.

Floatboating

The Snake is easy to get to, with U.S. Highway 89 roughly paralleling the river for much of the journey. Twelve boat ramps exist on the 130-mile-long section between Jackson Lake in Grand Teton National Park and Palisades Reservoir. Two floatable sections exist above Jackson Lake as well, but they're less popular. One reason is that the lower run necessitates a slow paddle on Jackson Lake to the Lizard Creek takeout.

Within Grand Teton National Park, the upper Snake is well-suited to canoes, but it's also floated by kayakers, rafts and drift boats. The first section, about 4.5 miles, is appropriate for beginners: Parts are almost currentless with few obstacles. Included in this section is a fine wildlife viewing area, the lakelike Oxbow. The takeout for this upper run is called Pacific Creek. The next section runs from Pacific Creek to Deadman's Bar, about 11 miles. Chances of seeing wildlife are excellent here, since the river parts ways with U.S. 89. Snags and braided channels are common. Neither this section nor the third, from Deadman's Bar to the Moose Visitor Center, are recommended for beginners. They look easy, but visitors get in trouble on them every year. In fact, the local craft rental shops may not rent a canoe to you if you say you're headed here. The 10-mile lower stretch has more current and more braiding, snags and logjams than the upper two. Statistically, this section is the most dangerous. Before you float, be sure to ask the rangers about which channels to stay in and any new obstacles that may have snarled themselves into existence.

If you plan to take out at Deadman's, Schwabacher or Moose, familiarize yourself with conditions at the takeout before you put in. Deadman's, for instance, is unobtrusive and easily missed; the Moose takeout has surprisingly fast current some times of year. Before launching, read the bulletin board at your put-in for latest information about water conditions. No motorized craft are allowed on this river within the park.

As the Snake River leaves Grand Teton National Park and meanders toward Wilson, Wyoming, then south down the wide valley floor, it grows gradually deeper and less braided. Eddies can be powerful, but for the most part, the river is forgiving, with regular waves, plenty of flat but generally fast-moving stretches and infrequent obstacles. This part of the Snake River is rated Class II.

From Moose to South Park Bridge, the river is controlled by dikes on both sides to prevent erosion. Most of the houses are concentrated in the 14-mile section between Moose and Wilson. Beyond Wilson Bridge the river moves through relatively undeveloped land for 13 miles to the next take-out point, South Park Bridge. Between South Park Bridge and the local whitewater run, called Alpine Canyon or Snake River Canyon (see the next section), are three possible take-outs: Astoria Hot Springs, East Table and West Table. The total distance between South Park and East Table is 18 miles. West Table is about a mile downstream of East Table.

Local whitewater paddling schools use the area between Wilson and South Park Bridge for beginner kayak instruction because it has plenty of manageable river features to play in and learn from. Jackson's Pole Peddle Paddle relay uses the South Park to Astoria section for its boating leg. Canoes, kayaks, dories and rafts all run the Snake in Jackson Hole. These stretches also see a lot of fishing traffic, so in season be prepared to share the river with the hook-and-line folks.

Snake River in Alpine Canyon

This 8-mile, Class III section is the local whitewater playground. Outfitters float raftloads of guests down it; thousands of private floaters ply it. Jackson, Wyoming, residents stop by after work for a couple of hours of hole riding and wave surfing. This is no secluded wilderness float — it's more like a whitewater highway.

The put-in is called West Table, and the takeout is Sheep Gulch. Because of heavy waves in rapids like Lunch Counter and Big Kahuna, the most common craft here are kayaks, whitewater canoes and rafts. At higher spring flows, some rapids become Class IV; intermediate floaters should think twice before trying this section when the water is running more than about 13,000 cubic feet per second.

Fishing Outfitters

Grand Teton Lodge Company at Colter Bay Village

U.S. Hwy. 89, Grand Teton National Park, Wyo. • (307) 543-2811

Fishing boats depart at flexible times from the marina at Colter Bay for a minimum of two hours. Fish Jackson Lake for lunker trout while the non-anglers in your party enjoy the scenery. Grand Teton Lodge Company will also rent you a 9.9-horsepower boat or an aluminum canoe if you don't need a guide. Make advance reservations for guided fishing. Reservations are not necessary for small craft rental.

Signal Mountain Lodge

Teton Park Rd., Grand Teton National Park, Wyo. • (307) 543-2831

Signal Mountain Lodge, perched on the shore of Jackson Lake, offers daily guided fishing trips on 425-foot-deep Jackson Lake. You may also simply rent your own fishing boat from these folks. Canoes and oar boats are available at $8 per hour; Signal Mountain also rents fishing skiffs with outboard motors. Reservations are suggested.

Floatboat Outfitters and Powerboat Tours

Float trips in Grand Teton National Park are on the Snake River. Expect most scenic tours to take two to four hours and cost in the neighborhood of $35 for one adult. Extras such as Dutch-oven dinners or private boats cost more. Read our previous descriptions of the three sections of the Snake below Jackson Lake. All but one of the outfitters listed here float one or more of these. Flagg Ranch floats the smaller, rockier Snake River above Jackson Lake.

Barker-Ewing Scenic Tours

Moose, Grand Teton National Park, Wyo. • (307) 733-1800, (800) 365-1800

A real raft-guiding old-timer, this company has been providing scenic raft tours in the park since 1963. Trips run from Deadman's Bar to Moose, a 10-mile float on Class II water. Some trips include a Dutch-oven cookout.

Flagg Ranch Float Trips

John D. Rockefeller Jr. Memorial Pkwy., Wyo. • (307) 543-2861

Flagg Ranch offers the only commercial trips on the upper Snake above Jackson Lake. The river is smaller and less traveled here. Both Class III whitewater and Class I and II scenic trips are available.

Grand Teton Lodge Company at Colter Bay Village and Jackson Lake Lodge

U.S. Hwy. 89, Grand Teton National Park, Wyo. • (307) 543-2811, (800) 628-9988

Some Snake River float trips include picnic lunches or dinners at Deadman's Bar. Several morning and afternoon departures from both Colter Bay and Jackson Lake Lodge are scheduled daily for the 10.5-mile scenic float. Transportation to the put-in is provided. Colter Bay also runs four regularly scheduled scenic cruises on Jackson Lake every day. Its most popular scenic cruise includes breakfast or dinner on Elk Island.

Signal Mountain Lodge

Teton Park Rd., Grand Teton National Park, Wyo. • (307) 543-2831

Signal Mountain Lodge, perched on the shore of Jackson Lake, offers scenic trips on the Snake below Jackson Lake Dam. You can also arrange for a guided fishing boat on 425-foot-deep Jackson Lake.

Triangle X — Osprey Float Trips

U.S. Hwy. 89, Grand Teton National Park, Wyo. • (307) 733-5500, (307) 733-6455

The Turner brothers, who also run a guest ranch called Triangle X Ranch, offer sunrise, afternoon and evening scenic floats on the Snake in Grand Teton National Park. Some trips travel the 10 miles between Deadman's Bar and Moose, but trips as short as 5 miles are possible, as are extra-long 20-mile floats. All trips are on Class I or II water. You can also arrange a dinner float.

Watercraft Rentals

Adventure Sports

Dornan's at Moose, Grand Teton National Park, Wyo. • (307) 733-3307

These folks rent stable canoes and kayaks for beginner boaters, anglers and families. These boats are intended for lake floating only, not for the Snake or any other area river. The full-day rate for a canoe is around $30. Adventure Sports is open seven days a week in summer, but hours can vary in spring and fall. In winter the shop is closed.

Grand Teton Lodge Company at Colter Bay Village

U.S. Hwy. 89, Grand Teton National Park, Wyo. • (307) 543-2811

Tour Jackson Lake in an aluminum canoe from Colter Bay Marina for $8 per hour. Reserve your craft in advance. Colter Bay also rents 9.9-horsepower motorboats. Guest buoys and other services for boaters are available.

Signal Mountain Lodge

Teton Park Rd., Grand Teton National Park, Wyo. • (307) 543-2831

Signal Mountain Lodge, perched on the shore of Jackson Lake, rents canoes and oar boats for about $8 per hour; fishing skiffs with outboard motors are available. So are pontoon boats and deck cruisers that can hold groups of 8 to 10. Deck cruisers rent for about $50 an hour or $225 for the day. Reservations are suggested. Guest buoys and other services for boaters are available.

Teton Boating Company

South Jenny Lake, Grand Teton National Park, Wyo. • (307) 733-2703

This is the only company renting motorized and nonmotorized boats on Jenny Lake. Teton Boating also runs a regular ferry service across the clear waters of the lake to the West Side boat dock and back. Climbers and hikers appreciate the shorter trip to the backside of Jenny Lake — West Side boat dock is only a short walk from one of the park's more popular attractions: Hidden Falls (see our Hiking and Backpacking chapter).

Jackson Hole

Wyoming fishing regulations apply throughout Jackson Hole, generally including Grand Teton National Park. Pick up regulations and other fishing information at the local office of the Wyoming Department of Game and Fish, 360 N. Cache Street, Jackson, Wyoming, (307) 733-2321.

Gros Ventre River and Lower Slide Lake

The narrow Gros Ventre is floated by whitewater enthusiasts and fished from shore by small-stream lovers. Its 80-mile length flows into Lower Slide Lake and then out the bottom of that lake's natural dam. Then it roars and riffles its way east to meet the Snake 5 miles north of Wilson. Lower Slide Lake formed in 1925 when one side of fractured, unstable Sheep Mountain tumbled into the Gros Ventre River. The natural reservoir is just outside Grand Teton National Park and only several minutes' drive from Jackson.

Fishing

The Gros Ventre offers good rainbow trout fishing, especially just below Lower Slide Lake, but cutthroat are the dominant trout. For part of its journey, the Gros Ventre has carved itself a respectable canyon that makes getting to the river a strenuous matter, but both the Gros Ventre River Road and U.S. Highway 89 cross the river at convenient access points. A dirt forest road parallels the upper reaches of the Gros Ventre. Slide Lake itself is also fishable. A free boat ramp is available at Atherton Creek Campground, and a dirt forest road provides access to the north shoreline. The bag limit on the Gros Ventre River is six fish per day; the season runs from May 21 to October 31.

Floatboating

The Gros Ventre drops through sharp-edged boulders for almost 3 miles of technical, continuous Class III and IV water. At high water, the section is solid class IV. Then the gradient levels and the next 2 miles are fast-moving Class II. On the lower section, shallow boulder gardens necessitate more maneuvering than you might generally associate with Class II. Put-in for the upper section is off the Taylor Ranch Road. Takeout is about 3 miles downstream at a turnout at the national park boundary. This is also the put-in for the lower section. The next takeout is at the town of Kelly. Private land abuts the road, so be thoughtful when you park vehicles and trailers.

This river is recommended for skilled paddlers only, particularly the upper section and most particularly at high water when the few eddies disappear, turning this run into one long stomping ride. Rafters don't find much

INSIDERS' TIP

Combine high elevation with the water's reflection and you've got a prescription for sunburn. Be sure to pack sunscreen.

maneuvering room here — this is primarily a kayakers' river.

Power Boating

Power boats have no place on the Gros Ventre, but Lower Slide Lake's location, just outside of Grand Teton National Park, means powerboaters can avoid park restrictions and tag requirements by boating here. The single boat ramp is at Atherton Creek (use is free), where you will also find camping, picnicking and restroom facilities. Be careful of the drowned trees still standing in many areas of the lake.

Hoback River

U.S. Highway 191 runs alongside this shallow river and provides ready access, although much of the lower Hoback is sandwiched by private land. The upper section runs beside a forest road nearly to its headwaters. The river runs rocky and shallow through sagebrush flats and faster through its narrow canyon section until it meets the Snake River at the bottom of Jackson Hole. Its total length is 43 miles.

Fishing

This bouldered mountain river is almost always fished from shore or by wading. Less well-known than the Snake, this is a river for anglers who like solitude more than they do fish (the fishing is not as good here as on more famous area waters).

Catch cutthroat and a few brook trout here. This river can be fished year-round. Anglers tend to focus on the lower section above the river's confluence with the Snake.

Floatboating

The 12-mile run between the Granite Creek put-in and the Hoback Junction takeout is a little sister to the Snake River's Alpine Canyon (see a previous description). The river is narrower and shallower. With the exception of logjams on some outside corners and underneath bridges, rapids are straightforward Class II and small Class III, with some rock dodging. You can shorten or lengthen your trip, since lower put-in points exist, as well as a second, lower takeout at Astoria Hot Springs on the Snake. This section is most popular with kayakers and whitewater canoeists. At higher spring flows, the river becomes solid Class III, and logjam obstacles more significant.

Fishing Outfitters

One thing worth knowing about the guided-fishing scene outside Grand Teton National Park is that minimal regulation has resulted in a local reservoir of anglers with boats who guide part-time, particularly on unregulated sections of the Snake. Although many are extremely capable anglers and oarsmen, they may or may not be insured. Ask lots of questions before you hire a guide in Jackson Hole. Or choose one of the guide services listed below. Each has a good local reputation and is conveniently associated with a fly shop.

High Country Flies

185 Center St., Jackson, Wyo.
• (307) 733-7210

Float the Snake River near Jackson, the New Fork and Green River to the south. Fish the famous waters of Yellowstone National Park, the Firehole and Madison rivers and Yellowstone and Lewis lakes. Shop owner James Jones worked as a guide for this fly shop and guide service before he bought the place in 1984. Jones can also arrange instructional trips that emphasize casting, entomology, knot tying, and playing and releasing fish. Trips are catch-and-release only. James runs a fly shop near town square in Jackson to complement his guide service.

Jack Dennis Fishing Trips

50 E. Broadway Ave., Jackson, Wyo.
• (307) 733-3270

Fishing celebrity Jack Dennis Jr. opened his fly shop and guide service here in 1967. Now Jack Dennis Sports is home to one of the better-known fishing guide services in town. Guides can take you to the brushy little New Fork, the Green, the rivers and lakes of Yellowstone National Park and the Upper Snake River through Jackson Hole. Through an Idaho outfitter, you can also book trips on eastern Idaho's South Fork Snake, famed for its native cutthroat fishery. Trips can be walk-in or float. This company also offers seminars

Big Springs National Water Trail

Imagine water so clear it slips over rocks like liquid light. Imagine an underwater forest of flowing green plants laced with lanes of clean gravel. Picture trout as long as your arm, so close you can watch their eyes swivel. Hear the sandhill crane's distant bellow, like seized-up machinery, then another that picks up the cry from just over there. You're on the Big Springs National Water Trail, a 5-mile-long section of the Henry's Fork that begins a mile after the river spills from the ground and ends at Mack's Inn, below the point where the Henry's Fork swallows the slightly cloudy water of Henry's Lake Outlet.

It's a river, but trail-like in that you can't get lost and the going is easy. The river runs shallow down an unbraided channel which requires no route-finding skills. You need only your binoculars, camera, warm clothes, fishing gear and snacks. Mack's Inn provides the rest: boat, oars or paddles, life jackets and a ride to the put-in. It also sells snacks, ice and beverages for the trip, and allows you to park in its lot. Craft available for rent include canoes, rowboats, flat-bottom skiffs and rubber rafts.

You're likely to see bald eagles, ospreys and kingfishers. Waterfowl of all descriptions paddle into startled flight as you sweep slowly around the river bends. You may see elk or moose. Come in the fall and, after you pass the Henry's Lake outlet, watch for the red-bodied, slope-faced kokanee salmon, a landlocked fish that, unlike his cousins the chinook and sockeye, doesn't need to reach the ocean to complete his life cycle. Water flows vary little during the year, since the main source of the flow above Henry's Lake is Big Springs itself. That's why the water is so ethereally clear, too: Little or no

— continued on next page

Photo: Jo Deurbrouck

A couple enjoys a quiet September trip on the clear waters of the Big Springs National Water Trail.

stream sediment is present. It's also why the trout are so large. The steady year-round water temperature is chilly enough to hold lots of dissolved oxygen and warm enough to support lots of food sources for trout. Less sediment means that the Henry's Fork provides the clean gravel beds that trout and salmon need to spawn in. Despite the enticing size of the fish, please don't wet a line until you pass Henry's Lake Outlet (you'll know because the water will become less clear and because you'll see a sign). In order to protect the fishery, fishing is not permitted above the outlet.

Expect to take about four hours if you stop much to fish or explore, or even if you simply float the current. If you row or paddle downstream and don't plan to stop, the trip will take about two hours. Depending on the craft you choose, you'll pay between $25 and $50 for two people, including shuttle costs. Mack's Inn offers unguided boat trips from as soon as the Big Springs Road is clear of snow, usually May, until October. If you own a craft and equipment appropriate to a cold, shallow river with slow-to-moderate current, you can just head for the put-in off Big Springs Road (watch for the sign on your left about 5 miles off U.S. Highway 20). Summer days on the Big Springs National Water Trail can be crowded, but even as early as September you can expect to have the whole glorious thing to yourself.

Check with Mack's Inn, U.S. Highway 20, Mack's Inn at Island Park, Idaho, (208) 558-7272. Reservations are a good idea.

---

and fly-casting instruction, besides organizing a well-known fishing event: a one-fly trout derby.

Westbank Anglers

3670 N. Moose-Wilson Rd., Teton Village, Wyo. • (307) 733-6483

This guide service maintains its own fly shop for your convenience. The shop carries outdoor clothing, poles, reels and waders to take with you on your fishing adventure. You can arrange fishing adventures for nearby Flat Creek and the Upper Snake in Jackson Hole, the South Fork of the Snake (in cooperation with an Idaho outfitter), the Firehole, Gibbon, Madison and Yellowstone rivers; Yellowstone and Lewis lakes in Yellowstone National Park; the Green and New Fork rivers in the Pinedale area; and several stretches of private water. Half-day, full-day and overnight trips are available.

Floatboat Outfitters

Commercial outfitters in Jackson Hole generally float a Class III stretch of the Snake called Alpine Canyon and/or a scenic Class I and II run just above Alpine Canyon. Each section is about 8 miles long. Outfitters charge between $25 and $35 per person for a run down one of these sections. Breakfast and dinner floats are available at higher cost. Most outfitters will help you rent cold-water gear, primarily wetsuits and booties, if you ask. If you get cold easily or it's June and the water's high, consider asking. Also inquire about the type of craft available and how many it will hold. Paddle rafts allow you to participate under the direction of a guide, oar rafts let you sit back and be taken down the river, and inflatable kayaks put you in the driver's seat with nobody to blame for your good time but you. Rafts generally hold between eight and 15 people. Smaller rafts will make the wave action more fun. Larger craft are stable and less likely to flip or toss people into the water.

Barker-Ewing Jackson Hole River Trips

45 W. Broadway Ave., Jackson, Wyo. • (307) 733-1000, (800) 448-4202

Paddle boats and oar boats are both available on Barker-Ewing's trips down Alpine Canyon. Other trips offered by this company include scenic floats through the Snake River's South Park area and scenic and whitewater combos that run 16 miles of the Snake, encompassing the 8-mile Alpine Canyon and the scenic Class II section above it. Breakfast and overnight trips run daily. This company has a solid regional reputation for their operation here and on other rivers.

Dave Hansen Whitewater

455 N. Cache St., Jackson, Wyo. • (307) 733-6295, (800) 732-6295

Alpine Canyon runs and scenic floats on the pretty stretch above the whitewater run are both popular. Sometimes the company runs a combined photo and whitewater trip on the entire 16 miles. At the end of the scenic run, guides pull the oar frames out of their crafts, turning their boats into whitewater paddle rafts. You can choose to ride in 12- to 14-person rafts or the smaller, more exciting eight-person craft.

Jackson Hole Whitewater

650 W. Broadway Ave., Jackson, Wyo. • (307) 733-1007, (800) 648-2602

A popular trip is the scenic/whitewater combo. Your guide hands each person a pair of high-powered binoculars with which to scan the shore for moose, beaver, coyote and other creatures. After lunch, you return the binoculars, cinch down your life jacket and run the 8-mile Alpine Canyon stretch. You can also choose a breakfast or a steak or chicken dinner with your whitewater adventure. Jackson Hole Whitewater runs a maximum of 10 guests per boat except at high water, and no more than two boats per trip. A local newspaper poll voted this one Jackson's favorite raft company in 1996 and 1997.

Lewis & Clark Expeditions

335 N. Cache St., Jackson, Wyo. • (307) 733-4022, (800) 824-5375

Lewis & Clark is a small company running Alpine Canyon and the 12-mile South Park scenic stretch of the Snake River. The company says it averages fewer people in its rafts: 11 in standard-size rafts and six in small rafts. Some trips are capped with a steak dinner at a riverside campsite.

Lone Eagle Whitewater

U.S. Hwy. 89/191, near Hoback Junction, Wyo. • (307) 733-1090, (800) 321-3800

Lone Eagle runs Alpine Canyon. Trips are paired with a hot breakfast, lunch or dinner cooked up at the company's outdoor kitchen and dining area on the Hoback River. The resort's hot tubs are waiting after your ride. Lone Eagle promises no more than eight to 10 guests per raft on the Alpine Canyon section. Scenic floats are also available. They put in at Wilson Bridge and float for about three hours.

Mad River Boat Trips

1255 S. U.S. Hwy. 89, Jackson, Wyo. • (307) 733-6203, (800) 458-7238

Special touches here include guaranteed self-bailing rafts (so you don't have to clear water out of your raft with a bucket), a riverside lunch or barbecue cookout dinner to cap off your whitewater adventure, and a stop at Mad River's River Runners Museum, a small collection of interpretive material designed to show you the roots of rafting in this region. Mad River's buses are air conditioned with video entertainment. Rental wetsuits are washed and dried in big commercial machines after every use.

Charlie Sands River Trips

110 W. Broadway Ave. and 1450 S. U.S. Hwy. 89, Jackson, Wyo. • (307) 733-4410, (800) 358-8184

This company's been in business since 1967, plying Class III Alpine Canyon. Private groups can arrange breakfast and cookout trips. Also by special arrangement, a group can take an overnight excursion, camping at Pine Bar in the Bridger-Teton National Forest. Sixteen-mile combined scenic and whitewater floats are available as well.

Craft Rentals

Leisure Sports

1075 S. U.S. Hwy. 89, Jackson, Wyo. • (307) 733-3040

This all-purpose rental shop has rafts and canoes, snowmobiles, trailers, autos and more. In summer rent Avon and Achilles rafts between 12 and 18 feet long. An 18-foot rental costs $90 per day. You can also rent Coleman canoes and inflatable kayaks. If you want to trailer your raft, these folks can rent you the equipment. If your vehicle doesn't have a hitch, they can rent you a car that does.

Rent-A-Raft/Jackson Hole Outdoor Center

Lewis Landing, 10925 S. U.S. Hwy. 89, Hoback Junction • (307) 733-2728

Rod Lewis has been in the river business for decades. Now from his riverside location he rents Achilles and Hyside rafts. Lewis's staff can also rent you a trailer or help you load your rented raft on top of your car. They can shuttle you up the Hoback (you'll take out on the grassy bank at Lewis's place) or down the Snake. Other services here include inner-tube, sit-on-top and inflatable kayak rentals.

Teton Aquatic Supply/Snake River Kayak and Canoe School

155 W. Gill Ave., Jackson, Wyo. • (307) 733-3127, (800) 529-2501

Besides operating a paddling school and watersports store, these folks rent canoes, inflatable kayaks, paddle and oar rafts and sea kayaks. Rafts made by Achilles, Sotar and Legacy rent for around $50 per day. You can rent a canoe by Sawyer, Dagger or Mohawk by the half-day or longer. The half-day rate is $20. Whitewater kayaks are by Wavesport and Perception.

Surrounding Areas

Southwestern Montana

Perched on the banks of the Madison River, the small town of Ennis displays a sign that reads, "Home of 640 people and 11 million trout." In the wadeable waters of the Madison, Gallatin and Yellowstone rivers, you'll see Robert Redford look-alikes casting their lines into the rippling waters, fishing and dreaming themselves into the script of *A River Runs Through It*, filmed on the Yellowstone and the Gallatin. Drift boats full of fly fishers sit in the water like stuckup ducks staking out their pieces of the river. Chances are good that even a beginning fly fisher will be rewarded with that hoped-for but always-surprising jerk on the line. Landing a wiggling, jumping rainbow or native cutthroat is the ultimate reward. But even if you don't get a nibble, fishing is a good excuse to stand in the river, to listen to its soothing hum, to forget about the world you left behind.

If you look at a map, you'll see that the Gallatin, the Yellowstone and the Madison rivers originate in Yellowstone National Park before flowing into Montana's valleys. Since most of their waters lie outside the park, we've listed them that way. Keep in mind, though, that there's excellent fishing in these rivers where they're within the park. Outside the park, you'll need a Montana fishing license, a set of regulations and someone to interpret them for you. Inside the park you'll need a permit.

Drop into almost any specialized sporting goods store in Bozeman, Montana, and the clerks there will likely tell you that the main reason they live in this town is because its location is central to an unlimited field of recreational opportunities. Watersports, especially river rafting, kayaking and canoeing rank high on their list of fun things to do. From Bozeman, they have easy access to the Madison, Gallatin and Yellowstone Rivers. For those who windsurf, Ennis, Dailey and Hebgen lakes are just a short drive away.

You'll find that southwestern Montana's rivers and lakes are easy to get to. And a long list of outfitters are available to treat you to thrills if you aren't into paddling your own vessel. If you're visiting and need to rent a boat and some gear, you'll also find plenty of places to meet your needs. We've listed some of the best in this section.

Hebgen Lake

Fifteen-mile-long Hebgen Lake, north of West Yellowstone, was formed in the early 1900s when an irrigation company dammed the Madison River. It wasn't long before Montana Power Company, which uses the multipurpose man-made lake as a reservoir for downstream hydroelectric power, bought the dam. More than 90 percent of the Hebgen's shoreline is public land managed by the Forest Service. That means there aren't a whole lot of homes or services on Hebgen.

Hebgen Lake is used for a bit of everything, including water-skiing, windsurfing and sailing. You can reach the water via three Forest Service boat ramps at Lonesomehurst and Rainbow campgrounds (see our Campgrounds and RV Parks chapter) and at an informal launch on the north shore. Four private resorts also have launch sites they'll let you use for a fee. (The Kirkwood Motel only charges $2.)

Fishing

You'll see plenty of people putt-putting around this man-made lake bait and lure fishing for rainbows and browns below the surface. Locals, though, don't bother because the catch rate for this kind of fishing is low. They also know that 20 miles down the road at Henry's Lake they can fish the same way and catch much bigger fish. Experienced fly fishers like Hebgen Lake, especially in the Madison Arm where the Madison River comes in and where the weed growth is good. Conditions are just right for good insect hatches. From about May 10, when the lake ice has melted, fish are cruising in packs looking for big midges. Their speed and spookiness combine to make spring fishing a challenge for the experienced and impossible for beginners. It's best to use a boat this time of year because you need some speed to find and catch up with the roving packs. By the end of May, the midges have gotten smaller, so use smaller flies.

As bugs go, so goes the fishing, so pay attention to insect hatches. And practice up on your Latin so their names roll off your tongue when you reach Yellowstone country. In late June, tricos start coming off the water early in the morning, while callibaetis hatch about 10:30 AM. This is a good time to take your boat or float tube to the Madison Arm. Fishing in this technical lake falls off about mid-September. A few people ice fish during the winter months, mostly at the mouth near the dam and close to the Happy Hour Bar on the north side of Hebgen Lake.

Floatboating

Exploring the shores of Hebgen by canoe or kayak, especially in the more protected Madison and Grayling arms, can lead you to wildlife that you might otherwise miss. In addition to waterfowl of all kinds, you're apt to see deer, elk, moose, bears and some of the smaller critters like coyotes, raccoons or weasels. The lake, a living pantry for land-loving wildlife, is also their drinking fountain. Animals like to tank up on water mornings and evenings, and lake waters are generally calmer at these times. Sailboats and windsurfers also raise their sails on summer days.

Powerboating

Powerboats and scenic cruisers as well as personal watercrafts zip across the lake's waters on warm days. There are three marinas on Hebgen's north shore: **Kirkwood Ranch Motel** at (406) 646-7200; **Yellowstone Holiday Resort** at (406) 646-4242, (800) 643-4227; and the **Happy Hour Bar** at (406) 646-7281. The **Madison Arm Resort and Marina** at (406) 646-9328 is on the south shore. Each rents slips, sells gas and rents boats ranging from rowboats to speedboats and party pontoons.

Quake Lake

Formed in 1959 when a mountain collapsed and blocked the Madison River after an earthquake, Quake Lake is more of a curiosity than a recreation attraction. Anglers, though, say its waters hold a surprising number of trout. (See our Attractions chapter for a longer account of the quake.) You'll find one Forest Service boat ramp here, used mostly by fishing parties. Stumps from drowned trees clutter the cold waters, and hair-raising winds howl up the canyon each day beginning just before noon. The lake is on U.S. Highway 287 downstream from Hebgen Lake and northwest of West Yellowstone, Montana.

Dailey Lake

This small lake (it's about 150 acres), just a few miles down Old Chico Road from Chico Hot Springs near Emigrant, is a local hot spot for windsurfers and anglers. A road runs along the lake's north and west sides as well as down the length of its eastern shore before continuing off onto private property to the southwest. Two campgrounds at Dailey Lake (on the north and east sides of the lake) contain about 30 informal sites. Each has a vault toilet and a boat ramp. Dailey Lake is home to rainbow, German browns and walleye. It is a popular ice-fishing lake. It's also popular with windsurfers.

Ennis Lake

Known by longtime locals as Meadow Lake (Forest Service mappers renamed it long ago), Ennis Lake was formed in 1905 when Montana Power built a dam on the Madison River at the head of the Bear Trap Canyon. The lake has since been slowly filling with silt, which means the water is warm — just right for water-skiing, particularly in the morning before the wind comes up, and windsurfing in the windy afternoon. About 3 miles square (the braided channels of the Madison River make it look much longer), Ennis Lake is surrounded almost entirely by private property, mostly ranches, and seems to be a management no-man's land. The Montana Department of Fish, Wildlife and Parks operates one primitive campground on the western end of the lake and another one along the river's channels south of the lake. The area has enough room for about 10 sites and has a vault toilet and an informal launch site at each. (The channel site, though, is used more as a takeout because the river shore downstream is entirely bordered by private property.)

Near the mouth of the lake, on the north side, the Bureau of Land Management acquired Sandy Beach, which has a vault toilet and informal camping. The **Lakeshore Lodge**, (406) 682-4424, on the north side of Ennis Lake has a boat ramp and a marina for guests. They also rent small motorboats for fishing. Each spring thousands of trumpeter swans land on Ennis Lake, then spend a few days there before flying on.

Fishing

Anglers haunt the lake looking for rainbow and brown trout. Cruising the undeveloped shoreline in a quiet canoe or kayak can pay high dividends when it comes to wildlife viewing.

Hyalite Reservoir

About 15 miles south of Bozeman and about a mile long, Hyalite Reservoir is the center of recreation for Bozemanites. A no-wake regulation means motorboaters must putt-putt on this lake, so mostly anglers boat here. But there's also some canoeing, kayaking and float tubing. A couple of campgrounds line the lake shore. You'll find a boat ramp at the Hood Creek Campground and an informal launch site near the Blackmore trailhead. Bring your own gas.

Madison River

The Firehole and the Gibbon rivers give birth to the Madison right at Madison Junction in Yellowstone National Park east of West Yellowstone, Montana. From there this world-renowned blue-ribbon stream winds its way like a seductive serpent through park meadows before flowing into (and out of) Hebgen Lake, the first of three reservoirs totalling 23 miles. (Hebgen, Quake and Ennis lakes are described elsewhere in this section.) After leaving Quake Lake, the Madison winds through narrow canyons, across wide open meadows, along U.S. Highway 287 and through a remote section of the Lee Metcalf Wilderness before dumping into the Jefferson River and then the Missouri. Just below the Madison Dam at the mouth of Ennis Lake is Bear Trap Canyon's whitewater stretch.

Fishing

In the spring, big rainbows swim from Hebgen Lake up the Madison to spawn. Browns do the same in autumn, stopped only by the waterfalls of the Gibbon and Firehole rivers. Within Yellowstone National Park, avoid wading in the sucking, silty muck in the marshy area above Seven Mile Bridge.

Below the lakes, the river flows through a canyon before streaming into the wide open spaces of the Madison Valley, where U.S. Highway 287 parallels it. Fishing and access along this stretch of the river is good, especially at hot spots such as the confluence of the West Fork and a 10-mile stretch from the Varney Bridge to Ennis. Rainbows, browns, brookies, grayling and whitefish all call these waters home. Until whirling disease reared its ugly head, anglers could count on catching several fish an hour in this stretch of the Madison, the hardest hit by the disease. Catch rates still average a bit more than one per hour, and fishing is improving.

About 10 miles below Ennis Lake, the water slows down. Four access sites, beginning with one near Norris Hot Springs, will get you near this mostly wadeable stretch of river. It's also a popular piece of water for drift fishing. If

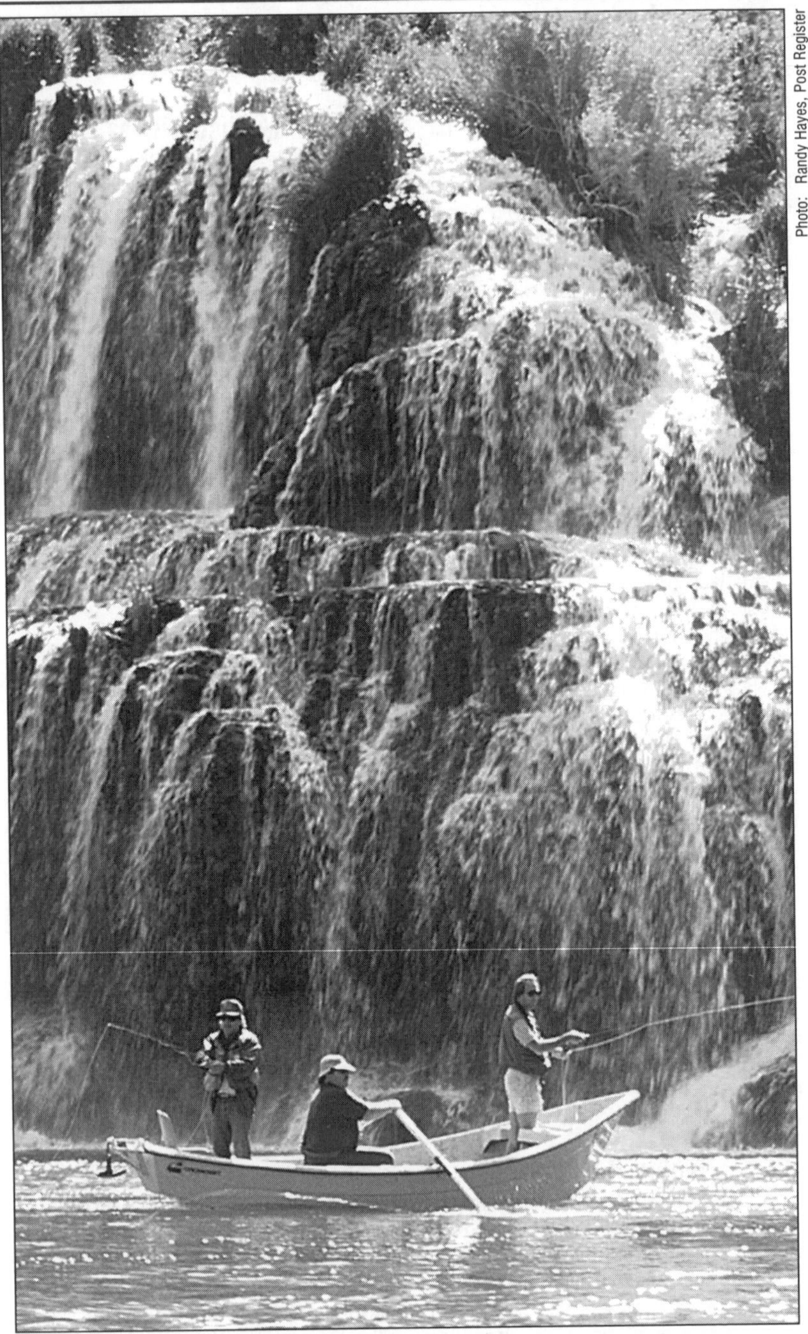

Photo: Randy Hayes, Post Register

These anglers ply the water of the South Fork of the Snake River below Fall Creek in Idaho's Swan Valley area.

you fish the Madison in the park, restrictions call for fly fishing only. Rainbow fishing is catch-and-release. But you can keep two brown trout smaller than 13 inches. There are some real whoppers in these waters.

Floatboating

The very popular 9-mile run of Class IV rapids in Bear Trap Canyon can be reached by driving the Ennis Lake Road, which runs east of the reservoir then into a narrow rocky canyon to Madison Dam. Water discharges from the dam vary hugely from 900 to 10,000 cfs. If you're new to the river (and even if you aren't) check the flow gauge up from the power plant before putting in. Portaging around the rapids is possible, but check with local experts to find out which side is best for each one. Unless you are highly skilled with a good raft or kayak, we recommend you float with a guide service. (Some folks tackle these rapids in whitewater canoes.) Some of the outfitters listed in this section run the Bear Trap. Below Bear Trap Canyon is the Mont. Highway 84 access, popular as a takeout because of its proximity to Norris Hot Springs. Below this point, the river lines out into 31 miles of calm water OK for practiced beginners to paddle. You'll find 24 launching sites on Madison River and numerous campgrounds along the river's length.

Gallatin River

The river follows U.S. Highway 191 most of the way, but wildlife is still abundant, as are campgrounds and public accesses, five of which are on the whitewater stretch in the canyon.

Fishing

Just outside the park is the confluence of Taylor Creek, which pretty much dictates fishing conditions by running either clear or muddy depending on the weather. Below Taylor Creek, the waters hold rainbows, browns and hatchery grayling. In Yellowstone National Park, you can add cutthroat and hybrids to that list. Fishing on the Gallatin in Montana is possible year-round. In the park, it's closed during the winter. In Montana you must release grayling; otherwise the limit is five trout, with only one longer than 18 inches allowed. In the park, it's catch-and-release for cutthroat, with a two-fish limit on rainbows and browns.

Floatboating

Technically, you can begin floating the Gallatin as soon as it leaves Yellowstone National Park, but most people who want to paddle this 20-mile, Class I stretch begin a few miles downstream at the Taylor Creek Access. (During low water, it's best to put in downstream at the Red Cliff Campground or the West Fork.)

Local river outfitters frequent a 13-mile stretch of Class III and IV that begins a few miles downstream from Big Sky at Deer Creek and ends at Squaw Creek. Over the next 23 miles, you'll face eight irrigation diversion dams, fences and logjams, all of which require a heads-up and some of which require portages. You'll encounter easier Class I and II water without obstacles on the last 19 miles of the Gallatin, beginning at the Central Park Access near the Interstate 90 bridge.

Yellowstone River

One of the longest undammed rivers in the United States, the Yellowstone begins as two small branches in Wyoming's Shoshone Mountain Range. It flows 12 miles through some of the wildest country in the United States, then into Yellowstone Lake. Surrounded by bogs, bugs, sloughs, marshes and mosquitoes, the Yellowstone's headwaters are a favorite haunt for grizzlies. From Yellowstone Lake this river spills off the Yellowstone Plateau into Montana's Paradise Valley before winding its way east across the prairies of Montana. The Yellowstone is the most popular river in Yellowstone National Park for angling and fish watching.

Fishing

When fishing season opens July 15 above the falls of the Yellowstone, the river's waters along a 9-mile stretch are dotted with almost as many anglers as trout. It's easy to understand why. Large native cutthroat 16 to 24 inches long lurk in these wadeable waters. From a quarter-mile upstream to 1 mile downstream of the Fishing Bridge, angling is permanently closed. Another half-mile stretch midway between the Fishing Bridge and Sulphur Cauldron is closed. Between Sulphur Cauldron and Alum Creek is another 6-mile closure. The only fish in the waters between Yellowstone Lake and the Upper Falls is the Yellowstone cutthroat. Once you get past the Grand Canyon where the Yellowstone crashes over two waterfalls before tearing through the bottom of the deep gorge, you'll find two more hotspots before this river leaves the park. One is in the canyon near Tower Fall, and the other is in Black Canyon where trails lead into the river. A 20-mile stretch from Emigrant to Pine Creek south of Livingston is a locals' favorite for drift and wade fishing. The Yellowstone River, a prolific insect factory, can be deceptively swift, so be aware when trying to wade it, especially upstream from the falls.

Floatboating

Since boating Yellowstone National Park rivers is prohibited, you won't be able to put in until Gardiner, Montana, where a 16-mile stretch of mostly Class III whitewater begins and runs through Yankee Jim Canyon. (There's a 5-mile piece of flatwater in the middle.) Easily handled by experienced rafters, kayakers and whitewater canoeists, this stretch from Queen of the Waters access to Carbella is frequented by river outfitters. Six accesses are available along this part of the Yellowstone.

Once you hit Carbella, you may want to trade your paddle for a fly rod. The water slows down (good water for practiced beginners) and turns into blue-ribbon fishing for cutthroat, browns and rainbow. Suitable for kayaks, rafts, dories and canoes, this 48-mile section of peaceful river runs through the bottomlands of the Paradise Valley. Even though the river mostly follows U.S. Highway 89, you can expect to see a variety of wildlife and waterfowl, despite the growing number of homes along the river. Local paddlers warn about a treacherous bridge just before Livingston. Because the river hits it at an angle, paddlers can get sucked into the bridge supports. Navigating this stretch is for only accomplished paddlers.

Fishing Outfitters

Until Robert Redford's *A River Runs Through It* shone its spotlight on fly fishing, the region had only a handful of well-known fishing outfitters, such as Livingston's Dan Bailey and West Yellowstone's Bud Lilly. Since the movie came out, outfitters and guides, some of them newcomers to the area with little fly-fishing experience, have set up shop on every other street corner. We have selected some of Greater Yellowstone's standouts for this book.

West Yellowstone, Montana

Blue Ribbon Flies

315 Canyon Ave., West Yellowstone, Mont. • (406) 646-7642

You won't find independent guides working out of Blue Ribbon Flies — just eight or so regulars with years of experience under their waders. Owner Craig Mathews and his staff try their darnedest to steer you into having a good time fishing. That doesn't necessarily mean fishing 10 hours a day and bagging every fish in the river. It does mean that they'll try to teach you about bugs and fish psychology so when you go fishing without a guide, you'll have a better idea of what you're doing. They'll also try to lead you into the finer art of fly fishing.

In addition to a staff of veteran guides, Blue Ribbon has a complete selection of top-of-the-line, hard-to-find fly-tying materials. Mathews and his partners at the store have written several books as well as a weekly (in the summer) column called "The Fish Wrapper." Blue Ribbon, open year-round, guides on the Madison and Gallatin rivers as well as all of the streams in Yellowstone. Blue Ribbon's 1998 fees are the same for wade and float fishing daytrips: $265 for one person, $285 for two and $350 for three people. Blue Ribbon also offers high-country packtrips that take you to the big ones.

Bud Lilly's Trout Shop

39 Madison Ave., West Yellowstone, Mont. • (406) 646-7801, (800) 854-9559

It's true. Bud Lilly's Trout Shop has been a household word among fly fishers for 45 years. Bud Lilly no longer owns this shop, but the staff strives to maintain his sterling reputation in the fishing and guiding world. Besides being able to load you up with every bit of gear and tackle you need, Bud Lilly's has six full-time guides who can lead you to smaller park streams or larger rivers in and out of the park. This is a busy place, so it's best to reserve a guide months ahead of time if you plan to be in the area during the peak season. Occasionally, though, you can walk in and catch a guide on pretty short notice even in the summertime. Float trips cost $310 per person, while a walk-and-wade guided daytrip is $265 for one person, $280 for two people and $290 for three people. This shop is open year-round.

Jacklin's Fly Shop

105 Yellowstone Ave., West Yellowstone, Mont. • (406) 646-7336

Bob Jacklin, who happens to own the oldest established fly shop in West Yellowstone, has been guiding fishing folks out of West Yellowstone since 1967. While he specializes in the Henry's Fork and Madison rivers, Jacklin knows and guides on all the rivers in Montana and Yellowstone National Park. Jacklin's, a full-service fly shop across from the old Union Pacific Depot, uses six to 10 guides each summer day. It'll cost you and your partner $325 to go fishing with one of Jacklin's guides. Lunch is included. Sunday evenings Jacklin gives free fly-casting lessons at 7:30 PM on his pond behind the police station (across the street from his shop).

Bozeman, Montana

R.J. Cain & Company Outfitters

23 E. Main St., Bozeman, Mont. • (406) 587-9111, (800) 886-9111

Besides employing several full-time guides, R.J. Cain uses contract guides throughout southwestern Montana. Operating out of their shop in Bozeman, owners Rod, Pam and Garry King tailor their guide service to your needs whether you're a beginner or a seasoned fly fisher. R.J. Cain offers lessons, guided float fishing on area rivers inside and outside the park, walk-and-wade trips and backcountry fly fishing trips by horseback.

In 1998, a day of guided float or walk and wade fishing cost $290 for one or two people. A third person could come along for an extra $75. You pay a $100 deposit when you book a trip.

Big Sky, Montana

Gallatin Riverguides

U.S. Hwy. 191, Big Sky, Mont. • (406) 995-2290

In business since 1981, Gallatin Riverguides is the longest-operating fly shop in Big Sky. Owners Steve and Betsy French offer a variety of low-cost casting clinics at their 2-acre pond behind the shop. The pond is equipped with a casting platform and target rings, not to mention some hefty rainbows. They employ eight guides, almost all of whom have at least five years of experience on southwestern Montana waters. (Some of the guides have been with the Frenches for more than a dozen years.)

Gallatin Riverguides fish the Madison, Yellowstone and Gallatin rivers and the rivers and streams of Yellowstone National Park. They also do overnight trips on the Beaverhead and Missouri rivers. A day of guided walk-and-wade fishing costs $275 for two people. Fishing from a drift boat costs more: $300 for two. Gallatin Riverguides also rents rods, reels and waders.

Livingston, Montana

George Anderson's Yellowstone Angler

U.S. Hwy. 89 S., Livingston, Mont. • (406) 222-7130

While Bud Lilly and Dan Bailey may have been the big fly fishing names of the past, George Anderson is giving them a run for their money these days. Operating out of a 4,500-square-foot shop stocked with a broad selection of trout and saltwater tackle and rods, Anderson uses about 15 guides. Each has an area of expertise: Some prefer spring creeks, while others like to fish Yellowstone National Park or the bigger rivers. In addition to fishing the Yellowstone, Anderson takes anglers to the Bighorn, Missouri, Boulder and West Boulder rivers as well as to the rivers and streams of Yellowstone National Park.

Anderson's 1998 fees for two were $300

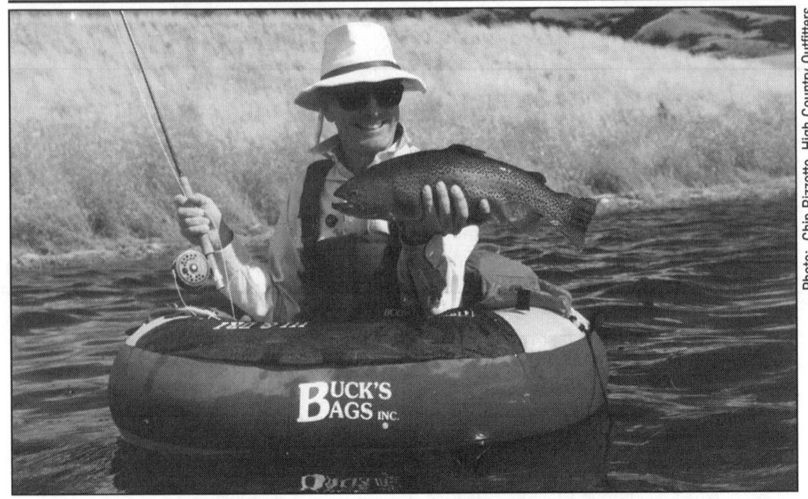

Photo: Chip Rizzotto, High Country Outfitters

A happy fisherman shows off a 4 pound trout he has just caught in a private high mountain lake near Emigrant, Montana.

for a day of float fishing and $285 for a walk-and-wade trip.

Dan Bailey's
209 W. Park Ave., Livingston, Mont.
• (406) 222-1673, (800) 356-4052

Dan Bailey's is synonymous with fly fishing. This hopping fly-fishers' hotspot taps into a battalion of independent guides to complement three or four in-house guides. You'll find that Bailey's guides mostly fish the Yellowstone River, the Madison River above Ennis and spring creeks in the Paradise Valley. It's best to reserve a guide ahead of time, although at times you may get lucky as a walk-in. Dan Bailey's, featured in our Shopping chapter, is a full-service fly shop.

Pray, Montana

High Country Outfitters
158 Bridger Hollow Rd., Pray, Mont.
• (406) 333-4763

This guide comes with a private cabin and casting pond, a lodge (Chip and Francine Rizzoto's home) and fine dining. While Chip takes you on a fishing experience tailored to your desires and your ability, Francine will cook up incredibly delicious meals in her country kitchen, then serve them when you're ready. She'll also tailor the menu to your tastes, keeping a computerized record of your favorite foods. It's no wonder *Sports Afield* ranked High Country among the top five best North American fishing lodges.

High Country offers a five-night, four-day package for two people that costs $3,140. The cabin comes complete with a queen-size bed and a set of bunkbeds, fly-tying equipment, a complete fishing library and a music system. In June, they hold a women's fly-fishing clinic and will take only four students. It costs $1,200. Each year, this lodge books 24 groups with no more than four people each. And they have a 75 percent return rate. Rizzoto says he's already taking reservations for the millennium.

High Country is at the base of the Absaroka-Beartooth Wilderness and is a six-minute drive from the Chico Hot Springs Lodge. (See our Resorts and Lodges chapter to learn more about Chico.)

Floatboat Outfitters

Because of the distance and logistics involved in operating on more than one river in Montana, most river outfitters specialize in running just one river. There are a few, though, that offer trips on two or more rivers.

Adventures Big Sky

U.S. Hwy. 191 at the Big Sky Resort entrance, Big Sky, Mont. • (406) 995-2324

Whitewater or flatwater? Take your pick because Adventures Big Sky offers both on the Gallatin River. Ride in a paddleboat, an inflatable kayak or a raft with a frame and oars. Barbara and Patrick Dillon offer half- and full-day trips with lunch. If you're at least 15 years old, for a bit more money you can paddle along in an inflatable kayak.

Canoe Montana and Montana River Expeditions

26 Cedar Bluffs Rd., Livingston, Mont. • (406) 222-5837, (800) 500 4538

Russell Young promises guests a "soft adventure" paddling canoes or touring kayaks (a special kind of kayak that's hard to roll) on quiet river waters in Greater Yellowstone. Instead of hooking you up to your adrenaline, Young aims to connect you to the river so it soothes your hurried soul. Young offers trips at dawn, sunset, by moonlight and overnight on a variety of rivers.

Geyser Whitewater Expeditions

47200 Gallatin Rd., Gallatin Gateway, Mont. • (406) 995-4989, (800) 914-9031

Located on U.S. Highway 191 just south of the Big Sky turnoff, Geyser Whitewater Expeditions runs half- and full-day floats on the upper and lower sections of the Gallatin River. In addition, Geyser offers half-day inflatable-kayak trips and a rafting and horseback-riding combo that includes some of each.

Montana Whitewater

Bozeman, Mont. • (406) 763-4465, (800) 799-4465

Montana Whitewater offers a menu of options including half- and full-day whitewater and scenic floats on the upper and lower Gallatin as well as dinner and breakfast floats. They also have a "Paddle and Saddle" package with a half-day of riding followed by a half-day float on the Gallatin. In addition they offer half- and full-day floats on the Yellowstone.

Beartooth Whitewater

Red Lodge, Mont. • (406) 446-3142, (800) 799-3142

Beartooth offers half- and full-day trips on a stretch of water that includes three rivers: the Rosebud, Stillwater and Yellowstone. The company conducts four regularly scheduled half-day trips each summer's day. It also has a three-hour trip on the Stillwater with one-person rafts.

Wild West Rafting

Yellowstone Outpost Mini Mall (Headwaters Angler), U.S. Hwy. 89, Gardiner, Mont. • (406) 848-7110, (800) 862-0557

Experienced river guides lead guests down the Yellowstone River on two types of trips: whitewater and gentle water. Their trips, offered daily during summer, are tailored for families. Ask about horseback riding, too.

Yellowstone Raft Company

406 Scott St., Gardiner, Mont. • (406) 848-7777, (800) 858-7781
Big Sky, Mont. • (406) 995-4613, (800) 348-4376

In business since 1978, Yellowstone Raft Company offers half-day and full-day trips on the Yellowstone and Gallatin rivers and a full-day raft trip through the Bear Trap Canyon Wilderness on the Madison. They also offer kayak instruction for a couple of hours or a full day. Ask about their guided fishing trips.

Floatboat Rentals

Army and Navy Economy Store

539 E. Main, Bozeman, Mont. • (406) 586-1919, (800) 822-0241

Army and Navy rents 12-foot rafts for $30 per day and 13-foot self-baling rafts with rowing packages for $60. Paddles, life jackets and a foot pump come with the rafts. Two-person inflatable kayaks rent for $30 a day.

Northern Lights Trading Company

1716 W. Babcock, Bozeman, Mont. • (406) 586-2225

In addition to offering camping, ice climb-

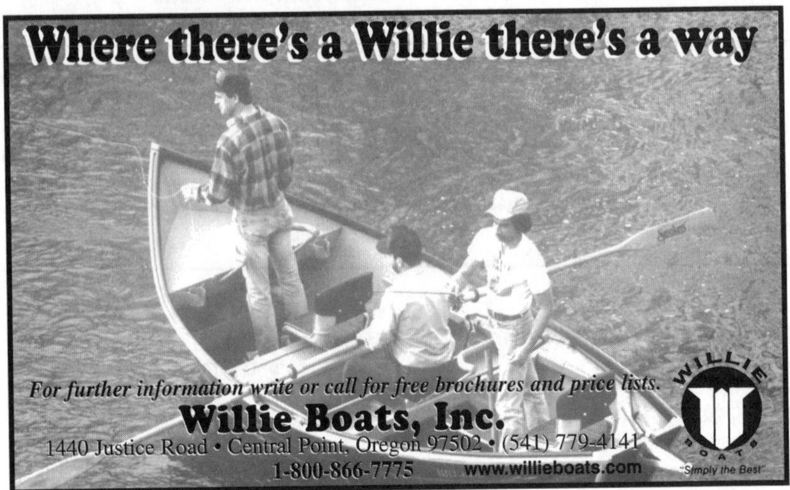

ing and cross-country skiing gear, Northern Lights rents canoes, kayaks and rafts. Canoe rentals range from $30 to $40 per day depending on the model; touring kayaks cost $20 to $40 per day. There are discounts for multiple-day rentals. You'll pay $100 to $200 per day for a whitewater raft. Sizes range from 12 feet to 17 feet. All come with rowing frames. Deposits range from $1,000 to $4,000, which can be "paid" by simply letting the rental shop hold your credit card until you return (with the raft). Northern Lights also rents watersports accessories such as paddles, wetsuits, paddle jackets, dry bags and helmets. In addition, each summer the folks here organize free weekly canoeing and kayaking get-togethers on local waters.

Panda Sport Rentals

621 Bridger Dr., Bozeman, Mont.
• (406) 587-6280

Panda rents 11- to 16-foot rafts for $35 to $75 per day depending on the style, and canoes for $20 a day. Rafts can be rented with or without frames.

Paradise Mercantile

U.S. Hwy. 89, Emigrant, Mont.
• (406) 333-4060

Right next door to the Emigrant General Store, the Mercantile rents Avon six-man rafts for $50 a day or $250 per week. These rafts come with paddles, life jackets and foot pumps. They aren't made for whitewater, but they're great for the flatwater stretches.

West Fork Cabin Camp

1487 U.S. Hwy. 287 N., Cameron, Mont.
• (406) 646-682-4802

Located at the confluence of the main and West Fork of the Madison River, West Fork Cabin Camp has a few rafts for rent in its fly shop.

INSIDERS' TIP

All of our region has 911 service and helicopter-transport capability. In many areas, dialing 911 on your out-of-state cellular phone will still hook you into emergency personnel.

Eastern Idaho

Idaho contains more than 2,000 lakes and 16,000 miles of streams; by a generous count, it's home to 39 species of game fish, including trout, mountain whitefish, chinook, kokanee salmon, bass, white sturgeon, steelhead trout, yellow perch, crappie and catfish. In the small chunk of Idaho that belongs to Greater Yellowstone, you'll find mostly trout, whitefish and kokanee. One exception is Ririe Reservoir near Idaho Falls, which is warm enough to host smallmouth bass and perch. Remember as you read that almost every lake and stream in eastern Idaho will reward your careful cast. We have little topnotch whitewater, but there are several fine scenic floats and reservoirs for canoeing, personal watercraft riding and powerboating. What we have in rich plenty is prime trout-fishing lakes, rivers and streams. What follows, in alphabetical order, are fishing and boating highlights for the region.

Anglers, it's a good idea to either hire a guide or talk to a local fishing shop, a local ranger or Idaho Fish and Game at 1515 Lincoln Road, Idaho Falls, Idaho, (208) 525-7290. The shop where you pick up your license should be able to provide you with information on regulations and limits that apply where you intend to fish. Some rivers allow only fly fishing. Most have bag limits; some don't allow anglers to keep any fish.

The rivers and lakes described below provide fantastic fishing in large part because anglers and regulatory agencies protect them. Boaters, you need to check local conditions as well. Use the resources numbers listed below or, for river and flow information, try these websites: http://www.webpak.net/~rafter/ and http://www.visitid.org/outdoor/RiverFlows97.HTML.

Bitch Creek, Canyon Run

Floatboating

This 12-mile-long, experts-only run seems a magical thing: a dramatic basalt canyon tucked beneath the rolling potato fields of Teton Valley. The whitewater is Class IV with two Class V drops. Logjams and blind corners are frequent. The put-in is at the Idaho Highway 32 bridge over Bitch Creek. Take-out is on the Teton River. Bitch Creek drops a steep 70 feet per mile. Below the confluence with the Teton, the canyon walls fall away a bit and the whitewater action slows. Get the confusing directions to put-in and take-out while you're soliciting more information about this run (see the resource phone numbers at the end of this chapter). If you don't like to share your whitewater with lots of wood, don't consider floating Bitch Creek. This is a kayakers' run.

Fall River

Floatboating

Depending on which map, sign or resident you believe, this river is called Falls River or Fall River. Either way, it's home to a fun Class III or III/IV whitewater run and a longer, fast-moving scenic float upstream of the whitewater section. A recently completed private diversion project pulls enough water from the 6-mile lower run to make it unfloatable most of the year, so catch this one during spring runoff. The upper run, called the Cave Falls run, is rated Class III but is mostly without defined whitewater. Its river bed is wide and gravelly, so even its 44-foot-per-mile gradient doesn't kick up a lot of waves. It does require several portages along its 16-mile length, however; it also holds a lot of wood. Put-in for the Cave Falls run is at Cave Falls Campground just south of Yellowstone National Park's only unroaded entrance. Takeout is at a C.C.C. bridge on 4525 E. near Ashton. This is also the put-in for the lower run. Takeout for the lower run is at the Kirkham Bridge spanning the river.

Rafts, dories, kayaks and whitewater canoes float the lower section. The upper run is best suited to kayaks because of the shallow sections, a few tight moves and the multiple portages. It's possible, especially on a weekday, that you'll have these runs to yourself.

Henry's Fork of the Snake River

This river winds across the Island Park Caldera, is impounded in two reservoirs and roars through scenic, waterfall-stepped Cardiac Canyon. About 120 miles downstream of its headwaters, the Henry's Fork joins the South Fork of the Snake to form the Snake River. For much of its length, the river is shallow, swift Class I or II, but some Class III exists, as well as a few spectacular waterfalls.

Fishing

The meandering, riffly Henry's Fork is world-famous for its monster rainbows and prime fly fishing; it also promises great wildlife watching. Wading and bank fishing are popular on this narrow, shallow river. Road access is good for the non-canyon sections of the river, as first Big Springs Road and then Idaho Highway 47 and U.S. Highway 20 run alongside the river for much of its length. Drift-boat fishing is common, too.

This river can be fished from Memorial Day weekend through November 30, except at Harriman State Park, where fishing season doesn't open until June 15, and Harriman Bird Sanctuary, which is open June 15 to September 30. From Vernon Bridge down, the river is open for fishing all year.

The catch is mostly big rainbows, plus browns and a few brook trout, cutthroat and cutthroat/rainbow hybrids called cutt-bows. Efforts to maintain the spectacular quality of the fishing here despite heavy use have created complex regulations. Limits and allowable fishing techniques vary from section to section. For instance, Box Canyon to Riverside Campground is catch-and-release only, and Harriman State Park is fly-fishing only. Check with the Ashton, St. Anthony or Island Park ranger stations for the most recent regulations before you drop a line in the water. (You will find their numbers in our Parks and Forests chapter.)

Floatboating

Twelve boat ramps allow trips of varying length. Drift-boat fishing is extremely popular, but a couple of sections are also good for scenic or whitewater floats. Check for boat ramp locations with the Ashton, St. Anthony or Island Park ranger stations. (You will find their numbers in our Parks and Forests chapter.) Two good runs are described in this section. Cardiac Canyon, with its spectacular waterfalls, is not floatable.

Henry's Fork, Big Springs National Water Trail

It's the prettiest Class I we've ever floated. Splash-full of waterfowl, trout and landlocked kokanee salmon, its water so clear you can imagine you're suspended on shimmering air, this 4-mile run is a scenic floater's dream. It's also heavily used in summer, to the point that concerns have been raised about damage to the local fishery. If crowds don't discourage you, turn to our Close-up on the Big Springs National Water Trail in this chapter.

Henry's Fork, Coffee Pot Run

Drift-boat anglers go to great lengths to get their oars into many sections of this blue-ribbon fishery, but if you want fun whitewater and convenient logistics, try Coffee Pot. This 6-mile run is the only Class III on the Henry's Fork without difficult portages or put-ins. Most of this stretch is fast, shallow Class I and II with a gravel bottom. The Coffee Pot stretch, however, includes about 1.5 miles of fun pool-drop Class III. Watch for logs. Most of the run is flat, but the scenery, the fishing and Coffee Pot Rapids make up for that.

Put in at Mack's Inn, where you can also get supplies or a meal. Take-out is at McCrea Bridge, a stone's throw from Island Park Reservoir on the McCrea Road. Kayaks, canoes, drift boats and rafts all float this stretch.

Henry's Lake

The Targhee, Centennial and Gravelly ranges arc round and bald eagles overfly the trophy-trout-filled waters of Henry's Lake. This natural lake, like Grand Teton National Park's Jackson Lake, has been enlarged by a dam at its outlet. It measures about 4 miles wide by 5 miles long. At its narrowest, it's 2 miles across. Henry's Lake is as well-known for its sudden winds and high waves as it is for its fishing, so keep an eye tipped skyward.

Fishing

The lake is best fished from boats or float tubes, since it is mostly surrounded by private land which limits lakeshore access.

Catch trophy cutthroat (about half are wild, half stocked from nearby hatcheries), rainbow/ cutthroat hybrids called cutt-bows, and brook trout. The limit is two fish, at which point you must stop fishing. You can fish Henry's Lake between Memorial Day weekend and October 31, daytimes only. The lake's tributaries are open only for the month of August except Hatchery Creek, which is closed to fishing.

Floatboating and Powerboating

Neither Henry's Lake nor its neighbor, Island Park Reservoir, are generally paddled by nonmotorized craft, mostly because of their large size. Anglers in motorized craft tend to gravitate toward the superb fishing in Henry's Lake; powerboaters, sailboaters and personal-watercraft enthusiasts generally head to Island Park Reservoir. If you do choose to canoe or kayak on Henry's Lake, be aware that its reputation for sudden winds and high waves is earned with regularity. Eight boat ramps exist on the lake. Half charge a fee for launches and sometimes for parking. One of the most convenient, Henry's Lake State Park, offers camping, a boat launch and shower facilities; in summer the entrance gates often host a long line of trucks with fishing boats in tow. Read more about Henry's Lake and Henry's Lake State Park in our Camping and RV Parks chapter. Contact the Island Park Area Chamber of Commerce, P.O. Box 83, Island Park, ID 83429, (208) 558-7755, for more information about Henry's Lake.

Island Park Reservoir

Of the two large lakes in the area, 8,400-acre Island Park Reservoir is the powerboater's choice. The other, Henry's Lake, draws more anglers; its often-rough, always-cold waters seem to discourage other forms of recreation. Camping, picnicking and hiking are available along Island Park Reservoir's heavily forested shores (see our Camping and RV Parks chapter). Anglers catch brook, cutthroat and rainbow trout, as well as coho and kokanee salmon. Boat ramps provide ready access for powerboats and personal watercraft.

Contact the Island Park Area Chamber of Commerce, P.O. Box 83, Island Park, ID 83429, (208) 558-7755, for more information about Island Park Reservoir.

Palisades Reservoir

Sixty miles east of Idaho Falls at the top of Swan Valley is 16,000-acre Palisades Reservoir, created by a dam across the South Fork of the Snake River. The area also offers seven camping facilities, plus parking and picnic areas and restrooms. U.S. Highway 26 runs along the upper shore of this long reservoir, making it easy to reach.

Floatboating and Powerboating

The shores of the reservoir are equipped with two paved boat ramps, Calamity and Blowout, and seven unofficial, unpaved access points. Stick to the paved ramps when the water is low or you may end up stuck in the mud. Much of the lower shoreline is unroaded; access there is primarily by boat. Anglers pull brown, lake, cutthroat and rainbow trout from these waters. Few floatboaters use this reservoir, primarily because of its large size. Contact Palisades Ranger District at (208) 523-1412 for more information.

Ririe Reservoir

Ririe, with water temperatures reaching into the 70s in summer, hosts not only several species of trout, but also warm-water fish like perch and smallmouth bass. Ririe Reservoir is not regular in shape but rather reaches every which way up what were once stream-cut basalt canyons. For boaters, this means plenty of interesting nooks and crannies to explore and plenty of scenic corners to turn. Ririe Reservoir consists of only 1,560 acres but seems much larger because from any one point, you can't see most of it.

Floatboating and Powerboating

Paved boat ramps are located at the dam, reached from Meadow Creek Road off Idaho Highway 26, and at Blacktail. Picnicking and camping facilities are available at both sites.

Most of the land surrounding the reservoir is public land, so although you won't find other developed sites for recreation, plenty of opportunity exists. You'll find powerboating much more popular here than floatboating, partly because with only two ready launch sites, paddlers often have to work hard to get where they want to go on this big, tentacled reservoir. For more information, contact Idaho Fish and Game, 1515 E. Lincoln Road, Idaho Falls, (208) 525-7290.

South Fork of the Snake River

The South Fork begins in Swan Valley, Idaho at the bottom of Palisades Reservoir. It's a broad Class II river that winds, with some braiding, through cottonwood flats into an increasingly steep canyon. Below its confluence with the Henry's Fork, Idahoans call it the Snake or mainstem Snake. Unimproved campsites and camping areas, some accessible by road, dot the banks at several-mile intervals. Moose and bald eagles are common sights.

Fishing

This big, high-volume river is dry-fly heaven and home to native cutthroat and record-breaking (but imported) brown trout. Rainbows and rainbow-cutthroat hybrids are also caught. Idaho doesn't stock this river with hatchery fish, so all the fish you catch are wild, if not all native (most Western waters were stocked at one time, either by official agencies or private sports enthusiasts.) Much of the river is road-accessible for those on foot, but drift boating is a popular way to fish this river.

Fish this river from Memorial Day to November 30, except the section from the Heise measuring cable to the Henry's Fork confluence, which is open for fishing all year. This river has a two-trout limit. Other regulations, such as wildlife closures, may apply.

Floatboating

The river has 11 public boat ramps in the 64 miles between Palisades Dam and the Henry's Fork confluence, so boating trips can be of various lengths. The Conant Valley section is particularly picturesque, with its dramatic basalt canyon walls, although most of those who float it are fishing more than looking. Limited road access makes some shuttles much longer than you'd expect; you may find that a paid shuttle driver is a luxury worth having. Call the Sandy-Mite at (208) 483-2609, or Julie's Shuttle Service at (208) 483-2903.

Teton River

The upper sections of the river run through scenic Teton Basin, with its flat valley floor, sandhill cranes and views of the Teton range. The lower section has carved a narrow canyon. Access to the Teton River is not as convenient as with most eastern Idaho rivers; it exists mostly at bridge crossings, since no road runs alongside.

Fishing

Drift-boat fishing is popular, although boating is not recommended between Idaho Highway 33 and Spring Hollow. You can put in at seven boat ramps between the Teton's start, where Pine Creek and Trail Creek combine, and its confluence with the Henry's Fork 75 miles downstream. Most access points allow wading and bank fishing, but the Rainey site is probably best.

Fish for cutthroat, wild rainbow and cuttbows (cutthroat-rainbow hybrids), as well as a few hatchery rainbows. This river is open Memorial Day weekend to November 30, except for Teton Creek and its tributaries, which can't be fished until July 1. There's a two fish limit on cutthroat. Other regulations may apply.

Fishing Outfitters

For information about Idaho's fishing guides and outfitters, write the Idaho Outfitters and Guides Association, P.O. Box 95, Boise, ID 83701, or call (208) 342-1438 or (208) 342-1919. Idaho was one of the first Western states to require that outfitters and their guides be licensed. In addition to the guide services listed below, check out our Resorts and Lodges chapter for fishing lodges that also provide guide services.

Henry's Fork Anglers

Last Chance in Island Park, Idaho
• (208) 558-7525

Mike Lawson was born in this area and

has fished here his whole life. In the off-season, he writes for fly-fishing magazines and presents lectures on the sport. But when the rainbows are biting on the Henry's Fork, he's off fishing. Mike and his guides also offer trips on the Madison, Firehole, Gibbon, Yellowstone and Gallatin rivers in Yellowstone National Park, as well as on Island Park Reservoir, Henry's and Hebgen lakes and a variety of small area streams. A full-service fly shop is on premises.

Hyde Outfitters Inc.

3408 N. Hwy. 20, Last Chance in Island Park, Idaho • (208) 558-7068

Hyde Outfitters uses local guides and locally built Hyde drift boats. These folks offer daytrips to the South Fork of the Snake, the Henry's Fork, Teton River, Henry's Lake, Palisades and Island Park reservoirs and even Yellowstone National Park, all for about the same price. Your base price includes the guide, lunch, a Hyde drift boat and transportation. Guides are often available on short notice, but don't count on it. Hyde's has a complete fly shop.

South Fork Lodge

40 Conant Valley Loop, Swan Valley, Idaho • (208) 483-2112, (800) 483-2110

South Fork Lodge was in Swan Valley native Spence Warner's family for more than 45 years, but he recently sold it. For the time being, he continues to run the operation. The South Fork of the Snake River winds past South Fork Lodge through cottonwood flats, literally jumping with trophy-size native cutthroats. Trips can involve float or wade fishing (or both), depending on your preference. Float trips vary between 8 and 15 miles in length. Spence recommends anglers make guide and accommodations reservations well in advance.

Photo: Robert Bower, Post Register

Fly fishing in the Firehole River is very popular in Yellowstone National Park.

The full-service fly shop probably carries everything you forgot.

Watercraft Rentals

Canyon Whitewater Supply

450 S. Yellowstone Hwy., Idaho Falls, Idaho • (208) 522-3932

This shop sells and rents Aire rafts; Prijon, Perception and New Wave kayaks; and Old Town Canoes. A range of rafting and kayaking accessories is kept in stock as well. (See our Shopping chapter for more on this shop.)

Mack's Inn Resort

U.S. Hwy. 20 at Mack's Inn in Island Park, Idaho • (208) 558-7672 Mack's Inn • (208) 558-7272 Henry's Fork Landing

Rent rafts, canoes and skiffs to float placid Big Springs National Water Trail. You'll pay between $25 and $50 for boat, life jackets and a ride up to the put-in. Reservations are a good idea. Mack's Inn is at the junction of the Henry's Fork and U.S. Highway 20. It also rents watercraft by the hour for paddling around the immediate vicinity.

Sports Korner Inc.

660 Northgate Mile, Idaho Falls, Idaho • (208) 528-7222

Rent Dagger, Wavesport and Necky whitewater kayaks; Maravia rafts and catarafts; and Dagger and Mad River canoes and sea kayaks. All rentals include everything you need to go paddling, including the straps to hold that boat on your car. Shop owner Andy Grover also runs the town's only whitewater kayaking school, called Snake River Whitewater. The shop is closed Sundays.

Northwestern Wyoming

The fishing here is as good as anyplace in Greater Yellowstone and you'll generally find the same species in Wyoming as in Yellowstone National Park. We've listed only one lake in this section, but there are several good fishing lakes in the Cody area. Ask about them at a local fly shop. And check with the Wyoming Game and Fish, (307) 777-4600 or (307) 527-7125, for regulations on waters within their state. Floatboating and other watersports are pretty much limited to the Shoshone and Clarks Fork rivers, with the exception of a few lakes.

North Fork of the Shoshone River

Originally called the Stinking Water by early day explorer John Colter, the North Fork of the Shoshone races out of the Absaroka Mountains like a locomotive running wild. U.S. Highway 20 parallels this cold, rushing river for 40 miles between Pahaska Tepee and Buffalo Bill Reservoir. This stretch of road, rimmed by red-rock spires and minarets reminiscent of an ancient Holy City, was used by Buffalo Bill Cody for his early day Yellowstone National Park tours.

Fishing

The North Fork of the Shoshone is easily accessed and very fishable. Open year-round, the North Fork spawns fair-size Yellowstone cutthroat and rainbows, with brook trout at the top end and browns down below. In spring, grizzlies coming out of hibernation take up fishing along the river's banks. An incredible number of tributaries flow out of the surrounding mountains into the North Fork from Pahaska to Wapiti. Some of these streams, such as the Grinell, Clearwater, Sweetwater, Elk Fork and Eagle creeks, also offer good fishing.

Below the reservoir, created in 1910 with the completion of the Buffalo Bill Dam, the North Fork runs through a deep rocky canyon that's difficult to access. You can catch and keep three trout per day; only one can be more than 20 inches.

Floatboating

While some very experienced river runners raft or kayak the upper stretches, it's characterized by frequent downfalls and logjams coupled with unexpected elevation drops. Early in the year, the rapids are rated anywhere from Class III to Class V depending on the stretch. The most popular rafting segment is from the Wapiti Valley near the Rimrock Ranch to a take-out 12 miles downriver just above the Buffalo Bill Reservoir. During highwater, this run can be rated as high as Class IV, but it quickly drops with the water.

By summer's end, it's pretty tame. Access to the river below the dam is difficult because of the narrow rocky canyon.

Shoshone River

A few very experienced kayakers put in at the Hayden Arch Bridge about a mile below the Buffalo Bill Dam, then take out 4 miles downstream at the Old Bronze Boot below the rodeo grounds. Saner rafters and professional outfitters use a combination of smaller whitewater that runs from the Old Bronze Boot (DeMaris Hot Springs) to a takeout just above Corbett's Crossing before the Powell Bridge. Just past the bridge, the river is blocked by an irrigation diversion. Wyoming River Trips has an exclusive right on the put-in at DeMaris (members of the public can put in there as long as they haven't rented the raft). It runs either half or all of the 11 miles of a Class III stretch (it tames to I and II late in the summer). From the Corbett's Diversion Dam, the Shoshone flows another 50 miles to Bighorn Lake east of Lovell where you'll find frequent diversion dams.

Clarks Fork of the Yellowstone River

This 140-mile river begins in the Beartooth Mountains above Cooke City, dips into Wyoming where it cuts its way through one of the most beautiful canyons in Yellowstone country, then curls back up into Montana. There it flows through an amazing number of diversions before reaching the Yellowstone River near Laurel, Montana. U.S. Highway 212 and then Wyo. Highway 296 follow the Clarks Fork from Colter Pass to Crandall Creek.

Floatboating

As the river enters the canyon, you'll encounter a 5-mile stretch of floatable whitewater used by some local rafters and kayakers. But at the end is a very dangerous stretch of Class V, so it's best not to tackle this run without a knowledgeable guide, lots of experience, plenty of nerve and a life-insurance policy for your family. The very rocky, bumpy Clarks Fork Canyon Road will take you to the put-in.

Red Canyon River picks up the Clarks Fork as it leaves the canyon and offers a scenic 12-mile float for those wanting to watch wildlife and learn about history. Once you reach the Montana border, the Clarks Fork is riddled with diversion dams that either cross a good portion of the river or block it entirely.

Fishing

From the Montana-Wyoming state line to Crandall Creek, you'll find a 16-mile stretch of fishable, mostly wadeable water winding through a high-mountain forested valley. From there the river disappears into a deep canyon then emerges to run across the sagebrush desert of the Bighorn Basin.

Since the regulations on this river vary considerably depending on which stretch you're fishing, we recommend you check with Wyoming Department of Game and Fish, (307) 777-4600 or (307) 527-7125, to find out the specifics. The upper Clarks Fork has mostly rainbow with a few cutthroat and brook trout; the canyon offers rainbows. In the lower stretch you'll find brown trout, cutthroat, rainbows and a few grayling. Crandall Creek holds good-size cutthroat, while Sunlight Creek has some hefty brookies.

Buffalo Bill Dam Reservoir

In the early 1980s, *Outside Magazine* included the Buffalo Bill Dam Reservoir on its list of the nation's top-10 windsurfing lakes. No sooner had *Outside* printed its list than the multicolored sails of diehard windsurfers began popping up on the icy waters of this 8-mile-long reservoir tucked into the beautiful North Fork Canyon. Ironically, a three-day event that attracted windsurfers from across the nation brought a quick end to the reservoir's popularity. For the full three days of the event, the wind refused to cooperate. A few diehard locals still windsurf (wearing wetsuits), and the wind continues to be capricious. Because of its frigid waters, this lake tends to be used mostly for fishing (including ice fishing). A sailboat also pops up on the lake from time to time.

To find the lake, take U.S. Highway 20 west 8 miles out of Cody, Wyoming.

Fishing

Those who fish here use both flies and bait. The mix of fish in the Buffalo Bill Reservoir includes rainbows, browns, cutthroats and

Photo: Rocky Barker

Rafters go through rapids on the Middle Fork of the Salmon River.

lake trout, which can grow up to 30 pounds. Browns run as high as 10 to 12 pounds, while rainbows and cutthroat weigh in from 2 to 8 pounds. Ice fishing is not good on this lake because of chinook winds that come through, often creating "rotten" ice. You'll find campgrounds and boat launches here.

Fishing Outfitters

North Fork Anglers
937 Sheridan Ave., Cody, Wyo.
• (307) 527-7274

Operating out of its store on Cody's main street, North Fork Anglers not only has a full-service fly shop with hand-tied flies customized for the area, but also offers a range of guided fishing trips in and out of Yellowstone National Park. Tuned into fishing conditions, Tim Wade and his guides weigh your needs and capabilities with hatches and high water. Wade also offers two weeklong "Cowboys and Cutthroats" horsepacking trips each July, as well as a "Cast and Blast" (fishing and hunting) trip in the fall.

Permitted to fish in Yellowstone National Park and the Shoshone National Forest, North Fork Anglers charges $275 per day (for two people) for drift fishing and $250 per day for walk-and-wade.

Floatboat Outfitters

Wyoming River Trips
233 Yellowstone Hwy., Cody, Wyo.
• (307) 587-6661, (800) 586-6661

Wyoming River Trips offers five different raft and kayak trips in the Cody area. Four of them, including an inflatable-kayak trip, are on the Shoshone River. A fifth is on the North Fork of the Shoshone. Trip lengths range from 1½ hours to a half-day. Wyoming River Trips operates out of two locations: The Holiday Inn complex on Sheridan Avenue and on the Yellowstone Highway west of Cody. They pride themselves on their experienced guides.

Red Canyon River Trips
1374 Sheridan Ave., Cody, Wyo.
• (307) 587-6988, (800) 293-0148

Red Canyon River Trips offers four different trips, including two-hour rafting and "Duckie" trips on the Shoshone River. (A Duckie is an inflatable kayak.) They also run an 11-mile trip on the North Fork of the Shoshone as well as a 12-mile trip on the Clarks Fork of the Yellowstone.

River Runners

1491 Sheridan Ave., Cody, Wyo.
• (307) 527-7238

River Runners operates seven days a week during the summer months from a blue and white building across from Wendy's on Cody's main street. The company offers three different trips on the Shoshone River ranging from 1½ hours to a half-day. River Runners, established in 1967 by Buffalo Bill Cody's grandson, is the oldest float company in Cody. River Runners' guides pride themselves on their family trips.

Paddling Schools

Rendezvous River Sports/ Jackson Hole Kayak School

1035 W. Broadway Ave., Jackson, Wyo.
• (307) 733-2471

Not only can you get yourself outfitted for whitewater fun here — you can learn what to do with all that gear. Jackson Hole Kayak School offers courses taught by American Canoe Association (ACA) certified instructors. They range from roll classes for non-boaters to private instruction to help you improve upon your current skill level, whatever that may be. You can also go kayak touring in Yellowstone National Park with Jackson Hole Kayak School guides. Tours last from three to five days and can accommodate beginners as well as experienced sea kayakers. All necessary gear can be rented from the shop.

Snake River Whitewater/Sports Korner Inc.

660 Northgate Mile, Idaho Falls, Idaho
(208) 528-7222

Get group or private roll lessons at the local indoor swimming pool, or join one of three or more training trips staged annually on nearby moving Class I-II water. Lessons are also staged at the Snake River Whitewater project on the Idaho Canal (also called the 12th Street Canal). The city of Idaho Falls and the Snake River Whitewater Project have created a little paddle park here, with a couple of playholes and slalom gates positioned over Class I-II water. Snake River Whitewater uses the canal for lessons and for its summer introductory paddling course for kids ($85 buys kids ages 10 to 18 lessons, equipment and use of the canal and pool). Call Andy Grover at Sports Korner for information about Snake River Whitewater, the kids' program, or possible fees for non-school-related use of the paddling park. Andy's shop is closed Sundays.

Teton Aquatic Supply/Snake River Kayak and Canoe School

155 W. Gill Ave., Jackson, Wyo.
• (307) 733-3127, (800) 529-2501

What makes this place really cool is the indoor training pool, used by both scuba and paddling schools. The 45,000-gallon pool is 12 feet deep. It's equipped with whirlpool jets to simulate a 4-mph current. The company conducts kayak roll clinics here; more advanced boating classes begin in the training pool and then move out onto the Snake River or a tributary.

The staff offers instruction for a variety of craft: hard-shell kayaks, inflatable kayaks, sea kayaks, canoes, oar and paddle rafts, and dories. Teton Aquatic Supply also conducts three-day guided sea kayak tours on Yellowstone Lake. The company supplies all meals, transportation and gear. Guides are also instructors who can fine-tune your paddling style as well as help you stay safe.

Scuba Outfitters

Diver Down Idaho

2457 N. Yellowstone Ave., Idaho Falls,

INSIDERS' TIP

Anglers remember...Panther, Obsidian and Indian creeks in Yellowstone National Park are reserved especially for bait fishing by children.

Photo: Post Register Photo Archive

On the water? Expertise and equipment become crucial to survival for whitewater kayakers.

Idaho • (208) 535-2962

This shop provides NAUI open-water training for $245. It also organizes about 12 charter trips annually to exotic dive sites like the Bahamas, Cancun and Belize, as well as driving trips to places like Washington's San Juan Islands or Arizona's Lake Mead. Rental gear includes scuba kayaks so you can paddle yourself and your gear to your dive site. Winter open-water dives happen at Homestead, Utah, in a large, partially enclosed cavern with 90-degree water, or at Sea Base (see the Inland Scuba Inc. entry). In summer, open-water dives are staged at Ririe and Palisades reservoirs, as well as Bear Lake on the Idaho/Utah border. Bear Lake has a dive park made up of sunken cars, boats and other objects for divers to explore underwater. Don't let his baby face fool you: Owner Chuck Webb has been certified since he was 12 and is a former commercial diver and underwater welder.

Inland Scuba Inc.

551 S. Capital Ave., Idaho Falls, Idaho • (208) 529-2636

This SSI (Scuba Schools International) facility fills air tanks, repairs dive gear and sells a small inventory of scuba and related gear and some used consignment merchandise, but mostly it's a place to learn how to breathe underwater. The company does winter open-water training dives at Tooele, Utah (pronounced tu-WILLA). Tooele's private dive facility is called Sea Base. It's geothermally warmed to 65 degrees in winter and stocked with colorful tropical fish and nurse sharks. The company also dives in the murky 92-degree waters of Belmont Springs, near the Idaho/Utah border. In summer, dives generally take place at Ririe Reservoir. Certification costs $235. This is a family-owned business.

Teton Aquatic Supply

155 W. Gill St., Jackson, Wyo. • (307) 733-3127, (800) 529-2501

Diving courses take place year-round in the 45,000-gallon indoor training pool. Class sizes range between four and 10. Open-water dives and guided dives are sometimes staged at Fremont Lake in Pinedale, Wyoming, with its crystal-clear water and huge underwater rock formations. Visibility at Fremont runs between 50 and 85 feet. Ririe Lake is another option, warmer but with about 20 feet of visibility. Belmont Springs or Homestead are both warm springs located a couple of hours south of Jackson. They're not large enough for satisfying recreational diving, but the warm water makes them perfect for instruction. You can become PADI licensed for $285.

Resources

Bureau of Land Management Idaho Falls District Office

1405 Hollipark Dr., Idaho Falls, Idaho • (208) 524-7500

These folks manage the South Fork of the Snake below Palisades Reservoir, so they always know what's going on down there.

Bureau of Reclamation

River and Reservoir Line • (800) 658-5771

This recorded information supplies water-level information on any river or reservoir in the Upper Snake drainage controlled by a Bureau of Reclamation dam (that's Jackson Lake, Grassy Lake, Palisades Reservoir, the Snake River and more).

Bureau of Reclamation River and Reservoir Line

• (800) 253-8737

Calling this number will get you the same type of information as the previous listing for the Buffalo Bill Dam and the Shoshone River, plus other areas not covered by this book.

Canyon Whitewater Supply

450 S. Yellowstone Hwy., Idaho Falls, Idaho (208) 522-3932

Dave Gonzalez, owner of this shop, has his finger on the pulse of local river levels. An avid rafter, he knows the best stretches of water around here.

Idaho Fish and Game

1515 Lincoln Road, Idaho Falls, Idaho • (208) 525-7290

Wyoming Game and Fish

360 N. Cache Dr., Jackson Wyo.

• (307) 733-2321

Most sporting goods stores that carry fishing licenses also have copies of regulations, but you can also get it from the horse's mouth.

Rendezvous River Sports

1035 W. Broadway Ave., Jackson, Wyo. • (307) 733-2471

This watersports store and school takes pride in having the latest information on area water, particularly whitewater runs. Staff can tell you about runs scattered throughout Greater Yellowstone, including some that have not yet been described in whitewater books.

U.S. Geological Survey

Helena, Mont. • (406) 449-5900

Call these folks for the latest stream flows on Montana's rivers. You can also get stream flow info updated hourly via the Internet at montana.usga.gov.

Living in the shadow of a time when Greater Yellowstone's human inhabitants depended for their survival on the bounty of the mountains, folks in this region are still very much tied to the idea — if not to the actuality — of the mountains being a living pantry.

Hunting

In the not-too-distant past, a few schools would close on the opening day of hunting season. Administrators knew there wouldn't be enough kids (or teachers) in school to bother with classes.

Living in the shadow of a time when Greater Yellowstone's human inhabitants depended for their survival on the bounty of the mountains, folks in this region are still very much tied to the idea — if not to the actuality — of the mountains being a living pantry. Locals trade elk sausage recipes, and children take homemade deer jerky to school in their lunches. Smoked fish makes a fine hors d'oeuvre, and cut-up elk sirloin is excellent in Chinese stir-fry. One mark of friendship here is the sharing of elk tenderloins, called backstrap. If a resident of Greater Yellowstone offers you some, consider yourself blessed. Then eat it.

When we talk hunting in Yellowstone country, we first think of wapiti — the mighty elk. Sure, there are plenty of other big-game animals in our neck of the woods, and we'll talk about those later. But the elk, bugling from across the meadow, herding his harem of cows, is the most sought-after big game in Greater Yellowstone. Besides being beautiful to behold, elk are elusive enough to require stalking and studying. And they live in country remote enough to make the hunt a challenge. Elk hunters not only have to exert themselves physically, but they also have to learn something about the wapiti to find him, then think like an elk to outsmart him.

Elk also make good eating. The meat is high on flavor, low in cholesterol and untainted by food additives. Having a freezer full of wild game is so much a way of life for many people in Yellowstone country that they can't rest until they've filled that freezer. In small rural towns where the economies have always been depressed, the wild game that haunts the nearby hills is insurance against lean times. Often dependent on seasonal work, people may not be able to pay their bills through the winter months, but their families won't go hungry when meat is so close at hand, especially if they've also raised and put up a big garden during the summer.

While many still look to game to supplement their larder, others simply relish the hunt: long days of hiking steep terrain in cold weather; stalking and outsmarting wild animals able to move much faster than a human being; making a clean shot. And bugling in a bull elk carries its own thrill. Headed your way, bugling back with blood in his eyes, he has mistaken your call for that of an intruding bull. His instincts aren't ruled by reason.

Shooting a trophy bull or buck has always been cause for celebration — for the household as well as the hunter. In stores, restaurants, homes, even medical clinics in Yellowstone country, you'll see mounted heads of elk, deer, moose, bear, bison and a whole

INSIDERS' TIP

The Idaho Outfitters and Guides Association maintains a Web site that gives you access to hunting regulations and the Web sites of many Idaho outfitters. Find them at: www.ioga.org. For 24-hour sportsman's information, call (800) 654-1178 in Wyoming and (406) 994-5700 in Montana. Idaho Fish and Game has no comparable service, but makes a world of sportsman's info available on their Web site: www2.state.id.us/fishgame.

slew of other animals. On main streets in small towns, clusters of men gather around a pickup truck, admiring an especially big bull filling the pickup bed. While an increasing number of locals and almost all out-of-state hunters now have their kill cut, wrapped and frozen by local butcher shops or packing plants, some still butcher their own, setting up an assembly line on the kitchen table at home. Old-timers used to use every scrap of meat. The neck and head, discarded these days as waste, were pressure-cooked before the meat was removed to be canned up as mincemeat. The ribs, also often discarded, were sawed into slabs and saved for barbecued ribs. The bones were saved for soup.

We pride ourselves on passing the hunting tradition on to the next generation. Young boys and girls are given guns at an early age — and taught how to use them responsibly. They can start hunting at age 12 after a course in hunter safety. Men and women drive pickup trucks with rifles mounted on racks across the back window. Guns in the window racks of pickup trucks during hunting season are so prevalent that a few years back, when a federal law outlawed guns on school grounds, students and their parents were outraged. Teenagers, especially those who live miles out of town, hunt on their way to and from school each fall.

For insights into why people in our region hunt, read *Bloodties* by Ted Kerasote. Kerasote, a Jackson, Wyoming, author, is one of the region's top environmental reporters writing for a number of national outdoor magazines. Kerasote makes a compelling study of the ancient human urge to hunt. He also makes a good case for hunting, gathering and eating those foods from within our bioregions rather than relying on fossil-fuel-dependent foods transported thousands of miles for our consumption.

Because Greater Yellowstone has such an extensive concentration of wild lands, it's a hunter's mecca. In addition to elk, Montana, Idaho and Wyoming all have fairly large mule-deer populations. Bighorn sheep, mountain goats, moose and mountain lions are scarcer. That means hunting for these species is limited to comparatively few permits each year. The same is true of black bears. Antelope, which are prevalent across Wyoming in general, are relatively rare on the Yellowstone Plateau. (A herd of about 230 roam the northern range near Gardiner, Montana.) Anywhere you find water in Greater Yellowstone, though, you'll likely find great duck and good goose hunting. Other game birds can be pretty plentiful depending on the year.

In this chapter we'll give you just a taste of hunting opportunities. For more information on hunting in Greater Yellowstone, we refer you to the Montana Department of Fish, Wildlife and Parks, P.O. Box 200701, Helena, MT 59620, (406) 444-2535, (406) 994-4042; the Wyoming Department of Game and Fish, Attention: Information Section, 5400 Bishop Boulevard, Cheyenne, Wyoming, (307) 777-4600; and the Idaho Department of Fish and Game, P.O. Box 25, Boise, ID 83707, (208) 334-3700.

Thinning the Elk Herds

Hunting is forbidden in Yellowstone National Park, and Grand Teton National Park has only a brief hunt. Outside Yellowstone's boundaries, battalions of hunters wait each fall to pick off migrating elk. To the north, where the country is more open and elk more plentiful, many animals seem to have learned from experience not to step over the boundary line. That means fewer of them are killed. It also means that more elk are staying longer on their summer range in the park, which some believe will cause habitat degradation. The reintroduction of wolves in 1995 will undoubtedly help curb the herd's growth.

In Yellowstone, the park's summer elk population ranges from 75,000 to 90,000, with about 18,000 of them calling the park's northern range their summer home. Except for a few isolated pockets of elk that hang out year-round near thermal areas, the rest of the elk in the park begin to trickle off the Yellowstone Plateau as soon as the first snows fall. To the south they head into Grand Teton National

Park and onto the Snake River Plain. To the west they migrate over Targhee Pass and into the Targhee National Forest. To the east, many are blocked by the towering Absaroka Range, but some find their way to the eastern slopes of the Absarokas and into Sunlight Basin.

When Yellowstone National Park was first formed, President Theodore Roosevelt recognized that the park's elk herds, though decimated at the time by poachers, would multiply so fast they would overpopulate the park if they weren't hunted. In 1951, Yellowstone National Park officials tried to reduce the northern herd size from 11,800 animals to 5,000, the number they felt the range could support. The same range today is currently carrying about 18,000 elk. Live-trapping and removal of the animals to other areas failed to fix the problem. In the winter of 1955-56 park officials removed more than 6,000 elk from the northern herd. Nearly 2,000 of them were shot. The program was wildly unpopular.

Management of the migrating herds, which comes under the jurisdiction of three state and federal agencies, is complicated. Yellowstone National Park manages for natural regulation by predators and winter kill. Outside the parks, state fish and game management agencies, tend to manage for high populations to meet hunters' demands. But if they sell too many elk tags, especially for cow elk, the public attacks them. The Forest Service, which manages the land, doesn't always take game into consideration. For example, much of its money lately is supposed to be used for burns. While a prescribed sagebrush burn may promote increased grass growth, it also wipes out the sagebrush, a winter food source for mule deer.

Grizzlies and Hunters

Before you head for the hills, a word about grizzlies: Hunters + *ursus horribilis* = trouble. In 1997, out of 13 known grizzly deaths, eight were by hunters during surprise encounters outside the parks. In 1998, the figures were better: A total of eight grizzlies died, only one at the hands of a hunter. Think about it. Except during hunting season, humans in Greater Yellowstone — and in the parks in particular — walk in groups on trails during the day and make a lot of noise. Grizzlies have figured out human behavior and so generally stay off trails during the day. Come hunting season, though, lone camouflaged hunters are sneaking around off-trail, sometimes in the predawn dark. While their intent is to sneak up on an elk, some end up surprising a grizzly — and scaring the heck out of themselves. To compound the problem, gut piles left by hunters and hanging elk carcasses in camp act as magnets to grizzlies.

The Interagency Grizzly Bear Committee offers the following advice for hunters:

- Travel in pairs.
- Use horses when possible.
- Make a wide circle around dead carcasses or gut piles. After you've made a kill, gut, pack and remove the carcass as soon as possible. Don't leave a gut pile near a trail.
- Hang the carcass if you have to leave it, but leave the carcass where you can see it from a distance or approach it from upwind. When returning to a carcass, be wary; if a grizzly has claimed it, let him have it.
- Keep a clean camp with food inaccessible to bears.

Guided Hunting

Hunting seasons vary by state, areas, species and weapon. And regulations, different in each state, are so complicated that it darn near takes an attorney to decipher them. Generally, the seasons begin with bow hunts in late August or early September. A general season that begins about October 1 is followed by late hunts for black-powder rifles and/or bow hunters that runs through December. Scattered throughout the seasons are special

INSIDERS' TIP

No motorized vehicles are allowed in designated wilderness areas. This includes snowmobiles, all-terrain vehicles and mountain bikes.

hunts. In some places where elk are overpopulated, state fish and game managers will extend a season if hunters haven't harvested enough animals. If you want the scoop on regulations and hunting licenses, we recommend you call the state agencies responsible for managing fish and game. They're listed at the end of the general introduction to this chapter.

When it comes to hunting, nonresidents pay for being outsiders. In Wyoming, it costs an out-of-stater $410 to hunt elk and $195 for deer. The same permits cost Wyoming residents $35 and $22. Each applicant is assigned a number. Numbers are thrown into a pot from which permits are drawn.

The Idaho Legislature is contemplating changes at this writing, but in early 1999, residents were paying $7.50 for a hunting license and $22.50 for an elk tag. Those same two items together run an out-of-state hunter $434.

In Montana, nonresidents will pay $478 for a big game combo license in 1999. Applicants are assigned a number, which is thrown into a pot for drawing. Nonresidents can bypass the drawing and secure a license by booking with an outfitter and paying $835 for a license. A regular nonresident license for deer alone is $478; outfitted, it's $745. Elk permits are priced the same. A nonresident bird license is $55.

If you're contemplating coming to Yellowstone country to hunt, we recommend you consider going with an outfitter. Most outfitters set up backcountry tent camps, often in the difficult-to-access wilderness. That means while many locals are combing national forest lands in their pickup trucks, you'll be tucked miles away from the nearest road. Outfitters not only know where to find the game, they have all the equipment (except the rifles and the clothing) you'll need for a hunt.

Montana, Idaho and Wyoming each have an Outfitters and Guides Association with lists of the licensed outfitters in their state (see the list later in this section). If you do come hunting in Yellowstone country, we recommend you arrive looking forward to all aspects of the hunt — the hike, the scenery, the fresh mountain air — rather than the kill or a trophy. It's amazing how many hunters ruin their own hunts because they've come all the way across the country believing they can't go home without a trophy elk or deer.

Guided hunts can be expensive. Weeklong guided elk hunts range from $1,500 to $3,800, while a guided bighorn sheep hunt can cost up to $8,000. *Your Guided Hunt*, written by veteran hunting guide Randy Blackburn of Cody, Wyoming, and featured in *Sports Afield*, is a must for folks embarking on their first guided hunt. Blackburn's hunting tales are not only interesting, but they'll also answer questions that most outfitters don't think to answer. To get a copy of Blackburn's book, write him at 84 South Fork Road, Cody, WY 82414. The cost is $14.95 (add 4 percent if you're a Wyoming resident), plus $3 for shipping.

By the way, if you call Fish and Game departments in any of Greater Yellowstone states, chances are good the first thing they'll tell you is, "Get in shape." The Rockies are steep. Their high elevations also mean your lungs will have a harder time finding oxygen in the air. And, if you target practice at home, you're less apt to miss your only shot at a big bull or a fat cow.

In the following sections, we tell you about a number of outfitters who guide in Greater Yellowstone. Cody alone has more than a dozen licensed hunting outfitters. We recommend you call the respective state's Outfitters and Guides Association for a complete listing. And we suggest that when you're trying to

INSIDERS' TIP

Property owners and livestock grazers are generally pretty nice folks. They don't mind, if their land isn't posted "no trespassing," when you pull their gate open and drive through. But one of the biggest social faux pas in our region is not to close that gate behind you!

Photo: Randy Hayes, Post Register

The South Fork of the Snake River flows through the Byington Landing area.

decide on an outfitter, you ask for (and check out) references. The associations are listed below.

Idaho Outfitters and Guides Association, P.O. Box 95, Boise, ID 83701, (208) 342-1438 or (208) 342-1919.

Montana Outfitters and Guides Association, P.O. Box 1248, Helena, MT 59624, (406) 449-3578.

Wyoming Department of Commerce, Wyoming State Board of Outfitters and Professional Guides, 1750 Westland Road, Cheyenne, WY 82002; call (307) 777-5323 or (800) 264-0981.

Jackson Hole

Jackson, Wyoming

Darwin Ranch

Jackson, Wyo. • (307) 733-5588

Loring Woodman hunts elk on horseback from the most comfortable of hunting camps: his private ranch surrounded by the Bridger-Teton National Forest. Loring has been guiding horseback hunting trips here since 1965. His experience and the fact that the area has a resident elk herd almost guarantee sightings. He estimates his hunters' success rate at 80 to 85 percent. (For more on the guest ranch itself, see our Guest Ranches chapter.)

Jackson Peak Outfitters

Jackson, Wyo. • (307) 733-3805

Charlie Petersen Jr.'s operation features comfortable, family-operated hunting camps, and limited numbers of clients. Hunts are for elk, deer, moose, bighorn and bear. Charlie, his wife and two grown sons usually put on five or six hunts a season in the Gros Ventre Wilderness and other areas east of Jackson. The family also hosts summer pack trips. Charlie began working as a hunting guide in 1952; he started his own business in 1967. He estimates his success for bighorns at around 80 percent. Elk success ranges from 70 to 75 percent.

Moran, Wyoming

Two Ocean Pass Outfitting

Moran, Wyo. • (307) 543-2309, (800) 726-2409

John Winter guides elk, deer, antelope, moose and bighorn sheep horseback hunts in the remote backcountry of the Bridger-Teton and Shoshone national forests. He's hunted

Bear Safety

When Bozeman, Montana, contractor Mark Matheny was attacked in 1992 by a grizzly, it changed his life and his career. Matheny now makes and markets UDAP Pepper Power, a high-powered pepper spray designed to repel bears. Matheny and a friend, who were bow hunting near Big Sky, were hiking the main trail back to their pickup truck after shooting an elk. They startled a sow grizzly feeding on a carcass with her three cubs. Within seconds she had charged the 35 yards between her and the two hunters and had Matheny's head in her mouth. Meanwhile, Matheny's partner managed to get to his 4-ounce can of pepper spray designed for law enforcement. A shot into the bear's mouth from 5 or 6 feet, sent her away — for a moment. It took a second shot (and the rest of the can) to send the sow packing after she returned and bit Matheny's arm.

When Matheny had recuperated, he tried to return to his contracting business but could think only of developing a pepper spray especially designed for bears. In addition to the spray itself, Matheny has designed quick-draw holsters.

While pepper spray is no substitute for being alert, knowledgeable and careful, evidence is mounting that it is an effective bear repellent in case of attack. Newspapers in Greater Yellowstone carry story after story of pepper spray each fall during hunting season. Near Bozeman, a hunting guide turned a sow and her cub away with pepper spray after they charged first his client and then him. Near Cody, Wyoming, a Forest Service crew sprayed a grizzly when it charged into their camp. After rolling around on the ground, the bawling bear got up and left. Near Jackson, a hunter surprised a grizzly in a berry patch. While the bear was biting his leg, the hunter shot it in the face with pepper spray that was attached to his belt. The bear fled.

Pepper spray has a 10- to 15-foot range and can be rendered ineffective by adverse weather conditions like rain and wind. It's also not much good if you don't know how to use it. (In other words, if you choose to carry it, practice using it in your yard.)

By the way, most human-bear encounters occur during hunting season when hunters are sneaking around alone in the woods. In 1997, hunters killed eight grizzlies in Greater Yellowstone after being charged by the animals.

Now that we have your attention, relax. Yellowstone country is not crawling with grizzlies, and not all grizzlies are going to charge you. They also aren't the only kind of bear that demands respect in Yellowstone country. Black bears, while less aggressive, can be equally dangerous if they learn not to fear humans. Mother bears that feel their cubs are being threatened will attack instantly. And black bear boars (male bears) have been known to be unpredictable during mating season. All bears will protect a kill. The vast majority of visitors will never see a bear. (A radio-collared male grizzly, tracked and studied in Montana over a period of years, once spent two peaceful days just 100 yards from the Dairy Queen in Big Fork, Montana. Only the trackers knew he was there.)

There are some things you can do to avoid close encounters. First of all, we recommend you read as much as possible about grizzlies and black bears if you plan to hike or camp in their territory. Bill Schneider, a Yellowstone Institute instructor and author of *Bear Aware*, says knowledge is your best weapon against bears. Another

— continued on next page

Photo: Robert Bower

A grizzly pauses to sniff the air and check out the situation as it forages.

good book is *Learning to Talk Bear* by Roland Cheek, an outfitter for more than 20 years in grizzly country. (See our Education chapter for information on the Yellowstone Institute).

Schneider and other bear experts recommend defensive behaviors. Be alert — look for bear sign such as tracks, droppings or diggings — and look ahead. Be noisy — talk, sing, or clap. And be social. A bigger group makes more noise and looks more formidable than a single person. Travel between 11 AM and 3:30 PM when wildlife is likely to be bedded down. Stay on trails, as bears tend to avoid them during the day because they know that that's where humans travel. If you happen to smell or see a dead carcass, steer clear. It could be a grizzly's food cache, which it will aggressively defend. If you see a bear cub, know that its mama is somewhere nearby. Back off. Avoid smelly foods or scented deodorants, etc.

In camp, you can do other things to discourage bear visits. Most serious injuries or fatalities occur at night in camps where attractants are present. To avoid these situations, hang your food from poles or from a tree. Next, pitch your tent at least 100 yards from your cooking site and your food cache. Don't cook in your tent or keep food in it — and don't wear your cooking clothes to bed. Don't leave food unattended during the day. People who sleep outside their tents are more likely to be attacked by a bear than those who sleep inside. If a bear does come into camp, especially during the day, be concerned. That's a clear indication that it has no fear of humans. If it has come into camp and gotten a reward, you can be sure it will return the next night expecting more. Move your camp.

If you encounter a bear, Yellowstone National Park officials recommend backing away slowly, talking quietly to the bear, refraining from sudden movements and avoiding eye contact with the bear. A bear can outrun you so don't run for a tree. Black

— continued on next page

bears, young grizzlies and some adults can also climb trees. If a bear charges you, a Yellowstone publication for campers recommends you freeze since charges often turn out to be bluffs. In the event of an actual attack, most authorities recommend dropping to the ground, putting your knees to your chest and your hands behind your neck and playing dead. Usually, a bear will bite and swat a couple of times before running off. Don't move until you are sure the bear is gone. If a bear comes into your camp at night, most experts say not to play dead in that situation.

Before you go into the backcountry, it's a good idea to check with the agency involved. In Yellowstone National Park, call the backcountry office at (307) 344-2160. In Grand Teton National Park, call (307) 739-3399. If you're planning to hike on public lands managed by the Forest Service, call the local ranger district that manages the area you'll be hiking. Forest maps indicate the ranger districts, and our Resources chapter lists the numbers of ranger districts in Greater Yellowstone.

between Cody and Jackson, Wyoming, since 1963. Except for one client back in 1993, his success rate on sheep has been 100 percent. He guesses his success with deer at 90 percent. The least experienced of John's guides have been working with him for three years. He personally oversees each of his hunting trips. He also runs summer pack trips for nonhunters.

Diamond D Ranch Outfitters

Buffalo Valley Rd., Moran, Wyo. • (307) 543-2479

Rod Doty operates a comfortable little guest ranch in summer, but during hunting season he's on horseback in the Bridger-Teton Wilderness, guiding clients to bighorn sheep, elk, moose and deer. (For more on Rod's guest ranch operation, see our Guest Ranches chapter.)

Turpin Meadows Ranch

Moran, Wyo. • (307) 543-2496, (800) 743-2496

At the top of Buffalo Valley just outside of Grand Teton National Park, this summer guest ranch becomes a comfortable base for your hunting expedition in the Bridger-Teton Wilderness. Dale Castagno and his three sons, Stan, Steve and Ryan, can show you elk, moose, bighorn sheep and deer. This family operation guides 30 to 50 hunters per season. (For more on their guest ranch operation, see our Guest Ranches chapter.)

Southwestern Montana

Cooke City, Montana

Beartooth Plateau Outfitters Inc.

U.S. Hwy. 212, Cooke City, Mont. • (406) 838-2328 June through Sept. Roberts, Mont. • (406) 445-2293 Oct. through May, (800) 253-8545

Operating from a pack station in Cooke City, Beartooth Plateau Outfitters offers early hunts: an early rifle bugling hunt from mid-September through the first week in October; an archery hunt from September 1 through mid-October; and a rifle hunt from October 1 through mid-October. The first hunt is in Montana, while the second two are just over the state line in Wyoming. Both are adjacent to Yellowstone National Park.

The best part about these hunts is you only have to ride horseback for two hours before reaching the base camp — a deluxe setup of wall tents housing sleeping, cooking and dining quarters. Outfitter Ronnie Wright offers later hunts near Dillon, Montana. Wright also offers day and overnight pack trips out of Cooke City. For more information, see our Other Recreation chapter.

Blue Ribbon Flies

309 N. Canyon St., West Yellowstone, Mont. • (406) 646-7643

Blue Ribbon Flies is the only licensed outfitter to offer waterfowl shoots in the West Yellowstone area. Most hunting takes place over decoys in remote coves of Hebgen and Quake Lakes. Jump shooting for snipe, ducks, and geese along nearby beaver ponds, sloughs and small streams is also very popular. Hunters are welcome to bring their own dogs. Blue Ribbon's season generally begins the first Saturday in October. When your hunt is over, your guide can take you fishing for the rest of the day. Because repeat clients reserve most of their dates, Blue Ribbon has few openings, so make your reservations early.

Bozeman, Montana

Medicine Lake Outfitters

Bozeman, Mont. • (406) 388-4938

Tom and Joan Heintz outfit in the Absaroka-Beartooth Wilderness north of Yellowstone National Park and the Madison Range to the west. While elk and mule deer are what most of their hunters are after, Heintz will also help you bag a moose, mountain goat or whitetail if you draw a permit for one. Heintz employs seasoned, professional guides whose average age is 40, and he operates with a string of 70 horses. During the summer months, Heintz leads pack trips into Yellowstone National Park, the Absaroka-Beartooth Wilderness and the Madison Range.

Livingston, Montana

Bear Paw Outfitters

136 Deep Creek Rd., Livingston, Mont. • (406) 222-6642

This family-run outfitting business operates out of Tim and Cindy Bowers' homeplace 8 miles south of Livingston. These days Tim specializes more in horseback rides in and out of Yellowstone National Park during the summer, but he does a good hunt from his ranch. After a day in the Absaroka Mountains, he'll take you home, Cindy will feed you, and you'll sleep in a warm, comfortable bed. Tim doesn't guarantee his hunters an elk. He does promise a rich hunting experience — and he promises to send you home well-fed and tired. For more information about Bear Paw's per-hour, daylong and overnight horseback rides, see our Other Recreation chapter.

Gallatin Gateway, Montana

Broken Hart Ranch

73800 Gallatin Rd., Gallatin Gateway, Mont. • (406) 763-4279

Lee Hart has been leading hunters to big game in the Gallatin since 1969. While his specialty is elk, he'll also guide you to bighorn sheep, moose or any other big game for which you hold a permit. See our Other Recreation chapter for information on horseback riding here.

Elkhorn Enterprises

302 E. Fourth St., Big Timber, Mont. • (406) 932-4482

Outfitter Pete Clark can't remember a time in his life when he wasn't guiding hunters. Clark's father began the outfitting business in 1950. These days, Clark takes only about 20 guests deer and elk hunting each year during the general season. His average group size is six. Hunter success is close to 100 percent for deer and half that for elk. Clark runs his hunts from a cabin accessed by four-wheel drive, but hunters head out each morning on horseback. His hunting area borders the Absaroka-Beartooth Wilderness.

Eastern Idaho

Idaho's hunting seasons run long: around 65 days. Success rates are high and permits

INSIDERS' TIP

The Foundation for North American Wild Sheep says that no state, including Alaska, has more Rocky Mountain bighorn habitat than Idaho. Numbers of bighorns in the state are low, but the potential for herd growth is tremendous.

generally not difficult to get. Idaho's public lands support a wide range of game animals, from elk, mule deer and bighorn sheep to pronghorn antelope, bear, moose, cougar, mountain goat, whitetail deer, upland game birds and waterfowl. In the past 15 years, elk populations have increased and elk harvests have quadrupled. Deer harvests have doubled in the past decade. Many believe the population growth and the increased hunter success are tied to a string of mild winters through the late 1980s and early '90s.

Anderson Outfitting

5646 Sorrell Dr., Pocatello, Idaho • days (208) 237-6544, evenings (208) 237-2664

Bob and Mary Anderson offer a range of outdoor activities, including trophy rifle and bow hunts for moose, cougar, grouse, deer, bear and elk in the Caribou National Forest of southeastern Idaho. They specialize in one-on-one hunts. Ask about their driftboat and jetboat fishing on the Snake River, too.

Beard Outfitters

Leigh Canyon, Wyo. • (307) 576-2694

Hunt with a Teton Basin native for elk, deer, moose and bear on the west slopes of the Teton range, as well as in the Jedediah Smith and remote Winegar Hole wildernesses. Lyle Beard and his brother, Bill, started this business in 1963. When Lyle's sons, Gary and Joe, became old enough to help, they joined the company. The younger Beards have hunted around here since they were children. Some of the Beards' clients have been coming back for more than 30 years. Summer horseback trips are also available.

Haderlie Tincup Mountain Guest Ranch

5336 Idaho Hwy. 34, Idaho • (208) 873-2368, (800) 253-2368

Vaughn Haderlie and son, David, lead archery, rifle and muzzle-loader hunts for elk, deer, moose and occasionally cougar and bear. They also offer summer trail rides and pack trips. The company has been in the family since 1968. You can hunt from the ranch Vaughn's granddad homesteaded in 1888 at the mouth of Tincup Canyon, or stay at a pack-in camp. The company takes 30 to 50 hunters every year. Lately the elk success rate has been about 60 to 70 percent, David says. The Haderlies hunt Swan Valley and Star Valley.

Northwestern Wyoming

At the turn of the century, antelope had almost taken their last dash across the prairie. Since then, though, Wyoming game managers have brought antelope populations back to nearly a half-million. And that's after about a third of the population was wiped out by the severe winter of 1992-93. Elk numbers are also at record highs with an estimated statewide population of 105,000. Wyoming is home to about 450,000 mule deer. In 1997, hunters harvested 23,000 elk, more than 26,000 mule deer and about 7,000 whitetails.

Wyoming Department of Game and Fish, which manages the state's wildlife, can be reached at 5400 Bishop Boulevard, Cheyenne, WY 82006; (307) 777-4600. Wyoming's elk-hunting seasons begin in September and run through most of December. Since the seasons vary hugely depending on the area and the type of weapon you're using, we refer you to Wyoming Game and Fish.

INSIDERS' TIP

Always ask a prospective hunting outfitter about his success rate with the species you're after. Also ask lots of questions about conditions in camp and the local experience of the company's guides. Ask for and call references to find out if the kind of trip this outfitter puts on is the kind you want to participate in.

Bliss Creek Outfitters

326 Diamond Basin Rd., Cody, Wyo.
• (307) 527-6103

Veteran outfitter Tim Doud offers wilderness hunts on the South Fork of the Shoshone River. While he specializes in elk hunts, he also guides moose, bighorn sheep and spring bear hunts. At one time or another, all his guides have been through Doud's four-week guide school held each summer at his ranch. That means that in addition to the usual necessary skills, they are trained in archery elk hunting. Maybe that's why Doud's archery hunters consistently have a shooting success rate of 75 percent. Rifle hunter success is a bit higher: 80 to 90 percent. The group size for Doud's hunt ranges from four to six.

Lost Creek Outfitters

31 Cedar Mountain Dr., Cody, Wyo.
• (307) 587-8584

You may never go back to tent hunting after a hunt with Lost Creek Outfitters operated by Greg "Griz" and Karla Turner. Midway between Yellowstone National Park and Cody, the Turners offer a wilderness elk hunt combined with luxury accommodations at the Bill Cody Ranch. While you're riding the mountains on horseback, stalking that trophy bull, folks at the Bill Cody Ranch will be plumping the pillows in your cabin and cooking up a hearty ranch supper. Well-known locally for his own guiding abilities, Griz Turner prides himself on having the best guides in the area and limits his trips — hunting, fishing and packing — to small groups.

He specializes in elk and mule deer hunts, but also guides spring bear hunts (both archery and rifle) as well as antelope hunts in the fall. In the summer, he guides two- to 10-day pack trips as well as overnight fishing trips.

Grizzly Ranch

North Fork Hwy., Cody, Wyo.
• (307) 587-3966

While you hunt with Rick Felts and his guides, Felts' wife, Kim, will be cooking up a homemade dinner so good that some hunters say it's her meals that keep them coming back year after year. Using his ranch as a base camp, Felts guides elk, deer, bighorn sheep and antelope hunts in the wilderness. At the end of a long day, you can wolf down one of Kim's famous dinners complete with homemade bread and desserts, then retire to your cabin for a few winks of sleep. Felts' deer and elk hunters reported more than a 60 percent success rate in 1998. He can accommodate six people at once.

Gary Fales Outfitters

2728 North Fork Hwy., Cody, Wyo.
• (307) 587-3970

A second-generation outfitter and guide, Gary Fales offers wilderness elk hunts in two places: the Thorofare at the headwaters of the Yellowstone River just outside Yellowstone National Park boundaries and Boulder Basin on the South Fork of the Shoshone River. Fales boasts an 85 percent success rate on his bull elk hunts. During the past few years, more than 60 percent of the bulls have been six-points or better. Fales also guides deer, antelope, sheep and moose hunts.

Yellowstone National Park contains more than 1,000 miles of designated, marked trail. Grand Teton National Park has a mere 200 miles, but off-trail hiking and mountaineering add nearly endless opportunity.

Hiking and Backpacking

It's been said that only about 3 percent of Yellowstone National Park is available to visitors who stay on park roads. If you want to see the rest, you have to enter the maze of trails that lace Yellowstone's backcountry. The added bonus is that you leave most of the crowds behind. Yellowstone National Park contains more than 1,000 miles of designated, marked trail. Grand Teton National Park has a mere 200 miles, but off-trail hiking and mountaineering add nearly endless opportunity.

If solitude is a high priority, leave the parks altogether. The seven national forests that surround Yellowstone and Grand Teton parks each have at least a couple of hundred miles of trails, and some much more.Trail-filled Gallatin, Bridger-Teton and Shoshone forests together have some 6,300 miles of designated hiking trails.

Both day-hiking and backpacking are popular in Greater Yellowstone. This chapter describes some of the better-known hikes in Yellowstone and Grand Teton parks and neighboring forest in Idaho, Montana and Wyoming. Several are appropriate for multiple-day treks. The fact that these trails are particularly well-known can mean they are also particularly busy. Our picks aren't your best bets for solitude. September clears the trails dramatically, and at any time of year, sunrise hikes allow you to enjoy even the most popular trails in near solitude.

Another way to find quiet is to seek what, for the most part, we've left out: hard-to-reach or longer trails. Learn about them from hiking books or ranger stations and visitor centers. We like Jerry Painter's books. He's an avid hiker and author of several books, including *The Tetons: Great Trails for Family Hiking* and *Back Country Hiking and Biking Trails in the Idaho Falls Area*. Painter suggested many of the hikes described in this chapter. You can find his books at the *Post Register* in Idaho Falls, 333 Northgate Mile, (208) 522-1800.

Remember: The more remote your chosen trail, the better prepared you should be with information, maps and equipment.

General Information

Backcountry Camping, National Forest Style

On national forest lands near paved roads, camping is typically restricted to designated campgrounds (see our Campgrounds and RV Parks chapter). Camping restrictions protect plant life, resources and scenic attractions from heavy use. Signs alongside the road will alert you to roadside camping restrictions.

Once you're in the backcountry, you may camp almost anywhere you choose. This places some responsibility on you. Choose a campsite others have used, rather than damaging vegetation in a new site. It's tempting to camp streamside, but your presence can cause bank erosion and prevent wild creatures from reaching water (restrictions at some high-use areas will push your site even farther from streamsides and lakes). Camp at least 100 feet from water (some high-use areas will require that your site be even farther from streamsides and lakes). Keep fires small and in existing fire circles, or better yet, don't build a fire at all unless somebody is chilled and needs warming. Some areas at some times of year don't allow fires, so bring and use a camping stove. Don't cut vegetation or trench your tent or modify the site in any avoidable way. As much as possible, leave no trace that you've been here: Pack out all garbage. Bury human waste 6 inches deep and at least 200 feet from any water source (toilet paper is not human waste and should be burned or packed out with the trash).

If you're in Greater Yellowstone, you're probably in bear country, so food and any sweet-smelling toiletries (toothpaste, for instance) must be stored appropriately. It's said that a grizzly bear can smell tuna inside an unopened can. Take bear precautions seriously for your own safety and the bears'. If you're not familiar with the safety rules for travel in bear country, read our Close-up on bear safety in our Hunting chapter. You can obtain additional information from ranger stations and national park visitor centers.

The groups you encounter in the backcountry probably shouldered their packs seeking solitude, so don't camp within sight or earshot of another group if you can help it. If you find yourself camping near others, be considerate and quiet. This goes double for pets: Leash or otherwise control your dog, for the sake of the dog (mountain lions and wolves are said to love dogs), for the sake of horse packers and other human travelers on narrow trails, and for the sake of wildlife that it may amuse your dog to disturb.

Check with the local ranger district or the national forest administrator's office before entering Greater Yellowstone's backcountry (see our Parks and Forests chapter). Ask about the varying maximum-stay regulations, special restrictions on fires and occasional trail closures. Special transportation restrictions apply in designated wilderness and some national forest lands. The trail you've chosen may restrict mountain biking or motorized vehicles. Motorized vehicles are allowed in some areas, but their use is restricted to established trails in order to limit damage.

Rangers can also provide maps and share key information like how voracious the mosquitoes and black flies have been, which stream crossings are difficult, how much snow remains at high elevations, which water sources have dried up, whether trails are too muddy to navigate without damaging them, etc. Find phone numbers and addresses for national forest ranger stations in our Parks and Forests chapter.

Backcountry Camping, National Park Style

Extremely heavy demand for backcountry sites in Grand Teton and Yellowstone national parks necessitates restrictions that don't apply elsewhere in Greater Yellowstone. For instance, no pets are allowed in national park backcountry. Neither are firearms (many visitors carry bear-repellent sprays, said to be safer and more effective than a gun). Other regulations apply, including maximum-stay limits for particular areas. Jackson Lake in Grand Teton National Park, for instance, carries a three-day maximum. In Yellowstone National Park, whole trails are closed at certain times to provide bears with solitude and to protect humans. Campsites near bear kills are routinely closed, since bears generally return to kills until the meat is gone.

A backcountry permit is required if you plan to stay out for more than a day. In Grand Teton National Park, this permit may be obtained in person at Moose, Colter Bay or Jenny Lake visitor centers. In Yellowstone National Park, pick up your permit at a park ranger station (and some entrance stations, if the ranger has time). Part of the reason for the permit system

INSIDERS' TIP

Even in the national parks, not all backcountry campsites have bear boxes, so be prepared with rope and an understanding of how to use it to stow packs and food safely.

Photo: Robert Bower

This waterlogged grizzly bear rests on a rock in West Yellowstone, Montana

is to give the rangers a chance to provide you with information about how to use the national park backcountry safely and responsibly.

Your campsite must also be reserved. In Grand Teton National Park, 30 percent of backcountry campsites are reservable in advance; the rest are first-come, first-served. Reservations may not be made by phone, so you need to write the Grand Teton National Park Permits Office, P.O. Box 170, Moose, WY 83012, or stop by the Moose Visitor Center. A new program for 1999 adds a $15 reservation fee. For more information about backcountry travel and camping in Grand Teton National Park, call park dispatch at (307) 739-3300 or stop by any park visitor center.

In Yellowstone National Park, the drill is similar. Advance Yellowstone campsite reservations may be made in person or by mail for a charge of $15. Write to Backcountry Office, P.O. Box 168, Yellowstone National Park, WY 82190. You can speed the process by calling (307) 344-2160 or (307) 344-2163 to request advance forms by mail. Not all Yellowstone sites are reservable in advance. If you wait until you arrive and book your site less than 48 hours in advance, the $15 fee is waived.

In both parks, rangers can help you select sites, but they appreciate your having several plans in mind. If navigating these requirements gets irritating, remember that they exist to make your backcountry experience more pleasant. Users would overrun more popular sites and trails in no time without some sort of turnstile at the trailhead.

Do Your Homework

A friend of ours has the following definition for adventure: When, in the middle of an experience, you're wishing you were safely home regaling your friends with it, that's an adventure. To avoid backcountry adventures, do your homework before hitting the trail. Novice hikers/backpackers should make use of available books that help beginners select and pack gear, plan trips and have maximum fun with maximum safety. One we recommend, although it contains more information than a casual hiker needs, is called *Mountaineering: The Freedom of the Hills* (see our Resources chapter). This is one of the most comprehensive resources available for backcountry travel. It's aimed mostly at climbers, but the first sections are applicable to any would-be backcountry traveler. It discusses how to find safe creek crossings, how to select hiking boots, how to plan menus for a longer trip, what kind of camp stove to buy and more. If you only plan to day-hike, the introduction to any good hiking book should provide most of the information you need. Also make sure you stop in at the nearest ranger station or visitor center before you hike, particularly if you've selected a longer or more challenging trail or if you're going in overnight. Be sure to pick up a map of the area you're planning to hike

Your preparation and knowledge will, in large part, determine whether you enjoy an exhilarating experience or fall victim to adventure. At least as important a reason to study up before you hit the trail is the fact that Greater Yellowstone's backcountry is rare and fragile. Few such wild places still exist in this country. Only a knowledgeable traveler can walk lightly and with the care required to protect the wonders that await.

Yellowstone National Park

Many of Yellowstone's hydrothermal attractions are reached by short, well-marked hikes. They range in length from several hundred feet to a couple of miles. To find these, simply use the map handed to you at the entrance gate or watch the signs on the side of the road. However, most of the 1,000-plus miles of trail are not so easily stumbled upon. What follows are some of the best shorter and longer hikes in the park. Most of these hikes are more memorable for their scenery, wildlife opportunities and wilderness than for hydrothermal features. Perhaps their biggest attraction is their quiet: Although it's not as easy as you might think to find real solitude in Yellowstone National Park, you can expect to leave 90 percent of park visitors behind when you get more than 2 miles from a road or parking area.

Much of Yellowstone National Park is grizzly country, particularly backcountry areas with few or no roads, such as the park's southeast and southwest corners. Learn appropriate precautions. Read about bear safety in our Hunting chapter, or pick up any of several bear safety brochures at visitor centers or ranger stations on neighboring national forest lands. Visitors planning to spend a night or more in the backcountry must register and reserve their site. Backcountry permits and site registration materials are available at all park visitor centers (see our discussion of backcountry site reservations above).

Mount Washburn
Off Canyon-Tower Rd.

Mount Washburn is one of those must-do short hikes. You'll hike 3 miles and climb 1,500 feet as you ascend. The payoffs are colorful wildflower meadows, a good chance that you'll see bighorn sheep, and summit views of Yellowstone Lake, the Tetons, the Yellowstone River and more. You'll find a hikers' wind shelter at the lookout tower atop the more than 10,000-foot-high mountain.

Two trails climb Mount Washburn, each about 6 miles round-trip; arranging a shuttle vehicle gives you the option of hiking up one and down the other. One trail starts at Dunraven Pass and the other at the Chittenden Road parking area. Both trailheads are reached via the Canyon-Tower Road.

Fairy Falls and Fairy Falls Trail
Fountain Flat Dr., 1 mile south of Firehole River Bridge

Of several quick approaches to Fairy Falls, we like this one best. It begins at the Imperial Meadows trailhead off Fountain Flat Drive (this road may be gated, adding about 1.5 miles to the trip) and meanders through green meadow alongside Fairy Creek (watch for elk), arcs up to visit restive Imperial Geyser, then meets another trail and heads east to the base of Fairy Falls. Round-trip distance is 6 miles. Two hundred feet high, the thin, delicate cascade of Fairy Falls is one of the tallest waterfalls in the park. You'll spend some time in lodgepole forest burned in the fires of 1988.

The long way into Fairy Falls is perhaps the most rewarding. You'll have to get a car to the far end of your hike, since you begin at the Biscuit Basin trailhead and emerge 13.5 miles away just south of Midway Geyser Basin. Fairy Creek Trail runs beside the Little Firehole River, loops through a bison summering area called Little Firehole Meadows then drops off the edge of the Madison Plateau. Watch for trail markers, since we hear people occasionally get lost on this steep stretch. Below the plateau, you pass Imperial Geyser and come to a fork in the trail. The northern route follows Fairy Creek to Fountain Flat Drive. The other takes you to the base of Fairy Falls and then the Midway Geyser Basin trailhead.

Canyon Rim Trails

Grandview or Artist Point

You were planning to stop here anyway; why not take the time to see this canyon's golden walls and thundering waterfalls from a few more angles? This hike starts at either Grandview or Artist Point and links together the North Rim and South Rim trails for a one-way distance of just under 4 miles. If you start at Grandview, you'll begin on the North Rim Trail. At just more than a mile, you'll reach the Upper Falls parking area. Just beyond it, cross the Yellowstone River on a highway bridge. Turn left and head downstream along the South Rim Trail which takes you to Artist Point.

Several interesting side hikes exist along your route. Three of the best are the scenic overlook at Red Rock Point, the spur trail to Crystal Falls, and Uncle Tom's Trail, which uses a steep stairway to reach an observation platform at the lip of the Lower Falls. Uncle Tom's Trail is worth doing by itself, although the steel platforms bolted to the canyon wall generally host a steady stream of hikers. Uncle Tom's Trail has its own parking area on the South Rim Trail about 1 mile before Artist Point. Park here and your one-way hike is only about .25 mile. You'll drop 500 feet below the canyon rim in that distance though, so this is not a casual stroll. Nor is it likely to be appreciated by those fearful of heights.

Hellroaring Creek

Tower Junction

This 10-mile out-and-back hike begins at Tower Junction. Start by heading northwest on the dirt road used for stagecoach rides. After about 1.5 miles the trail turns north (right) and descends toward the Yellowstone River. A steel suspension bridge takes you across the narrow gorge cut by the Yellowstone. From there the trail crosses sagebrush flats, then runs alongside Hellroaring Creek before ending at Hellroaring Ranger Station.

Fishing for cutthroats is excellent along Hellroaring Creek. If you want to spend more time here, wander upstream of the ranger station about a half-mile. You'll find a footbridge that will allow you to safely cross the boisterous creek and continue exploring. Backcountry campsites are available to make this into a short overnight trip.

Shoshone Lake and Shoshone Geyser Basin

DeLacy Creek Trailhead off West Thumb Rd.

This 20-mile hike makes a perfect two-day backpacking trip, taking you past lovely Shoshone Lake and Shoshone Geyser Basin (which many call the park's best backcountry thermal site). The 10-mile days are only moderately strenuous, even with full packs, because the trail is well-maintained and generally level. Find the DeLacy Creek Trailhead at a pullout 9 miles south of Old Faithful on the road to West Thumb. The trail follows DeLacy Creek, reaching Shoshone Lake after about 3 miles. Turn right at the fork in the trail and continue along the north side of Shoshone Lake, passing several backcountry campsites. At 11 miles the trail forks again. To your right is the route you'll follow to leave; a couple of minutes' walk down the left fork is Shoshone Geyser Basin.

After you've checked out the geyser basin, head back to the fork and turn onto the main trail. You can either follow this trail all the way to Old Faithful on the Howard Eaton Trail, or, when you reach another fork at about 17

INSIDERS' TIP

Be sure to tuck an all-purpose bandanna or two into your pack. These handy squares of fabric can be used for slings or bandages and as sweat bands. They can also be used to tie back your hair or to protect it from wind and dust. On a hot day, if you dip your bandanna in water, you can tie it loosely around your neck. The evaporating water on your neck will help cool you. We even know someone who has used a bandanna for makeshift sunglasses. He cut two slits big enough to see through while keeping out the bright light.

miles, turn right. Your trail becomes an old road that runs beside the Firehole River, passing Lone Star Geyser before coming out at the Lone Star Geyser Trailhead, 2 miles east of Old Faithful. Either way you'll need to arrange a shuttle for your vehicle.

Thorofare Trail and Parts Beyond

East Entrance Rd., 9 miles from Fishing Bridge Junction

Thorofare Trailhead connects to a nearly endless array of remote, longer multiple-day hikes, including a couple of loop hikes. The Thorofare Trail itself is one of the easiest ways to access the remote reaches of the Upper Yellowstone Valley. AmFac Parks and Resorts makes it easier yet with a boat shuttle on Yellowstone Lake that cuts some 9 miles off your trail at a cost of about $60 per hour. From mid-May to late September, call AmFac's marina on Yellowstone Lake at (307) 242-3876.

Thorofare Trail begins by hugging the shore of Yellowstone Lake's southeast arm. At Terrace Point, the trail leaves the lake, offering panoramic views of the Upper Yellowstone Valley. Not far south of Terrace Point, you begin to have choices, many of which will have led you to shuttle a vehicle to the point at which you plan to exit the backcountry, possibly as far as Pahaska, Wyoming, or Pacific Creek Road in Grand Teton National Park, or the Heart Lake Trailhead on Yellowstone's South Entrance Road. Many of the forested areas from Terrace Point south are burned, but don't let that keep you off these long wilderness trails.

At about 19 miles, Thorofare Trail intersects Trail Creek Trail, which can take you to lovely Heart Lake and from there out to Heart Lake Trailhead on the South Entrance Road. You can also build a loop out of Trail Creek, Two Ocean Plateau and South Boundary trails and return the way you came on Thorofare Trail. Or continue beyond Trail Creek Trail to the next loop possibility, which swings around Bridger Lake before returning to Thorofare for the more than 30-mile journey back to your starting point.

If you stay on Thorofare Trail, you'll pass the backcountry Thorofare Ranger Station at about mile 32, cross the park boundary a few minutes later and head toward the Continental Divide and Grand Teton National Park or continue along Thorofare Creek east and then north over Ishawooa Pass. On this route, the first road you intersect is Wyo. Highway 291, which runs from Cody to its dead end here in the Absarokas.

Many other options exist among the trails that intersect Thorofare. The important thing to know about these hikes is that they're remote — there are no roads in the southeast corner of Yellowstone National Park — and they involve long distances. Be sure to ask lots of questions when you sign up for your backcountry campsites, and be sure you carry good topographic maps.

Grand Teton National Park

Hikes in Grand Teton National Park are of two types: shorter loop trails on the valley floor, often encircling lakes, and strenuous longer loops that lasso steep-sided mountain canyons, traverse ridgelines or thread through mountain passes. The ease of the valley floor trails makes them popular — and crowded — on summer days. The best way to lose the crowds is to head into the mountains, but some care is required. Mountain trails in Grand Teton National Park start at about 6,800 feet, then go up. Though exhilarating, these trails should be approached with care and planning. Weather changes, route-finding problems, ex-

INSIDERS' TIP

Since it's more difficult for horses (especially pack strings) to step off the trail, they have the right of way. Step off to let them pass, and don't make any sudden movements while they're angling by you. We've seen some hellacious wrecks caused by spooked mules and horses.

haustion or poor timing can turn a day's outing into an overnight fiasco. Snow can be encountered on mountain pass trails any time of year.

Bears are more commonly seen in Grand Teton National Park's backcountry, mountain and valley, than near its roads. Learn appropriate precautions. See our Close-up on bear safety in the Hunting chapter, or pick up any of several bear safety brochures at visitor centers or ranger stations on neighboring national forest lands. Visitors planning to spend a night or more in the backcountry must register and reserve their site at a park visitor center (see discussion earlier in this chapter).

Swan Lake and Heron Pond

Off U.S. Hwy. 89 at Colter Bay Village

This 3-mile hike is a perfect dawn or dusk excursion. You may see moose, elk, beaver, sandhill crane, bald eagles, pelicans and other waterfowl. Swan Lake is so named because it has nesting swans, so be sure to look for them. This easy hike is also popular with horseback riders, so don't expect to have the trail to yourself during the day in summer. You'll loop down the west shore of Swan Lake and back beside the east shore of Heron Pond. Elevation gain is nearly zero.

Many options exist for longer hikes, including a trek out to Hermitage Point (a backcountry campsite exists along this route on the shore of Jackson Lake) or looping east of Swan Lake. The Hermitage Point hike is about 10 miles long on level trails; it's suitable for novice hikers.

To find this hike, pull into the Colter Bay Village complex from U.S. Highway 89. Turn left at the visitor center. The trailhead is at the south end of the marina parking lot. In summer the visitor center provides free maps to the maze of trails in this area.

String Lake Trail

Jenny Lake Loop Road

Scattered at the base of the Tetons like jewels, Jenny, Leigh and String lakes provide plentiful opportunities for hikes. The shortest, easiest hike loops around shallow String Lake for 3.4 miles. Longer hikes head out past Leigh Lake to Bearpaw Lake and Trapper Lake (about 9 miles one way), or completely encircle lovely Jenny Lake, passing Hidden Falls and Inspiration Point, two of Jenny Lake's more popular scenic stops (see hike description in this chapter). None of these hikes offers much solitude except in spring and fall or in early morning.

The String Lake hike is particularly nice for families. It's partially paved and has two footbridges, one across the lake's inlet and the other across its outlet. Elevation gain/loss is about 200 feet. On warm summer days, kids swim and innertube the placid shallow water and families picnic on the shores. A segment of String Lake's east shore is paralleled by a road that links the trail's two parking and picnic areas, so access is good.

Jenny Lake, Hidden Falls and Inspiration Point

Near Jenny Lake Visitor Center

You can do this trail a couple of ways: Either you hike the 6.6-mile loop completely around the pretty glacial lake or you use the ferry to shorten the journey. From the East Shore boat dock to the watery veils of Hidden Falls is 2.5 miles. Inspiration Point, an overlook that allows you to view Jenny Lake, Jackson Hole and the Gros Ventre River range, is another half-mile beyond the falls. If you hike up to see the falls and look out over Jenny Lake, you'll gain and lose about 220 feet. Otherwise elevation gain is minimal.

You can pick up maps at the Jenny Lake Visitor Center and at the trailhead. This hike is wildly popular, as is the ferry ride. You could almost imagine the park service installing passing lanes and traffic lights. But don't let that discourage you from taking this hike: The scenery is marvelous, and in late summer the huckleberries are sweet.

Find this trailhead near the East Shore boat dock below the Jenny Lake Visitor Center. You can also reach this hike from the String Lake loop trail (see previous above). There are no backcountry campsites on the perimeter of Jenny Lake.

Two Ocean Lake

Two Ocean Rd., off Pacific Creek Rd.

This trailhead off Pacific Creek Road leads to several loop trails, two of which trace the perimeters of Two Ocean and Emma Matilda lakes. Lake views, wildflower meadows, beaver dams, fishing and wildlife viewing are attractions, but the biggest reason to hike here is that few do. The dirt road that takes you to the trailhead means that, compared to other trails in Grand Teton National Park, these are quiet.

The hike around Two Ocean Lake is flat and about 7 miles long. A short connecting trail takes you to the more popular Emma Matilda Lake trail, about 8 miles around. Horseback riders from the stables at nearby Jackson Lake Lodge make frequent use of parts of this trail because it can also be reached from the lodge.

Find the trailhead by turning east off U.S. Highway 89 onto Pacific Creek Road. After about 1.3 miles turn left (north) on gravel Two Ocean Road. Two more miles takes you to a picnic area and trailhead. Two Ocean Road can be impassable after heavy rain or snow.

Surprise Lake and Amphitheater Lake

South Jenny Lake Junction on Teton Park Rd.

This is a classic Teton hike: The trail rises nearly 1,000 feet per mile, and before about mid-July you're likely to find yourself walking through patches of snow. The prizes at the end of your trek are two lovely mountain lakes — Surprise and Amphitheatre — invisible from below. On the way up, enjoy eagle's-eye views of Jenny, Taggart and Bradley lakes. Check out the creek fed by Teton Glacier, its waters opaque and bluish from rock particles ground to chalk beneath the glacier's inexorable weight.

Twice you'll pass left-forking trails. One takes you to Bradley Lake and beyond. The other is the Garnet Canyon climbers' trail, which heads up sheer-walled, waterfall-stepped Garnet Canyon and is considered "off-trail" hiking. Backcountry campsites exist between Surprise Lake and Amphitheatre Lake less than a half-mile beyond, so this trip can be made into an overnighter. The round-trip distance is about 10 miles.

This hike is not recommended for young children. Find the trailhead by turning onto an unpaved road a mile south of the South Jenny Lake Junction. About 1.5 miles in, a restroom and parking area mark the trailhead.

Cascade Canyon and Lake Solitude

East Shore Boat Dock at Jenny Lake

The hike up glacier-carved Cascade Canyon offers several options. You can begin from Jenny Lake's East Shore boat dock or, for a small fee, shave 2 miles each way by hopping on the ferry. From Inspiration Point near the West Shore boat dock, a moderately strenuous 4.5 mile hike brings you to the forks of Cascade Canyon. You gain more than 1,000 feet in elevation and enjoy views of Teewinot and Mount Owen, and of cascading waterfalls. In late summer, allow a little time for berry picking. You can turn back at the forks, but if you're backpacking or looking for a more strenuous day's adventure, you have two choices.

Hiking up South Cascade Canyon beyond the forks can take you eventually to the Teton Crest Trail which traverses the southern half of the Teton range. This allows the possibility of a long backcountry trek. Or you can turn up the North Fork Trail, which climbs another 1,200 feet in just under 3 miles one way and carries you to alpine Lake Solitude, surrounded by sheer rock. Don't let the name fool you: This hike is popular, and solitude is not likely at your destination. Camping is available near the lake.

INSIDERS' TIP

We have friends who never hike with watches. They say they're escaping their schedule-bound lives. Sounds great, but people who know how long they've been hiking can better guess how far they've come. This makes it easier to use maps or to make plans if you become lost. And in an emergency people can make better decisions if they know exactly how much daylight remains.

Emergency Gear: Think Ahead, Be Prepared

We think of it as plan-B gear. It goes in the backpack before tent, cookstove or clothing. It lives behind the car seat and gets tossed into our daypacks before a hike. Exactly what it consists of varies, but the principle is always the same: Plan-B gear answers the "what if" questions: What if the car breaks down? What if I get sick? What if I fall and hurt my ankle? What if we get lost and have to spend the night?

If you looked in our daypacks before a typical all-day summer hike in Yellowstone backcountry, the plan-B gear would probably consist of:

- a flashlight (preferably a headlamp with an elastic headband that allows us to work or walk with hands free)
- a knife, pliers and nylon cord for various repairs and projects
- matches and firestarter
- a watch, compass and good map of the area
- at least one extra piece of warm, non-cotton clothing, plus a wool or fleece hat
- water-repellent jacket
- extra water (or water purification tablets) and extra high-calorie food
- a first-aid kit

All plan-B gear, first-aid kit included, should vary from person to person and trip to trip. Two good rules for plan-B gear are: Don't pack it if you don't know how to use it; and don't pack it if something else you've already packed could make do. The farther into the backcountry you plan to go, the harsher the weather or the longer your stay, the more carefully and thoroughly you should pack your plan-B gear. For instance, we take winter backcountry travel seriously, so for a full day in winter backcountry, we'd almost certainly add to the above list:

- a head-to-toe extra non-cotton set of warm clothes, including extra gloves. Extra doesn't include the clothes we plan to wear. If we start with one warm shirt but plan to wear two, we bring three.
- spare batteries for that flashlight
- chemical hand-warmer packets
- a bivy sack or "space blanket"
- duct tape for ski and other repairs
- tools for adjusting ski bindings
- even more extra food — without fuel the human machine can't produce heat.

As first-aid kits go, ours is minimal because we've found that heavy first-aid kits tend to get left in the car where they can't do much good. Besides, when minor backcountry injuries occur, there are often items in our packs or jacket pockets from which solutions can be improvised, eliminating the need for specialty items in the first-aid kit. For instance, we don't carry commercial splinting devices: A padded stick or ski will do. And we don't pack much medication unless we plan to be in the backcountry for several days or weeks. What our kit almost always contains are recently checked and replenished supplies of the following:

- standard-size, water-resistant Band-Aids (to protect a wound that has been

— continued on next page

cleaned and disinfected)

•knuckle and/or fingertip bandages (tabs on these bandage styles allow good coverage for wounds on fingers, toes and heels)

•sterile gauze pads, about 4 inches square (to scrub out and cover larger wounds or injured eyes)

•athletic tape (sticks better than medical tape and can be used to make makeshift butterfly bandages or wrap sprains and strains)

•povidone-iodine solution for disinfecting wounds

•individually wrapped antiseptic towelettes (to wash hands before treating a wound, to clean the area around a wound, etc.)

•moleskin for treating blisters and blisters-to-be. To slow down a developing blister, use moleskin when you start to feel a "hot spot." Duct tape from your plan-B kit is a good last step here: it holds moleskin on and decreases friction because it's slippery against your sock.

•6-inch athletic wrap (for sprains, strains, attaching splints or use as a constricting band in case of snake bite)

•safety pins (for removing splinters, attaching the athletic wrap, securing a sling, fixing a broken pack strap, etc.)

•sharp scissors (not a razor blade — scissors are a safer tool in shaky hands)

•tweezers

It's a good idea to add a book on backcountry medicine. We recommend Buck Tilton and Frank Hubbell's *Medicine For the Backcountry* if you're going on a longer trip. Short booklets that would be more appropriate for a day-hiking first-aid kit are also available. Such books and booklets are even more useful if you re-read them periodically to refresh your memory.

The North Fork Trail can be made into a loop hike. You can continue beyond Lake Solitude over Paintbrush Divide, past Holly Lake, down to String Lake on the valley floor and back along the shore of Jenny Lake to the West Shore boat dock. This loop hike is extremely strenuous — it climbs another 1,700 feet above Solitude and generally involves crossing large snowfields. Ice axes are often required. Talk to the rangers at Jenny Lake before heading up to Lake Solitude or the Paintbrush Divide loop.

Jackson Hole

Ski Lake Trail

Off Wyo. Hwy. 22 west of Wilson, Wyo.

Getting to see pretty alpine lakes generally involves strenuous hiking, but not at Ski Lake near Wilson, Wyoming. This hike is easy to moderate and only 4.6 miles round-trip. You hike through wildflower meadows, enjoy great views of Jackson Hole and the Gros Ventre range and, only 2 miles from your car, relax by the crystal-clear waters of Ski Lake. The trailhead is often busy, since it's also a popular access point for the Teton Crest Trail, a long trail which traverses the southern half of the Teton range. To access the Teton Crest here, take the right fork to Phillips Pass when the trail divides about one mile in. To get to Ski Lake, take the left.

Find the trailhead by driving 4.5 miles west out of Wilson on Wyo. Highway 22. At the sign for Phillips Canyon, pull off into a parking lot on the south side of the road. Walk up the Jeep trail for about .3 mile. You'll see the trailhead sign on your left. For more information, call the Jackson Ranger District at (307) 739-5400.

Gros Ventre Slide Nature Trail

Off Gros Ventre River Rd.

This easy interpretive hike makes a great addition to a day of picnicking, swimming and fishing at Lower Slide Lake outside Grand Teton National Park. Lower Slide Lake created itself in 1925 when the north side of Sheep Mountain sheared off and tumbled into the Gros Ventre River. Within a few minutes, 50 million cubic yards of debris had buried the river and created a natural dam. Frequent signs along the half-mile loop trail describe common plants, the slide itself and other points of interest.

Find the trailhead by turning east on Gros Ventre River Road from U.S. Highway 89. After 6 miles, watch the south side for the Slide display. The trail starts near the restrooms below the interpretive signs. For more information, call the Jackson Ranger District at (307) 739-5400.

Surrounding Areas

Southwestern Montana

Before heading out onto southwestern Montana's trails, check in with your local Forest Service office. On the Beaverhead Forest, call the Madison Ranger District office west of Ennis at (406) 682-4253. For trails on the Gallatin Forest, check in with the recreation specialist at the Bozeman Ranger District Office, (406) 587-6920. Many of the trails numbered on Forest Service maps aren't necessarily numbered the same way or at all on the ground. Take along good maps and a compass to help find your way around this mountainous terrain.

Beaverhead National Forest, Madison Ranger District and Gravelly Range

Elk River Trail #79
Off U.S. Hwy. 287 on F.S. Rd. 209

This 18-mile round-trip hike climbs gently through the timber paralleling Elk River, then heads up onto Lobo Mesa where the timber opens into grasslands. Elk, bear, moose, and mule deer frequent these meadows, which are loaded with idyllic campsites. (Be sure to read sections on low-impact camping in this chapter and in the Campgrounds and RV Parks chapter if you plan to stay overnight.) If you're really fit and get an early start, you can hike this in a day. We recommend spending the night on top.

Those with four-wheel-drive, high-clearance vehicles can begin their hike at the end of the Elk River Road. Others should park at the Elk River trailhead at Miller Flat up the West Fork of the Madison River Road (#209 on the Forest Service map), a high-standard gravel road. It is about 10 miles from U.S. Highway 287 to the trailhead, from which hikers should strike out across the sagebrush flat, heading west along the fence line to join the Elk River Road less than a mile from the trailhead. Follow the road past mature stands of aspen and rolling meadowlands another 4 miles where the road ends and trail #79, the Elk River trail, begins. This point is a good first-night camp spot for those not in a hurry.

The trail starts as a gentle climb through stands of spruce, Douglas fir, and lodgepole pine, following Elk River. After 2.5 miles of relatively easy hiking, the trail comes to a junction with the Little Elk River Trail #29, the route that takes you up — and we do mean up — to Lobo Mesa, climbing 1,500 feet over the next 3.5 miles. This vertical climb is the price of admission to the upper world of the Gravelly Range. Camping in the Little Elk River Basin, where water is plentiful, before ascending to the top of Lobo Mesa, where it is scarce, is recommended unless you can carry enough water to meet the needs of a dry camp on top. The reward of a dry camp is the opportunity to see the sun rise and set over the jagged landscape of the Rockies with ranges rising up like rows of shark's teeth as far as the eye can see. On a clear day you can see the Tetons.

The trip back to the trailhead, east across Lobo Mesa, is mostly a gentle descent through open grasslands. The Lobo Mesa portion of the trail is open to ATVs, and hikers should be prepared to share the trail. However, motorized use along Lobo Mesa is not common, and hikers, especially those visiting during midweek, will likely encounter no motorized

INSIDERS' TIP

Yellowstone National Park trails are marked with square orange metal markers which the National Park Service has nailed to trailside trees.

visitors. The Lobo Mesa trail terminates at the Elk River Trailhead on Miller Flat, your starting point. If you left a vehicle at the end of the Elk Lake road, a shuttle vehicle will save you a 5-mile hike, reducing this round-trip hike from 18 to 13 miles.

Gallatin National Forest/ Bozeman Ranger District

Hyalite Lake Trail #427

Hyalite Reservoir, 15 miles south of Bozeman, Mont.

This 10-mile round-trip trail takes off from the head of Hyalite reservoir and climbs 1,800 feet to Hyalite Lake. Along the way, you'll pass 11 waterfalls. For the first 1.5 miles, the trail is wide and wheelchair-accessible. It's also very busy. Don't let that discourage you. Once you get past the first waterfall, the traffic thins out dramatically. In addition to seeing people, your chances are good of seeing lots of wildlife including a bear or two.

To get to the trailhead, take the right fork of the Hyalite Canyon Road at the head of the reservoir. You'll find some parts of this trail are pretty steep, but it is well worth reaching the top. If you feel inclined to keep on going once you reach the lake (we wouldn't), you'll have all kinds of options for continuing on. To do this, though, means you'll have to plan ahead and leave a vehicle at another trailhead. Included among the trail options are a few that head into the Yellowstone Valley to the east. For more detailed information we suggest you contact the Bozeman Ranger District at 3710 Fallon Avenue, Bozeman, Montana. The phone number is (406) 587-6920. And take a map.

Lee Metcalf Wilderness (Spanish Peaks Unit), Gallatin National Forest

Spanish Lakes Trail #407 and #411

Spanish Creek Rd. off U.S. Hwy. 191

This 14-mile round-trip hike will take you into the beautiful Spanish Peaks. About 20 miles south of Bozeman on U.S. Highway 191, you'll come to the Spanish Creek Road headed west. Follow this road until you come to the trailhead. Trail #407 is the main thoroughfare for a whole system of trails leading into the wilderness. About 3 miles up, the trail forks. Stay to the left. About 1.5 miles farther, the trail forks again. This time stay to the right. Just a little ways farther, you'll come to another fork in the trail. Stay left. Now you're on your way, and it isn't all that much farther — about 2.5 miles.

From the Spanish Lakes there are several options for loops. They all take off from Trail #412, which heads north from Spanish Lakes.

A couple of trails (#401 and # 410) will add only a few miles and new vistas to your trek.

Absaroka-Beartooth Wilderness

The Absaroka-Beartooth Wilderness — Montana's third-largest with 943,377 miles — is legendary for its ruggedness, its alpine beauty and a multitude of mountain lakes filled with hungry trout. Twenty-seven peaks in this wilderness exceed 12,000 feet. Hundreds of miles of trail lead across huge alpine meadows, across breathtaking (literally) mountain passes and to more than a thousand lakes. One of the unique things about this wilderness is that in many places from Cooke City to Red Lodge, you can practically step out of your car and be within the wilderness boundaries. (See our chapter on Parks and Forests to read about special restrictions in wilderness areas and to read more about the Absaroka-Beartooth Wilderness.)

While it's a known fact that the deeper you go into wilderness, the fewer people you'll see, there are still plenty of beautiful, relatively people-free trails fairly close to the road. Following are a few either within or adjacent to the wilderness. Remember — and signs in the area won't let you forget — even though they're outside Yellowstone National Park, the Beartooths are still very much in grizzly country. Before heading off into the Beartooths, stop and pick up a map and carry a compass. We've given you the trail numbers as they're marked on the Gallatin National Forest Map, but on the ground, trails often aren't marked by number. To add to the confusion, different maps put out by the Gallatin Forest use different numbers for the same trail. We also recommend checking with the local ranger district for information on creek crossings, especially in early summer during runoff. If there's a problem bear in the area, they'll also tell you about that. To make contact with the ranger district, you'll have to think ahead. The office is more than 50 miles away in Gardiner, Montana.

Kersey Lake Trail

Trailhead 6 miles east of Cooke City, Mont., at Chief Joseph Campground on U.S. Hwy. 212

If you don't have much time, you can consider several options on this trail for in-and-out day hiking or camping combined with great fishing. Two miles in is Kersey Lake and another 2 miles down the trail is Rock Island Lake. Both offer good fishing and easy day hiking. For a longer version, you'll need a shuttle but it's well worth the extra planning, since this 14-mile trail takes you gradually downhill through mostly timbered country with open meadows and past lots of trout-filled lakes. If you're a strong hiker and want to do it in a day, you can. But it's a beautiful easy hike with lots of great views and excellent fishing, so we recommend you turn it into at least a two-day jaunt.

This well-signed trail (#567) begins at the parking lot across from the Colter Pass campground east of Cooke City on U.S. Highway 212. If you take the whole trail, it ends at the spectacular Crazy Creek Falls adjacent to the same-named campground on U.S. Highway 212 (about 7 miles east of where you'll start). About 3 miles into the hike, though, you'll intersect trails #3 and #565. Here's where you'll have to make your first decision. If you take #565, it will lead you 1.5 miles to Rock Island Lake. Chances are good you'll catch enough brook trout or cutthroat to make a meal. Trail #3 — the main trail you'll be following for the rest of your hike — leads to the Crazy Lakes, so named because they are connected by the white waters of Crazy Creek. About 4 miles from the trailhead and a mile or so east on trail #624, timber-framed Fox Lake, elevation 8,055 feet, is full of brook and rainbow trout.

INSIDERS' TIP

Planning to treat your drinking water with purification tablets? Carry a powdered sport drink mix as well: It'll mask the chemical taste and provide you with additional carbohydrates.

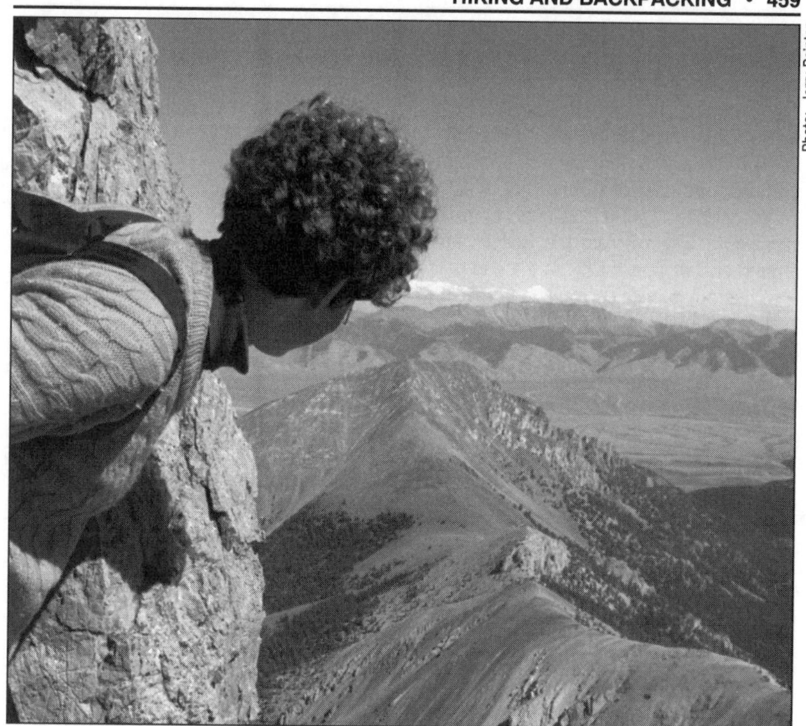

Photo: Jerry Painter

A hiker surveys the scene from atop Ten Peaks.

Another 1.5 miles down the trail (about the halfway mark of your trek) is Widewater Lake — 100 acres big and full of brookies. From there the trail meanders past Big Moose Lake on the Montana-Wyoming line. Ivy Lake (elevation 7,998 feet), is 4 miles from U.S. Highway 212 and pretty much the last fishable lake on your journey. You'll need a Wyoming fishing license here, though. (You can buy a one-day Wyoming license for $3.) Once you pass Little Moose Lake (it's hard to fish and plagued with mosquitoes, so keep on going), the rest of the trail winds through sagebrush grasslands with scattered timber and aspen patches.

Glacier Lake Trail #160

End of the Rock Creek Rd. southwest of Red Lodge, Mont.

This 2-mile hike is not for the faint of heart, literally. It begins at the end of the Rock Creek Road and makes a steep ascent to Glacier Lake, the queen of a string of alpine lakes ranging from 9,800 to 10,040 feet in elevation. If you're a low-lander, travel slowly to avoid altitude sickness (a major headache, nausea and lethargy caused by a lack of oxygen). Fields of alpine flowers, old wind-carved trees still standing after many years of fire and a spectacular view of the Beartooths make the climb well worth the effort.

Tucked into the base of a steep talus rock mountain, Glacier Lake is home to some lunker brook trout as well as rainbows and browns. A few campsites are available near the outlet (there's an irrigation dam here) at the eastern end of the lake. If you cross the outlet, you'll find a clump of trees that act as a windbreak. You'll also be pretty close to Emerald Lake, which is just a stone's throw from Glacier. If you follow the northern shore of Glacier, you'll reach the inlet creek. Follow the trail up the drainage to find Triangle, Mountain Sheep and Mountain Goat lakes. The weather at these lakes can change quickly for the worse, so take extra clothes. And take your fishing pole. By the way, Emerald Lake is in Wyoming, but Montana fishing licenses are honored here.

Grasshopper Glacier (Trail #569)

Off U.S. Hwy. 212 near Colter Campground east of Cooke City, Mont.

Jeep Road 3230 heads north from U.S. Highway 212 just before the Colter Campground east of Cooke City. At the end of the road (about 6 miles) you'll come to the trailhead of Trail #569. From here it's about a 3.5 mile climb to Grasshopper Glacier. This giant snowfield facing the Rosebud River is worth seeing.

Eastern Idaho

Teton Valley

South Darby Canyon Wind Cave

Off Idaho Hwy. 33

This is a well-made but steep trail that climbs 1,800 feet in its 3.4-mile, one-way length. About 3 miles in, the trail forks. The unmaintained trail that continues along the creek joins eventually with the Fox Creek Trail. The main trail continues past a monument erected in memory of five people killed here by lightning. Your destination is just beyond: a cave that runs for about .75 mile through the mountain. The mysterious wind that rushes from its mouth is the result of air pouring in from holes farther up the canyon — as the air cools, it rolls downhill toward where you stand.

Negotiating the cave itself involves technical rock and ice climbing, but its entrance can be examined by hikers with flashlights. If the steep scramble to the cave's mouth is still snow-covered, skip it and view the cave from more stable footing below, especially if you're hiking with kids.

Find the trailhead by turning east off Idaho Highway 33 onto a paved road marked with signs for Darby Girls Camp. After 1.5 miles, the road, now gravel, forks. Follow the right fork about 6 miles to a parking area. Your trail heads up the south fork of Darby Creek. For more information, call Teton Basin Ranger District at (208) 354-2431.

Table Mountain

Off Ski Hill Rd. near Teton Campground

One of the area's most popular and strenuous short hikes, the Table Mountain hike is 12.5 miles round-trip, with an elevation gain of more than 4,000 feet. To enjoy this hike, you need to be in good condition and allow plenty of time. The payoff is at the top of a nontechnical scramble onto the flat top of Table Mountain, elevation 11,106 feet, just below the razor-edged summits of the Teton range. With binoculars, you can watch from your rocky vantage as climbers challenge the Grand Teton — with nothing between you and them but thin mountain air. Most people do this as a day hike, but nice campsites exist along the north fork of Teton Creek.

Find the trailhead by turning right from Ski Hill Road, which leads to Grand Targhee Ski and Summer Resort, onto a dirt road marked with a sign for Teton Campground. Drive 5 miles to the trailhead parking area at one end of a Forest Service campground. For more information, call Teton Basin Ranger District at (208) 354-2431.

Alaska Basin

Off Ski Hill Rd. near Teton Campground

Alaska Basin is one of the loveliest backpacking and horsepacking trails in the Tetons. The last 4 miles up to a lake-studded alpine basin are steep and strenuous. It is possible to add 2.5 miles to this 8-mile hike by heading past the Basin Lakes to Sunset Lake and beyond to Hurricane Pass. This adds significant elevation gain to the 2,400 feet you already climbed to reach the basin, but from the top of Hurricane Pass the views of the stark Teton range are breathtaking. Head back the way you came or take the loop that winds down

INSIDERS' TIP

In Grand Teton National Park, most hiking trails start at about 6,800 feet and then go up. If you're not accustomed to high altitude, give yourself extra time.

the Devils Stairs (a narrow, steep trail not recommended for children), returning to the main trail after about 4 miles. If you don't mind arranging a shuttle, a longer route crosses over Hurricane Pass, hooks up with the Cascade Canyon trail and back to civilization at Jenny Lake in Grand Teton National Park. At a little more than 20 miles, this makes a comfortable three-day trip or a strenuous two-day one.

Find the trailhead by turning right from Ski Hill Road, which leads to Grand Targhee Ski and Summer Resort, onto a dirt road marked with a sign for Teton Campground. Drive 5 miles to the trailhead parking area at one end of a Forest Service campground. For more information, call Teton Basin Ranger District at (208) 354-2431.

Swan Valley

Palisades Creek Trail

Palisades Creek Rd. off Idaho Hwy. 26 near Irwin, Idaho

Ask folks in Swan Valley for a good hike and they're going to point you toward this one. Your destinations are Lower and Upper Palisades lakes, although if you hike beyond the upper lake the options become nearly endless. Travel also becomes more difficult — the creek crossings in particular can require care — and travelers much less common. Both lakes offer good trout fishing and pleasant campsites, although the popularity of this trail means that the lower lake's sites get snatched up fast, particularly on weekends. Bridges over creek crossings on the way to the lower lake make this hike particularly pleasant for families, bike riders and horseback riders. One-way distance to Lower Palisades Lake is 4 miles; the upper lake is 7 miles from the trailhead, with an elevation gain of about 1,000 feet.

Find the trailhead by turning northeast onto tiny Palisades Creek Road from Idaho Highway 26 near Irwin. The road runs up the canyon for about 2.5 miles before ending at a small Forest Service campground (see our Campgrounds and RV Parks chapter). Palisades Creek Trail takes off from just beyond the campground. Park in the parking area just outside the campground on the far side of Palisades Creek. To learn more, call the Palisades Ranger District at (208) 523-1412.

Bear Creek Trail

Off Idaho Hwy. 26 near Palisades, Idaho

Bear Creek is a great trail system for folks who don't like to retrace their steps. You have at least four ways to make this journey a loop and even more options for building a multiple-day trip. The first few miles parallel pretty, fishable Bear Creek with a level, well-maintained trail (you must wade the shallow creek in a couple of places). After about 4 miles the trail divides to follow the creek's north and south forks; families with young children or hikers not looking for strenuous activity should pack up their fishing poles and head back. Travel becomes more difficult, with more stream crossings and steeper stretches. The side trails off the North and South Fork trails are steeper yet as they climb out of Bear Creek Canyon and can involve route-finding difficulties. This keeps most mountain bikers and horseback riders on the main trails.

Find the trailhead by turning off Idaho Highway 26 to cross Palisades Reservoir Dam near the tiny town of Palisades. About 6 miles after crossing the dam you'll see Bear Creek. Follow the road a quarter-mile north of the creek past the campground. Park among the willows at the trailhead parking lot. To learn more, call the Palisades Ranger District at (208) 523-1412.

INSIDERS' TIP

We haven't included a detailed description of the popular Teton Crest Trail here. It's hiked several different ways, but one is a 28-mile, two- or three-night trip from the Jenny Lake Ranger Station to the Granite Canyon Trail parking area. Some hikers save a stiff climb out of Granite Canyon by riding the Jackson Hole ski area tram to 10,400 feet.

Island Park, Idaho

Coffee Pot Rapids Trail

Off U.S. Hwy. 20 at Upper Coffeepot Campground

This hike begins at Upper Coffeepot Campground and wanders alongside the dimpled, crystal-clear waters of the Henry's Fork for about 2.5 miles. At Coffeepot Rapids, the river gets to show its teeth. You'll travel through lodgepole and subalpine fir. In late summer look for huckleberries along the sides of the trail. You may also find our favorite flower, the sego lily. It's a creamy cuplike bloom on a slim stem with grass-blade leaves.

This is an out-and-back trail suitable for families with young children. Find the trailhead near Mack's Inn by turning from U.S. Highway 20 onto the road marked for Upper Coffeepot Campground, a small and often quiet Forest Service facility. At the entrance to the campground is day-use parking for anglers and hikers. Call the Island Park Ranger District (208) 558-7301 for more information.

Old Railroad Bed Trail

Various access points

Along the Union Pacific's old tourist-train route to Yellowstone National Park now runs one of the easiest hiking and biking trails in the area. The gentle grade required by trains makes for mellow walking, if not for fascinating terrain. Sometimes short sections are boggy and crossed by downed timber early in the season, but by late summer this trail is a backcountry sidewalk. The 55-mile-long route parallels the Warm River for 6 miles, leaves it and then returns for several more. It crosses Toms Creek and the Buffalo and Henry's Fork rivers, slips over the Continental Divide and drops into West Yellowstone, Montana. It winds through lodgepole forest and open meadows, over trestle bridges and even through a tunnel long enough that you can't see the end from the beginning. It gains about 400 feet in the 10 or so miles between West Yellowstone and the divide, then loses about 1,500 feet as it gradually drops toward the trailhead at Warm River Campground.

Pick up a map at the Island Park or Ashton ranger districts to see how you can break this hike into short or long pieces by leaving a shuttle vehicle at any of several spots where the trail meets or parallels various forest roads. If you plan an out-and-back hike, try the section above Warm River Campground. Another short scenic section starts at the Black Canyon Loop Road and heads downhill to Big Springs.

You get to the Warm River trailhead from Warm River Campground just off of Idaho Highway 47, the Mesa Falls Scenic Byway. Reach the Black Canyon Loop Road from Big Springs Road which meets U.S. Highway 20 at Mack's Inn. For more information, call the Island Park Ranger District (208) 558-7301 or the Ashton Ranger District at (208) 652-7442.

Northwestern Wyoming

Chain Lakes Trail

Trailhead on Beartooth Hwy. (U.S. Hwy. 212) east of Island Lake

This 12-mile loop takes you on a pretty gradual up-and-down hike through beautiful open alpine plateaus dotted with lakes and timbered pockets. You can see many of the lakes from the road which, for more timid hikers, is encouraging. Don't be so encouraged, though, that you forget to take a day pack filled with extra food, clothing and matches. A snow storm or fog can blow in any month of the year.

Once you're off the road, you'll forget about the world of cars above. The hillsides, covered with every wildflower imaginable — lupine, arrow-leaf balsamroot, asters, buttercups, monkey flowers — dip and climb between 9,650 and 9,200 feet. Across the highway from

INSIDERS' TIP

Are you going hiking or backcountry camping with kids? We suggest you give your children loud whistles to use if they get lost. Tell them that, if lost, they are to stay put and blow the whistle until help comes.

Long Lake (you can't miss it) you'll see an old Jeep trail (#120) heading down the hill. The old road leads to Duck Lake about 3 miles below Long Lake. From Duck, you can head south to Sawtooth Lake or east to Top Lake. We're taking you past Top Lake, so stick with us. The nice thing about this country is, except for a few draws that you drop into, you can really see where you're going. Follow the trail past Top Lake. Just after the creek crossing, there's a trail (#613 1A) that heads north to Stockade, Loosekamp, Solar and Hauser lakes. The fish bite at these lakes — some are catch-and-release while others are catch-and-keep. Be sure to check the regulations first. This trail also takes you back to U.S. Highway 212. It reaches the highway about a mile east of the Jeep road where you parked your car. If you're short on time, you can start the hike in reverse and hike in and out of Hauser, Loosekamp and Solar lakes with plenty of time for fishing.

Beartooth Lake Trails

Beartooth Lake Campground, about 20 miles east of Cooke City, Mont., on U.S. Hwy. 212

While this hike is in Wyoming, it's only 20 miles east of Cooke City, Montana, just south of the Absaroka-Beartooth Wilderness. Again, the options in this neck of the woods are endless and the views stupendous. This 5-mile loop leads up Beartooth Creek and past several lakes including Grayling, Beauty and Crane lakes. Park at the Beartooth Lake Campground. The fishing is good and the mirrored view of Beartooth Butte is a bonus. Hike up Trail #619 around the marshy east side of Beartooth Lake. At the north end, cross Beartooth Creek (before July, this can be challenging if not treacherous). About 2 miles up the trail — it's a gradual ascent through meadows with rock outcroppings — you'll come to a junction with Trail #620, which heads east past Grayling and Beauty lakes. Each of them offers good fishing.

On the north end of Beauty Lake, you'll come to Trail #621. If you go left, you'll head northeast to Island Lake. (It's outstanding, with a campground and a whole new set of trails leading into the Beartooths.) If you turn right on #621, the trail will follow the eastern shore of Beauty Lake, heading south back to the Beartooth Lake campground. This hike can easily be done in a day. If you want to fish and explore, though, make it an overnighter and be sure to take your rod and your mosquito dope.

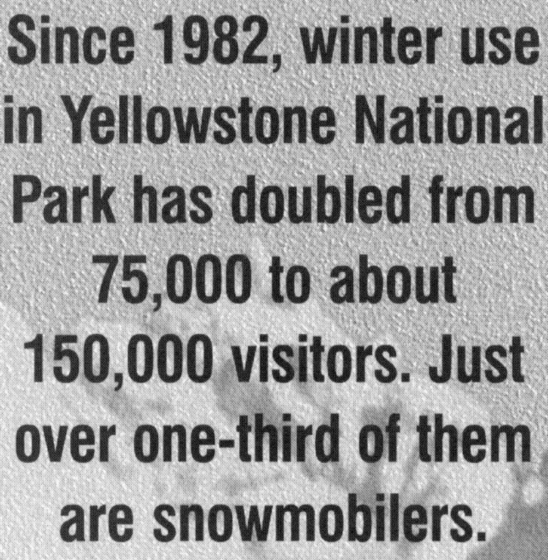

Since 1982, winter use in Yellowstone National Park has doubled from 75,000 to about 150,000 visitors. Just over one-third of them are snowmobilers.

Winter Sports

Winter lowers the curtain on frenetic summer activity in Yellowstone and Grand Teton National Parks. One by one, tourist facilities and park gates close. About November the snow begins to fall in earnest until it covers the parks 2 to 8 feet deep.

Just as elk and bison, alerted by age-old signals, begin to head down off the Yellowstone Plateau toward lower, less snowy wintering grounds, another call of the wild goes up across the land: "Let the winter sports begin!"

Since 1982, winter use in Yellowstone National Park has doubled from 75,000 to about 150,000 visitors. Just over one-third of them are snowmobilers. On a winter's day, you might see 1,500 snowmobiles heading from West Yellowstone, Montana, through the park's west entrance to spend the day riding the 150 miles of park roads. A blue haze from the two-stroke snowmachine engines hovers above West Yellowstone streets and the roads into the park. Yellowstone National Park still shuts down each November 1, but it re-opens to accommodate winter recreationists on a limited basis from mid-December until the first week in March. In the heart of the park, the Old Faithful Snow Lodge is a hub of winter recreation including cross-country skiing, snowmobiling, snowshoeing and snowcoach touring. The Mammoth Hotel also opens.

Outside the park, winter recreation has grown just as much. While 1,500 snowmobilers are heading from West Yellowstone into the park, an equal number are heading onto the 400-plus miles of trails in the Gallatin National Forest. The tiny town of Cooke City, which experiences nine months of winter, is also packed with snowmobilers each winter. In addition, backcountry skiing has grown so much that Bill Blackford, owner of the Bike Shack, runs two snowmobiles each winter carting skiers into the backcountry so they can ski downhill to their accommodations in Cooke City. Throughout Greater Yellowstone you'll find snowmobile and cross-country ski trails, often groomed by local clubs.

Snowmobiling is big business here. The Chamber of Commerce in West Yellowstone, which bills itself as the Snowmobile Capital of the World, spends $80,000 annually to maintain 400 miles of groomed snowmobile trails and another $40,000 to groom the world-class Rendezvous cross-country ski trails adjacent to town. The Park Service grooms another 200 miles in Yellowstone. Once the snow falls, snowmobiles become the primary mode of transportation in and out of West Yellowstone and in the parks. Visitors can walk out of their motel rooms, fire up their snowmobiles and head off into the snowy hinterlands on more than 1,000 miles of mostly groomed trails that lead into the park, to Idaho and to Lander, Wyoming.

Avalanches

Increased use of the backcountry by cross-country skiers, snowshoers, snowboarders and snowmobilers has raised concerns about avalanche danger. According to Kim Schlenker of the Southwestern Montana Avalanche Center, headquartered at the Supervisor's Office of the Gallatin National Forest in Bozeman, more people are venturing into avalanche country. Many are unaware they're in potential danger once they get off the trail.

The Avalanche Center employs one part-time and two full-time experts to monitor avalanche conditions in the Madison and Gallatin national forests, near Cooke City, northern Yellowstone National Park and the Lionhead portion of the Gallatin near West Yellowstone. The Center has three hotline numbers folks can call to learn avalanche and weather conditions each morning before heading out. They are (406) 587-6981 in Bozeman, (406) 646-7912 in West Yellowstone and (406) 838-2341 in Cooke City. Advisories are updated each day before 7 am mid-November through mid-April. Bridger-Teton National Forest also has an avalanche hotline, (307) 733-2664. Although not specifically an avalanche line, Grand Teton National Park also offers recorded daily weather information. Call (307) 739-3611.

Experts say that four out of five avalanches occur during or just after a storm. Sudden temperature changes can also trigger slides, as can heavy winds that deposit unstable snow loads on lee aspects of mountains. Slopes angled between 30 and 45 degrees are the most likely originators of avalanches, although slopes as low as 25 degrees have been known to slide. Angles greater than 55 degrees are generally too steep to accumulate enough snow to cause an avalanche.

Looking at a snowy slope can't tell you if it's safe, since composition of the snowpack also plays a part in avalanche probability. For example, frigid temperatures can turn the top snow layer to dry crystals called hoarfrost. These crystals function much like an ocean of marbles: Snow layers that later accumulate on this unstable foundation can begin to slide.

The best way to minimize the risk of getting caught in an avalanche is to stay at home immediately after a fresh snowfall, get an expert opinion about the current safety of the snowpack in the area you plan to visit, and stay on established trails.

Weather and Safety

Miles of white snow and blue sky can lull winter recreationists into a false sense of security. Storms can and do blow into Yellowstone country without warning. For that reason it's best to prepare for emergencies, including an unexpected overnight stay outdoors. Here are a few important safety tips:

- Travel in a group.
- Dress for extreme cold.
- Stay within the capabilities of the weakest person in your group.
- Carry extra food, matches and a first-aid kit.
- Know locations of warming huts, visitor centers and public phones.
- Check weather conditions before starting your trip.
- Practice caution, particularly on the most likely avalanche terrain: slopes between 30 and 45 degrees. Avoid these slopes when avalanche risk is high, such as during or right after heavy snowfall, heavy winds, or rapid temperature changes.
- Don't approach wildlife.
- Use extreme caution when crossing any body of water.
- Drink plenty of water to avoid dehydration.
- Learn as much as you can about winter survival. See our Resources chapter for some books to start with.

Ski Areas

Mix mountains with snow and you've got a powerful, powderful combination. In all, Greater Yellowstone has eight downhill ski areas, each with its unique claim to fame. Several are expanding like mad.

Big Sky Ski and Summer Resort

One Lone Mountain Trail, Mont.
• (406) 995-5000, (800) 548-4486

The brainchild of former newscaster Chet Huntley, Big Sky Ski and Summer Resort has grown into a world-class ski area with a list of amenities to amaze even the most jaded skier. Big Sky encompasses 3,500 acres and has 85 miles of named runs on two separate mountains. Of the 78 runs, the longest is 6 miles. The vertical drop is 4,180 feet — one of the highest in the country — and skiing ranges from groomed runs to knee-deep powder. The average snowfall is more than 400 inches, and the average winter daytime temperature is 20 degrees Fahrenheit.

Big Sky also has nearly wait-free lift lines and the capacity to handle 20,000 skiers per hour. A 15-passenger tram takes skiers (and non-skiers) to the summit of 11,166-foot Lone Peak. In addition, three high-speed quads, a gondola, a quad chair, two triple chairs, three double chairs and four surface tows keep skiers moving and dispersed.

Nearby Lone Mountain Guest Ranch offers 65 kilometers of cross-country ski trails along with nordic ski rentals and sales. (For more information, refer to our Resorts and Lodges chapter and the cross-country skiing section in this chapter.)

Children are not only welcome at Big Sky, but also expected. Up to two youngsters 10 and younger can ski free with each adult. A single-day lift ticket costs $48, while a half-day costs $40. Kids 11 to 17 and college students ski all day for $40. A standard ski package that includes boots, skis and poles rents for $24. You'll find an international ski school for young and old alike and a day-care center for kids who don't want to ski. Children can ski for a half-day and spend time in day care for the rest of the day. Snowboarders will appreciate the new snowboarding terrain complete with piped-in music and a slopeside bar.

Off the hill you'll find a range of accommodations including the 200-room Huntley Lodge, the 96-suite Shoshone Condominium Hotel and seven other condominiums in the Mountain Village (see our Resorts and Lodges chapter). You'll also find some shopping and an array of restaurants and bars in the resort complex as well as in the villages below the ski hill.

Big Sky Resort is open for the winter season from mid-November until mid-April. A free, scheduled shuttle service stops at various locations in the Meadow and Mountain Village subdivisions, as well as at the Canyon on U.S. Highway 191.

Bridger Bowl Ski Area

15795 Bridger Canyon Rd., Bozeman, Mont. • (406) 587-2111, (800) 223-9609 Central Reservations

This "steep and cheap" ski area ranked seventh among *Snow Country Magazine's* 1996 top-50 ski resorts in North America. Sixteen miles north of Bozeman, Bridger Bowl has 350 inches of annual snowfall, a 2,000-foot vertical drop and six chairlifts with a carrying capacity of 7,300 skiers per hour. The longest run in this 1,200-acre ski area is 2.5 miles. Longtime Bozeman residents like to boast Bridger is where extreme skiing and modern telemark skiing got their best start. Montana State U. students (and dropouts) have long made a habit of climbing into hair-raising chutes for a few seconds of adrenaline rush, and telemark was cool here long before most ski magazines even knew what it was.

Lift tickets for adults cost $30 for a full day and $25 for a half-day. Children 12 and younger ski for $13 a day. Seniors ski for $25 per day, and seniors 72 and older ski free. Ski rental packages are $15 for adults, $10 for children and $8 for senior citizens. Bridger Bowl also offers a variety of ski lessons and lesson packages for all ages. For a fee, an on-site day-care center will watch your non-skiing children (ages 18 months to 6 years) while you ski. You'll have to call ahead for a reservation, though.

You'll find food and drink at two cafeterias (one of them is the new Deer Park Chalet at midmountain) as well as Jimmy's Bar and Grill.

You won't find accommodations at the ski area, but you will find a well-organized central reservation service that can set you up with area motels, condominiums and guest houses. A few of the condominiums are within a quarter-mile of the ski hill, but there are no ski-in and ski-out accommodations. Bridger Bowl also offers a variety of ski packages that include accommodations.

Bridger Bowl is a nonprofit organization started in 1954 by local skiers who first built a tow and a ski lift. For ski and weather information call (406) 586-2389.

Grand Targhee Ski and Summer Resort

Ski Hill Rd., Alta, Wyo. • (307) 353-2300, (800) 827-4433

Clouds roll in from the Pacific, and 10,200-foot Fred's Mountain scoops the snow out, a powdery blanket freshly laid, it seems, nearly every morning. Grand Targhee averages 43 feet of cumulative snowfall per season.

This consistent, heavy snowfall means that Targhee gets good snow when nobody else does — you're most likely to encounter lift lines here on the days other ski hills in the region languish in bad snow blahs.

Once primarily a locals' hill where area families and "pin-heads" waved to each other as they cruised downhill in Scotch-Guarded jeans, Grand Targhee's prime powder draws increasing attention from destination travelers. The resort grooms 300 of its 1,500 acres. Three lifts and one rope tow serve all runs on the mostly intermediate terrain (only 10 percent is beginner and 20 percent expert). A neighboring peak, slated to be lift-served by winter 1999-2000, is also used as a snowcat-served powder preserve.

Situated 2,200 feet below Fred's summit are Grand Targhee's five restaurants, shopping, spa, ski service/rentals and ski school (with child-care facilities). For après-ski action, try Trap Bar, where the band is generally good and the burgers better. Accommodations range from motel-style units to condos. Below the village, 15 kilometers of nordic trails loop through meadows and forest; other activities are available.

In 1998-99, adult lift tickets cost $41. Grand Targhee opens around Thanksgiving and closes in mid-April.

Jackson Hole Mountain Resort
Teton Village, Wyo. • (307) 739-2753

Twelve miles northwest of Jackson on Wyo. Highway 390, Jackson Hole is known for its heart-thumping steep shots, which bomb through cliff bands and down gullies and ridges, and for its 4,139 feet of vertical. Beginners and intermediates will find plenty to do here, too: The resort has nine lifts and one rope tow on two mountains, Rendezvous and Après Vous. The altitude at the top of Rendezvous, by far the bigger peak, is 10,450 feet. Lifts serve 75 runs and a total of 2,500 skiable acres. You can buy snacks or meals at four locations on the mountain. A full range of services is available at the base, called Teton Village: condos, several sporting goods stores that rent ski and snowboard gear, repair shops for skis and snowboards and other shopping opportunities. Teton Village also has motels, restaurants and the Mangy Moose, an award-winning après-ski bar (see our Nightlife chapter).

Jackson Hole Ski and Snowboard School offers both instruction and child care. The Bridger Gondola transports 2,000 skiers per hour from the base of the mountain to the Headwall. The ride up is comfortable — you're completely enclosed — and fast, about 7 minutes. A few main trails are equipped with snowmaking machines.

Lift tickets for winter 1998-99 cost $51 for adults. Jackson Hole opens in early December and closes in mid-April.

Kelly Canyon Ski Resort
400 Market, Ririe Idaho • (208) 538-6261

This locals' ski hill is attractive both for its reasonable lift prices and for its short lift lines. Terrain is beginner and intermediate, consisting largely of stair-stepping runs to the base area. Base amenities include a ski school, cafeteria and ski rental shop. Four lifts and a rope tow serve 740 skiable acres. Base elevation is 5,800 feet and summit elevation 6,700, so low-elevation snowstorms make for the best skiing at Kelly Canyon. Adult lift tickets for winter 1998-99 cost $25. Night skiing, available Tuesday through Saturday, cost $18.

Red Lodge Mountain Resort
101 Ski Run Rd., Red Lodge, Mont. • (406) 446-2610, (800) 444-8977

Open from mid-November until mid-March, Red Lodge Mountain has a 2,400-foot vertical drop, 60 trails (the longest is 2.5 miles) and seven ski lifts including two high-speed detachable quads. In the heart of the Beartooth

INSIDERS' TIP

New telemark skiers or those who want to improve their technique should check out a slim paperback, *Allen and Mike's Really Cool Telemark Tips: 109 Amazing Tips to Improve your Tele Skiing*. The authors are Teton Valley locals. Both work for NOLS, the National Outdoor Leadership School. Winter NOLS courses use another book of theirs, *Mike and Allen's Really Cool Backcountry Ski Book*. Find both at area bookstores.

Mountains, Red Lodge Mountain's Grizzly Peak juts 9,416 feet into the sky and collects an average of 250 inches of snow each winter. An expansion in 1996 added 12 intermediate and expert runs and two high-speed quads to the ski area's list of amenities. The expansion increased the area's capacity to 10,640 skiers per hour.

What didn't increase much was the reasonable lift rates: $33 per day for adults, $27 per day for juniors (ages 13 to 18) and $12 a day for children 12 and younger. Adults and juniors pay $15 to rent a ski package, while children pay $10.

A 10-year master plan includes new base lodges and services, cross-country trails, a year-round restaurant atop Grizzly Peak and on-site lodging with conference facilities. For now, though, you'll have to stay at one of a dozen local motels or bed and breakfast inns in Red Lodge. Red Lodge Mountain operates on a special use permit from the Custer National Forest.

Photo: Randy Hayes, Post Register

The ride was fast, but the jump at the bottom of the hill provided the thrill.

Sleeping Giant Ski Resort
348 Yellowstone Hwy., Wapiti, Wyo.
• (307) 587-4044

This little family-run operation near the east entrance of Yellowstone National Park has a T-Bar and a chairlift accessing 17 trails. A busy day at Sleeping Giant, used only by locals, means about 300 skiers are gliding down its trails. On Sleeping Giant's busiest day of all time, 675 skiers showed up. Sleeping Giant has a lunch counter and a ski school. It also offers ski and snowboard rentals. An all-day ticket for the 1998-1999 season cost $18 for adults; children 12 and younger can ski for $8.

Snow King Resort
400 E. Snow King Ave., Jackson, Wyo.
• (307) 733-5200, (800) 522-5464

This hill is a bit short on vertical and skiable terrain — 1,571 vertical feet and 400 skiable acres are served by three chairs and one rope tow. But its location right in Jackson makes it long on convenience. Snow King also offers night skiing, a real treat with the lights of Jackson sparkling below.

Base elevation is 6,237 feet. Most runs are groomed, and 50 percent of groomed runs have snowmaking capacity. Terrain tends to be difficult: 60 percent of the mountain is expert terrain, and only 15 percent is beginner. The mountain generally opens by the end of November and closes in late March. A ski school is on-site.

The resort facility provides other extras, such as an ice-skating rink, a tubing hill, restaurants, a gift shop, an après-ski bar and more.

In 1998-99, adult lift tickets cost $30. Night skiing was $14. Discounts are available to resort guests.

Cross-Country Skiing

In this magnificent snowscape, you can head out almost anyplace and blaze your own trail, if that's your bag. For your convenience, though, we've compiled a short list of groomed trails or at least well-established ski trails in and out of the national parks. We also describe a few of the companies that offer equipment rentals and/or guided ski tours in and around the most popular areas. If you want to get out onto trails or untracked snow but aren't sure you want to do it with skis on your feet, most shops that rent ski gear also rent snowshoes, and most trail systems that allow skiers also welcome snowshoeing. Snowshoes have become lighter and more convenient than they once were, but particularly in deep snow, expect to expend more effort than you will on skis.

Ski Trails

Yellowstone National Park

Except for the Northwest Yellowstone Ski Trails listed here, all the cross-country ski trails described in this section are reachable by snowcoach tours or shuttles. In the Northeast Corner, along the Gardiner-Cooke City Road, trails can be reached either by private auto or by AmFac van shuttles. One outfitter, Yellowstone Expeditions, has a yurt camp at Canyon, which is used as a base camp for overnight ski expeditions there. For more information about these, refer to subsequent sections in this chapter: Ski Tours and Snowcoach Tours.

Canyon Ski Trails

This area has three moderate ski trails ranging from 2.5 to 6 miles. A fourth trail on Mount Washburn is more difficult. The only one that is ever machine-set is the portion of the Canyon Rim trail that follows the Rim Road. This area is reachable only by snowmobile or snowcoach.

Northeast Yellowstone Ski Trails

Two easy marked trails and a very difficult one await skiers in this area of the park where deep snow softens the natural contours. None of them are groomed. Two follow along close to the road. The third, the Pebble Creek Trail, is for very experienced skiers only and is often done as a two-day trip.

Old Faithful Ski Trails

This system of 11 trails is hard to beat for sheer beauty. The combination of geothermal steam and freezing temperatures turns the trees here into lacy winter guardians. AmFac operates a couple of snowcoach shuttles from the Old Faithful Snow Lodge. And Alpen Guides out of West Yellowstone drops skiers off in Biscuit Basin where they can ski 2.5 miles through the geyser basin before eating lunch at the lodge. The hoary thermal features are heavenly. Once again, you can't drive to Old Faithful in the winter, which means you'll either have to spend the night or make a very long day of it. If you're planning to stay overnight at Old Faithful, you'll need to reserve a room months ahead of time.

Tower Junction Ski Trails

Several trails begin in the Tower Junction area where a shuttle from the Mammoth Hotel makes three regular stops. Tower Fall trail, a 5-mile moderate ski, follows the unplowed Tower Canyon road for about 2.5 miles. A longer trail (5 miles) past Lost Lake offers beautiful scenery and a variety of terrain. The other two trails, Chittenden Loop and Black Plateau Trail, are difficult. All but the Lost Lake Trail are machine-set when weather permits. AmFac offers a shuttle from Mammoth to the trails.

Upper Terrace Loop

Early in the day, when the hoarfrost is still on the trees, is the best time to ski this moderate 1.5-mile trail that follows the Upper Terrace Road south of the inn at Mammoth Hot Springs. This trail is groomed. The Upper Terrace Loop is one of six trails in the Mammoth area.

Grand Teton National Park

Grand Teton National Park doesn't groom any of its roughly 40 miles of cross-country and snowshoe trails, but it does mark them with flags and provide descriptive brochures. Most trails are popular, so they're usually well-packed and easy to follow. Trail markers are for days when fresh snow has obliterated the tracks of previous parties. Trails range in difficulty, with some routes friendly enough for the most cautious beginner.

Cross-country skiing and snowshoeing are not limited to trails, several of which are described in this section, but if you plan to explore, be sure you know which areas are closed to human traffic (mostly river bottoms where wildlife seeks winter refuge). Also carry good maps, which can be purchased at sporting goods stores in Jackson or at the Moose visitor center. Learn more about trails and park regulations by stopping by the Moose Visitor Center or by calling the park's dispatch at (307) 739-3300. Learn about the approximately 10 miles of mapped but ungroomed trails around Flagg Ranch Resort in the John D. Rockefeller Jr. Memorial Parkway by calling the Park Service number listed here, or by calling the resort at (307) 543-2861. The trails listed in this section are some of the most popular.

Swan Lake-Heron Pond Loop

You're here to view Jackson Lake and the northern peaks of the Teton range decked out in their snowy best. This easy trail winds through level terrain among lodgepole forest, splits to loop the east shore of Heron Pond and the west shore of Swan Lake; the best views are from the edge of Heron Pond. This 3-mile round-trip trail begins at Colter Bay Visitor Center.

Jenny Lake Trail

Another easy trail with spectacular views, the Jenny Lake loop is long enough to give you a full day's adventure. You begin at the Taggart Lake parking area and ski north along pretty Cottonwood Creek through a series of large meadows and gentle climbs. You'll skirt the base of the Tetons and end at an overlook of Jenny Lake. Return on the mostly level trail for a 9-mile trip.

Signal Mountain

This 10-mile round-trip ski requires moderate skill and provides panoramic views. Park at the end of the road near Signal Mountain Lodge (it's closed this time of year, but there are bathrooms and pay phones available). Ski south along a snowmobile trail for about a mile until you see the Signal Mountain Road winding up and east. It's a gradual 4-mile climb to the summit. Enjoy eagle's-eye views of the ice-choked Snake River on the valley floor and peer up at Mount Moran and other peaks still far above you. Then zip up your coat and enjoy the long downhill glide back to your car.

Phelps Lake Overlook

This moderate trail begins at a little parking area about 3 miles south of Moose on the Moose-Wilson Road. Its first 1.7 miles run along a narrow road, gradually ascending to the Death Canyon trailhead. Gradient increases as the trail climbs through lodgepole forest and over open slope to reach the Phelps Canyon Overlook. The Park Service does not recommend continuing past this point because of high avalanche danger. The return trip, all downhill, can be very fast when the trail is packed down; less experienced skiers will feel more comfortable on this trail after a snowfall. The trail is 5 miles round-trip.

Jackson Hole

The Jackson area has both groomed and ungroomed skiing, but skiing the groomed trails costs money. So if you're cheap or you like less structured skiing, two of the most popular free, ungroomed trails near Jackson are on the Snake River Dike and in Cache Creek Canyon. They're used often enough that there's generally a trail to follow.

The Snake River Dike ski starts 5 miles west of Jackson on Wyo. Highway 22 just as it crosses the Snake River. Skiers, snowmobilers and snowshoers use the flat trail, which can be made into a several-mile ski. Moose, deer and a variety of bird life are common sights. So are people.

Cache Creek Canyon is reached by driving up Cache Creek Drive east of Jackson until you reach a parking area. Simply ski in as far as you like, then ski back to your car. The farther you go, the steeper and more chal-

INSIDERS' TIP

Backcountry skiers in the Bridger-Teton National Forest can pick up an avalanche report, updated early each morning, on the Internet at www.untracked.com or by calling (307) 733-2664.

lenging the terrain becomes. The trail can be made to loop back to U.S. Highway 191 in order to avoid retracing steps, but talk with a knowledgeable skier at one of the local sporting goods shops if this sounds interesting, as you'll be crossing terrain with moderate avalanche risk. Many more ungroomed options exist. Call Skinny Skis (below) to learn about them, or pick up a recent edition of Skinny Skis' area trailguide, called *Trailhead*.

To learn about the area's groomed ski trails, read on.

Jackson Hole Nordic Center
Moose-Wilson Rd. at Teton Village, Wyo. • (307) 739-2629

This is the largest system of groomed trails in the valley. The rental center can supply skate or diagonal skis, snowshoes and telemark gear. Instruction is available. The location at the base of Jackson Hole's biggest ski resort is convenient; Teton views and forested sections of trails also make it attractive. A one-day pass costs $8 for adults, or you can trade your lift ticket in for a free nordic trail pass on the same day.

Spring Creek Resort
Spring Gulch Rd., Jackson, Wyo. • (307) 733-1004

Spring Creek Resort is tucked into the hills overlooking the National Elk Refuge. In winter the resort grooms 10 kilometers of skating and diagonal trails with sections suitable for beginner, intermediate and advanced skiers. Your trail pass costs $8. If you don't own your own gear, rental packages cost $9 for a half-day and $12 for a full day. Snowshoes rent for $10 per day; snowshoe enthusiasts get their own separate trails that run along about 5 kilometers of a summer horse trail. These folks also offer ski tours of Grand Teton National Park.

Teton Pines
3450 N. Clubhouse Dr., Jackson, Wyo. • (307) 733-1005, (800) 238-2223

This Arnold Palmer-designed golf course turns into cross-country ski trails in winter, with 14 kilometers of terrain groomed for both skaters (skating lanes are extra-wide) and diagonal skiers. Sandwiched between the Tetons and the Snake River, the course offers lovely views. Warm up in the clubhouse after your ski; the lobby area, with its massive fireplace, a bar and fine-dining restaurant are all available. An all-day trail pass costs $8. Ski equipment can be rented at Teton Pines for around $12. Ski tours of Grand Teton National Park are available.

Surrounding Areas

Southwestern Montana

Northwest Corner Ski Trails

Four trails lead from U.S. Highway 191 into Yellowstone National Park. At Mile Post 18, on the west side of U.S. 191, you'll find the Telemark Meadows. At Mile Post 20, a small parking lot marks the beginning of Bighorn Pass Trail. This trail heads east across a flat, then follows the Gallatin River. Watch for moose, elk, eagles and coyotes.

At Mile Post 22, the popular Fawn Pass Trail takes off from a large parking lot. The trail crosses the Gallatin River then climbs up through woods and meadows. It connects with the Bighorn Pass Trail at 8 kilometers. Specimen Creek Trail follows the creek from Milepost 27. This is another good trail for wildlife viewing. Keep your eyes peeled for standing petrified trees.

Rendezvous Ski Trails

Used each November by national, collegiate and international ski teams, the 30-plus-kilometer Rendezvous Trails begin just two blocks off Yellowstone Avenue in West Yellowstone. Just ski through the log arch at the edge of the parking lot at the junction of Geyser and Obsidian Streets, and you'll be on your way. Once you get on the trail, you can choose from five different loops depending upon your skill and your mood. The 6-kilometer Rendezvous Loop leads across gently rising trails through a pine forest with several short cutoffs. You'll find a warming hut at the Biathlon Range.

Volunteer Loop, 2.3 kilometers, includes several options for lengthening or shortening your ski. The loop traverses rolling hills and offers spectacular views of the Gallatin Range. Two other loops, the Windy Ridge and the

Dead Dog, offer longer, more challenging trails.

Most of these loops are groomed from early November through April with both diagonal stride tracks and a 12-foot skating lane.

Riverside Ski Trail

Look for the orange trail marker between the snow piles at the intersection of Boundary and Madison Streets on the east edge of West Yellowstone. This trail consists of two loops: the 2.5-kilometer Upriver Loop and the 5.9-kilometer Downriver Loop. This trail generally follows the Madison River and offers exceptional wildlife viewing opportunities.

Bohart Ranch Cross Country Ski Center

16621 Bridger Canyon Rd., Bozeman, Mont. • (406) 586-9070

A hop, skip and a ski from Bridger Bowl Ski Area, the Bohart Ranch offers 25 kilometers of groomed and tracked trails on private and Forest Service lands. Facilities include a biathlon range for year-round training and competition. Services and amenities include rentals, lessons, snacks and a warming cabin. Trails are open in summer for walking, running, mountain biking and horseback riding. Be sure to ask about the 18-Hole Frisbee golf course. The Bohart Ranch charges $8 per day for use of its facilities.

Lindley Park Trail

Downtown Bozeman, Mont.

This 1.5-mile-trail loops around Lindley Park in downtown Bozeman. Day and night, you'll see folks skiing their way around this loop when there's enough snow.

Lone Mountain Ranch

Lone Mountain Rd., Big Sky, Mont. • (406) 995-4644, (800) 514-4644

Founded in the 1970s as a cross-country haven, Lone Mountain Ranch's ski facilities are known far and wide. In addition to a meticulously groomed 65-kilometer trail system, Lone Mountain Ranch offers guided backcountry ski tours into Yellowstone National Park and the Spanish Peaks Wilderness.

INSIDERS' TIP

Yellowstone country saw skiers as early as the 1870s, but their gear looked nothing like today's. Called snowshoes, skeys or skees, early skis were huge — 9 to 15 feet long and at least 4 inches wide. Saturated with wax and oil, each ski weighed at least 10 pounds.

For more information about Lone Mountain Ranch, refer to our Guest Ranches chapter.

Red Lodge Nordic Center
Mont. Hwy. 78, 2 miles west of Red Lodge, Mont. • (406) 446-9191

From mid-December until the end of March, you can ski the 15 kilometers of groomed trails at the Red Lodge Nordic Ski Center for $6 per day for adults and $3 for kids. This day-use area has a warming hut and about 50 pairs of cross-country skis for rent. An adult rental package costs $10 ($8.50 for kids). Snowshoes rent for $10.

Wade Lake Resort
About 8 miles south of U.S. Hwy. 287, Cameron, Mont. (406) 682-7560

Thirty-five kilometers of groomed trails and five old-fashioned secluded cabins await you at the Wade Lake Resort. Trails follow the shorelines of Wade and Cliff lakes, part of the Hidden Lake chain in the Beaverhead National Forest. One trail leads to a hilltop with a stupendous view. Others offer excellent wildlife and bird-watching opportunities. The trails are groomed by the owners of the Wade Lake Resort, where you'll find five cozy cabins tucked into a secluded nook above Wade Lake.

Eastern Idaho

The rolling terrain and plentiful public land that make up much of eastern Idaho create endless opportunities for cross-country skiing. Any summer dirt road is a likely candidate for winter skiing, as it's probably not plowed. Many hiking trails, including trails and back roads in the Kelly Canyon area and around Ririe on the South Fork of the Snake, make interesting challenges for more experienced skiers. Groomed trail systems also exist. A few are described in this section.

The Big Holes
Targhee National Forest • (208) 356-3101

The Big Holes are a mountain range on the Targhee National Forest between Rexburg and Teton Basin. The area is home to 240 miles of groomed, mapped trail used mostly by snowmobilers. These trails see around 200 to 300 users per day in winter. Cross-country skiers don't use them much, but if you want to, go on a weekday. Snowmobile traffic will be thinner.

Grand Targhee Ski and Summer Resort
Ski Hill Rd., Alta, Wyo. • (307) 353-2300, (800) 827-4433

Enjoy 15 kilometers of groomed skate and ski track. Beginner, intermediate and advanced loops stretch west and north of the ski village at the base of Fred's Mountain. Trails loop through open meadows and snow-blanketed forest. Maps are available. If you're staying at the resort, you may use the trails free. Otherwise you'll pay $8 per person for the day. You can rent all the gear you need. Lessons are available.

Harriman State Park
U.S. Hwy. 20, Island Park, Idaho • (208) 558-7368

Fifteen miles of mechanically groomed cross-country ski trails await you at Harriman State Park just south of town. Island Park is a snowmobile mecca. Most popular winter trails get a lot of snowmachine traffic, but not in Harriman: No snowmobiles are allowed here.

Harriman provides great wildlife viewing in winter. Its open water attracts trumpeter swans and other creatures. One pleasant beginner route, called the Ranch Loop, takes skiers into the historic Railroad Ranch. The clusters of buildings and corrals here are still part of a

INSIDERS' TIP

The methyl alcohol in blue wiper fluids helps detergent evaporate quickly and lowers its freezing temperature, making it less likely your vision will be obscured by ice crystals.

Photo: Randy Hayes, Post Register

It's fun in the sun as two skiers zoom down Chief Joseph Bowl at Grand Targhee.

working cattle operation in summer. Stop in at the Jones House warming hut to thaw your hands by the fire. Then ski along the north side of Silver Lake, watching for wildlife, before returning to the main trail. Park literature describes seven other loops of varying lengths and levels of difficulty.

A $3 fee allows entrance to the park. Skis can be rented north of the park at Last Chance Texaco, (208) 558-7399.

For information about other cross-country ski opportunities in the Island Park area, call Island Park Ranger District, (208) 558-7301, or the Ashton Ranger District, (208) 652-7442.

Kelly Canyon

Near Ririe, Idaho • No phone

Kelly Canyon has about 20 miles of ski trails, which begin from the Kelly Canyon ski area parking lot. A trail map and trail descriptions are available at Idaho Mountain Trading in Idaho Falls (see its entry in this section). Some of these trails are periodically groomed. All are signed and marked periodically with blue diamonds. The shortest is about 1 mile long. Steeper trails afford good views of the Snake River range and Kelly Canyon. Easy trails often wind through heavy forest. Some trails are used by snowmobilers.

Moose Creek Road

Off Idaho Hwy. 33, Victor, Idaho • No phone

Almost every canyon emptying into the Teton Basin offers cross-country ski possibilities. Many see little or no snowmobile traffic, either because they head into the Teton Wilderness where snowmobiles aren't allowed, or because they opt for the ease of trails groomed for them in the Big Hole Mountains. One of our favorites starts at the end of Moose Creek Road, off Idaho Highway 33 on Teton Pass. Park across from Moose Creek Ranch and head up Moose Creek on a trail that will probably be snowed in but visible. Side trails, which may be difficult to spot, leave the main trail at intervals. One of them leads to a mountain yurt available for rent to skiers. Moose are common along the creek. The farther you go, the steeper the trail becomes, but the first mile or two is nearly level. For more information, contact the Teton Basin Ranger District at (208) 354-2312 or Yöstmark, listed in the next section and in the Shopping chapter.

Tautphaus Park and Community Park

Idaho Falls, Idaho • (208) 529-1480

Local skiers occasionally enjoy groomed

areas around Tautphaus Park and Community Park. Idaho Falls Parks Department grooms these parks any time enough heavy snow falls to prevent damage to the grass. Skiing at these parks is free. Pinecrest Golf Course is occasionally groomed, although most years there's not enough snow to ensure that the grooming machines won't harm the grass. In years that the course is groomed, a $10 pass allows you to ski here for the season.

Teton Canyon Road

Off Ski Hill Rd., Alta, Wyo.

This popular trail offers a pleasant downhill grade into an almost endless array of ski options. The area is used often enough that you'll probably find a trail at least for the first couple of miles. Odds are there'll be cars in the parking area at the intersection of Teton Canyon Road and Ski Hill Road. Four miles in, you'll find yourself at Teton Canyon Campground. From there, trails begin to climb toward Table Mountain or Alaska Basin, depending on your choice of routes. For more information, contact the Teton Basin Ranger District at (208) 354-2312 or Yöstmark, listed in the next section and in the Shopping chapter.

Northwestern Wyoming

Pahaska Trails

Cody folks have to drive a ways to find enough snow for skiing. One of their favorites is the Pahaska Trails. About 20 kilometers of groomed trails maintained by the Park County Nordic Ski Association begin at Pahaska Tepee, 3 miles east of Yellowstone National Park's east entrance. Two ungroomed backcountry trails, the Cow Creek Trail and the Sunlight Wilderness Trail, lead off the groomed trail. For a map and more information, contact Pahaska Tepee at (307) 527-7701, (800) 628-7791.

Ski Rentals

Yellowstone National Park

AmFac Resorts and Services

Mammoth, Yellowstone National Park • (307) 344-7311

AmFac, Yellowstone National Park's main concessionaire, rents cross-country skis at Mammoth and Old Faithful. In 1998-99, the rental rates were $14 for a full day and $9 for a half-day. AmFac also offers guided ski tours from Mammoth and Old Faithful to the Grand Canyon, DeLacy Creek near Shoshone Lake and a ski in the Lamar Valley combined with lunch in Cooke City. AmFac also offers ski drops from Mammoth and Old Faithful to and from a few popular ski trails.

Jackson Hole

Flagg Ranch Resort

U.S. Hwy. 89 (John D. Rockefeller Jr. Memorial Pkwy.) • (307) 543-2861

Rent cross-country ski packages for $12 per day and snowshoe packages for $10. Lessons are available, as are guided trips on the area's approximately 10 miles of ungroomed trails, most of which are of beginner/interme-

INSIDERS' TIP

Looking for a new winter activity? Try one of the oldest: snowshoeing. Guided snowshoe tours are available at Grand Targhee Ski and Summer Resort and through the ranger-naturalists at Grand Teton National Park. Ranger-naturalist tours and loaner snowshoes are free; the tours at Grand Targhee, which include instruction, cost around $30 plus a few bucks for snowshoe rental. For more information, call Grand Teton National Park at (307) 739-3300; contact Grand Targhee at (307) 353-2300, or (800) 827-4433.

diate difficulty. You can also pick up trail maps for this area, as well as for Grand Teton National Park to the south.

Skinny Skis

65 W. Deloney Ave., Jackson, Wyo. • (307) 733-6094

Skinny Skis is Jackson's snowshoe and diagonal and skate ski headquarters in winter. Staff at this 24-year-old business tend to be practitioners of the sports for which they sell and rent equipment. Snowshoes rent for $8 per day; cross-country gear costs $12 for a full day. Skate and touring gear are both available. While you're there, pick up a copy of *Trailhead*, published twice a year. It'll steer you to area trails and attractions and provide you with simple maps to help find them.

Teton Mountaineering

170 N. Cache St., Jackson, Wyo. • (307) 733-3595, (800) 850-3595

You can rent skis and backcountry camping gear here. Skate- and diagonal-ski packages cost $12 for a full day. Telemark and snowshoe rentals are available as well.

Surrounding Areas

Southwestern Montana

Bangtail Bicycle and Ski

508 W. Main St., Bozeman, Mont. • (406) 587-4905

Named after the Bangtail Mountains, a hotspot for mountain bikers near Bozeman, this shop rents bikes in the summer and cross-country skis in the winter. A ski package will cost you $8 the first day and $5 for succeeding days. By the way, the Bangtails are a favorite snowmobiling area, but skiers don't go there.

Bud Lilly's Ski Shop

39 Madison Ave., West Yellowstone, Mont. • (406) 646-7801, (800) 854-9559

In addition to having about 30 pairs of cross-country skis for rent, Bud Lilly's also rents snowshoes. The charge is $15 per day for skis ($10 per half-day).

Cooke City Bike Shack

U.S. Hwy. 212, Cooke City, Mont. • (406) 838-2412

This place rents cross-country and telemark skis, snowshoes and accessories. Ski rentals range from $12 to $17.50, depending on the type of ski. For $15, owner Bill Blackford will also snowmobile you up to Daisy Pass so you can ski down to town. And for $45 per day, he will act as your guide in the backcountry. Blackford is a member of Professional Ski Instructors of America, works with the Southwestern Montana Avalanche Center and has been skiing the Cooke City area for 15 years.

Free Heel and Wheel

40 Yellowstone Ave., West Yellowstone, Mont. • (406) 646-7744

The Free Heel and Wheel rents a variety of cross-country skis including touring, performance skate or classic and race skate or classic skis. The rates are $15, $20 and $25, respectively. The shop also rents snowshoes for $15 per day. If you only want to ski for a couple of hours, the Free Heel and Wheel also offers hourly rates. When you're done, you can belly up to the coffee counter and warm up with a hot coffee and a treat from Nancy P's Bakery.

Grizzly Outfitters

145 Center Lane, Unit H, Big Sky, Mont. • (406) 995-2939

In the summer, Grizzly rents bikes. When the snow flies, though, owner Ken Lancey puts away the bikes and pulls out the skis. Skis here rent from $10 to $25 per day. Lancey has reduced rates for multiple-day rentals. Snowshoe rentals are $8 for half a day.

Northern Lights Trading Company

1716 W. Babcock St., Bozeman, Mont. • (406) 586-2225

Not only will you find skis to rent here, but you'll find a staff loaded with Insiders' tips on where to go and how to get there. Ski packages range from $10 to $25 per day, with discounts for multiple-day rentals. Northern Lights also rents snowshoes for $8 per day.

Parks' Fly Shop

U.S. Hwy. 89, Gardiner, Mont. • (406) 848-7314

Parks' pulls out about 20 pairs of cross-country skis for rental each winter. A set of skis in 1999 rented for $9.50 for the day. Weekends Parks' gives a discount: three days for the price of two.

The Round House Ski and Sports Center

1422 W. Main St., Bozeman, Mont. • (406) 587-1258
15795 Bridger Canyon Rd., Bozeman, Mont. • (406) 587-2838

In town and at the ski hill, The Round House has a complete selection of ski rentals, both for downhill and cross-country. Add snowboards and snowshoes to that list, as well as waxing and reconditioning. Cross-country skis and snowshoes rent for $8 per day.

Eastern Idaho

Teton Valley

Grand Targhee Ski and Summer Resort

Ski Hill Rd., Alta Wyo. • (307) 353-2300, (800) 827-4433

A complete nordic ski package at Grand Targhee costs around $17 for a full-day rental. Lessons are available for additional charge.

Yöstmark Mountain Equipment

12 E. Little Ave., Driggs, Idaho • (208) 354-2828

This shop specializes in telemark, cross-country, snowshoe and snowboard equipment for the backcountry. You can rent both touring and skate skis and collect some good advice about where to take them. Nordic and telemark packages rent for $16.

Island Park, Idaho

Last Chance Texaco

U.S. Hwy. 20 at Last Chance in Island Park, Idaho • (208) 558-7399

You won't find many places in Island Park that rent ski gear, but this is one. Nordic packages cost $10 per day. The store also sells ski equipment, both new and used.

Idaho Falls, Idaho

Idaho Mountain Trading

474 Shoup Ave., Idaho Falls, Idaho • (208) 523-6679

Rent alpine, telemark and nordic skis, as well as snowboards. A repair shop is on-site. Diagonal packages cost $8 for the day and $12 for the weekend.

Northwestern Wyoming

Foote's Mountaineering

1280 Sheridan Ave., Cody, Wyo. • (307) 527-9937

Check with Foote's Mountaineering for backcountry telemark skis and associated equipment like telescoping avalanche poles and beacons. Ski rentals range from $15 to $20, and plastic boots cost the same.

Pahaska Tepee

183 Yellowstone Hwy., Cody, Wyo. • (307) 527-7701

Pahaska rents cross-country skis for $10 per day and $6 for a half-day.

Sunlight Sports

1251 Sheridan Ave., Cody, Wyo. • (307) 587-9517

Sunlight Sports, Cody's oldest sporting goods store, rents nordic skis for $8 to adults and $5 to kids. Snowshoes rent for $9 a day.

Ski Tours

Teton County/Jackson Parks and Recreation

155 E. Gill St., Jackson, Wyo. • (307) 739-9025

These folks offer four kinds of refreshingly inexpensive winter outings. On Tuesdays join a one-day cross-country ski tour to various locations, usually in Grand Teton or Yellowstone National Parks. The $7 fee covers transportation and guides, but not gear or park entry fees. For most trips the maximum number is 22; trips typically involve 5 or 6 miles of skiing. Routes vary in degree of difficulty. A couple of times each winter, moonlight ski tours are planned. These tours typically involve a 3-mile ski over mostly level terrain.

Snowshoe tours are also available; they, too, cost $7. Snowshoes are not provided. Some previous experience is required.

Teton County/Jackson Parks and Recreation usually plan one three-day cross-country ski trip into Yellowstone National Park, Harriman State Park, Idaho, or a similar destination. Reservations and advance payment are required for any of these ski tours. Detailed itineraries are available, including information to help you decide if the tour is within your skill level.

Yellowstone Expeditions

511 Gibbon Ave., West Yellowstone, Mont. • (406) 646-9333

For a little more than $100 per day, you can ride a snowcoach to a yurt camp at Canyon, stay for two to eight days, and ski to your heart's content. At camp, you'll find two large communal yurts (living room and kitchen) surrounded by seven individual yurtlets. One of these will be your home for the stay. Evenings, when you're not skiing the backcountry, you'll be treated to gourmet meals (à la yurt), warm living and sleeping quarters and an on-site sauna and shower. During the day, expect to see lots of wildlife and magnificent scenery.

Snowmobiling

It's no accident that West Yellowstone is called the Snowmobile Capital of the World. You can walk out of your motel room, hop on your sled and drive more than 1,000 miles across glorious white snow. Almost every motel in town offers bed-and-sled packages that include your motel room and use of a snowmachine or two (depending on whether you and your partner want to ride together or separately.) Aggressive competition leads motel owners to throw in such extras as a prime rib dinner, continental breakfast and the park entrance fee. Because January is the slowest month, you can sometimes find better deals and less traffic during this time. You might even find a last-minute opening at the Old Faithful Snow Lodge. (Refer to our Hotels, Motels and Cabins chapter.)

At the edge of town, 400 miles of groomed trails take off into the Gallatin National Forest. Several of these trails top mountain passes and hook up with another 600 miles of groomed trails in Idaho's Targhee Forest. Another 200 miles of trails wind through Yellowstone National Park to the east. If you head south into Grand Teton National Park you can drive clear to Lander, Wyoming, if that's your pleasure.

In this chapter, we'll highlight some of the more popular trails, then leave the rest up to you. In West Yellowstone, Island Park and other snowmobile meccas you'll find trail maps in every store, motel and restaurant. And you'll encounter plenty of folks willing to help you on your way. In Jackson, you have to drive or be driven from your motel to the Flagg Ranch or some nearby place where you can then unload your sled and take off into the wild white yonder.

Before you head into the forest or the parks, it's a good idea to know the rules. For example, both Yellowstone National Park and the Gallatin Forest have 45 mph speed limits. In Yellowstone National Park, no offroad sledding or sidehilling is permitted. You must also have a valid driver's license to operate a snowmobile. Snowmachine use has increased so dramatically that park officials liken the experience to highway driving with fast cars and heavy traffic. In January 1999, a visitor died in a snowmobile accident. It was her first time on a snowmobile. Park officials say inexperience, excessive speed and wildlife encounters cause most accidents.

While we're at it, here are a few guidelines for avoiding wildlife: If you encounter a bison walking toward you, pull over and let it pass. And if an animal is standing in the road, stop 25 yards away, assess the animal's state of mind, then proceed past cautiously unless the animal is agitated. Remember that pressured animals can suddenly charge you. If you plan to leave well-established, frequently traveled trails (you must stay on the roads in the parks), carry a repair kit and know how to use it. The least you should have — and know how to replace — are extra spark plugs and a drive belt. You should also carry the clothes and equipment necessary to walk out or spend the night.

Another good wildlife rule to remember is this: If you're close enough that the animal is reacting to you, you're too close.

Snowmobile Trails

Yellowstone National Park

Inside Yellowstone National Park you'll find nearly 200 miles of groomed trails that follow the park's roads leading to almost all the major attractions. While most of the 50,000 snowmobilers who go into the park drive to Old Faithful and back to West Yellowstone, at least half of them take the Lower Loop road through West Thumb, Fishing Bridge, Canyon, Norris and Madison. You'll find six warming huts along the way, and all but one of them is open 24 hours a day. Four of the huts have at least some kind of snack available.

Gasoline is available at Old Faithful, Fishing Bridge, Canyon and Mammoth. In addition, Yellowstone National Park service stations at Old Faithful, Canyon and Fishing Bridge sell drive belts, spark plugs and some accessories.

Off-trail sledding or sidehilling is not permitted in the park. And the speed limit, strictly enforced, is 45 miles per hour. Snowmachines whose engines exceed noise restrictions may be denied entry into the park.

Grand Teton National Park

Riding in Grand Teton National Park is far less popular than on the snowmobile-filled trails of Yellowstone to the north. Nevertheless, some trails exist. The most popular is a segment of the groomed Continental Divide Scenic Trail (CDST), which runs alongside U.S. Highway 287 through the park. This allows a 26-mile, easy ride from Moran Junction to Flagg Ranch. More challenging riding is possible on Toppings Lake Road and Shadow Mountain Road along the eastern perimeter of the park. The Teton Park Road, unplowed in winter, also provides snowmobile terrain. From the parking area at Taggart Lake near the Moose visitor center to Signal Mountain on this road is 15 miles.

Gas is not available inside the park, but Flagg Ranch just north of Jackson Lake, and Grand Teton National Park RV Resort 6 miles east of the Moran entrance do sell gas and provide other services. Pay phones are available at the Moran entrance station, Signal Mountain Lodge and Flagg Ranch. To learn more, stop by the Moose visitor center for a brochure, ask your snowmobile provider for maps and information, or call Grand Teton National Park at (307) 739-3300.

Jackson Hole

Jackson Hole is not the snowmobile mecca West Yellowstone, Montana, or Island Park, Idaho, are, mostly because you can't just jump on your sled and ride out of town. If you're willing to drive between 10 and 70 miles, though, extensive trail systems await.

Folks looking for shorter trips close to the town of Jackson often head for Granite Hot Springs; the trail is actually a well-marked 10-mile-long road ending at a commercial hot springs pool (see our Attractions chapter for more on the joys of soaking in Granite Hot Springs). This trip begins east of Hoback Junction on U.S. Highway 191. We're told that snowmobiling on this road is faster and more comfortable than driving its rutted summer surface in a car. Another popular short trip takes you into the Gros Ventre Mountains along the unplowed Gros Ventre River Road just south of Grand Teton National Park. Wildlife such as moose and elk are commonly seen from this trail.

Limited rides are also possible in Grand Teton National Park itself (see the previous section).

Longer, farther away, but still popular are the groomed trail systems of Yellowstone National Park, the Continental Divide Snowmobile Trail, the Togwotee Pass area (a popular section of the CDST) and trails south of Jackson Hole adjacent to the Grey's River. Both Togwotee Pass and the Grey's River trails pro-

INSIDERS' TIP

For information about snow conditions at Big Sky Ski and Summer Resort, call (406) 995-5900.

vide easy access to powder fields for off-trail play.

The CDST, which runs between Lander, Wyoming, and West Yellowstone, Montana, through both Grand Teton and Yellowstone national parks, would be a two- or three-day trip if you tried to ride the whole thing. Most people choose to bite off 20- and 30-mile chunks, which is easy to do because the trail has many access points. In the Jackson Hole area, you can reach this popular trail from Grand Teton National Park RV Resort in the Buffalo Fork Valley, Signal Mountain Lodge in Grand Teton National Park or at Flagg Ranch just south of Yellowstone National Park. You can also jump onto the trail from the Gros Ventre River Road.

People unfamiliar with the area usually choose to be guided rather than striking out on their own, in large part because of the distances involved in getting to trailheads. Look in the following section for providers of guided snowmobile trips in the area, as well as a couple of snowmobile rental companies for those who want to go it alone. Be sure you ask at the rental company for recommendations and trail maps. The state of Wyoming produces a fine series of snowmobile trail maps that most area snowmobile providers carry.

Photo: Randy Hayes, Post Register

A skier crosses an open meadow with a sled filled with winter gear in tow.

Surrounding Areas

Southwestern Montana

Big Sky, Montana

Amazingly, you won't find that many groomed snowmobile trails around Big Sky. Most people travel the Buck Creek Ridge Road, which runs east to west south of the Big Sky Ski Area. This trail is suitable for inexperienced snowmobilers and can be reached from U.S. Highway 191 to Buck Creek Ridge. Also, you may hear rumors about the Big Sky Trail running north to south from Bozeman to West Yellowstone. We talked to many people about this trail and each described it much differently — some even said it didn't exist. Others said part of it has been closed to snowmobile traffic in order to protect wintering elk. Some said it was groomed in parts. If this trail really exists, it is strictly for the experienced. If you're in search of the trail, we advise you find an expert who has traveled it recently. A groomed trail runs beside U.S. 191 from the Big Sky entrance south to the Buck Creek Ridge Trail.

West Yellowstone, Montana

Four major trails lead away from West Yellowstone's city limits into Gallatin National Forest. All are joined by loops, and most connect to Idaho trails leading to Island Park, Idaho. Each has its own beauty, but probably the most popular is Two Top, a 30-mile loop described below under the Eastern Idaho header. Other trails, such as the Lionhead Loop, offer opportunities for off-trail play, but be aware that you're in avalanche country here.

Cooke City, Montana

Cooke City, known as the Black Diamond of off-trial snowmobiling, doesn't have the groomed trail system that West Yellowstone has. Check with any local business to find out where the groomed trails are. And remember that the danger of avalanche increases greatly every time you leave the trail.

Eastern Idaho

The Big Holes

There are lots of riding options around here, but the best known are the Big Holes trails. The Big Holes offer 240 miles of groomed trails used mostly by snowmobilers, although in theory cross-country skiers and snowshoers are welcome. Located on the Targhee National Forest between Rexburg and Victor, Idaho, the Big Holes trails will someday be connected to the roughly 600 miles of snowmobile trails in the Island Park area. Right now the Big Holes trails see around 200 to 300 users per day in winter. Terrain varies from open, rolling valley floor to tree-lined mountain roads. Trails are well-marked. Call (208) 356-3101 for more information.

Island Park, Idaho

Island Park is eastern Idaho's snowmobiling mecca. Its generally high altitude — around 6,000 feet — keeps annual precipitation high. Most of this moisture falls as snow in December and January. Snow depths of 6 feet or more are typical.

Island Park maintains more than 400 miles of groomed main trail on top of 200 miles of irregularly groomed backcountry trails. These trails connect to the even larger maze of trails around West Yellowstone, Montana, which in turn lead to snowmobiling routes within Yellowstone National Park. The local trail maps are detailed and trails so well-marked that if you have basic winter survival and snowmachine repair skills, you'll have little need of a guide.

One popular destination is 8,710-foot-high Two Top Mountain, only about 9 miles from the northern end of Island Park. This trail is suitable for beginners, but experts find plenty of challenge in the off-trail bowls. The combination, plus the view from the top, attracts some 80,000 visitors a winter.

A shorter, easier daytrip takes you out to Upper Mesa Falls near Ashton. This trail is flat and fast, and at the end of your 30-mile trip from northern Island Park you're rewarded with the sight of water cascading over icicles and mist freezing into sparkles in the air over the 110-foot-high falls.

A pleasant half-day trip for beginners takes you out Big Springs Road to Big Springs, where you can feed the lunker rainbows and marvel at the river of clear, iceless water welling from the ground. Continue on Big Springs Road to loop back to U.S. Highway 20.

Another easy option is the Old Railroad Bed Trail, used by nordic skiers in winter and hikers and bikers in summer. Read about this pleasant beginner ride in our Hiking and Backpacking chapter.

Your adventures here are made more pleasant by the fact that every Island Park business you could want to get to can be reached by snowmobile. Also, warming huts are available on the Gallatin and Targhee national forests. For information or a trail map, try the Island Park Ranger District at (208) 558-7301.

Idaho Falls, Idaho, Area

More than 200 miles of marked and groomed trails lace the hills around the dryland farming community of Bone east of Idaho Falls on the Bone Road. From the perspective of the visiting snowmobiler, Bone consists of the Bone Store, a gas station and a cafe dropped in the middle of windswept miles of hills and plateaus. The rocky hills are cut by narrow canyons and softened by pockets of aspen.

Bonneville County maintains the trails, which are popular with locals. The volume of traffic can build sequences of hilly bumps on trails, forcing riders to slow. You can get trail maps from the snowmobile rental companies listed below or from the Eastern Idaho Visitor Information Center at 505 Lindsay Boulevard in Idaho Falls, (208) 523-1010.

Northwestern Wyoming

Cody snowmobilers can find groomed trails an hour's drive from town in three different locations. The Chief Joseph Highway (U.S. Hwy. 276) to the northwest leads to 57 miles of groomed trails and unlimited powder sledding in the Beartooth Mountains. To the west is Yellowstone National Park. The groomed trail, which begins at Pahaska Tepee, connects snowmobilers to the rest of Yellowstone Park's groomed trails. If you want to keep on going, you can go to the Flagg Ranch in Grand Teton National Park, or hook up to the Continental Divide Snowmobile Trail. To the east, in the Bighorns, you'll find miles of groomed trails.

Snowmobile Rentals

Yellowstone National Park

AmFac Parks and Resorts Mammoth Hotel Snowmobile Shop

Mammoth Hot Springs • (307) 344-7311

Old Faithful Snow Lodge Snowmobile Shop

Old Faithful • (307) 344-7311

For $115 per day ($130 for two) you can rent a snowmobile at either Mammoth or Old Faithful. Clothing rents for $16 per day. Children younger than 11 ride free as a double rider.

Jackson Hole

Flagg Ranch Resort

U.S. Hwy. 89 (John D. Rockefeller Jr. Memorial Pkwy.) • (307) 543-2861, (800) 443-2311

Rent 1998 Polaris 440s and 1999 Polaris 440s, 488s and 550s. The package price of $140 also includes a one-piece snowsuit, snowmobile boots, mittens and a helmet. One-day and multiple-day rentals are available. So are guided tours, but they're not popular, since the well-marked, well-mapped roads of Yellowstone National Park make self-guided snowmobiling easy.

The 90-mile trip to Old Faithful Inn and back generally takes a full day. Other visitor needs available here include lodging, a grocery store and a gas station.

Grand Teton National Park RV Resort

17800 E. U.S. Hwy. 287, Moran Wyo. • (307) 733-1980

Rent snowmobiles just 6 miles from the east entrance to Grand Teton National Park. Here you're poised to roll up Togwotee Pass to the Continental Divide Snowmobile Trail, other groomed terrain on Togwotee Pass, and to its endless powder bowls and meadows. Or head through Grand Teton National Park and up into Yellowstone's popular snowmobile trails.

Rentals are available with or without guides. Machines are 1998 Polaris 488s. Protective clothing and gear is included. With no guide, you pay $109 for a single rider. With a guide you pay $155.

Jackson Hole Snowmobile Tours

1000 S. U.S. Hwy. 89, Jackson, Wyo. • (307) 733-6850, (800) 633-1733

Machines are new every year. In 1998-99 they were Polaris Indy Trails. If you want someone else to do the thinking for you, these folks are ready. They'll pick you up in the morning, outfit you with all the necessary gear, teach you a few snowmobile basics and then guide you to Yellowstone National Park, Granite Hot Springs, the Togwotee Pass area or a custom two- to seven-day extended tour. All trips include a hot lunch cooked up by your guides. Trips range between $130 and $150 for the first rider; an additional adult rider costs $75.

Leisure Sports

1075 S. U.S. Hwy. 89, Jackson, Wyo. • (307) 733-3040

These folks rent 1999 Ski-Doos for $120 to $130 per day, depending on whether the machines hold one rider or two. Leisure Sports is situated 10 to 70 miles from the trailheads you'll be aiming for; if you don't have a trailer to transport your rented machines you can rent one here. If your vehicle is not four-wheel-drive or you lack a trailer hitch, you can rent the appropriate vehicle as well.

Eagle Rent-A-Car

375 N. Cache St., Jackson, Wyo. • (307) 739-9999, (800) 582-2128

This is one of two companies in Jackson that rent snowmobiles for unguided trips. In the winter of 1998-99, the rental fleet consisted of 1999 Polaris Trail RMKs and 700 RMKs. New machines are generally purchased every year. Rates are around $115 to $145 per day, depending on the machine and number of riders. Included in the base rate is your protective clothing and, if you rent two or more machines, your trailer rental.

Togwotee Snowmobile Adventures

650 W. Broadway Ave., Jackson, Wyo. • (307) 733-1418

The owners of the Cowboy Village Resorts in Jackson and on Togwotee Pass also run guided snowmobile tours and snowmobile/accommodations packages. The fleet consists of more than 200 1999 Polaris 488 Indy Trails and Polaris RMK 600s and 700s, the latter two being powder-performance sleds with larger engines, longer tracks and wider paddles.

Rides out of Jackson cost $155 per person; the second rider on a sled costs $75. Tours go to Yellowstone National Park, the Gros Ventres, nearby Granite Hot Springs and along the Grey's River south of Jackson Hole. Box lunches or lodge meals are provided. If you go to Granite Hot Springs, your admission to the hot pool is also included.

Surrounding Areas

Southwestern Montana

Backcountry Adventures

224 Electric St., West Yellowstone, Mont. • (406) 646-9317, (800) 924-7669

Rent a snowmobile with or without a guide at Backcountry Adventures snowmobile rentals. Jerry Johnson, owner of Backcountry, features a fleet of up-to-date Polaris snowmachines that rent from $79 to $134 per day depending on the model. He also rents clothing for $15 per day. If you're one of the 10 percent who want a guided trip into Yellowstone National Park, then Jerry can help you. His guides, knowledgeable about the park, will take you along for $175 per day.

Cooke City Exxon and Polaris/Ski-Doo

U.S. Hwy. 212, Cooke City, Mont. • (406) 838-2244

If you find yourself in this little burg without a sled, Cooke City Exxon has about 16 rentals that will run you from $125 to $150 per day, plus gas. A full suit of clothing and gear will cost you $30 for the day.

Gallatin Ridgetop Adventures

U.S. Hwy. 191, 1 mile south of Big Sky, Mont. • (406) 995-3333

Mike Schmidt, owner of Gallatin Ridgetop Adventures, has 30 Ski-Doo snowmobiles for rent during the winter. Although he doesn't guide snowmobile trips, he does know a lot about the trails in the area. Renting Schmidt's double-rider machine for one person costs $89; there's an additional $10 charge for a second rider. A higher-end single-rider costs $109 per day.

Travelers' Snowmobile Rentals

Madison Ave. and Electric St., West Yellowstone, Mont. • (406) 646-9561, (800) 548-9551

Owner Glen Loomis has a fleet of 200 mostly Polaris snowmachines. They rented from $89 to $149 per day in 1998. The faster you want to go, the more you'll pay. Loomis also rents snowmobile outfits and has bed-and-sled packages to go with his sleds.

Yellowstone Adventures

131 Dunraven St., West Yellowstone, Mont. • (406) 646-7735, (800) 231-5991

If you're looking for a bed-and-sled package, Yellowstone Adventures specializes in finding just what you want. Besides being a Ski-Doo dealer, Yellowstone Adventures offers clothing and snowmobile rentals. In 1998, its sleds rented for $79 to $156, which included your first tank of gas. This company has been around longer than any other snowmobile outfit in West Yellowstone.

Yellowstone Arctic/Yamaha

208 Electric St., West Yellowstone, Mont. • (406) 646-9636, (800) 646-7365

Mostly associated with three motels in town, the Yellowstone Arctic/Yamaha rents two kinds of snowmachines to walk-ins. It has a fleet of 140 machines in a range of models made by Arctic Cat and Yamaha. A snowmobile will cost you from $94 to $134 for a day. A complete snowmobile outfit rents for $17. The company offers a discount for bed-and-sled packages.

Yellowstone Tour and Travel

1211 Yellowstone Ave., West Yellowstone • (406) 646-9310, 646-9636 Oct. 1 to April 1, (800) 221-1151

Affiliated with three motels in town (the West Yellowstone Conference, The Three Bears, and the Big Western Pine), Yellowstone Tour and Travel books guided trips into and out of Yellowstone National Park. For out-of-park trips onto as many as 1,000 miles of groomed trails of national forest lands, Yellowstone Tour and Travel offers guides for an extra fee. The price of the package depends on the number of people in your party, the kind of sleds you choose, where you're going and where you stay.

Eastern Idaho

Action Motor Sports

1355 E. Lincoln Rd., Idaho Falls, Idaho • (208) 522-3050

Rent Polaris 440 Sports and Sport Touring models, plus a range of performance machines. Rates are cheaper on weekdays than on weekends, ranging from $65 to $120 per machine per day. If you rent two or more machines, the company will waive the $15 trailer rental fee. Pick up trail maps for Bonneville, Bingham and Fremont counties.

All Season Sports

160 W. Main St., Rexburg, Idaho • (208) 356-9245

Rent newer Arctic Cat and Yamaha snowmobiles from $75 to $100 per day. Trailers rent for around $20 unless you rent two machines, in which case the trailer is free. While you're here, make sure you pick up trail maps for the two most popular area destinations: the Big Holes trail system and the Island Park trails.

Basin Auto Snowmobile Rental

180 N. Main St., Driggs, Idaho • (208) 354-2297

This is the oldest company in the basin offering unguided snowmachine rentals. Rent brand-new snowmobiles for $119 per day. You can also rent trailers and snowmobile clothing and arrange a shuttle for your car or a drop-off for you and your sled. Ask about group rates and other discounts. Trail maps are available here; so is free information, since the employees are riders themselves. If you're not comfortable without a guide, these folks are happy to find you one, although they offer no guided trips of their own. Call to find out more about occasional special events such as Poker Runs and about the hundreds of miles of groomed snowmobile trails nearby.

Teton Mountain View Lodge

Idaho Hwy. 33 at Tetonia, Idaho • (208) 456-2741, (800) 625-2232

You can arrange for guided trips with a snowmobiler in Tetonia, but the well-marked, well-mapped Big Holes trail system starts practically outside the door of this unpretentious newer motel on the edge of Tetonia. Rent 1997 and 1998 Yamahas for between $85 and $124. Free maps of the Big Holes are available.

Northwestern Wyoming

Pahaska Tepee

183 Yellowstone Hwy., Cody, Wyo. • (307) 527-7701, (800) 628-7791

Pahaska has a fleet of snowmobiles that rent for $97 to $125 depending on the make, model and year of the snowmobile. The shop also rents clothing and gear. Situated at the east entrance of Yellowstone National Park, Pahaska Tepee offers a variety of snowmobile packages into the park. Among the packages available are three- and five-day guided and unguided trips, which include overnight stays not only at Pahaska, but also at Old Faithful or West Yellowstone or both.

Snowcoach Touring

Imagine a giant, glassed-in snowmobile, big enough to seat 10 people. That's a snowcoach. Another kind of snowcoach is a regular 13-person van mounted on snow tracks.

Yellowstone National Park

AmFac Parks and Resorts

AmFac Parks and Resorts offers regularly scheduled snowcoach tours between Old Faithful and South Gate, Mammoth Hot Springs and West Yellowstone, Montana. AmFac also has several sightseeing and skiing tours that last from three hours to all day. Besides wildlife viewing, snowcoach tours come with an informed guide who can tell you about what you're seeing.

Snowcoach passengers are limited to two

pieces of luggage plus cross-country ski equipment. Prices for scheduled ski drops in 1998-99 ranged from $6.50 to $10. All-day tours cost as much as $84 for adults and half that for children 11 and younger.

Jackson Hole

Flagg Ranch Village

U.S. Hwy. 89 (John D. Rockefeller Jr. Memorial Pkwy.) • (307) 543-2861, (800) 443-2311

All winter, snowcoaches run between Flagg Ranch Village and Old Faithful about 45 miles away. The daylong trip includes a hot lunch at Old Faithful Inn and interpretive talks from your guide. Children younger than 6 aren't allowed, primarily because they tend not to find the bumpy snowcoaches very comfortable. The price is $100 for adults.

Surrounding Areas

Southwestern Montana

West Yellowstone, Montana

Alpen Guides

555 Yellowstone Ave., West Yellowstone, Mont. • (406) 646-9591

With a fleet of seven snowcoaches, Alpen Guides will take you anyplace you want to go in Yellowstone National Park. Alpen offers daily tours from West Yellowstone to Old Faithful. Skiers have the option of being dropped off at Biscuit Basin, then skiing 2.5 miles through the geyser basin to the Old Faithful Lodge. Alpen also has daily tours to Canyon as well as a special wildlife tour that includes a two-night stay in West Yellowstone and a night at the Old Faithful Snow Lodge. On Wednesdays, Alpen will take you and your skis deep into the park for a day of cross-country skiing. A daily tour of Old Faithful costs $79 for an adult, while a Grand Canyon Tour costs $99.

Yellowstone Tour and Travel

1211 Yellowstone Ave., West Yellowstone, Mont. • (406) 646-9310, 646-9636 Oct. 1 to April 1, 800) 221-1151

Yellowstone Tour and Travel has a fleet of three snowcoaches that come with guides well-versed in area geology, ecology and biology. They'll take you almost anyplace in the park you want to go. See a previous entry for more information about Yellowstone Tour and Travel.

Sleigh Riding

Lone Mountain Ranch

Lone Mountain Rd., Big Sky, Mont. • (406) 995-4644, (800) 646-4644

This renowned cross-country ski center offers weekly sleigh rides over the creek and through the woods to their North Fork cabin where they can feed as many as 55 people a gourmet meal in a rustic setting. They take non-guests, but you'll have to make a reservation. Refer to our chapter on Guest Ranches for more information.

320 Guest Ranch

205 Buffalo Horn Creek, Gallatin Gateway, Mont. • (406) 995-4283, (800) 243-0320

For $28, adults can ride one of two ranch sleighs out to a camp set up in a wall tent. Once there, the folks in this woodstove-heated tent will serve you hors d'oeuvres like cowboy chili and popcorn, as well as hot drinks. If you want your hot chocolate spiked with Peppermint Schnapps, just ask. Rides leave the ranch at 5:30 and 7 PM and last for about an hour. The address is confusing because the 320 is actually south of Big Sky and nowhere near Gallatin Gateway near Bozeman.

INSIDERS' TIP

If you're traveling in Yellowstone country in winter, carry a little digging-out insurance in your trunk. Always pack a shovel and for traction add salt, kitty litter or sand. Salt will actually melt ice if the ambient temperature is greater than about 25 degrees. Kitty litter and sand provide gritty traction at any temperature.

Ice-Skating

Yellowstone National Park

Mammoth Hotel

Mammoth Hot Springs, Yellowstone National Park, Wyoming • (307) 344-7311

Each winter AmFac floods a rink near the hotel. The whole family can rent skates at the Mammoth Hotel for $1 per hour each or $4 per day.

Jackson Hole

Snow King Center Ice Rink

100 E. Snow King Ave., Jackson, Wyo. • (307) 733-5200

This big indoor ice rink operates from August to mid-April. Skate rentals, snacks and warm beverages are available on-site. Adults pay around $6 for the regularly scheduled public skate sessions. A less expensive Saturday session is often available. But call first: The rink hosts many sporting and other events, so ice times can change.

Surrounding Areas

Southwestern Montana

Beall Park

Villard and Black Sts., Bozeman, Mont.

You'll find recreational skating here most times and broomball on Tuesdays and Thursdays. This rink is open from 10 AM until 10 PM on weekends and noon until 10 PM on weekdays.

Bogert Park

325 S. Church, Bozeman, Mont.

This rink is reserved for hockey after 4 PM. Check the schedule for open-hockey use times.

Skate Palace

2015 Wheat Dr., Bozeman, Mont. • (406) 586-7770

Hockey and skating are big in Bozeman, and this is one of the town's busiest skating venues. Call to find out free skating hours.

Southside Park

West College Ave. and S. Fifth Ave., Bozeman, Mont.

This rink, open from noon until 10 PM weekdays and 10 AM to 10 PM weekends, offers recreational skating and hockey in an enclosed area.

West Yellowstone Skating Rink

Electric St., West Yellowstone

City officials flood an area for skating on Electric Street each winter.

Eastern Idaho

Idaho Falls, Idaho

Idaho Falls Hockey Shelter

Rollandet Ave. and Rogers St., Tautphaus Park, Idaho Falls, Idaho • (208) 529-0941

The Tautphaus (say it TOFF-us) Park hockey rink tries to schedule public skate time most days in winter, but they recommend you call and check before you drive over. This indoor rink is open November through March. Rink admission is around $3; skate rental is around $2.50. Although the rink doesn't have a snack concession, food and drink vending machines are available.

Horseback riding, mountain biking, golf, technical climbing — the Yellowstone region is a playground for these pastimes and more.

Other Recreation

You've come to a place where outdoor recreation is a key part of local culture. Look in residents' closets and basements and you'll find toys, toys and more toys. Even those of us who don't play hard figure we'll get around to it one of these days, maybe next weekend or next summer. And because so many of us are hooked either on the reality or the idea of enjoying outdoor recreational opportunities, you won't have trouble finding people who are happy to share what they know in order to hook you, too.

So on top of previous chapters' lures — skiing, snowmobiling, whitewater rafting, hiking, hunting and fishing adventures — this chapter takes some parting casts. What follows are a few more of the many recreational opportunities available in Greater Yellowstone: horseback riding, mountain biking, golf and technical climbing. Go ahead, take the bait. We all did.

Horseback Riding

There's something about climbing onto a half-ton of horse that's irresistible to some and unthinkable for others. If you happen to be one of those folks who dreams about riding the range on horseback, there are plenty of outfits glad to take you for a ride. Most offer a variety of options that includes one- and two-hour tours close to the corral and half- or full-day rides into some spectacular mountain country. Some will take you to a mountain lake for a few hours of fishing. Or they'll pack you in for a night or a week. Along the way, most outfitters will teach you things about Yellowstone country that you most likely wouldn't learn any other way.

Throughout Greater Yellowstone you'll see and hear plenty of advertisements for horseback riding. Climbing atop a horse is a wonderful way to travel up and into the backcountry. If you're on an overnight trip, chances are you'll sleep in a wall tent and eat food cooked over a campstove.

No matter where you ride in this neck of the woods, it's a cinch you'll climb a mountain on longer rides. Climbing or descending a steep mountain trail can be thrilling and scary. Outfitters select their horses for surefootedness and calm dispositions. Still, horses are powerful and unpredictable animals, and it's impossible to control all the variables that could cause accidents. Horses can be spooked by rolling rocks, mountain bikes and sudden movements. They can trip and tumble just like the rest of us. We have listed just a few outfitters that operate in the region. Wherever you are, we recommend that you do your own checking. Start by asking the local chamber of commerce if it has had complaints about a particular outfit.

Rates for horseback riding generally run between $15 and $20 per hour for the first hour. Most stables offer a range of rides, from an hour to a day or more. Unguided trips are sometimes possible and tend to be less expensive, but guided rides are more common. Horses and riders can be matched to riders' abilities; make sure the guide knows your ability level. Reservations are a good idea, particularly in summer. In addition to the stables listed below, many dude ranches (see our Guest Ranches chapter) offer day rides to nonguests. Few if any stables provide rides in winter. Most close down in September or October and open again in June.

Yellowstone National Park

AmFac Parks and Resorts
Mammoth, Yellowstone National Park
• (307) 344-7311

AmFac, Yellowstone National Park's largest concessionaire, leases 150 horses and hires more than 50 wranglers each summer to stock their three stables in the park. At Mammoth, Roosevelt and Canyon you can rent and ride a horse for one or two hours. In 1998, $19 bought a one-hour ride and $30 bought a ride twice that long. Wranglers will lead you and as many as 24 other riders on the trails surrounding the corrals.

AmFac also offers stagecoach rides for $5.95. Children ages 2 to 11 can ride for $4.95. Old West Cookouts, on which you can either ride a chuckwagon or horseback to the evening feast, cost $36 to $46 for horseback riders and $20 for those who ride in the wagon.

Grand Teton National Park

Colter Bay Village and Jackson Lake Lodge Corrals
Grand Teton National Park
• (307) 543-2811

The Grand Teton Lodge Company operates two riding corrals in Grand Teton National Park. A variety of park rides begin at these two stables, including breakfast rides, evening campfire rides and rides in horse-drawn wagons. All rides last one or two hours; all are guided. Reservations are strongly recommended. If you have kids, ask about the minimum age and size restrictions.

Scott's Jackson Hole Trail Rides
Teton Village, Wyo.
• (307) 733-6992, (307) 739-2753 Teton Village Guest Service Center

Choose from one-hour to all-day guided rides in Grand Teton National Park. This stable is located near the Moose-Wilson Road entrance to the park, which sees less traffic than other park roads. The Scott family has provided trail rides in various Jackson Hole locations since the early 1960s.

Jackson Hole

Many area guest ranches and some hunting outfitters also provide guided or unguided dayriding and multiple-day packtrips. The stables included below are not the only game in town. For more options, try our Resorts and Lodges, Guest Ranches or Hunting chapters.

A/OK Corral
U.S. Hwy. 89 near Hoback Junction, Wyo. • (307) 733-6556

Ten minutes south of Jackson enjoy guided trail rides, cowboy breakfast rides, evening steak dinner rides and covered wagon rides with a ranch family that's been breeding and raising horses around here since the 1870s. The Billings family will also take you horseback into Yellowstone National Park for a day or more. Transportation to and from Yellowstone is provided by the ranch. You can also ride directly from the ranch into the Gros Ventre Wilderness for one- to 10-day guided trips. Horseback fishing trips are also available.

Snow King Stables
400 E. Snow King Ave., Jackson, Wyo.
• (307) 733-5781

Ride an hour or all day out of these stables, which are located at the edge of Jackson in the Snow King Resort complex. Breakfast, lunch and evening steak rides can be arranged. Unguided rides can, too, at wranglers' and management's discretion. A one-hour ride will take you onto the flanks of Snow King

Mountain, with a view of Jackson Hole, the Tetons and Flat Creek winding through the National Elk Refuge. Two or three hours will take you to the top of the mountain and back. These folks have been in business here since the mid-1980s.

Two Ocean Pass Outfitting

Moran, Wyo.
• (307) 543-2309, (800) 726-2409

John Winter stages packtrips in the remote backcountry of the Bridger-Teton and Shoshone national forests and Yellowstone National Park. Trips can last from two days to 10. A typical trip has six to eight guests, but up to 20 is possible. Private trips can be arranged. John runs a hunting business in winter and has crisscrossed this area, summer and winter, since 1963. He is proud of his guides' levels of experience: The newest have been with him three years. He personally tries to spend at least a day with every packtrip.

Surrounding Areas

Southwestern Montana

West Yellowstone, Montana

Parade Rest Guest Ranch

7979 Grayling Creek Rd., West Yellowstone, Mont.
• (406) 646-7217, (800) 753-5934

Why ride from a corral next to the highway when you can drive a mere 8 miles to ride at the Parade Rest Guest Ranch? At Parade Rest, you'll find a variety of rides across flower-filled meadows, through timbered forests, below towering mountain peaks and beside beautiful Hebgen Lake. Parade Rest will fix you up with a horse suited to your ability, then take you riding for one to six hours, depending on what you want. Listen for their regular ads on the local radio station.

Gardiner, Montana

Hell's A Roarin' Outfitters

Jardine Rd., Gardiner, Mont.
• (406) 848-7578

In addition to one- or two-hour rides, Warren and Susan Johnson will take you for a half-day or full-day ride in the Absaroka-Beartooth Wilderness. Warren, born and raised in Jardine, knows the area well. He also leads multiple-day packtrips, which cost $200 per person per day. Daylong fishing trips are also an option, and cost $125 to $250.

Cooke City, Montana

Beartooth Plateau Outfitters

U.S. Hwy. 212, Main St., Cooke City, Mont. • (406) 838-2328 June through September, (800) 253-8545
Roberts, Mont.
• (406) 445-2293 October through May

While Beartooth Plateau Outfitters specializes in overnight packtrips into Yellowstone National Park during the summer and hunting in the fall, it is possible — and worth your while — to day-ride into the park. Occasionally, if you're having a lucky day, you can even walk in and find an empty saddle for the next day's ride. See our Hunting chapter for more information on this outfitter.

Bozeman, Montana

Broken Hart Ranch

73800 Gallatin Rd., Gallatin Gateway, Mont. • (406) 763-4279

During the summer, Lee Hart leads horseback riders on day and multiple-day trips in the Spanish Peaks Wilderness and the Gallatin Range. Lee, who has been outfitting since

INSIDERS' TIP

Your bike, boat, boots and broncs can bring foreign weed seeds, tiny snails or whirling disease from one place to another. Before entering national forest and national park lands or waters, think ahead and hose off your toys to avoid spreading weeds, disease or other problems in the ecosystem.

1969, offers folks customized trips that include daytrips into the backcountry, packtrips and sightseeing trips that take guests horseback to a cluster of private backcountry cabins in grizzly country. Hart's rates are among the most reasonable: A daytrip costs $200, which means if there are two of you, you'll each have to pay $100 for the day. If there are three of you, it will cost you each only $75.

Big Sky, Montana

Diamond K Outfitters Inc.

Rainbow Ranch Lodge, U.S. Hwy. 191 south of Big Sky, Mont.
• (406) 995-4132, (406) 995-4103

Operated by licensed Montana outfitter Chuck Kendall (he's also an elected member of the Montana Wilderness Council and a fifth-generation Montanan), Diamond K Outfitters runs trail rides out of a corral adjacent to the lovely Rainbow Ranch Lodge. (See our Resorts and Lodges chapter for more information on the Rainbow Ranch Lodge.) In addition to two-hour, half-day and daylong rides, Kendall features dinner rides, riding lessons, fishing trips and overnight packtrips.

Two-hour rides cost about $60, and half-day rides are $75 per person. Full-day rides and fishing trips cost $150 per person; for three people it's $130 per person. A two-hour Western horsemanship lesson will cost you $75, the same as an evening dinner ride. Kendall is licensed to pack into Yellowstone National Park backcountry. He specializes in tailoring his trips to your wants, needs and ability, and takes time for lighthearted education along the way.

Jake's Horses

U.S. Hwy. 191, 3 miles south of Big Sky, Mont. • (406) 995-4630, (800) 352-5956

Jake's Horses, owned by Jake and Katie Grimm, has been around longer than the Big Sky Ski Area. They've been leading guests down the trail on horseback since 1976. Jake's takes about 4,000 people a year for rides ranging from an hourlong tour to all-day and overnight packtrips in the wilderness and Yellowstone National Park. He also does dinner rides during the summer and sleigh rides (no dinner) in the winter. If that's not enough, he'll take you fishing at a high-mountain lake.

Jake uses 50 horses and about seven employees (including wranglers). He also runs a second horseback riding operation out of the Cinnamon Lodge south of Jake's on U.S. Highway 191.

A one-hour ride at Jake's with tax will cost you $23, while a full day will cost $105. Hayrides are $15 per person, and dinner rides are $53. Overnight packtrips range from $175 to $450 per person per day, depending on the number in your party and the duration of your trip. (The more people and the longer you stay, the less it is per day.)

Livingston, Montana

Bear Paw Outfitters

136 Deep Creek Rd., Livingston, Mont.
• (406) 222-5800, (406) 222-6642

Operated by the Bowers family from their ranch south of Livingston, Bear Paw offers horseback rides ranging from one-hour tours for $20 to overnighters into Yellowstone National Park for $200 per day. Bowers also has a deluxe summer tent camp high in the Absaroka mountains. Among the other options he offers are two-hour, half-day and full-day rides. (A day of riding and fishing in Yellowstone will cost you $160.) If you've got a hankering to ride through the park or pack into Slough Creek, these people are a good bet. Bowers has his guests meet him at the trailhead. (For information on Bear Paw's fall hunting operation, see our Hunting chapter.)

INSIDERS' TIP

Sport climbers can find well-protected basalt cragging just outside Idaho Falls near Heise Hotsprings. Local climbers call the area Paramount. Routes start at around a difficulty rating of 5.8. Near Jackson, sport climbers can ask about routes on Blacktail Butte or an area near Hoback Junction called The Shields. Both are on limestone; difficulty is mostly 5.10 and up.

Photo: Randy Hayes, Post Register

Golfers at Teton Pines enjoy a spectacular view of the Tetons.

Eastern Idaho

Teton Valley

Bustle Creek Outfitters

Ski Hill Rd., Alta, Wyo.
• (307) 353-2300, (800) 827-4433

Ride for an hour or three days; learn Western or English-style riding. Rides and riding lessons are booked with and originate from Grand Targhee Ski and Summer Resort.

Beard Outfitters

Leigh Canyon, Wyo.
• (307) 576-2694

Joe Beard, born and raised in Teton Valley, guides hourlong or daylong rides from the family ranch and out onto the west flank of the Tetons. You'll ride the same horses he and his family use for winter commercial hunting trips. Call a week in advance to make sure Joe and his horses are available.

Island Park, Idaho

Harriman State Park

Off U.S. Hwy. 20, south of Island Park, Idaho • (208) 558-7077, (208) 624-7777

Tom Angell of St. Anthony's Halo Ranch brings some of his working ranch horses to Harriman State Park every summer. He and his guides offer a variety of rides ranging from steep, high-altitude trail riding to a gentle loop around game-rich Silver Lake. Dinner rides begin about 4 PM and last until dusk. You'll stop at the headwaters of Golden Lake for a Dutch-oven feast of spare ribs, scalloped potatoes and hot scones. Reservations are recommended but not required for any ride except the Dutch-oven dinner trip. Tom's 14-year-old business is the only stable authorized to conduct trail rides in wildlife-rich Harriman.

Idaho Falls, Idaho, Area

Granite Creek Guest Ranch

U.S. Hwy. 26 east of Idaho Falls, Idaho
• (208) 538-7140

This little family-owned guest ranch just a short drive out of Idaho Falls offers guided trail rides and cattle drives; rides accommodate all skill levels. Half-hour pony rides for kids are also available.

Northwestern Wyoming

Bill Cody Ranch

2604 Yellowstone Hwy., Cody, Wyo.
• (307) 587-6271

Midway between Cody and Yellowstone

National Park, the Bill Cody Ranch offers regular ranch rides from two hours to a full day. Owners Jamie and John Parson maintain a herd of 60 horses and use 14 different mountain trails leading into the Shoshone National Forest. All-day rides include lunch. If you plan ahead, you can have dinner at the end of the day in the ranch's old-fashioned dining room. See our Guest Ranches chapter to learn more about this popular ranch.

Gateway Ranch
Yellowstone Hwy., Cody, Wyo.
• (307) 587-6507, (307) 527-5981

Speed Spiegelberg has been taking folks for rides since 1955. Located halfway between Cody and the Stampede Rodeo Grounds west of town, Spiegelberg employs a wrangler these days to lead trips either into the canyon below the ranch or up onto the mountain. Hourlong trips head downhill; the rest head up. Spiegelberg charges $15 per hour for rides up to four hours. Check with him on his rates for longer rides. If you can't reach him at the numbers listed above, try his cell phone at (307) 272-2555 from 6 AM to 5 PM.

Mountain Biking

Mountain biking opportunities abound in Greater Yellowstone, mostly outside Yellowstone and Grand Teton parks. Below are general overviews for some of the better mountain biking areas in the region, as well as information on shops that sell or rent gear.

Rentals generally cost between $15 and $25 for a full day. Hourly or half-day rates are often available. Be sure you ask what comes with your rental; generally you can expect a bike pump and helmet. Some shops throw in a spare tube, maps and even water bottles. Also be sure you are paying for the kind of bike you want. Performance bikes will have different gear ratios and suspension systems than standard bikes. They'll also rent for up to twice as much. If you plan to simply cruise around on level dirt roads, you probably don't need to pay for the whistles and bells.

Bike shops are fine sources of information about area trails; most welcome your call. They may also provide guided tours or be able to suggest a reputable company that does. Competent bikers probably need little more than directions and a spare inner tube, but beginners or those who've never mountain biked in remote settings may be comforted by the presence of an instructor/guide. Restrictions and weather-related trail obstacles may exist, so be sure to ask locally about your chosen route, even if it's one described below. We've provided you with phone numbers to assist your information gathering.

Yellowstone National Park

Except for early spring and late fall, when the park is closed to motorized vehicles and roads are free of snow, biking on today's park roads is generally discouraged because many of the roads are barely wide enough for vehicles without adding bicycles to the equation. The updated roads are improved with a few feet of shoulder, but remember that there are lots of oversized recreational vehicles on the road and many drivers are busy looking for wildlife — not bicyclists. These riding obstacles don't discourage some riders, especially Europeans. If you're one of those determined to bike the park during the peak of tourist season, we recommend you check in with the local experts to learn every possible tip for surviving the highways of Yellowstone. Otherwise, try biking the park during the in-between

INSIDERS' TIP

Some experts believe that mountain biking in bear country is made safer by noisemaking devices on your bike (remember that card you slipped between the spokes when you were a kid?) because otherwise you're moving so fast and so silently that bears may be taken by surprise. A surprised bear can be dangerous.

seasons. In spring, when grizzlies coming out of hibernation are concentrated in the area, bikers aren't allowed to travel the road between Madison Junction and Old Faithful. That time of year, the road between Madison and Norris is also pocked with potholes.

There are no offroad biking opportunities in the park. You can pedal on the few one-way side roads depicted on park maps, as well as a 1-mile trail to the natural bridge at Bridge Bay. Yellowstone National Park bike passes cost $10.

Grand Teton National Park

Like those in cars, bicyclists need a park pass to enter Grand Teton National Park. Bike passes cost $10. Once inside, you must stay on designated roads and trails. Off-trail riding is not permitted, and the park offers very little single track for bikers. This means if you're looking for technical riding, you'll fare better on surrounding national forest lands. Grand Teton National Park's roads are more bike-friendly than Yellowstone's, mostly because road shoulders are more generous. It helps, too, that drivers seem a tad less likely to be staring out the passenger side window at a bison instead of at you and the road.

One pleasant beginner ride is the Antelope Flats loop, a flat 12-mile ride that, unfortunately, runs mostly on narrow, poorly shouldered roads. It takes you past historic Mormon Row, including the famous Moulton barn, which by now you've seen on local postcards and posters. One leg of this ride is on gravel road.

A better (read: wider) road for a flat loop ride is the Jenny Lake loop. This 15-mile ride, all on pavement, leaves the Teton Park Road adjacent to String Lake and loops down toward lovely Jenny Lake. You'll be pedaling almost at the feet of the spectacular Tetons. Remember that those fabulous views also distract the many drivers passing you.

A third option, which takes you away from the main park thoroughfares, is Shadow Mountain, a 7-mile loop ride on gravel road that climbs and loops its namesake mountain. Good technical mountain bikers should ask about the single-track route that drops off the top of Shadow Mountain, rejoining the main route near the starting area.

For more information, call Grand Teton National Park (307) 739-3300, or the folks at Adventure Sports (listed below).

Adventure Sports

Dornan's at Moose, Grand Teton National Park, Wyo. • (307) 733-3307

Mountain bikes by Diamond Back, Cannondale, Giant and Marin are available for rent or sale. Rentals are the current year's models. Bikes are available for half- and full days. Staff can provide area maps and ideas for rides suitable to your skill and fitness levels. They'll also provide shuttle, pickup and dropoff services if you're renting their gear.

Adventure Sports is open seven days a week in summer, but hours can vary in spring and fall. In winter it's closed.

Jackson Hole

Outside Grand Teton National Park it's easier to find technical biking. Old logging roads provide miles of two-track; hiking trails make for even more single track. Be aware that any trail open to bikers is typically open to horseback riders as well. If you encounter horses, move off the trail to let them pass. Horses can be made extremely nervous by new and unpredictable things.

One popular but strenuous and technical loop is the 18-mile-long Cache Creek ride, which goes up Cache Creek Road, turns single track and includes a steep ascent and matching technical descent. You return to Jackson on Game Creek Road.

Another strenuous, less technical ride is the Old Teton Pass Road. It roughly parallels Wyo. Highway 22's ascent of Teton Pass between Idaho and Wyoming. This 11-mile route is extremely popular with both bikers and hikers, so don't look for solitude here. A good beginner ride is an out-and-back trip of whatever length you like on the Elk Refuge's dirt road, accessed from Broadway in Jackson. Runners and bikers are the main users of this road in summer, although the occasional passing car will kick up some dust.

For more information, call any of the bike

and bike rental shops listed below in this section.

Hoback Sports

40 S. Millward St., Jackson, Wyo. • (307) 733-5335

Rent Specialized, Trek and Voodoo performance mountain bikes, including full-suspension bikes, pick up area trail maps or sign up for a mountain bike tour here. Fat Tire Tours ride directly from the store either to the Elk Refuge or use lift-assist to get up Snow King Mountain. This second, more technical ride descends the backside of Snow King Mountain on a single track trail.

Teton Mountain Bike Tours

Jackson, Wyo. • (307) 733-0712, (800) 733-0788

This company will rent you a mountain bike and deliver it free to your Jackson area motel or condo, but their specialty is guided tours. Tour Yellowstone and Grand Teton national parks and the Bridger-Teton National Forest. Tours range from three to nine hours, cost roughly $10 per person per hour, and accommodate all skill levels. Families can even rent Burley child trailers and bring along kids too young to ride. Instruction is available for beginners.

Wilson Backcountry Sports

Fish Creek Center, Wilson, Wyo. • (307) 733-5228

Only 10 minutes from Jackson, you can ride out of this shop at the base of Teton Pass and right onto the trails that loop through the area. Bikes are this year's Gary Fishers. You can also pick up local trail maps and lots of free advice here, as well as bike clothing and accessories. Bike repair is available.

Surrounding Areas

Southwestern Montana

West Yellowstone, Montana

Mountain biking is getting to be a popular pastime in West Yellowstone. The chamber sponsors two annual races: One early in October is in the park; the other, in April, goes past Hebgen, Wade and Henry's lakes, over Targhee Pass and back into West Yellowstone. Both begin at the Chamber of Commerce. The array of biking options in and around West Yellowstone is way too long to list here. We assume if you're a mountain biking mogul you'll bring your own bike and head for the nearest bike shop to find out what's what. For those of you who are more casual, the Rendezvous Ski Trails bordering town are used for biking during the summer months. This 40-kilometer trail system loops over and around rolling hills and through timber for riding that will pump up your heart.

Local bike shops listed below can supply you with maps outlining a whole series of popular local loop roads and trails. We also recommend that you check with the Hebgen Lake Ranger District, U.S. Highway 191 N., West Yellowstone. The phone number is (406) 646-7369.

Free Heel 'n Wheel

40 Yellowstone Ave., West Yellowstone, Mont. • (406) 646-7744

Owners Kelli Criner and Melissa Buller rent new Trek and Specialized bikes. Occasionally, you'll find a women's ride out of the shop. These two are avid riders and go-getters. They can tell you where to go depending on your ability.

Yellowstone Bicycles

132 Madison Ave., West Yellowstone, Mont. • (406) 646-7815

Leslie and Gay McBirnie have been selling and renting bicycles in West Yellowstone since 1967. Not only do they have a variety of bikes for rent, including recumbents and tandems, but also packs come free of charge with an extended rental for touring the park.

Bozeman, Montana

Bozeman is a mountain biking mecca with as many options as there are old logging roads and trails. Two of the hot spots in the area, though, center around the Bridger Mountains to the north and Hyalite Basin to the south. (See our Fishing and Watersports chapter for more about Hyalite Reservoir.) Hyalite, about 15 miles south of Bozeman, offers so many rides you could take a different one each day for weeks. Some of the more popular trails are loaded with hikers, bikers and horseback riders, while on others you'll barely see another soul.

For specific information about trails, we recommend you stop in at one of the rental shops listed below or the Bozeman Ranger District office at 3710 Fallon, Bozeman, or call (406) 587-6920. Another good place to start is reading *Fat Tracks of Bozeman: 39 Great Mountain Bike Rides* by Will Harmon (Falcon Press).

Bangtail Bicycle and Ski

508 W. Main St., Bozeman, Mont.
• (406) 587-4905

For bike (and ski) sales, rentals and information, Bangtail is a great place to stop. During the summer, Bangtail rents Rockhoppers. They don't offer guided rides here, but check at the shop to see about scheduled weekly rides. In 1998, Bangtail organized a regular Monday-night ride. On Wednesdays women rode together, and on Thursdays it was the men's turn. Bangtail sells Trek and Specialized bikes. For information about Bangtail's cross-country ski rentals, see our Winter Sports chapter.

Panda Sports Rental

621 Bridger Dr., Bozeman, Mont.
• (406) 587-6280

This convenience store/gas station rents bikes, river rafts, canoes, skis, and avalanche transceivers.

Big Sky, Montana

Mountain biking around Big Sky, where the Madison and Gallatin ranges wall in the narrow Gallatin Canyon, can be extreme with plenty of old logging roads and trails from which to choose. Trails on Porcupine Creek, in the Beehive Basin and the North Fork Drainage are among local favorites. To get the inside scoop on trails — new ones seem to pop up as soon as someone tries, likes and talks about them — we recommend you talk to someone in a local bike shop or to someone at the Bozeman Ranger District, 3710 Fallon, Bozeman, Montana, (406) 587-6920.

Grizzly Outfitters

1700 Big Sky Rd., Big Sky, Mont.
• (406) 995-2939

Big Sky's only full-service bike shop, Grizzly Outfitters offers 40 bikes for rent. Owner Ken Lancey is also a storehouse of information about mountain biking in the area. Rentals range from standard mountain-bike to high-performance-bike packages. Grizzly also offers a reduced rate for kids' packages ($6 per hour), as well as Burley bike trailers for (two) tots. Grizzly rents downhill and cross-country skis, too (see our Winter Sports chapter).

Gallatin Alpine Sports

3090 Pine Dr., West Fork Meadows,
Big Sky, Mont. • (406) 995-2313

In addition to bike rentals, this loaded-to-the-gills sport shop also rents camping, skiing, and canoeing gear. Bikes — all top of the line — rent from $23 to $30 per day depending on what kind of cycle you want to pedal up the mountain. Gallatin Alpine is open year round, seven days a week.

Livingston, Montana

When it comes to biking, Livingston is a little lacking, not because of the terrain, but because access to the mountains is pretty much blocked by private property. Most dedicated riders (there are about a dozen in the area) have to load up their bikes and haul them somewhere, often to the Gallatin Valley, to find a challenging or accessible trail.

Chico Hot Springs

Chico Rd., Pray, Mont. • (406) 333-4933

At the Chico Hot Springs Lodge barn you can rent bicycles. Roads and trails lead away from the lodge, or you can load up your bike and head for other trails in the area. Shop

INSIDERS' TIP

Check out any outfitter or service provider's complaint record with the Better Business Bureau. In Greater Yellowstone, the number is (800) 657-6450.

manager Melissa Taylor knows the area well and can steer you in the right direction.

Saddle Sore Cycles

117 W. Callender St., Livingston, Mont.
• (406) 222-2628

Storrs Bishop sells, repairs, rides and rents mountain bikes. The more days you keep a bike, the less he charges by the day. Bishop mostly rents to out-of-towners who want to fly in, ride through the park, then over 11,000-foot Beartooth Pass. If you want to know what's up with biking in the area, Saddle Sore Cycles is the place to start.

Eastern Idaho

Teton Valley

Teton Valley is bikers' heaven, if you don't mind climbing. Lift-assisted technical rides can be had at Grand Targhee Ski and Summer Resort. For the less daring, Grand Targhee has easy trails that wind through the wildflower meadows of Rick's Basin. On the valley floor, loops can be built from the dirt roads that crisscross the valley, taking you through rolling farmland and past recreational cabins. Valley rides offer views of the peaks that ring Teton Basin. Some carry you past scenic Teton River and its wildlife viewing opportunities. In the Big Holes and the Tetons themselves, old logging roads and newer hikers' trails offer challenging, strenuous riding.

The Horseshoe Canyon area west and northwest of Driggs offers three good beginner or intermediate rides. The Big Hole Challenge trail is single-track with few obstacles, so it's suitable for intermediates. The trail begins as a gravel road, becomes two-track then single track. The first part of the 12.5-mile ride is uphill; the downhill is fairly steep but not very technical. Enjoy good Teton views and heavily forested sections. The Grand View Point intermediate ride is a bit longer. It takes off from the end of Packsaddle Road. Since it's mostly two-track, some beginners may enjoy this ride as well, but they may find themselves walking parts of the climb. You'll ride through forest and wheat field and stop for panoramic views of the Snake River Plain and the Teton range. The Horseshoe Canyon loop itself is a good beginner ride. It begins where Packsaddle Road ends. Cross the cattleguard and simply pedal up the Forest Service road beyond. Cars occasionally use this road. Trails branch off to provide additional options for more advanced riders. The Horseshoe Canyon loop, like most rides in Teton Valley, involves climbing. You can complete it in about two hours.

For more information, call Grand Targhee Ski and Summer Resort at (307) 353-2300, (800) 827-4433 or one of the businesses listed below.

Peaked Sports

70 E. Little Ave., Driggs, Idaho
• (208) 354-2354, (800) 705-2354

Peaked is the valley's Schwinn headquarters in summer. The shop rents mountain bikes (included are helmet, extra tube, seat pack, pump, patch kit, bottle cages and advice about where to go). Two-hour, four-hour, per-day and multiple-day rates are available. You can rent standard or performance Schwinn models. You can also rent bike trailers so you can haul small children along. And since many rides necessitate a drive to the start point, the shop rents mount-on-your-car bike racks. Bike repair is also available. Peaked closes Sundays in summer.

Teton Teepee Lodge

Ski Hill Rd., Alta, Wyo.
• (307) 353-8176, (800) 353-8176

Teton Teepee Lodge (see our Resorts and Lodges chapter) rents Research Dynamics mountain bikes by the hour, half-day and day. The shop also provides a guide service that includes transportation, bike rental and snacks. They can personalize tours to your skill level and interests. Bike tours cost about $30 per hour. Teton Teepee Lodge is just inside the Wyoming border near Driggs, Idaho.

Swan Valley, Idaho

The biking terrain around mountain-walled Swan Valley is mostly steep. Both single and double track are available. Plenty of good riding exists on Pine Creek Pass between Teton Valley and Swan Valley. For instance,

5-mile-long gravel Rainey Creek Road travels along a ridge between the pass and the top of the North Fork of Rainey Creek. Here it connects to a maze of technical single-track trails that can drop you down into Swan Valley or past Fourth of July Peak and down into Teton Valley.

Other, shorter two-track roads along Idaho Highway 31 on Pine Creek Pass include the road up Mike Spencer Canyon and one that heads up Fleming Canyon. Some folks like to ride the lower stretches of the Palisades Lakes Trail, which originates on the valley floor. Read about this popular trail in our Hiking and Backpacking chapter.

For more information on mountain biking in the Swan Valley area, call the Palisades Ranger District, (208) 523-1412, or Idaho Mountain Trading in Idaho Falls, Idaho, at (208) 523-6679.

Island Park, Idaho

What in winter is hundred of miles of snowmobile trails becomes, in summer, nearly endless opportunity for mountain bikers. Much of what is available is two-track and fairly level because much of Island Park is a gently rolling plateau. Often you'll find yourself on dirt roads also used by cars. To avoid traffic, bike in early mornings, on weekdays or in the fall.

One place you won't encounter cars is the Old Railroad Bed Trail. Read the description of the 50-plus miles of this gently graded trail in our Hiking and Backpacking chapter. The Old Railroad Bed Trail connects the Warm River in Idaho with West Yellowstone, Montana. In early summer, downed trees and boggy spots create a bit of hassle for riders, but by midsummer and into fall, riding this trail is like riding on soft sidewalk through lodgepole forest, wildflower meadow, over trestle bridges and even through an old railroad tunnel. If you start at the Black Canyon Loop Road or Big Springs Road, you can ride some 30 miles of almost continuous, mostly gentle downhill track to Warm Springs.

At Harriman State Park south of Island Park, enjoy some 20 miles of trails designated for nonmotorized use only. Both steep and level riding are available here. To learn about Harriman's hiking/biking trails, call (208) 558-7368.

For information on other rides in the area, call the Island Park Ranger District at (208) 558-7301, or the Island Park Chamber of Commerce, (307) 558-7755.

Idaho Falls, Idaho, Area

Idaho Falls seems flat as Kansas, so it may surprise you to learn that the surrounding area is laced with mountain biking trails. Trails are clustered around Taylor Mountain, Kelly Canyon near the South Fork of the Snake, Tex Creek and the tiny town of Bone. Most of these roads involve pleasant combinations of moderate or extreme climbs up out of canyons and long, mellow plateau or canyon-floor sections. Sometimes roads become deeply rutted by autos that travel them too soon after spring runoff or heavy rains.

Trails around Kelly Canyon are named and well-marked. Their difficulty ranges from beginner to upper-intermediate. One popular beginner/intermediate ride called Buckskin Morgan follows the ridge directly across from the Kelly Canyon ski hill. It's a two-hour ride offering great views from the ridgetop and the strong possibility that you'll see moose. In the same area, several intermediate but very strenuous rides climb to the radio tower at the top of Kelly Mountain. From there you can see Palisades Dam, Idaho Falls and the Snake River as it winds between the two. Within riding distance of town, check out rides that range from beginner to expert around Black's Canyon. Black's Canyon is between Foothill Road

INSIDERS' TIP

The nine-hole Livingston Golf Club may have been the first to be established in what is now called the Greater Yellowstone area. It was created in 1900 and was called the Yellowstone Golf Club. You'll find it along the Yellowstone River on View Vista Drive in Livingston. The phone number is (406) 222-1031, and the greens fee is $14.

Photo: Robert Bower, Post Register

A mountain climber takes a practice climb near the town of Jackson, Wyoming, not far from the Grand Teton Mountain Range

and the Bone Road. Rides start at the little parking area atop Lincoln Hill; the canyon is just south. Two-track beginner rides run along the canyon floor and at the rim. Advanced trails link the two, mostly along the north wall. Use them to build loops that range from 2 to 12 miles.

For more information on rides in the area, call the bike shops, listed in this section.

Bill's Bike Co.

805 S. Holmes Ave., Idaho Falls, Idaho • (208) 522-3341

Rent Specialized front or full suspension mountain bikes, usually this year's models. You can rent bike trailers and buy local trail books here, as well. This shop also provides maintenance on all makes, including BMX and road bikes. They sell Specialized, Trek, Raleigh and Haro mountain bikes. Most of Bill's employees are riders and can tell you about area trails. The shop is closed Sundays.

Idaho Mountain Trading

474 Shoup Ave., Idaho Falls, Idaho • (208) 523-6679

Rent Fisher mountain bikes, both standard and high-end full-suspension models. Bike and in-line skate mechanics are on duty to handle your repair problems and to keep the rentals serviced regularly. The shop has been selling and renting outdoor toys since 1978.

Northwestern Wyoming

Mountain biking in the Cody area is growing as fast as everywhere else. Among the favorite biking haunts is the McCullough Peak area about 7 miles east of town. Managed by the Bureau of Land Management (BLM), this is both a wild-horse management area and a wilderness-study area. That means mountain bikers must ride the boundary trails and roads, which are intersected by scattered chunks of private property, some of which offer public access and others of which do not. To be sure about where you're going, we suggest you stop in at BLM's Cody Resource Area office at 1002 Blackburn, Cody, Wyoming, or call (307) 587-2216.

Other biking areas include trails on the North Fork of the Shoshone (U.S. Highway 20 west of Cody) and Carter Mountain south of town. For the latter ride, locals have a friend shuttle them to the top so that they can coast down through the trees, across streams and over meadows.

You'll find a strong women's biking group in Cody, mostly centered around Olde Faithful Bicycles. We recommend you stop in at Olde Faithful Bicycles, listed below; the BLM listed earlier in this entry; or the Wapiti Ranger District Office, 203 Yellowstone Avenue, Cody, (307) 527-6921, for more information about mountain biking in the Cody area.

Also, to keep up on pedaling in the Cody area, you can subscribe to Olde Faithful's *Chainletter* (see the entry below for more information).

Olde Faithful Bicycles
1362 Sheridan Ave., Cody, Wyo.
• (307) 527-5110

Olde Faithful Bicycles rents, sells and fixes bikes of all kinds. Doug and Leslie Shinaver, owners of this busy biking hub, not only rent mountain bikes, but they also know every good trail or road in the area. The Shinavers publish *Chainletter*, an occasional newsletter full of humor, bike-maintenance tips and information about races and good mountain-biking trails. Behind the store is the Cody BMX Track.

Technical Climbing and Mountaineering

Technical climbing is defined as any rock climbing where ropes or other devices are used to protect climbers or to assist them in their ascent. Devices include bolts drilled into rock, pitons that climbers hammer into rock, or ice axes they carry. Mountaineering is climbing and more: It involves route-finding and other backcountry skills as well as technical rock — and often ice or snow — climbing. Many mountaineering routes take two or more days to complete. Climbing and mountaineering should only be undertaken by individuals in good physical condition, equipped with the right skills, the proper gear and knowledge of the area.

Although interesting technical climbing areas exist all over Greater Yellowstone, the region is best known for the granite, ice and snow climbs of the Tetons. Many are serious, multiple-pitch mountaineering routes. Some are world-class, drawing skilled climbers from all over the planet. The sheer peaks of the Teton range offer so much opportunity for classic climbs that some routes are still waiting to be put up.

Several books are available on Teton climbs. The most comprehensive is probably Leigh Ortenburger and Reynold Jackson's *A Climber's Guide to the Teton Range*. It details routes but also describes the climbing history of these famous peaks.

Beginners and less experienced climbers can and do experience the exhilaration of Teton climbing. Smart ones use a competent guide. Some experts argue that even highly skilled climbers new to the Tetons should hire a guide

INSIDERS' TIP

Most of Yellowstone country is 6,000 feet or higher above sea level. If you live at low altitude and are older, or if you suffer from heart or respiratory difficulties, it's a good idea to consult your doctor before you come here. Even the physically fit and healthy may find themselves unusually short of breath for several days.

their first time or two out, especially if they're planning big ascents like the Grand Teton. Either of the well-known climbing schools listed in the next section offer both instruction and guiding services.

Climbing is discouraged in Yellowstone National Park because of the loose, crumbling rock. It is outlawed altogether in the Grand Canyon of the Yellowstone River area.

Climbing Schools and Guide Services

Exum Mountain Guides

South Jenny Lake, Grand Teton National Park, Wyo. • (307) 733-2297

In summer, Exum offers basic and intermediate classes daily near Hidden Falls on the backside of Jenny Lake. Climbers can arrange guided trips up the Grand or any other peak in the Tetons, summer or winter, on ice, rock or snow. The company also leads climbs and treks into the remote Wind River Range. Exum is named after Glenn Exum, who as a young man in 1931 made a dramatic solo ascent of the Grand Teton along a ridge that now also bears his name.

Jackson Hole Mountain Guides

165 N. Glenwood St., Jackson, Wyo. • (307) 733-4979, (800) 239-7642

These folks offer daily climbing classes year-round on rock, ice and snow. They'll also take individuals or small groups up any skill-appropriate route in the Tetons. Beginners who wish to summit the Grand Teton may like the four-day climbing program: Hike to 11,000 feet one day, spend the next training and practicing, take another day to reach the summit and on the last day return to the valley floor. Each night is spent on the mountain's flank, so you also get accustomed to altitude. This company offers sport climbing classes in the area, as well as small-group climbing trips into the Wind Rivers.

Climbing Gyms

Jackson, Wyoming, hosts a fine climbing gym, as do Idaho Falls, Idaho, and Bozeman, Montana. Climbing gyms provide vertical and overhung walls pegged with rocklike hand- and footholds for climbing practice. They're made safe with ropes attached to chains at the ceiling and, of course, by your friend or instructor, who "belays" from the working end of the rope. Grand Targhee Ski and Summer Resort puts up holds on a lift tower close to the base lodge every summer. Any of the four are fine places to try out a new sport.

Teton Rock Gym, 1116 Maple Way, Jackson, Wyoming, (307) 733-0707, and **Stone Walls**, 751 S. Capital Avenue, Idaho Falls, Idaho, (208) 528-8610, both offer instruction as well as a place for serious climbers to hone their skills or get a winter workout. Both are described in our Attractions chapter.

Bozeman Climbing Center, 1408 Gold Avenue, Bozeman, Montana, (406) 582-0756, varies its hours according to the season and offers a variety of classes for people of all ages.

For more on Grand Targhee's outdoor climbing wall, call the resort at (307) 353-2300 or (800) 827-4433.

Golf

Golf is not what most people think of when they start packing for a Greater Yellowstone vacation, but the region is not without good reasons to bring those spikeless shoes. Municipal courses, some pleasantly mature, others relaxed and funky, allow play for prices

INSIDERS' TIP

National Forest trails can change dramatically due to weather or lack of maintenance — especially with federal budget cutbacks. To avoid encountering problems, be sure to check with a local national forest ranger district office or visitor center about trail conditions.

that may surprise you — some are as reasonable as $10. The region's resort towns are home to award-winning courses (with the higher greens fees you'd expect). Greater Yellowstone courses often make use of the lovely mountain scenery to enhance the beauty of their courses. In winter, many of these courses are laced with cross-country ski trails (see our Wintersports chapter). Below are a few highlights to pique your interest and convince you to toss those shoes in the suitcase.

Jackson Hole

Jackson Hole Golf and Tennis Club
5000 N. Spring Gulch Rd., Jackson, Wyo. • (307) 733-3111

Like the fine dining and fine art galleries of this little resort valley, Jackson Hole's golf courses are world-class. *Golf Digest* says this one is among the top-10 resort courses in the country. Course designer Robert Trent Jones built water hazards on 11 of 18 holes. Each hole provides fine views of the mountain ranges that ring this valley.

The par 72 course is rated 72.5 with a slope of 126 from the championship tees. It measures 6756 from the white tees. Reserving tee times is recommended. No metal spike shoes are allowed. Greens fees range between $50 and $100, depending on season and time of day.

Teton Pines Resort and Country Club
3450 N. Clubhouse Dr., Jackson, Wyo. • (208) 733-1733 for tee times

This award-winning course just 6 miles west of Jackson off Teton Village Road was designed by Arnold Palmer. It was built in 1987. Teton Pines is open to the golfing public in summer and to nordic skiers in winter. The 18-hole, par 72 course is rated 74.8 with a slope of 137 from the gold championship tees. It measures 6330 from the white tees.

Please wear spikeless shoes; if you don't have any, a few complimentary pair are available for use. Soft-Spikes™ conversions are also available for a small fee. Greens fees range between $50 and $140 depending on season and day. Lodge guests receive a discount. Lessons are available for $65 to $80 per hour. Reservations are strongly recommended.

Surrounding Areas

Southwestern Montana

Bozeman, Montana

Bridger Creek Golf Course
2710 McIlhattan Rd., Bozeman, Mont. • (406) 586-2333

Voted by *Golf Digest* as one of the 10 best courses in Montana, the Bridger Creek Golf Course combines the best of town and country. It's situated at the base of the Bridger Mountains and is still only minutes from downtown Bozeman. The trout-filled East Gallatin River and Bridger Creek bisect or border the lower holes. The upper holes feature views of the Gallatin Valley as well as four of Montana's more spectacular mountain ranges. At the clubhouse you'll find a pro shop with cart rentals ($10 for nine holes), space for catered group outings, and friendly service. Greens fees for nine holes are $14 weekends and $12 weekdays. For 18 holes, the fees are $24 and $22. Bridger Creek Golf Course is open from about April 1 to November 1.

Big Sky, Montana

Big Sky Ski and Summer Resort
Mountain Village, Big Sky, Mont. • (406) 995-5000, (800) 548-4486

Big Sky Resort managers have plans for adding 18 more challenging holes to this beautiful golf course designed by Arnold Palmer. While the Big Sky course is so far not a destination golf course, it's hard to beat for pure setting. On the course you're apt to see moose, deer, elk, an occasional bear and a few hard-headed anglers casting their lines into the stream that flows through it. The golf course, located in Meadow Village, is part of the Big Sky Resort complex. The pro shop has a complete line of golf rentals.

Photo: Randy Hayes, Post Register

The log clubhouse at Pinecrest Golf Course in Idaho Falls, Idaho, was built of logs hauled to town from the Targhee National Forest.

Red Lodge, Montana

Red Lodge Mountain Resort Golf Course

828 Upper Continental Drive, Red Lodge, Mont. • (406) 446-3344

Tee off from a 40-foot cliff. Down below is the green — an island surrounded by water. Those in the know bring extra balls to the Red Lodge course, not just for the floating green. With two creeks, two irrigation ditches and a half-dozen ponds, 13 of the course's 18 holes have some sort of water obstacle lurking nearby. The emphasis here is accuracy, not distance. Built in the mid-1980s, the Red Lodge course was bought in 1995 by the Red Lodge Mountain Resort. The complex includes a beautiful clubhouse with an upstairs restaurant that overlooks the golf course and the Beartooth Mountains in the distance. A snack bar and the pro shop are downstairs. The Red Lodge golf course is open from about mid-April to early October.

Northwestern Wyoming

Olive Glenn Golf and Country Club

802 Meadow Ln., Cody, Wyo. • (307) 587-5551

Golf Digest ranks Olive Glenn as the fifth-best golf course in Wyoming. In addition to the 18-hole, par 72 course, Olive Glenn has a fully staffed golf shop, club and cart rental, Mulligan's restaurant (lunch and dinner only), tennis courts, a swimming pool and a weight room. Fun for any level golfer, Olive Glenn offers a beautiful view no matter which way you turn. Olive Glenn hosts many Wyoming Golf Association events and in 1997 hosted the Girls' Junior America Cup tournament — the first international golf tournament to be held in Wyoming. The buy-in membership at Olive Glenn costs $2,500, and monthly dues are $105 (per family). Visitors can play by paying a $28 greens fee.

INSIDERS' TIP

Mountain biking is limited to established roadways in Yellowstone and Grand Teton national parks.

Eastern Idaho

Ashton, Idaho, Area

Aspen Acres

4179 E. 1100 N., Ashton, Idaho
• (208) 652-3524

Thirty years ago, Arthur and Velma Anderson began to create this anomaly among the potato fields outside Ashton. They retired from full-time ranching, contracted golf fever and built a three-hole course to treat the symptoms. Friends began coming to play, and before they knew it, Arthur and Velma's golf course had taken on a life of its own.

Unlike many courses, Aspen Acres grew organically, following existing contours of the land, shaping itself around the aspen groves. The result is a pleasantly eccentric, relaxed family course that offers lots of chipping practice as well as the opportunity to occasionally view moose and bear from your golf cart. And you have the chance to drive your cart right to your campsite, because Aspen Acres is also a full-hookup RV park and campground (see our Camping and RV Parks chapter).

A small pro shop and snack bar are on the premises. Golf carts are available to rent. No tee-time reservations are necessary. The cost for 18 holes of play is $10.

Rexburg, Idaho, Area

Teton Lakes Golf Course

N. Hibbard Hwy., Rexburg, Idaho
• (208) 359-3036

The groundskeepers must work overtime here: The greens are always well-maintained and immaculately cut, and you couldn't find a divot to save your life. The front nine, built in 1978, is open and features trees; each hole in the more recently built back nine has water in play. Yardage off the white tees is 5900. The par 71 course is rated 66.6 from the white tees with a slope of 112.

Greens fees are about $12; plan to arrange your tee time two days in advance. This is a spikeless course.

Idaho Falls, Idaho

Pinecrest Golf Course

701 E. Elva St., Idaho Falls, Idaho
• (406) 529-1485

This municipal course — one of three in Idaho Falls — is a locals' favorite. It's the oldest in the area, with stately old trees that screen players ahead of you from sight. A gentle contour to many of the holes adds challenge. The par 70, 18-hole course totals 6394 yards. No spikes are allowed. Greens fees run around $13.50. Tee times must be arranged one day in advance.

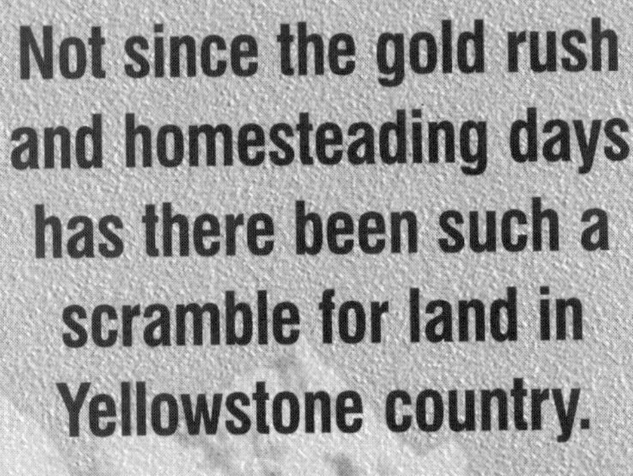
Not since the gold rush
and homesteading days
has there been such a
scramble for land in
Yellowstone country.

Real Estate

Mountain retreat. Fisherman's Fantasy. Perfect Private Paradise. Magnificent Mountain Estate. Recreational Hideaway.

The list of properties for sale in Greater Yellowstone is long. From 1992 until mid-1996, it seemed as if every piece of property on the market would be snatched up no matter what the price. In some places, ranches and recreational properties sold and resold, and tripled in value during the five-year period. Not since the gold rush and homesteading days has there been such a scramble for land in Yellowstone country.

Throughout Yellowstone country, where once we saw nothing man-made to interrupt the landscape, new homes and roads have appeared. There are still plenty of wide open spaces, but the recent buying and building boom, combined with general accelerated growth since the 1970s, has left enough of a mark on the land to worry newcomers and old-timers alike.

Until fairly recently, ranchers wouldn't have thought of selling or subdividing their ranches. But the average age of ranchers in Greater Yellowstone is approaching 60. Tempted by land prices and tired of enduring the rigors of ranching, the graying ranchers of Yellowstone country have sold or subdivided their ranches by the dozens.

Cities, counties, conservationists, newcomers and even ranchers have been grappling with ways to manage growth so it doesn't interfere with the views, consume the productive farmlands, reduce the wildlife habitat or degrade the water quality of Greater Yellowstone. For example, 20 years ago Big Sky Resort was a secluded ranch. Homes and lodges now stand in the middle of prime elk and grizzly bear habitat. Agencies fear, too, that septic and sewage from the community may be tainting the Gallatin River. Big Sky's new comprehensive management plan allows for 20,000 residents, more than twice as many as the community currently accommodates.

To protect the wide open spaces and the environment, landowners are beginning either to sell or donate conservation easements. For a hefty sum of money, property owners basically sell forever their right to develop or subdivide their property, but they retain ownership of the land and are allowed to continue working it. More than 200,000 acres in Greater Yellowstone are protected by easements set up through land trusts.

In this chapter we briefly describe communities and their markets. For more detailed information about them, we provide the names of a few real estate agencies throughout the region. Within each area, we generally chose those agencies that have been around the longest. As you will note from our entries, we have also included a few that handle specialized or unique properties. See our Area Overviews chapter for additional community information.

Greater Yellowstone Communities

Jackson Hole

Most of Teton County, Wyoming, is owned by the state or federal government. In a valley so pretty and famous that everyone wants to own a piece, that guarantees top-dollar property values. The average three-bedroom house sells for $450,000 to $500,000. A lot in Jackson Hole, if you can find one, will probably command at least $130,000. Larger lots outside of town come dear, too. Start looking for 2-acre lots at around $250,000.

If those numbers startle, consider that figures run higher in desirable locations. Property on the west side of the Snake River — an area locals call the West Side — is pricier. It's out of the hubbub of Jackson, much of it shaded with cottonwoods, aspens and pine, and it's close to golf courses, tennis courts, Jackson Hole Mountain Resort and other recreational facilities. Particularly popular, and expensive, is the tiny West Side town of Wilson at the base of Teton Pass.

One proviso about these high numbers: Realtors caution that "average selling prices" can be misleading in Jackson Hole. There are so many homes sold for more than $1 million — some for as much as $8 million — that averages don't necessarily mean much.

Out toward Hoback Junction, 13 miles south of Jackson, land costs a bit less — not as much less as you might think, but enough that if you can afford a home in Jackson, you can get that home on a small acreage in Hoback.

Once upon a time, folks who worked in Jackson but couldn't afford to buy here purchased their homes in Teton Valley, just over the Idaho border. Many still do, commuting over Teton Pass. Plentiful supply keeps Teton Valley prices from skyrocketing, but at one-third to one-half Jackson's prices, real estate in that increasingly popular valley is no longer a steal.

No one knows exactly how many people live in the tourist mecca that is Jackson Hole. Seminomadic locals, part-time recreationists and seasonal employees come and go too fast to be reliably counted. Best guesses usually fall around 6,000 for Jackson and perhaps 15,000 for the whole county. Upwards of 3 million visitors pass through town every summer, most of them in July and August. Residents willing to work in the service sector don't lack for jobs in season. Jackson Hole is largely a second-home market, but local Realtors think their buyers may spend more time in their Hole second homes than is typical in other recreational areas.

Southwestern Montana

West Yellowstone, Montana

If it's a 10-acre parcel with trees and a stream running through it that you want, chances are you won't find it in West Yellowstone. Carved out of a lodgepole pine forest and corralled by national forest and park boundaries, West, as it's often called, is a booming tourist town 90 miles south of Bozeman with no place to sprawl. That means land is getting scarce. While West boasts only about 1,000 full-time residents, it has more than 50 motels to accommodate the million-plus tourists that visit the town each year.

The lack of available land, combined with the need for employee housing and the demand for both commercial and recreation property, has driven property prices so high that locals are often unable to afford it. In 1997, a business owner paid $500,000 for an older 11-unit motel in order to provide housing for his employees. Quarter-acre residential lots in the Madison Subdivision (there are only a few left) sell for $20,000 to $30,000 dollars. Commercial lots (if you can find one) are priced as high as $170,000 each. A two-bedroom, two-bath, 1,000-square-foot, ranch-style home on Hebgen Lake starts at $120,000.

Gardiner, Montana

Of all the entrance communities to Yellowstone, Gardiner has most retained its small-town, Western atmosphere. You won't find world-class shopping, paved streets or

INSIDERS' TIP

Individuals at land trust offices in Greater Yellowstone can put you in touch with conservation real estate brokers. Among the land trusts you can contact are: Montana Nature Conservancy, 32 S. Ewing Street, Helena, Montana 59601, (406) 443-0303; Wyoming Nature Conservancy, 258 W. Main Street, Lander, Wyoming 82520, (307) 332-2971; Teton Valley Land Trust, P.O. Box 247, Driggs, Idaho 83422, (208) 726-3007; and Montana Land Reliance, P.O. Box 355, Helena, Montana 59624, (406) 443-7027.

other signs of "dressing up for the tourists" here. You will find big-hearted, hard-working residents who are glad to have retained their easy-going lifestyle.

Once the grand entrance for tourists traveling on the Northern Pacific Railway and now the only year-round entrance to Yellowstone National Park, Gardiner ranks third in numbers of visitors entering the park. Just 5 miles from Mammoth, where permanent park employees live all year, Gardiner is home to the warehouses of park concessionaires. Gardiner, which sprang up in the 1880s as a supply town for Fort Yellowstone soldiers, is still a supply town and bedroom community for those who work in the park.

Like West Yellowstone, growth in Gardiner is limited by national forest and national park boundaries. Available land is as scarce as in West Yellowstone. And, despite the fact that a gold mine near Jardine shut down in 1996, homes don't come on the market very often. A two-bedroom, one-bath house on a 50-foot by 100-foot lot cost around $100,000 in 1998, while a three-bedroom, two-bath home on the same size lot ran about $155,000. A four-bedroom, three-bath home on a 1-acre lot brought about $195,000.

Silver Gate and Cooke City, Montana

At 7,600 feet above sea level, winter comes hard and early to Silver Gate and Cooke City, sister communities just outside the northeast entrance of Yellowstone National Park. About mid-October, depending on the snow depth, the Beartooth Highway is closed for the winter, so the only access to Cooke City is via Yellowstone National Park from Gardiner. While Cooke City is gradually becoming a winter recreation destination, it isn't until the snow melts (usually in June) that the streets come alive and the town's population grows from 90 to 300. Then Main Street becomes a moving stream of people and cars. Silver Gate's population grows from a handful to about 100 each summer.

Silver Gate, 3 miles west of Cooke City and a mile from the northeast entrance of Yellowstone National Park, was founded in 1932. The town's founders hoped to create a rustic Western theme for tourists and buyers of recreation homes.

Both towns are squeezed into a narrow canyon, and — you may have already guessed — they, too, are bordered by Yellowstone National Park and the Absaroka-Beartooth Wilderness in the Gallatin National Forest. While the boundaries may limit growth in the canyon, they make for easy access to the park and to countless recreation opportunities. You can literally walk out your door and, within minutes, be in the wilderness.

A 1-acre lot near Cooke City was listed in 1998 as a "steal" at $37,900. A Cooke City restaurant with a beer and wine license as well as several small cabins was listed at $350,000.

Bozeman, Montana

First, there's Montana State University, once a cow college now a university with diversity. Then there's a lively arts community that began at MSU and then moved into the community. Next there's Bridger Bowl Ski Area just up the canyon. If that's not enough, about 40 miles to the south is Big Sky Ski and Summer Resort. And 90 miles to the south is Yellowstone National Park. In between are millions of acres of public lands and miles of trout-bearing river.

It's easy to see why Bozeman, population 28,000, is one of the fastest growing towns in Montana — and why it has some of the highest-priced real estate in the state: Bridger Bowl Ski Area is just north of town, Hyalite Basin recreation area is about 15 miles south, and three whitewater rafting rivers are within an hour's drive. In town, beginner homes start at about $115,000. The hottest-selling new homes in a subdivision south of town range from $185,000 to $235,000.

Livingston, Montana

Founded in 1882 as a railroad town for the Northern Pacific Railroad, Livingston was the gateway through which early-day tourists passed on their way to Yellowstone National Park. These days Bozeman is the favored northern jumping off point for the park. And Livingston is a quiet — almost quaint — little town (population 7,500) still unspoiled by development. Residents like the small town life with easy access to recreation and to all that Bozeman has to offer. Compared to Bozeman, you'll see fewer subdivisions and lower prices in town.

Livingston is the humming hub of Paradise Valley in a county with an average income of $22,658. Popular with movie stars and other celebrities, Paradise Valley property has become very dear, especially recreational properties close to Yellowstone National Park or Emigrant, midway between Livingston and the park. For example, we saw a 124-acre parcel with 1,900 feet of Yellowstone River frontage for $375,000. A two-story stone and wood all season recreational retreat on 3 acres a half-mile from Yellowstone National Park was priced at $375,000. Take heart, though, we also saw a cute two-bedroom town home with hardwood floors, a fenced back yard and a garage for $59,900.

Big Sky, Montana

In 1969, the late NBC newsman Chet Huntley and a group of investors bought what is now known as the Big Sky Ski and Summer Resort. Trailer parks have been outlawed, and that "little cabin in the woods" might sell for $400,000. A studio apartment that used to sell for $35,000 now sells for $70,000. A 20-acre parcel, depending on where it is, runs from $150,000 to $500,000. A 1-acre lot in the Meadow will cost you $150,000, while a quarter-acre lot right on the golf course may go for $90,000.

Despite the high prices, Big Sky property continues to be in demand, mostly because the Gallatin Canyon is a recreation mecca. Generally, new development is west of U.S. Highway 191, along the road leading to the Big Sky Ski Area or in one of the Big Sky villages, especially Mountain Village at the foot of the ski hill.

Ennis, Montana

Cattle ranching, a large talc mine and tourism share the economic pie in Ennis, population 1,000. Situated in the heart of the wide and often-windy Madison Valley, Ennis is a popular fishing destination with plenty of recreational properties for sale. As in other Greater Yellowstone communities, properties that border public lands and that have good hunting access are hot sellers. Five-acre subdivision parcels cost $10,000, while 20-acre parcels cost from $30,000 to $150,000 depending on their amenities. Property with trees, creek frontage, year-round access and power are hard to find and very dear. Town homes are priced from $85,000 to $250,000.

Red Lodge, Montana

There is plenty of property for sale in Red Lodge, population 2,300, but if you think you might want to live here year round, you'd better be prepared to like winter and lots of snow. At an elevation of 5,555 feet, Red Lodge averages 150 inches of snowfall per year, with an average of 105 frost-free days. During the winter, the Beartooth Highway — U.S. Highway 212 between Red Lodge and Cooke City, which crawls over an 11,000-foot summit — is buried by snow so deep that even in July, motorists pass snowbanks beside the road. Sixty miles to the north lies Billings, the main supply town for Red Lodge residents, who have one grocery store in their town.

Because of the climate, though, and because of nearby Red Lodge Mountain Ski Area, this town is an up-and-coming family resort town. In addition to winter sports, Red Lodge is the gateway to the Beartooth Mountains. Real estate prices that have leveled off in other areas appear to be holding strong in Red Lodge, but compared to a town like Jackson, they're still a bargain. Five years ago, you could buy almost any house in town for $30,000.

INSIDERS' TIP

Many conservation organizations purchase conservation easement; easements allow a landowner to retain ownership while giving up some rights in order to guarantee wildlife habitat and undeveloped space. To learn about the Rocky Mountain Elk Foundation's conservation easement program, call (800) 225-5355.

Now those same houses are selling for $80,000. In the past two years, the cost of raw land has nearly doubled.

An older 1,300-square-foot split-level home in town was listed in 1998 for $79,000, while a 100-foot-by-125-foot lot on Rock Creek, with city water and sewer, commanded $49,500. A two-story Victorian home in Red Lodge's historic "High Bug" district was listed at $235,000. Lots surrounding the Red Lodge Country Club range from $24,900 to $75,000, depending on their location and size. If you look, you can still find that cabin in the woods or on the river at an affordable price. In 1998, we saw a two-bedroom cabin on the Rosebud River for $125,000.

Eastern Idaho

Teton Valley, Idaho

Locals call it "the quiet side of the Tetons." Teton Valley (a.k.a. Pierre's Hole) is what Jackson Hole could have been: a mountain valley in the midst of recreational heaven, its feet still solidly planted in reality. The valley is surrounded on three sides by mountains. It contains three small agricultural communities, Tetonia, Victor and Driggs, and is increasingly ringed by recreational properties tucked into the wooded foothills. Alta, Wyoming, its fourth community, is a quality-of-lifer heaven worn on the valley's mountainous cuff.

Changes are coming. In 1996, valley population was just more than 5,000. Figures commonly touted around here list Teton as the sixth-fastest growing county in the nation. Property used to run through peak-trough cycles, regularly losing and regaining value. Now it rises, plateaus and then rises again.

The most affordable property lies in the lower valley, around Victor and Tetonia (residents of Teton Valley might dispute that Tetonia is in Teton Valley). More expensive recreational property is found on the valley perimeter, particularly to the north, in the desirable forested areas. Another high-priced area is in Alta, where restrictive zoning in effect since 1979 has left land in larger parcels. These days, new subdivisions in rural Alta can't exceed a ratio of one home per 35 acres.

The dream cabin on dream land — a hand-hewn, tree-shaded log house of modest size, say 1,000 square feet — doesn't sell for less than $200,000. And that's if you can find it at all. Easier to find are uniform-turned log homes and frame or manufactured homes on the treeless valley floor. Turned-log homes start around $160,000. The high cost is partly explained by the equally high cost of construction here. Houses must be built to withstand an 80-pound snow load, high winds and deep-freeze winters.

Swan Valley, Idaho

Most of what's available in this still-undiscovered recreational haven are building lots rather than homes or cabins. If you're willing to purchase land away from the river, you can find property from $2,000 to $10,000 per acre. The prime Swan Valley properties, though, are along the South Fork of the Snake, tucked into the cottonwoods. For one of those, multiply the asking price by 10 — if anything's available.

Much of the rest of the valley is open and treeless. Some of it has winter access problems, since not all valley roads are plowed in winter. Valley residents say the flip side is that winter brings welcome quiet.

Right now, especially if your waterfront dream home can be on a parcel with an irrigation canal running through it, property is still plentiful and affordable in Swan Valley. But that is probably changing. This puts little Swan Valley, population 950, in line with a trend seen all over our region: Folks from other regions are beginning to notice what the area has to offer in terms of recreation and quality of life.

Island Park, Idaho

Island Park and its 33-mile-long main street are entirely enclosed by Targhee National Forest. What this means to prospective buyers is that although the area is definitely gathering steam as a vacation-home market, it'll be hard for developers to build it to death, since only about 11 percent of the land is in private hands.

Island Park boasts two large lakes — Henry's Lake and Island Park Reservoir — and more than 75 miles of river and stream. This is good since local Realtors say everybody's dream cabin has a creek burbling through it. Of course, you pay for the waterfront. A lot with a distant view of Henry's Lake might cost you $20,000; that same lot on the lake will go for $100,000.

Although there's a little of everything in the Island Park area, most of what's available (and what's in greatest demand) are best called cabins. They are log or log-sided, rustic and cozy, and, depending on size and accessibility to water, they go for anywhere from $60,000 to $1.5 million. Lots can be had starting at around $8,000.

Realtors like to say that Island Park is just being discovered. Part of the fuel is the bountiful recreational opportunities, such as fishing and snowmobiling. The location is attractive, too: You can be in Yellowstone before you finish that cup of coffee you bought at Island Park Lodge. Another impetus of development here is the fact that nearby resort areas like Big Sky and Jackson Hole have priced themselves out of reach for middle-class buyers.

One last word about Island Park and its reasonably priced recreational property: Don't expect it to last. Real estate prices have been climbing at a rate of 10 percent annually for the past few years. Several years ago you could pick up an acre lot for $2,400. Those days are gone.

Ashton, Idaho

Drive through unassuming little Ashton, seed potato capital of the world, and you'll feel you're as far from booming tourism and vacation property as it is possible to be. You're not. Although tourism is mostly of the drive-through kind here, there's plenty of that: Ashton is only a couple of dozen miles from Yellowstone National Park. The town claims the only roadless access point to Yellowstone, at a place called Bechler. And fly-fishing heaven is not much more than a good cast from town on the Fall River, Henry's Fork, Warm River and others.

The first recreational subdivision was constructed in 1970—Ashton is young as a vacation home area. So while there's plenty of recreational land for sale, you'll generally do the building. Most sales of already-constructed houses are in town; usually eight or nine are on the market.

New residents may have difficulty finding employment. Principal employers in the area are the Forest Service and small businesses looking for service personnel. Some residents commute to Rexburg or even Idaho Falls, a 45-minute drive on dry pavement. Before buying your dream home here with plans for commuting out of the Ashton area, think access: In winter, roads close two or three times per season for a day or more.

You'll pay $4,500 to $10,000 for a 7,000-square-foot lot, depending on how developed it is and what amenities it offers. For example, Teton views affect the price; so do trees (the more mature the trees are on a lot, the higher the price). Lots in town are generally very reasonable, running about $1 per square foot.

A final tip: The water table is deep around here. If you have to sink a well, you may be looking at another $10,000 to $15,000.

Rexburg, Idaho

Rexburg offers the charms of a stable, economically thriving small town right out of *Leave it to Beaver*, coupled with the fantastic recreational opportunities of Greater Yellowstone. The town, population 14,000, is nearly unique in a region where most small communities make their living from tourism, leaving the "real" jobs and industries to cluster in cities like Idaho Falls and Bozeman.

Much of the town's charm comes from its strong Mormon influence. If the town seems to you like a place where children walk the streets at night without looking over their shoulders, it is. Mormon communities tend to be strongly family-oriented, and this one is no exception.

Ironically, the other significant cause of Rexburg's tidy hometown look was a disaster.

INSIDERS' TIP

All log homes are not created equal: factory-turned logs produce a uniform look that costs much less than the unique, rougher look of hand-hewn log. Some even cheaper "log" homes are actually frame houses with log siding attached to the outside.

Photo: Robert Bower, Post Register

This haystack house was built on the south edge of the town of Jackson, Wyoming.

In 1976, the newly built Teton Dam crumbled, releasing a massive flood that nearly wiped out several towns, including Rexburg. That's why buildings more than 20 years old are scarce, even though Rexburg is one of the oldest townships in the region.

Local real estate agents say folks are sometimes surprised by what their money doesn't buy in this predominantly rural area. A smaller three-bedroom, one- or two-bathroom home will sell for \$80,000 to \$85,000. Sometimes this causes an affordability problem for first home buyers. Nevertheless, this midrange property moves quickly.

Idaho Falls, Idaho

Idaho's third-largest town sits in the middle of the Snake River Plain. It's uncompromisingly flat, with rich farmland and mountains that float like distant mirages on the horizons. Nearly 50,000 people call it home.

Property in Idaho Falls is still a bargain and easy to find. Typically a Realtor can show you at least 50 homes in the \$70,000 price range. Average selling prices in town were about \$91,700 in 1998 (\$85,000 outside the city limits). Bonneville County real estate magazines generally carry at least 500 listings for condos, townhouses, homes and residential acreages. Popular in 1997 were more expensive homes in the area around Sage Lakes Golf Course on East River Road north of town. The town annexed the area and brought city services out to these newer rural homes. In 1998, areas south and east of town, like Stonebrook and Victorian Village, sold well.

Areas that seem to hold value include what locals call "the numbered streets," a neighborhood of older (some historic) residences with mature trees on quiet streets adjacent to downtown. East and south of town, beyond Ammon, you'll find many acreage properties with stable property values. Some of the highest prices are found among the newer homes south of town — $150,000 to more than $1 million.

Northwestern Wyoming

Cody, Wyoming

Don't let the location or the size of this 8,500-person town fool you. Located in the middle of the Big Horn Basin's high desert, Cody is an oasis in the land of cowboys. On Sheridan Avenue, Cody's main street, upscale shopping and dining are common fare. And a budding collection of art galleries adds to the cosmopolitan feeling of this small town. If that isn't enough, you'll find the town full of energetic, enthusiastic folks who love to show visitors a good time. At the center of their show are two attractions: the Buffalo Bill Historical Center and the Cody Nite Rodeo, which runs from June through August. (See our Rodeo chapter.) You'll also find medical and educational facilities that aim for quality.

While many other Greater Yellowstone communities saw real estate sales level off in 1996, the lull in Cody was brief. Sales picked up in the fall of 1998 and have been brisk ever since. Non-irrigated property on the South Fork of the Shoshone, though, could cost you from $5,000 to $12,000 per acre — if you can find a piece for sale. North of Cody, near Clark, bare land can be had for much less. And near Greybull, 60 miles east of Cody, you can still buy irrigated ground for $800 to $1,200 per acre.

Real Estate Companies

Jackson Hole

Century 21 Art Hazen Real Estate
140 N. Cache St., Jackson, Wyo.
• (307) 733-4339, (800) 227-3334

Part of the largest real estate organization in the world, these folks can hook you into any place from any other. Agents pride themselves on knowing the Jackson psyche. Agent Bob LaLonde is an example of what this brokerage offers in the way of local understanding: He has been a planning and zoning commissioner, a Wyoming state senator and president of the Jackson Chamber of Commerce. Century 21 doesn't focus heavily on high-end properties.

Jackson Hole Realty
185 W. Broadway Ave., Jackson, Wyo.
• (307) 733-9009, (888) 733-9009

Founded in the '60s by Paul McCollister, the guy who began development of a ski hill in Teton Village, this brokerage is a Jackson Hole institution. At least 12 of its agents have sold real estate in the valley for more than 15 years, including Greg Prugh and Jackie Montgomery. Jackson Hole Realty is also the largest real estate agency in Wyoming, with 17 partners, eight offices (including one in Driggs, Idaho) and about 40 agents.

Jackson Hole Realty handles a bit of everything, including commercial properties, condos and lots. Its specialty, though, is high-end second homes, so if you're looking for your castle in the mountains, call these folks.

Prime Properties of Jackson Hole
1230 Ida Ln., Wilson, Wyo.
• (307) 733-7440, (800) 800-6455

Broker Bruce Simon moved to Jackson Hole in 1968. He began selling real estate here 10 years later. His brokerage is unique in its Wilson location — most real estate companies base themselves in Jackson or Teton Village. Prime Properties has a niche in subdivision development, although the agency also sells recreational and residential real estate as do other valley brokerages.

Real Estate of Jackson Hole
110 E. Broadway Ave., Jackson, Wyo.
• (307) 733-6060, (800) 443-6130

These folks have a local reputation for selling higher-end properties, but what they pride themselves on is their wide-ranging listings and experience. Listings and branch offices are scattered from Driggs, Idaho, to Alpine, Wyoming. The company has roughly 40 agents, many of them natives to Jackson or other Wyoming areas, whose job is to know those areas and their listings.

Southwestern Montana

All Seasons Realty

303 Canyon St., West Yellowstone, Mont. • (406) 646-7714

Real estate agent Don Stanley recently bought this full-service year-round agency along with Yellowstone Realty. Though new to the field of real estate, Stanley knows West Yellowstone well. He has lived in West 30 years and worked at a variety of jobs including running a cable TV business, working in a lumber mill, driving a tour bus and feeding the bears at Grizzly Discovery Center. He handles all types of real estate.

Arrow Real Estate

219 E. Main St., Ennis, Mont. • (406) 682-4290, (800) 497-4290

Arrow Real Estate, formerly FNI Real Estate, is the oldest real estate company in the Madison Valley. Founded by Jess Armitage, who holds one of the lowest-numbered real estate licenses in Montana, Arrow is now owned by Don and Toni Bowen. Armitage and the Bowens bring a total of 65 years experience to their business. They combine old-fashioned service with high-tech resources, and carry "properties to fit every dream."

Big Sky Properties

3091 Pine Dr., Big Sky, Mont. • (406) 995-2318, (800) 799-2919

Big Sky Properties is a small agency operated by husband-wife team Tim Cyr and Cathy Gorman. Cyr began coming to Big Sky with his parents when he was a small boy. Now he and Gorman bring friendly, personal service to a market that could easily drive another real estate agent to hurry you through a search or a sale. Big Sky Properties handles resort properties because that's mostly all there is in Big Sky.

Bridger Realty

85 W. Kagy Blvd., Bozeman, Mont. • (406) 586-7676, (888) 586-7676

Bridger Realty, established in 1980, is one of the top real estate sellers in Bozeman. They have 20 full-time sales professionals and a relocation specialist on staff. Bridger Realty's specialties include in-town residential, commercial building and development, investment properties, building sites and acreage.

Century 21 Payne Realty and Housing Inc.

124 W. Lewis St., Livingston, Mont. • (406) 222-6377, (800) 637-7911

Brokers Bob and Dee Payne have been selling real estate in Livingston for 25 years. A full-service agency, Payne Realty works with 16 licensees selling farm and ranch properties as well as commercial, recreation and residential properties in Livingston and the surrounding area, including the Yellowstone Valley. They are consistently among the leaders in sales in the Livingston area.

C Mor Real Estate

110 S. Broadway, Red Lodge, Mont. • (406) 446-2123, (800) 752-2499

Red Lodge's oldest and largest real estate agency, C Mor has eight agents knowledgeable about the area, including the natural world. That means they know important things like how deep the water is, how it runs underground and how the idiosyncrasies of the immediate environment might affect you, your family and your home. Mostly older than 50 and longtime residents, C Mor's agents pride themselves in their community involvement. For more than 20 years, this agency has sold

INSIDERS' TIP

The Corporation for the Northern Rockies prints "Welcome to the West," a guide to private land conservation for people considering the purchase of real estate in the Northern Rockies. To learn more about this publication, write: Corporation for the Northern Rockies, P.O. Box 1448, Livingston, MT 59047, or call (406) 222-0730.

all types of real estate. It also provides a relocation service.

Coldwell Banker/Maverick Realty
125 E. Callender St., Livingston, Mont. • (406) 222-0304, (800) 676-8189

Broker-owner Michelle Goodwine was born and raised in Livingston and has been with Maverick Realty since 1986. While she sells all kinds of properties, including ranches and businesses, she sells more small acreages and homes than anything else. In fact, Coldwell Banker/Maverick Realty has been the leader in residential sales in the Livingston area for the past four years. The agency has seven sales associates, a licensed assistant and a full-time property manager.

Fay Fly Fishing Properties Inc.
Bozeman, Mont. • (406) 586-4001, (800) 238-8616

Owner Gregory W. Fay and associate James Esperti have taken their passion for fly fishing into the real estate market. Since 1992 Fay has found and sold prime properties along Montana's rivers and streams to conservation-minded fly fishers. Fay handles various size ranches and works extensively with conservation easements as a means of ensuring preservation of the natural landscape. He and Esperti also offer a buyer brokerage service, researching unlisted properties and those listed by other companies.

Gardiner Office, Century 21 Payne Realty
Outpost Mall, Gardiner, Mont. • (406) 848-7904

Associate Broker Karen Hayes, who handles the Gardiner area for Century 21 Payne Realty, has been selling real estate in the area for several years. If you're bent on buying property in Gardiner, it's best to keep in touch with Hayes, since property is snapped up quickly once it goes on the market.

Jacobs Western Land Brokerage Inc.
3504 Good Medicine Way, Bozeman, Mont. • (406) 586-8575

If it's a ranch you're after or a large recreational parcel, the odds are excellent that Ken Jacobs knows the property. Jacobs came west with Chet Huntley's Big Sky and has been handling land transactions since 1971. Jacobs has marketed many of Montana's finest prop-

Photo: Susan Short

The exterior of the Original Buffalo Bill Cody House in Cody, Wyoming is decorated with flags and bunting.

erties over the last 26 years, and brings his intimate knowledge of the region to his job.

The Real Estate Agency

15 Madison Ave., West Yellowstone, Mont. • (406) 646-9523, (800) 438-5263

West Yellowstone's oldest established agency, The Real Estate Agency sells all types of property all year round. Owned and operated by Rob Klatt, this agency welcomes dreamers and others with questions about real estate in the West Yellowstone area.

Triple Creek Realty

47650 Canyon Rd., Big Sky, Mont. • (406) 995-4848, (800) 548-4632

The oldest established realty company in Big Sky, Triple Creek Realty is first in listings and sales in Big Sky and the Gallatin Canyon. In addition to selling residential, recreational and commercial properties in the Big Sky area, Triple Creek handles vacation condo rentals. With two offices, one in Gallatin Canyon and the other in Mountain Village, Triple Creek is staffed with 10 sales people.

Yellowstone Realty

303 Canyon St., West Yellowstone, Mont. • (406) 646-7575

Yellowstone Realty is a full-service agency owned and operated by Don Stanley. For more information about this agency, refer to the previous entry for All Seasons Realty.

Eastern Idaho

American Realty West

189 N. Main St., Driggs, Idaho • (208) 354-2348

Locally owned and operated, American Realty West is the oldest and largest brokerage in the Teton Valley. All of its agents are local property owners. They know the people here, which is an important part of doing business in a small, close-knit community. Broker John McKellar and associate broker Brooke Saindon are the office old-timers. McKellar was already here when the clean air and cleaner lifestyle drew Saindon to Teton Valley in 1978.

Another strength of this brokerage is that it sells property only in Teton Valley and Alta, Wyoming. This helps ensure a good working knowledge of any piece of valley property you may want to see.

Century 21 Hathaway-Genta

305 W. Main St., Rexburg, Idaho • (208) 356-0588, (800) 807-0588

This brokerage has around 11 agents, several of whom go way back in this area. Nancy White, a Rexburg native, has been with the agency for a decade. Sharon Schindler, born 13 miles away in St. Anthony, has sold area real estate for 14 years. Broker Barry Genta, a third-generation local, began selling real estate in 1974.

Hathaway-Genta sells 120 to 130 properties a year, which makes it the biggest seller in Rexburg.

Green Tree, Realtors

796 Memorial Dr., Idaho Falls, Idaho • (208) 524-5401

This is a unique little brokerage. Co-owners Nila Briggs and Joy Simmons are its only agents. Both have been selling real estate on the Snake River Plain for more than 20 years (Briggs for more than 30). They decided to leave the larger franchise brokerages they worked for 12 years ago because they wanted a small, personal office.

Green Tree specializes in homes, residential acreages and small land parcels. Briggs has been a certified real estate instructor for more than 20 years. She says teaching a few classes a year keeps her current on new property issues.

Harrell Realty

416 Main St., Ashton, Idaho • (208) 652-7436

Jim Harrell started this company in 1957,

INSIDERS' TIP

Montana, Wyoming and Idaho are all "open range" states. That means if your neighbor has livestock, it's your responsibility to build a fence if you want to keep them off your land.

and he's still the guy most likely to answer the phone if you call. There's been a brokerage on this spot since the early 1900s. Up until a few years ago, Harrell was the only real estate professional with an office in Ashton. Harrell Realty focuses on residential and recreational properties.

Island Park Realty

Valley View at Island Park, Idaho • (208) 558-7332

Two full-time and three part-time agents staff the oldest real estate agency in town. Broker/owner Lenyce Zenk has worked at this agency since 1976. In 1995, she and her husband bought it. Like other area brokerages, Island Park Realty specializes in what sells around here: vacation and recreational lots and cabins.

Rainbow Realty

3376 U.S. Hwy. 20, Last Chance in Island Park, Idaho • (208) 558-7116, (800) 853-7420

Six real estate agents work in this office, whose greatest strength is combined experience in the Island Park area. Because Island Park is primarily a second-home market, Rainbow says they spend more time showing homes than trying to hard-sell them: Folks buying their dream cabin know what they want when they see it, apparently.

The Real Estate Office

30 S. Second W., Rexburg, Idaho • (208) 356-5050

Dale Walker and Mary Hill are the office old-timers. Mary's been selling real estate in this town since 1976; she's the broker. Dale, an Idaho native now in his early 80s, specializes in commercial property. Other agents at The Real Estate Office focus mostly on residential property.

RE/MAX Homestead Realty

1301 E. 17th St., Ste. 1, Idaho Falls, Idaho • (208) 529-5600, (800) 729-5601

Idaho Falls has several franchise brokerages; we've included this one because RE/MAX does things a bit differently than most. In many brokerages, agents split their commissions in return for paying little or no overhead. At RE/MAX agents keep their commissions but pay out of pocket their share of office overhead. This means an agent who doesn't sell property can't afford to be there — good news for the client.

South Fork Properties

40 Conant Valley Loop, Swan Valley, Idaho • (208) 483-2112, (800) 483-2110

Spence Warner was born and raised in Swan Valley. He inherited his fly-fishing lodge in Conant Valley from his dad. He's one of only two real estate agents selling nothing but Swan Valley real estate; most agents showing Swan Valley property are based in Idaho Falls, 40-odd miles away.

Warner handled more than half of the 50 or so Swan Valley lots and acreages sold from 1994 to 1997. The Warners work with a few farms and businesses, but their bread and butter comes from the sale of recreational property.

Teton Valley Realty

40 N. Main St., Driggs, Idaho • (208) 354-2439

Owner Mark Rockefeller has been in business in this valley since 1976. He's the only valley broker who is also a developer. In addition to selling recreational and residential lots and houses, he creates subdivisions.

His favorite parts of the valley to work in are the wooded foothills at the valley perimeter. There, rolling terrain and habitat requirements make subdividing complicated but rewarding. Rockefeller says he prides himself

INSIDERS' TIP

The Montana Department of Natural Resources and Conservation has put out a booklet called "Tips on Land and Water Management for Small Farms and Ranches in Montana." To get a copy, write: Conservation Districts Bureau, Department of Natural Resources and Conservation — CARDD, P.O. Box 201601, Helena, MT 59620-1601, or call (406) 444-6667.

on being able to divide acreages so that every lot is a great house site.

Rockefeller takes his housing projects from start to finish, from designing and installing roads to organizing homeowners' associations. He's finished more than a dozen in the area, each consisting of from eight to 44 lots.

Wackerli Realty

255 B St., Ste. 300, Idaho Falls, Idaho
• (208) 522-7784, (800) 924-7784

Both Dick Clayton Sr. and the company he started with his brother 50 years ago are local icons. Wackerli is the oldest brokerage in town; at one point not long ago, Clayton owned much of the property in downtown Idaho Falls.

One of the company's strengths is its diversity. Clayton specializes in commercial property; his son, Dick Clayton Jr., and Dean Hansen work mostly in ranch and agricultural property. Other agents on staff specialize in recreational property in Island Park, Swan Valley and Teton Valley. Wackerli also operates a property management service.

Northwestern Wyoming

Homestead Realty/LC/Better Homes and Gardens

1273 Sheridan Ave., Cody, Wyo.
• (307) 587-4750

Founded in 1995 by two Cody natives, Louis Kousoulos and Stan Siggins, Homestead Realty had 13 sales agents in 1997 and is one of the area leaders in sales. Kousoulos began selling real estate in 1985 after retiring from 35 years in the food business. Siggins began his career in real estate in 1990 after retiring from the dude ranch business. This agency has an energetic staff that sells every kind of property.

Western Real Estate

1143 Sheridan Ave., Cody, Wyo.
• (307) 587-4926, (800) 538-5122

Established in 1969, Western Real Estate is a full-service agency with six full time agents who operate in well-organized teams specializing in farm, ranch and recreational properties as well as building lots, homes and commercial property in and out of town. The agency is staffed mostly by longtime residents of Cody and is owned by Shirley Lehman, a fourth-generation native, and Ed Higbie, a second-generation native to the area. Western Real Estate, once the only agency selling recreational property in the area, still sells the lion's share of it.

Real Estate Publications

Montana and Idaho each have publications advertising regional properties for sale. They are crammed with offerings, and if you're really interested in Yellowstone country property, these publications carry a good representation of the best. Each requires a mailing and handling fee. We'll give you their names and addresses. The rest is up to you.

Idaho Land Magazine, Rocky Mountain Publishing, P.O. Box 6062, Pocatello, ID 83205-6062

The Montana Land Magazine, P.O. Box 30516, Billings, MT 59107 (See the Media Chapter for more information about the Montana Land Magazine.)

Greater Yellowstone's larger communities offer good medical and emergency facilities and a long menu of resources and opportunities especially designed for seniors.

Retirement

For retiring baby boomers, Yellowstone country is a dream come true. It is a land of mountains to climb, streams to fish, places to camp, wildlife to watch and big game to hunt. It's an oasis of clean air, pure water, wide-open spaces and myriad natural mysteries.

On the other hand, for older retirees especially, Greater Yellowstone can quickly become a very inhospitable place with the advent of winter. Even for those of us who grew up here, the winters can be long, hard and tedious. The rigors of battening your house against arctic weather, stoking the fire, shoveling snow and navigating icy, snow-packed roads can take their toll. Even in the 1990s, the maladies associated with a bad case of cabin fever have driven many a golden-ager to the warmer climate of the South, if not forever, then for at least long enough to avoid Jack Frost.

Greater Yellowstone's larger communities offer good medical and emergency facilities and a long menu of resources and opportunities especially designed for seniors. Amenities such as senior centers, public transportation for seniors and paved streets in larger towns make life easier for older citizens. In smaller towns such as Gardiner and Ennis, Montana, and Irwin, Idaho, you won't find any senior center at all. Emergency medical care is provided by trained volunteers, side streets are unpaved, the towns pretty much shut down for the winter, and the nearest hospital is miles away. We know older residents whose failing health forced them to move elsewhere to be closer to modern medical facilities.

For anyone contemplating retiring in Greater Yellowstone, we recommend researching the facilities in your area of interest. Staffed senior citizen centers in Bozeman, Livingston, Jackson, Idaho Falls and Cody are good places to start. The next sections provide descriptions of these centers' programs and others. For your convenience, we have provided the following clearinghouse numbers where you can get all the information you need before you make your decision: Gallatin County Council on Aging in Bozeman, (406) 586-2421; Cody Council on Aging, (307) 587-6221; and Idaho's Region VII Council on Aging, (800) 632-4813.

Another good resource is *Prime Time News*, published monthly by High Country Independent Press, 220 S. Broadway, Belgrade, Montana, (406) 388-6762. This publication is chock-full of news, columns and calendars related to older adults in Gallatin County, Montana. Seniors looking for volunteer slots to fill in the community can find them listed in *Prime Time*. Its pages also contain descriptions of upcoming events at Bozeman, Belgrade, Manhattan and Three Forks senior citizen centers and monthly menus for each center.

Jackson Hole

Senior Center of Jackson Hole
830 E. Hansen Ave., Jackson, Wyo.
• (307) 733-7300

Like other area senior centers, the Senior Center of Jackson Hole serves lunch daily (a $2 donation is requested) to those 60 and older. Reservations are required. The center also provides home care and delivers meals to the homebound. If you want to learn more about these folks and the services they offer, ask for a copy of their fact-packed monthly newsletter. It includes an activities calendar and a menu for that month's lunches.

Teton County Parks and Recreation Department/Recreation Center
155 E. Gill St., Jackson, Wyo.
• (307) 733-5056

Teton County Parks and Recreation manages a well-equipped recreation center with an eight-lane lap pool, a therapy pool, hot tub, sauna, gym and giant water slide. The center offers courses in step aerobics, yoga and low-impact water aerobics. The water aerobics course is a favorite with seniors. Course participants meet three times weekly for one-hour sessions. In 1998, the cost was $4 to $8 for drop-ins. Another favorite pastime is the Bridge Club, which meets Monday nights at the Recreation Center. Participants' pocket change creates a kitty for the high scorer.

Programs specifically geared to area seniors include the weekly senior walks. Every Friday, Parks and Recreation provides transportation and a guide for a short (3-mile maximum) hike in the Jackson area. Senior hikes are free and run May through September. Every Christmas, Teton County loads up buses with interested seniors for a one-day shopping spree in Idaho Falls' Grand Teton Mall, 80 miles away. Every September, a Parks and Recreation bus takes seniors up to Yellowstone National Park for the day to watch Old Faithful blow its top and to check out area gift shops. These programs charge participants a refreshingly affordable $5.

Southwestern Montana

West Yellowstone Senior Social Center

West Yellowstone • (406) 646-7311

The West Yellowstone Senior Social Center launched its first meal and afternoon activity hour in May of 1997. The center has no building to call home yet, but it meets each Wednesday for a noon meal at the Bear's Den Cinema at 15 Electric Street. The meals are $2. Summer residents make up the bulk of the patrons of the meals and field trips. During winter, local seniors who are busy working during the summer look forward to meeting there. This center allows anyone of any age to join. If you happen to be 50 or younger, though, don't expect to vote. The 14-passenger West Yellowstone Foundation/Galavan bus carries passengers from West to Bozeman. It leaves from the Chamber of Commerce parking lot at the corner of Canyon Street and Yellowstone Avenue at 8 AM each Tuesday and Thursday from October until May and each Thursday the rest of the year. It returns about 5 PM. To reserve a seat on the bus, seniors must call the West Yellowstone Police Station at (406) 646-7600.

Bozeman Senior Citizen Center

807 N. Tracy, Bozeman, Mont. • (406) 586-2421

Since the completion of a new addition — its second in four years — the Bozeman Senior Citizen Center has one of the best senior facilities in Montana. A beehive of activity, the center has 1,600 members who work, play, socialize and dine there. A few hundred more older adults gather in Belgrade, Manhattan and Three Forks under the auspices of the Bozeman Senior Center. In addition to the noon meals served Monday through Friday, the center serves a Sunday dinner once a month. The dining room seats 300, and reservations for meals should be made a day in advance. Meals-on-wheels (about 120 of them each weekday) also roll out of the center's kitchen.

The Bozeman Senior Center also has a well-organized and active travel program, including at least one trip per year to Yellowstone National Park and an every-other-year tour of the Beartooth Highway (see our Attractions chapter). In addition, volunteer seniors organize any number of fund-raisers, including dinner, style and craft shows as well as dances in the new dining room which features a roll-out stage and 3,300 square feet of dancing room. The Bozeman Senior Center also has regular health screenings and clinics including those for blood pressure, foot care, health education, nutrition counseling and immunizations.

The center is open from 8:30 AM to 3:30 PM Monday through Friday. Membership costs $7.50 per year and is open to anyone 50 years or older.

Galavan, a seniors bus service that transports rural seniors from outlying areas to Bozeman, operates out of the Bozeman Senior Center. Buses are equipped with wheelchair lifts and will often take passengers from their doorsteps to the doctor's office, beauty parlor, grocery store or anyplace else in Bozeman. In Belgrade, Galavan leaves from the Price Rite Drug Center every Tuesday. For reservations and more information, call (406) 587-2434.

Belgrade Senior Citizen's Friendship Club

92 Cameron Ave., Belgrade, Mont. • (406) 388-4711

Monday, Wednesday, Thursday and Friday, seniors gather here for a noon meal at the cost of a small donation. Affiliated with the Bozeman Senior Center, this center has an annual craft sale and garage sales.

Senior Citizens' Center of Park County

206 S. Main, Livingston, Mont. • (406) 222-9995

In the 1960s, Livingston seniors used grant money to buy the fire-damaged Yellowstone Hotel in downtown Livingston. Today, more than a decade after they paid off the mortgage, the board of this center has 26 apartments that provide low-income housing for seniors. Staffed by several part-time paid employees, the Senior Citizens' Center of Park County has 300 members (they've had as many as 600) who pay a $5 membership fee. An in-house thrift store grosses $2,000 to $4,000 per month. Besides serving noon meals Monday through Friday, the center offers card parties, dances, bingo, a pool table, exercise and wellness clinics. The facility prohibits the practice of politics or religion on the premises. It's open Monday through Saturday and publishes a monthly newsletter.

Red Lodge Senior Citizens' Center

207 S. Villard Ave., Red Lodge, Mont. • (406) 446-1826

This volunteer-run center serves three meals a week: soup and sandwiches at noon on Wednesday, a full meal on Thursday at 11:30 AM and a Friday noon meal. The center has 150 members who pay a $5 fee to belong. You'll also find regular card parties, bingo, a blood-pressure clinic and a foot clinic.

Eastern Idaho

Teton Valley

Community Outreach

283 N. First E., Driggs, Idaho • (208) 354-2383, Ext. 164

Lesley Baer, Community Outreach director at Teton Valley Hospital, says her job is to bring needed services to the community. Some of the services she can hook you into are the Stretch, Flex and Tone senior fitness classes sponsored by Teton Valley Hospital. Then there's the AARP-sponsored 55 Alive driving class; this two-day course addresses how changes associated with aging affect driving safety. Community Outreach also assists with transportation for seniors. Baer's newest project, an adopt-a-grandparent program, pairs trained teens and young adults with area seniors for the benefit of both sides of the generation gap.

Teton County Senior Citizens

P.O. 466, Driggs, ID 83422 • No phone

For seniors 60 and older, dinner is served at Driggs' American Legion Hall on Wednesdays and Thursdays. Thirty to 60 people generally attend. Meals for the 10 to 15 people who can't make it into town are delivered, in cooperation with Teton Valley Hospital Community Outreach. Another critical service in this rural area is the CART bus, which takes senior citizens to doctors' appointment and the grocery store. It also brings them into town for those Legion Hall dinners. Other services sponsored through the Area VI Agency on

INSIDERS' TIP

If you're older than 62 and heading for Grand Teton or Yellowstone national parks, make sure you buy a Golden Age Passport. It costs $10 and buys you lifetime entrance to all national parks.

A member of the Idaho Falls Old Tyme Fiddlers entertains seniors at Tautphaus Park.

Aging may be available from time to time in this area (see our entry on Idaho Falls' Area VI services later in this chapter).

Ashton, Idaho

Ashton Senior Center

Main St., Ashton, Idaho • (208) 652-3594

Ashton is a small town, and its senior center is small, too. Nevertheless, these folks serve lunches to seniors two days a week. About once a month a speaker comes in to share health or finance related information. The Ashton Seniors quilting circle has been meeting for at least 10 years; they quilt on Tuesdays and Wednesdays. Other services sponsored through the Area VI Agency on Aging may be available from time to time in this area (see our entry on Idaho Falls' Area VI services later in this chapter).

Madison County Senior Citizen Center

40 S. Second W., Rexburg, Idaho • (208) 356-0080

The annual influx of what locals call "sunbirds" — more than 2,000 retirees from the hot-weather states who rent Ricks College's student housing for the summer months —

INSIDERS' TIP

Adults older than 55 are eligible for educational programs sponsored through Boston-based Elderhostel, available at several sites in Greater Yellowstone. One-week courses focus on natural history or outdoor recreation. Adults older than 55 can bring a younger companion. To learn more, call Elderhostel toll-free (877) 426-8056.

keeps this senior center hopping. Cook Darla Mower has been turning out what we're told are exceptional lunches for many years. These inexpensive meals are served at the center; about 40 lunches are delivered to shut-ins Tuesday through Saturday. Thursday is bingo. Once a month, the center brings in an area physician to discuss seniors' health issues. Various organizations sponsor tours and activities to area attractions for center seniors during the busy summer months.

Idaho Falls, Idaho, Area

Area VI Agency on Aging
357 Constitution Way, Idaho Falls, Idaho • (208) 522-5391, (800) 632-4813

Emily Hoyt coordinates assistance programs for older people in nine eastern Idaho counties, including Jefferson, Bonneville, Madison, Fremont and Teton. This makes her a one-stop resource for anyone who wants to know what is available for older adults in Idaho Falls, Rigby, Rexburg, Ashton, Island Park, Swan Valley and Teton Valley. Services vary by area and availability of funds and volunteers, but most programs are available in Idaho Falls; some operate in other communities as well.

Among its programs are those that assist older folks with employment, health and safety problems. Homemaker, shopper and chore workers help frailer seniors with difficult household tasks. Respite is a program that provides full-time caregivers of homebound adults occasional breaks from their responsibilities. Legal services are available, as is adult day care. Nearly every community within Area VI offers home-delivered and communal meals, as well as transportation for older people who have no other way to get to doctors or grocery stores. Call for more information, especially since program availability may change.

Senior Citizens' Community Center Inc.
535 W. 21st St., Idaho Falls, Idaho • (208) 522-4357

This large and active senior center has a membership of 4,500 and a full-time paid staff that keeps the center open from 8:30 AM to 4:30 PM Monday through Friday. The center sponsors a range of health services from cholesterol and glaucoma checks to a monthly foot clinic. Regular seminars offer information on topics such as investments, fraud and fitness. The center serves lunch Monday through Friday and is the setting for Thursday afternoon dances and Tuesday morning singalongs paired with afternoon bridge games. The center has a large library with more than 5,000 titles. You can learn more about these folks from their monthly newsletter or from the community calendar in the local paper. And pay attention to center travel plans: The Senior Citizens' Community Center sponsors regular (and affordable) summer trips to places such as Lava Hot Springs, Jackson Hole and Yellowstone National Park.

Northwestern Wyoming

Cody, Wyoming

Cody Senior Citizens' Center
613 16th St., Cody, Wyo. • (307) 587-6221

The hub of senior citizen activity in Cody, the Cody Senior Center claims to have the best cook in town. While other cooks in town may dispute that boast, it is a known fact that at the Cody Senior Center, you'll find meals just like your grandma used to cook. The meals are served in a dining room that accommodates 200, but usually there are about 90 diners. A crew of volunteers operates a thriving thrift shop Monday through Saturday from 10 AM until 3 PM. Sales accounted for $20,000 of the center's 1998 budget. The Cody Senior Citizens' Center has no membership fees.

You'll also find a senior bus service operating out of the center for Cody seniors and the handicapped. Medical and personal services and meals are also offered here. The Cody Senior Citizens' Center is open from 8 AM until 4 PM Monday through Friday.

All areas of Greater
Yellowstone, including
the parks, have 911
service.

Healthcare

Greater Yellowstone is about the size of Maine, yet towns are few and far between. Towns, separated by long distances, generally lie within the valleys and, with few exceptions, are small rural communities. Many have only clinics to serve the everyday health needs of local residents, and some of the smaller towns have no medical services at all. Despite their isolation, clinics are well-connected with the regional hospitals. And because of their remoteness, clinics are staffed with doctors or nurse practitioners who have a wide range of emergency and everyday medical expertise.

All of the region's hospitals, with the exception of Lake Hospital in the center of Yellowstone National Park, lie anywhere from 53 to 109 miles from the park's boundaries. That means life-threatening injuries or illnesses that strike you while you're in Yellowstone may require one or two ambulance transfers to get you to a hospital. If the emergency is extreme, an air ambulance likely will fly you to one of several regional hospitals listed later in this chapter.

All areas of greater Yellowstone, including the parks, have 911 service. Many individuals with emergency medical technician (EMT) status inside and outside the parks are trained for backcountry rescues. Except for the larger towns like Bozeman, Billings and Idaho Falls, EMTs are volunteers who will leave their jobs, families and beds at a moment's notice to rush to your aid. We hope you won't need emergency medical attention while you're in Yellowstone country, but if you do, you'll find fast, efficient help.

As in other areas across the country, various forms of alternative healthcare are taking root in Greater Yellowstone. In the larger towns like Bozeman, Idaho Falls and especially Jackson, you will find several individual homeopaths, holistic medicine practitioners, massage therapists (some even make house calls) and certified midwives who offer home births. Even in small towns, where cowboys have pitched too much hay or have been pitched from one horse too many, chiropractors hang up their shingles. For more information about alternative healthcare, hospice, home healthcare, special health services or veterinarians, we suggest you consult the Yellow Pages.

In this chapter, we'll tell you where the hospitals and clinics are and what services they provide. Because of the size of Greater Yellowstone, we suggest you call either the clinics or the hospitals listed in your area for information about emergency dental care or doctor referrals.

In the Parks

Two clinics and a hospital in Yellowstone National Park and a single clinic in Grand Teton serve the 3 million visitors who pass through the parks each summer. In Yellowstone National Park, between 75 and 100 of the rangers each year have at least EMT status. About 10 of those will be trained medics, and a couple

INSIDERS' TIP

Between the strong high-altitude sun and the low humidity, you won't notice yourself sweating — even if you are. Dehydration is no fun, but it easily can be prevented by drinking lots of water — 2 quarts per day is recommended — and keeping your alcohol consumption down. Dehydration is such a common problem around here that if you have a headache after a day outside, water is probably going to fix you faster than aspirin.

may actually be paramedics. Grand Teton has about as many EMTs, including 16 park medics.

Steve Sarles, emergency medical services coordinator in Yellowstone, reports that each year the Yellowstone Park Service gets from 700 to 800 emergency calls as a result of illness and injury. (They're evenly split.) Of those calls, about 250 end up needing ambulance services. In Grand Teton, emergency medical services were activated about 232 times in 1996. The vast majority were a result of motor-vehicle accidents. Once you get to Yellowstone, you'll know why. The roads are narrow, congested and winding. Roadside attractions can quickly become distractions that lead to unhealthy auto interactions. Take your eyes off the road and you're liable to rear-end the last car in what Insiders call a "bear jam."

Since the Yellowstone Park Service changed its bear-management policy, minor injuries from belligerent begging bruins have dropped dramatically. Before, when bears regularly foraged at open dumps and waited by the roadside for tidbits from tourists, minor bear-related injuries were common. Bear sightings have dropped correspondingly. Sarles reports that hospital and clinic staff also treat burns on folks who step off the boardwalks near geysers and hot pools. And a fair number of visitors need medical attention because they've snagged themselves with a fishhook.

Yellowstone National Park

Lake Hospital

Lake Village, 713 Lake, Yellowstone National Park • (307) 242-7241

Lake Hospital, managed by West Park Hospital in Cody (see subsequent entry), is the only seasonal hospital in the United States. Each May, the doors to this 10-bed hospital open with a new crew of healthcare professionals who offer round-the-clock care to park visitors. From mid-May until mid-September you can count on finding one doctor at the hospital and another on call. Three — occasionally, four — doctors share the work load. While the staff at this hospital gives quality care, emergency capabilities are limited not only by equipment, but also by the number of individuals on hand to help. A three-patient emergency would tax this hospital to the max, says its manager. Most emergency cases treated here are the result of either auto accidents or altitude-aggravated cardiac problems.

Mammoth Clinic

Mammoth Village, Yellowstone National Park • (307) 344-7965

Visitors to the Mammoth Hot Springs Clinic are apt to find elk grazing on the front lawn. Inside, though, they'll find a friendly doctor and several helpful nurses. The Mammoth Clinic, built in the 1960s, is the only year-round medical facility in Yellowstone National Park. The clinic serves not only park employees, but also the residents of Gardiner and Cooke City. It has X-ray equipment and an emergency room, but no pharmacy.

Mammoth Clinic is generally open seven days a week between Memorial Day and Labor Day weekends, and Monday through Friday the rest of the year. Check with either the clinic or the Park Service (see our Resources chapter) for specific times, which vary depending on the season.

Old Faithful Clinic

Old Faithful, Yellowstone National Park • (307) 545-7325

Imagine watching Old Faithful erupt while you're waiting to see the doctor. You can do just that at the Old Faithful Clinic, where walk-ins are not only welcome, but also expected. The clinic, built in 1996 to replace the old one housed in a dinky trailer next to the ranger station, has a big picture window facing Old Faithful geyser.

Old Faithful Clinic follows the openings and closings of the Inn and is open from early May until late October. During the spring and fall, the clinic is closed on Mondays and Tuesdays, but you'll find the Mammoth Clinic open on those days. Check with the Park Service for hours, which can vary.

Grand Teton National Park

Grand Teton Medical Clinic
Jackson Lake Lodge, Grand Teton National Park
• (307) 543-2514

At the only clinic in Grand Teton National Park, the physician's assistants not only write your prescription, but often can fill it. This is pretty handy since the nearest pharmacy is an hour's drive away (sorry, they can't fill a prescription they didn't write). They can X-ray that bum ankle and then sell you crutches if necessary.

Grand Teton Medical Clinic is owned by Emerg+a+Care in nearby Jackson, so these capable folks get on the phone with Emerg+a+Care's Dr. Blue when they need consultation. The clinic is open seven days a week from mid-May to mid-October. After hours or off-season, call park dispatch at (307) 739-3300 or St. John's Hospital in Jackson, (307) 733-3636 (see the previous entry in this chapter). The clinic can bill Medicare, but does not bill regular insurance.

Jackson Hole

Gooder Family Care
545 W. Broadway Ave., Jackson, Wyo.
• (307) 733-7003

Only a few blocks from town square on one of Jackson's main drags, Gooder Family Care is convenient and easy to find. Also convenient are the clinic's extended hours and seven-day weeks. No appointments are necessary; just come on in. These folks can do lab work and X-rays on-site, which might save you a trip to St. John's, the town's hospital (see this chapter's entry). Doctors Brent and Ron Gooder are a father/son team.

Jackson Hole Medical Clinic
988 U.S. Hwy. 89 S., Jackson, Wyo.
• (307) 739-8999

Dr. Rivers is a board-certified family physician with 22 years of emergency room experience. His clinic is equipped for minor surgery and orthopedic care. He even maintains a small on-site pharmacy so he can fill the prescriptions he writes.

The clinic keeps regular hours Monday through Friday. Dr. Rivers' staff have been known to locate accommodations for patients' families when a hospital stay was required. Dr. Rivers' specialty is asthma and allergy problems; he also speaks Spanish and a bit of German.

St. John's Hospital
625 E. Broadway Ave., Jackson, Wyo.
• (307) 733-3636

This is a hospital with history: It first opened its doors in 1916 in a four-room cabin; three years later, the cabin was expanded to eight rooms. Only 6 years old in its new location, St. John's now has 102 beds, five trauma rooms and the capacity to deal with everything from plastic surgery and advanced cardiac care to infectious diseases. Some of the top orthopedic surgeons in the nation practice here. The hospital focuses on community and outpatient services.

A transitional-care unit was built to help prepare patients to go home; the SurgiCenter was remodeled to better handle outpatient surgeries; and rehabilitation programs have been strengthened. St. John's other goal is to save area residents the long drive to Idaho Falls or

INSIDERS' TIP

West Park Hospital's lobby has an extensive museum-quality display of old-time drugs dispensed by Dr. M.F. Smith, an early-day pharmacist. If you're in Cody and happen to be touring the Buffalo Bill Historical Center, swing into the West Park Hospital right across the street. By the way, West Park Hospital manages the medical services in Yellowstone National Park.

Salt Lake City. Toward that end, the hospital has grown into a remarkably large and complete facility for such a rural area. The most recent addition was a new MRI unit for medical imaging.

In cooperation with Jackson Hole Mountain Resort, the hospital built a big new clinic at Teton Village. Called Teton Village Medical Clinic, the four-room trauma facility will eventually be open year round. In the short term it exists primarily to serve skiers; it was due to open December 1998.

Surrounding Areas

Southwestern Montana

Beartooth Hospital and Health Center

600 W. 21st St., Red Lodge, Mont. • (406) 446-2345

Owned by the community since 1993, this facility changed its name in 1997 from Carbon County Memorial Hospital and Nursing Home to the Beartooth Hospital and Health Center. This 22-bed hospital has an attached nursing home and offers 24-hour emergency care. In addition, it offers a range of outpatient surgeries, including knee surgeries, plastic surgery, mastectomies and appendectomies. The facility includes a day-care center and a pharmacy. Obstetrics, cardiac rehabilitation and community health education are also among this hospital's services. Mountain View Medical Center, a private clinic across the street from the hospital, encourages appointments but will accommodate walk-ins.

Bozeman Deaconess Hospital

915 Highland Blvd., Bozeman, Mont. • (406) 585-5000

Bozeman Deaconess Hospital, which opened its doors in 1986, is a full-service hospital with 86 beds. Deaconess offers an inpatient and retail pharmacy, radiology, physical therapy, cancer treatment and cardiopulmonary rehabilitation services as well as a full range of surgical services. A third medical office building was added in 1997 to the two that already adjoin Deaconess. The original two clinics are occupied by 49 doctors in 16 different groups. The medical staff is comprised of physicians representing a range of specialties.

Clinic at West Yellowstone

236 Yellowstone Ave., West Yellowstone, Mont. • (406) 646-7668

The folks at this cozy little clinic treat everything from sore throats to life-threatening emergencies. Managed until April 30, 1999 by Eastern Idaho Regional Medical Center in Idaho Falls (see separate entry), it is owned and staffed by two physician's assistants, two registered nurses and a friendly office crew with direct access to additional medical needs. The Clinic at West Yellowstone is open year round, Monday through Saturday from 8:30 AM until 5 PM, closing for an hour at noon. Patients needing acute emergency care are either flown via helicopter to Idaho Falls' EIRMC or taken by ambulance to hospitals in Bozeman, Rexburg or Idaho Falls.

Occupying a building that is now part of West Yellowstone's Historical District, the clinic was once part of an Oregon Short Line Railroad dining hall. On the exterior, the log-sided building carries the look of yesteryear. A recent remodeling has polished the interior, but you'll still see evidence of the clinic's Western frontier spirit, like a photo of a doctor and a Discovery Center veterinarian with an unconscious 9-month-old grizzly bear X-rayed at the clinic in 1996. Elsie, the cow elk — she's stuffed — presides over an outside waiting room.

Deaconess Billings Clinic

2800 10th Ave. N., Billings, Mont. • (406) 657-4000

Deaconess Hospital and Billings Clinic joined forces in 1993 and are now called Deaconess Billings Clinic. Don't let the name fool

INSIDERS' TIP

The effects of alcohol are increased at high altitudes. So are the symptoms of hangovers.

you — this is a hospital. It is a 272-bed nonprofit regional clinic, hospital and trauma center recognized for its patient-focused care. Services include emergency, trauma and walk-in care, family practice, internal medicine, obstetrics and gynecology, cardiology, renal dialysis, psychiatric and behavioral health services, orthopedics and sports medicine, neurology and women's health services. Since opening in 1927, the hospital has evolved from a family-oriented 58-bed facility to a regional medical center employing more than 1,000 people. Deaconess operates DEACARE/ALS, a fixed-wing air-ambulance service that uses two prop jets.

Livingston Memorial Hospital

504 S. 13th St., Livingston, Mont.
• (406) 222-3541

Livingston Memorial Hospital, built in 1955, is a nonprofit facility that offers a full range of care and is licensed for 45 beds.

Madison Valley Hospital and Madison Valley Clinic

217 N. Main St., Ennis, Mont.
• (406) 682-4222

This nine-bed, nonprofit hospital staffs three full-time and two part-time physicians as well as a physician's assistant and a family nurse practitioner. The staff here offers family medicine, gynecological services (but no obstetrics), X-rays, lab testing, cardiology and world-class orthopedics. Madison Valley Hospital provides urgent emergency care 24 hours a day, seven days a week. The clinic attached to the hospital provides general family medicine. The 46-bed Madison County Nursing home is next door to the hospital.

The Medical Clinic of Big Sky

Mountain Village, Big Sky, Mont.
• (406) 995-2797

Until 1994, folks from Big Sky had to drive miles to see a doctor. Now the Medical Clinic of Big Sky, a year round urgent-care center at the base of the Lone Mountain ski run, has a doctor and a paid emergency medical technician on staff. During the winter, when the clinic also serves injured skiers, staff size increases. The clinic is equipped for general family medicine including X-rays and casting. More extreme emergencies are stabilized, then sent either by ambulance, helicopter or airplane to Bozeman Deaconess Hospital or Saint Vincent Hospital in Billings (see previous entries), depending on the nature of the emergency. Dr. Jeff Daniels is on call 24 hours a day.

Saint Vincent Hospital and Health Center

1233 N. 30th St., Billings, Mont.
• (406) 657-7000, (800) 762-8778

Billings' first hospital has been providing medical care for the people of the region for more than a century. Saint Vincent has 302 beds and offers a range of services including a neonatal intensive-care unit, cancer care, the Sports Medicine Institute, The Women's Center, an emergency helicopter air service and Ask-A-Nurse, a 24-hour service that provides free healthcare information, and can help you find a physician. Fifteen clinics in and around Billings are part of Saint Vincent Primary Care Network.

Eastern Idaho

Ashton Family Practice Center

23 S. Eighth St., Ashton, Idaho
• (208) 652-7471

This is Ashton's only medical clinic. It's open during business hours Monday through Friday. The clinic's owner, Dr. Larry Curtis, also runs the Teton Valley Clinic in Driggs (see subsequent entry), 40 miles away. Although a doctor is on-site only one day a week, you'll get competent care here: Rural nurse practitioners and physician's assistants do a lot more than administer aspirin. Staff operate the in-house lab, X-ray and EKG equipment. Doctors are in constant contact when consultations are necessary. Ashton has no inpatient facilities. Minor maladies that require hospital admission will land you in Idaho Falls, Driggs or Rexburg.

Eastern Idaho Regional Medical Center

3100 Channing Way, Idaho Falls, Idaho
• (208) 529-6111

This 318-bed facility is the largest hospital in Yellowstone country. The reason? Even though Idaho Falls is home to only about

50,000 people, the hospital's service area includes 200,000 to 300,000. EIRMC (say it ER-mac) has the area's only open-heart-surgery program as well as the only bone bank (a bone bank stores donated human bones for transplant into those who might otherwise lose limbs or use of a joint). The hospital hosts a neurosurgery program and a breast-biopsy machine that saves women from surgeries to learn if their breast lumps are benign.

Driving time between an injured or ill person and a hospital can be measured in hours not minutes in this region, so EIRMC also owns a jazzy helicopter, designed to fly at speeds in excess of 150 mph and at high altitudes — two things most helicopters don't do well. The EIRMC rescue helicopter is the only one licensed to fly into Yellowstone National Park to transport victims of medical emergencies. Another program, called Fast Track, allows physician's assistants to treat minor emergencies and save you ER waiting time and expense. Fast Track is available 10 AM to 10 PM seven days a week.

Family Emergency Centers

East, 1995 E. 17th St., Idaho Falls, Idaho • (208) 529-5252
West, 250 S. Skyline Dr., Idaho Falls, Idaho • (208) 525-2600

Unlike many walk-in clinics, you won't be seen by a physician's assistant here. The centers' doctors and nurses handle the gamut of minor emergencies and are equipped to do lab work, X-rays and drug screening. They make life easy for travelers because they accept no appointments; just walk in (you can call in advance to see what the wait might be; usually it's short). The 17th Street clinic keeps extended hours seven days a week; Skyline is open six days. Family Emergency Center East was the first freestanding urgent-care clinic of this type in Idaho. It's been doing business since 1980.

Madison Memorial Hospital

450 E. Main St., Rexburg, Idaho • (208) 356-3691

If you need medical help in Rexburg, you'll come here. Large for a town of only 20,000 people, this 53-bed hospital is growing even larger. Emergency-room beds recently increased from seven to 11. Three additional surgical suites are planned, along with a new women's center that will house labor and delivery rooms, a postpartum program and other kinds of female surgery. The hospital delivers about 900 babies a year. Twenty-five full-time physicians staff the hospital, and the emergency room is staffed by doctors 24 hours a day. The reason Rexburg has such a complete and growing hospital is largely because this is a college town; every winter the population swells by about 8,000, or nearly a third.

Teton Valley Clinic

283 N. First E., Driggs, Idaho • (208) 354-2302

Driggs' clinic shares a building with the local hospital. This means you can have lab tests done or be admitted to the hospital without stepping outside. Call ahead Monday through Friday during business hours and on Saturday mornings (if your problem is not a serious emergency) and let the clinic save you big bucks over the hospital's emergency room. The clinic does accept walk-in patients on a case-by-case basis, but they appreciate it when you make an appointment.

Two family-practice doctors, a physician's assistant and two nurse practitioners staff the clinic. One of the doctors is always on-site or

INSIDERS' TIP

***Doc* (Lyons and Burford, 1994), written by Ennis family practitioner and internationally known orthopedic surgeon Ron "Doc" Losee, captures the pioneering spirit of the West and tells the story of doctoring in a small town. Losee, who often had to work with rudimentary equipment, is the kind of doctor about whom movies are made. *Doc* takes you right into the heart of the West, where wits are still sometimes the best — and only — medical tools available.**

nearby. This rural clinic also serves residents of Swan Valley and Island Park since these areas have no clinic of their own.

Teton Valley Hospital & Surgicenter
283 N. First E., Driggs, Idaho
• (208) 354-2383

This 13-bed facility recently underwent a $3.7 million renovation/expansion, paid for almost completely by community fund-raising. The little hospital can handle pretty much everything you'd expect from a hospital: surgery, medical imaging including CAT scans, respiratory and physical therapies, lab work and obstetrics. Patient services and community outreach are major focuses. The facility has a home healthcare program — a nurse comes to a patient's home. Staff offer a hospice program and a range of community education classes including prenatal and childbirth, grief support, fitness, blood-pressure monitoring and CPR training.

The hospital has a 24-hour acute-care emergency room with a doctor on call.

Northwestern Wyoming

Cody Family Practice
225 W. Yellowstone Ave., Cody, Wyo.
• (307) 527-7561

This clinic has three physicians on staff and welcomes walk-ins during regular daytime office hours. After hours you'll have to head for the emergency room of West Park Hospital.

West Park Hospital
707 Sheridan Ave., Cody, Wyo.
• (307) 527-7501, (800) 654-9447

West Park Hospital has 24-hour emergency/ambulance services and the latest technology, including MRI and renal dialysis equipment. West Park is well staffed with physicians specializing in family practice, general surgery, gynecology, internal medicine, obstetrics, orthopedic surgery, pediatrics and urology. The hospital is responsible for medical services within Yellowstone National Park, and patients requiring more care than park facilities can manage are often sent to West Park Hospital by helicopter or ambulance. The Coe Medical Center, attached to the hospital, accommodates up to 22 physicians. The 12-bed inpatient Chemical Dependency Center is one of only four resident facilities in Wyoming. For more information about medical services in Cody, call West Park Hospital Public Relations at the listed number and ask for extension 299.

West Park Urgent Care Clinic
702 Yellowstone Ave., Cody, Wyo.
• (307) 587-7207

Conveniently situated near Wal-Mart on the west end of town, this clinic welcomes walk-ins seven days a week from 9 AM until 7PM, except on Sundays when they close at 5 PM. Opened in June of 1998, the West Park Urgent Care Clinic is operated by West Park Hospital (see the entry above) and is staffed year round by a doctor, physician's assistants and a registered nurse.

Opportunities abound to help you gain insight into the issues, landscape, inhabitants or recreational opportunities of the region.

Education

Greater Yellowstone is a special place, and the opportunities afforded here for learning and growth can be pretty special, too. In this chapter we describe educational programs that help you gain insight into the issues, landscape, inhabitants or recreational opportunities of the region. We hope you are tempted to sample one of these offerings. New understanding is a better souvenir than all the snapshots in the world.

Yellowstone National Park

The Yellowstone Institute
Mammoth, Yellowstone National Park
• (307) 344-2294

Formed in 1976 to provide visitors with in-depth, on-the-ground educational experiences, the Yellowstone Institute treats about 850 students each year to an array of multiple-day classes aimed at enrichment, education and, let's face it, entertainment. In 1998, the Yellowstone Institute, the education arm of the nonprofit Yellowstone Association, listed more than 80 different classes in its catalog. (For more information on the Yellowstone Association, Yellowstone Park's partner in education and research, see our Shopping chapter.) All but a handful of these classes took place between June 1 and September 1.

The classes, based at the Buffalo Ranch, take students into the field to learn about the flora, fauna, geology, ecology, history and mystery of Yellowstone country. Many offer college credits. A peek at last year's catalog is likely to drive you to spend your entire summer sampling the institute's menu of offerings. At the very least, you might decide to join the growing group of regulars who come each summer from New York to learn a little bit more about the wilds and wherefores of Yellowstone country.

Past classes have included "Lakes of Yellowstone by Canoe," "The Bison of Yellowstone," "Family Horsepacking — Doing Things Together," "Mammal Tracking," "Wildflowers of Yellowstone," "Family Days in the Thermal Basins," "Autumn Wildlife Photography" and "Fly Fishing in the Fall," among many others. In addition, the institute offers nature-inspired writing, art and photography courses. To teach its courses, the institute uses various modes of transportation including vans, hiking, backpacking, llama packing, horsepacking, canoeing and cross-country skiing. Instructors are mostly from the Northwest and have a wealth of outdoor experience and expertise in their course subjects. Many of them are veteran teachers at the institute.

Facilities at the Buffalo Ranch include sleeping cabins, a historic bunkhouse and a communal kitchen. Situated on the year-round Gardiner-Cooke City Road, the Yellowstone Institute is accessible by road during the winter and is therefore able to offer a few winter courses. If we've tempted you with these field classes, we recommend you write the institute at P.O. Box 117, Yellowstone National Park, WY 82190, and ask for the 1999 catalog. We also suggest you sign up for their classes as soon as possible, since the institute gets a lot of class reservations from old-timers who know that some courses fill up fast.

Ranger-Naturalist Programs
• (307) 344-7381

Yellowstone National Park employs a battalion of ranger-naturalists each summer who guide walks and give programs tailored to their expertise and interests. *Yellowstone Today*, a publication handed to park visitors at each entrance, contains a schedule and descriptions of these programs. For an in-depth description of the ranger-naturalist program in Yellowstone, refer to the entry that follows on the Grand Teton National Park ranger-naturalists. The two parks' programs are very similar.

Grand Teton National Park

Ranger-Naturalist Programs

Grand Teton National Park visitor centers and other locations • (307) 739-3399

In 1916 when the National Park Service was established, so were ranger-naturalists. Back then, talking to and educating the public was part of every ranger's job. Now, although all rangers wear the same uniform, their ranks include backcountry rangers, law enforcement rangers, visitor-use assistants (they'll take your money at the park entrance) and ranger-naturalists. The job of the ranger-naturalist is to help you appreciate the complexity and wonder of their national park.

Three kinds of programs are offered in Grand Teton National Park: evening programs, talks and walks. Programs are greater in number and variety in summer — about 30 ranger-naturalists work here in summer, and about five in winter — but all year, you can bet something good is going on. Evening programs happen in each campground's outdoor amphitheater. They're about 45 minutes long, usually accompanied by slides and music. Presentation topics vary according to the individual ranger's interests and areas of expertise. Learn about fire ecology, birds of prey, wolves, bears and more. Talks are scheduled at various places and times. Often they provide overview information about the park, as well.

At Moose, orientation talks often make use of the detailed relief map that dominates the visitor center. Orientation talks are given several times a day at both Colter Bay and Moose visitor centers. Hikes vary in length, but usually take no more than a couple of hours. They're not physically demanding. For instance, the popular Inspiration Point hike focuses on area geology. It involves a pleasant boat trip across Jenny Lake, followed by a leisurely hike (less than a mile) past Hidden Falls to Inspiration Point, 400 feet above the lake. You walk back down at your own pace after asking the ranger every question you can think of. The cost of the boat ride is $4, but the hike itself is free.

Twilight hikes focus on wildlife. It's not uncommon on these hikes to see moose, black bears, red squirrels, pikas and marmots. June and July wildflower walks meander through sagebrush flats like those around Taggart Lake. You learn to identify flowers and see relationships between these lovely plants and the plant and animal communities to which they belong. You'll also learn about edible and medicinal plants. One very popular ranger-led activity occurs only in September and only out of Moose visitor center. A car caravan, limited to 10 vehicles (carpooling is encouraged) leaves the visitor center during the prime evening wildlife viewing hours. You visit three or four locations, learning about the types of wildlife that frequent them. You'll generally see animals, but even if you don't, you'll have learned their addresses.

Another popular fall activity is simply to meet the ranger-naturalist at Oxbow Bend turnout, a rich area for game, particularly moose, and use binoculars or spotting scopes to observe whatever is there to be observed. Fall is perfect for this activity because the mating season is on, which stirs things up.

In winter, rangers conduct snowshoe hikes out of Moose on old-style wood snowshoes. They even provide the snowshoes. The focus of these hikes is winter ecology and plant and animal adaptations to cold weather. Unlike Yellowstone National Park which is so popular with snowmobilers, Grand Teton National Park tends to be quiet in winter, which makes for pleasant hiking.

In general, there is no limit to participant numbers, and reservations are not necessary for ranger-led activities or ranger talks. Exceptions are snowshoe hikes, car caravans and the Inspiration Point hike. Call park dispatch or stop by any visitor center for a schedule of current ranger-naturalist activities.

Teton Science School

Ditch Creek Rd. off Kelly Rd., Grand Teton National Park • (307) 733-4765

More than 5,000 students ages 8 to 90

www.insiders.com
See this and many other
Insiders' Guide®
destinations online.
Visit us today!

attend the school each year. They come from all over the world, but about 80 percent live in the Intermountain West. Courses are taught at the campus, an aspen-ringed former guest ranch at the edge of Grand Teton National Park. Instruction also moves out into Grand Teton and Yellowstone parks and the Bridger-Teton National Forest.

TSS is a natural science center with a mission: Instructors believe that responsible management of fragile resources like those that make Greater Yellowstone precious is best accomplished by people with an educated, involved appreciation. They also believe that experience teaches. So school programs, teacher-education programs, community outreach and Elderhostel programs all focus on giving you opportunities for hands-on understanding of the natural world.

The school is open year-round; opportunities range from residential courses to one-day seminars. Some courses can be taken for college credit. School kids get involved in real research, like the bird banding project that, since 1991, has banded more than 51 species for monitoring. Other kid research includes radio telemetry studies of pronghorn antelope and coyotes. Students also work with the extensive collection of animal specimens collected by noted field biologists Olaus and Adolph Murie and explore the Muries' field journals and sketches.

Opportunities available to the general public include the four-day "Entomology for Flyfishers," co-taught by an entomologist and a noted fly-tier and fly-fisherman. The course teaches you how to identify and understand insects important in trout diets. Then you learn imitative patterns and fly-tying tips. Then you go fishing.

You can take advantage of popular short courses for birders and wildflower enthusiasts. Animal lovers learn how to identify and interpret the signs animals leave behind or learn more about specific species like coyotes or bears. You can canoe the Oxbow Bend of the Snake River in Grand Teton National Park and learn about the inhabitants of that rich riparian area.

Every year, longer residential programs are available to the public. For instance, summer 1999 marks the third year that TSS and adult students follow the Lewis and Clark Trail from eastern Montana to the Oregon coast, visiting expedition sites and taking part in scientific and historical explorations based on the jour-

INSIDERS' TIPS

See our Getting Around chapter for step-on guides and tours that can teach you a lot about Yellowstone country in just a day.

nals of Lewis and Clark. The 16 slots for this 2½-week odyssey fill fast.

Courses are reasonably priced starting at about $50 for a one-day class.

Jackson Hole

Great Plains Wildlife Institute
Jackson, Wyo. • (307) 733-2623

These folks have three goals: 1) They offer you the chance to do some of what wildlife biologists do; 2) they help you give back to the region's wildlife in return for the pleasure you receive from watching; and 3) they provide local jobs for researchers, paid for by concerned and involved tourists. When you sign up for a daylong safari, you and a maximum of five other guests spend the morning with a staff biologist in the institute's four-wheel-drive customized Suburbans, getting oriented and learning about the region's ecology, observing wildlife through institute-provided spotting scopes and binoculars. In the afternoon, you help the researcher gather data. Usually, this means you observe and record what you see. Often it means working with radio locating devices. Projects this year include radio-collar studies of coyotes and pronghorn antelope. The institute calls it citizen scientry; staff emphasize that although these research projects are real, participating in them requires no expertise and no hardbody stamina. In fact, if you're a family with kids, they'll bring the whole experience down to the kids' level of understanding. (If you don't have kids, you won't be paired with a family that does.)

Daytrips run year round and cost around $140 per person. In winter, the institute provides the snowshoes you'll probably end up on. Sunrise and sunset outings are available in the busy summer months, but the institute doesn't recommend those: You'll probably see wildlife, but you won't have much time to get involved in the research. Longer trips, including the Wolf Weekend Safari in Yellowstone National Park in May, are also available. Twelve weeklong programs are scheduled through the year. These long safaris take you through Yellowstone and Grand Teton national parks as well as surrounding land, mixing old-fashioned tourist sight-seeing with research. Call for scheduled dates.

Surrounding Areas

Southwestern Montana

A Naturalist's World
206 Fifth St. W., Gardiner, Mont. • (406) 848-9458

James Halfpenny, author of *A Field Guide to Tracking in North America* and *Winter: An Ecological Handbook*, leads several multiple-day workshops featuring wolves, bears, tracking and ecology. An ecologist and educator, Halfpenny has led several research projects across the nation and is very knowledgeable about Yellowstone's wild inhabitants. Halfpenny's workshops run from late December through June. Workshop costs vary.

Montana State University
120 Hamilton Hall, Bozeman, Mont. • (406) 994-0211

Founded in 1893, Montana State University was the first public institution of higher education in Montana. A land-grant college, it specialized in agriculture and mechanical arts

INSIDERS' TIPS

Each summer the Greater Yellowstone Coalition, a conservation organization formed in 1983 to protect and preserve Greater Yellowstone, leads a half-dozen educational trips somewhere into the region. In addition to summer tours, GYC offers dozens of educational workshops each year at its annual spring meeting the weekend after Memorial Day. For more information about GYC's classes and educational newsletters, write: 13 S. Willson Ave., Bozeman, MT 59715, or call (406) 586-1593.

Photo: Kirsten Burns

Teton Science School provides outdoor educational experiences.

back then. These days, though, the number of colleges at this 12,000-student university has expanded to eight: Arts and Architecture, Business, Agriculture, Education, Health and Human Development, Engineering, Letters and Science, Nursing and Library.

Many MSU professors use Montana's national forests and parks (Yellowstone National Park included) for their outdoor laboratories in the pursuit of such sciences as plant pathology, earth science, biology, sociology and paleontology. Paleontology students are attracted to MSU, where the Museum of the Rockies, an extension of the university, owns the only complete T. Rex collection in the state of Montana. (See our Attractions chapter for more information on the Museum of the Rockies.)

Northern Rockies Natural History

Bozeman, Mont. • (406) 586-1155

There is no better place in the world to watch wild wolves than Yellowstone National Park. And wildlife biologist Ken Sinay can lead you to them. He can also interpret their behavior while you watch them through binoculars or a spotting scope. Sinay specializes in leading small groups of people (his group size averages three or four) "off the asphalt," then showing and telling them about the mysteries and history of Yellowstone country. Tour the geysers with him and learn astounding facts about what lies beneath the surface of their bubbling, spraying waters. Walk a ways off the road and watch a bear bathing in the river. Or, if you must, stay in the car, and he or one of his guides will ride along and tell you what they know.

If you're inclined to leave your car, he won't have to lead you far for you to see what you never imagined you might see. For example, Sinay offers a daylong river float on the slow waters of the Madison, Gallatin or Jefferson rivers. You will sit in chairs on a 16-foot, flat-bottomed boat, slip into back channels, pull over in eddies and scope out wildlife. Along the way, you might observe muskrats, pelicans, cranes, eagles, river otter playing on the banks, mink, coyotes, osprey catching fish, beaver and deer.

After nine years in the business, Sinay offers his guests well-rounded insights into the historical, cultural and scientific aspects of the Greater Yellowstone ecosystem. You'll come away from one of his tours with a greater understanding of Yellowstone country and a desire to know more about what's going on in your own backyard. Sinay charges $125 per day per person for his float trips (there's a discount for additional people) and $410 per day for one person and $730 for two people for personally guided tours. You need to call ahead to make arrangements for a tour, because Sinay is often booked far ahead of time.

Off the Beaten Path

27 E. Main St., Bozeman, Mont.
• (406) 586-1311, (800) 445-2995

Working like a finely conducted orchestra, this company's army of staff members custom- designs vacation experiences intended to give you a local's insights into the culture, history, flora, fauna and science of Greater Yellowstone. The staff, veteran travelers and locals, themselves have scoured the region for the very best places, guides, outfitters and accommodations to make the most of your time. Each year they lead several expeditions into Yellowstone National Park. Past trips have included the eight-day "Bears and Wolves of Yellowstone"; "Tracing the Flight of the Nez Perce," a 12-day trek that follows the Nez Perce Trail through Montana and Idaho; and "Winter in Yellowstone Wonderland," an eight-day, cross-country trip that will lead you across pristine ski trails, through thermal basins and to wildlife.

Symbiosis Yellowstone Wildlife Tours

Gardiner, Mont.
• (406) 344-6555, (888) 436-4576

Nathan Varley grew up in Yellowstone National Park. Now 30, he is a wildlife biologist who works as a volunteer for the Yellowstone Wolf Project when he isn't leading photographers and film crews to wolves and other wildlife. Varley is also editor of *Wolf Tracker Magazine*. (See our Media chapter.) If you want to learn about Yellowstone wolves, Varley is a good bet. He charges $180 per day.

Yellowstone Ecosystem Studies

13 S. Willson Ave., #9, Bozeman, Mont.
• (406) 587-7758

Imagine watching a pack of coyotes trying to pick off and kill a single calf among five cow elk, or watching while coyotes (or wolves) devour an elk carcass, or witnessing territorial disputes between wolves and coyotes — both canids. Yellowstone Ecosystem Studies, a nonprofit, nonpolitical research and education organization, leads weeklong "Wild Dog" research trips in Yellowstone National Park. If you sign up for one of their trips, you will become a part of the research team. A team of biologists and zoologists will train you to observe canids, gather information and record what you see. After each day in the field, you and your fellow researchers will review and compare field notes. This trip, held seven times throughout the summer, costs $1,300 per person. It includes lodging in Cooke City and three squares a day.

Yellowstone Ecosystem Studies, led by canid biologist Bob Crabtree, shares its research with Yellowstone National Park to track the relationship between coyotes and wolves since wolves were re-introduced to the park in 1995. Crabtree has been studying coyotes in Yellowstone since the early 1980s.

Eastern Idaho

Teton Valley

Targhee Institute

Ski Hill Rd., Alta, Wyo.
• (307) 353-2233

Adults older than 55 and their companions can learn about Western water issues, outdoor photography, the geology of the Yellowstone region and more. Hosted by the Targhee Institute and Boston-based

INSIDERS' TIP

At motels, hotels and campgrounds in West Yellowstone, look for "Audio Auto Tours," a set of four cassettes produced by Dennis Paterson, a 25-year veteran tour-bus driver in Yellowstone National Park. These cassettes, which sell for $6 each, contain colorful details about the nooks and crannies of Yellowstone.

Photo: Robert Bower, Post Register

A Ricks College student takes a moment in the sun to review assignments before heading off for the next class.

Elderhostel, these residential courses generally run one week at a cost of around $450. Winter courses focus on teaching you to cross-country ski, snowshoe and track winter wildlife. The institute runs some programs without Elderhostel, such as its one-week natural-history-oriented day camps for 6- to 12-year-olds, available in summer.

Targhee Institute is in the Targhee National Forest at Grand Targhee Ski and Summer Resort. To learn about Elderhostel and the courses it offers in cooperation with Targhee

Institute, call (877) 426-8056. To learn about other programs, call the number listed above.

Rexburg, Idaho

Ricks College

U.S. Hwy. 20, Rexburg, Idaho • (208) 356-2011

Owned and operated by the Church of Jesus Christ of Latter-day Saints, Ricks is the largest two-year college in the country. Enrollment is held to 8,600 students, about a third of whom are from Idaho. Courses are taught by more than 300 full-time faculty members, nearly all of whom have either master's degrees or doctorates. Ricks also has an active continuing education program. On the main Rexburg campus, short-term, noncredit courses for the general public are available, mostly in summer; most focus on the natural or human history of the area. One final thing about Ricks: It adheres to the strictures of the Mormon faith and asks that while you're on campus you do the same. That means no caffeine, tobacco, alcohol, shorts or miniskirts.

Idaho Falls Area

Idaho State University/University of Idaho at University Place

1776 Science Center Dr., Idaho Falls, Idaho • (208) 535-7800

Question: How do you earn a college degree when your town has no university? Answer: With a little help from your friends. Idaho Falls is the largest town in Idaho with no university of its own. So Pocatello's ISU and Moscow-based U of I have combined forces to provide more than 500 academic courses to locals. Nearly 2,500 students per semester, most of them degree-seeking, take general-education courses or obtain bachelor's and graduate degrees through this cooperative program.

Eastern Idaho Technical College

1600 S. 25th E., Idaho Falls, Idaho • (208) 524-3000, (800) 662-0261

The focus here is vocational training. Health occupations, mechanical trades and business are well represented, with the business department attracting nearly 50 percent of student enrollment. Computer training courses are popular. The full-time enrollment of the college is small, around 450 students. Requests from local health facilities led to a recent expansion of health and medical programs. A sense of good fun led to summer and fall fly-fishing courses for the general public in 1998, offered in conjunction with Hyde Driftboats and All Seasons Anglers.

BYU-Ricks Center

1776 Science Center Dr., Idaho Falls, Idaho • (208) 523-4682

Ricks, a large Mormon Church-owned junior college in Rexburg, provides an important service to degree-seeking students in Idaho Falls. Every semester the school offers a selection of general-education requirements in English, math and social sciences to students in Idaho Falls. The instructors are generally Ricks faculty who drive down to teach these evening courses to students enrolled in degree programs through University of Idaho or Idaho State University who sometimes scramble to meet general-education requirements without having to leave town.

Community Education, Idaho Falls School District #91

601 S. Holmes Ave., Idaho Falls, Idaho • (208) 525-7748

This very active community education program deserves special notice. And it's getting it: 500 to 700 people a semester notice how much fun taking one or more of the program's 80-odd offerings can be. Prices range from $12 to $103 for courses that last from one day to 10 weeks.

INSIDERS' TIPS

Check with chambers of commerce in Red Lodge, Montana, and Cody, Wyoming, for top-quality teen workshops teaching classical and jazz music.

Northwestern Wyoming

Northwest College

231 West Sixth St., Powell, Wyo.
• (307) 754-6111

Located in Powell, about 70 miles from the east entrance of Yellowstone National Park and about 90 miles south of Billings, Montana, Northwest College is a two-year, residential college with about 2,000 students. It has come a long way since it began in 1946 as the first satellite branch of the University of Wyoming, with seven instructors teaching on the second floor of Powell High School. Northwest College offers transfer programs based on traditional arts and sciences and other programs that have strong educational requirements.

The college also operates the Mickelson Field Station in the Absaroka Mountain Range on Dead Indian Hill just off the Chief Joseph Scenic Highway (Wyo. Highway 296). This year-round facility includes a lodge with three buildings containing a total of 12 cabins. Reservations are filled on a first-come, first-served basis and may be made up to two years in advance. The length of stay is usually limited to five nights.

Summer Classes

Buffalo Bill Historical Center, Cody, Wyo.
• (307) 578-4061, (307) 578-4007

July through August, the BBHC offers nearly nonstop single and multiple-day workshops for children and teens. Themes include art, Native American cultures and hands-on history. Registration for the classes is usually the first of July, and reservations are required for each class. The fee is nominal.

Backcountry drives for the whole family

IDAHO Byways

Adventure roads from the Panhandle to the central mountains, the Snake River Plain and the Continental Divide

BY TONY HUEGEL

Media

Fierce local pride, a thirst for local news and a relative dearth of other media sources make the Yellowstone country newspaper business volatile. Every Yellowstone country community wants its own paper. Sometimes every faction within a community wants its own paper. That's how Teton County, Idaho, and Teton County, Wyoming, each ended up with two weekly papers serving their tiny towns (Idaho's *Teton County Independent* recently folded, however).

Tough luck for journalists, but a windfall of print information sources for residents. For you it's even better, because all those community newspapers and specialty magazines are a series of tiny windows straight to the syncopated heart of our region.

Radio and television reception can be iffy in this mountainous country. Most communities are cut off from neighboring towns' radio or television stations by mountains. This means local broadcast media choices can be limited. For many Yellowstone country residents, in fact, the only way to get pretty pictures on that glass-eyed box is a cable or satellite hookup. That's why the motels you've looked at advertise cable TV and not just TV. That's also why video rental stores are nearly as ubiquitous as gas stations.

What follows is a quick tour through the print and broadcast media of Yellowstone country.

Newspapers and Periodicals

In the Parks

Teewinot
Moose, Wyo. • (307) 739-3600

Grand Teton National Park's biannual publication is named for one of the peaks in the Teton Range. Its original purpose was to supply essential safety information to visitors, but you'll also find information about visitor resources, schedules of events, maps and discussions of wildlife and park issues in this 12-page newspaper. *Teewinot* is produced by park staff and published by the nonprofit Grand Teton Natural History Association, which also operates bookstores and visitor centers throughout the park and in neighboring national forest. About 500,000 copies are distributed annually.

Yellowstone Today
Mammoth, Yellowstone National Park • (307) 344-2258

As you enter Yellowstone National Park, a park ranger will give you a copy of *Yellowstone Today*, a 20-or-more-page newspaper that carries enough information about the park to get you on your way. Except for a five-year interruption from 1980 to 1985, Yellowstone National Park has had some sort of newspaper since 1974. Called the *Yellowstone Explorer* from 1974 to 1979, the park's quarterly publication became *Yellowstone Today* in 1986, after the Park Service put together a patchwork of funding to resurrect the newspaper. The Park Service hands out about a million copies of *Yellowstone Today* to visitors entering the park.

The summer issue is the largest of the year with about 20 pages, and it is full of all the information you'll need to get you started. *Yellowstone Today* includes maps showing locations of lodging, campgrounds, medical services, visitor centers and other facilities in both Yellowstone and Grand Teton parks. The rest of the publication highlights rules, campgrounds and lodging, concessionaire activities, safety, road construction schedules and information about fishing in Yellowstone National Park. An eight-page version, the *Yellowstone Guide*, is sent to those requesting an information packet from the Park Service.

The Yellowstone Wolf Tracker

Holladay, Utah • (801) 272-2981

This magazine may be published in Utah, but it's about Yellowstone National Parks' wolves reintroduced in 1995 and 1996. Those original wolves, now overflowing out of the park onto private lands and into Grand Teton National Park, have grown to a population of more than 100. They've also become very visible and popular among visitors. That's why the nonprofit Wolfstock Foundation puts out *The Yellowstone Wolf Tracker* six times a year, written mostly by volunteers. A year's worth of *Wolf Trackers* can be had for a $35 donation to the Wolfstock Foundation.

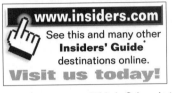

Dailies

Billings Gazette

401 N. Broadway Ave., Billings, Mont. • (406) 657-1200

With a Sunday circulation of 62,000, the *Billings Gazette* is Montana's largest newspaper. The *Gazette* has an incredibly wide circulation. It covers 90,000 square miles from the Canadian border to central Wyoming and from the western Dakotas to Helena, Montana. It supports bureaus in Cody, Wyoming, and Bozeman and Helena, Montana. Each year the *Gazette* publishes 60 special sections including a tab on Yellowstone National Park and guides to hunting and fishing.

Bozeman Daily Chronicle

32 S. Rouse Ave., Bozeman, Mont. • (406) 587-4491

The *Bozeman Daily Chronicle*, a morning paper published seven days a week by Big Sky Publishing, LLC, employs a full-time staff writer to cover Yellowstone National Park year-round. In addition to park coverage, the *Chronicle* puts out an annual publication called *Explorer*, a guide to outdoor recreation and activities in Yellowstone country, as well as an annual fishing guide for Southwestern Montana. The *Bozeman Daily Chronicle*, first published in 1911, covers national and regional news, local color and regional sports. The *Chronicle* has a daily circulation of 13,500 and a Sunday circulation of 15,000. The daily paper costs 50¢, and the Sunday edition is $1.25.

Livingston Enterprise

401 S. Main St., Livingston, Mont. • (406) 222-2000

The *Livingston Enterprise*, published every weekday, has been in continuous publication since the first issue was put out on June 4, 1883, in an office above Frank White's Saloon in the Orschel Building on E. Park Street. Since that time, the paper has changed hands several times, switched back and forth from a daily to a weekly and changed location at least four times. Owned by the super-big and politically powerful copper-mining Anaconda Company from 1919 to 1959, the *Enterprise* was bought by Lee Newspapers then sold to William and Helen Hornby in 1971. The *Enterprise*, which has a circulation of 3,800, carries several features each issue and offers diverse news coverage. In the same day, you might read on one page about a presidential visit to Yellowstone National Park and on the next page about who went to dinner at whose home in Wilsall. The *Enterprise*, generously supplemented with Associated Press stories, gives good coverage to Yellowstone National Park issues. The paper costs 50¢.

Post Register

333 Northgate Mile, Idaho Falls, Idaho • (208) 522-1800

Idaho Falls' newspaper is the media anchor for the west side of Yellowstone country. It distributes 28,000 copies daily between Pocatello, Idaho, and West Yellowstone, Montana, and between Salmon, Idaho, and Freedom and Afton, Wyoming. The Post Company also owns Local News 8, KIFI-TV. By Idaho standards, it's a regular publishing giant, producing recreation and travel guides (including this one!), a small stable of magazines and several weekly newspapers. The *Post Register's* pedigree dates to 1880, when the *Blackfoot Register* was first published by William Wheeler. Since 1925, the paper has been owned by the Brady family, many of whom live in Idaho Falls.

The *Post Register*, along with several other Idaho dailies, won a national award in 1998 for a cooperative project which examined the state's prison spending and its spending on education. The *Post Register* is a seven-day morning paper. Its newsstand price is 50¢ on weekdays and $1.50 on Sundays.

Semiweeklies

Cody Enterprise

1549 Sheridan Ave., Cody, Wyo. • (307) 587-2231

Founded by Buffalo Bill Cody in 1899, the *Cody Enterprise* is the oldest business in Cody. This award-winning newspaper, published Monday and Wednesday afternoons, reflects the community's general attention to quality. The *Enterprise* sports top quality photos as well as features and general news about Cody and the surrounding area. In addition to lively news reporting, the paper is peppered with local weekly columns such as "Quade's Quips," "Tracks Trails and Tidbits" and "Streamside." The *Cody Enterprise* has a circulation of 6,025; it costs 50¢.

Fremont County Herald Chronicle

St. Anthony, Idaho • (208) 624-4455

This decade-old consolidation of three Fremont County weeklies is published on Mondays and Wednesdays by *The Rexburg Standard Journal* in Madison County. Like Rexburg's paper, the *Herald Chronicle* is owned by a local family, the Porters; it shares both a philosophy and some of its pages with the larger Rexburg publication. Both try to provide broader coverage than most weeklies, mixing regional and national news of local interest with strictly local news. Like the Rexburg paper, the *Fremont County Herald Chronicle* is a wire-service paper, unusual for a small weekly. This paper is available by subscription and for 50¢ at countywide newsstands. It has about 1,500 subscribers.

Rexburg Standard Journal

Rexburg, Idaho • (208) 356-5441

Folks in Rexburg like their paper. The roots of this award-winning independent biweekly stretch back a century in its pin-neat farming town. Unlike many smaller papers within range of Idaho Falls' big daily, the *Rexburg Standard Journal* provides some regional and national news, although its focus is still the community. The paper prints 4,400 copies. It's published on Mondays and Wednesdays and costs 50¢ at newsstands throughout Madison County.

Weeklies

Carbon County News

202 S. Hauser St., Red Lodge, Mont. • (406) 446-2222

If a picture is worth a thousand words, there's plenty to read between the lines in the *Carbon County News*. Loaded with top-quality interesting photos (even the mug shots are good), you'll swear Editor Shelley Beaumont has a team of photographers scouring the countryside for prize-winning snapshots. The photos and the copy in this weekly, owned by News Montana Inc., mirror the diversity of Red Lodge and the surrounding area. The *Carbon County News*, first published in 1907 as the *Red Lodge Pickett-Journal*, has a staff of seven and a circulation of 3,000. It's published on Wednesdays and costs 75¢.

The Fremont Current

37 W. Main St., St. Anthony, Idaho • (208) 624-4500

This weekly, which hits newsstands every Thursday, is a locals' local. It runs no national wire copy. Its writers live and work in Fremont County, and stories are about Fremont County. Editor Cathy Koon was born in the county seat of St. Anthony. Born in July of 1997, *The Fremont Current* is an experiment, a merging of weeklies based in St. Anthony, Ashton and Island Park. Subscribe for $26 per year, or pick up a newsstand copy almost anywhere in the county for 50¢. The paper has about 2,000 subscribers.

Gardiner Community Newsletter

233 Main St., Suite A, Gardiner, Mont. • (406) 848-7971

Printed 52 weeks a year for more than 15 years by the Gardiner Chamber of Commerce, the *Gardiner Community Newsletter* hits the streets each Wednesday morning. Printed on both sides of legal-size paper, this free newsletter is for both locals and tourists. It contains brief news about business summer hours and sales as well as reminders to locals about the date, time and location of the next visit by the Schwann's delivery truck. The newsletter also announces the times and dates of meetings and contains a section of classifieds, including rentals, jobs and yard sales. Look for the *Gardiner Community Newsletter* at most local businesses.

High Country Independent Press

220 S. Broadway St., Belgrade, Mont. • (406) 388-6762

The *High Country Independent Press* began as the *Belgrade Independent Press* in 1979. After several ownership changes, *High Country* was bought in 1987 by Glenn and Devon Sorlie. In 1989, this weekly, which is published every Thursday, switched from a free to a paid-for publication. It quickly grew from a sometimes-12-page paper to its current 18 to 24 pages with a circulation of just less than 3,000. Covering Belgrade, Big Sky, Bozeman, Manhattan and Three Forks, this paper contains an array of community news. The extensive and detailed Sheriff's Log and Belgrade Police Log make fascinating reading. The newsstand price is 50¢.

Island Park News

(208) 558-0267

This weekly prints no wire-service copy: It's for and about the Island Park area. Copublisher Elizabeth Laden says *Island Park News* has subscribers in all 50 states, however. Tourists who care about the area come through in the summer, pick up a free newsstand copy and decide they want to keep hearing about Island Park after they go home, she says. The paper prints between 2,500 and 10,000 copies per week, depending on the season and what's happening in the area. This is interesting in light of the fact that Island Park has only 400 year-round residents. *Island Park News* is distributed from Idaho Falls to Billings, Montana, in retail stores and visitor centers.

Jackson Hole Guide

185 N. Glenwood St., Jackson, Wyo. • (307) 733-2430

Born in 1952, *Jackson Hole Guide* is Jackson's oldest newspaper. It publishes a thick weekly edition and a slimmer daily version. The weekly has a circulation of 8,000, and the daily's distribution is 5,000. The paper has subscribers in all 50 states and is available on newsstands from Jackson to Pinedale and from Victor and Driggs to Star Valley.

The *Guide* is not Jackson's only paper, though. For years it was seen as a conservative paper, so the *Jackson Hole News* stepped in to tell the liberal story. Those political labels no longer seem accurate, but what is still true is that the competition between two newspapers in such a small market has made both topnotch. Both routinely win national awards. Both are read, sort of interchangeably, by area residents. *Jackson Hole Guide* costs 75¢ on newsstands; it comes out on Wednesdays. The daily edition, mostly ad copy, is free.

Jackson Hole News

1225 Maple Way, Jackson, Wyo. • (307) 733-2047

Jackson's residents tend to be well-educated and very interested in area issues. So it's no surprise that the typical Jackson resident reads two local weekly newspapers. But headlines about local issues — how grizzlies and bison should be managed or winter recreation conflicts in Yellowstone National Park, for instance — are often compelling to those from outside the region as well.

The *News* is about 26 years old. In 1996 it was named best in its class by the National Newspaper Association, but it started getting attention long before that. In the mid-1980s, the University of Missouri picked little *Jackson Hole News* from every other paper in the country for its effective use of photos. The weekly edition is available on area newsstands for

50¢; like the *Guide* (see previous entry), the *News* comes out on Wednesdays. It circulates about 8,000 copies. A slimmer daily edition, mostly ad copy, is free.

The Jefferson Star

134 W. Main St., Rigby, Idaho
• (208) 745-8701

Jefferson County's weekly dates to 1903. It has been owned since 1988 by Terry and Kenneth J. Carr, originally from Texas. Circulation is around 2,000, mostly in Jefferson and Clark counties. *The Jefferson Star* readers often subscribe also to the area's daily, the *Post Register*. This gives the *Star* the freedom to focus on the local news the *Post Register* can't provide. You can pick up a copy of *The Jefferson Star* at area newsstands for 50¢; it comes out Wednesday mornings.

Here's a great trivia tidbit about *The Jefferson Star*: Back when it was called *The Rigby Star*, this tiny paper in a backwater farming area of a backwater state was home to a columnist whose work was syndicated across the country. Vardis Fisher was an acclaimed novelist (and during his stint as a college professor, the instructor of Pulitzer Prize-winner Wallace Stegner). Fisher's best-known book is *The Mountain Man*.

Lone Peak Lookout

Meadow Village Center, Big Sky, Mont.
• (406) 995-4133

Big Sky is a happening place, and the Lone Peak Lookout is just the publication to take you into the nooks and crannies of everyday life in the Canyon. This award-winning independent, purchased in 1998 by Big Sky Publishing, LLC, has served Gallatin Canyon and Big Sky since 1982. A free publication, it is jam-packed with articles and columns that represent the spectrum of life in the Canyon. The *Lookout* can be found at newsstands almost anyplace in Greater Yellowstone; it's published on Thursdays. This paper has 700 subscribers nationwide, with a total circulation of between 3,500 and 5,500.

Park County Weekly

306 S. Main St., Livingston, Mont.
• (406) 222-9500

Sharon Walker first began the *Park County Weekly* on April Fool's Day, 1986, right at the beginning of an economic downswing. Six months later, she put the free publication to rest and moved to Seattle where she started a printing and graphics business. Seven years later, she returned to Livingston and brought her business with her. Three years after that, in 1996, she resurrected the *Park County Weekly* by popular demand. Walker now employs eight people and publishes 8,000 copies each Tuesday. Dubbed "the paper that's read from cover to cover," the *Park County Weekly* is filled with down-home, warmhearted, interesting reading about people, places and events in Park County.

Teton Valley News

80 E. Little Ave., Driggs, Idaho
• (208) 354-8101

In 1909, *Teton Valley News* fired up its

INSIDERS' TIP

Don't let the newspaper scene in Jackson confuse you. It works like this: Jackson is home to two weekly papers. Most residents read both. Each weekly also publishes a daily edition available in area stores and restaurants. Many residents read neither. The reason? The dailies carry mostly advertising and regional and national wire service copy of interest to tourists. The well-researched local stories that Jackson residents crave are almost all found in the weekly editions, which come out on Wednesdays. You'll know you're picking up a "real" newspaper if you have to pay for it, since their daily versions are free. As a visitor to the area, you'll find the dailies' restaurant guides and ads useful. But if you want a window into Jackson's character, make sure you buy a weekly paper, too.

presses and became Teton Basin's first and only newspaper. It has had competition off and on from other weeklies, but the *News* is still the voice of tradition (and the traditional voice) of Teton Valley. It prints 2,500 copies. Only 1,600 of the paper's subscribers are valley residents, reflecting wider interest in the little mountain valley. Of course, it doesn't hurt that the Idaho Press Club regularly singles the *News* out for excellence in a variety of areas, including General Excellence awards in 1994 and 1997. This Thursday weekly is available at local newsstands for 50¢.

West Yellowstone News

309 Canyon St., West Yellowstone, Mont. • (406) 646-9719

The *West Yellowstone News*, which bills itself as the "Biggest Little Paper in the West," took a big upswing in 1997. This homey little paper will tell you what's going on in West Yellowstone. It also carries news about Yellowstone National Park issues, especially those that relate to the welfare of West Yellowstone. Several columns, including the "Fish Wrapper" by John and Craig of Blue Ribbon Flies, offer insider information on the community in general and fishing in particular. The circulation is 2,500, and it costs 50¢.

Periodicals

Arts Alive!

498 A St., Idaho Falls, Idaho • (208) 522-0471

This 16- to 20-page newsprint magazine is published by the Idaho Falls Arts Council three times a year. You can pick it up free in coffee shops and restaurants from Idaho Falls, Idaho, to Jackson, Wyoming. Expect to find news about local performing and visual arts throughout Eastern Idaho. Perhaps the most useful item is the calendar, which includes not only art shows and festivals, but also community events, rodeos, storytelling festivals and fairs.

Big Sky Journal

101 E. Main St., Bozeman, Mont. • (406) 586-2712, (800) 417-3314

A high-gloss, nonpolitical, coffee-table magazine mostly about Montana, *Big Sky Journal* has been published five times a year since 1993. In a single issue, you might find an article on Montana's Hutterites, mountain men, Montana writers or Western photographer Barbara Van Cleve. Somewhere in those pages you'll find a couple of essays on ranching, maybe a photo feature on Yellowstone National Park and always some tips on "Eating Around Montana." Special departments in the *Big Sky Journal* include Ranch Life, Western Designs, In Place and Time, Backcountry and The Back Forty. *Big Sky Journal* also includes reviews of several books relevant to the Rockies. The newsstand price is $5.95; a subscription for five issues is $24.

Caldera

Jackson, Wyo. • (307) 733-2995

Caldera is a place for "news of the imagination," as one former editor puts it. Kendra Day, editor and publisher for the next several issues, explains that the volunteer job of editor has traditionally changed hands with every issue. One issue in 1998 was midwifed by students from the local alternative high school. Ads, grants and private donations pay for printing costs. The mag is about living in Jackson Hole, about stewardship of the land, about people in relation to place. Material ranges from poetry to personal reflection, sketches to photography and commentary to fiction. *Caldera* comes out irregularly once or twice a year. The cover price ranges between $3.95 and $4.95 in area bookstores, Albertson's grocery stores and other locations in and around Jackson Hole.

Crone Chronicles: A Journal of Conscious Aging

Kelly, Wyo. • (307) 733-5409

Wisdom is the result of paying attention to your experience, believes editor and co-publisher Ann Kreilkamp. Her 9-year-old quarterly publication is a forum for people to glean from their experience and share what they find. The magazine prints 5,000 copies an issue. Subscriptions are available for $21. The magazine's readers are scattered across the country, as are its contributors of personal reflections, essays, poetry and images. Issues are themed:

Past emphases include war and peace, power and presence, emergence and emergency, soul and money, and journeys. In Jackson, you can pick up a copy for around $7 at Harvest, the Herb Store, Teton Book Shop and Valley Bookstore.

Intermountain Farm and Ranch Magazine

333 Northgate Mile, Idaho Falls, Idaho • (208) 522-1800

A 7-year-old weekly newsprint magazine with a circulation of 15,000, Farm and Ranch prints news farmers can use. It is inserted into *Post Register* deliveries on rural routes. You can also pick it up free on magazine racks in Southwestern Montana, Western Wyoming, Northern Utah and Eastern Idaho as far north as Lemhi County. In 1996 The Post Company surveyed *Intermountain Farm and Ranch* readers to learn that 3,400 are full-time farmers, 2,200 are full-time ranchers, and 1,700 work part-time or are retired from agricultural jobs. Editor John Thompson plans a dozen themed issues for 1999; topics will include farm-related law, the region's horse industry and irrigation technology.

Montana Free Press

Red Lodge, Mont. • (406) 446-1906

The *Montana Free Press* changed ownership in 1998 after eight years in business. Current publisher/editor Rick Cosgriffe hasn't changed the content or format of this popular regional publication. The *Montana Free Press*, billed as "the journal of rural Montana," regularly exceeds 50 pages. Since its early days, the *Free Press* has evolved into a vehicle for recording the oral histories of individuals and their communities. Cover stories feature various rural communities throughout Montana and Wyoming. The *Montana Free Press* has a circulation of 10,000. Postal patrons in Carbon and Stillwater counties receive free copies via third-class postage.

Montana Land Magazine

1364 Valley Heights Rd., Billings, Mont. • (406) 259-3534

Known as the real-estate bible of Montana, the *Montana Land Magazine* may be the largest real-estate publication in the country. Gordie Dangerfield, a Billings real estate agent, got the idea for the magazine one day as he was driving through Big Sky country dreaming and scheming. Since 1982, when he put out the first 40-page issue, the *Montana Land Magazine* has grown so much that it takes a semi-truck to haul the 125,000 issues distributed in Montana and five other states each summer. Distributed free to the public at 900 locations, this quarterly publication is widely read and has subscribers in several foreign countries.

Snake River Echoes

Rexburg, Idaho • (208) 356-9101

This biannual publication of the Upper Snake River Valley Historical Society in Rexburg is published out of the same building that contains Rexburg's Teton Flood Museum. Like the museum itself, the magazine is about remembering. Contents include poetry, reminiscence and first-person accounts of events from Eastern Idaho's history. Only about 750 copies are printed, but they end up in libraries as far away as Seattle, Washington; Battle Creek, Michigan; and the Smithsonian Institute in Washington, D.C. You can purchase current and back copies at the museum. Current copies sell for $5.

SnowAction

520 Park Ave., Idaho Falls, Idaho • (208) 524-7000

Smaller than *SnoWest* (see subsequent listing), this Harris Publishing Company magazine is for snowmobile racers and racing fans. It covers grass and asphalt drags (yes, people really do race on asphalt with specially modified snowmobiles), ovals and hillclimbs and snowcross races. Each issue includes a useful calendar of races nationwide. The magazine is published eight times a year, with five issues saturating the peak racing season, January through March. Subscribers pay around $15 a year for eight issues of 40 to 60 slick pages full of photos and color. You can't buy this magazine on newsstands, but some snowmobile dealerships handle it. *SnowAction* prints around 22,000 copies per issue.

SnoWest

520 Park Ave., Idaho Falls, Idaho • (208) 524-7000

SnoWest is one of two snowmobile magazines published by family-owned Harris Publishing (the other is *SnowAction;* see previous listing) and one of seven recreational and agricultural publications Harris owns. Aimed at recreational riders, this magazine features travel destinations, industry information and consumer reviews of snowmobiles and new products. *SnoWest* focuses on mountain riding. *SnoWest* is published eight times a year at a cover price of around $4. Circulation is 170,000, but subscription is the best way to get ahold of this publication.

Top to Bottom

189 N. Main St., Driggs, Idaho • (208) 354-3466

Not your typical tourist guide, this glossy magazine tries to include something for all, from the third-generation valley native to the drive-by visitor. Writers and photographers are usually valley residents. Regular departments include Field Notes, a natural history column; Familiar Faces, a profile of a valley resident; Clubhouse, which focuses on kid issues; and Back When, which looks at area history. Fiction, poetry and visual art are also featured. Toward the back, you'll find the usual — and useful — calendar and dining/lodging guides. The magazine, produced twice a year, has subscribers in 33 states. Newsstand copies are complimentary; you can subscribe for $9.95 per year.

The Tributary Magazine

14 S. Willson Ave., Ste. 2, Bozeman, Mont. • (406) 586-0744

First published in 1992 by two Montana State University art students bent on covering the arts in Bozeman, *The Tributary*, "Montana's Source Beyond the Main Stream," was then called *Happenings*. Now owned by publisher Carter G. Walker, *The Tributary* is a free monthly publication packed with poetry, profiles, essays, fiction and photographs aimed at capturing the evolving community that is the Old and the New West. Outsider, newcomer, Insider and old-timer swap stories and insights across *The Tributary's* pages, dancing briefly with the shifting tide of change. An in-depth centerfold events calendar outlines the coming month, and "Harper's Index" at the end of each issue is a reminder of the ludicrous and the outrageous beyond Bozeman. *The Tributary*, published the first of each month, can be found in coffee shops and restaurants. It's free.

Wyoming Magazine

Jackson, Wyo. • (307) 739-4646

This publication, launched in January 1997, covers events and issues from across the Equality State. You'll enjoy the window into the "real" Wyoming. The calendar is also useful: Every calendar generally includes at least one item for every major town in the state. The magazine is published biannually. Subscribe for $16 per year, or pick up an issue for $3.50 at newsstands and bookstores across the state. Circulation is around 10,000.

Yellowstone Journal

431 Main St., Lander, Wyo. • (307) 332-2323

If you want to keep up on what's happening in Yellowstone country year in and year out, the *Yellowstone Journal*, published in Lander, Wyoming, is the newspaper for you. This lively paper is loaded with color photos and crammed with interesting stories about people, places and things to do mostly in Yellowstone and Grand Teton national parks. The *Yellowstone Journal* features the finer details of the parks, the things the average person would bypass without ever knowing them.

Editor/publisher Shelli Johnson and her husband, Jerry, created the *Yellowstone Journal* in 1993 with the tourist in mind. Its pages will take you into the world of insects and antelope, into the office of Yellowstone National

INSIDERS' TIP

In Yellowstone country, if your accommodations choice doesn't offer cable or satellite TV, don't plan on much in the way of selection or quality reception.

Park Superintendent Mike Finley, through museum exhibits, deep into a geyser, into a wolf den and straight to a hidden waterfall or high mountain lake. The *Journal* sells for $1 in Yellowstone and Grand Teton national parks as well as at various locations in entrance and gateway communities to both parks. The paper has subscribers in all 50 states and numerous foreign countries.

Television

Until the 1970s, when cable service brought more channels and better reception to rural television viewers in Yellowstone country, those beautiful Rocky Mountains translated into poor TV reception for those of us who live in rural towns. For Greater Yellowstone's rural residents, it was cable service provided by small companies that brought the "outside world" — for better or worse — into our living rooms.

Cable Companies

Gateway Cable Company

76405 Gallatin Rd., Gallatin Gateway, Mont. • (406) 763-4777

This tiny cable company 13 miles southwest of Bozeman has no phone, no fax and only 64 customers who can tune in to 14 channels. Put together in 1987 by the owners of the Gallatin Gateway Inn, a resurrected railroad hotel, Gateway Cable was initially designed only to serve the Inn's guests. Additional customers were added to the system when neighbors asked to be hooked up to the service.

High Mountain Communications Inc.

303 Canyon St., West Yellowstone, Mont.

When High Mountain Communications brought cable to West Yellowstone residents in 1979, television viewing jumped from one static-riddled channel to 14. Today, High Mountain supplies more than 300 households and 1,500 motel rooms with cable service providing up to 32 channels. High Mountain has to lay temporary cables across the top of the snow during the winter to accommodate new hookups.

North Yellowstone Cable Television

Third St. and Park St., Gardiner, Mont. • (406) 848-7561

Owned by George Buffington, North Yellowstone Cable Television was the first cable company to service a national park. In 1983, one year after creating the company, Buffington; his father, Ken Dixon; and a third partner, Dave Lane, ran a cable line from Gardiner to Mammoth to serve Yellowstone National Park's permanent employees. Cable service increased their reception from three fuzzy channels to 15 sharp ones. North Yellowstone Cable serves 260 subscribers.

TCI Cablevision of Idaho

1480 Lincoln Rd., Idaho Falls, Idaho • (208) 523-4567

TCI first brought cable service to eastern Idaho about 21 years ago. The largest cable provider in the area serves from St. Anthony to Idaho Falls and Blackfoot and east to Teton Valley.

TCI Cablevision of Montana Inc.

511 W. Mendenhall St., Bozeman, Mont. • (406) 586-2089

TCI Cablevision of Montana serves the cities of Billings, Bozeman, Livingston and Butte.

TCI Cablevision of Wyoming Inc.

3575 S. Park, Jackson, Wyo. • (307) 733-6030
2432 Sheridan Ave., Cody, Wyo. • (307) 587-2219

This company is made up of autonomous offices scattered across the state of Wyoming, each offering service to a relatively small area. The Jackson office serves around 6,000 subscribers in Teton Village, Wilson and Jackson. The Cody office serves mostly viewers within Cody's city limits, with a couple of out-of-town exceptions. Other communities in Jackson Hole, like little Kelly and Hoback Junction, do not have cable service. It's more cost-effective for them to access TV through satellite services.

Stations and Network Affiliates

The following major television stations are listed along with their network affiliate:

KCTZ Channels 7 and 20 (FOX), Bozeman, Mont.

KFXP Channel 31, (Fox) Pocatello, Idaho

KHMT Channel 4 (FOX), Billings, Mont.

KIDK Channel 3 (CBS and Fox), Idaho Falls, Idaho

KIFI Channel 8 (ABC), Idaho Falls, Idaho

KISU Channel 10 (PBS), Pocatello, Idaho

KJWY Channel 2 (NBC), Jackson, Wyoming

KPVI Channel 6 (NBC), Idaho Falls, Idaho

KSVI Channel 6 (ABC), Billings, Mont.

KTVM Channels 6 and 42 (NBC), Butte, Mont.

KTVQ Channel 2 (CBS), Billings, Mont.

KULR Channel 8 (NBC), Billings, Mont.

KUSM Channel 9 (PBS), Bozeman, Mont.

KWYB Channel 8 (ABC), Butte, Mont.

Radio

Depending on where you are, what kind of weather it is and whether it's night or day, you can pick up any number of stations that broadcast in Yellowstone country. Unless the station has a huge transmitter or a translator to help send its sound waves across the mountains, its signal can fade in and out pretty fast while you're driving along.

There is one notable exception to the rule: Yellowstone Public Radio, which broadcasts from the Joseph S. Sample Studios at Montana State University-Billings. It has the largest geographic coverage of any public radio station in the country. The station, which began as a 10-watt student station, expanded in the late 1970s after getting federal grants. Yellowstone Radio, which can be picked up in the northern part of Yellowstone National Park, sends its programs over the air as far north as Cutbank, Montana, east to Glendive and southeast to Thermopolis, Wyoming.

You can pick up the West Yellowstone stations KWYS 102.9 FM and KEZQ 92.9 AM throughout both Yellowstone and Grand Teton national parks, as well as south to Blackfoot, Idaho, and north to Big Sky and Ennis in Montana. Cody's KODI 1400 AM station carries a community call-in show each morning that not only lets you know what's happening in the area, but also lets you peek into the local culture.

Adult and Soft Contemporary

KADQ 94.1 FM, Rexburg, Idaho
KBMJ 95.5 FM, Billings, Montana
KGTM 98.1 FM, Idaho Falls, Idaho
KLCE 97.3 FM, Idaho Falls, Idaho
KMXE 99.3 FM, Red Lodge, Montana
KOHZ 103.7 FM, Billings, Montana
KOSZ 105.5 FM, Idaho Falls, Idaho
KTAG 97.9 FM, Cody, Wyoming
KYYA 93.3 FM, Billings, Montana
KZJH 95.3 FM, Jackson, Wyoming

Christian

KGVW 640 AM, Belgrade, Montana
KULR 730 AM, Billings, Montana

Contemporary

KCTR 102.9 FM, Billings, Montana
KFTZ 103.3 FM, Idaho Falls, Idaho

Continuous Favorites

KSCY 96.7 FM, Bozeman, Montana

Country

KDWG 970 AM, Billings, Montana
KGHL 790 AM, Billings, Montana
KID 96.1 FM, Idaho Falls, Idaho
KIDX 98.5 FM, Billings, Montana
KPOW 1260 AM, Powell, Wyoming
KPRK 1340 AM, Livingston, Montana
KSGT 1340 AM, Jackson, Wyoming
KUPI FM 99.1 FM, Idaho Falls, Idaho
KWYS 102.9 FM, West Yellowstone, Montana
KZBQ 93.7 FM, Idaho Falls, Idaho
KZLO 99.9 FM, Bozeman/Livingston, Montana

Full Service

KBOZ 1090 AM, Bozeman, Montana

News/Talk/Sports

KBLG 910 AM, Billings, Montana
KID 590 AM, Idaho Falls, Idaho
KMMS 1450 AM, Bozeman, Montana

Golden Oldies

KKBR 97.1 FM, Billings, Montana
KOBB 1230 AM, Bozeman, Montana
KOBB 93.7 FM, Bozeman, Montana
KODI 1400 AM, Cody, Wyoming
KUPI 980 AM, Idaho Falls, Idaho

Public Radio

KEMC 91.7 FM, Billings, Montana
KGLT 91.9 FM, Bozeman, Montana
KRIC 100.5 FM, Rexburg, Idaho (reaches Idaho Falls, Rexburg, Fremont County and Teton County, Idaho; in Dillon, Montana, try 105.5; in Jackson and Afton, Wyoming, look at 104.9; and in Freedom, Wyoming, 103.9.)

Rock — Album/Alternative/Classic

KEZQ 92.9 AM, West Yellowstone, Montana
KLZY 92.5 FM, Powell, Wyoming
KMMS 95.1 FM, Bozeman, Montana
KMTN 96.9 FM, Jackson, Wyoming
KRKX 94.1 FM, Billings, Montana
KPKX 97.5 FM, Bozeman, Montana

Spanish Language Radio

KRXK 1230 AM, Rexburg, Idaho

Travelers' Information

WBEY 530 AM, Bozeman, Montana

The connection between the natural world and religious worship is so strong throughout the Greater Yellowstone region that you'll find several simple chapels here — their doors unlocked during the summer months — inviting travelers to step inside and worship.

Worship

In Yellowstone country, where the natural landscape is largely uninterrupted by man-made structures, we only have to walk out our doors or to the edge of town, drive to the mountains or walk into the wilderness to find spiritual inspiration.

Just look at the mountains, capped with snow deeper than the average church and whiter than sun-bleached bones. Like omniscient sentinels, they jut into the blue firmament, so clear that from the valley below you can see the wind whipping the peaks' snow into rooster tails.

Feel the breath-sucking, will-sapping midafternoon heat in a hot, dry, silent sagebrush-strewn draw. Know that this afternoon, this evening, maybe minutes from now, angry storm clouds can gallop over the horizon, dumping damnation and buckets of bale down this same dry draw. We call them gully washers. News folks call them flash floods. Whatever you call them, they are but a flash in the pan of terrifying and terrific natural wonders that often drive us to dwell on the divine.

All around us, pure, winking water bubbles from its hidden and mysterious source deep within the earth. Rainbows of wildflowers — deep-blue larkspur, lavender lupine, yellow arrow-leaf balsamroot, sunny mule ears, cream-colored camas, red Indian paintbrush — follow the melting snow from the valley floor to the highest peaks. Birds call, elk bugle, wolves howl, antelope snort, cougars scream and the elements rage.

The connection between the natural world and religious worship is so strong throughout the Greater Yellowstone region that you'll find several simple chapels — their doors unlocked during the summer months — inviting travelers to step inside and worship. Summers, the priests at the Chapel of the Sacred Heart, near Signal Mountain Lodge in Grand Teton, leave the door unlocked for those who want to stop. Father Putka, now retired after 17 summers at the chapel, used to say Yellowstone country is so beautiful that people are often moved to commune with their Maker. While some prefer to do so outside, many seek the sanctuary of these chapels. Several of them feature picture windows behind the altars. In each, if the tip of the cross on the altar were a gun sight, it would be perfectly aligned with the very top of a spectacular mountain in the distance. We think these chapels are so charming — and so unique — that we briefly discuss them and their locations at the end of this chapter. If you're near one of them on a Sunday morning, we encourage you to stop and worship with others. Otherwise, feel free to stop at any time.

Ironically, it is not only the beauty of the mountains but also their impenetrability and unpredictability that has kept us deeply connected as neighbors and communities. Huddled at the feet of the mighty mountains that even now defy modern communication and transportation, our very survival depends on forgiveness and goodwill — and if all else fails, common decency. If a rancher falls ill or is injured, his neighbors finish putting up the hay. If we are injured in a car wreck, or our houses catch fire, our neighbors come as volunteers to help us. If our homes burn to the ground and we lose everything, we know that

INSIDERS' TIP

Schedules and locations of worship services in Yellowstone and Grand Teton national parks are posted on bulletin boards outside all visitor centers. Times and locations change according to demand and availability of staff. Be sure to check.

tomorrow, food, clothing and temporary shelter will appear at our doorstep.

Nurtured by isolation and fertilized by hardship, both economic and physical, these roots are the foundation of community churches. In towns surrounding the parks, there are plenty of churches from which to choose. And, if the number of churches in a town are any indication, those of us who do attend regular services are particular about the way we worship. For example, Ennis (population 660) has 13 churches. The 8,000 residents of Cody, on the other hand, can choose from 29 churches and chapels, and that doesn't include the Bighorn Basin outside Cody where there are more churches, including 10 chapels of the Church of Jesus Christ of Latter-day Saints.

Generally, you won't find us particular, though, about what we wear to church. An advertisement by the Presbyterian Church of Jackson sums up the general churchgoing dress code in Greater Yellowstone: "We don't care what you wear to church. And considering he walked around in a sheet, Jesus probably won't either." You'll also find that some churches, too small to finance a building, assemble on Sundays in public buildings such as schools, motel conference rooms or library basements.

Except in the larger towns, you will likely find only a menu of Christian denominations. In the larger towns — Bozeman, Billings, Idaho Falls and Jackson — you also might find Unitarian, Jewish, Quaker and Christian Science houses of worship. New Age groups are popping up here and there as well. For more information about churches in your area, we suggest you consult either the Yellow Pages or a local newspaper for listings. For information about worship specifically in Yellowstone and Grand Teton national parks, read on.

A Christian Ministry in the National Parks

Today, thanks to a program called A Christian Ministry in the National Parks, those who live in, work in and visit Yellowstone and Grand Teton national parks can find interdenominational services at park amphitheaters, lodges and chapels from Memorial Day until Labor Day. The program — headquartered in Boston, Massachusetts, and recognized by more than 40 denominations — serves 65 national parks, monuments, recreation areas and national forests across the country. In 1998, 53 volunteers provided services in Yellowstone National Park, while about a dozen ministered to those in Grand Teton National Park. Look for worship schedules posted at hotel front desks, activity desks, and at campground offices and amphitheater bulletin boards.

Evolution of Worship

A Christian Ministry in the National Parks, formed in 1953, took root at the Yellowstone National Park Chapel in Mammoth, after the Rev. Warren Ost enlisted Princeton theological students to help staff regular church services in 1950, about 85 years after the first missionary entered the Greater Yellowstone area. According to *The Yellowstone National Chapel* by author Aubrey Haines, Fr. Francis Xavier Kuppens, a Belgian Jesuit working as a missionary among the Blackfeet Indians, was the first man of the cloth to enter Yellowstone

INSIDERS' TIP

The Mormon temple in Idaho Falls is the largest in the region outside Salt Lake City. The temple itself is not open to the public, but a nearby visitor center is. Stop in to learn more about the religion that has had such a dramatic impact on the history of this region.

country. Kuppens came to the Yellowstone region in 1865, seven years before it would be set aside as the world's first national park. Accompanying a band of Blackfeet, he no doubt said Mass someplace within today's park boundaries.

It wasn't until 1873, though, that William Wesley Van Orsdel, known as "Brother Van," held an official service in Lower Geyser Basin. Brother Van's visit to the park led to the appointment of Methodist minister George Comfort to serve the Upper Yellowstone Valley. Headquartered in Livingston — then the only gateway to Yellowstone National Park — Comfort held services in a Northern Pacific Railroad box car in the rail yards. By 1886, Methodist circuit riders were traveling up and down the Yellowstone Valley, preaching wherever congregations would assemble — in homes, under trees, perhaps even in saloons.

In 1897, ministers returning from a religious conference in San Francisco toured Yellowstone National Park. One of them, F.T. Proctor of Utica, New York, offered to build a chapel for the soldiers guarding the park. His offer, though, was rejected as impractical, given the park management's limited financial resources. About 1900, the Episcopalians arrived on the scene. John F. Pritchard, an Episcopalian minister, settled near Emigrant, about midway down the valley. Serving the settlements up and down the valley, Pritchard would catch the train, ride it to the end of the line in Gardiner, then borrow a saddle horse or a buggy, serving up sermons, baptizing babies, ministering to the sick and burying the fallen wherever he could. Pritchard, also chaplain to the Fort Yellowstone soldiers at Mammoth, held services in the mess hall. By 1909, he had convinced the Secretary of War that money was needed for a chapel at Fort Yellowstone. Before Congress could approve appropriations, though, the commanding officer at Fort Yellowstone was replaced by S.B.M. Young, the same officer who had rejected Proctor's chapel proposal in 1887. Construction of the chapel would be delayed another four years.

Finally, in the spring of 1912, Gagnon and Co. of Billings, Montana, began construction on the Gothic chapel. Native sandstone was quarried from the bluffs overlooking the Gardner River. Douglas firs were felled, cut into timbers for the roof and sliced into boards for the floors and interior walls. Covering the whole was a steeply sloping slate roof.

By 1923, several denominations were using the chapel. Episcopalians as well as the English and Norwegian Lutheran churches had scheduled services. The Congregationalists, Baptists and Catholics used the chapel sporadically for services. All denominations shared the cost of the building's upkeep. During the summer, services were more regular. In winter, when deep snow and bitter cold made the park less accessible, services were held less often.

World War II brought change to the chapel. No services were held for three years during the war because it had caused a shortage of men in general and preachers in particular. After the war, the stream of visitors to Yellowstone National Park began to grow steadily. Eager to find a way to provide Sunday worship services for park employees and visitors, the Park Service formed the Superintendent's Church Committee in 1949. That same year, the committee recruited young men from eastern theological seminaries to help lead worship services. Young Princeton seminarians were the first to respond. The success of their first two years of service led to the formation of A Christian Ministry in the National Parks.

The Latter-day Saints

No mention of the development of organized religion or the settlement of greater Yellowstone can exclude the Church of Jesus

INSIDERS' TIP

A few worship services in Yellowstone and Grand Teton national parks include Sunday schools for children. Consult worship schedules posted at visitor centers to learn more.

Christ of Latter-day Saints (a.k.a. the Mormon church). Like the volcanic eruptions and subsequent flows that helped shape the Yellowstone landscape eons ago, a swell of Latter-day Saints seeped into the plains and valleys of the Greater Yellowstone region. Like the rippling aftershocks of an earthquake, they moved from their epicenter: the Holy City, New Jerusalem, Zion in the Valley of the Mountains, Salt Lake City. Now the center of what its chamber of commerce likes to call the Intermountain Empire, Salt Lake City was the gathering place for Latter-day Saints. Whole families — brothers, sisters, aunts, uncles, cousins, in-laws, grandparents — tens of thousands of them, followed the Mormon Trail west to the Great Salt Lake Valley. Bound by an organized framework for command and bolstered by faith, they lost lives and limbs in their zeal to reach Zion. For many, arriving was not the end of the trail, but rather the beginning. As soon as they arrived, some began planting and digging irrigation canals, while others were sent forth to colonize the valleys to the north, south, east and west.

The first church in Jackson Hole was built in 1905 by the Mormons; the first Mormon homesteader in that area was James May, who settled east of Black Butte in 1894. May and those who followed laid out a community with the grid-like orderliness found in Mormon towns in Utah and eastern Idaho in what is now Grand Teton National Park. It came to be known as Mormon Row, both for its "un-Jackson-like" neatness of design and for the religious preference of its inhabitants.

In eastern Idaho, the Mormon influence is still present — and strong. Mormon settlers went there in the late 1860s as hardscrabble farmers. Their forte was cooperation, a requirement in this harsh land where dry farming was a poor bet and irrigation a community project. Even today, meandering canals carry Snake River water across a landscape agriculturally productive in large part because of early Mormon farmers and their canal-building efforts.

Some, like the 100 Mormon families who settled the Bighorn Basin near Cody, Wyoming, came by gubernatorial invitation. In 1900, Wyoming's governor solicited aid from the Utah Saints who colonized the Bighorn Basin. After some investigation, LDS President Snow agreed to send his people, who promptly set to work digging 27 miles of canal still in use today. It took them four years. Shortly after they arrived, the Burlington Northern Railroad paid the Bighorn Saints $80,000 to lay 23 miles of track. The money laid the foundation for the solid LDS community that still thrives there today.

Roadside Chapels

Grand Teton National Park

Chapel of the Sacred Heart, a half-mile north of Signal Mountain Lodge, (307) 733-2516, is an unassuming brown log structure. Yet people from all over the world come here Saturdays and Sundays, June through August. Part of the parish of Our Lady of the Mountains Catholic Church in Jackson (in fact, that's where the phone number rings), the little chapel was built in 1935 to serve the park's visitors.

Scheduled services are offered once on Saturday and twice on Sunday. But the chapel is unlocked 24 hours a day for those with an unscheduled desire for prayer. Commune a while and then sign the guest book (be sure to scan the addresses of other signers; you'll be amazed at how many nations are represented). One of the old building's odd quirks

INSIDERS' TIP

From 1937 until 1954, Catholics from the Gardiner area and the Upper Yellowstone Valley celebrated Mass in the traveling St. Paul Chapel Car. The 84-foot-long chapel on wheels, a specially fitted railroad car built in 1914, contained an altar and enough pews to seat 70 people. Since moved to the Midwest, the chapel car has become part of a national traveling exhibit.

Photo: Randy Hayes, Post Register

Yellowstone country is so beautiful that people are often moved to commune with their maker, says Father Putka, after 16 years at Chapel of the Sacred Heart.

is the resident bats. You won't know they're there — they spend their days quietly sleeping under the eaves — but the folks who clean up after them wish they would find a new home. Trouble is, neither the Park Service nor the Catholic Church has been able to convince them to leave.

The second of two chapels in Grand Teton National Park, the rustic **Chapel of the Transfiguration**, on U.S. Highway 89 near Moose, Wyoming, (307) 733-2603, is built of log; its pews are aspen. The big picture window above the altar frames the Tetons. What better place to meditate upon the beauty of creation? The chapel is associated with St. John's Episcopal Church in Jackson.

The idea for Chapel of the Transfiguration was born one night in 1920 among a group of campers, tired after a long trek to Jackson for worship. The land on which the chapel now sits was donated by a local woman to save others the long ride. From late May through September, Holy Eucharist and a morning prayer service are offered here every Sunday. The chapel is available during those months for baptisms, weddings and memorial services. Call the St. John's church office (the number above) to make arrangements.

Southwestern Montana

The **Mt. Republic Chapel** is just 2 miles from the Northeast Entrance to Yellowstone National Park on Mont. Highway 212 between Silver Gate and Cooke City. Built in the 1970s, it serves as a year-round place of worship for local residents. Windows behind the altar frame the towering peak of Mt. Republic. While services are held here each Sunday between Memorial Day and Labor Day (thanks to A Christian Ministry in the National Parks), during the winter locals worship here only once a month when a minister from Gardiner comes to town. Visitors are welcome. Call the church at (406) 838-2397 summer, (406) 838-2359 winter.

When we first saw **The Soldiers Chapel** at Big Sky, (406) 995-2777, just west of Mont. Highway 191, we had no choice but to make a quick U-turn. A nondenominational church, this picture-perfect log and native stone chapel was built in 1955 as a memorial to the World War II fallen comrades of the 163rd Infantry. It was built by Col. Nelson Story III, a former member of the 163rd. A huge picture window behind the altar frames 11,000-foot Lone Mountain, home to the ski runs of Big Sky Ski and Summer Resort (see our Winter Sports chapter). Guests are welcome at worship services. The chapel doors are open continuously throughout the summer months for meditation and prayer. Tidy homestyle restrooms with real paper towels (none of those electric blowdriers) sit at the edge of the property. This is a popular wedding chapel.

The **Big Sky Chapel** in Meadow Village on the Big Sky road should be completed by the summer of 1999. In winter, residents of Big Sky worshipped first in homes, then in commercial locations such as the Golden Eagle Lodge. Built entirely through volunteer work and donations, this beautiful chapel is a lovely addition to the region's roadside chapels. A spectacular picture window featuring Lone Peak is complemented by stained glass windows. For information, call (406) 995-4294.

Meditation Chapel is a small frame building situated atop a knoll right next to the only rest area on Mont. Highway 89 between Livingston and Gardiner. This tiny chapel — it has only eight chairs — has a window behind the altar that frames Emigrant Peak. A Bible — it was opened to Genesis when we visited — sits at the front of the chapel. Next to the door, you will find a guest book filled with a wide range of religious writings. Chapel keepers

INSIDERS' TIP

Motorists can still find Prayer Rock beside Wyo. Alternate Highway 14, between Powell and Byron. A sign tells the story of how the rock, which blocked canal construction and was too big to blast apart, mysteriously broke apart 24 hours after the construction foreman prayed for divine help.

George and Ira Feswick of Bozeman say an occasional wayfarer spends the night here. Call (406) 587-7911 for more information.

Northwestern Wyoming

The outdoor **Wayfarer's Chapel** is situated high above Wyo. Highway 14/16/20, about 10 miles from Yellowstone National Park's East Entrance. Built in the 1960s as an outreach to travelers, the chapel is composed of a beautiful stone altar with a semicircle of split-log benches. From mid-June until the end of August, prayer services are held by lay members of the congregation. This chapel is a popular site for weddings. Road construction during summer 1997 tore up the area and forced members of the Christ Episcopal Church to move the chapel's site. Look for the sign on the north side of the highway. A dirt parking lot is available beside the road, and a path leads up the hill and through the trees to the chapel. We think this is a rest area worth visiting.

For more information on Wayfarer's Chapel, call the Christ Episcopal Church in Cody, Wyoming, at (307) 587-3849.

To help you build your Yellowstone library, we've added a bibliography drawn from the best of what's on our own bookshelves and the best resources we discovered as we researched this guide.

Resources

For additional information on communities, area businesses and attractions, try these visitors centers, government offices and chambers of commerce. See our Parks and Forests chapter for information on contacting a Forest Service ranger station. To help you build your Greater Yellowstone library, we've added a bibliography drawn from the best of what's on our own bookshelves and the best resources we discovered as we researched this guide.

Organizations

Regional Information

Jackson Hole

Jackson Hole Chamber of Commerce — (307) 733-3316; 990 W. Broadway Avenue, Jackson, Wyoming.

Jackson Hole/Greater Yellowstone Information Center — 540 N. Cache Street, Jackson, Wyoming.

Wyoming Game and Fish — (307) 733-2321; 360 N. Cache Street, Jackson, Wyoming.

Wyoming Travel Commission — (800) 225-5996

Southwestern Montana

Big Sky Chamber of Commerce — (406) 995-3000, (800) 943-4111; Box 160100, Big Sky, MT 59716

Bozeman Chamber of Commerce and Visitor Center — (406) 586-5421, (800) 228-4224;1205 E. Main Street, Bozeman, Montana

Cooke City Chamber of Commerce — (406) 838-2495; Box 1071, Cooke City, MT 59020

Ennis Chamber of Commerce — (406) 682-4388; Box 291, Ennis, MT 59729

Gardiner Chamber of Commerce — (406) 848-7971; Box 81, Gardiner, MT 59030 (located on U.S. Highway 89).

Livingston Chamber of Commerce and Visitor Center — (406) 222-0850; 212 W. Park Street, Livingston, Montana.

Red Lodge Chamber of Commerce — (406) 446-1718; U.S. Highway 212 north of Red Lodge, Montana.

West Yellowstone Chamber of Commerce — (406) 646-7701; Canyon Street and Yellowstone Avenue, West Yellowstone, Montana.

Eastern Idaho

Ashton Chamber of Commerce — (208) 652-3987 (City Building); 64 N. 10, Ashton, Idaho.

Ashton Visitor Center — (208) 652-7520; 801 N. U.S. Highway 20, Ashton, Idaho.

Bureau of Land Management — (208) 525-7500; 1405 Hollipark Drive, Idaho Falls, Idaho.

Eastern Idaho Visitor Information Center — (800) 634-3246; 505 Lindsay Boulevard, Idaho Falls, Idaho. Included in this center are the Chamber of Commerce, (208) 523-1010; Bureau of Land Management, (208) 523-1012; and the Forest Service (208) 523-3278

Idaho Fish and Game — (208) 525-7290; 1515 Lincoln Road, Idaho Falls, Idaho.

Idaho Sport Fishing Information Line — (800) ASK-FISH

Island Park Chamber of Commerce — (208) 558-7755; P.O. Box 83, Island Park, ID 83429.

Rexburg Chamber of Commerce — (208) 356-5700; 420 W. 4 S., Rexburg, Idaho.

Teton Valley Chamber of Commerce — (208) 354-2500; Main Street, Driggs, Idaho.

Northwestern Wyoming

Cody Country Chamber of Commerce — (307) 587-2777; 836 Sheridan Avenue, Cody, Wyoming.

Other Sources

Greater Yellowstone is home to several groups that can be reached for information about the region's unique features.

Blue Ribbon Coalition — (208) 233-6570.

Bureau of Reclamation river/reservoir line — (800) 658-5771. This number reaches a recorded message with up-to-date water level information on any river or reservoir in the Upper Snake drainage controlled by a Bureau of Reclamation dam (that's Jackson Lake, Grassy Lake, Palisades Reservoir, the Snake River and others).

Grand Teton Natural History Association — (307) 739-3606. This nonprofit sells a range of books and maps that relate to Grand Teton National Park and the Yellowstone region. Some of their offerings would be difficult to find elsewhere.

Greater Yellowstone Coalition — (208) 522-7927; 1740 E. 17th, Idaho Falls, Idaho; (406) 586-1593; P.O. Box 1874, Bozeman, MT 59771

Henry's Fork Foundation — (208) 652-3567; P.O. Box 852, 604 Main Street, Ashton, ID 83420. These folks run research and stewardship programs and supply information about the waters of the Henry's Fork drainage.

Rocky Mountain Elk Foundation Visitor Center — (406) 543-4545; 2291 W. Broadway Avenue, Missoula, Montana.

Sportsman's Information Number in Wyoming — (800) 654-1178.

Books

Yellowstone National Park

The Geysers of Yellowstone, by T. Scott Bryan. University Press of Colorado, Niwot, Colorado, 1991: 299 pages. You won't find beautiful photographs in this book, but it's chock-full of fascinating information about Yellowstone's geysers. Bryan, a seasonal ranger-naturalist in the park for years, has a Master of Science degree from the University of Montana. This is his first book.

Greater Yellowstone: The National Park and Adjacent Wildlands, by Rick Reese. American and World Geographic Publishing, Helena, Montana, 1991; 103 pages. This beautifully illustrated book takes the reader quickly through Yellowstone's birth, its ecology, its politics and its present threats. A former director of the Yellowstone Institute, Rick Reese is part of Yellowstone's story.

Yellowstone, by Fred Hirschmann. Graphic Arts Center Publishing Company, Portland, Oregon, 1990; 88 pages. This book is fun to read both for its informative descriptions of Yellowstone National Park's most interesting features and for the firsthand accounts Hirschmann pulls from his five years of rangering there. Hirschmann is a nature photographer as well as a writer; his striking images salt the text.

Yellowstone: 125 Years of America's Best Idea, by Michael Milstein. Billings Gazette, Billings, Montana, 1996; 112 pages. Milstein has been covering Yellowstone issues since 1989 and it shows. This informative, well-written book is packed with interesting anecdotes about Yellowstone. Historic and modern photographs make this book as pleasant to leaf through as it is to read.

Yellowstone: A Wilderness Besieged, by Richard A. Bartlett. The University of Arizona Press, Tucson, Arizona, 1989. A history of Yellowstone National Park, Bartlett digs into the archives and brings to light the intricate relationships between Yellowstone National Park officials, politicians, concessionaires, railroaders and poachers. A teacher of the westward movement and a professor of history at The Florida State University in Tallahassee, Bartlett has written several history books.

Yellowstone Ecology: A Road Guide, by Sharon Eversman and Mary Carr. Mountain Press Publishing Company, Missoula, Montana, 1992; 242 pages. Ecology explores connections between living things and their surroundings. This book is organized so that you can read about the unique connections that shape the lives and places you visit as you stand there with that ground under your feet.

Yellowstone On Fire!, by Robert Ekey and staff of *Billings Gazette*. Billings Gazette, Billings, Montana, 1989; 128 pages. Beautiful photos and lively text capture the nightmare of Yellowstone's 1988 fires. For anyone interested in the fires, this book is a must. The photos

Photo: Robert Bower, Post Register

Bret Zollinger keeps the spirited Mackay rodeo bucking herd headed in the direction on the rodeo grounds.

alone, taken by the *Billings Gazette* staff, tell a compelling story.

Yellowstone Place Names, by Lee H. Whittlesey. Montana Historical Society Press, Helena, Montana, 1988; 178 pages. Written by Yellowstone National Park historian Lee Whittlesey, this book is full of interesting anecdotes about how places in the park got their names. It's also illustrated with some great old photos. Whittlesey began working in the park in the early 1970s and has held just about every park job imaginable along the way.

The Yellowstone Story: Volumes One and Two, by Aubrey L. Haines. University Press of Colorado, Niwot, Colorado, 1996; 385 pages and 543 pages. Retired Yellowstone National Park historian Haines researched these books for years. Now they are the bible when it comes to Yellowstone National Park history. Haines meanders through the subject matter, coloring it with volumes of anecdotes and interesting facts.

Grand Teton National Park

Crucible for Conservation: The Struggle for Grand Teton National Park, by Robert W. Righter. Colorado Associated University Press, 1982; 192 pages. Righter argues that Grand Teton's piecemeal construction is a story of conservation success. This book presents a fascinating, if somewhat academic, picture of the complex politics that led to the park's creation. If Western politics intrigues you, you'll find this a worthwhile read.

For Everything There is a Season, by Frank Craighead: 207 pages. The Craighead name winds through Greater Yellowstone issues, politics and recent history. Frank is a field biologist who studied grizzlies in the region. He's been instrumental in attempts to define Greater Yellowstone. This book looks at this region's mysteries and natural patterns.

Interpreting the Landscape: Recent and Ongoing Geology of Grand Teton and Yellowstone National Parks, by John Good and Ken Pierce. Grand Teton Natural History Association: 58 pages. A fast but thorough sketch of the forces that sculpted the region.

Outdoor Recreation

A Climber's Guide to the Teton Range, by Leigh Ortenburger and Reynold Jackson. The Mountaineers, Seattle, Washington, 1996; 415 pages. This book is interesting reading for mountain lovers as well as mountain climbers. The book not only carefully pictures and describes climbing routes in the Teton Range, but it also includes a fascinating climbing history of the Tetons. There are sections on the geology of the region and each of the region's peaks. Ten years in the writing, this book is the product of two longtime Teton climbers, one a dedicated historian of the area.

Floating and Recreation on Montana Rivers, by Curt Thompson. Pub. Curt Thompson, Lakeside, Montana, 1993; 370 pages. Thompson takes the reader down all 81 Montana rivers. Along the way, he tells in an organized fashion about floating, fishing and other recreation opportunities. You'll find a simplified map of each river, as well as some entertaining black-and-white photos. Thompson is an avid outdoorsman with degrees in recreation and biology. Thirty years of floating Montana's rivers (and finding no information about them) led Thompson to write this book.

Greater Yellowstone Fly Fisher's Stream Guide, by Ken Retallic. GBH ink, Idaho Falls, Idaho, 1996; 78 pages. This slim volume covers Greater Yellowstone's fly-fishing hot spots. Retallic even has suggestions for what kinds of flies to use when in which streams, information you would otherwise only get at the local fly shop.

Hiking Yellowstone National Park, by Bill Schneider. Falcon Publishing Inc., Helena, Montana. 1997; 335 pages. Two features make this guidebook a little different. One is that hikes are categorized a variety of ways, like "Trails to Avoid if You Don't Want to See Horses," or "For a Good Chance of Seeing a Bear." The other is that each hike's elevation gain and loss is charted on a mile-by-mile graph, so you can see exactly what you're getting into before you're in.

Mountaineering: The Freedom of the Hills, 5th Edition, edited by Don Graydon. The Mountaineers, Seattle, Washington, 1992; 447 pages. This book is one of the most comprehensive resources available for backcountry travel, with a long history of offering good advice (the book was first published in 1960). We recommend *Freedom of the Hills* for anyone interested in serious mountaineering, as well as technical rock, ice and snow climbing. The book also has excellent sections for backpackers and other backcountry travelers on issues such as snowpack and avalanche, route-finding, gear, backcountry cooking and more.

Idaho, The Whitewater State, by Grant Amaral. Watershed Books, 1990; 315 pages. Of the several books available on runnable rivers in Idaho, we like this one best. Amaral is a serious kayaker; his river descriptions are particularly well-suited to kayakers.

The Yellowstone Fly-Fishing Guide, by Craig Mathews and Clayton Molinero. Lyons and Burford, New York, New York, 1997; 164 pages. Mathews and Molinero have more than 30 years of combined fishing time in Yellowstone National Park waters. Rather than focusing on just the well-known waters, these two give a streamlined, easy-to-read lowdown on 200 lakes and streams in every nook and cranny of the park. Besides telling you what kind of fish you'll find, the authors also tell you about wildlife to watch for, how to get to the site, what insects are hatching and when. Mathews is owner of Blue Ribbon Flies. Molinero has guided in Yellowstone for more than a decade.

Yellowstone Trails: A Hiking Guide, by Mark C. Marschall. The Yellowstone Association, Yellowstone National Park, Wyoming, 1995; 172 pages. After more than two decades as a park ranger, Marschall has updated this book several times and is still humble about his knowledge of the park. The book includes helpful information about caring for the park and yourself, bear attacks, water treatment and backcountry camping. It also includes topographic maps and detailed descriptions of more than 70 trails ranging from easy to difficult and short to long.

First Aid and Backcountry Medicine

Medicine for the Backcountry, by Frank Hubbell and Buck Tilton. ICS Books Inc., Merrillville, Indiana, 1990; 155 pages. This is an easy-to-read resource to start you thinking about how medical problems and emergencies should be approached in the backcountry, with an emphasis on common sense and planning. No book is a substitute for adequate training, but this is a first step.

Medicine for Mountaineering, by James Wilkerson. The Mountaineers, Seattle, Washington, 1973. More important than gear in your first-aid kit is information, so pack a good wilderness medicine book like this one with your Band-Aids and athletic tape.

Idaho

In Mountain Shadows: A History of Idaho, by Carlos Schwantes. University of Nebraska Press, Lincoln, Nebraska, 1991: 292 pages. The author is a professor of history at Moscow's University of Idaho. He describes his book as "an extended essay on the character of Idaho." We found it an entertaining and enlightening read about a state whose development has encompassed every major issue of the West, from wars with Native Americans and gold rushes to lumber booms, water wars and outdoor recreation-based tourism.

The Snake River: Window to the West, by Tim Palmer. Island Press, Washington D.C., 1991; 320 pages. If you fall in love with the Snake River or you want to learn more about the water issues that are such beautiful windows into Western politics — or if you are intrigued with the state of Idaho — this thoroughly researched, well-written book will repay your time.

Field Guides

Animal Tracks, a Peterson Field Guide, by Olaus Murie. Houghton Mifflin Company, New York, 1982; 375 pages. If you're observant, you'll see the signs that animals leave behind much more frequently than you'll see the animals themselves. Murie's book teaches how understanding can be gained from animal tracks, scat and other signs. We like this book over other tracking books because it's comprehensive, but even more because Olaus Murie was a longtime Jackson Hole resident. The book's line drawings, mostly created in the field, are his. The animal behaviors he describes are from firsthand experience.

A Field Guide to Wildflowers of the Rocky Mountains, by Carl Schreier. Homestead Publishing, Moose, Wyoming, 1996: 224 pages. Schreier understands how many words a picture is worth and includes hundreds of lovely color images in this trim field guide. No trying to identify plants by artists' sketches!

A Field Guide to Yellowstone's Geysers, Hot Springs and Fumaroles, by Carl Schreier. Homestead Publishing, Moose, Wyoming, 1992; 122 pages. Like Schreier's *A Field Guide to Wildflowers of the Rocky Mountains* by the same publisher (and also in our library), this book is thorough, stuffed with lovely photos and intelligently organized. If you'd like to understand the geothermal features you stared at in the park, you'll appreciate Schreier's book.

Stokes Field Guide to Birds, by Donald and Lillian Stokes. Little, Brown and Company, New York, 1996; 519 pages. Of all the bird identification guides we've looked at or owned, this one is the most complete. It's organized so non-birders can locate information on their bird by general appearance. Best of all, each species is illustrated with at least two high-quality photographs.

Miscellaneous

Bloodties: Nature, Culture and the Hunt, by Ted Kerasote. Kodansha International, New York, 1994; 277 pages. Worth reading both for its well-researched, thoughtful approach to the question of why people in a supermarket society might choose to kill their own meat and for the final section, which focuses on Kerasote's life in Jackson Hole and his reasons for hunting.

Greater Yellowstone National Forests, by Todd Wilkinson. Falcon Publishing, Inc., Helena, Montana, 1991; 104 pages. Part of the National Forests of America series, this resource provides interesting factoids about area forests, plus attractions, campgrounds, trails, phone numbers and maps.

Journal of a Trapper, by Osborne Russell; edited by Aubrey L. Haines. University of Nebraska Press, Lincoln, Nebraska, 1955; 191 pages. Written by 1840s trapper Osborne Russell and edited by Yellowstone expert Aubrey Haines, this book is the historian's main link to the days of trapping in the wilderness. Besides being a general journal of travel and trapping, Russell's account of the years from 1834 to 1843 in the Yellowstone Country provide astounding glimpses into his everyday life.

Index of Advertisers

Index

Symbols

A

B

C

G

H

I

M

P

Q

R

T

U

V

W

Y

Z